同等学力人员申请硕士学位全国统一考试辅导丛书

全国同等学力统考命题研究组 组编

英 语

词汇分频速记

（最新版考试大纲配套用书）

北京理工大学出版社
BEIJING INSTITUTE OF TECHNOLOGY PRESS

版权专有 侵权必究

图书在版编目（CIP）数据

英语词汇分频速记 / 全国同等学力统考命题研究组组编 . —北京：北京理工大学出版社，2018.9（2019.8 重印）

（同等学力人员申请硕士学位全国统一考试辅导丛书）

ISBN 978-7-5682-6336-8

Ⅰ.①英… Ⅱ.①全… Ⅲ.①英语 – 词汇 – 硕士 – 水平考试 – 自学参考资料 Ⅳ.① H313

中国版本图书馆 CIP 数据核字（2018）第 210717 号

出版发行 /	北京理工大学出版社有限责任公司
社　　址 /	北京市海淀区中关村南大街 5 号
邮　　编 /	100081
电　　话 /	（010）68914775（总编室）
	（010）82562903（教材售后服务热线）
	（010）68948351（其他图书服务热线）
网　　址 /	http://www.bitpress.com.cn
经　　销 /	全国各地新华书店
印　　刷 /	天津东辰丰彩印刷有限公司
开　　本 /	787 毫米 × 1092 毫米　1/32
印　　张 /	24.75
字　　数 /	618 千字
版　　次 /	2018 年 9 月第 1 版
	2019 年 8 月第 2 次印刷
定　　价 /	49.80 元

责任编辑 / 梁铜华
文案编辑 / 梁铜华
责任校对 / 周瑞红
责任印制 / 边心超

图书出现印装质量问题，请拨打售后服务热线，本社负责调换

百分百系列编委会成员

(按姓氏拼音排序)

陈能军:中国人民大学经济学博士,深圳大学理论经济学博士后,广东省金融创新研究会副秘书长,广东省国际服务贸易学会理事,安徽大学创新管理研究中心研究员,中合博士后智库科研研究院研究员。主要从事文化金融、国际经济的研究。

褚建航:北京理工大学管理学硕士,学苑教育青年辅导教师。独立出版《实用面试技巧》《新富滚钱术》等数本经济、管理类著作,具备咨询工程师、基金和证券从业资格。拥有多年工商管理同等学力申硕考试辅导经验,熟悉各学科知识框架与重点、难点。

黄卫平:中国人民大学教授,博士生导师,中国世界经济学会理事,中国欧盟研究会理事,中美经济学教育交流委员会执行主任。国际经济关系、国际经济学、发展经济学为其主要研究领域。

李自杰:对外经济贸易大学国际工商管理学院副教授,经济学博士,对外经济贸易大学海尔商学院执行副院长。企业理论、产权理论、管理经济学和管理理论为其主要研究领域。

刘刚:中国人民大学商学院副教授,商学院院长助理,MBA项目中心主任,管理学博士,中国企业管理研究会常务理事。企业战略与文化、市场营销、供应链管理与物流、危机管理、产业竞争、艺术市场为其主要研究领域。

吕随启:北京大学经济学院金融学系副主任,中国金融研究中心副主任,经济学博士,副教授。金融学为其主要研究领域。

舒燕飞:中央民族大学经济学院副教授,经济学博士,中国宏观经济管理教育学会理事。经济增长、宏观调控和西方经济制度为其主要研究领域。对同等学力考试分析独特,具有丰富的教学经验。

宋华:中国人民大学教授,经济学博士,日本京都大学博士后,中国物流学会理事,南开大学现代物流研究中心兼职研究员。物流与供应链管理、企业战略管理为其主要研究领域。

宋莉莉:北京大学应用心理学博士,学苑教育青年辅导教师,北京大学人格与社会心理学研究中心理事。曾参加多项国家自然科学基金项目的研究,成功参与并完成国家863计划项目子课题,现从事973计划项目课题研究,所在科研团队获得2016年度北京市科技进步一等奖。在学苑教育多年的教学中,积累了丰富的辅导经验,能精准把握考点,深谙答题技巧,学员通过率高,口碑极佳。

孙杰:北京外国语大学英语语言文学硕士,学苑教育英语研究小组核心成员。擅长在职人员英语考试语法、完形、翻译等题型,参与编辑同等学力申请英语应试教材。

孙茂竹:中国人民大学教授,全国高校财务理论研究会理事。著有《管理会计》《企业会计学》《公司理财学》《审计学》等。财务管理、管理会计为其主要研究领域。

王蕙:中国青年政治学院杰出的青年教师,英语语言学硕士,京城著名在职英语"王牌组合"的"二王"之一。著有多部在职英语教科书及辅导用书。

王利平:中国人民大学商学院教授,管理学博士。先后出版《管理学原理》《经济管理基础》《商业企业经营学》《现代企业管理基础》等专著和教材。管理理论、企业理论、企业战略管理、连锁经营管理为其主要研究领域。

闫相国:中国人民大学管理学硕士,北京大学心理学硕士,《广州日报·求学指南》专家顾问团成员,学苑教育教学研究中心主任。企业战略管理和公司财务管理为其主要研究方向。

学苑教育简介

学苑教育自1997年建立以来,作为全国最早的在职研究生考试辅导培训机构,以其优异的师资团队和完善的教学服务,20余年来帮助数万名考生通过了在职研究生考试,顺利获得硕士、博士学位。教研中心拥有自己的专职教师队伍、专业教学研发团队和自行研发出版的学员用书,同时与数百位国内外管理专家以及多家国内外知名的管理培训机构建立了紧密的合作关系,共同推出了各个系列的培训课程及图书教材,并在此基础上打造了学苑教育(www.xycentre.com)、学苑教育在线(www.xycentre.org)等多个服务性培训网络平台。学员和社会的认可,愈发证明学苑已成为在职培训领域中的领跑者。我们将始终以"智力服务于中国,提高企业与个人整体竞争力"为目标,用我们恒久不变的真诚与努力,与您共同"启迪广袤思维,追求卓越表现,迈向成功之路"。

前 言

对于英语学习者来说,词汇的重要性是毋庸置疑的。对于参加同等学力的考生来说更是如此。英语最新考试大纲(第六版)规定同等学力考生最低应掌握6 000个英语词汇和700个常用词组。对其中的2 800个核心词汇要求熟练掌握,即能在会话、写作和翻译中准确地运用;其余词汇则要求能在阅读中识别和理解。此次新大纲的调整较之第五版大纲有了很大的变动,仅词汇方面,大纲新增核心词汇约440个,词组100多个。这无疑增加了考试的难度,同时对同等学力的考生提出了更高的要求。

同等学力考生的共同特点是复习时间短、基础知识遗忘严重且久离考场,因此考试的通过率比较低。考虑到考生的实际特点,《英语词汇分频速记》将大纲词汇按照考试出现的频率分为4个等级:核心词汇(即积极词汇)、认知词汇、大纲新增词汇和词组用法,帮助考生更好地掌握英语学科的考试特点和学习方法,助其备考成功!

本书的主要特色:

1. 词汇分频,层次记忆

本书将新大纲中的词汇按重要程度和使用频率分为4个等级:核心词汇(即积极词汇)、认知词汇、大纲新增词汇和词组用法。

核心词汇:大纲规定的2 800个积极词汇,考生必须熟练掌握,并能在会话、写作和翻译中准确地运用。

认知词汇:仅要求考生看到单词能理解其词义,并在阅读中识别和理解。

新增词汇:将大纲新增词汇进行专项归纳和细致讲解。本部分是本手册的重点部分,目的是方便考生对新增词汇进行重点复习备考。

词组用法:对大纲中规定的所有词组及新增词组的用法给予详解。

2. 收词全面,释义权威

本书收录最新大纲的全部词汇,词条释义的选择均来自相关权威的辞典,充分体现其权威性。

3. 巧记速记,考点分析

本书在单词的记忆方法上博采众长,根据每个单词的不同特点,综合运用了各种记忆方法,如语境记忆法、词缀词根法、联想记忆法、派生词、同义词、反义词记忆法等。目的是通过这些记忆方法的综合运用,彻底掌握每个词的用法。同时,我们对每个单词的考点进行了提炼,对单词的固定搭配、习惯用语及词义辨析等给予分析,以帮助考生快速掌握词汇的含义。

4. 经典例句,提分秘籍

本书例句均来自权威辞典,取材广泛,内容新颖,信息量大。经典的例句不断重复使用大纲中的词汇,让考生做到"温故而知新"。精彩的例句不但能帮助考生在实际的环境中记忆单词,而且还能够扩展知识,增强学习兴趣,甚至提高考生的阅读和写作能力。

5. 真题演练,有的放矢

根据语言专家的研究,一个单词重复出现5~10次,学习者才能记住。为此,在核心词汇部分我们精心设计了配套真题练习,通过真题记忆的方式,增加单词重复出现的次数,帮助考生循序渐进,从而达到记忆和活用的效果。

本书在编写过程中得到了学苑教育(www.xycentre.com)的大力支持,在此我们表示感谢,同时对参与本书编写的老师及编辑人员表示由衷的感谢。

我们衷心希望广大考生通过本书的学习,在考试中取得优异的成绩。由于编写时间有限,书中难免会有纰漏,希望广大考生和相关领域的专家及老师给予批评指正,以帮助我们不断地改进和提高。

编　者

核心词汇精解/1
● Word List 1—Word List 50

认知词汇扫描/549
● A—Z

大纲新增词汇/655
● A—Z

词组用法详解/693
● A—W

Word List 1

a/an [ə, eɪ/ən, æn] *art.* 一(个);每一(个);(同类事物中的)任何一个

[语境] A triangle has three sides.
三角形有三条边。
We met once a week.
我们每周见面一次。
A child needs love. 儿童需要爱。

abandon[4] [əˈbændən] *vt.* 放弃,抛弃,离弃

[巧记] 派生词:abandoned (*a.* 被抛弃的,被遗弃的); abandonment (*n.* 放弃,放任)

[语境] We decided we'd have to abandon ship.
我们决定弃船。
The old man abandoned himself to grief.
那老人悲痛欲绝。

[考点] abandon oneself to 沉溺于……; with abandon 放任地,放纵地,纵情地

ability [əˈbɪlɪtɪ] *n.* 能力,本领;才能,才识

[巧记] 反义词:inability (*n.* 无能,无力); disability (*n.* 无能力,残疾)

[语境] The visual ability of cats is much better than that of dogs at night.
晚上猫的视觉比狗的要好得多。

Education develops potential abilities.

教育能开发人的潜能。

[考点] to the best of one's ability 竭尽全力

able ['eɪbəl] *a.* **有能力的；有本事的，能干的**

[巧记] 派生词：ability (*n.* 能力)；enable (*v.* 使能够)；反义词：unable

[语境] The President had to quit his job for he wasn't able to deal with the crisis.

总统因为不能处理这起危机而只好辞职。

I consider him to be a very able student.

我认为他是个很能干的学生。

[考点] be able to do sth. 能做，会做

aboard [ə'bɔːd] *ad. /prep.* **在船/车/飞行器上；上船/车/飞行器**

[巧记] 派生词：board *v. /n.* 上车(船、飞机等)；木板

[语境] We must not take combustible goods aboard.

我们切不可带易燃物上车。

Everyone was soon aboard the plane.

大家很快登上了飞机。

[考点] go aboard 上船/车/飞机等

about [ə'baʊt] *prep.* **在……周围；关于，对于** *ad.* **附近，周围，到处；大约**

[语境] My mother often spoke to me about you.

家母常和我谈起你。

She likes to walk about.

她喜爱四处走走。

[考点] be about to 即将(做)

above [ə'bʌv] *prep.* **在……之上，高于** *ad.* **在上面** *a.* **上述的**

[巧记] 同义词：on, up, upon；反义词：below

[语境] The moon is now above the trees.

月亮正位于树梢上。

There are snowy peaks above.

上面是白雪皑皑的群峰。

abroad [ə'brɔ:d] *ad.* 到国外,在国外;在传播,在流传
 [巧记] 同义词:overseas(*ad.* 在国外);反义词:home(国内)
 [语境] The man went abroad, leaving his wife and children to shift for themselves.
  那男人去了海外,留下妻子儿女自谋生计。

absence ['æbsəns] *n.* 缺乏,不存在;缺席,不在;缺席的时间
 [巧记] 反义词:presence(*n.* 出席,到场)
 [语境] Please look after my house during my absence.
  我不在时,请帮我看房子。
  We must invent an excuse for our absence.
  我们必须为缺席编造一个借口。
 [考点] in the absence of 缺乏……时;当……不在时

absent ['æbsənt] *a.* 缺席的;缺乏的,不存在的;心不在焉的
 [巧记] 派生词:absentation(*n.* 缺席);absently (*ad.* 心不在焉地,茫然地)
 [语境] He was absent from class and he gave an incredible excuse.
  他没来上课,提出的借口令人难以置信。
  To preserve a friend three things are required: to honour him present, praise him absent, and assist him in his necessities.
  维持友谊需要三点:当面尊重他,背后赞扬他,需要时帮助他。

absolute[4] ['æbsəlu:t] *a.* 绝对的,完全的;确实的,肯定的
 [巧记] 派生词:absoluteness (*n.* 绝对, 完全, 专制)
 [语境] If I were president I must be given absolute power.
  如果我是总统,我必须拥有绝对的权力。
  I have told them with absolute certainty there'll be no change.
  我明白无误地告诉他们不会有什么变化。
 [考点] by absolute necessity 万不得已

absorb[7] [əb'sɔ:b] *vt.* 吸收;使全神贯注,吸引……的注意
 [巧记] 派生词:absorbable (*a.* 易被吸收的);absorbability (*n.* 吸收,可吸收性)
 [语境] Plants absorb minerals and other nutrients from the soil. 植

物从泥土中吸收矿物质和其他养料。

Plants can absorb carbon dioxide and release oxygen.

植物可以吸收二氧化碳释放氧气。

[考点] be absorbed in 专心于……，一心从事，热衷于；absorb sb.'s attention 吸引某人注意

abstract ['æbstrækt] *a.* 抽象的 *n.* 摘要，梗概 *vt.* 提取；摘录要点

[巧记] abs(离开) + tract(拉)→从……拉出→抽象。派生词：abstractly(*ad.* 抽象地)

[语境] Modern art is often rather abstract.

现代艺术往往相当抽象。

In the end she abstracted the most important points from her long speech.

最后她从自己的长篇演说中提取出最重要的几点。

abuse [ə'bjuːz] *n.* 滥用；虐待；辱骂；陋习，弊端 *vt.* 滥用；虐待；辱骂

[巧记] 村干部把职权 abuse(滥用)，秋菊开始 muse(沉思) 想到法律的 use(用途)

[语境] Overweight children are being placed in foster care on the grounds that they are victims of child abuse.

那些肥胖的孩子因为遭受虐待将被寄养安置。

You must never, never abuse him any more!

你必须永远、永远不再虐待他了！

academy[8] [ə'kædəmɪ] *n.* 学院；学/协会；研究院

[巧记] 派生词：academic (*a.* 学术的；学院的)

[语境] He passed into the Military Academy with no difficulty.

他毫无困难地获准就读军事学院。

The lecture was given under the auspices of the Academy of Sciences.

这次报告会是由科学院主办的。

accent ['æksənt] *n.* 重音；口音

[巧记] ac(与……对照，和着……) + cent(唱歌) →口音

[语境] He speaks English with an American accent.

他说英语有种美国的腔调。

It is her American accent that distinguishes her.
她的特征是说话带美国口音。

accept[15] [əkˈsept] vt. 同意,认可;接受,领受

[巧记] 派生词:acceptable(a. 可接受的); acceptability(n. 可接受性); acceptance(n. 接受, 认可)

[语境] It is generally accepted that smoking is harmful to our health. 吸烟有害健康,这是大家公认的。

The police are not allowed to accept rewards.
警察是不允许接受酬金的。

[考点] receive, accept, take 辨析:receive 只表示被动地接受;accept 总表示主动而且高兴地接受;take 所表示的接受包含着有人赠给之意

acceptable[4] [əkˈseptəbəl] a. 值得接受的,可接受的

[巧记] 反义词:unacceptable(a. 不能接受的;不受欢迎的)

[语境] Compliments are always acceptable.
恭维话总是受欢迎的。

We must make it clear from the very beginning that competitive quotations are acceptable.
必须一开始就讲清的是,有竞争力的报价可以接受。

access[15] [ˈækses] n. 接近,获得(机会等);入口通道 v. 存取

[语境] I can't access the file on your company because I've forgotten the code.
我无法取出贵公司的文件,因为我把代码忘了。

As her private secretary he has access to all her correspondence.
他是她的私人秘书,能接触到她所有的信件。

[考点] have[gain, get, obtain] access to 接近(会见;进入;使用)

accident[19] [ˈæksɪdənt] n. 事故;意外的事,偶然的事

[语境] They ranked her for the traffic accident.
他们要她对这次交通事故负责。

They blamed the accident on him.
他们把这个意外事故归咎于他。

accommodation [əˌkɒməˈdeɪʃən] n. (pl.) 住处;膳宿

[语境] Have you found accommodation?

找到住处没有?

according to [əˈkɔːdɪŋ tuː] *prep.* 据/照……(所说、所写);按……,视……

[语境] History books are usually written in narrative style, describing political and social changes according to time order.

历史书通常以叙述体来写,根据时间顺序叙述政治和社会的变迁。

accordingly [əˈkɔːdɪŋlɪ] *ad.* 因此,从而

[语境] Accordingly, we have no obligation to pay any of these demands.

因此,我们没有义务履行其中的一切付款要求。

account[16] [əˈkaʊnt] *n.* 账户;说明,叙述 *vi.* (for) 解释

[巧记] 派生词:accountability (*n.* 有责任,有义务)

[语境] He has been asked to account for his conduct.

他被要求解释他的行为。

His illness accounts for his absence.

他因为生病,所以才缺席。

[考点] account for 说明原因,解释; by one's own account 据某人自己说

accurate [ˈækjʊrət] *a.* 准确的,精确的

[巧记] 派生词:accurately (*ad.* 正确地); accuracy (*n.* 精确,精准);反义词:inaccurate

[语境] My aim was accurate. 我瞄得很准。

The new salesgirl is accurate at figures.

新来的女售货员计算正确无误。

[考点] accurate, correct, exact 辨析:accurate 表示"准确的,精确的",指"通过努力,使事情达到正确"; correct 为一般用语,指"正确的"; exact 表示"确切的""精确无误的",指"与事实完全相符"

accuse [əˈkjuːz] *vt.* (of) 谴责;指控,告发

[巧记] 派生词:accused(*n.* 被告); accuser(*n.* 原告,控告者)

[语境] He was accused of incompetence.
他被指责为不称职。
Why couldn't he even accuse her?
他为什么连责骂她都不能呢?

[考点] accuse sb. of... 指控某人……

accustomed [əˈkʌstəmd] *a.* (to) 惯常的,习惯的

[语境] I am accustomed to a spare diet.
我习惯于简单的饮食。

[考点] get accustomed to something 习惯……

ache [eɪk] *n. /vi.* 疼痛,酸痛

[巧记] headache (*n.* 头痛); stomachache (*n.* 肚子痛,胃痛)

[语境] My head still ached dizzily.
我的头仍疼得发晕。

achieve[25] [əˈtʃiːv] *vt.* 实现,完成;达到,得到 *vi.* 达到预期目的

[巧记] 派生词: achievement (*n.* 成就,成绩); achievable (*a.* 可完成的,可有成就的)

[语境] We should do our best to achieve our goal in life.
我们应尽全力去达成我们的人生目标。
Try to achieve a better balance between work and play.
要努力使工作和娱乐更好地平衡。

acid [ˈæsɪd] *n.* 酸,酸性物质 *a.* 酸的,酸味的;尖刻的

[语境] Lemons have an acid taste. 柠檬有酸味。
The acid burnt a hole in the carpet. 酸把地毯烧了个洞。

acquaintance [əˈkweɪntəns] *n.* 熟人,相识(的人)

[语境] The son of an acquaintance of mine has recently landed a good job on a national newspaper.
我一位熟人的儿子最近在一家全国性报社找到了一份好工作。

[考点] make someone's acquaintance 与(某人)初次相识;结识(某人)

acquire[9] [əˈkwaɪə(r)] *vt.* 取得,获得,学到

[巧记] 派生词: acquirement (*n.* 取得,获得)

[语境] We admired his intellectual providence to acquire vast stores of dry information.

我们钦佩他收集大量原始资料的远见卓识。

How did he acquire his wealth?

他的财富是怎样得来的?

[考点] acquire, learn 辨析:acquire 指(经由努力而)获得,学得知识、学问等;learn 指养成、学会习惯等

acre[ˈeɪkə(r)]*n.* 英亩

[语境] That was in 1958, and the government paid sixty dollars an acre.

那是在1958年,政府以六十美元一英亩的价格付了款。

across [əˈkrɒs]*prep.* 横过,越过;在……的对面 *ad.* 横过,穿过

[语境] Anyone travelling across the bridge has to pay a toll.

过这座桥的人都要付通行费。

They canoed across the river.

他们划着小舟过河。

act [ækt]*v.* 表演;举动;起作用 *n.* 行为,法令;一幕

[语境] He acted Othello at the Royal Theater that evening.

那天晚上他在皇家剧院扮演奥赛罗。

Would you tell us something about the new Education Act?

请你给我们讲讲新的教育法好吗?

[考点] act against 违反;act as 担任,充当;起……作用;act for 代理,代表;act on 对……起作用;奉行,按照……而行动

action [ˈækʃən]*n.* 行动,动作;作用;运转;行为;战斗

[巧记] 派生词:actionless(*a.* 不采取行动的,静止不动的);actionist(*n.* 行动主义者)

[语境] The quick action of the firemen saved the building from being burned down.

消防队员行动及时,该建筑物方免遭焚毁。

[考点] out of action 失去作用;put into action 实行,实施

active [ˈæktɪv]*a.* 活跃的,敏捷的,积极的;在活动中的

[巧记] 同义词:dynamic, energetic;反义词:inactive

[语境] Mount Vesuvius is an active volcano.
维苏威是一座活火山。
He became an active social reformer.
他成了一位积极的社会改革家。

activity [æk'tɪvɪtɪ] *n.* 活动;活力;能动性

[巧记] act 活动 + -ivity 状态(名词后缀)→活动状态

[语境] The school offers many recreational activities for the students.
该校为学生提供了很多娱乐活动。

actor [ˈæktə(r)] *n.* 男演员

[语境] Which actor do you like best?
你最喜欢哪个男演员?

actress [ˈæktrɪs] *n.* 女演员

[语境] The famous actress is now appearing at the Capital Theatre.
目前这位著名女演员正在首都剧场演出。

actual [ˈæktʃʊəl] *a.* 实际的;现实的,真实的,目前的

[巧记] 派生词:actually(*ad.* 实际上);actuality(*n.* 现实,现实性)

[语境] His designs, for the most part, corresponded with the actual needs.
他的设计绝大多数情况下都符合实际需要。

actually[21] [ˈæktʃʊəlɪ] *ad.* 事实上

[语境] Actually there is no need to up staff.
实际上没有必要增加员工。

[考点] 辨析 indeed, really, truly, actually, 这些副词均有"确实地,真正地"之意。indeed:一般用于肯定或证实对方所说的话,多承接前言,也用来加强或肯定自己说话的语气。really:主要用于强调与事实或现实不相违背,也可表示不快、惊奇或某种含蓄的怀疑。truly:强调客观存在的真实性,没有任何虚假。actually:侧重于实际的事,而不是凭空想象或推测的事

ad = advertisement [ədˈvɜːtɪsmənt] *n.* 广告,宣传;公告;出公告,做广告

· 9 ·

[语境] I notice that the advertisement misses out the price of the product.

我注意到,广告漏写了产品的价格。

adapt[10] [ə'dæpt] *vt.* (to)使适应;改编

[语境] You must adapt to the norms of the society you live in.

在社会中生活就要遵循社会行为准则。

This machine has been specially adapted for underwater use.

这机器是为水下使用而特别改装的。

[考点] adapt oneself to 适应……;adapt...for 修改

add [æd] *vt.* 加;增加(进);进一步说/写 *vi.* (to)增添

[巧记] 同义词:increase, join, attach;反义词:subtract

[语境] Add some wine to the gravy.

请在肉汁里加点酒。

The snowstorm added to our difficulties.

暴风雪增加了我们的困难。

[考点] add on 加上;附加;包括;add to 增加,加到;add up to 总计共达;(总起来看)等于说;意味着

addition[8] [ə'dɪʃən] *n.* 加,加法;附加部分,增加(物)

[巧记] 派生词:additional (*a.* 附加的);additive (*n.* 添加物)

[语境] In addition to giving a general introduction to computer, the course also provides practical experience.

课程除了介绍一般电脑知识外,还提供实际操作的机会。

The little girl is not very clever at addition.

这个小女孩不太善于做加法。

[考点] in addition 加上,又,另外;in addition to 除了……以外

address [ə'dres] *n.* 地址,通信处 *vt. /n.* 致辞,讲话 *vt.* 致函;写地址

[语境] Take his address down.

把他的地址记下来。

I am delighted to be here and address the World Economic Forum Annual Meeting 2009.

我很高兴出席世界经济论坛2009年年会,并发表特别致辞。

You should address the envelope.

你应该在信封上写上姓名和地址。

adjust[7] [əˈdʒʌst] *vt.* 调节,调整;校对 *vi.* (to) 适应于
　[巧记] ad-表示 to + just 刚好,正确→弄正确→调整
　[语境] He can't adjust himself to the whirl of modern life in this big city.
　他无法适应这个大都市的现代生活的忙碌。
　Could you teach me how to adjust the iris of the camera?
　你能教我怎么调照相机的光圈吗?
　[考点] adjust oneself to 使自己适应;adjust to sth. 适应于某事

administer[ədˈmɪnɪstə(r)] *vt.* 管理;执行;给予 *vi.* 给予帮助;担当管理人
　[语境] They had the right to administer their own internal affairs.
　他们有权管理他们自己的内部事务。
　The courts administer the laws.
　法院执行法律。

administration[ədˌmɪnɪˈstreɪʃən] *n.* 管理;行政,行政机关;政府
　[语境] The enterprise has been put under local administration.
　这个企业已划归地方管理。
　The teachers are responsible to the school administration.
　教师向学校行政负责。

admire [ədˈmaɪə(r)] *vt.* 钦佩,赞赏,羡慕;称赞,夸奖
　[巧记] 反义词:despise (*vt.* 轻视,鄙视)
　[语境] We all admire their dogged efforts.
　我们都很钦佩他们坚持不懈的努力。

admit [ədˈmɪt] *vt.* 承认,供认;准许……进入,准许……加入
　[巧记] 派生词:admittable(*a.* 具有进入的资格的); admission (*n.* 准许进入); admissible(*a.* 可容许的,可接纳的)
　[语境] She freely admits that what he said was wrong.
　她坦率地承认她说错了。
　No one but ticket-holders was admitted.
　只有持票者方可入内。
　[考点] admit, acknowledge, confess 辨析:admit 通常指因外界压

11

力、良心或判断而承认某事的存在或真实性,含"不情愿"之意;acknowledge 指"公开承认",常用于过去隐瞒或否认之事;confess 着重承认自己的过错或罪恶,因此有"忏悔""坦白"的含义

adopt[6] [ə'dɒpt] *vt.* **采用,采纳;收养**
[巧记] 派生词:adopted(*a.* 被收养的,被采用的);adoptable(*a.* 可采用的,可收养的);adoptability(*n.* 采纳性)
[语境] Most countries adopt metric system.
大多数国家采用米制。
We should adopt the consumers' suggestion.
我们应该接受用户的建议。

adult[15] [ə'dʌlt, 'ædʌlt] *n.* 成人 *a.* **成年的,成熟的**
[语境] They have an adult son.
他们有一个儿子已经成年。

advance[19] [əd'vɑːns] *vt.* **推进,促进;提升,提高** *vi.* **前进,进展** *n.* **前进,进展;预付**
[语境] The report advances the suggestion that safety standards should be improved.
该报告建议安全标准应该改进。
It is a popular show, so advance booking is essential.
这是个很受欢迎的演出,所以一定要提前订票。
[考点] in advance 预先,事先;in advance of 在……前面,比……进步

advanced[12] [əd'vɑːnst] *a.* **超前的,先进的;高级的;开明的;前进的**
[语境] Ancient Greece was an advanced civilization.
古希腊是个先进的文明国家。
My younger brother studied advanced math.
我弟弟学过高等数学。

advantage[15] [əd'vɑːntɪdʒ] *n.* **优点,有利条件;利益,好处**
[巧记] 反义词:disadvantage(*n.* 不利,劣势,短处)
[语境] Earthenware has an advantage over wood in being more easily kept clean.

陶器的优点在于比木器更容易保持清洁。

Rich has an advantage over you since he can speak German.

理奇比你占优势,因为他会讲德语。

[考点] advantage over sb./sth. 和人或物相比有优势;take advantage of 利用别人的弱点占便宜;欺骗;to sb.'s advantage 对……有利

考点集训

1. The Labor Party's electoral strategy, based on an _____ with other smaller parties, has proved successful.
   A. acquaintance   B. integration
   C. alliance   D. curious

2. In calculating the daily calorie requirements for an individual, variations in body size, physical activity and age should be _____.
   A. brought into practice   B. taken into account
   C. thrown light on   D. looked down upon

3. It is too early to say whether IBM's competitors will be able to _____ their products to the new hardware at an affordable cost.
   A. adapt   B. stick
   C. yield   D. adopt

4. The author was required to submit an _____ of about 200 words together with his research paper.
   A. edition   B. editorial
   C. article   D. abstract

5. I'd _____ his reputation with other farmers and business people in the community, and then make a decision about whether or not to approve a loan.
   A. take into account   B. account for
   C. make up for   D. make out

6. There's the living room still to be _____, so that's my next project.
   A. abandoned   B. decorated

· 13 ·

C. dissolved   D. assessed
7. The writer was so _____ in her work that she didn't notice him enter the room.
   A. absorbed   B. abandoned
   C. focused   D. centered
8. I suggested he should _____ himself to his new conditions.
   A. adapt   B. adopt
   C. regulate   D. suit
9. He is quite sure that it's _____ impossible for him to fulfill the task within two days.
   A. absolutely   B. exclusively
   C. fully   D. roughly
10. For professional athletes, _____ to the Olympics means that they have a chance to enter the history books.
    A. access   B. attachment
    C. appeal   D. approach
11. There is no _____ to their house from the main road.
    A. access   B. avenue
    C. exposure   D. edge
12. The statistical figures in that report are not _____. You should not refer to them.
    A. accurate   B. fixed
    C. delicate   D. rigid
13. The author of the report is well _____ with the problems in the hospital because he has been working there for many years.
    A. informed   B. acquainted
    C. enlightened   D. acknowledged
14. He soon received promotion, for his superiors realized that he was a man of considerable _____.
    A. ability   B. future
    C. possibility   D. opportunity
15. If people feel hopeless, they don't bother to _____ the skills

they need to succeed.

A. adopt
B. acquire
C. accumulate
D. assemble

16. Mr. Jones holds strong views against video games and _____ the closing of all recreation facilities for such games.

A. assists
B. acknowledges
C. advocates
D. admits

17. The London Marathon is a difficult race. _____, thousands of runners participate every year.

A. Therefore
B. Furthermore
C. Accordingly
D. Nevertheless

答案与解析

1. C 工党的竞选策略是与其他较小的政党结盟，答案是 C(结盟)。

2. B 在计算一个人每天所需要摄入的卡路里的标准数量时，我们必须考虑到由于身体尺寸、活动多少和年纪的不同所造成的一些差异。brought into practice"投入到实践中";taken into account"考虑到";thrown light on"使……清楚些";looked down upon"藐视,瞧不起"。

3. A 现在断言IBM的竞争对手能否让其产品适应新的硬件的要求,尚且还早。A 适应;B 坚持;C 收获,屈服;D 采用。故选 A。

4. D 作者被要求提交大约200字的摘要和它的研究论文。A 版本,版次;B 编辑的;C 文章;D 摘要。故选 D。

5. A 我想先考虑下他与社会上其他农民和商人的关系,然后再决定是否通过贷款申请。A 把……考虑在内;B 解释,说明;C 弥补;D 理解,假装,辨认出,填写表格。故 A 为正确答案。

6. B 根据题干中 the living room 和 so that's my next project,再结合四个选项,abandon 表示"放弃,遗弃";decorate 表示"装饰";dissolve 表示"溶解";assess 表示"估定,评定"。只有 decorated 符合题意,答案为 B。

7. A 因为作家全神贯注地在工作,她没注意到他进入房间。be absorbed in sth. 全心全意做某事,故选 A。

8. A　我建议他调整自己适应新环境。A 调整,调节;B 采用;C 管理;D 适合。故 A 为正确答案。

9. A　他十分清楚在两天内完成这份工作是绝对不可能的。A 绝对地;B 专门地,专有地;C 完全地;D 大概地。因此正确答案为 A。

10. A　对专业运动员而言,参加奥林匹克运动会意味着他们的名字有机会载入史书。A 进入;使用权;B 附件;C 恳求,呼吁,吸引力;D 方式,方法。故选 A。

11. A　从主干道没法去他们家。A 通道;B 大街,大道;C 暴露;D 边缘。故 A 为正确答案。

12. A　那份报告里的数据不准确,你不要参考它们。A 准确的;B 固定的;C 精致的;D 僵化的。故 A 为正确答案。

13. B　作报告的人对医院的问题很清楚,因为他在那里工作了很长时间。A 告知;B 清楚,熟悉;C 启迪,启蒙;D 承认,感激。故 B 为正确答案。

14. A　没过多久他就升职了,因为他的上级意识到他是一个很有能力的人。A 能力;B 将来;C 可能性;D 机会。故 A 为正确答案。

15. B　如果人们绝望的话,他们不愿意去掌握成功需要的那些技巧。A 采用;B 获得;C 积累;D 组装。故 B 为正确答案。

16. C　琼斯先生强烈反对视频游戏,提倡关停这些游戏的所有娱乐设施。A 帮助;B 承认,感激;C 支持,拥护;D 承认。故选 C。

17. D　根据题干中前后两句的逻辑关系,得知空格处填入的词应该表示转折关系。therefore 表示"因此";furthermore 表示"此外,而且";accordingly 表示"因此,从而";nevertheless 表示"然而,不过"。答案为 D。

Word List 2

adventure [əd'ventʃə(r)] n. 冒险,冒险活动,奇遇 vt. 大胆进行
[巧记] 派生词:adventurer (n. 探险家);adventurism(n. 冒险主义)
[语境] Reading adventure stories quickened my imagination. 阅读

冒险故事激发了我的想象力。

advertise[4] [ˈædvətaɪz] *vt.* 公告,公布;为……做广告 *vi.* 登广告

[巧记] 派生词:advertisement[4](*n.* 广告); advertising(*n.* 广告业)

[语境] If you want to sell your product you must advertise it.
如果你要推销自己的产品,你就必须做广告。

[考点] advertise for 登招请[待聘等]广告

advice [ədˈvaɪs] *n.* 劝告,忠告,(医生等的)意见

[巧记] 同义词:counsel,suggestion,recommendation

[语境] His advice has been invaluable to the success of the project.
他的建议对这一工程的成功起了无法估量的作用。
He disregarded my advice.
他无视我的忠告。

[考点] ask advice of 向……征求意见,请教; follow sb.'s advice 接受某人的意见

advise [ədˈvaɪz] *vt.* 忠告,劝告,建议;通知,告知

[语境] The doctor advised him specifically not to eat fatty food.
医生特别劝他不要吃多脂肪的食物。

[考点] advise sb. of 把……报告[通知]某人

aeroplane = airplane

[语境] He played a searchlight upon the aeroplane.
他向飞机打探照灯。

affair[5] [əˈfeə(r)] *n.* [*pl.*]事务;事情(件);(个人的)事

[巧记] af(= to) + fair(集市):反复不断地去集市→事务多

[语境] The premier deals with important affairs of state.
总理处理国家重要事务。

affect[28] [əˈfekt] *vt.* 影响;感动;(疾病)侵袭

[巧记] 派生词:affection(*n.* 喜爱,爱); affected (*a.* 受影响的,受侵袭的); affecting(*a.* 令人感动的)

[语境] He was much affected by the sad news.
这个悲惨的消息使他非常难过。
The climate affected his health.
气候影响了他的健康。

afford[4] [əˈfɔːd] *vt.* 提供,给予;供应得起,负担得起
[巧记] 派生词:affordable(*a.* 负担得起的)
[语境] I can't afford a holiday this summer.
今年夏天我无法度假。
These trees afford a pleasant shade.
这些树提供了阴凉。
[考点] afford 通常和 can/could/be able to 连用,表示省出或找到足够的时间或金钱

afraid [əˈfreɪd] *a.* 害怕的,恐惧的;犯愁的,不乐意的
[巧记] 同义词:cowardly, fearful, frightened, scared
反义词:bold, brave
[语境] She was afraid that she might lose her job.
她担心会丢掉工作。
I'm afraid what you're saying now is off the point.
恐怕你现在所说的有些离题。
[考点] be afraid of 害怕; be afraid to do sth. 不敢做某事

Africa [ˈæfrɪkə] *n.* 非洲
[语境] The giraffe ranges in Africa.
长颈鹿生长在非洲。

African [ˈæfrɪkən] *a.* 非洲(人)的
[语境] A large number of independent African countries emerge at a historic moment.
一大批非洲独立国家应运而生。

after [ˈɑːftə(r)] *prep.* 在……以后;在……后面 *ad.* 以后,后来
[语境] After a fierce battle the enemy was forced to retreat.
激战之后,敌人被迫撤退了。
They arrived shortly after.
不久以后他们抵达了。
[考点] After you! [口] 您先请!

afternoon [ˌɑːftəˈnuːn] *n.* 下午,午后
[语境] He dozed away the afternoon.
他打了一下午的瞌睡。

[考点] in the afternoon 在下午

again [ə'gen] *ad.* 再次,另一次;重新;除此,再,更,还

[语境] I have explained again and again, but even now they don't understand.

我已经解释了一遍又一遍,尽管如此,他们还是不明白。

[考点] again and again 一次又一次地,反复地;ever and again 不时地;时时地;now and again 间或,不时地;once again 再次;over and (over) again 一再地,翻来覆去;time and (time) again 多次,一再地

against [ə'genst] *prep.* 对着,逆;反对;违反;紧靠着;对比

[巧记] 同义词:in opposition to, versus;反义词:for

[语境] The people rose against their leaders.

人民起来反抗他们的首领。

Against all expectations, the play was greatly welcomed.

出乎意料的是,那出戏大受欢迎。

[考点] over against 在……对面;与……成鲜明的对比

age [eɪdʒ] *n.* 年龄;时代;老年;长时间 *v.* (使)变老

[语境] People of the Stone Age used rude tools.

石器时代的人使用粗糙简陋的工具。

The whisky has aged for twenty-five years.

这种威士忌酒已存放了二十五年了。

[考点] at the age of 在……岁时;for ages 很长的时间,很久

agency[13] ['eɪdʒənsɪ] *n.* 代理(处),代办(处)

[语境]The agency places about 4,000 young persons per annum.

该代理机构每年为4 000名年轻人安排工作。

agenda [ə'dʒendə] *n.* 议事日程,记事册

[巧记] 联想记忆:代理处(agency)每天都要有日程(agenda)

[语境] What's on your agenda today?

你今天有哪些工作要做?

agent['eɪdʒənt] *n.* 代理人,经办人

[语境]They are trawling London for an agent.

他们正在伦敦搜罗一个代理人。

ago [ə'gəʊ] *ad.* (常和一般过去时的动词连用)以前,……前
[语境]The dinosaurs disappeared long ago.
恐龙很久以前就绝种了。
[考点]long ago 很久以前,从前;some time ago 不久前

agree [ə'griː] *vi.* 答应,赞同;适合,一致;商定,约定
[语境] They agreed to give the matter top priority.
他们同意优先考虑这件事。
The two sides agreed on a cease-fire.
双方达成了停火协议。
[考点] agree on/upon 对……达成协议;对……取得一致意见;
agree to sth. 同意某事;agree with 同意……的意见;与……一致

agreeable [ə'griːəbl] *a.* 使人愉快的;欣然同意的;适合的
[巧记]agree(同意,赞同) + 后缀-able(表示可以的)→能得出一致意见或想法的→适合的;令人愉快的
[语境]I have really spent the most agreeable evening.
我确实过了最令人愉快的夜晚。
I regard them as my most agreeable companion.
我把它们看作我最称心如意的伴侣。

agreement [ə'griːmənt] *n.* 协定;协议;契约;达成协议;同意,一致
[巧记] agree(同意,赞同) + 后缀-ment(表示行为,行为的过程或结果)
[语境] We clinched the agreement with a handshake.
我们握手达成协议。
[考点] make an agreement with 与……达成协议

ahead [ə'hed] *ad.* 在前面(头);向(朝)前;提前
[语境] We must look ahead before we make a decision.
我们做出决定之前必须想得远一点。
[考点] ahead of 在……前头;早于;超过

aid[8] [eɪd] *n.* 援助,救护;助手,辅助物 *vi.* 援助,援救
[语境] They offer financial aid with no strings attached.
他们无条件提供财务援助。

[考点] aid, assist, help 辨析：aid 是正式用词，指帮助他人脱离危险或战胜困难，着重强者对急需帮助的弱者的帮助。assist 强调在提供帮助时，以受助者为主，所给的帮助起第二位或从属的作用。help 是最普通用词，含义广泛。指一般性的或迫切需要的帮助，侧重积极地为他人提供物质、精神或其他方面的帮助

aim[16] [eɪm] *n.* 目的；瞄准 *vi.* (at) 目的在于 *vt.* 把……瞄准

[语境] The aim of a university should be the advancement of learning.
大学的目标应是促进学术。
We'll aim for quality.
我们将力求提高质量。

[考点] aim at 向……瞄准；旨在，针对；志在

air [eə(r)] *n.* 空气；(复数) 神气 *vt.* (使) 通风；晾干

[语境] Air is a medium for sound.
空气是声音的传播媒介。
The sheets were aired on the line.
床单都晾在绳上。

[考点] by air 乘飞机；up in the air 悬而未决，慌乱

airline ['eəlaɪn] *n.* 航空公司；(飞机的) 航线

[巧记] air(空) + line(线) → 空中的线条 → 航线

[语境] About 20 percent of airline revenues comes from air freight.
航空公司大约 20% 的收入来自航空运输。
The airplane from the airport flies along its airline.
从机场上开出的飞机，沿着航线飞行。

airplane ['eəpleɪn] *n.* 飞机

[语境] The airplane cracked up in landing.
这架飞机在着陆时坠毁。

airport ['eəpɔːt] *n.* 机场

[语境] He drove me to the airport.
他开车送我到机场。

alcohol ['ælkəhɒl] *n.* 酒精，乙醇

[语境]He was stupefied with alcohol.

他喝酒喝得神志不清了。

alike [əˈlaɪk] *a.* 相同的,相似的

[语境] The sisters are as alike as two peas.

两姐妹长得一模一样。

No two people think alike.

没有两个人的想法是一样的。

[考点] alike 只能作表语,不能用在名词前。还可以用作副词,表示"同样地,相似地"

alive[10] [əˈlaɪv] *a.* 活着的;存在的;活跃的;(to)敏感的

[语境] The injured man is unconscious but still alive.

受伤的人不省人事但仍活着。

Although he is eighty, he is still very much alive.

他虽有八十岁了,但仍然充满了活力。

[考点] alive,live,living 辨析:均有"活着的,活的"之意。alive,其反义词为 dead,指生命从奄奄一息到精力旺盛的各种状态。live 通常作定语,指活生生的、生气勃勃的,还可以表示现场直播的。living,其反义词为 dead,指包括人和动植物的生命没有消失、仍然存在的状态

all [ɔːl] *a.* 全部的;非常的 *ad.* 完全地,很 *pron.* 全部

[语境] All governments should make a concerted effort to stop the drug trade.

各国政府应协调一致努力阻止毒品交易。

[考点] above all 表示"最重要的是,首先;尤其是"; after all 表示"毕竟,终究,归根结底"; over all 表示"到处,遍及;总的说来"; all but 表示"几乎,差一点;除……外全部"

allow[37] [əˈlaʊ] *vt.* 允许,准许;承认;给予;(for)考虑到

[巧记] 都(all)低下(low)头,表同意

[语境] Swimming is not allowed at this beach.

这片海滩禁止游泳。

A true democracy allows free speech.

真正的民主国家允许言论自由。

[考点] allow for 估计到，考虑到；allow of 容许；许可

almost [ˈɔːlməust] *ad.* 几乎，差不多

[巧记] 同义词：close to, just about, nearly

[语境] It is almost impossible to skirt the knotty problem.

想回避这个棘手的问题几乎是不可能的。

alone [əˈləun] *a.* 单独的，孤独的 *ad.* 单独地，独自地；仅仅

[语境] Peace alone could not bring bread to the masses.

和平自身并不能给大众带来必需的食品。

[考点] all alone 独自一人，孤零零地；let alone 至于……更不必说

along [əˈlɔŋ] *ad.* 向前；和……一起，一同 *prep.* 沿着，顺着

[语境] Ivy creeps along the fence.

常春藤攀着篱笆生长。

[考点] along with 和……一起[一道]，随着；除……以外（还）

aloud [əˈlaud] *ad.* 出声地，大声地

[巧记] 反义词：quietly, silently

[语境] The English teacher stressed the importance of reading aloud.

英语老师强调了朗读的重要性。

[考点] aloud, loud, loudly 辨析：均含有"高声地、大声地"之意。aloud 强调出声，能让人听见，无比较级。用于修饰 cry, call, shout 等动词时，有"高声"之意。loud 指声音响亮，高声说话，一般放在所修饰的动词后面。loudly 与 loud 含义相同，可放在动词之前或之后，用以说明声音的强度，含"喧闹"的意味

already [ɔːlˈredɪ] *ad.* 已，已经，早已

[巧记] all（所有）+ ready（准备好）→所有都准备好了→已经

[语境] This plant is already conditioned to the northern climate.

这一作物已适应了北方气候。

also [ˈɔːlsəu] *ad.* 而且（也），此外（还）；同样地

[语境] The president is also the chief of the armed forces.

总统也是三军的统帅。

[考点] as also 同样（也），照样（又）

· 23 ·

although [ɔːlˈðəʊ] *conj.* 尽管,虽然……但是
  [语境] Although there is a parliament, the army is in effective control of the country.
  虽然有议会存在,但实际上军队控制着这个国家。

altogether [ˌɔːltəˈɡeðə(r)] *ad.* 完全,总之,全部地;总共;总而言之
  [语境] Altogether, exports are looking up.
  总的说来,出口贸易在好转。
  [考点] for altogether 永久地;一劳永逸地

always [ˈɔːlweɪz] *ad.* 总是,无例外地;永远,始终
  [语境] We always trust in her cautiousness.
  我们一向相信她办事谨慎。

amazing [əˈmeɪzɪŋ] *a.* 令人惊讶的,令人吃惊的
  [语境] One of the amazing things about life, for me, is that we have a choice in everything we do.
  对于我来说,生活让人惊讶的是,我们在做每一件事时都可以做出选择。

ambassador [æmˈbæsədə(r)] *n.* 大使
  [巧记] embassy(*n.* 大使馆)ambassadress(*n.* 大使夫人)
  [语境] She agreed to accompany the ambassador.
  她同意陪大使。

ambition [æmˈbɪʃən] *n.* 雄心;野心
  [语境] Ambition winged his spirit.
  雄心驱策他进取。
  Her ambition knows no limit.
  她的野心没有限度。
  [考点] ambition 指不畏艰险,从事困难工作的进取精神和事业心,可用于褒义,也可用于贬义

ambitious [æmˈbɪʃəs] *a.* 有抱负的,雄心勃勃的;有野心的
  [巧记] 派生词:ambitiously(*ad.* 雄心勃勃地);ambitiousness(*n.* 不凡的抱负)
  [语境] She is an ambitious woman.
  她是一个雄心勃勃的女人。

ambulance [ˈæmbjʊləns] *n.* 救护车

[巧记]谐音记忆法:我不想死→救护车

[语境]The old man had hopped off when the ambulance reached the hospital.

当救护车开到医院时,那老人已经死了。

America [əˈmerɪkə] *n.* 美洲;美国

[语境]She scampered in London then went back to America.

她在伦敦匆忙地游览了一番,然后回到了美国。

American [əˈmerɪkən] *a.* 美洲(人)的;美国(人)的 *n.* 美洲人;美国人

[语境]He operated in an American company.

他在一家美国公司供职。

among/amongst [əˈmʌŋ; ˈəmʌŋst] *prep.* 在……之中;在一群(组)之中;于……之间

[语境]Rivalry among business firms grew more intense.

公司间的竞争变得更加激烈了。

考点集训

1. He is quick to _____ himself to new circumstances.
   A. adopt   B. adore
   C. adapt   D. adept

2. You can not see through a telescope unless it is correctly _____ to your sight.
   A. adapted   B. adjoined
   C. adjusted   D. adjudged

3. _____ pollution control measures tend to be money consuming, many industries hesitate to adopt them.
   A. Although   B. However
   C. When   D. Since

4. But what's the _____ of using nuclear power?
   A. interest   B. benefit
   C. profit   D. advantages

5. Without computer network, it would be impossible to carry on _____ any business operation in the advanced countries.
   A. practically   B. preferably
   C. precisely   D. possibly
6. He _____ that a combination of recent oil discoveries and the advance of new technology will lead to a decline in the price of crude oil.
   A. predicts   B. compels
   C. arranges   D. disputes
7. The rain will _____ our plan for a picnic.
   A. affect   B. influence
   C. effect   D. infect
8. We can't afford to let the situation get worse. We have to take _____ to put it right.
   A. decisions   B. advantages
   C. sides   D. steps
9. The twins are so much _____ that it is difficult to tell one from the other.
   A. similar   B. alike
   C. same   D. likely
10. He has a/an _____ from the government for travelling expenses.
    A. tuition   B. fee
    C. allowance   D. pension
11. She often _____ her clothes according to the latest fashion.
    A. changes   B. varies
    C. alters   D. alternates
12. He _____ me by his wonderful speech.
    A. admired   B. amazed
    C. wondered   D. advised
13. The statement completely laid bare their _____ for world conquest.

A. enterprise B. ambition
C. aspiration D. admiration

14. Many youngsters have heard their parents say "You'll never amount to _____ anything if you keep daydreaming that way!"
    A. be equal to B. accomplish
    C. add up to   D. pursue

15. The shy girl felt quite _____ and uncomfortable when she could not answer the interviewer's question.
    A. amused   B. sensitive
    C. curious D. awkward

16. Norman Davis will be remembered by many with _____ not only as a great scholar but also as a most delightful and faithful friend.
    A. kindness B. friendliness
    C. warmth   D. affection

17. My brother's plans are very _____; he wants to master English, French and Spanish before he is sixteen.
    A. arbitrary   B. aggressive
    C. ambitious   D. abundant

18. Only those who can _____ to lose their money should make high-risk investments.
    A. maintain B. sustain
    C. endure   D. afford

答案与解析

1. C 他很快就会适应新环境。adopt 采纳,采取;adore 敬爱;adapt 适应;adept 熟练的。

2. C 除非你把望远镜调节得完全适合你的眼力,否则你看不见。adapted 修改和做大的改变;adjoined 毗邻;adjusted 调整;adjudged 判决,宣判。

3. D 由于控制污染措施需花费大笔资金,因此许多厂家迟迟不采用它们。

27

4. B　可是利用核电的优点在哪里？interest 常用作复数,表示"利益";benefit 和 profit 都是指好处,profit 尤其指金钱上的好处。

5. A　如果没有计算机网络,在发达国家进行商业操作几乎是不可能的。

6. A　他预言最近石油的发现和科技进步的结合将导致原油价格下跌。predict 预测;compel 驱使,迫使,逼迫,操纵;arrange 安排;dispute 争论,争执,吵架。

7. A　下雨会影响我们的郊游计划。influence 指通过做出行动或榜样以影响别人,左右他人的思想和情感。effect 是名词,infect 感染,传染。

8. D　我们担负不起让形势继续恶化下去,我们必须采取措施纠正错误。take steps/measures 表示采取措施,采取手段。

9. B　这对双胞胎长得非常像,使你无法辨认。likely 可能的;similar 类似的,说外表像常用 similar in。

10. C　他可以得到政府发给的旅游津贴。fee 指付给专业人员的酬金、报酬等;tuition 指大学或学院的学费;pension 养老金,退休金。

11. C　她常根据最流行样式修改服装。change 指的是换衣服;vary 并不表示质上的变化;alternate 交替变化。

12. B　他出色的演讲使我十分惊奇。admired 钦佩,佩服;wondered 感到惊奇,诧异,多与 at 连用;advised 提议。

13. B　这句话充分地暴露了他们要征服世界的野心。enterprise 进取精神;aspiration 愿望,希望,期望;admiration 赞赏,钦佩。

14. B　许多年轻人经常听到父母这样说:如果还这样做白日梦,你将一事无成。accomplish 实现/完成。

15. D　这个害羞的女孩答不出记者的提问,她感到十分尴尬和不舒服。awkward 尴尬的;curious 古怪的,好奇的;sensitive 敏感的。

16. D　许多人会永远铭记诺曼·达维斯的,因为他不仅是一位伟大的学者,也是一位和蔼可亲、值得信赖的朋友。with affection 热情洋溢,固定搭配,故选 D。

17. C　我弟弟的计划很宏大,他想在 16 岁前掌握英语、法语和西班牙语。A 随意的;B 侵略性的,雄心的;C 有雄心的,宏伟的;

D 大量的。故 C 为正确答案。
18. D 只有承受得起亏钱的那些人才应该做高风险的投资。A 保持；B 持续；C 忍受；D 支付，承受。故选 D。

Word List 3

amount[24] [əˈmaʊnt] *n.* 数量，数额，总数 *vt.* (to) 合计，相当于，等同

[语境] It all amounts to a lot of hard work.
那一切意味着大量艰苦的工作。
The amount of unemployed capital is very large.
未被利用的资金数量很大。

[考点] in amount 总之，总计； amount to 总计

amuse [əˈmjuːz] *vt.* 给……提供娱乐；使开心

[巧记] 派生词：amused (*a.* 愉快的，好玩的)；amusing (*a.* 好笑的，有趣的)

[语境] The boys amuse themselves by drawing caricatures of their teacher.
男孩子以画老师的漫画取乐。
The actors were really hamming it up to amuse the audience.
这些演员为博观众一乐，表演得实在太过火了。

[考点] amuse sb. by sth. 用……逗乐某人

analysis[9] [əˈnæləsɪs] *n.* (*pl.* analyses) 分析；分解

[巧记] 反义词：synthesis 综合

[语境] Your critical analysis helped me a great deal.
你的评论分析对我帮助很大。

analyze/-yse [ˈænəlaɪz] *vt.* 分析，解析

[语境] Let's analyze the problem and see what went wrong.
让我们分析一下这道题，看什么地方出错了。
Analyze the sentence into its constituent parts.
把这个句子的各个成分加以分析。

ancient[8] [ˈeɪnʃənt] *a.* 古代的,古老的

[语境] This stone axe is a relic of ancient times.
把石斧是古代的遗物。
Soldiers in ancient times used escutcheon to fight.
古代的士兵用饰有花纹的盾作战。

[考点] ancient, old, antique 辨析:这些形容词均含"古代的,古老的"之意。ancient 指很久以前发生或存在的事物。用于描述历史时,指远古时代。old 指长期以来一直存在着的事物,与 times 连用指古代,与 days 连用时指从前或旧社会。antique 指已经很古老或颇有古风的事物,一般都具有较高价值

and [ənd, ænd] *conj.* 和,与,而且;那么;接连,又

[语境] Adam and Eve are the first man and the first woman in the *Bible*.
亚当和夏娃是《圣经》中的第一个男人和女人。

anger[4] [ˈæŋgə(r)] *n.* 愤怒,气愤 *vt.* 使发怒,激怒 *vi.* 发怒

[巧记] 派生词:angerly(*ad.* 愤怒地)

[语境] His anger was unreasonable, a storm in a teacup.
他发怒毫无道理,只是小题大做。

[考点] bluster oneself into anger 勃然大怒

angry [ˈæŋgrɪ] *a.* 生气的,愤怒的;(天气)风雨交加的

[语境] She was so angry that she actually tore up the letter.
她一气之下竟然将信撕碎了。

animal [ˈænɪml] *n.* 动物,野兽,牲畜 *a.* 动物的,野兽的

[语境] I kept my friend back from the dangerous animal.
我不让我的朋友靠近那个危险的动物。

annoy[5] [əˈnɔɪ] *vt.* 使烦恼,使生气,打搅

[语境] We can annoy the enemy by raids.
我们可用袭击骚扰敌人。
A fly kept annoying me.
一只苍蝇老在打搅我。

[考点] be annoyed at 对……烦恼;生气

annual[16] [ˈænjʊəl] *a.* 每年的,年度的 *n.* 年鉴,年刊

[巧记] 派生词：annually (*n.* 一年一次，每年)

[语境] Many garden plants are annuals.

许多观赏植物都是一年生的。

How much is his annual salary?

他的年薪是多少？

another [əˈnʌðə(r)] *a.* 另一个，又，再 *pron.* 另一个，类似的一个

[语境] There was another rainfall early this morning.

今天清晨又下了一场雨。

[考点] one after another 相继地

answer [ˈɑːnsə(r)] *n.* 回答，答复，答案 *v.* 回答，答复，响应

[语境] Her answer was affirmative.

她的回答是肯定的。

He answered that he knew nothing about it.

他答道他不知道这件事。

[考点] in answer to 为了回答；为了响应

anticipate [ænˈtɪsɪpeɪt] *vt.* 预料；期望；预先考虑；抢先；提前使用

[巧记] 派生词：anticipated (*a.* 预先的；预期的)

[语境] It is impossible to anticipate when it will happen.

不可能预料这事何时发生。

anxiety [æŋˈzaɪətɪ] *n.* 挂念，担心；渴望，热望

[语境] The doctor's report removed all their anxieties.

医生的报告消除了他们的一切忧虑。

It proved difficult to disguise his anxiety.

他的焦虑难以掩饰。

[考点] in anxiety 担忧着，挂念着；with anxiety 焦虑地

anxious [ˈæŋkʃəs] *a.* 焦虑的，担心的；急于（得到的），渴望的

[巧记] 派生词：anxiously (*ad.* 忧虑地，不安地)

[语境] We're anxious for your safe return.

我们盼望你平安归来。

[考点] be anxious for 渴望，期盼；be anxious to 渴望要……

any [ˈenɪ] *a.* (用于否定句、疑问句等) 什么，一些；任何的

[语境] Without any hesitation, he jumped into the river to save the drowning child.

他毫不犹豫地跳下河去救溺水的孩子。

anybody ['enɪˌbɒdɪ,-bədɪ] *pron.* [否定、疑问、条件句中]任何人；[肯定句中]随便哪一个人

[语境]She swore me not to tell anybody about my secret.

她向我发誓不把我的秘密告诉任何人。

anyhow ['enɪhaʊ] *ad.* 无论如何,不管怎样；不管以什么方法；总之

[语境]Anyhow Tony intended to acknowledge him as his son.

不管怎样托尼打算承认他为自己的儿子。

anyone = anybody

anything ['enɪθɪŋ] *pron.* [否定、疑问、条件句中]任何事(物)；无论什么事(物)

[语境]She bawls for anything she wants.

她要什么东西总是大喊大叫。

anyway = anyhow

[语境]We can only ever do one step at a time anyway.

不管怎样,我们只能一步一个脚印往前走。

anywhere ['enɪweə(r)] *ad.* 无论哪里；(用于否定、疑问等)任何地方

[语境]He never got anywhere in politics. He's just an also-ran.

他在政治上毫无进展,他只是一位失败者。

apartment [ə'pɑːtmənt] *n.* 一套房间

[语境]We leased an apartment from the school.

我们从学校租到了一套公寓住房。

apologize/-ise [ə'pɒlədʒaɪz] *v.* (to,for)道歉,认错

[语境]I won't apologize unless she apologizes first.

除非她先道歉,否则我不道歉。

[考点]apologize to sb. 向某人道歉

apology [ə'pɒlədʒɪ] *n.* 道歉,歉意

[巧记]派生词:apologetic (*a.* 表示道歉的); apologize (*v.* 道歉)

[语境]Your allegations are completely untrue, and I demand an immediate apology.

你的说法完全不真实,我要求你立即道歉。

The Finance Director sends her apology and is unable to attend the meeting.

财务总监派人带话说,她因不能出席会议而向大家道歉。

appear [ə'pɪə(r)] *vi.* 出现,出场,问世;好像是

[巧记] 派生词:appearance (*n.* 出现,现身)

[语境] A truck appeared over the hill.

一辆卡车在山丘上出现。

Mr. Green had to appear before the committee to explain his behavior.

格林先生必须在委员会上出面解释他的行为。

appetite ['æpɪtaɪt] *n.* 食欲,胃口;欲望,性欲;爱好,趣味

[语境] Exercise gave her a good appetite.

运动使她胃口大增。

apply[10] [ə'plaɪ] *vi.* (for) 申请 *vt.* (to) 运用,应用

[语境] In this way they can better apply theory to practice.

这样他们就能更好地把理论运用到实践中去。

This rule cannot be applied to every case.

这项规则不是所有情况都适用。

[考点] application (*n.* 申请)经常和 for 连用,当表示"运用"时,经常和 to 连用。apply oneself to 努力进行,致力于;apply to sb. 适用于;apply for sth. 申请得到

appoint [ə'pɔɪnt] *vt.* 任命,委派;指定,约定(时间、地点等)

[巧记] ap(= to 到) + point(点):到某一地点去,即指定

[语境] He was appointed ambassador to France.

他被任命为驻法国大使。

appointment[5] [ə'pɔɪntmənt] *n.* 约会,约见;任命,委派

[巧记] appoint (*vt.* 任命,委派)

[语境] Rose had forgotten all about their appointment.

罗斯把他们的约会全忘掉了。

The whole family felicitated John on his new appointment.

全家为约翰新的任命向他表示祝贺。

appreciate [əˈpriːʃIeIt] *vt.* 感激,感谢;评价,欣赏,赏识

[巧记]派生词:appreciation(*n.* 感激,欣赏)

[语境] We appreciate your helping us.

我们感谢你们的帮助。

[考点] appreciate 后面如果跟动词作宾语,要使用动名词形式

approach[7] [əˈprəʊtʃ] *n.* 接近;看法,观点;办法 *vi.* 临近,接近 *vt.* 走近,接近;处理,对待

[语境] All approaches to the city were blocked.

通往这座城市的所有道路都被封锁了。

There are several ways of approaching the problem.

处理这个问题有好几种方法。

[考点] make approach to 想法接近(认识)某人

approval [əˈpruːvəl] *n.* 批准,通过;赞成,同意

[巧记]反义词:disapproval

[语境] The plan had the approval of the school authorities.

计划得到学校当局的认可。

[考点] give one's approval to 批准;nod one's approval 点头同意;meet with sb.'s approval 得到某人的赞同

April [ˈeIprəl] *n.* 四月

[语境]The workers were hustled to finish the work before April by the master.

老板催他的工人在四月前完成任务。

Arab[ˈærəb] *n.* 阿拉伯人 *a.* 阿拉伯的

[语境]They do these things well in the Arab world.

在阿拉伯世界,他们在这方面做得很好。

Arabian [əˈreIbIən] *n.* 阿拉伯人的 *a.* 阿拉伯的

[语境]Arabian work influenced it much without doubt.

阿拉伯人的工作无疑对其产生过重要的影响。

area[ˈeərIə] *n.* 地区,区域,面积,方面

[语境]This meadow epitomizes the beauty of the whole area.

这块草地是整个地区的美景之缩景。

The area of the bedroom is larger than that of the sitting room.

卧室的面积比起居室的面积大。

argue[14] [ˈɑːgjuː] *vi.* 辩论,争论 *vt.* 论证;说服

[语境] The United States should, he argues, attempt to remain aloof.

他认为,美国应保持超然态度。

[考点] argue for/against 赞成/反对; argue with sb./about sth. 与……争论

argument[11] [ˈɑːgjʊmənt] *n.* 争论(吵),辩论;理由;论证

[语境] The argument darkened her mood.

那场争吵弄得她心情很不愉快。

arise [əˈraɪz] *vi.* 出现,起来,升起

[语境] A heavy mist arose from the lake. 湖面起了浓雾。

Unexpected difficulties arose in the course of their experiment.

在他们进行实验的过程中出现了意想不到的困难。

考点集训

1. The food was _____ and found to contain amount of poison.
   A. anticipated			B. analogized
   C. alternated			D. analyzed
2. Floods have _____ the foundation of the ancient bridge.
   A. weakened			B. reached
   C. spoiled			D. covered
3. A warm sunshine _____ the coming of spring.
   A. declares			B. announces
   C. proclaims			D. publishes
4. The audience, hostile at first, were greatly _____ by her excellent performance.
   A. annoyed			B. encouraged
   C. impressed			D. depressed
5. The new automobile factory is expected to _____ around 30,000 to 50,000 vehicles annually in the first three years.
   A. assemble			B. service

C. supply D. repair
6. As his confidence in his work increased, his _____ about it diminished.
   A. concern B. anxiety
   C. expectation D. anticipation
7. But to _____ for their apparent laziness, they are actually very intelligent.
   A. compensate B. provide
   C. search D. account
8. Another important difference is that adults frequently must apply their knowledge in some _____ fashion in order to learn effectively.
   A. probable B. practical
   C. modern D. routine
9. The teacher _____ me to call the roll.
   A. appreciated B. approached
   C. approved D. appointed
10. I really appreciate _____ to help me, but I am sure that I can manage it myself.
    A. you to come B. that you come
    C. your coming D. how you come
11. Both approaches require that the actor _____ his or her own personal values as well as the character's.
    A. must understand B. should understand
    C. has to understand D. need to understand
12. How can we express our _____ for your help?
    A. appreciation B. compliment
    C. comprehension D. apprehension
13. Herman's success is due to his hard work and his ability to _____ plans which will get work done efficiently.
    A. fulfill B. approve
    C. conceive D. conduct

14. A major goal of the state travel agency is to _____ more people to visit its country at the turn of the century.
    A. reduce   B. expect
    C. arouse   D. induce

15. Arriving anywhere with these possessions, he might just as easily _____ for a month or a year as for a single day.
    A. arrange   B. manage
    C. last   D. stay

16. He informed _____ while carrying out his instructions.
    A. his arrest to the editor
    B. the editor his arrest
    C. the editor of his arrest
    D. the editor that his arrest had been

17. Many a player who had been highly thought of has _____ from the tennis scene.
    A. disposed   B. disappeared
    C. discouraged   D. discarded

18. It _____ without saying that consumers would be happier if prices were lower.
    A. takes   B. appears
    C. makes   D. goes

答案与解析

1. D 对这种食物进行了分析化验,发现了一定量的有毒成分。anticipated 预料,预感;analogized 类比为;alternate 交替,更替。

2. C 洪水已经使这座古桥失去了作用。spoil 破坏,毁坏;weaken 使变瘦弱,变弱小;reach 到达。

3. B 温暖的阳光预示着春天即将来临。declare 正式场合宣布官方的立场或态度;proclaims 官方宣布申明;publish 以口头或印刷的形式让人们知道。

4. C 她精彩的表演给一开始有些不满的观众留下了深刻的印象。annoyed 乏味的;encouraged 鼓励的;depressed 不振作的。

· 37 ·

5. A 人们期待这家新的汽车制造厂在前三年每年能生产30 000~50 000辆车。

6. B 随着对工作信心的增加,他的担心也随之消失。concern 关心,挂念;expectation, anticipation 期望。

7. A 为了弥补他们表面的懒惰,他们学习东西很快。compensate 补偿,弥补;provide 提供;search 搜寻;account 账目,数数。

8. B 另外一个重要的不同点是,成年人为了有效地学习,经常把知识应用在一些实用的时尚领域。probable 可能的;modern 现代的;routine 日常的,例行的,正常程序的。

9. D 老师指派我点了名。appreciated 感激;approached 走过,靠近;approved 证明;appoint sb. to do sth. 指派某人做某事。

10. C 非常感谢你来帮我,但是我认为我自己就行了。appreciate 后面跟动词作宾语,一定要用动名词形式。

11. B 两种方法都要求演员应该不仅要理解自身的价值,还要理解角色的价值。

12. A 我们该如何表达对你的感激之情呢?compliment 称赞,赞美;comprehension 理解,领悟;apprehension 忧虑,理解。

13. C 赫尔曼的成功依赖于他辛勤的工作和构想计划的能力,辛勤的工作和构想计划的能力使工作能够高效完成。fulfill 履行;approve 赞成;conduct 做。

14. D 国家旅行社的一个主要目的就是让更多的人在世纪之交到他们国家观光。induce 说服,促使;reduce 减少;expect 希望,期望;arouse 唤醒。

15. D 有了这些物品,不管到了什么地方,他都能很容易地待上一个月或一年就像待一天一样。arrange 安排;manage 管理;last 持续;stay 停留,暂住。

16. C 他通告编辑被捕了,这是在执行命令。固定短语:inform sb. of sth. 告知某人某事。D 中用的是宾语从句,但是句子不完整。

17. B 曾受到高度表扬的网球选手已经从网球界消失了。A 处理;B 消失;C 泄气;D 丢弃。故选 B。

18. D 是一个短语题,答案是 D,这个是固定搭配,表示毋庸置疑的意思。

Word List 4

arm [ɑːm] *n.* 手臂,臂状物;(*pl.*) 武器 *vt.* 武装,装备

[语境] He snatched at my arm.

他一把抓住了我的胳臂。

Driven beyond endurance, they led the villagers to arm themselves and prepare for action.

他们忍无可忍,领导乡亲们拿起武器准备行动。

It will not wait for you to arm yourself.

它不会等你武装好自己才来临。

around [əˈraʊnd] *ad.* 在……周围,到处 *prep.* 在……四周(或附近)

[语境] Ann travelled around Europe for a few months.

安妮在欧洲各地旅游了数月。

[考点] all around 四周,到处,处处

arouse[4] [əˈraʊz] *vt.* 唤醒,唤起,激起

[巧记] a(加强语气的前缀) + rouse(激起)→唤醒,唤起

[语境] Diana aroused them just before dawn.

戴安娜在黎明前唤醒了他们。

His sufferings aroused our sympathy.

他的痛苦引起了我们的同情。

arrange [əˈreɪndʒ] *vt.* 安排,整理,排列 *vi.* 安排,准备

[巧记] 派生词:arrangement (*n.* 安排)

[语境] I arranged the flowers in the vase as soon as I came back home.

一回到家里,我就把花插好在花瓶里。

I have arranged with him to meet at the restaurant.

我和他约好在饭馆见面。

arrangement[8] [əˈreɪndʒmənt] *n.* 安排,准备工作;整理,准备

[语境] I agree to this arrangement.

我同意这个安排。

Data arrangement is an important part of an information system.

数据整理是信息系统的重要组成部分。

[考点] make an arrangement for 为……做好安排

arrest [ə'rest] *vt./n.* 逮捕,拘留

[巧记] ar(向,朝) + rest(休息)→让一个人去反复不断休息→逮捕

[语境] The riot led to the arrest of three young men.

暴乱导致3个年轻人被捕。

The police arrested the thief.

警察逮捕了小偷。

arrive [ə'raɪv] *vi.* 到达;(时间、事件)到来,发生;达到

[语境] Mary arrived punctually at ten o'clock.

玛丽十点钟准时到达。

[考点] come, arrive, reach 辨析:这些动词均含"到达"之意。come 是普通用词,含义广泛,强调到达的动作或进程,不侧重是否到达目的地。也可用于比喻意义。arrive 侧重到达目的地或达到某一目标。也可用作比喻。reach 既可指到达目的地,又可指到达途中的中间站。强调经过的周折或付出的努力

article ['ɑːtɪkəl] *n.* 文章,论文;条款,条文;物件;冠词

[语境] The article was severely cut up by some critics.

那篇文章曾受到一些评论家严厉的抨击。

The article is a part of speech in the English language.

冠词是英语的一种词类。

artificial [ˌɑːtɪ'fɪʃəl] *a.* 人工的,人造的;做作的,不自然的

[巧记] 派生词:artificially (*ad.* 人工地); artificiality (*n.* 人工,不自然,人造物)

[语境] This orange drink contains no artificial flavourings.

这种橙汁饮品不含人工调味料。

Artificial heating hastens the growth of plants.

人工供暖能促进植物生长。

as [əz, æz] *ad.* 同样地 *conj.* 由于;像……一样 *prep.* 作为

[语境] Their friendship was as close as ever it had been.
他们的友谊跟以往一样亲密。
His job as a diplomat was just a screen for his life as a spy.
他做外交官的工作只不过是间谍生涯的一种掩护。

[考点] as for 至于;就……方面说来;as if/though 好像……似的;仿佛……一样;as it is 事实上,实际上;照现在的样子;as it were 仿佛,好像,可以说;as to 谈到;关于;至于

ashamed [əˈʃeɪmd] *a.* 惭愧的,羞愧的

[语境] He was ashamed that he had lied.
他很惭愧,他说了谎。
The poor boy was ashamed of his ragged cloths.
这个穷孩子为自己的破衣服感到难为情。

[考点] be ashamed of 以为……是耻辱;feel ashamed for sb. 替某人感到羞愧;be ashamed to do sth. 以干……为耻

Asia [ˈeɪʃə, ˈeɪʒə] *n.* 亚洲

[语境] The teacher chalked out a map of Asia on the blackboard.
老师用粉笔在黑板上画了一张亚洲地图。

Asian [ˈeɪʃən, ˈeɪʒən] *n.* 亚洲的

[语境] About half of its Asian sales come from China.
该公司在亚洲的销售额,约有一半来自中国。

aside [əˈsaɪd] *ad.* 在旁边,到一边 *n.* 旁白;离题的话

[语境] He stepped aside to let them pass.
他站到一旁让他们通过。

[考点] aside from 除了……以外

ask [ɑːsk; æsk] *vt.* 问,询问;请求,要求;邀请,约请

[语境] Ann asked many questions and I did my best to answer them.
安妮问了许多问题,我尽可能地回答。

[考点] ask, demand, inquire, question 辨析:这些动词均含有"问,询问"之意。ask 是普通用词,可与 demand, inquire 和 question 换用,但 ask 用于口语中,指提出问题让人回答。demand 指根据自己的权利、职责或身份认为有必要弄清情况

而正式发问,常隐含命令对方回答的意味。inquire 为较正式用词,指为得到真实情况而详细询问或调查了解。question 指因感到可疑或为了解情况,弄清究竟而发问,有时指一连串的发问

asleep [əˈsliːp] *a.* 睡着的,麻木的

[巧记]反义词:awake

[语境]He soon fell asleep and began to snore.
他很快睡着并开始打起鼾来。

[考点]sleepy, asleep 辨析:均含有"欲睡的"之意。sleepy 是常用词,指人昏昏欲睡,或沉睡时的寂静状态。asleep 作表语,多用于非正式的英语里,指处于睡着的状态,侧重动作的结果

aspect[8] [ˈæspekt] *n.* 样子,面貌;(问题、事物等的)方面

[语境]The whole scheme began to take on a more practical aspect.
整个计划开始具有更切合实际的性质。

I am a beginner in this aspect.
在这方面,我是一个生手。

[考点] all aspects 各个方面

assignment[7] [əˈsaɪnmənt] *n.* (分派的)任务,(指定的)作业;分配,指派

[巧记] assign (*v.* 分配,指派)

[语境] I begged off that assignment.
我恳求免除分派的那个任务。

Today I have an assignment for you.
今天,我要分配给你一个任务了。

[考点] job assignment 工作分工

assist [əˈsɪst] *vt.* 协助,帮助,促进 *vi.* 帮忙,参加

[巧记] 同义词: aid, help, support; 反义词: oppose, resist

[语境] She refused to assist at the reception for reasons unknown.
不知什么缘故她不肯出席招待会。

associate[6] [əˈsəʊʃieɪt] *vt.* 使发生关系,使联合 *vi.* 交往,结交 *a.* 合伙的,有联系的 *n.* 合伙人,同事

[巧记] 派生词:association (n. 协会,组织); associated (a. 联合的, 有关联的, 联想的)

[语境] I got a new job and a new set of work associations.
我有了新工作和一班新同事。
I don't want to associate myself with them any more.
我不愿再和他们交往了。

[考点] associate oneself with 加入；参与；与……发生联系；associate with 和……来往，联系

association[10] [əˌsəʊsɪˈeɪʃən] n. 联盟,协会,社团;交往,联合;联想

[语境] Have you joined the teachers' association?
你加入教师协会了吗?
I benefited much from my association with him.
我在跟他的交往中获益匪浅。

[考点] in association with 与……联合[结交, 有关联]

assume[5] [əˈsjuːm] vt. 假定,设想;承担,接受

[巧记] 派生词:assumption(n. 假定；承担)

[语境] I assumed you can speak French fluently.
我以为你能讲流利的法语。
I made a mistake and I will assume responsibility for it.
我错了,我愿为此承担责任。

assure [əˈʃʊə(r)] vt. 使确信,使放心;保证,担保

[巧记] as(to) + sure(确定):一再确定→肯定

[语境] We book early to assure ourselves of seats.
我们及早订票以确保有座。
Her success as an actress was now assured.
她当演员很成功,已毋庸置疑了。

astonish [əˈstɒnɪʃ] vt. 使大吃一惊

[巧记] 派生词:astonishing (a. 令人惊异的); astonishingly (ad. 令人吃惊地); astonishment (n. 惊讶, 惊奇)

[语境] I was astonished at the news of his escape.
听到他逃之夭夭的消息,我感到惊讶。
She astonished me with her beautiful handwriting.

她秀丽的书法使我惊异。

astronaut [ˈæstrənɔːt, -nɑt] *n.* 宇航员,太空人

[巧记] astro(宇宙) + naut(人)→翱翔宇宙的人→宇航员

[语境] Yes, I have wanted to be an astronaut.
是的,我想过要成为一个宇航员。

at [æt, ət] *prep.* (表示价格、速度等)以,达;在……方面

[语境] We arrived at the airport at four.
我们四点到达了机场。
He is an expert at troubleshooting.
他是位排解争端的能手。

atmosphere[8] [ˈætməsfɪə(r)] *n.* 空气;大气,大气层;气氛

[语境] Industrial wastes are poisoning the atmosphere of the country.
工业废物在污染着该国的大气。
The talks proceeded in a friendly atmosphere.
会谈在友好的气氛中进行。

atom[5] [ˈætəm] *n.* 原子

[语境] Might be an atom there.
可能这里有一个原子。

attack[14] [əˈtæk] *vt./n.* 攻击,袭击;(病)发作

[语境] The enemy attacked during the night.
敌人在夜间发动攻击。
The disease had already attacked the central nervous system.
疾病已侵犯了中枢神经系统。

[考点] under attack 遭袭击;make an attack 攻击,抨击

attempt[12] [əˈtempt] *vt./n.* 企图,试图

[巧记] a(= to) + tempt(引诱):尝试去引诱→企图

[语境] He attempted the exam but failed.
他试图通过考试,但失败了。
My early attempts at learning to drive were unsuccessful.
我曾经几次打算学开车,却都没有学成。

attend[7] [əˈtend] *vt.* 出席,参加;照顾,护理 *vi.* 注意;伴随

[语境] Danger attended everything he did.

他所做的每一件事都有危险。

They had a quiet wedding only a few friends attended (it).

他们的婚礼静悄悄的——只有几个朋友参加。

[考点] attend on 服侍,照料;陪,随从;attend to 倾听,注意,照料,关心

attention[26] [əˈtenʃən] *n.* **注意,注意力;立正;特别照顾;照料**

[巧记] 反义词:inadvertence(*n.* 不注意,漫不经心)

[语境] His whole attention was centered on this matter.

他的全部注意力都集中在此事上。

She gave her aging parents much attention.

她悉心照料年迈的双亲。

[考点] draw attention 引起注意;pay attention to 注意,重视,倾听;with attention 留心地,注意地

attitude[18] [ˈætɪtjuːd] *n.* **态度,看法**

[巧记] 同义词:opinion, position, standpoint, viewpoint

[语境] What is your attitude to the question?

你对这个问题的态度是什么呢?

It's not his work that bothers me; it's his attitude.

困扰我的不是他的工作,而是他的态度。

attract[18] [əˈtrækt] *vt.* **吸引,引诱**

[巧记] 派生词:attractable(*a.* 可被吸引的);attractability(*n.* 吸引性)

[语境] The flower show attracted large crowds this year.

今年的花展吸引了大批观众。

Do any of these designs attract you?

这些设计中有使你感兴趣的吗?

attractive [əˈtræktɪv] *a.* **有吸引力的,诱人的**

[巧记] 派生词:attractively (*ad.* 动人地,迷人地);attractiveness (*n.* 魅力,吸引力)

[语境] I think she is a very attractive girl.

我认为她是很有魅力的女孩。

Ice cream is attractive to children.

冰淇淋对孩子们非常有吸引力。

audience[13] [ˈɔːdjəns, ˈɔːdɪəns] *n.* 听众,观众

[巧记] audi(听) + ence(人)→听的人→听众

[语境] The audience reacted readily to his speech.

听众对他的演说立即做出反应。

audio [ˈɔːdɪəʊ] *n./a.* 声音(的),听觉(的);音频(的),音响(的)

[语境] I recommend you to use those sources that have both audio and transcripts.

我推荐你使用那些既有音频又有文本的资源。

August [ˈɔːɡəst] *n.* 八月

[语境] He moved to another city last August.

去年八月,他搬到另一座城市。

aunt [ɑːnt] *n.* 伯母,姑母,姨母

[语境] I was brought up by my paternal aunt.

我是由姑姑拉大的。

Australia [ɒˈstreɪlɪə] *n.* 澳洲;澳大利亚

[语境] Her children have gone to Australia, and she missed them very much.

孩子们去了澳大利亚,她非常惦记他们。

Australian [ɒˈstreɪlɪən] *a.* 澳洲的;澳大利亚的 *n.* 澳大利亚人

[语境] The Australian team had the added ingredient of perseverance.

澳大利亚队另外还具备了顽强的意志。

author [ˈɔːθə(r)] *n.* 作者

[语境] The author bared his heart to the world.

作家向全世界敞开他的心扉。

[考点] author, writer 辨析:这两个名词均有"作者,作家"之意。author:泛指用自己名字或笔名发表过作品的人,不强调是否以写作为主职业。writer:含义广泛,一般指以写作为职业的人

auto(mobile)[6] [ˈɔːtə(ˈməʊbɪl, -mə-)] *n.* 汽车

[语境] The parts of an automobile are standardized.

汽车零件是标准化了的。

autumn [ˈɔːtəm] *n.* 秋季,秋天

[语境] Leaves turn yellow in autumn.

树叶在秋天变黄。

[考点] in autumn 在秋天

available[22] [əˈveɪləbəl] *a.* 可利用的,可提供的

[巧记] 派生词:availability(*n.* 可用性, 实用性)

[语境] Do you have a room available?

你们有空房间吗?

Several cars are available within this price range.

在这个价格范围内,有好几种汽车可供选购。

[考点] available 常常指现成可利用的,可得到的

average[22] [ˈævərɪdʒ] *n.* 平均,平均数;一般水平,平均标准

[语境] The average age of the boys in this class is fifteen.

本班男生的平均年龄是十五岁。

Tom's work at school is above the average.

汤姆的功课是中上水平。

[考点] on an/the average 平均起来,一般来说

avoid[31] [əˈvɔɪd] *vt.* 避开,避免

[巧记] a 朝向, void 空→空城计→避开

[语境] The boy avoided punishment by running away.

那个男孩逃跑以逃避惩罚。

She tried to avoid answering my questions.

她试图避而不答我的问题。

[考点] avoid 后面跟动词要用 doing 形式

award [əˈwɔːd] *n.* 奖,奖品 *v.* 授予,将给

[语境] This new invention won the highest award.

这项新发明获得最高奖。

The general decided to promote him and award him with medals of bravery and honor.

将军决定提升他的官职并授予他英雄荣誉勋章。

[考点] award somebody something 授予某人某物

award, reward 辨析:这两个动词均有"给予奖励"之意。award:侧重指官方或经正式研究裁决后对有功者或竞赛优胜者所给予的奖励。reward:指对品德高尚和勤劳的人所给予的奖励;也可指为某事付酬金

aware[15] [əˈweə(r)] *a.* 意识到的,觉察到的

[巧记] 派生词:awareness(*n.* 知道,晓得)

[语境] We are fully aware of the gravity of the situation.
我们十分清楚形势的严峻性。
Are you aware that you are sitting on my hat?
你知道你坐在我的帽子上了吗?

[考点] be aware of 知道,意识到

away [əˈweɪ] *ad.* 在远处;离开;渐渐远去;一直;去掉

[语境] Don't loaf away your time. 别虚度光阴。

awful [ˈɔːful] *a.* 糟糕的,极坏的

[语境] They were devastated by the awful news.
那可怕的消息把他们吓坏了。

awkward [ˈɔːkwəd] *a.* 尴尬的,别扭的;笨拙的;使用不便的,难处理的

[巧记] 派生词:awkwardly(*ad.* 尴尬地);awkwardness(*n.* 笨拙,不雅观)

[语境] Your refusal puts me in an awkward predicament.
你的拒绝让我感到十分为难。
The heavy ax was awkward to use.
这把重斧头不好用。

考点集训

1. He asked us to _____ them in carrying through their plan.
   A. provide   B. arouse
   C. assist   D. persist

2. Tomorrow the mayor is to _____ a group of Canadian businessmen on a tour of the city.

A. coordinate   B. cooperate
C. accompany   D. associate

3. The ship's generator broke down, and the pumps had to be operated _____ instead of mechanically.
   A. artificially   B. automatically
   C. manually   D. synthetically

4. The mayor _____ the police officer a medal of honor for his heroic deed in rescuing the earthquake victims.
   A. rewarded   B. awarded
   C. credited   D. prized

5. Niagara Falls is a great tourist _____, drawing millions of visitors every year.
   A. attention   B. attraction
   C. appointment   D. arrangement

6. In a sudden _____ of anger, the man tore up everything within reach.
   A. attack   B. burst
   C. split   D. blast

7. Tryon was extremely angry, but cool-headed enough to _____ storming into the boss's office.
   A. prevent   B. prohibit
   C. turn   D. avoid

8. This is the nurse who _____ to me when I was ill in hospital.
   A. accompanied   B. attended
   C. entertained   D. shielded

9. The shy girl felt quite _____ and uncomfortable when she could not answer the interviewer's question.
   A. amused   B. sensitive
   C. curious   D. awkward

10. Research shows heavy coffee drinking is _____ a small increase in blood pressure, but not enough to increase the risk for high blood pressure.

A. compared with B. associated with
C. attributed to D. referred to

11. He was proud of being chosen to participate in the game and he _____ us that he would try as hard as possible.
    A. insured B. guaranteed
    C. assumed D. assured

12. Three university departments have been _____ $600,000 to develop good practice in teaching and learning.
    A. promoted B. included
    C. secured D. awarded

13. The courses aim to give graduates an up-to-date grasp of their subject and _____ laboratory skills.
    A. superficial B. subjective
    C. structural D. sophisticated

答案与解析

1. C 他让我们帮助他们实施他们的计划。A 提供；B 唤起；C 帮助；D 坚持。故选 C。

2. C 明天市长要陪一群加拿大商人游览城市。A 协作，协同；B 合作；C 陪伴；D 结交，联合。故选 C。

3. C 船的发动机坏了，不得不手动操作水泵代替机器推动。A 人工地；B 自动地；C 手动地；D 综合地，以综合方法。故选 C。

4. B 鉴于这位警官在拯救地震受害者时的英勇表现，市长授予他荣誉金牌。A 回报，报答；B 授予；C 归功于，相信，记入贷方；D 表扬，奖励。故选 B。

5. C 尼亚加拉大瀑布是一个著名的旅游观光景点，每年吸引了上百万的游客。A 注意力；B 有吸引力的地方；C 约会；D 安排，布置。从意思上来看，C 为正确答案。

6. B 这个人脾气大发，扯烂了所有他可以接触到的东西。A 攻击，袭击；B 短暂的突然发作；C 分开；D 爆炸。故 B 为正确答案。

7. D 尽管 Tryon 非常生气，但是他头脑很清醒，没有冲进老板的办公室。A 阻止;B 禁止;C 转向;D 避免。故 D 为正确答案。

8. B 这就是那位在我生病住院期间照看我的那位护士。A 陪伴;B 照顾,关心;C 娱乐,招待;D 遮蔽,包庇。故 B 为正确答案。

9. D 那个害羞的女孩在回答不出面试官的提问时感到非常尴尬,不舒服。A 愉快的,开心的;B 敏感的;C 好奇的;D 糟糕的。根据 and 和句子意思,这里选和 uncomfortable 意思相近的词。

10. B associate with "和……来往,和……共事,同……联合;(在思想上)同……联系在一起"。干扰项 C 后面应该连接的是原因,主语只能是人。

11. D 被选中参加比赛,他很骄傲,他向我们保证他会尽全力的。A 确保,保证,给……上保险;B 保证;C 认为,承担;D 向……保证。故选 D。

12. D 大学三个系因他们在教学和学习方面的开拓性实践获赠 60 万美元。A 提升,提高;B 包括;C 确保;D 授予,给予。故选 D。

13. D 这些课程的目的是让毕业生掌握他们所学专业的最新的知识和一些复杂的实验技能。superficial "肤浅的,浅薄的";subjective "主观的";structural "结构的";sophisticated "复杂的,久经世故的"。

Word List 5

baby [ˈbeɪbɪ] *n.* 婴儿,孩子

back [bæk] *a.* 后面的 *ad.* 向后 *v.* 倒退;支持 *n.* 背;后面

[语境] My mind flashed back to last Christmas.
忽然回想起去年圣诞节的情景。

A severe back injury plagued him all his life.
严重的背伤终身折磨着他。

[考点] back and forth 来回;往复

background[5] [ˈbækgraʊnd] *n.* 背景,经历;幕后

[巧记] back(背后)+ ground(场地,场景)→背后的地是背景,对人是经历

[语境] It is wrong to differentiate between pupils according to their family background.

按家庭出身区别对待学生的做法是错误的。

bad [bæd] *a.* 坏的;低劣的;不舒服的;腐败的;严重的

[语境] Bad customs and laws ought to be abolished.

不良的习俗和法规应予以废除。

bag [bæɡ] *n.* 袋,提包,背包

[语境] I have subjected your bag to your driver.

我早把你的包交给你的司机了。

baggage [ˈbæɡɪdʒ] *n.* 行李

[语境] They ticketed my baggage at the airport.

在机场,他们给我的行李贴了行李条。

[考点] baggage,luggage 辨析:这两个名词均可表示"行李"之意。baggage:不可数名词,在英式英语指大而重的行李,在美式英语泛指一切行李。luggage:多用于英国,指旅行者的行李

bake [beɪk] *v.* 烤,烘,焙;烧硬,焙干

[语境] There's a knack to baking a good cake.

烘烤美味的蛋糕是有窍门的。

balance[10] [ˈbæləns] *n.* 平衡,均衡;秤,天平 *v.* (使)保持平衡;(收支)相抵

[语境] You have to balance the advantages of living in a big city against the disadvantages.

你必须权衡住在大城市的利与弊。

All the parts of the building are in perfect balance.

建筑物的各部分都显得非常匀称。

[考点] keep one's balance 保持某人的平衡,一般指的是身体的平衡,也可以指使人冷静。on balance 总的来看。in the balance 不能确定的

bald [bɔːld] *a.* 秃头的；单调的

[语境] Men who are going bald often wear baseball caps.
秃顶的男人通常会戴棒球帽。

The job will be very bald, can you adapt yourself to the job?
那里的工作会很单调，你能适应吗？

[考点] bare, naked, bald 辨析：这些形容词都含"裸露的"之意。bare：指缺少必要的遮盖物。用于人时，多指身体的部分裸露。naked：指全身一丝不挂，暴露无遗。bald：指头上无发，山坡无树无草，树顶无叶

ball [bɔːl] *n.* 球，球状物；大型舞会

[语境] The ball drifted on the water.
那只皮球在水面上漂荡。

They silently split off the ball.
他们悄悄地离开了舞会。

banana [bəˈnɑːnə] *n.* 香蕉

[语境] The area is under banana cultivation.
这个地区种植香蕉。

band[5] [bænd] *n.* 乐队；一伙；带，箍；频道，波段

[语境] The children banded together to buy a present for their teacher.
孩子们合起来为他们的老师买了一件礼物。

A band of robbers held up the train.
一群强盗抢劫了火车。

[考点] band together 联合；结合

bank [bæŋk] *n.* 银行；岸，堤 *vi.* 存入(经营)银行；信赖

[语境] The bank folded up during the recent economic crisis.
在最近的经济危机中，这家银行倒闭了。

banker [ˈbæŋkə(r)] *n.* 银行家

[巧记] bank(银行) + er(人) → 开银行的人 → 银行家

[语境] He has applied to the banker for a loan.
他向银行家请求贷款。

bar[57] [bɑː(r)] *n.* 条，杆，闩；酒吧；栅，障碍(物) *v.* 闩上，阻拦

[语境] The monkey reached out a hand through the bars and took the banana.

猴子从栏杆里伸出爪子拿走了香蕉。

[考点] behind bars 关在监牢里

bare [beə(r)] *a.* 赤裸的;极少的,仅有的

[语境] Just give us the bare facts of the case.

你只要向我们提供案件最低限度的事实真相就行。

The trees are bare in the winter.

冬天的时候,树上的叶子全掉光了,光秃秃的。

base[44] [beɪs] *n.* 基(础),底(座);基地 *vt.* (on) 把……建立在……基础上

[语境] The harbour is an important naval base.

该港是一个重要的海军基地。

He based his conclusions on the evidence given by the captured prisoners.

他根据被俘囚犯提供的证据得出了这个结论。

[考点] base...on... 以……为基础

basic[13] [ˈbeɪsɪk] *a.* 基本的,基础的

[巧记] base(基础)+ -ic ……(的)→基础的

[语境] These poor people lack the basic necessities of life.

这些穷人缺乏生活的基本必需品。

basically [ˈbeɪsɪkəli] *ad.* 基本地,根本地

[语境] The situation is basically sound.

情况基本上是健康的。

basketball [ˈbɑːskɪtbɔːl] *n.* 篮球

[巧记] basket(篮子)+ ball(球)→篮球

[语境] We love playing basketball.

我们爱打篮球。

bath [bɑːθ] *n.* 沐浴,洗澡;浴室(池,盆) *v.* (给……)洗澡

[语境] She was bathed in the spring sunlight.

她沐浴于春日的阳光。

bathroom [ˈbɑːθrʊm, -ruːm] *n.* 浴室;盥洗室

[巧记]bath(洗澡) + room(房间)→洗澡的房间→浴室
[语境]The water shed from the bathroom.
水是从浴室中溢出来的。

battle ['bætəl] *vi./n.* 战斗,作战

[语境] The two fighters battled for half an hour.
两个拳击手战斗了半小时。
They died in the Battle of Waterloo.
他们战死于滑铁卢战役。

be [biː, bɪ] (现在式 am, are, is; 过去式 was, were; 过去分词 been; 现在分词 being) *v.* (就)是,等于;(存)在;到达,来到,发生

[语境]There must be immediate action if chaos is to be averted.
要避免混乱就必须立即采取行动。

beach [biːtʃ] *n.* 海滩,海滨

[语境]They love to run about on the beach.
他们喜欢在海滩上跑来跑去。

bear [beə(r)] *n.* 熊;粗鲁、笨拙的人 *vt.* 忍受,经得起;承担,负担;怀有(爱、憎等感情)

[语境] The ice is too thin to bear your weight.
冰太薄,承受不住你们的重量。
Her husband is such a bear that nobody likes him.
她丈夫很粗暴,没人喜欢他。
These are matters that bear on the welfare of the community.
这些都是与社会福利有关的问题。

[考点] bear down on sb. 向某人逼近;bear on sth. 和某事有关,对某事有影响;bear out 证实某事,为某人作证;bear up 处理,对付,不气馁

beat [biːt] *n.* 敲打;(心脏等)跳动 *v.* 打败;(心脏等)跳动

[语境] My heart beat thick in the course of the interview.
在面试过程中我的心跳得厉害。

[考点] beat down 击败,压倒;镇压;摧毁

beautiful ['bjuːtɪfəl] *a.* 美的,美丽的;出色的,完美的

[巧记] beauty 美 + -ful 充满……的；此词用来指女人，说男人漂亮时用 handsome 或 good-looking

[语境] The beautiful scenery inspired the composer.
美丽的景色使作曲家灵思泉涌。

because [bɪˈkɒz] *conj.* 因为，由于

[语境] Reception improved because of the new antenna.
接收效果因有新天线而得到改善。

become [bɪˈkʌm] *vi.* 变成，开始变得 *vt.* 适合，同……相称

[语境] The sky became suddenly covered with dark clouds.
天空突然变得乌云密布。

[考点] become of 遭遇；发生

bed [bed] *n.* 床，床位；苗圃，花坛；河床，海底

[语境] He offered me a bed.
他提供我一个床位。

Countless billions of minute sea creatures and plants lived and sank to the sea bed.
数亿的微小海洋动物和植物繁衍生殖并沉到海底。

[考点] a bed of roses 称心如意的境遇；安乐窝

bee [biː] *n.* 蜜蜂

[语境] He was stung by a bee.
他被蜜蜂蛰了。

beef [biːf] *n.* 牛肉

[语境] Take the beef out of the refrigerator to defrost.
把牛肉从冰箱里拿出来解冻。

beer [bɪə(r)] *n.* 啤酒

[语境] The beer is brewing in these vats.
啤酒正在这些桶里酿造着。

before [bɪˈfɔː(r)] *prep.* (指时间)在……以前，在……前面，在……之前

[巧记] 反义词：after，behind

[语境] Before giving evidence you have to swear an oath.
在作证之前你得先发誓。

begin [bɪˈgɪn] *v.* (began, begun) 开始,着手

[语境] The concert began with a Mozart quartet.

音乐会以莫扎特的一首四重奏曲开始。

[考点] to begin with 首先;第一点(理由)

beginning [bɪˈgɪnɪŋ] *n.* 开始,开端;起源,早期阶段

[语境] A good beginning is half done.

良好的开端是成功的一半。

behave [bɪˈheɪv] *v.* 举止,举动,表现;运转,开动

[巧记] be 表示动作 + have→[一个人]拥有的动作→举动

[语境] Not all kings behave in a kingly way.

并非所有国王都有王者风范。

behavio(u)r[18] [bɪˈheɪvjə(r)] *n.* 行为,举止;(机器等)运转情况

[巧记] 同义词:action, conduct, manner; 反义词:misbehavior

[语境] Every student is required to conform his behavior to the rules.

每个学生都必须遵守校规。

[考点] behavior,conduct,manner 辨析:这些名词均含有"行为,举止"之意。behavior 是普通用词,侧重指某人在特定场合对他人或在他人面前的行为、举止。conduct 较正式用词,泛指某人的行动,侧重根据社会道德标准和责任感。manner 主要用来指人的习惯行为

behind [bɪˈhaɪnd] *prep.* 在……的背后,(遗留)在……后面;落后于

[语境]There is a garden behind the house.

屋后有个花园。

[考点]behind the times 落伍;赶不上时代

belief[17] [bɪˈliːf] *n.* 信任,相信,信念;信仰,信条

[语境] He explained the beliefs of Taoism to us.

他向我们讲解了道教教义。

believe[37] [bɪˈliːv] *vt.* 相信,认为 *vi.* 相信,信任,信奉

[语境] Christians believe in Jesus.

基督徒信仰耶稣。

[考点] believe in 相信;信奉,信仰

belong [bɪ'lɒŋ] v. (to) 属于,附属,隶属;应归入(类别、范畴等)

[巧记] 派生词:belongings (n. 动产;财物)

[语境] Keeping what belongs to another amounts to stealing.

将他人之物占为己有等于偷窃。

below [bɪ'ləʊ] prep. 在……下面,在……以下 ad. 在下面,向下

[语境] His family lives below the poverty line.

他的一家生活极端艰苦。

beneath[5] [bɪ'niːθ] prep. 在……下边,在……之下 ad. 在下方

[巧记] 同义词:below, under;反义词:on

[语境] The ship sank beneath the waves.

轮船沉没于波涛下面。

benefit[22] ['benɪfɪt] n. 利益,好处 vi. 得益 vt. 对……有利,有益于……

[巧记] 反义词:damage, lose, loss

[语境] I have benefited a lot from extensive reading.

广泛的阅读使我受益匪浅。

This project is of great benefit to everyone.

这项工程对每个人都大有好处。

[考点] for the benefit of 为了……的利益

beside [bɪ'saɪd] prep. 在……旁边,在……附近;和……相比

[语境] Her beauty seemed pale beside Mary's.

她的美貌与玛丽的相比似乎显得黯然失色。

besides [bɪ'saɪdz] prep. 除……之外(还) ad. 而且,此外

[语境] The play was badly acted, besides being far too long.

这出戏除了太长之外,演得也不好。

I haven't time to see the film, besides, it's had dreadful reviews.

我没有时间去看这部影片,再说,影评也诸多贬斥。

best [best] a. 最好的 ad. 最好地

[语境] Which do you like best?

你最喜欢哪一个?

[考点] at (the) best 充其量;至多

at one's best 处于最佳状态,在巅峰时期

make the best of 充分利用,尽量利用,善于处理(不幸、损失等)

better ['betə(r)] *a.* 较好的 *ad.* 更好(地) *v.* 改良 *n.* 较佳者
[语境]Working conditions have bettered a lot.
工作条件已大为改善。

between [bɪ'twiːn] *prep.* 在……之间,在(两者)之间 *ad.* 在中间
[巧记]betweenness *n.* 介乎两者中间(的状态或性质)
[语境]The relationship between these two countries has eased.
两国之间的关系有所缓和。

bike/bicycle *n.* 自行车
[巧记]bi(两个)+cycle(圈)→有两个圈的车→自行车
[语境]My bike spanked down the hill.
我的自行车疾驶滑下了山坡。

big [bɪg] *a.* 大的;重要的;宽宏大量的;大受欢迎的
[语境]Big earrings are the rage now.
大耳环是现在流行的东西。

bill [bɪl] *n.* 账单;招贴,广告;(人员、职称等的)表;钞票
[语境]This bill does not agree with your original estimate.
这张账单与你当初的估计不符。

bind [baɪnd] *v.* 捆,绑,包括,束缚
[语境]She bound the parcel with a cord.
她用细绳捆绑包裹。

bird [bɜːd] *n.* 鸟,禽
[语境]A large bird flew past us.
一只大鸟从我们这儿飞过。

birth [bɜːθ] *n.* 出生;出身;起源
[语境]He falsified his birth certificate to get a passport.
为了取得护照,他伪造了出生证明。
This was the birth of astronomy.
这就是天文学的起源。
[考点]give birth to 生孩子,产子

birthday ['bɜːθdeɪ] *n.* 生日

[巧记]birth(出生) + day(日子)→出生的日子→生日

[语境]Can you ever forgive me for forgetting your birthday?

我忘记了你的生日，你能原谅我吗？

[考点]birthday party 生日派对

bit [bɪt] *n.* **一点，一些；小块，少量；片刻；[计]位，比特**

[语境] A bit of music will cheer you up.

听会儿音乐会使你的心情愉快起来。

[考点] a bit (of) 有点；稍微

考点集训

1. It is reported that Uruguay understands and _____ China on human rights issues.
   A. grants   B. changes
   C. abandons   D. backs

2. Companies are struggling to find the right _____ between supply and demand, but it is no easy task.
   A. equation   B. formula
   C. balance   D. pattern

3. Some people believe that since oil is scarce, the _____ of the motor industry is uncertain.
   A. terminal   B. benefit
   C. fate   D. estimate

4. Reading _____ the lines, I would say that the Governments are more worried than they will admit.
   A. behind   B. between
   C. along   D. among

5. We have planned an exciting publicity _____ with our advertisers.
   A. struggle   B. campaign
   C. battle   D. conflict

6. Not only the professionals but also the amateurs will _____ from the new training facilities.

A. derive　　　　　　　　B. acquire
C. benefit　　　　　　　 D. reward

7. Could you take a _____ sheet of paper and write your name at the top?

   A. bare　　　　　　　　B. vacant
   C. hollow　　　　　　　D. blank

答案与解析

1. D 据报道,乌拉圭在人权问题上理解并支持中国。A 授予;B 改变;C 抛弃;D 支持。故选 D。

2. C 公司想尽力保持供求平衡,但这绝非易事。A 方程式,等式;B 公式;C 平衡;D 模式,花样。故选 C。

3. C 根据题干中 oil is scarce 和 motor industry 之间的关系,再结合四个选项——terminal 表示"终点站,终端";benefit 表示"利益,好处";fate 表示"命运,运气";estimate 表示"估计,估价,评估",可知,只有 fate 符合题意,答案为 C。

4. B 我敢说,政府人员读出了其弦外之音后,会比外表看起来忧虑得多。固定搭配 between the lines 弦外之音,故正确答案为 B。

5. B 我们和广告商一起谋划了一场激动人心的战役。A 挣扎;B 战役;C 战斗;D 冲突。故选 B。

6. C 不仅专业人员,业余人员也会从新的培训设备获益。A 来源;B 习得,获得;C 获益;D 回报。故选 C。

7. D 请拿出一张空白纸,在纸的上方写上你的名字。A 光秃的;B 空着的,未被占用的;C 中空的;D 空白的。故选 D。

Word List 6

bitter [ˈbɪtə(r)] *a.* 有苦味的;辛苦的,辛酸的;严寒的,刺骨的

[语境] I had to take the herb tea although it's bitter.
虽然汤药很苦,我还是不得不喝了。

False friends are worse than bitter enemies.

[谚]明枪易躲,暗箭难防。

[考点] a bitter pill 难以忍受的,不愉快的或丢脸的;to the bitter end 拼到底

black[17] [blæk] *a.* 黑色的 *n.* 黑人,黑色

[语境] Those black shoes clash with that white skirt.

那些黑鞋与那条白色的裙子很不协调。

blame[8] [bleɪm] *n.* 责任,责备 *vt.* 责备,(on)把……归咎于

[语境] We were ready to take the blame for what had happened.

我们准备对所发生的事承担责任。

The driver was not to blame for the accident.

这次事故怪不着司机。

[考点] blame for sth. 归因于[某物]; blame sth. on sb. 将某事归因于某人; be to blame for 应受谴责,应负责任

bleed [bli:d] *v.* 出血,流血

[语境] All the young soldiers are ready to bleed for the country.

所有的年轻战士都愿意为祖国洒热血。

bless [bles] *v.* 祝福,保佑

[语境] I bless him for his kind-heartedness.

我为他的仁慈而祝福他。

blind[6] [blaɪnd] *a.* 盲的,瞎的;盲目的 *vt.* 使失明 *n.* 百叶窗

[语境] The blind people live in a dark world.

盲人生活在黑暗的世界里。

[考点] blind to 看不见……; 对……熟视无睹

block[8] [blɒk] *vt.* 阻塞,封锁 *n.* 街区;路障,阻碍物;大块(木料、石料)

[语境] The trees outside the window blocked off the sun.

窗外的树木挡住了阳光。

We live on the same block.

我们住在同一个街区。

[考点] block in 塞满……;使受限制[受阻]; block out 遮住,挡住

blood [blʌd] *n.* 血,血液;血统,血亲

[巧记] bloody (a. 血腥的,暴力的;血淋淋的)

[语境] Blood started out of his wound.

血从他的伤口涌了出来。

He has oriental blood in his veins.

他是东方血统。

blow [bləu] vi. **吹,吹气,打气;吹奏;爆炸** n. **打,打击**

[语境] He blew out the candle and went to bed.

他吹熄蜡烛,上床睡觉。

The blow dazed me, but I wasn't hurt.

这一击使我头晕目眩,但我并未受伤。

blue [blu:] a. **蓝色的,沮丧的,忧郁的** n. **蓝色**

[语境] The blue dress show you off.

那条蓝裙子使你光彩夺目。

Why do you look so blue?

你为什么看上去如此的沮丧?

board [bɔ:d] n. **板,木板,全体委员;伙食** v. **上船(车、飞机)**

[巧记] boardman (n. 搞布景的人)

[语境] Pirates boarded the vessel and robbed the passengers.

海盗登上船只,抢劫旅客。

[考点] on board 在[到]船、飞机或车上; go on board 上船;上飞机,上火车

boast [bəust] n. **自夸的话,可夸耀的事** vi. (of, about) **夸耀,说大话** vt. **以有……而自豪,自夸**

[巧记] 派生词:boaster n. 自诩者; boastful a. 好自夸的

[语境] Don't believe him, he is just boasting.

别相信他,他只是在吹嘘罢了。

It is one of their proudest boasts that they have halved the death rate from typhoid.

他们使伤寒病人的死亡率降低了一半,这是他们最感骄傲的事之一。

boat [bəut] n. **船** v. **划船**

[语境] Our boat gently dropped down with the tide.

我们的小船慢慢随潮顺流而下。

boil [bɔɪl] *v.* (使)沸腾,煮(沸)
[语境] When water boils, it passes into steam.
水达到沸点时变成蒸汽。

bold [bəʊld] *a.* 大胆的,冒失的;鲜明的,醒目的,(线、字等)粗的
[巧记] boldly *ad.* 大胆地,显眼地;boldness *n.* 大胆,冒失,勇敢
[语境] May I be so bold as to ask how old you are?
可否冒昧问一下您多大年纪?
He is a bold thinker, with lots of original ideas.
他是个敢于思考的人,富有创新观点。

bone [bəʊn] *n.* 骨,骨骼
[语境] The dogs were fighting over a bone.
那些狗为了一块骨头而争斗。

book [bʊk] *n.* 书,书籍 *vt.* 订(票、座位、房间等),预订
[语境] Mary has booked a flight from New York to London.
玛丽已预订了从纽约到伦敦的飞机票。
[考点] book in 签到;(旅馆等)登记旅客姓名等;book up 预订(车、船、飞机票、旅社房间等)

boom [buːm] *n./v.* (发出)隆隆声;繁荣,兴隆起来
[语境] He made his pile during the property boom.
在房地产生意兴隆期间他发了大财。

boot [buːt] *n.* 靴子
[语境] He angrily swished his boot.
他气愤地嗖嗖地抽打他的靴子。

border [ˈbɔːdə(r)] *n.* 边界,国界;边(沿) *v.* 交界,与……接壤;接近
[巧记] borderer *n.* 边境居民;borderism *n.* 边境居民的特殊语言、习惯
[语境] Their efforts toward the settlement of the border dispute are praiseworthy.
他们为解决边界争端所做的努力是值得赞扬的。
[考点] border on/upon 与……接壤[相邻];类似;非常像

核心词汇精解

boring [ˈbɔːrɪŋ] *a.* 令人厌烦的

[语境] His long boring story made me yawn.
他的冗长的故事听得我直打哈欠。

born [bɔːn] *a.* 出生的,产生的;天生的,十足的

[语境] Good memory is your born gift.
良好的记忆力是你与生俱来的天赋。

borrow [ˈbɒrəʊ] *vt.* 借,借入;(思想、文字等)采用,抄袭

[语境] These words were borrowed from French.
这几个词是从法语引进的。

boss [bɒs] *n.* 老板,上司

[语境] I myself agree with you, but I can't speak for my boss.
我同意你的提议,可我的话并不能代表我的老板。

both [bəʊθ] *prep.* 两者(都),双方(都) *a.* 两个……(都)

[巧记] 反义词:neither

[语境] Both sides observed the cease-fire.
双方都遵守停火协议。

bother [ˈbɒðə(r)] *vt.* 烦扰,麻烦 *vi.* 担心,烦恼 *n.* 烦恼,焦急

[语境] Her baby sister bother her for candy.
她的小妹妹缠着她要糖果。

My cold still bothers me.
我的感冒仍然困扰着我。

Don't bother about me.
别为我担忧。

[考点] bother to do something 操心,费力做某事

bottle [ˈbɒtl] *n.* 瓶子

[语境] He filled the bottle with wine.
他用酒装满了那只瓶子。

bottom [ˈbɒtəm] *n.* 底部;屁股,臀部 *a.* 底部的

[语境] This bottom of bucket has worn through.
这个桶底已经磨穿了。

You can download the examples from the download section at the bottom of this page.

您可以从本页底部的下载小节中下载这些示例。

[考点] at the bottom of 是……的真正原因;是……的根源;在……的底部

bowl [bəʊl] *n.* **碗,钵**

[语境] He plopped the bowl on the table.

他把碗重重地往桌上一放。

box [bɒks] *n.* **盒子,箱** *v.* **装……入盒中**

[语境] Please lift the box down from the shelf for me.

请帮我把这只箱子从搁板上抬下来。

boxing ['bɒksɪŋ] *n.* **拳击**

[语境] He wants to take on that boxing champion.

他想和那个拳击冠军较量。

boy [bɔɪ] *n.* **男孩**

[语境] She had a boy by her first husband.

她与她的第一个丈夫有一男孩。

brain [breɪn] *n.* **脑(子),脑髓;(*pl.*) 心智,智力**

[语境] The difficult question tasked my brain.

这个难题让我大费脑筋。

The music is his brain child.

这首乐曲是他的智力产物。

branch [brɑːntʃ] *n.* **(树)条,分支;分店;(学科)分科,部门;支流**

[巧记] branchy *a.* 多枝的,枝繁的

[语境] English is a branch of the Germanic family of languages.

英语是日耳曼语系的一个分支。

brave [breɪv] *a.* **勇敢的** *v.* **勇敢地面对(危险等)**

[巧记] braveness *n.* 勇敢,华饰

[语境] They braved the storm to rescue their sheep.

他们冒着暴风雨抢救羊群。

break [breɪk] *vt.* **打破;中止;违反** *vi.* **破(裂)** *n.* **休息时间**

[语境] She broke the world record for the broad jump.

她打破了跳远的世界纪录。

[考点] break away 突然离开;逃走;脱离;放弃

break down 毁掉；拆除；损坏；瓦解；崩溃
break forth 突然发出，迸发
break in 闯入；破门而入；训练；打断
break into 闯入；潜入；破门而入；插入；打断
break off 突然停止；暂停；休息一下；折断；绝交
break out 发生；爆发
break through 突破；克服；打破

breakfast ['brekfəst] *n.* 早餐

[语境] He wolfed down his breakfast and went to school.
他狼吞虎咽地吃了早饭上学去了。

[考点] have breakfast 吃早餐

breakthrough ['breɪkθruː] *n.* 突破；突破性的发现

[语境] Yet in one sense it is a breakthrough.
然而，在某种意义上这是一个突破。

[考点] make a breakthrough 取得重大发展或突破

breath [breθ] *n.* 呼吸，气息

[语境] I'm out of breath after running up the stairs.
奔上楼梯我气喘吁吁。

[考点] out of breath 喘不过气来

brief [briːf] *a.* 简短的，简洁的；短暂的 *vt.* 简单介绍

[语境] To be brief, she was happy with that result.
总之，她对那个结果非常的高兴。

The Air Commodore briefed the bomber crew on their dangerous mission.
空军准将向轰炸机机组下达执行危险任务的各项指示。

[考点] to be brief 简言之；in brief 简单地说，简而言之

bright [braɪt] *a.* 明亮的，辉煌的；聪明的；欢快的，美好的

[巧记] brightly *ad.* 明亮地

[语境] The bright light made him wink.
强烈的光使他直眨眼睛。

He is full of bright ideas.
他足智多谋。

bring[32] [brɪŋ] *v.* 拿来,带来;产生,引起;使处于某种状态

[语境] Fatigue brought on dark rings under her eyes.
劳累使她眼睛下部出现了黑圈。

[考点] bring forth 引起;提出;产生;致使 bring forward 提出;出示;展示

British [ˈbrɪtɪʃ] *a.* (大)不列颠(人)的;英国(人)的 *n.* 英国人

[语境] British kings are crowned in Westminster Abbey.
英国国王都在威斯敏斯特教堂加冕。
These are all reasons why the British are different.
这些都是英国人与众不同的原因所在。

broad [brɔːd] *a.* 宽的,广阔的;广大的;宽宏的,豁达的

[巧记] broadness *n.* 广阔,明白,粗野

[语境] Broad prairies stretch out as far as the eye can see.
辽阔的草原一望无边。

brother [ˈbrʌðə(r)] *n.* 兄弟

[语境] He looked to his brother for help.
他希望得到他兄弟的帮助。

[考点] sisters and brothers 兄弟姐妹

brown [braʊn] *a.* 褐色的,棕色的 *n.* 褐色,棕色

[语境] The blue curtains clash against the brown furniture.
蓝色窗帘与褐色家具很不协调。

brush [brʌʃ] *n.* 刷(子),毛刷;画笔 *v.* 刷,擦,掸,拂;掠过

[语境] The wind blew lightly, brushing through her hair.
微风轻轻吹过她的头发。

build [bɪld] *vt.* 建造,建筑;建设,建立 *vi.* 增大,增强

[语境] You should build your arguments on facts.
你的论点应建立在事实的基础上。

building [ˈbɪldɪŋ] *n.* 建筑物,大楼

[语境] It was rebuilt on the site of the old building.
它是在原来建筑物的旧址上重新建造的。

burden [ˈbɜːdən] *n.* 负担;负荷,载重;义务,责任

[语境] In the old times, farmers took great burden on their shoulder.

在旧社会,农民的负担很重。

I don't want to burden you with my problem.

我不想让我的问题给你添麻烦。

[考点] lighten/relieve a burden 减轻负担;carry a burden 负载重物;share a burden 分担负担;shoulder a burden 肩负重担

burn [bɜːn] *v.* 燃烧,烧着;烧毁;灼伤 *n.* 烧伤,灼伤

[语境] He burnt his finger when he lit a cigar.

他点雪茄烟时烫了手指头。

bury [ˈberɪ] *v.* 埋(葬),安葬;埋藏,遮盖

[语境] She buried her face in the roses, drinking in the fragrance.

她把脸埋在玫瑰里,吸入芳香。

[考点] bury (oneself) in 埋头于;专心于

bus [bʌs] *n.* 公共汽车

[语境] The passengers disembarked from the bus.

旅客从公共汽车上下来。

business [ˈbɪznɪs] *n.* 商业,生意;事务,业务,职责

[语境] When business is depressed, there is usually an increase in unemployment.

商业不景气,失业率往往会随之上升。

[考点] on business 因公,有事

busy [ˈbɪzɪ] *a.* 忙,忙碌的;热闹的,繁忙的;(电话)占线

[语境] Politicians are busy near election time.

在接近选举的时候政治家们都很忙。

but [bət, bʌt] *conj.* 但是 *prep.* 除……以外 *ad.* 只,才,仅仅

[语境] Nothing but a miracle can save her life.

只有奇迹才能挽救她的生命。

buy [baɪ] *vt.* 买,买得;向……行贿,收买 *vi.* 购买东西

[语境] He bought the house at a budget price.

他以低廉的价钱买下这所房子。

by [baɪ] *prep.* 被;凭借;经由;由于 *ad.* 在近旁;经过

[语境] I passed the examination by learning everything by rote.

· 69 ·

我凭死记硬背通过了考试。

[考点] by and large 总的说来，基本上

考点集训

1. Blacks and American Indians _____ less than 10% of students in the top 30 business schools, while they are about 28% of the U. S. population.
   A. make up B. take up
   C. reach out D. turn out

2. Susan never took any cookery courses; she learned cooking by _____ useful tips from TV cookery programs.
   A. picking up B. bringing up
   C. putting up D. pulling up

3. All the key words in the article are printed in _____ type so as to attract readers' attention.
   A. dark B. dense
   C. black D. bold

4. You shouldn't have written in the _____ since the book belongs to the library.
   A. interval B. border
   C. margin D. edge

5. Then in June 1967 the country _____ diplomatic relations with Israel after the outbreak of the Six Day War.
   A. broke away B. broke off
   C. cut out D. cut down

答案与解析

1. B take up 占,占据;make up 编造、补足;reach out 延伸、扩展;turn out 关灯,结果是。

2. A 从后半句话看,它是通过电视里面的烹饪节目所讲的一些好方法学会了烹饪,这个表示自然而然的去学会某种知识,或者

养成某种习惯,应选 A pick up,表示自然而然养成习惯,自然而然地学习知识和语言;而 B 带大,养大;C 竖起;D 拽起,拔起,不合此语境。
3. D 这篇文章的所有关键词都是用粗体印的,这样可以引起读者的注意。A 黑暗的;B 密集的;C 黑色的;D 粗体。故 D 为正确答案。
4. C 你真不应该在书的边缘写东西,因为这本书是图书馆的。A 间隔,幕间休息;B 边境;C 边缘;D 边。in the margin 在边缘,为固定搭配。故选 C。
5. B break off 断交,停止;break away 突然离开,突然挣脱,与……决裂,从……退出;cut out 剪裁,取代;cut down 削减。

Word List 7

cake[keɪk] *n.* 饼,糕,蛋糕
  [语境]He tasted of the cake.
    他吃了几口蛋糕。
calculate [ˈkælkjʊleɪt]*vt.* 计算;推测,估计;打算
  [巧记] calcul(计算) + ate(使):计算
  [语境] The new regulations are deliberately calculated to make cheating impossible.
    新的法规旨在杜绝诈骗行为。
    The scientists calculated when the spacecraft would reach the moon.
    科学家推算出宇宙飞船抵达月球的时间。
  [考点] calculate on 依靠,指望;calculate to 计划或设计
call[35][kɔːl]*vt.* 叫,喊;打电话 *vi.* 叫;访问 *n.* 叫;号召
  [语境] If anyone calls, tell him I'll be back about three o'clock.
    如果有人来电话,就说我三点左右回来。
  [考点] call after 依……名字而命名;追呼其后;call at 访问;拜

访；停泊

calm [kɑ:m] *a.* (天气、海洋等)静的 *n.* 平静 *v.* (使)平静

[语境] The high wind passed and the sea was calm again.
大风过后,大海又风平浪静。

[考点] calm down 使平息,使平静

camera [ˈkæmərə] *n.* 照相机

[语境] How do you thread the camera?
你怎么给这个照相机上胶卷?

camp [kæmp] *n.* 野营,营地,帐篷 *vi.* 设营,宿营

[语境] Jack and Harry bunked together at camp.
杰克和哈里在军营里合铺。
At night you'll camp beside the river on white sand beaches.
晚间你将在河流旁的白色沙滩上扎营。

[考点] concentration camp 集中营

campus [ˈkæmpəs] *n.* (大学)校园

[语境] He rarely mingles with other students on the campus.
他很少和校园里的其他学生交往。

[考点] on the campus 在校园里

can [kən, kæn] *aux./v.* 能;可以 *n.* 罐头;容器 *vt.* 把……装罐

[语境] He can imitate his father to the life.
他能惟妙惟肖地模仿他父亲的样子。

[考点] can, may 辨析:这两个情态动词均含有"能,可能,可以"之意。can 和 may 常被错用,应注意3点:①can 表示体力或智力方面的能力。may 没有这种功能。②can 和 may 都可表示请求允许做某事,前者较口语化,最常用;may 用于正式文体,多含尊敬之意。③can 和 may 都可表示可能性,前者表理论上的可能性,而后者表示现实的可能性。在这种用法中,can 一般不能用来表将来的可能性,多用在否定和疑问句中表现在的可能性,而 may 既可表现在又可表将来的可能性

Canada [ˈkænədə] *n.* 加拿大

[语境] Canada produces high-guality wheat.
加拿大出产优质小麦。

Canadian [kəˈneɪdɪən] *a.* 加拿大(人)的 *n.* 加拿大人

[语境] I do love being a Canadian.

我喜欢做一个加拿大人。

cancel [ˈkænsəl] *vt.* 取消,删去

[语境] The match had to be cancelled because of bad weather.

比赛因天气不好只得取消。

These arguments cancel each other out.

这些争论彼此势均力敌。

cap [kæp] *n.* 帽子,盖子

[语境] If the cap fits, wear it.

如果帽子合适,就戴着吧。

capable[8] [ˈkeɪpəbəl] *a.* (of) 能干的,有能力的,有才能的

[语境] He is a very capable doctor.

他是一个很高明的医生。

Our position is capable of improvement.

我们的地位可以改善。

[考点] be capable of = having the power or ability or inclination 有某种能力或倾向

capital [ˈkæpɪtəl] *n.* 首都;资本,资金;大写字母 *a.* 资本的;重要的;大写的

[语境] The criminal was sentenced to capital punishment.

罪犯被判处死刑。

London is spelt with a capital L.

London 一词中 L 是大写的。

[考点] gain political capital 获取政治资本;lose moral capital 丧失道义上的资本;labour and capital 劳资双方;capital outflow 资金外流;make capital out of 利用

captain [ˈkæptɪn] *n.* 船长 *v.* 率领,指挥

[巧记] 有钱(capital)的人多半是船长(captain)。

[语境] The captain cares the safety of both the crew and the passengers.

船长为船员和旅客们的安全操心。

He captained the siege of Berlin.

他指挥了围攻柏林的战役。

car [kɑː(r)] *n.* 汽车,车辆,车;(火车)车厢

[语境] Car bombs have become essential terrorist weapons.

汽车炸弹已经成为恐怖分子主要的武器。

card [kɑːd] *n.* 卡片,纸牌

[语境] He listed all the members' names on the card.

他把所有会员的名字都记在卡片上。

care [keə(r)] *n.* 小心;关怀,照料 *v.* (about) 关心,介意,计较

[语境] He cares very little for fame and gain.

他对名利很淡薄。

[考点] care about 关心,担心;care for 喜欢;想要;关心,关怀;take care of 照料;关怀;处理

careful ['keəful] *a.* 小心的,仔细的;细致的,精心的

[巧记] carefully *ad.* 小心地,谨慎地;carefulness *n.* 仔细,慎重

[语境] Be double careful when you cross the street.

你过街时要加倍小心。

careless ['keəlɪs] *a.* 粗心的,草率的;随便的,不介意的;不关心的,冷漠的

[语境] She's careless about her clothes.

她对穿着一点都不讲究。

carry[17] ['kærɪ] *v.* 运送,搬运;传送,传播;领,带

[语境] She carries with her the charm that comes natural to her.

她身上有一种天生的魅力。

[考点] carry on 继续开展,进行下去;carry out 开展,实现,完成,进行到底

case[16] [keɪs] *n.* 箱,盒,容器;情况,事实;病例;案件

[语境] This case is beyond this court's competence.

此法院无权受理这宗案件。

[考点] in case 假使,如果,万一;a case in point 佐证;恰当的例子

cash [kæʃ] *n.* 现金,现钱 *vt.* 兑换成现金

[语境] I have no ready cash on me. Can I pay you tomorrow?
我身上没带现钱,明天付你行吗?

I'm short of cash at the moment.
我现在缺钱。

[考点] hard cash 硬币;in cash 用现金付账;petty cash 零用钱;ready cash 现金;spot cash 现金交易

casual[16] [ˈkæʒjuəl] *a.* 偶然的,随便的,非正式的,漫不经心的

[语境] We are the casual acquaintance of a long railway journey.
我们是在火车长途旅行中偶然结识的朋友。

I love to go to casual parties.
我喜欢参加非正式的派对。

cat [kæt] *n.* 猫,猫科动物

[语境] Our cat eats out of her own dish.
我们的猫吃自己盘子里的食物。

catch[8] [kætʃ] *v.* 捕捉,捕获;赶上;感染;理解,听到

[语境] I catch colds frequently because my resistance is low.
我经常得感冒,因为我抵抗力差。

[考点] catch up with 追上,赶上,与……并驾齐驱

cattle [ˈkætl] *n.* (总称)牛,牲口,家畜

cause[39] [kɔːz] *n.* 原因;事业 *vt.* 造成,引起

[语境] Don't complain without good cause.
没有充分的理由就不要抱怨。

What caused his illness?
是什么使他生病?

celebrate [ˈselɪbreɪt] *vt.* 庆祝,赞美

[巧记] 派生词:celebrated *a.* 著名的,驰名的;celebration *n.* 庆祝仪式;celebrant *n.* 参加庆祝的人;celebrater *n.* 庆祝的人;celebrity *n.* 名人

[语境] People in the city held a great party to celebrate their victory.
本市的市民举行了盛大的晚会以庆祝他们的胜利。

Let's celebrate!

让我们好好庆祝一下吧!

cent[sent] *n.* 分,分币;[作单位的]百

[语境]He turned all his pockets inside out but found no cent whatever.

他把所有口袋都翻了出来,但一分钱都没找到。

center/-tre[12] ['sentə(r)] *n.* 中心,中央,中间 *vt.* 集中 *vi.* 以……为中心

[语境] Their talks always center around politics.

他们的谈话总是围绕着政治。

central ['sentrəl] *a.* 中心的,中央的;主要的,首要的

[语境] Such values are central to our way of life.

这些价值对于我们的生活方式是至关重要的。

My house is very central.

我的家非常靠近市中心。

century ['sentʃərɪ] *n.* 世纪,百年

[巧记]cent(百) + tury(名词后缀)→一百年→世纪

[语境]The century produces many great men.

这个世纪出了许多大人物。

ceremony ['serɪmənɪ] *n.* 典礼,仪式,礼节,礼仪

[语境]The ceremony proceeded in a solemn atmosphere.

仪式在庄严的气氛中进行。

certain ['sɜːtən] *a.* 某,某一,某些;(of)一定的,确信的,可靠的

[语境] In certain religions hell is believed to be the place where wicked people are punished after they die.

在某些宗教中,地狱被认为是恶人死后受惩罚的地方。

[考点] for certain 肯定地,确凿地

certainly ['sɜːtənlɪ] *ad.* 一定,必定,无疑;当然,行

[巧记] 反义词:perhaps

[语境] It is certainly important to distinguish between right and wrong.

明辨是非当然要紧。

chain [tʃeɪn] *n.* 链(条);(*pl.*) 镣铐;一连串 *v.* 用链条拴住

[语境] The dog was fastened to a post by a chain.

那条狗被链条拴在柱子上。

[考点] in chains 上着镣铐，在囚禁中；当奴隶

chair [tʃeə(r)] *n.* 椅子，席位，讲座

[语境] He dragged a chair across the room.

他把椅子拖到房间另一边。

This paper is a chair about expert system.

本文是有关专家系统的一个讲座。

chairman ['tʃeəmən] *n.* 主席，会长

[巧记] chair(席位) + man(人)→坐在主席台座位上的人→主席，会长

[语境] They made the appointment of Peter as chairman of the union.

他们任命彼得为工会主席。

challenge[15] ['tʃæləndʒ] *vt.* 向……挑战 *n.* 挑战

[语境] Nowadays no one will challenge the fact that the earth is round.

现在没有人会对地球是圆的这一事实提出异议。

This career offers a challenge.

这份职业具有挑战性。

[考点] challenge to sb. 质问，怀疑某人

chance[13] [tʃɑːns] *n.* 机会；可能性；偶然性，运气 *v.* 碰巧，偶然发生

[语境] I chanced to meet an old friend in the park today.

今天我在公园碰巧遇见一位老朋友。

[考点] chance, opportunity, occasion 辨析：这些名词均含"机会"之意。chance 侧重指偶然或意外的机会，有时也指正常或好的机会。opportunity 侧重指有利或适合于采取行动，以达到某一目的或实现某种愿望的最佳时机或机会。occasion 指特殊时机或良机，也指时节

change [tʃeɪndʒ] *n.* 改变，变化；零钱 *v.* 更换，调换，交换；改变

[语境] The abrupt change of schedule gave me lots of trouble.

行程突然改变给我造成许多麻烦。

[考点] change into 变为;使改变; change over (大幅度)改变;完全改变

channel[5] ['tʃænəl] *n.* 海峡;频道;渠道,管道

[语境] What's your favourite channel?

你喜欢哪个电视台?

Ships must follow the channel into the port.

船只必须沿航道进入港口。

This channel comes on the air every morning at 7 am.

这个频道每天早晨7点钟开始播放。

[考点] change the channel 改变频道,转变话题

chapter ['tʃæptə(r)] *n.* 章,回,篇

[语境] The opening chapter gives a brief historical overview of transport.

第一章是运输史的简要回顾。

character[6] ['kærɪktə(r)] *n.* 个性,性格;特征;人物,角色

[语境] He is firm in character.

他性格坚强。

It is out of character to do that.

那样做不合适。

[考点] be in(out of) character 是(不是)本来的性格

characteristic[8] [ˌkærɪktə'rɪstɪk] *a.* 特有的,典型的 *n.* 特性,特征,特色

[语境] Windmills are a characteristic feature of the Mallorcan landscape.

风车是马略卡岛风光的一大特色。

Genes determine the characteristics of every living thing.

基因决定每个生物的特征。

[考点] be characteristic of (品质、特点)明显的,显著的,典型的

charge [tʃɑːdʒ] *vt.* 收费,索价;控告,指挥;装满;充电 *n.* 负荷,电荷;负责;指控;收费

[语境] As long as you've paid in advance we won't charge you for delivery.

只要你预先付款,我们就不收你送货费。

He became his uncle's charge after his parents died.

他在父母去世后,由叔父抚养。

[考点] free of charge 免费;in charge of 负责;in the charge of 由……管;leave in charge of 交由……管;put sb. in charge of 让某人负责;take charge of 负责管理

chase [tʃeɪs] *v./n.* **追赶,追逐**

[语境] Why do modern people chase material possessions?

为什么现在的人们追求物质财富?

They caught the puppy after a long chase.

他们追了很久才把小狗逮住。

[考点] chase about(all over) 跑来跑去(到处跑);chase after 追逐;chase up 设法(迅速)找到

cheap [tʃi:p] *a.* **便宜的;低劣的,不值钱的**

[语境] The coat may be expensive but looks cheap.

那件大衣也许很贵,但是看起来很粗劣。

cheat [tʃi:t] *vt.* **欺骗,诈取** *vi.* **作弊,欺诈** *n.* **欺骗行为;骗子,不诚实的人**

[语境] He is a shameless cheat.

他是个无耻的骗子。

You can cheat in no circumstances.

在任何情况下你都不能欺骗。

[考点] cheat sb. (out of sth.), cheat(in/at sth.) 欺骗,骗取

check/cheque[10] [tʃek] *vt.* **检查,校对;控制** *n.* **检查,核对;控制**

[语境] Have you checked all your luggage?

你的全部行李都检查了吗?

They checked their steps.

他们突然停住脚步。

[考点] check in 登记,报到;check over 再检查一遍;check up 检查,校对;check with 和……查对;check out 付账后离开;check through 查看,校对

chemical[8] [ˈkemɪkəl] *a.* **化学的** *n.* *(pl.)* **化学制品,化学药品**

[巧记] 派生词:chemicalize(*v.* 以化学品处理);chemically(*ad.* 用化学,以化学方法)

[语境] He devoted his life to chemical research.

他一生从事化学研究。

chicken [ˈtʃɪkɪn] *n.* 鸡,鸡肉;胆小鬼

[语境] He finished off two bowls of chicken noodles soup in no time.

他很快吃了两碗鸡汤面。

I'm scared of the dark. I'm a big chicken.

我怕黑,是个十足的胆小鬼。

chief [tʃiːf] *a.* 主要的,首席的 *n.* 元首,领导

[巧记] 派生词:chiefdom *n.* 首领的地位 chiefless *a.* 没有首领(或领袖等)的

[语境] The chief of the police department demanded severe punishments for criminals.

警察局局长要求严惩罪犯。

What is the chief town in Norway?

挪威的主要城市是哪一个?

child [tʃaɪld] *n.* 小孩

[巧记] children *n.*(复数形式)小孩们

[语境] The child sitting on the ground yowled.

那个小孩坐在地上大哭大叫。

childhood [ˈtʃaɪldhʊd] *n.* 童年,幼年

[巧记] child(孩子) + hood(抽象名词后缀)→童年,幼年

[语境] All memory of the childhood faded from her mind.

她儿时的记忆从她脑海中逐渐消失。

China [ˈtʃaɪnə] *n.* 中国

[语境] This ship was made in China.

这艘轮船是中国制造的。

Chinese [ˌtʃaɪˈniːz] *a.* 中国(人/话)的 *n.* 中国人,汉语

[语境] Wang is a very common Chinese surname.

王是一个很常见的中国姓。

So the Chinese have skin in this game.

因此,中国人在这个游戏中也有参与。

choice [tʃɔɪs] *n.* 选择(机会),抉择,选择项;入选者 *a.* 精选的

[巧记] choiceless *a.* 没什么选的 choicely *ad.* 精选地,挑三拣四地,审慎地 choiceness *n.* 精选;优良;精巧;绝好

[语境] You may have your choice between these two positions.
在这两个职位中,你有权选择其一。

[考点] at one's own choice 随意挑选,自由选择

choose [tʃuːz] *v.* 选择,挑选;甘愿

[巧记] 反义词:decline, reject

[语境] The way we choose to bring up children is vitally important.
选用何种方式抚养子女是极其重要的。

circle [ˈsɜːkəl] *n.* 圆,圆周;集团;周期,循环 *v.* 环绕,旋转

[语境] A circle without a center is inconceivable.
一个没有圆心的圆是无法想象的。

circumstance[5] [ˈsɜːkəmstəns] *n.* 环境,详情,境况

[巧记] circum(=circle 周围),stance 位置,站立的姿势:周围的位置——环境

[语境] Different circumstances call for different tactics.
不同的情势需要不同的策略。

[考点] under all circumstances 无论如何

city [ˈsɪtɪ] *n.* 城市,都市

civilize [ˈsɪvəlaɪz] *v.* 使文明,使开化

[语境] Those facilities are intended to civilize people.
那些设施的目的在于教化民众。

考点集训

1. By a strange _____, both candidates have come up with the same solution to the problem.

   A. coincidence   B. encounter
   C. chance   D. overlap

2. As we can no longer wait for the delivery of our order, we have to

_____ it.
A. postpone B. refuse
C. delay D. cancel

3. He always did well at school _____ having to do part-time jobs every now and then.
   A. in spite of B. regardless of
   C. on account of D. to case of
4. This article _____ more attention to the problem of cultural interference in foreign language teaching and learning.
   A. calls for B. applies for
   C. cares for D. allows for
5. In the Chinese household, grandparents and other relatives play _____ roles in raising children.
   A. incapable B. indispensable
   C. insensible D. infinite
6. The decline in moral standards, which has long concerned social analysts, has at last _____ the attention of average Americans.
   A. clarified B. cultivated
   C. characterized D. captured

答案与解析

1. A 很巧合,两位候选人提出了解决问题的相同方案。A 巧合; B 碰面;C 机会;D 重叠。固定搭配,A 为正确答案。
2. D 因为我们再也等不了订购的货物,我们不得不取消订单。A 推迟;B 拒绝;C 延迟;D 取消。故 D 为正确答案。
3. A 尽管他时不时要做兼职工作,但是他在学校表现总是很好。A 尽管;B 不管,不顾;C 由于,因为;D 项不存在此短语。
4. A 这篇文章呼吁人们更多地去关注文化因素对外语教学和学习的影响。A 要求,呼吁;B 申请;C 喜欢;D 考虑。因此正确答案为 A。
5. B 在中国家庭里面,祖父母和其他亲人在抚养孩子方面扮演了不可或缺的角色。A 不能的;B 不可或缺的,不可缺少的;C 不理智的;D 无限的。故 B 为正确答案。
6. D capture the attention 是固定用法,表示引起关注之意。

Word List 8

claim [kleɪm] *vt.* 声明,主张;要求,索取 *n.* 权力,主张,要求

[巧记] 派:claimable *a.* 可要求的;可索取[赔]的 claimee *n.* 被索赔人

[语境] He set up a claim to the throne.
他自称王位是属于他的。
The government would not even consider his claim for money.
政府甚至不考虑他的赔款要求。

[考点] claim back 要求收回;make a claim for 对(赔偿等)提出要求……

class [klɑːs] *n.* 班级,阶级,年级;种类;(一节)课

[语境] You have to work hard to keep ahead in your class.
要想在全班保持成绩领先,你就必须努力学习。
Could any other class of molecules have substituted for proteins?
任何其他种类的分子能够代取代蛋白质吗?
I have to bat out a term paper before class.
我必须在上课前赶出一篇学期论文。

classic [ˈklæsɪk] *n.* (*pl.*) 杰作,名著 *a.* 第一流的,不朽的

[巧记] class(级别) + ic(的):第一流的

[语境] *War and Peace* is a literary classic.
《战争与和平》是一部经典文学著作。

classmate [ˈklɑːsmeɪt] *n.* 同班同学

[语境] He acquainted his classmate with my sister.
他把我妹妹介绍给他的同班同学。

classroom [ˈklɑːsruːm, -rʊm] *n.* 教室

[语境] The boy bounced out of the classroom.

那男孩突然从教室里奔出去。

clean[12] [kliːn] *a.* 清洁的,干净的 *v.* 除去……污垢,把……弄干净

[语境] The house is clean within and without.

这幢房子里里外外都很干净。

[考点] clean away/off 清除;擦去 clean up 收拾干净

clear [klɪə(r)] *a./ad.* 清晰的(地) *vt.* 清除;使清楚 *vi.* 变清澈

[语境] The horse cleared all the jumps.

那匹马越过了所有的障碍物。

[考点] clear up 整顿,清理,收拾

clever [ˈklevə(r)] *a.* 聪明的,伶俐的,机敏的,精巧的

[巧记] cleverish *a.* 有小聪明的,灵巧的

[语境] A clever politician knows how to manipulate his supporters.

机敏的政客懂得如何操纵自己的支持者。

client [ˈklaɪənt] *n.* 顾客,委托人 *n.* 客户

[语境] It is impossible for the client to recover.

该诉讼委托人不可能胜诉。

The client left his visiting card on his desk.

客户将自己的名片留在他的桌上。

climate [ˈklaɪmət] *n.* 气候,风气,气氛

[语境] These two regions differ greatly in climate.

这两个地区气候差异很大。

climb[6] [klaɪm] *v./n.* 攀登,爬

[巧记] climbable *a.* 可攀登的,爬得上去的

[语境] We climbed to the top of the mountain with grim determination.

我们怀着坚强的决心爬上山顶。

clinic[9] [ˈklɪnɪk] *n.* 诊所

[语境] He detoxed at a clinic.

他在诊所里戒毒。

[考点] at a clinic 在诊所里

clock [klɒk] *n.* 时钟,计时器

[语境] This clock neither gains nor loses.

这钟走得既不快也不慢。

close[16] [kləʊz] *v./n.* 关;结束 *a./ad.* 近的(地);紧密的(地)

[语境] His factory closed down during the period of economic recession.

他的工厂在经济衰退时期关闭了。

Please pay close attention to where they go.

请密切注意他们将去何处。

[考点] close down (工厂等的)关闭,停歇;封闭; close in 围拢;迫近,围上来

cloth [klɒθ] *n.* 布

[语境] The shop laid the cloth by for a customer.

商店为一个顾客保留着这些布料。

clothes [kləʊðz] *n.* [总称]衣服

[语境] Your clothes fit well.

你的衣服很合身。

cloud [klaʊd] *n.* 云,忧色,云状的烟

[语境] The rocket ascended into the cloud.

火箭高高飞入云端。

club[6] [klʌb] *n.* 俱乐部

[语境] We affiliated ourselves with their club.

我们加入了他们的俱乐部。

coal [kəʊl] *n.* 煤

[语境] Our stock of coal has not renewed yet.

我们的煤炭储存量还没有补充过。

coat [kəʊt] *n.* 外套,上衣;涂层 *v.* 涂上,包上

[语境] He hung up my coat.

他把我的外套挂起来。

Coat the fish with seasoned flour.

用拌有佐料的面粉将鱼裹上。

cock [kɒk] *n.* 公鸡,公鸟 *v.* 耸立,耸起

[语境] The cock was announcing the start of a new day.

雄鸡正在报晓。

The dog cocked its ears suddenly.
这条狗忽然把耳朵竖起来。

coffee [ˈkɒfɪ] *n.* 咖啡

[语境] She brewed some coffee for me.
她为我煮了些咖啡。

coil [kɔɪl] *n.* 卷,盘绕 *v.* 盘绕,卷

[语境] The burnt coil should be renewed.
烧穿的线圈应换新的。

It will coil itself around the egg, he said.
他说它自己会盘绕在蛋周围。

cold [kəuld] *a.* 冷的,寒冷的;冷淡的 *n.* 冷,寒冷;伤风

[语境] His cold manner holds people off.
他冷淡的态度使人无法接近。

colleague[9] [ˈkɒliːg] *n.* 同事,同僚

[巧记] col(一起) + league(联盟):一起在联盟里→同事

[语境] His dedication to teaching gained the respect of his colleagues.
他专心致力于教学的精神赢得了同事们的尊敬。

collect[18] [kəˈlekt] *vt.* 收集 *vi.* 聚集,堆积

[语境] This department collects information on political extremists.
这个部门搜集有关政治极端分子的情报。

We are collecting money for the famine victim.
我们在为遭受饥荒的灾民募捐。

college [ˈkɒlɪdʒ] *n.* 学院;大学;学会

[语境] She enrolled in college yesterday.
她昨天注册入大学。

[考点] college entrance examination 高考

colo(u)r [ˈkʌlə(r)] *n.* 颜色 *v.* 给……着色,染

[语境] What colo(u)r is this taxi?
这辆出租车是什么颜色?

She coloured the pictures with a yellow crayon.
她用黄色炭笔把这些画涂上颜色。

combine [kəmˈbaɪn] *v.* (使)结合,(使)合并;(使)化合

[语境] We can't always combine work with pleasure.
我们并不总是能在工作中享受到乐趣。
He combines creative imagination and true scholarship.
他同时具有创造性的想象力和真正的治学严谨学风。

come[43] [kʌm] *v.* 来;出现于,产生;是,成为;开始,终于

[语境] All wealth comes ultimately from human labor.
一切财富归根到底来源于人类的劳动。

[考点] come about 发生,产生;come across 不期而遇;come out 算出,显现,出版;come to 苏醒;共计;come up 出现,走上前来;come up with 提出

comfort [ˈkʌmfət] *vt.* 使安慰,使舒服 *n.* 安慰,安逸,舒适

[语境] My husband was a great comfort to me when my son was ill.
我儿子生病时,丈夫给了我极大的安慰。
He spoke a few words of comfort to me before leaving.
走之前,他向我说了几句安慰的话。

[考点] give comfort to 安慰,给……安慰

comfortable[5] [ˈkʌmfətəbəl] *a.* 舒适的,舒服的;感到舒适的,安逸的

[巧记] 反义词:discomfortable,uncomfortable

[语境] It's only human nature to want a comfortable life.
人的本性就是要过舒服的生活。

command [kəˈmɑːnd] *vt./n.* 命令,指挥;掌握,控制

[语境] com(共同)+mand(命令):全部下命令
The general commanded his men to attack the city.
将军下令部下攻城。
The army is under the king's direct command.
军队由国王直接统率。

[考点] at one's command 由本人支配(使用);at/by sb.'s command 听某人支配,服从某人指挥;in command of 指挥,控制;take command of 开始指挥

commence [kəˈmens] *vt.* 开始 *vi.* 获得学位

[语境] The bull-fight was to commence in twenty minutes.

斗牛在20分钟后开始。

[考点] commence on 着手 commence with 从……开始

comment[5] [ˈkɒment] vi. (on) 评论 n. 评论, 意见

[语境] What comments do you have about my son's behaviour?

你对我儿子的行为有什么意见?

The king refuses to comment on the election results.

国王拒绝评论选举的结果。

[考点] any comment 在口语中用来征求别人的看法或观点, 是个比较正式的用法; no comment 无可奉告

commit [kəˈmɪt] vt. 犯(错误、罪行等); 把……托付给, 提交

[语境] The girl was committed to the care of an aunt.

这女孩被交给姨母照顾。

She committed herself to philanthropy.

她专心从事慈善事业。

[考点] commit suicide 自杀; commit oneself 承担义务, 作出承诺

commitment[8] [kəˈmɪtmənt] n. 承诺, 许诺, 保证; 承担的义务

[语境] I felt I did not have to make such a commitment to them.

我觉得我没有必要对他们作出那样的承诺。

common[38] [ˈkɒmən] a. 普通的, 寻常的; 共同的, 共有的

[语境] Rabbits and foxes are common in Britain.

兔子和狐狸在英国很常见。

Does the common man oppose the ideas of political union between European countries?

一般人是不是反对欧洲国家政治联合的构想呢?

[考点] in common 共同的, 共用的; as common as an old shoe 平易近人的; common ground 共同利益; common touch 平易近人的; out of common 不同寻常的; common sense 常识, 头脑, 见地

communicate [kəˈmjuːnɪkeɪt] v. 交际, 交流(思想等); 传达, 传送通信, 通信

[语境] I can't communicate with them; the radio doesn't work.

我无法和他们联系, 无线电坏了。

He has communicated his wishes to me.
他已经把他的愿望告诉了我。

［考点］communicate with... 与……联系，与……交往

community[11] [kəˈmjuːnɪtɪ] n. 社团，社区

［语境］He worked in a community welfare department.
他在社会福利部工作。

Everyone should invest some time in community service.
每个人都应该花些时间在社区服务上。

company[36] [ˈkʌmpənɪ] n. 公司；陪伴；宾客；连（队），（一）群，队，伙

［语境］The company made an adjustment in my salary.
公司对我的薪金作了调整。

compare [kəmˈpeə(r)] vt. (to, with) 比较；(to) 把……比作 vi. 相比

［语境］He compared the girl to the moon in the poem.
他在诗中把那姑娘比作月亮。

［考点］compare to 比拟，比作；compare with（可）与……相比

comparison [kəmˈpærɪsən] n. 比较，对比，比喻，比拟

［语境］He is quite tall in comparison with his classmates.
与他的同学相比，他相当高。

［考点］by comparison 比较起来，用比较方法；in comparison with 和……比较起来

compete [kəmˈpiːt] vi. 竞争，竞赛

［语境］Several companies are competing for the contract.
几家公司正为争取一项合同而互相竞争。

We have limited funds and several competing claims.
我们的基金有限而争相申请的却有几处。

［考点］compete with... 和……竞争，竞赛；compete against 和……争；compete for 为……争夺

competition[6] [ˌkɒmpəˈtɪʃən] n. 竞争，比赛；角逐，较量；［总称］竞争者

［语境］Everyone in modern society faces the keen competition.
现代社会的每个人都面临着激烈的竞争。

complain[9] [kəmˈpleɪn] vi. 抱怨，投诉

[语境] Don't complain without good cause.

没有充分的理由就不要抱怨。

You've got nothing to complain about.

你没什么可抱怨的。

[考点] complain to sb. of (about) sth. 向某人抱怨……; complain about/against/of 控告，申诉

complaint [kəmˈpleɪnt] *n.* **抱怨,诉苦,发牢骚**

[语境] The road-works caused much complaint among local residents.

修路引起周围居民很多怨言。

I have a number of complaints about the hotel room you've given me.

我对你给我的旅馆房间有几点不满意见。

考点集训

1. Researchers at the University of Illinois determined that the _____ of a father can help improve a child's grades.

   A. involvement　　　　　　B. interaction

   C. association　　　　　　D. communication

2. Is the theory of evolution in direct _____ with religious teachings, or does it leave room for debate?

   A. comparison　　　　　　B. distinction

   C. disturbance　　　　　　D. contradiction

3. _____ energy under the earth must be released in one form or another, for example, an earthquake.

   A. Accumulated　　　　　　B. Gathered

   C. Assembled　　　　　　D. Collected

4. Some people apparently have an amazing ability to _____ the right answer.

   A. come up with　　　　　　B. look up to

   C. put up with　　　　　　D. live up to

答案与解析

1. A 伊利诺伊州大学的研究人员研究发现,父亲的参与对提高孩子的成绩有帮助。A 参与;B 互动;C 联系;D 交流。故选 A。
2. D 进化论跟宗教说教完全矛盾吗,还是留有讨论的空间? A 比较;B 特别;C 打扰;D 矛盾。故 D 为正确答案。
3. A 积累在地下的能量必须通过一种或另一种方式得到释放,例如,地震。A 积累;B 收集,搜集;C 组装;D 收集。在这里动词的过去分词充当定语,因此 A 为正确答案。
4. A 有些人很显然有一种惊人的能力,能够很快得到正确答案。come up with "提出,找到"; look up to "尊敬,仰望"; put up with "容忍,忍受"; live up to "依照……行事"。

Word List 9

complete[70] [kəmˈpliːt] *vt.* 完成,结束 *a.* 完整的,全部的;完成的,终结的;彻底的

[语境] I only need one volume to complete my set of Dickens's novels.

我那套狄更斯小说只差一卷就配齐了。

When will the railway be completed?

铁路何时竣工?

[考点] complete with 包括,连同

complicated [ˈkɒmplɪkeɪtɪd] *a.* 结构复杂的

[语境] The situation in Lebanon is very complicated.

黎巴嫩的情况十分复杂。

component[5] [kəmˈpəʊnənt] *n.* (尤指机器或系统的)组成部分,组件,成分 *a.* 构成的,组成的

[语境] Those are the components of an engine.

那些是发动机的部件。

Surprise is an essential component of my plan.
我的这项计划主要就是想让大家惊喜一下。

compound [ˈkɒmpaʊnd] *n.* 混合物,化合物 *a.* 混合的,化合的 *vt.* 混合

[语境] Carbon is an element, while carbon dioxide is a compound.
碳是元素,而二氧化碳是化合物。

compromise [ˈkɒmprəmaɪz] *n.* 妥协,折中 *vi.* 妥协 *vt.* 危及,放弃(原则等)

[语境] His reluctance to compromise is an obstacle to his political success.
他不肯妥协是他政治上成功的一个障碍。

[考点] compromise with on 在……方面同……妥协

compute [kəmˈpjuːt] *v./n.* 计算,估计

[语境] The losses caused by the floods were beyond compute.
洪水造成的损失难以估量。

[考点] calculate, count, compute, reckon 辨析:这些动词均含有"计算"之意。calculate 通常指要求细致精确和复杂的计算,以解决疑难问题,多用于自然科学、生产部门或要求专门计算的场合。count 指逐一计算而得出总数。compute 一般指已有数据的、较简单但数字长的数学运算。reckon 通常指较简单的数学计算,也可指心算

conceal [kənˈsiːl] *vt.* 隐藏,隐瞒

[语境] He concealed himself behind the tree.
他藏在树后。

It is wrong for a man to conceal things from his wife.
一个男人对妻子隐瞒事情是不对的。

[考点] conceal sth. from sb. 对某人隐藏或隐瞒某事

concentrate[6] [ˈkɒnsəntreɪt] *vt.* 集中;浓缩 *vi.* 集中,专心

[语境] The crowds concentrated round the palace.
人群汇集在宫殿的四周。

The threat of going bankrupt is very unpleasant but it certainly concentrates the mind.

即将破产的威胁虽令人极烦恼,但确实也能逼迫人开动脑筋。

[考点] concentrate on/upon 聚精会神

concept[16] [ˈkɒnsept] *n.* **概念,观念,思想**

[语境] I can not understand the so abstract concept.
我无法理解如此抽象的观念。
This concept is at the very core of her theory.
这个概念是她的理论的核心。

concern[12] [kənˈsɜːn] *vt.* **关心,担心** *n.* **所关切的事,(利害)关系**

[语境] How much money I earn is none of your concern.
我挣多少钱与你无关。
These problems concern all of us.
这些问题影响到我们每一个人。

[考点] as far as...be concerned 就……而言;concern oneself with/about 关心,关注;be concerned for 担心,操心;have a concern in 在……中有利害关系;of concern 重要的

concert [ˈkɒnsət] *n.* 音乐会;一致;和谐

[语境] We are queuing up to buy tickets for the concert.
我们正在排队等候买音乐会的入场券。
The teacher told them to act in concert with one another.
老师告诉他们行动要一致。

[考点] in concert 一致;协力;(音乐表演者)现场演出

conclude[5] [kənˈkluːd] *vt.* **结束,完结;下结论,断定**

[巧记] conclusion (*n.* 结论);conclusive (*a.* 决定性的,令人信服的)

[语境] They concluded the meeting at 6 o'clock in the afternoon.
他们于下午六点结束了会议。
We may reasonably conclude that the meeting has been postponed.
我们有理由可以断定,会议推迟了。

conclusion[11] [kənˈkluːʒən] *n.* **结论,推论;结尾;缔结,议定**

[语境] Our conclusion is based entirely on fact.

我们的结论完全是实事求是的。

[考点] come to/draw/reach a conclusion 得出结论,告一段落; in conclusion 最后,总之

condition[16] [kənˈdɪʃən] *n.* 条件,状况,环境 *vt.* 决定;支配;训练

[语境] These bad conditions have given rise to a lot of crime.

这些恶劣的环境已造成了许多犯罪行为。

[考点] on condition that 条件是

conduct [ˈkɒndʌkt] *n.* 行为,表现,品行 *v.* 引导,指挥;处理,管理; 传导,导电(热)

[语境] The reporter was accused of unprofessional conduct.

那位记者被控有违反职业道德的行为。

Copper conducts electricity better than iron does.

铜的导电性比铁强。

conditioner [kənˈdɪʃənə(r)] *n.* 调节装置,空调

[巧记] condition(气温条件) + er(设备)→调节室内气温的装置 →空调

[语境] This new style of air conditioner is noiseless.

这种新型空调没有噪声。

conduct[9] [ˈkɒndʌkt, -dəkt] *vt.* 引导,指挥;传电,传热 *n.* 行为,品行

[巧记] conduction *n.* 传导,输送 conductive *a.* 有传导力的,传导性的

[语境] Actors may hire agents to conduct their affairs.

演员可以雇用经纪人掌管他们的事务。

Most plastics do not readily conduct electricity.

大多数塑料都不容易导电。

Can you justify your conduct to me?

你能向我证明你的行为是正确的吗?

conductor [kənˈdʌktə(r)] *n.* 售票员;导体

[语境] The bus conductor forgot to remind him to get off at that station.

公共汽车售票员忘记提醒他在那一站下车了。

Wood is a poor conductor of heat and electricity.

木头是热和电的不良导体。

confidence[11] [ˈkɒnfɪdəns] *n.* 信心,信任

[语境] The servant enjoyed his master's confidence.

这个仆人深得主人的信赖。

She has great confidence in her success.

她充分相信自己能成功。

[考点] put/have/place confidence in/that 相信,信赖;in confidence 秘密地,私下地;take sb. into one's confidence 对……说知心话

confident[5] [ˈkɒnfɪdənt] *a.* (of, in) 确信的,自信的

[巧记] confidently *ad.* 信赖地,安心地

[语境] He is quite confident that he will pass the examination.

他很有信心通过考试。

confirm [kənˈfɜːm] *vt.* 证实,确认;批准;使坚固

[巧记] confirmable *a.* 可确定的, 能证实的; 可批准的

[语境] He looked around to confirm that he was alone.

他四处张望,以确定周围没人。

She was baptized when she was a month old and confirmed when she was thirteen.

她出生一个月时受洗礼,十三岁时行坚信礼。

conflict [ˈkɒnflɪkt] *n.* 冲突,关键,争执 *vt.* 抵触,冲突

[语境] The long drawn-out conflict between the employers and workers led to the strike last week.

劳资之间旷日持久的纠纷导致了上周的罢工。

There has always been some conflict between the sexes.

两性之间总是有矛盾。

[考点] in conflict(with) 和……有矛盾,不一致;conflict with 和……发生冲突

confront [kənˈfrʌnt] *vt.* 使面对,使遭遇

[语境] They confronted the prisoner with his accusers.

他们让犯人与原告对质。

A soldier often has to confront danger.

士兵常常要身临险境。

[考点] be confronted with 面临……(困难、危险等)

confuse[5] [kənˈfjuːz] vt. **使混乱,使困惑**

[语境] Please don't confuse Australia with Austria.
别把澳大利亚和奥地利混淆了。
They asked so many questions that they confused me.
他们问了许多问题,把我弄糊涂了。

congratulate [kənˈgrætʃuleɪt] v. (on) 祝贺,向……致贺词

[语境] I congratulate you on your great discovery.
我祝贺你的伟大发现。

[考点] congratulate oneself on 庆幸,感到幸运

connect[7] [kəˈnekt] vt. 连接;与……联系,接通(电话) vi. 连接

[语境] The bridge connected the island with the mainland.
这座桥把这个岛屿与大陆连接起来。

[考点] connect up 连起来,接上;connect with 和……有联系,和……有关

conquer [ˈkɒŋkə(r)] vt. 征服,占领;克服,改正(恶习等)

[巧记] 反义词:surrender

[语境] When will scientists conquer cancer?
科学家们什么时候才能征服癌症呢?
He set out to conquer the literary world of London.
他决心赢得伦敦文学界的赞誉。

conscience [ˈkɒnʃəns] n. 良心,良知

[巧记] conscienceless a. 没良心的,没道德的

[语境] I got nothing to hide. My conscience is clear.
我没有什么隐瞒的。我问心无愧。

conscious [ˈkɒnʃəs] a. 觉出的,意识到的;有知觉的,处于清醒状态的;有觉悟的,自觉的

[语境] He was very conscious of his shortcomings.
他对自己的缺点十分清楚。
He was badly hurt, but he still remained conscious.
他伤得很重,但仍未失去知觉。

consider [kən'sɪdə(r)] v. 考虑,细想;体谅,顾及;认为,把……看作
　　[语境] He considered that it was better for him to sit on the fence during the quarrel.
　　他认为在这场争吵中自己还是保持中立为好。

consist[5] [kən'sɪst] vi. (in)存在于,(of)由……组成,构成,包括
　　[语境] The United Kingdom consists of Great Britain and Northern Ireland.
　　联合王国由大不列颠和北爱尔兰组成。
　　The beauty of Venice consists largely in the style of its ancient buildings.
　　威尼斯的美很大程度上在于它那古代建筑的风格。

constant[7] ['kɒnstənt] a. 不断的,持续的;始终如一的;坚定的,恒定的,经常的
　　[巧记] constantly(ad. 不变地;经常地;坚持不懈地 = frequently)
　　[语境] The fear of being discovered was his constant companion.
　　他总提心吊胆的,担心被人发现。
　　The children's constant chatter was irritating.
　　那些孩子们喋喋不休的说话声使人心烦。

考点集训

1. Not having a good command of English can be a serious _____ preventing you from achieving your goals.
　　A. obstacle　　　　　　B. fault
　　C. offense　　　　　　D. distress

2. It's very _____ of you not to talk aloud while the baby is asleep.
　　A. concerned　　　　　B. careful
　　C. considerable　　　　D. considerate

3. The test results are beyond _____; they have been repeated in labs all over the world.
　　A. negotiation　　　　　B. conflict
　　C. bargain　　　　　　D. dispute

4. I'm _____ enough to know it is going to be a very difficult situa-

tion to compete against three strong teams.
   A. realistic　　　　　　　B. conscious
   C. aware　　　　　　　　D. radical
5. He found the _____ media attention intolerable and decided to go abroad.
   A. sufficient　　　　　　　B. constant
   C. steady　　　　　　　　D. plenty
6. We need to create education standards that prepare our next generation who will be _____ with an even more competitive market.
   A. tackled　　　　　　　　B. encountered
   C. dealt　　　　　　　　　D. confronted
7. The school arranged road trip appears to _____ the spring break.
   A. conform to　　　　　　B. coincide with
   C. consist in　　　　　　　D. collide with
8. Young people are not _____ to stand and look at works of art; they want art they can participate in.
   A. conservative　　　　　B. content
   C. confident　　　　　　　D. generous
9. Dr. Smith was always _____ the poor and the sick, often providing them with free medical care.
   A. reminded of　　　　　B. absorbed in
   C. tended by　　　　　　D. concerned about

答案与解析

1. A　不掌握流利的英语，你的目标难以实现。A 障碍；B 错误；C 冒犯；D 悲痛，危难。故选 A。

2. D　孩子睡着的时候，你说话很小声，你真体贴人。A 关心的；B 细心的；C 大量的；D 贴心的，贴切的。故选 D。

3. D　测试结果无可争议，世界范围内的实验室得出同样的结论。beyond dispute 毫无争议，故选 D。

4. B　我很清楚跟三个强敌竞争的艰难处境。A 现实的；B 有意识的,清楚的;C 意识到的;D 激进的,根本的。故选 B。

5. B 他难以忍受媒体的频繁关注,决定出国。A 足够的;B 频繁的,不断的;C 稳定的;D 大量的。故选 B。

6. D 我们要有教育标准,使要面对激烈竞争的下一代做好准备。A 处理,解决;B 相遇,碰见,不期而遇;C 处理,常与 with 连用;D 使面对,面临。故选 D。

7. B A 符合,遵照;B 与……一致,同时发生;C 存在于……中;D 与……冲突。

8. B 年轻人不满足于站着看艺术作品,他们想要有他们参与的艺术品。A 保守的;B 满足的;C 有信心的;D 慷慨的,大方的。故 B 为正确答案。

9. D 根据题干中 often providing them with free medical care,再结合四个选项——be reminded of 表示"被提醒,使记起";be absorbed in 表示"全神贯注于,专心于";be tended by 表示"被照顾";be concerned about 表示"关心,挂念"可知,只有 concerned about 符合题意,答案为 D。

Word List 10

consult [kənˈsʌlt] *vi.* **商量,咨询,会诊** *vt.* **请教,咨询,查阅;就诊**

[语境] I have consulted a number of law books in the British Museums.

我查阅了大英博物馆里许多法律书籍。

I consulted with a friend on a matter.

我和朋友商量了一件事。

[考点] consult with 和……商议,向……征求意见;consult on 向某人请教某个问题或事情;consult about 向某人请教比较一般或笼统的问题

contact[20] [ˈkɒntækt] *n.* **联系,接触** *vt.* **联系,接触,交往**

[语境] Have the children been in contact with disease?

孩子们同这种疾病有过接触吗?

We made contact with the ship by radio.

我们通过无线电同那只船保持联系。

[考点] have contact with 接触到,和……有联系；lose contact with 和……失去联系,离开；make contact with 和……接触[联系]

context [ˈkɒntekst] n. (文章等)前后关系；(事件等发生的)背景

[语境] We can often tell the meaning of a word from its context.

我们往往可以从一个字的上下文知道它的意思。

continue[20] [kənˈtɪnjuː] v. 继续,连续,延伸

[巧记] continued a. 连续的,继续的,不断的

[语境] Land will continue to appreciate.

土地将继续增值。

continent [ˈkɒntɪnənt] n. 大陆,洲

[语境] He traversed alone the whole continent of Africa from east to west.

他只身长途跋涉,从东向西横穿整个非洲大陆。

continue [kənˈtɪnjuː] v. 连续,继续

[巧记] continuous (a. 继续的,连续的)；continual (a. 不断的；频繁的；连续的)

[语境] The strike continued for several days.

罢工持续了几天之久。

contract[9] [ˈkɒntrækt] n. 契约,合同,包工 v. 收缩；感染；定约

[语境] The city contracted for a library with their firm.

市政当局和他们公司订立了修建图书馆的合同。

Marriage is, first of all, a contract which must be governed by justice.

婚姻首先是一种契约,它必须以公正为制约。

[考点] make a contract with 与……签订合同；contract oneself out of 约定使自己不受……的约束；退出(契约、协议等)

contradict [ˌkɒntrəˈdɪkt] v. 反驳；同……矛盾,同……抵触

[巧记] contradictable a. 可反驳的；contradictor n. 反驳者；相矛盾

的人;抵触者

[语境] The facts contradict his theory.

那些事实与他的理论相悖。

contrary [ˈkɒntrərɪ] *n.* **反面,相反**

[语境] My sister's taste in dresses is contrary to my own.

在服装方面,我妹妹的爱好和我完全不同。

The players on the contrary side now took their places.

双方运动员开始各就各位。

[考点] contrary to 与……对立;on the contrary 正相反

contrast[8] [ˈkɒntrɑːst] *n.* **对照,对比;对立面;反差** *vt.* **使对照,使对比** *vi.* **(with) 和……形成对照**

[语境] The black furnishings provide an interesting contrast to the white walls.

黑色家具和白色墙壁形成很有意思的对比。

The coastal areas have mild winters, but by contrast the central plains become extremely cold.

沿海地区的冬天天气暖和,可是相比之下中部平原却异常寒冷。

[考点] in contrast with 与……相对比,与……相对照

contribute[15] [kənˈtrɪbjuːt] *v.* **捐赠(款项);投稿;贡献**

[巧记] con 全部, tribute 给予→全部给予→捐献

[语境] Honesty and hard work contribute to success and happiness.

诚实加苦干有助于成功和幸福。

She asked him to contribute a biweekly article on European affairs.

她约他每两周写一篇有关欧洲情况的文稿。

[考点] contribute to 有助于,促成,捐献

contribution[8] [ˌkɒntrɪˈbjuːʃən] *n.* **贡献;捐款,捐献物;投稿**

[语境] The invention of paper was a great contribution to human civilization.

纸的发明是对人类文明的一大贡献。

[考点] make a contribution to 捐赠;作出贡献

control[37] [kən'trəʊl] *vt. /n.* 控制，操纵

[语境] At that time the Romans controlled a vast empire.
那时罗马人统治着一个很大的帝国。
The car went out of control and crashed.
汽车失去控制，撞坏了。

[考点] out of control 失去控制；under control 处于控制之下；be in control of 指挥，管理或支配；bring sth. under control 使……被控制住

controversial [ˌkɒntrə'vɜːʃəl] *a.* 引起争论的，有争议的

[巧记] contro 反，vers 转→跟别人反着转→引起争论的

[语境] Many of the new taxes are controversial.
许多新税收都是有争议的。

convenience [kən'viːnjəns] *n.* 便利，方便

[语境] We must consult his convenience.
我们必须考虑到他的方便。

convenient[5] [kən'viːnɪənt] *a.* 方便的

[巧记] 反义词：inconvenient, unhandy

[语境] Will it be convenient for you to come in the morning?
你上午来方便吗？
A bicycle's often far more convenient than a car in busy cities.
在热闹的都市里骑自行车往往比坐汽车方便得多。

convention[14] [kən'venʃən] *n.* 习俗，惯例；(正式)会议；公约，契约

[巧记] 派生词：conventional *a.* 依照惯例的，约定俗成的

[语境] The convention looms as political battle.
这场大会将是一场政治角斗。
Convention requires that such meetings open with prayer.
惯例上要求这样的集会应当以祈祷开始。

conversation[24] [ˌkɒnvə'seɪʃən] *n.* 会话，谈话

[语境] He is easy in conversation and graceful in manner.
他谈吐从容，举止优雅。

[考点] have/hold a conversation with 和……交谈[会谈]；in conversation with (在)和……谈话

核心词汇精解

convince[5] [kən'vɪns] *vt.* 使确信,使信服;使知错

[语境] He convinced me of his sincerity.
他使我确信他的真诚。
Your argument is too weak to convince me.
你的论点太薄弱了,说服不了我。

[考点] convince sb. of 使某人承认,使某人信服

cook [kʊk] *v.* 煮,烹调,烧 *n.* 炊事员,厨师

[巧记] 厨师(cook)做菜要用厨具(cooker)。

[语境] She cooked her meals on a gas range.
她在煤气灶上做饭。
They dismissed the cook.
他们把厨师解雇了。

cool [kuːl] *a.* 凉的,凉快的,酷的 *n.* 凉快 *v.* 使变凉

[语境] The cool autumn wind clarified my mind.
凉爽的秋风使我的头脑清醒过来。
This place remains cool all summer.
这个地方整个夏天都凉爽。
The rain has cooled the air.
这场雨使空气凉爽了。

cooperate [kəʊ'ɒpəreɪt] *vi.* 合作,协作

[语境] Everything cooperated to make our holiday a success.
这一切凑合起来使我们的假期圆满过去。
We want to cooperate with you greatly.
我们非常愿意与你们合作。

[考点] cooperate with sb. (in doing sth./to do sth.) 和某人合作

copy ['kɒpɪ] *n.* 抄本,摹本;(一)本 *vt.* 抄写;考试中抄袭

[语境] The reporter had copied down every word spoken by the minister.
记者已把部长讲的话一字不漏地全记下来了。

corporation [ˌkɔːpə'reɪʃən] *n.* 公司,团体

[巧记] corporation(公司)是由人组成的,其运转需要员工们的协作(cooperation)

103

[语境] The president disbanded the corporation.
总裁解散了公司。

correct [kəˈrekt] *a.* 正确的,恰当的,端正的 *v.* 改正,纠正,矫正

[巧记] 反义词:incorrect, wrong

[语境] Her analysis was correct to the nail.
她的分析极其正确。

correspond[93] [ˌkɒrɪˈspɒnd] *vi.* (to)相当于,(with)与……一致,相符合;通信

[语境] Does the name on the envelope correspond with the name on the letter inside?
信封上的名字与里面信上的名字是否相同?

[考点] correspond with sb. 和……通信;correspond to 相等,相当于

corrupt [kəˈrʌpt] *vt.* 腐蚀,使堕落 *a.* 堕落的,腐败的,贪赃的

[语境] She wrote a book declaiming against our corrupt society.
她写了一本书抨击我们这腐败的社会。

Democracy substitute election by the incompetent many for appointment by corrupt few.
民主主义以由无能的大多数作出的选举来代替腐败的少数作出的委任。

corruption [kəˈrʌpʃən] *n.* 堕落;腐化;腐败;贿赂;腐烂

[巧记] corruptionist *n.* 贪污腐化分子,行贿受贿分子

[语境] His integrity stood out in relief from the corruption of certain officials.
某些官员腐化堕落,相形之下他的廉正更引人瞩目。

cost[20] [kɒst] *n.* 成本,费用,代价 *v.* 价值为,花费

[语境] Climbing cost of cotton squeezes mill profits.
上涨的棉花价格减少了纺织厂的利润。

[考点] at the cost of 以……为代价,用……换来的;丧失;牺牲;cost of living 生活费用

costly [ˈkɒstlɪ] *a.* 昂贵的,代价高的

[语境] Actions need not be complex or costly.

行动不需要多么复杂或昂贵。

cough [kɒf] *v./n.* 咳嗽

[语境] Coughing at a concert can be a real embarrassment.

在音乐会上咳嗽真令人难堪。

could [kʊd] *v./aux.* (口语)(表示许可或请求)可以……,行

[语境] She could play the violin when she was five.

她五岁时便能拉小提琴了。

count [kaʊnt] *v.* 数,计算;算入;看作,认为 *n.* 计数,总数

[语境] Please count me out from tomorrow's basketball match.

明天的篮球比赛请不要把我算在内。

counter ['kaʊntə(r)] *n.* 柜台;计数器 *a./ad.* 相反的(地) *v.* 反对,反击

[语境] Our neighbor's opinion was counter to that of my parents.

我家邻居的意见与我父母的意见相反。

[考点] run counter to 与……相抵触,违反

考点集训

1. Please _____ dictionaries when you are not sure of word spelling or meaning.
   A. seek   B. inquire
   C. search   D. consult

2. There are several factors _____ the rapid growth of sales promotion, particularly in consumer markets.
   A. resorting to   B. appealing to
   C. applying to   D. contributing to

3. It is our _____ policy that we will achieve unity through peaceful means.
   A. consistent   B. continuous
   C. considerate   D. continual

4. In Britain people _____ four million tons of potatoes every year.
   A. swallow   B. dispose
   C. consume   D. exhaust

5. John doesn't believe in _____ medicine; he has some remedies of his own.
   A. standard   B. regular
   C. routine   D. conventional
6. Workers in the fine arts _____ thoughts and feelings through their creative works.
   A. transmit   B. elaborate
   C. convey   D. contribute
7. Even after reading it for three lines, he couldn't _____ the meaning of that letter.
   A. conceive   B. consult
   C. contrast   D. concern
8. Science and technology have _____ in important ways to the improvement of agricultural production.
   A. attached   B. assisted
   C. contributed   D. witnessed
9. The native Canadians lived in _____ with nature, for they respected nature as a provider of life.
   A. coordination   B. acquaintance
   C. contact   D. harmony

答案与解析

1. D 你要是不确定单词的拼写或意思,请查阅词典。A 寻求;B 询问;C 搜查;D 咨询,求助于。故选 D。

2. D contribute to 有助于;resort to 诉诸,采取;appeal to 向……请求,对……有吸引力;apply to 涂抹,向……请求。

3. A 通过和平手段解决统一问题是我们一贯坚持的原则。A 一贯的,坚持的;B 连续不断的;C 贴心的,贴切的;D 频繁的,不停的。因此,A 为正确答案。

4. C 英国人每年消耗掉 400 万吨土豆。A 吞咽;B 处理;C 消费,消耗;D 使筋疲力尽。故 C 为正确答案。

5. D 约翰不相信传统的药物,他有自己的救治方法。A 标准;B

有规律的,定期的;C 日常的;D 传统的。故 D 为正确答案。
6. C 艺术工作者通过他们的创造性工作传递他们的思想和情感。A 传输,传送;B 详尽说明;C 传达;D 有助于。故选 C。
7. A 尽管已经阅读了三行,他还是不能理解这封信的意思。conceive"想出,构想出";consult"请教,咨询";contrast"对比";concern"涉及,关系到"。只有 A 项与句意相符。
8. C 科学技术的进步从很多方面促进了农业产量的提高。A 附属;B 帮助;C 促进;D 目睹。故选 C。
9. D 加拿大本土人与自然和谐相处,因为自然为其生活提供了必需品,所以他们尊重自然。A 协调,协作;B 认识;C 联系;D 和谐。故选 D。

Word List 11

country [ˈkʌntrɪ] *n.* 国家;农村,乡下
 [语境] The two countries disputed for years over a small strip of land on their border.
 这两个国家为了边界上一块土地已经争执多年。
 [考点] host country 东道国

countryside [ˈkʌntrɪsaɪd] *n.* 乡下,农村
 [语境] I prefer the quiet countryside to the noisy cities.
 我喜欢安静的乡村胜过喧闹的城市。

couple [ˈkʌpəl] *n.* (一)对,双;夫妇 *v.* 连接,结合
 [语境] The young couple decided to start their tour immediately.
 那对年轻夫妇决定立即开始旅游。
 [考点] a couple of 两三个,(少数)几个; be coupled with 和……联合,结合

courage [ˈkʌrɪdʒ] *n.* 勇气,胆量
 [巧记] 同义词:boldness, bravery;反义词:coward, timidity
 [语境] It takes courage to break the bonds of convention.

打破传统的束缚需要勇气。

course[22] [kɔːs] *n.* 过程,进程;课程,教程;(一)道(菜) *v.* 快速地流动

[语境] Events took their natural course.
事态依自然进程发展。
The blood coursed through the arteries.
血液在动脉血管中循环。

[考点] in the course of 在……期间,在……的过程中; of course 当然

court [kɔːt] *n.* 法院,法庭;球场;院子;朝廷

[语境] The court of King Solomon was noted for its splendor.
所罗门国王的宫廷以其华丽著称。
The young man courted the young lady by bringing her flowers every day.
年轻人通过每天给那女子送花而向她求爱。

[考点] clear the court 禁止旁听,命旁人退席; go to court 上朝,朝见君主;上法院;打官司; in court 在法庭上

cousin [ˈkʌzn] *n.* 堂(或表)兄弟(姐妹)

[语境] He feeds on his cousin.
他靠他的表兄生活。

cover [ˈkʌvə(r)] *v.* 覆盖,包括,涉及 *n.* 盖子,套子;(书的)封面

[语境] The valley was covered with a blanket of snow.
山谷白雪如毯。

[考点] take cover 藏身,躲避,避难; under cover 在遮蔽处;附在信中;秘密地,暗中

crazy [ˈkreɪzi] *a.* 疯狂的,古怪的,蠢的;(about)狂热的

[语境] He was crazy and set the house on fire.
他疯了,放火烧了房子。

[考点] be crazy about 热衷于,醉心于;爱上,迷恋着; be crazy over 热衷于,醉心于;爱上,迷恋着; be crazy for 渴望,痴想

create[16] [kriˈeɪt] *vt.* 创造,产生

[语境] This decision creates a dangerous precedent.

这个决定开创了一个危险的先例。

We've tried to create the ambience of a French bistro.

我们想尽量创造出法国小餐馆的气氛。

creative[9] [kriːˈeɪtɪv] *a.* **有创造力的,创造性的**

[巧记] creativeness *n.* 创造力;艺术创新

[语境] Creative, two-way learning between teachers and pupils can take place.

教师和学生之间创造性的双向学习是可以实现的。

[考点] be creative of 产生

creature [ˈkriːtʃə(r)] *n.* **人,动物;生物**

[巧记] creaturely *a.* 生物的,动物的

[语境] These tiny creatures are hardly visible to the naked eyes.

这些微小的生物肉眼几乎看不见。

credit[5] [ˈkredɪt] *n.* **信贷,赊欠;信用,信誉;学分;荣誉,功劳** *vt.* **信任;(to)把(钱款)记入,存入(账户中)**

[语境] The bank refused further credits to the company.

银行拒绝再贷款给这家公司。

His improved performance does credit to his trainer.

他的表演有进步,这应该归功于他的教练。

[考点] reflect credit on 使……感到光荣; on credit 赊购; give credit to 相信;信任;称赞,赞扬

crime[21] [kraɪm] *n.* **罪,犯罪**

[巧记] crimeless *a.* 无罪的

[语境] Murder is a vile and loathsome crime.

谋杀是邪恶而令人发指的罪行。

It's a crime to neglect such a lovely garden.

让这么可爱的花园荒废是极不应该的。

[考点] a capital crime 死罪; commit a crime 犯罪; bring a criminal to justice 把罪犯带到法庭上

crisis [ˈkraɪsɪs] *n.* **危急关头,(政治、经济上的)危机,决定性的时刻;转变期**

[语境] Her fever passed its crisis.

她发烧已经过了危险期。

They suffered huge losses in the financial crisis.

他们在经济危机时遭受了巨大的损失。

[考点] at a crisis 在紧急关头；bring to a crisis 使陷入危机；face a crisis 面临危机；pass a crisis 渡过危机，脱离危险期

critic ['krɪtɪk] n. 批评家，评论家

[语境] Critics acclaimed the new play.

批评家们盛赞这出新戏。

critical[11] ['krɪtɪkəl] a. 批语的；爱挑剔的；重大的，决定性的

[语境] I think the chastisement to him is too critical.

我认为对他的惩罚太严厉了。

In the current critical climate her work is not popular.

在当前评论风气影响下，她的作品不怎么受欢迎。

[考点] at critical 在临界状态下；be critical about 爱挑剔

criticism ['krɪtɪsɪzəm] n. 评论性的文章，评论；批评，指责，非难

[语境] His criticism on my mistakes is dead on the target.

他对我的错误提出批评，真是一针见血。

criticize/-ise[5] ['krɪtɪsaɪz] v. 批评，评论

[巧记] 反义词：admire, praise

[语境] It's hard to criticize one's own work.

评价自己的工作并非易事。

crop [krɒp] n. 农作物，庄稼；收成

[语境] The land is out of crop.

这块土地未种庄稼。

cross [krɒs] n. 十字(架)；苦难 a. 交叉的；发怒的 v. 穿过

[语境] I'll keep my fingers crossed for you.

我将为你祝福。

[考点] get cross (对……)生气，发脾气；be cross with (对……)生气，发脾气

crowd [kraʊd] n. 人群；一群，一伙 v. 聚集，群集；挤满，拥挤

[语境] A crowd gathered at the scene of the accident.

出事地点聚集了一群人。

[考点] a crowd of 一群,一堆; be crowded with 满是…… follow the crowd 随大流,从众; crowd about 围住,包围; crowd out 挤出,推开,驱逐; crowd up 拥[挤]上

crowded [kraʊdɪd] *a.* 拥挤的

[语境] We are all bunched together in the crowded elevator.
在拥挤的电梯里我们聚拢在一起。

[考点] be crowded with 充满,挤满

cruel [kruəl] *a.* 残忍的,残酷的

[语境] Destiny is sometimes cruel.
命运之神有时是残酷的。

crush [krʌʃ] *n./v.* 压碎,压坏 *v.* 压服,压垮

[语境] Their plot to overthrow the government was crushed.
他们企图推翻政府的阴谋被粉碎了。

[考点] crush out 镇压;榨出;扑[熄]灭; crush up 捏成一团;粉[碾]碎

cry [kraɪ] *vi.* 哭,流泪 *v.* 叫,喊 *n.* 哭泣,哭声,叫喊,喊声

[语境] A baby's cry can be expressive of hunger or pain.
婴儿的啼哭可能是表示他饥饿或疼痛。

culture ['kʌltʃə(r)] *n.* 文化,教养,种植

[语境] It is impossible to dissociate language from culture.
把语言与文化分离是不可能的。

Sod-culture is the effective way to solve this problem.
生草栽培正是解决这一问题的有效途径。

cup [kʌp] *n.* 杯子

[语境] He flumped his cup on the table.
他砰地把杯子放在桌上。

cure [kjʊə(r)] *v.* (of) 治愈,医治;矫正 *n.* 治愈,痊愈;良药

[巧记] 同义词:heal, remedy, restore

[语境] She tried every means to cure her child of the bad habit.
她想尽一切办法试图改掉她孩子的这个恶习。

curiosity[5] [ˌkjʊərɪ'ɒsɪtɪ] *n.* 好奇(心)

[语境] I had to explain the reasons to satisfy his curiosity.

我只好解释原因来满足他的好奇心。

Curiosity is part of the children's nature.

好奇是儿童的天性。

curious[7] [ˈkjʊərɪəs] *a.* **好奇的，求知的，古怪的，爱挑剔的**

[语境] There are curious parallels between medicine and law.

在医学和法律之间有着奇特的相似之处。

[考点] be curious about 对(某事物)感到好奇；be curious to (do) 很想(做)；渴望(做)

current[16] [ˈkʌrənt] *a.* **现时的，当今的；通用的** *n.* **(水、气、电)流；趋势，倾向**

[语境] This word is no longer in current use.

这个词现在已经不再使用。

Nothing disturbs the peaceful current of life in the village.

没有任何事干扰村里一向平静的生活。

[考点] current 指的是目前存在的情况，可能是暂时的。而 recent 指的是不久前发生的事情，可能现在已经结束；也可指不复存在的事情

custom[11] [ˈkʌstəm] *n.* **习惯，风俗；(the Customs) 海关；(*pl.*) 关税**

[巧记] customable *a.* 可征收关税的 customize *vt.* 为顾客定制

[语境] It took us only a few minutes to get through the customs.

我们的海关检查只花了几分钟时间。

She followed her usual custom of spending Sunday at her villa at the seaside.

她按照通常的习惯，在海滨别墅度过了星期天。

customer[7] [ˈkʌstəmə(r)] *n.* **顾客，主顾**

[巧记] 顾客(customer)最终要为关税(customs)买单

[语境] The shop laid the cloth by for a customer.

商店为一个顾客保留着这些布料。

cut [kʌt] *n./v.* **切，割，削；削减，删节** *n.* **切口，伤口**

[语境] To cut a long story short, I decided to stay.

简而言之，我决定留下。

The workers had to take a cut in pay.

工人们只得同意削减工资。

[考点] short cut 捷径,近路;cut about 乱切,乱砍;cut across 走捷径,穿过去;cut down 削减,压缩;砍倒;cut in 插进来说,插嘴;干预;cut off 切断,停掉;隔绝,挡住

cycle ['saɪkəl] *n.* 自行车;周期,循环 *v.* 骑自行车;循环

[语境] He studied the cycle of events leading to the Great Depression.

他研究了导致大萧条的一系列事件。

考点集训

1. The local people were joyfully surprised to find the prices of vegetables no longer _____ according to the weather.
   A. evaluated   B. converted
   C. fluctuated   D. modified

2. After long negotiations, the firm _____ to build a double-purpose bridge across the river.
   A. contracted   B. contacted
   C. consulted   D. convinced

3. We want to _____ with you greatly.
   A. operate   B. corporate
   C. cooperate   D. co-ordinate

4. Retail sales volume in local urban and rural areas rose 57.8% and 46.8% _____ last year.
   A. individually   B. respectively
   C. correspondingly   D. accordingly

5. Next semester, Susan must take three _____ compulsory courses.
   A. formal   B. voluntary
   C. practical   D. required

6. The dishes _____ to the floor.
   A. falled   B. crashed
   C. smashed   D. broke

7. Many proverbs _____ in ancient Greece and Rome and in medieval Europe, spreading from country to country in Latin texts.
   A. designated   B. descended
   C. originated   D. created
8. He has failed me so many times that I no longer place any _____ on what he promises.
   A. faith   B. belief
   C. credit   D. reliance
9. She went to Europe on vacation but her happy time ended in _____ when their hotel caught fire.
   A. tragedy   B. crisis
   C. drama   D. misfortune
10. Why are you always so _____ ?
    A. critical   B. critic
    C. typical   D. logical
11. He _____ that a combination of recent oil discoveries and the advance of new technology will lead to a decline in the price of crude oil.
    A. predicts   B. compels
    C. arranges   D. disputes
12. She _____ him for ruining her life.
    A. accused   B. bruised
    C. scolded   D. cursed
13. Isn't it _____ when you learn something you've never known before?
    A. cool   B. crazy
    C. cold   D. cute
14. I'm _____ about how you discovered my website, and am very glad if you enjoy it.
    A. mysterious   B. furious
    C. serious   D. curious

答案与解析

1. C 当地人民惊喜地发现蔬菜的价格不再根据天气的不同而改变。evaluate 评估,评价;fluctuate 波动,涨落,起伏;modify 被修改,被修饰。

2. A 经过长时间的协商,公司签订合约决定建设一座两用桥。contract 合同,契约,婚约;contact 接触,联络;consult 商议,磋商。

3. C 我们非常愿意与你们合作。operate 手术,操纵;corporate 社团的,共同的;co-ordinate 平等的。

4. B 去年零售量在当地城市和农村分别上升57.8%和46.8%。

5. D 下学期开始,苏珊有三门必修课程。formal 正式的;voluntary 自愿的,志愿的;practical 实践的,实际的;required 必需的;compulsory 义务的,必修的。

6. B 碗碟哗啦一声掉在地板上。fall 指因为重力的作用或失去平衡而自由落下;smash 猛烈击碎或撞碎;break 打破;crash 指猛撞、坠毁,常伴有撞击声,和 into 或 to 连用。

7. C 许多谚语起源于古希腊、罗马以及中世纪欧洲,以拉丁文的形式传向世界。designate 指出,指示,标明;descend 下降,传下来,出自;originate 起源,追溯到。

8. D 他让我失望了这么多次,我不会再相信他的任何诺言了。faith 信任,信心,宗教信仰;belief 信念,观念;reliance 信赖,依赖的人。

9. A 她到欧洲度假,结果宾馆着火使原本快乐的时光在悲剧中结束了。tragedy 悲剧,惨案;drama 戏剧,戏剧作品;misfortune 不幸,坏运气,灾祸。

10. A 你怎么总是这样吹毛求疵?critical 后接 of 或 about 意思为"找茬";typical 典型的,象征性的;logical 合乎逻辑的。

11. A 他预言最近石油的发现和科技的提高将导致原油价格下跌。

12. D 她诅咒他,说他毁了她的一生。accuse 控告,常和 of 连用;bruise 受伤,伤害;scold 责备。

13. A cool 酷,很棒;crazy 疯狂的;cold 寒冷的;cute 可爱的。

14. D 这个本身是一个固定搭配:对什么东西很好奇,be curious about,答案是D。

Word List 12

daily [ˈdeɪlɪ] *a.* 每日的 *ad.* 每日,天天 *n.* 日报
 [语境] Daily practice is the trick in learning a foreign language.
  每天练习是学会一门外语的诀窍。

damage[20] [ˈdæmɪdʒ] *vt.* 损害,毁坏 *n.* 损害,毁坏;(*pl.*)损害,赔偿费
 [语境] The court awarded 5,000 pounds(in)damages to the injured man.
  法院判给伤者5 000英镑损害赔偿费。
  The flood did a lot of damage to the crops.
  洪水毁坏了大量农作物。

dance [dɑːns] *n.* 舞(蹈);舞曲,舞会 *v.* 跳舞;跳动
 [语境] Flags danced in the wind.
  旗帜在风中飘舞着。

danger [ˈdeɪndʒə(r)] *n.* 危险;威胁;危险事物
 [巧记] dangersome *a.* 非常危险的
 [语境] Apes are in danger of extinction.
  猿类正处于绝种的危险之中。
 [考点] in danger 在危险中; out of danger 脱离危险; run the danger of 冒……的危险

dangerous [ˈdeɪndʒərəs] *a.* 危险的,不安全的
 [语境] It's dangerous to be so near to the tiger.
  离老虎那么近是很危险的。
  Many dangerous diseases are carried by insects.
  许多危险的疾病是由昆虫传播的。

dare [deə(r)] *v.* 敢,胆敢
 [语境] We dare not play jokes on him lest he should become angry.

我们不敢开他玩笑,生怕他动气。

[考点] I dare say[作插入语用]我想,大概,可能,或许;I dare swear[作插入语用]我确信,一定

dark [dɑːk] *a.* 黑暗的,深(色)的;隐秘的 *n.* 无光,黑暗

[语境] Dark glasses is an effective shield against the glare.
墨镜有效地阻隔强光保护眼睛。

[考点] in the dark 在暗处;完全不知道

data ['deɪtə] *n.* 资料,材料

[语境] The data stored in a computer can be protected.
存储在计算机里的数据能被保护起来。

daughter ['dɔːtə(r)] *n.* 女儿

[语境] May I speak with your daughter?
我可以同你的女儿谈话吗?

day [deɪ] *n.* 白天

[语境] The day draws near.
这一天临近了。

[考点] all day (long) 一天到晚

day and night 日日夜夜

day by day 成天,天天

every other day 每隔一天

one day (过去或将来)某一天

some day (将来)总有一天,(日后)某天

the other day 前几天

dead [ded] *a.* 死的;无生命的;死气沉沉的 *ad.* 完全地

[语境] A dead body is without sensation.
死人是没有感觉的。

deadline ['dedlaɪn] *n.* 最后期限,截止交稿日期

[语境] I hope we can finish this before the deadline.
我希望我们能在最后期限之前完成这项工作。

[考点] meet the deadline 赶上截止日期;break a deadline 打破最后期限

deal[13] [diːl] *v.* 处理;做买卖,经营;分配;对待 *n.* 交易

[语境] The store deals in sporting goods.

这家商店经营运动服装和器具。

[考点] deal in 从事于;经营,做……买卖;deal out 分配;deal with 与……交往(有生意往来);应付,对付;处理

dear [dɪə(r)] *a.* 亲爱的 *int.* 啊,哎呀 *n.* 亲爱的人

[语境] I read that our dear premier had died of cancer in today's newspaper.

我在今天的报纸上获悉我们亲爱的总理死于癌症的消息。

death [deθ] *n.* 死亡,死;消失,毁灭

[语境] The court absolved him of guilt in her death.

法庭赦免了他在她的死亡中所犯的罪。

[考点] death toll 死亡人数

debate[5] [dɪˈbeɪt] *n./vt.* 争论,辩论

[语境] After a long debate the bill was passed.

经长时间的辩论,议案获得通过。

This is a question that they have often debated.

这是个他们常讨论的问题。

debt [det] *n.* 债,欠债

[语境] Getting out of debt must be placed before buying anything new.

必须先还清债务然后再置办物品。

I took her to court for repayment of the debt.

我为索取债务而起诉她。

[考点] be in/out of debt 欠(不欠)债;get/run into debt 负债;get out of debt 还清债

deceive [dɪˈsiːv] *v.* 欺骗,蒙骗

[语境] You are deceiving yourself if you still believe that she loves you.

你如果还相信她爱你,你就是在欺骗自己。

It's not honorable to deceive them.

欺骗他们是不光彩的。

[考点] be deceived in 对……感到失望,发现受骗;deceive into

欺骗使……

December [dɪˈsembə(r)] *n.* 十二月

[语境] My little daughter was born in December.
我的小女儿是十二月出生的。

decide[31] [dɪˈsaɪd] *v.* 决定,裁决

[语境] Don't decide on important matters too quickly.
不要过于匆忙地对重要的事情作决定。
He decided to get married.
他决定结婚。

decision[8] [dɪˈsɪʒən] *n.* 决定,决心;决议;决策

[语境] This decision represents a complete break with tradition.
这一决定完全打破了以往的惯例。

[考点] make a decision 决定下来,作出决定;下决心

declare [dɪˈkleə(r)] *vt.* 宣布,声明;断言,宣称;申报

[语境] The customs asked me if I had anything to declare.
海关人员问我是否有要报税的东西。
Britain declared war on Germany in 1914.
英国在1914年向德国宣战。

[考点] declare for/against sth./sb. 表示赞成/反对某人或某物

decline[12] [dɪˈklaɪn] *vi.* 减少,下降;衰落;婉言拒绝

[巧记] declining *a.* 倾斜的;衰退的

[语境] I wish prices would decline.
但愿物价下降。
The wall declined slightly on account of the earthquake.
墙壁因地震而倾斜。

[考点] on the decline 在减少,在衰退中;fall/go into a decline 开始衰落

decrease[7] [dɪˈkriːs] *v./n.* 减少,减小

[语境] His interest in this subject gradually decreases.
他对这门学科的兴趣逐渐减退。
They are making further efforts to decrease military spending.
他们正在做进一步的努力来减少军费开支。

[考点] on the decrease 在减少;decrease in sth. 在……方面减少

deep[20] [di:p] *a.* 深的,深长的;深奥的;强烈的 *ad.* 深入地,迟

[语境] His personality left a deep impression on us.

他的人品给我们留下了深刻的印象。

defeat [dɪ'fi:t] *vt. /n.* 战胜,挫败

[语境] He has been soundly defeated at chess.

他在国际象棋比赛中一败涂地。

The enemy was defeated in a decisive battle.

敌人在一场决定性的战斗中被击败。

defend [dɪ'fend] *vt.* 保卫,防守;答辩

[巧记] defendable *a.* 可防御的

[语境] This was his fatal defect;he was of feeble will.

这是他致命的弱点,他意志薄弱。

How can you defend the killing of animals for pleasure?

你怎么能为杀死动物取乐的行为辩护呢?

[考点] defend against 保卫;抵抗;defend from 保护,保卫(使不受伤害)

defense/-ence [dɪ'fens] *n.* 防御,保护;防务工事;辩护

[巧记] 反义词：assault, attack, offense

[语境] The defenses of the city must be strengthened.

这个城市的防御工事必须加强。

degree [dɪ'gri:] *n.* 度,程度;等级;学位

[语境] Water freezes at 0 degrees Celsius.

水在摄氏零度结冰。

They cannot be trusted in the slightest degree.

对他们一点也不能相信。

[考点] by degree 逐步地；with a degree of certainty 有一定的把握；to a certain degree 在某种程度上

delay[5] [dɪ'leɪ] *v. /n.* 推迟;耽搁,延误

[语境] After much delay, he finished his paper at last.

拖了那么久,他终于完成了论文。

We decided to delay our wedding until next year.

我们决定把婚礼推迟到明年。

[考点] without delay 赶快,立刻

delicate ['delɪkət] a. **优美的,美精的,精致的;微妙的,棘手的;灵敏的,精密的**

[语境] The scientist needs some delicate instruments.

这位科学家需要一些精密的仪器。

He persecuted me with various delicate questions.

他用种种微妙的问题把我难倒了。

delicious [dɪ'lɪʃəs] a. **美味的;美妙的;使人愉快的**

[巧记] de(低)lic(舔 lick) + ious(形缀):想低头去舔,太美味了

[语境] She can produce delicious meal from very simple ingredients.

她能用简单配料烹调出美味的饭菜。

delight[5] [dɪ'laɪt] n. **快乐,高兴** v. **(使)高兴,(使)欣喜**

[语境] Her eyes twinkled with delight.

她一双眼睛闪烁着喜悦的光芒。

[考点] take delight in 喜爱,以……为乐

deliver[10] [dɪ'lɪvə(r)] vt. **交付,递送;释放,解救;发表,表达**

[巧记] deliverly ad. [古]很快地;巧妙地

[语境] Newspapers are delivered every day.

报纸每天都送来。

The doctor delivered her baby.

医生给她接生。

[考点] deliver the goods 交货,履行诺言; deliver oneself of 阐述自己的观点; deliver oneself to 向……投案,向……自首; deliver over 交出,移交

demand [dɪ'mɑːnd] vt./n. **要求,需要**

[语境] This work demands your immediate attention.

这件工作急需你立即处理。

These developments have created a great demand for home computers.

这些发展促使家用电脑的需求量增大。

[考点] in demand 非常需要的,受欢迎的;make demand of/on sb. 需要某人用很高的技巧、很大的气力;on demand 一经要求

democratic [ˌdeməˈkrætɪk] *a.* 民主的

[巧记] democracy(*n.* 民主);democratically(*ad.* 民主地)

[语境] They pledged to fight for democratic rights.

他们誓为争取民主权利而斗争。

demonstrate[5] [ˈdemənstreɪt] *v.* 论证,证实;演示,说明

[巧记] 派生词:demonstration(*n.* 示范;实证);demonstrable(*a.* 可论证的)

[语境] The loyalties demonstrated their love for the country.

这些忠诚的行为显示了他们对祖国的爱。

dense [dens] *a.* 密的,稠密的,浓密的

[巧记] 反义词:sparse(*a.* 稀疏的),sparsely(*ad.* 稀少地,稀疏地)

[语境] The temple lay deep within the dense forest.

寺庙在密林深处。

deny [dɪˈnaɪ] *v.* 否定,否认;拒绝,谢绝

[语境] The accused man denies that he has ever met her.

被告否认曾经遇到过她。

I was denied the chance of going to university.

我得不到上大学的机会。

[考点] deny oneself to 拒绝见某人

department [dɪˈpɑːtmənt] *n.* 部,部门,系

[语境] The department offers four specialities.

这个系有四个专业。

depend [dɪˈpend] *v.* (on) 取决于,依靠,信赖,相信

[语境] Health depends on good food, fresh air and enough sleep.

健康依靠的是良好的食物、新鲜的空气和充足的睡眠。

[考点] depend on/upon 依靠;由……而定,取决于;depend from 悬挂,垂下来;it all depends 这很难说

depth [depθ] *n.* 深,深度,深奥,深刻

[语境] Scientists used to believe that there was no life in the depths of the ocean.

科学家过去认为海洋深处没有生物。

[考点] in depth 深入地;彻底地,广泛地

describe[25] [dɪˈskraɪb] *vt.* **描述,形容**

[语境] The falling star described a long curve in the sky.

流星在空中划出了一道长长的弧线。

The police asked me to describe exactly how it happened.

警察让我描述一下这事是怎样发生的。

[考点] describe as 说(某人)如何,认为

description[6] [dɪˈskrɪpʃən] *n.* **描写,形容;种类**

[语境] His gift for description adds color to his stories.

他擅长描写,这使得他的故事生色不少。

[考点] beyond description 难以描写,难以形容; give a description of 描述

考点集训

1. The jury's _____ was that the accused was guilty.
   A. verdict   B. sentence
   C. trial   D. debate

2. Libraries are an investment for the future and should not be allowed to fall into _____.
   A. dissolution   B. decay
   C. decline   D. depression

3. Britain has the highest _____ of road traffic in the world—over 60 cars for every mile of road.
   A. popularity   B. density
   C. intensity   D. prosperity

4. During the process, great care has to be taken to protect the _____ silk from damage.
   A. sensitive   B. tender
   C. delicate   D. sensible

5. I suffered from mental _____ because of stress from my job.
   A. damage   B. release

C. relief D. fatigue
6. Many people lost their jobs during the business _____.
   A. desperation B. decrease
   C. despair D. depression
7. Yor can hire a bicycle in many places. Usually you'll have to pay a _____.
   A. deposit B. deal
   C. fare D. fond
8. They were _____ admission to the military exhibition because they were foreigners.
   A. denied B. declined
   C. deprived D. rejected
9. Critics believe that the control of television by mass advertising has _____ the quality of the programs.
   A. lessened B. declined
   C. affected D. effected
10. Our neighbor Uncle Johnson is a stubborn man. Needless to say, we tried _____ to make him change his mind.
    A. in short B. in secret
    C. in vain D. in danger

答案与解析

1. A verdict(陪审团的)裁决,裁定;sentence 宣判,判决;trial 审判,审理;debate 争论,争吵。

2. C 图书馆是未来投资的方向,我们应大力支持。A 溶解;B 腐烂;C 下降;D 萧条;(心情)沮丧。故 C 为正确答案。

3. B 在世界上英国道路交通车辆密度最高,每英里有超过 60 辆汽车。A 人口;B 稠密;C 强度;D 繁荣。故 B 为正确答案。

4. C 在这个过程中,必须特别当心,以保护精致的丝绸免于损害。A 敏感的;B 柔软的;C 精致的;D 理智的。故选 C。

5. D 因为工作压力,我精神疲惫。A 毁坏;B 释放;C 减轻;D 疲劳,劳累。故选 D。

6. D 在商业萧条时期,许多人失去了他们的工作。A 绝望;B 减少;C 失望;D 萧条,不景气。故选 D。

7. A 根据题干中 hire a bicycle,可推断空缺处应填入表"押金"的词。deposit 表示"押金,保证金";deal 表示"交易,待遇";fare 表示"费用,食物";fond 表示"喜爱的,宠爱的"。答案为 A。

8. A 因为他们是外国人,所以无权参加军事展览。A 拒绝,否认;B 拒绝,委婉的拒绝;C 剥夺;D 回绝。故选 A。

9. C 批评家认为大量广告影响了电视节目的质量。A 减少;B 下降,拒绝;C 影响;D 引起,使产生。故选 C。

10. C 我们的邻居约翰逊是一个很倔的人,很显然,我们再怎么劝他改变决定也是白费力气。可选出 C 为正确答案。

Word List 13

desert [ˈdezət] *n.* 沙漠,不毛之地 [dɪˈzɜːt] *vt.* 离开,抛弃;从……开小差

[巧记] deserted(*a.* 荒芜的;为人所弃的);deserter(*n.* 背弃者;逃亡者);desertion(*n.* 丢掉;遗弃;逃亡)

[语境] The baby's mother deserted him soon after giving birth.
那个母亲生下他后不久就把他遗弃了。
The writer decided to live in the Sahara desert for some time.
那位作家决定去撒哈拉沙漠住一段日子。

deserve [dɪˈzɜːv] *vt.* 应受,值得

[语境] You've been working all morning, you deserve a rest.
你已经干了一个上午了,该休息一下了。
He deserved to be punished.
他应当受到惩罚。

[考点] rightly deserve 完全应得(惩罚)

design[14] [dɪˈzaɪn] *v.* 设计;构思;绘制;图案;企图 *n.* 设计,图样

[语境] His designs, for the most part, corresponded with the actual needs.

他的设计绝大多数情况下都符合实际需要。

[考点] by design 故意地,蓄意地

desirable [dɪˈzaɪərəbəl] *a.* 合乎需要的,令人满意的

[巧记] desire(渴望,愿望)+ able(可……的,能)

[语境] It is desirable that atomic energy should be used for peaceful purpose.

原子能应该为了和平的目的而使用,这是合乎情理的。

It isn't really desirable to have him working here.

其实没必要让他在这里工作。

desire[8] [dɪˈzaɪə(r)] *v./n.* 愿望,欲望,要求

[语境] There is a desire for peace universally.

全世界都渴望和平。

desk [desk] *n.* 书桌,服务台,办公桌

[语境] He brushed against the desk.

他触到了那张书桌。

despair [dɪˈspeə(r)] *vi./n.* 失望,绝望

[语境] He gave up the attempt in despair.

他绝望之下放弃了尝试。

He has been in the abyss of despair.

他已陷入绝望的深渊。

[考点] fall into despair 陷入绝望;in despair 绝望地

destroy[6] [dɪˈstrɔɪ] *vt.* 破坏,摧毁;消灭,扑灭;打破,粉碎

[语境] We want to nurture the new project, not destroy it.

我们要支持这个新工程,而不是破坏它。

A tunnel dug to intercept and destroy an enemy's min.

对抗地道截断或破坏敌人坑道而挖的地道。

detail[11] [ˈdiːteɪl] *vt.* 详述,详谈 *n.* 细节,详情;枝节,琐事

[语境] He told us the accident in detail.

他详细地把事故讲给我们听。

Could you detail all your expenses on this form?

请把你的各项开支列在这张表格上,好吗?

[考点] go into detail 详细叙述;in detail 详细地

detailed [ˈdiːteɪld] *a.* 详细的

[语境] "We have no detailed plans," he said.
"我们还没有详细的计划,"他说道。

detect[6] [dɪˈtekt] *vt.* 觉察,发现

[语境] I seemed to detect some anger in his voice.
我似乎在他的声音中听出一些怒气。
They detected no defect in the product.
他们没发现产品有任何问题。

[考点] detect 指的是发现、察觉、找出或注意到,也可以指用仪器等手段发现某物的存在或发现罪犯的身份、住所等。

detection[27] [dɪˈtekʃən] *n.* 察觉,发觉,侦查,探测

[语境] How did he imagine that things like that could escape detection?
他怎么会认为像那样的事情可以不被发觉呢?
He said some secrecy was important to avoid detection by the two governments.
他表示为避免两国政府侦查发现,保密工作很重要。

[考点] detection device 检测仪

determine[17] [dɪˈtɜːmɪn] *v.* 决心,决定;确定,限定

[语境] Demand determines supply.
需求决定供给。

[考点] be determined to do sth. 决心做某事

develop[16] [dɪˈveləp] *v.* 发展,进展;开发,研制;显现;发育,生长;进化

[语境] The machine developed the same fault again.
这台机器又出现了同样的毛病。
Modern music was first developed in Italy.
现代音乐最初是在意大利发展起来的。

development[25] [dɪˈveləpmənt] *n.* 发展,生长;新阶段,新事态;新产品,新发明

[语境] Foreign investments help our economic development.

外国投资有助于我们的经济发展。

[考点] development, evolution 辨析：这两个名词都表示"发展"或"进化"之意。development 强调通过一系列自然过程或人工方法使某物潜在的或隐藏的可能性显露出来，得以实现。evolution 侧重指事物由简到繁，由低级到高级的连续发展，强调变化或演变

device[8] [dɪˈvaɪs] *n.* 装置，设备；方法，设计

[语境] They use television advertising as a device for stimulating demand.

他们利用电视广告作为刺激需求的方法。

Her illness is merely a device to avoid seeing him.

她所谓的生病只不过是避免见他的花招而已。

devote[4] [dɪˈvəʊt] *v.* (to) 奉献，致力

[语境] Don't devote too much to games.

不要在游戏上浪费太多时间。

[考点] devote to 把……献给；把……专用于；devote oneself to 致力于，献身于；专心于

devotion [dɪˈvəʊʃən] *n.* 奉献，献身，忠诚；热爱，挚爱

[巧记] devotional *a.* 虔诚的；祈祷的；专心的

[语境] We were deeply moved by their devotion.

我们为他们的献身精神所感动。

diagnose [ˈdaɪəɡnəʊz] *v.* 诊断

[语境] The doctor diagnosed the illness as pneumonia.

医生诊断此病为肺炎。

[考点] diagnose...as... 把……诊断为……

dialog(ue) [ˈdaɪəlɒɡ] *n.* 对话

[巧记] dia(两个) + logue(说话)→两个人说话→对话

[语境] In this dialog, you can only open an artifact in the editor.

在这个对话框中，您只可以在编辑器中打开一个工件。

dictionary [ˈdɪkʃənəri] *n.* 词典，字典，辞典

[巧记] diction(措辞) + nary(表处所)→措辞集中的地方→词典

[语境] She bought an English dictionary for me.

她给我买了一本英语词典。

die [daɪ] *vi.* 死,死亡;(草木)枯萎,凋谢;渴望

[语境] He died in the service of his country.

他为国捐躯。

[考点] die,decease,expire,perish,pass away 辨析:这些动词或短语动词均有"死"或"死亡"之意。die 是普通用词,指某人或某物失去生命而永远不存在。decease 是正式用词,多指法律上的用语。expire 是委婉用词。从本义"从肺部吐出气来"引申为吐出最后一口气,断气而死。perish 书面用词,多指夭折或不幸暴亡。pass away 是 die 的委婉用语

differ [ˈdɪfə(r)] *vi.* 不同,相异

[语境] Although our looks differ, we are both attractive.

尽管我俩相貌不同,但都讨人喜欢。

They differ in size but not in kind.

这些东西的区别只是大小不同而实质一样。

[考点] differ from 和……不同的;differ in 在……方面不同

difference[22] [ˈdɪfrəns] *n.* 差别,差异,分歧

[语境] There is a notable difference between his earlier and later writings.

他的早期作品和后期作品之间有明显的差异。

[考点] make a difference 有很大差别,有很大的关系[影响]

different[43] [ˈdɪfrənt] *a.* 差异的,不同的

[语境] People have different interpretations of the passage.

人们对这一段文字有不同的解释。

[考点] be different from 与……不同

difficult[34] [ˈdɪfɪkəlt] *a.* 困难的,艰难的

[巧记] 反义词:easy,simply

[语境] A difficult situation can call forth a person's best qualities.

困境能唤起一个人最好的品格。

difficulty[5] [ˈdɪfɪkəltɪ] *n.* 困难,困境,难题

[语境] I encountered great difficulties in learning English grammar.

我在学习英语语法时遇到了很大困难。

[考点] without difficulty 容易地，毫不费力地

dig [dɪg] *v.* 挖，掘

[语境] It takes a lot of work to dig a deep well.

　　挖一口深井很费事。

[考点] dig through 挖穿；挖通(隧道等)；dig up 挖起；挖出；dig at [口]挖苦[嘲笑]某人；dig down 挖去；掘倒；dig for 发掘；搜集(资料、事实等)

dinner [ˈdɪnə(r)] *n.* 吃饭；正餐，主餐；宴会

[语境] We asked her round for dinner on the weekend.

　　我们在周末请她到家里来吃饭。

dip [dɪp] *v./n.* 浸，蘸

[语境] She dipped her finger in the water to see if it's hot.

　　她把手指浸入水中，看水热不热。

[考点] dip into 把……浸入(液体)中

direct[7] [dɪˈrekt, daɪˈrekt] *a./ad.* 径直的(地) *v.* 管理，指导；(at, to)指向

[语境] His remarks were not directed at you.

　　他的话不是针对你的。

[考点] direct at 把……对准；direct to 把(注意力、精力)贯注在……上

direction [dɪˈrekʃən, daɪˈrekʃən] *n.* 方向，方位；指令，说明

[语境] The direction of the thrust of the rockets is controlled by computer.

　　火箭推力的方向是由电脑控制的。

[考点] in all directions 四面八方；各方面；in every direction 向各方面，向四面八方；in the direction of 朝……方向

directly [dɪˈrektlɪ, daɪ-] *ad.* 直接地，直截了当地；立即，马上

[巧记] 近义词：immediately, at once 立刻，马上

[语境] The second question directly concerns children's safety, so it should be solved at once.

　　第二个问题与孩子们的安全有直接关系，所以必须立即解决。

Do only the things that benefit you directly.

只做能让自己马上受益的事情。

dirty ['dɜːtɪ] *a.* 弄脏的；下流的 *v.* 弄脏，玷污

[语境] The neck of a shirt gets dirty easily.

衬衫领口很容易弄脏。

disabled[26] [dɪs'eɪbəld] *a.* 伤残的；丧失劳动[战斗]力的；损坏的，不能使用的

[语境] Old age disabled him for hard labour.

年迈使他不能干繁重的工作。

disadvantage [ˌdɪsəd'vɑːntɪdʒ] *n.* 不利，劣势，短处

[巧记] disadvantaged *a.* 社会地位低下的；被剥夺了基本权利的

[语境] His lack of education was a disadvantage when he looked for a job.

他缺少教育,这在找工作时是一个不利条件。

[考点] to sb.'s disadvantage 对某人不利, 使某人吃亏

disappear[4] [ˌdɪsə'pɪə(r)] *v.* 不见，消失

[巧记] dis 不 + appear 出现→不出现→消失

[语境] Many beautiful fish are fast disappearing because of the severe pollution.

因为污染严重,许多美丽的鱼类正在面临绝种。

disappoint [ˌdɪsə'pɔɪnt] *vt.* 使失望，使扫兴

[巧记] 反义词：encourage

[语境] I'm sorry to disappoint your plans.

我很抱歉妨碍了你的计划。

The tenor disappointed us by singing flat.

那位男高音歌手调门儿唱得很低,十分扫兴。

disaster[12] [dɪ'zɑːstə(r)] *n.* 灾害，灾祸，灾难

[语境] They had led the country into economic disaster.

他们把国家带入了经济灾难中。

Thousands died in the disaster.

数千人死于这场灾祸。

discount ['dɪskaʊnt] *vt.* 打折扣 *n.* 折扣；贴现(率)

[语境] We give 10 percent discount for cash.

现金付款,我们九折优惠。

You can discount what Jack said; he's a dreadful liar.

杰克说的话你不必当真,他可是个说谎大王。

[考点] discount for cash 现金付账打折;without discount 无折扣

discover [dɪˈskʌvə(r)] *v.* **发现,显示**

[巧记] 去掉(dis)覆盖物(cover)→发现

[语境] Some ancient manuscripts were discovered in the temple.

在寺院里发现了一些古代的手稿。

discuss[7] [dɪˈskʌs] *vt.* **讨论,商议**

[巧记] 派生词:discussible *a.* 可讨论的,可商议的

[语境] They discussed how to promote cooperation between the two countries.

他们讨论如何促进两国间的合作。

[考点] discuss with sb. 和某人谈话

disease[38] [dɪˈziːz] *n.* **病,疾病;社会弊病**

[语境] The poor man has a serious disease of the liver.

这个可怜的人患有严重的肝病。

The disease is still in its primary stage.

疾病仍然处在初发阶段。

[考点] catch/suffer from/take a disease 患病

考点集训

1. I had been a university student for three years, but not until this afternoon had I felt the thrill of _____.
   A. confusion   B. disappointment
   C. sensation   D. fulfillment

2. Operations which left patients _____ and in need of long periods of recovery time now leave them feeling relaxed and comfortable.
   A. exhausted   B. abandoned
   C. injured   D. deserted

3. Eating too much fat can _____ heart disease and cause high blood pressure.

A. contribute to B. attribute to
C. attend to D. devote to

4. The lawyer advised him to drop the _____, since he stands little chance to win.

A. event B. incident
C. case D. affair

答案与解析

1. B 我成为一名大学生已经有三年了,但直到今天下午,我才感到万分失望。confusion"混乱,困惑";disappointment"失望";sensation"感觉";fulfillment"履行,实行"。thrill"激动,震撼",据语义应选 B。

2. A 虽然手术让病人筋疲力尽,需要很长时间才能恢复,但是手术让他们感到轻松舒适。A 劳累的,筋疲力尽的;B 抛弃的;C 受伤的;D 遗弃的,离弃的。故 A 为正确答案。

3. A 食用过多的脂肪会导致心脏病,引起高血压。A 导致,有助于;B 归因于;C 照顾,关心;D 投身于……故 A 为正确答案。

4. C 律师建议他放弃这个案子,因为它打赢的可能性很小。A 活动;B 小事件;C 案件;D 事件,事情。故 C 为正确答案。

Word List 14

dish [dɪʃ] *n.* **盘子,碟;菜肴**

[语境] Our cat eats out of her own dish.
我们的猫吃自己盘子里的食物。
The waiter brought up the next dish.
服务员把下一碟菜端了上来。

dismiss [dɪsˈmɪs] *vt.* **不再考虑;免职,解雇,开除;解散**

[语境] She was dismissed as a dreamer.
人们认为她是个空想家而不予理睬。

133

At first she threatened to dismiss us all, but later she relented.

起初她威胁要解雇我们所有的人,但是后来她态度软化了。

[考点] be dismissed from school 被学校开除

display[4] [dɪˈspleɪ] *v./n.* **陈列,展览,显示**

[巧记] dis(否定) + play(玩):橱窗里陈列的东西不能拿出玩的→展览

[语境] All exhibitors displayed their best products.

所有参展者展示了他们的最好的产品。

dispute [dɪˈspjuːt] *n.* **争论,争端** *v.* **争论,辩驳,争吵**

[语境] They are disputing about the rights and wrongs of the case.

他们正在激烈争论这个事件的是非曲直。

His honesty is beyond dispute.

他的诚实是无可争议的。

distance [ˈdɪstəns] *n.* **距离,间隔,远方,路程**

[语境] Time and distance often sunder friends.

朋友久别远离常产生隔阂。

[考点] at a distance 隔一段距离;距离稍远一些; in the distance 在远处

distant [ˈdɪstənt] *a.* **远的;遥远的;疏远的;不亲近的**

[巧记] dis(分散) + stant(stand 站):分开站→遥远的

[语境] We heard the distant bay of the hounds.

我们听到远处一群猎犬的吠声。

distinct [dɪˈstɪŋkt] *a.* **不同的;清楚的,明显的,显著的**

[语境] There is a distinct possibility that she'll be your teacher next term.

她下学期当你们的老师的可能性非常大。

[考点] be distinct in...from... 在某方面与……不同

distinguish[11] [dɪˈstɪŋgwɪʃ] *v.* **区别,辨别,辨认出**

[语境] Speeches distinguish human beings from animals.

人类和动物的区别在于人会说话。

He distinguished himself by his courage.

他因英勇而扬名。

[考点] be distinguished by 以……为特征;be distinguished for 以……而著名;be distinguished from 不同于;与……加以区别;distinguish...from... 辨别,识别;把……和……区别开;distinguish oneself 使自己杰出

distribute[7] [dɪˈstrɪbjuːt] *vt.* **分发,分送,配给;分布**

[语境] The mother distributed candy among children.
母亲给孩子们发糖果。
The books in the library were distributed according to subjects.
图书馆里的藏书按科目分类。

[考点] distribute...over... 把……配给[分配到,散布于]……;distribute over 散布,分类

district[6] [ˈdɪstrɪkt] *n.* **地区,行政区;美国各州的众议院选区**

[语境] The city has several shopping districts.
这个城市有几个商业区。

disturb[8] [dɪˈstɜːb] *vt.* **扰乱,妨碍;打扰,使不安**

[语境] Don't disturb the paper on my desk.
别乱动我桌上的文件。
They took the phone off the hook so no calls would disturb them.
他们摘下电话听筒,以免电话打扰他们。

[考点] disturb 指人的行动或某物妨碍了他人的工作、学习或生活等正常的顺序,使他人感到焦虑、心理不平衡或心慌意乱

diverse [daɪˈvɜːs] *a.* **不同的,多种多样的**

[语境] The program deals with subjects as diverse as pop music and Beijing Opera.
节目涉及从流行音乐到京剧这样形形色色的题材。
They are the people from diverse cultures.
他们是些有着不同文化背景的人。

diversity [daɪˈvɜːsɪtɪ] *n.* **多样化,差异,变化**

[巧记] diversify (*v.* 使多样化)
[语境] That is the advantage of diversity.
这就是多样性的优势。
How do you explain the diversity of jobs you've had?

你怎样看待你曾做过的工作之间的差异?

divide [dɪˈvaɪd] v. 分,划分,分开;分配;(by) 除

[语境] The human brain is divided vertically down the middle into two hemispheres.

人脑从中央垂直地分为两半球。

[考点] divide by 用……除(尽);因……分裂; divide from 把……分开; divide into 分成

divorce [dɪˈvɔːs] n./v. 离婚,离异;分离

[语境] She got a divorce after years of unhappiness.

经过多年的不幸之后,她终于离了婚。

do [dʊ, duː] aux./v./vt. 做,干,办,从事;引起 vi. 行动

[语境] You can do what you want to do, but never follow the crowd.

你想做什么就做什么,可别随大流。

doctor [ˈdɒktə(r)] n. 医生

[语境] Which doctor do you go to?

你要找哪一位医生?

document[6] [ˈdɒkjʊmənt] n. 文件,公文

[语境] He tampered the document.

他篡改了文件。

dog [dɒg] n. 狗,卑鄙的人

[语境] Suddenly my dog spit at the door.

突然,我的狗朝着门低吠起来。

He did such a thing. He was a yellow dog.

他做出这样的事情来,他是一个卑鄙可耻的人。

dollar [ˈdɒlə(r)] n. 美元

[语境] She bummed a dollar off me.

她向我讨了一美元。

door [dɔː(r)] n. 门

[语境] She pocketed her wallet and door keys.

她把钱包和门钥匙放进了口袋里。

double[4] [ˈdʌbəl] n. 两倍 a. 两倍的,双重的 vt. 使加倍 vi. 加倍

[语境] I'll give you double pay for working overtime.

你加班我付你双倍工钱。

doubt[5] [daʊt] *n.* 怀疑,疑问,疑惑 *v.* 怀疑,不相信

[语境] No doubt he means to help, but in fact he just gets in the way.

他确实是想帮忙,然而事实上却只是帮倒忙。

He was troubled by religious doubt.

他因对宗教的疑惧而十分烦恼。

[考点] without doubt 毫无疑问;beyond/past doubt 毫无疑问地;in doubt 怀疑地;make no doubt of 确信,对……不怀疑

down [daʊn] *ad.* 下;由大到小 *prep.* 沿着……而下 *a.* 向下的

[语境] The machine slowed down and stopped.

机器转速逐渐减慢,终于停住了。

download [ˌdaʊnˈləʊd] *v.* 下载

[语境] How can I improve my download speed?

如何提高下载速度?

dozen [ˈdʌzən] *n.* 一打,十二个

[语境] This store often charges only 65 US cents a dozen for large eggs.

一打大鸡蛋在这家店里常常仅卖六十五美分。

[考点] dozens of 许多的

drag[13] [dræg] *v.* 拖,拖曳

[语境] The battle dragged and the rainy season set in.

战争拖延着,雨季却来临了。

drain[4] [dreɪn] *n.* 排水沟,阴沟,消耗,负担 *v.* 排去,放干

[巧记] drainless *a.* 无排水设备的;取之不尽的

[语境] The country suffered from a continual brain drain because of bad economy.

那个国家因经济不景气,人才不断外流。

drama [ˈdrɑːmə] *n.* 剧本,戏剧

[语境] The other drama is the unfolding of Apple's story.

另一个剧本展开了苹果的故事。

dramatic [drəˈmætɪk] *a.* 戏剧性的,引人注目的,给人深刻印象的

[语境]The story lends itself to dramatic presentation.

这则故事适合以戏剧的形式来呈现。

The backdrop for the debate is one of dramatic progress.

这场辩论的背后是一项引人注目的科学成就。

draw[10] [drɔː] *v.* 拉;画;汲取;引出;(to)挨近 *n.* 平局;拖曳

[语境] They drew different conclusions from the facts.

他们从这些事实中引出了不同的结论。

[考点] draw away 拉开,引开,离开;draw back 收回(已付关税等);往回跑;退却;draw up 写出;草拟,制订

dream[11] [driːm] *n./v.* 梦,梦想,幻想

[语境] He dreamed of becoming a movie star when he was young.

他年轻时向往着成为电影明星。

[考点] dream of 梦见;梦想

dress[17] [dres] *n.* 服装,童装,女装 *v.* 穿衣,打扮

[语境]The dress was shaped to her figure.

这件连衣裙做得很适合她的身材。

drink [drɪŋk] *v.* (drank,drunk)喝,饮 *n.* 饮料;喝酒

[语境]Drink was his father's ruin and it will be the ruin of him too!

酗酒是他父亲死亡的原因,他也将遭同样的厄运!

drive [draɪv] *v.* 开(车);驱;驱动,把(钉,桩)打入 *n.* 驾驶

[语境] He blotted his driving record by having an accident.

他因发生一次事故而在驾驶记录上留下污点。

driver ['draɪvə(r)] *n.* 驾驶员,司机

[语境]I have subjected your bag to your driver.

我早把你的包交给你的司机了。

drop[20] [drɒp] *n.* 滴;落下;微量 *v.* 落下;下降;失落

[语境] As the temperature dropped abruptly, the campers were shivering all over with cold.

由于气温骤降,野营者冷得浑身发抖。

[考点] drop back 退后,后撤;恢复(旧习惯等)(into);drop behind 落伍,落后,落在……之后;drop by [美]顺便访问一下

drown [draʊn] *v.* 淹死,淹没

138

[语境]Many towns and villages drowned.

许多城乡被淹没了。

[语境] He saved the girl from drowning at the cost of his own life.

他舍身把溺水的姑娘救出来。

[考点] like a drowned rat 像落汤鸡一样

drug [drʌg] *n.* 药物;麻醉剂;毒品

[语境]An overdose of this drug can kill.

这种药服用过量可引起死亡。

dry [draɪ] *a.* 干(旱)的;干渴的;枯燥的 *vt.* 使干燥,晒干

[语境] The paint should have dried off by this time tomorrow.

油漆到明天这个时候就应该已经干了。

dull [dʌl] *a.* 单调的;迟钝的,愚笨的;不锋利的

[语境] The book's opening is dull, but the last chapters are interesting.

那本书的开始部分枯燥乏味,但最后几章很有意思。

dump [dʌmp] *v.* 倾倒,倾卸 *n.* 垃圾场

[语境] He dumped all the refuse into the garbage can.

他将全部垃圾倒入垃圾桶。

during [ˈdjʊərɪŋ] *prep.* 在……期间

[语境]During the most productive time in her career, she wrote five novels.

在她创作生涯中最多产的时期,她写了五本小说。

duty [ˈdjuːtɪ] *n.* 义务,责任;职务;税

[语境] Legislation is the duty of a congress.

立法是国会的职责。

[考点] off duty 下班;on duty 值班;值日;值勤;上班

考点集训

1. He _____ to his customers and halved the price.

   A. leaked   B. drew

   C. quoted   D. yielded

2. All human beings have a comfortable zone regulating the _____

they keep from someone they talk with.

A. distance B. scope
C. range D. boundary

3. A culture in which the citizens share similar religious beliefs and values is more likely to have laws that represent the wishes of its people than is a culture where citizens come from _____ backgrounds.

A. extensive B. influential
C. diverse D. identical

4. It is important to _____ between the rules of grammar and the conventions of written language.

A. determine B. identify
C. explore D. distinguish

5. During the lecture, the speaker occasionally _____ his point by relating his own experiences.

A. illustrated B. hinted
C. cited D. displayed

6. We don't know why so many people in that region like to wear dresses of such _____ colors.

A. low B. humble
C. mild D. dull

答案与解析

1. D 他向顾客妥协了,货物半价出售。A 流出,滴漏;B 牵引;C 引用;D 屈服,顺从。故 D 为正确答案。

2. A 每个人都有令自己舒适的区间,这个区间控制着他们与谈话人的距离。A 距离;B 范围;C 幅度;D 界限。故选 A。

3. C 具有相似的宗教信仰和价值观的市民文化,与有不同信仰和价值观的市民文化相比,更可能出台体现大家意志的法律。A 广泛的;B 有影响力的;C 多样的;D 相似的。故选 C。

4. D 区分语法规则和书面语言规则非常重要。A 决定;B 识别;C 探测,勘察;D 区分。故选 D。

5. A　演讲期间,演讲人时不时用自己的亲身经历来阐释自己的观点。A 说明;B 暗示;C 引用;D 陈列,展览。故选 A。
6. D　我们不明白为什么那地区的许多人喜欢穿暗色的衣服。A 低的,矮的;B 谦虚的,卑微的;C 温和的;D 暗色的,迟钝的。故选 D。

Word List 15

each [iːtʃ] *a./pron.* **各,各自的,每**

[语境] Each partner has a cut of the profits.

每个合伙人都可分到一份利润。

[考点] each and all 每人都,个个,全部; each other 互相,彼此

eager [ˈiːgə(r)] *a.* **热切的,渴望的**

[语境] He is eager for you to meet his friends.

他热切希望你见见他的朋友。

The company is eager to expand into new markets.

那家公司急欲开辟新的市场。

[考点] be eager for/about 渴望,渴求,争取; be eager to do 渴望做……

early [ˈɜːlɪ] *a.* **早的,早期的,及早的** *ad.* **早,在初期**

[语境] His early experiences turned him into a passionate social reformer.

他早年的经历使他变成了一个狂热的社会改革者。

[考点] early or late 迟早,早晚

earn[8] [ɜːn] *vt.* **赚得,赢得,获得**

[巧记] 派生词:earnings (*n.* 所得,收入)

[语境] His skill in negotiating earned him a reputation as a shrewd tactician.

他的谈判技巧使他赢得了精明战略家的名声。

He has earned a lot of money in this month.

141

这个月他已经赚了好多钱了。

[考点] earn one's living 谋生,挣钱生活

earth [ɜːθ] *n.* 地球;土壤;土地

[语境] The moon rotates around the earth.

月球围绕着地球旋转。

They tamped down the earth around the apple tree.

他们把苹果树周围的泥土夯实。

east [iːst] *a.* 东方的 *ad.* 向东方 *n.* 东,东方

[语境] The lighthouse bears due east.

灯塔位于正东方某处。

[考点] Middle East 中东;Far East 远东

easy[19] [ˈiːzɪ] *a.* 容易的,不费力的,安逸的,宽裕的

[语境] It's easy to pick him out in a crowd because he is very tall.

很容易从人群中辨认出他,因为他个子很高。

[考点] take it easy 沉住气,不紧张,慢慢来

eat [iːt] *vt.* 吃,喝 *vi.* 吃饭,吃东西

[语境] You eat too much candy. It's bad for your teeth.

你糖吃得太多了。这对你的牙齿不好。

[考点] eat up 吃光,吃完,耗尽

ecology[ɪˈkɒlədʒɪ] *n.* 生态学

[巧记] eco(表示"环境""生态""生态学的") + logy(学)→生态学

[语境] Basic ecology has similarly been ignored in many agricultural schools and universities.

同样,许多农学院和农业大学也忽视了基础生态学。

economy[10] [ɪˈkɒnəmɪ] *n.* 节约,经济

[巧记] economic(*a.* 经济的,经济学的); economical (*a.* 节约的,经济的,合算的)

[语境] They will make economies by hiring fewer part-time workers.

他们将通过减少雇用兼职工人来节省开支。

Agriculture is still the mainstay of the country's economy.

农业仍然是这个国家经济的主要支柱。

educate [ˈedjʊkeɪt] vt. 教育,培养,训练

[巧记] educated a. 受过教育的

[语境] He had paid out much money to educate his daughter at a boarding school.

他花了很多钱让他的女儿在寄宿学校接受教育。

She educated her younger daughter at home.

她在自己家里教育她的小女儿。

education[64] [ˌedjʊˈkeɪʃən] n. 教育,培养,训练

[语境] Mass education is essential in promoting democracy.

民众教育对提倡民主是非常重要的。

effect[52] [ɪˈfekt] n. 效果,作用,影响

[语境] A new system of taxation will be brought into effect next year.

新的税收制度将于明年实行。

The advertising campaign didn't have much effect on sales.

这些广告攻势对销售额并没有起到多大作用。

[考点] be of no effect 无效;come into effect 开始生效;have an effect on 对……有影响;in effect 实际上;take effect 见效

effective[25] [ɪˈfektɪv] a. 有效的,生效的

[语境] That's rather an effective use of color.

这种使用颜色的手法效果相当好。

Their efforts to improve the production have been very effective.

他们提高生产力的措施卓有成效。

efficiency[5] [ɪˈfɪʃənsɪ] n. 效率, 功效

[语境]The production efficiency is lamed by the old machines.

生产效率受到破旧机器的影响而无法提高。

efficient [ɪˈfɪʃənt] a. 效率高的,有能力的

[考点] 派生词:efficiently(ad. 有效率地,有效地); efficiency(n. 效率)

[语境] This is a highly efficient new heating system.

这是个高效的新取暖系统。

effort[23] [ˈefət] n. 努力,尽力

[语境] It's quite an effort to lift this heavy box.

抬起这只沉重的箱子要花费相当大的力气。
Put more effort into your work.
你要更加努力地工作。

eighty [ˈeɪtɪ] *num.* 八十

[语境] I got an eighty something.
我考了八十几分。

eight [eɪt] *num.* 八;八个

[语境] He slept eight hours.
他睡了八个小时。

eighteen [ˌeɪˈtiːn] *num.* 十八

[语境] The ages of the students of our class range from fifteen to eighteen.
我班同学的年龄在十五岁到十八岁之间。

either [ˈaɪðə(r)] *pron.* (两者中)任何一方,任何一个 *ad.* (与 not 连用)也(不);(与 or 连用)或……或……,不是……就是……

[语境] You may take either of the roads.
两条路你随便走哪一条。
Either we will find a supply, or we will make the goods.
我们或是寻求供货,或者自己制造。
A unit of measurement is equal to the length of either of these instruments.
测量单位等于这两种工具长度任一种的一个测量单位。

elder [ˈeldə(r)] *a.* 年长的,资格老的 *n.* 长辈

[巧记] 同义词:older, senior;反义词:junior, younger
[语境] Children should be taught to show honor to their elders.
我们应该教育孩子尊敬长者。

elect[7] [ɪˈlekt] *vt.* 推选,选举 *n.* 被选的人;上帝的选民;特殊阶层

[语境] The President elect will be installed next week.
候任总统将在下周正式就任。
They elected him chairman.
他们选他做主席。

election [ɪˈlekʃən] *n.* 选举，当选，推举

[语境] Her election to the board of directors caused great surprise.

她被选进董事会，令人大为吃惊。

electricity[5] [ɪˌlekˈtrɪsɪtɪ] *n.* 电，电流；电学

[语境] Most metals conduct electricity.

大多数金属能导电。

electronics [ɪˌlekˈtrɒnɪks] *n.* 电子学

[语境] He wants to brush up his knowledge of electronics.

他想温习他的电子学知识。

elegant [ˈelɪgənt] *a.* 优雅的，精美的，俊美的

[巧记] elegance (*n.* 优美，典雅)；elegantly (*ad.* 优雅地，典雅地)

[语境] She was an elegant and accomplished woman.

她是位优雅的才女。

element [ˈelɪmənt] *n.* 成分，要素，元素

[语境] Magnesium is the nutrient element in plant growth.

镁是植物生长的营养要素。

elephant [ˈelɪfənt] *n.* 大象

[语境] It's obvious that a man isn't strong enough to lift an elephant.

很明显，一个人是不能举起大象的。

eleven [ɪˈlevn] *num.* 十一

[语境] Television closed down for the night after eleven o'clock.

晚上11点过后，电视台停止播放节目。

else [els] *ad.* 其他，另外，别的；[与 or 连用] 否则

[语境] He always tries to shift the blame to someone else.

他总是试图将过错推卸给别人。

[考点] nothing else than 只不过；仅有；or else 否则，不然

emerge[10] [ɪˈmɜːdʒ] *vt.* 显现，浮现；暴露；形成

[巧记] emergence (*n.* 浮现；露出；出现)

[语境] Nothing emerged from the bilateral talks.

双边会谈没有结果。

emergency[13] [ɪˈmɜːdʒənsɪ] *n.* 紧急情况，突然事件

[语境] The rioting grew worse and the government declared a state of emergency.

骚乱恶化,政府只得宣布进入紧急状态。

It is important to keep/stay calm in an emergency.

在紧急情况下保持镇静是很重要的。

[考点] in an emergency (= in case of emergency) 遇到紧急情况,在紧急关头

emit [ɪˈmɪt] *vt.* **发出,发射;散发(光、热、气味等)**

[巧记] e(出去) + mit(发送) →发出,发射

[语境] The new device emits a powerful circular column of light.

新设备发出明亮的圆形光柱。

It is unlawful for factories to emit black smoke into the air.

现在,工厂往空气中排黑烟是违法的。

emotion[15] [ɪˈməʊʃən] *n.* **情感,情绪**

[语境] Love, joy, hate, fear and grief are all emotions.

爱、喜、恨、惧、悲都是情感。

He appealed to our emotions rather than to our reason.

他诉诸我们的情感而非我们的理智。

[考点] stir up emotion 激起感情;conflicting emotion 矛盾的心情;mixed emotions 复杂的心情;deep/sincere emotion 真挚的情感

emphasis[4] [ˈemfəsɪs] *n.* **强调,重点**

[语境] Our English course places great emphasis on conversational skills.

我们的英语课程非常重视会话技能。

Restraint or lack of emphasis in expression, as for rhetorical effect.

轻描淡写的陈述在表达上受限制或缺乏强调,如为了修辞作用。

[考点] put emphasis on 强调,重视;with emphasis 强调,加强,用力

emphasize/-ise[4] [ˈemfəsaɪz] *v.* **强调**

[语境] The speaker emphasized the cardinal importance of building a party to lead the country.

演讲者强调了建立一个政党来领导该国的根本重要性。

核心词汇精解

employ[9] [ɪmˈplɔɪ] *vt.* 雇佣,使用

[语境] The police had to employ force to break up the crowd.
警察不得不使用武力驱散人群。
The children were employed in weeding the garden.
孩子们忙着给花园除草。
Our company employed about one hundred people.
我们公司雇用了大约一百人。

employment[5] [ɪmˈplɔɪmənt] *n.* 雇用;使用;工作,职业

[语境] I got this job through an employment agency.
我通过职业介绍所找到了这份工作。

[考点] be out of employment 解雇,失业; lose employment 失业

empty [ˈemptɪ] *a.* 空的;空洞的 *v.* 倒空,使成为空的

[语境] Her words were quite empty of meaning.
她的话实在没有意义。

[考点] be empty of 毫无,没有,缺乏

enable[17] [ɪˈneɪbəl] *vt.* 使能够,使可能

[语境] The collapse of the strike enabled the company to resume normal bus services.
罢工的失败使公司恢复了正常的公共汽车营业。
A rabbit's large ears enable it to hear the slightest sound.
兔子耳朵大,能听到极微小的声音。

[考点] en-前缀,在名词或形容词前面,构成动词,表示"使成……;使能够……", enable sb. to do 使人能(做)……

encourage[7] [ɪnˈkʌrɪdʒ] *vt.* 鼓励,助长,促进

[巧记] encouraging(*a.* 鼓励的,给予希望的,振奋人心的)

[语境] Her success encouraged me to try the same thing.
她的成功鼓励我尝试同样的事。
High prices for farm products encouraged farming.
农产品价格的提高有助于农业的发展。

end[9] [end] *n.* 末端,端,梢;目标,目的 *v.* 终止,结束

[语境] By the end of the game, the stadium was almost vacant.
到比赛结束的时候,体育馆几乎空了。

[考点] bring to an end 结束，完成，终止；by the end of 到……末

考点集训

1. Showing some sense of humor can be a(n) _____ way to deal with some stressful situation.
   A. effective   B. efficient
   C. favorable   D. favorite
2. With demand continuing to rise in _____ economies such as China and India, energy traders believe that oil futures are a good bet.
   A. employing   B. emerging
   C. embracing   D. emitting
3. A fire engine must have priority as it usually has to deal with some kind of _____.
   A. precaution   B. crisis
   C. emergency   D. urgency
4. The beam that is _____ by a laser differs in several ways from the light that comes out of a flashlight.
   A. emitted   B. transported
   C. motivated   D. translated

答案与解析

1. A 幽默感对处理紧张的局面很有效。A 有效的；B 高效的；C 有利的；D 最喜欢的。故选 A。
2. B emerging 正在涌现的；employ 利用，雇佣；embrace 拥抱，包含；emit 发出，放出。
3. C 消防车拥有道路行驶优先权，因为通常它要处理某些紧急事件。A 预防措施；B 危机；C 紧急事件；D 紧迫，急迫，急事，紧要。故选 C。
4. A 激光器放射出的光束与手电筒放出的光，在几个方面有所不同。A 放射出；B 运输；C 激励；D 翻译。故选 A。

Word List 16

endure [ɪnˈdjʊə(r)] *vt.* 耐久,忍耐,容忍,持久,持续

[巧记] endurance (*n.* 忍耐,忍受力)

[语境] They could endure much pain.

他们能忍受很多痛苦。

His plays have endured for more than two centuries.

他的戏剧经历两个多世纪而不衰。

[考点] endure cold 耐寒

enemy [ˈenəmɪ] *n.* 敌人

[语境] We delivered him from the enemy.

我们把他从敌人手中解救出来。

energy[67] [ˈenədʒɪ] *n.* 活力,精力;能,能量

[语境] Don't expend all your energy on such a useless job.

不要把你的精力全花在这无益的工作上。

engage [ɪnˈgeɪdʒ] *vt.* 使从事,使忙于;占用(时间等);雇用,聘用;使订婚 *vi.* (in) 从事于,参加

[语境] I engaged the clutch and the car moved forwards.

我踩下离合器,汽车便朝前开了。

Politicians should not engage in business affairs that might affect their political judgement.

政治家不应该参与那些可能会影响其政治判断力的商业事务。

[考点] engage for 担保,对……负责;engage in 从事 engage upon 开始某种职业;be engaged with 和……有事商谈

engineer[18] [ˌendʒɪˈnɪə(r)] *n.* 工程师

[语境] The engineer explained the plane's technical capabilities.

工程师讲解了该飞机的技术性能。

[考点] engineer in chief 总工程师

England [ˈɪŋglənd] *n.* 英格兰

[语境]The teacher told us his experiences in England.

老师给我们讲了他在英格兰的经历。

English [ˈɪŋlɪʃ] *a.* 英语的,英国(人)的 *n.* 英语,英国人

[语境]She bought an English dictionary for me.

她给我买了一本英语词典。

enjoy [ɪnˈdʒɔɪ] *vt.* 享受……的乐趣;欣赏;喜爱

[巧记] 派生词:enjoyable *a.* 可爱的,令人愉快的,有趣的

[语境] Everybody enjoyed themselves on vacation.

假期里大家都过得很愉快。

[考点] enjoy oneself 享乐,过得快乐[愉快];尽情地玩

enough [ɪˈnʌf] *a.* (for)足够的 *n.* 足够,充分 *ad.* 足够地

[语境] Oddly enough, he didn't seem to remember his own birthday.

说来也奇怪,他似乎不记得自己的生日。

[考点] adequate, enough, sufficient 辨析:这些形容词均含"足够的,充足的"之意。adequate 指数量上足够,质量上适当。enough 是普通用词,口语、书面语可用,较侧重分量或数量的足够,多指希望的满足。sufficient 正式用词,侧重数目或数量或程度达到某一特定要求或需要

ensure [ɪnˈʃʊə(r)] *v.* 确保,保证;使安全

[巧记] en 使 + sure 确信,即担保

[语境] These are safety devices to ensure workers against accidents.

这些安全设施是为了保护工人不出事故。

enter [ˈentə(r)] *vt.* 进入;参加,加入;写入 *vi.* 进去,进来

[语境] Competition among youths to enter the best colleges is intense.

年轻人想进一流大学的竞争是很激烈的。

[考点] enter into 进入,参加;enter on 开始,着手

entertainment[7] [ˌentəˈteɪnmənt] *n.* 娱乐

[语境] He fell into the water, much to the entertainment of the onlookers.

他跌进水中,旁观者大乐。

There are few entertainments in that town.

那个镇上几乎没有娱乐设施。

[考点] to the entertainment of 使……感到有趣的是

enthusiasm [ɪnˈθjuːzɪæzəm] *n.* **热心,热情,积极性**

[巧记] enthusiastic (*a.* 有热情的)

[语境] He commended them for their enthusiasm.
那个称赞他们的热情。

[考点] with great enthusiasm 兴致勃勃地

entire[12] [ɪnˈtaɪə(r)] *a.* **完全的,全部的,完整的**

[语境] I've wasted an entire day on this.
我为此事浪费了一整天的时间。

We are in entire agreement with you.
我们完全同意你的意见。

entitle [ɪnˈtaɪtəl] *v.* **给以权利(或资格);给……称号(题名);授权**

[巧记] entitlement *n.* 权利

[语境] Employees are entitled to an annual paid leave of fifteen days.
职员一年可享受十五天带薪的假期。

[考点] be entitled 叫作,称为,题目

entrance [ˈentrəns] *n.* **入口,门口;进入;入学,入会**

[巧记] 反义词:exit

[语境] The enemy mined at the entrance to the village.
敌人在村口布了地雷。

envelope [ˈenvələʊp] *n.* **信封,信皮;封套**

envious [ˈenvɪəs] *a.* **羡慕的;嫉妒的**

[巧记] envy (*v.* 羡慕,嫉妒)

[语境] All my friends were happy for me and envious.
我所有的朋友都为我感到高兴和羡慕。

[考点] be envious of 嫉妒,羡慕……

environment[56] [ɪnˈvaɪərənmənt] *n.* **环境,四周,外界**

[语境] Children need a happy home environment.
孩子需要一个幸福的家庭环境。

She is not used to the new environment.

她对新环境不习惯。

envy [ˈenvɪ] *v./n.* 妒忌,羡慕

[语境] They envy him his good fortune.

他们羡慕他的好运气。

He's the envy of the whole street.

整条街的人都很羡慕他。

[考点] lost in envy 非常嫉妒

equal[13] [ˈiːkwəl] *a.* 同等的,相等的;平等的;胜任的 *n.*(地位等)相同的人,匹敌者 *vt.* 等于,比得上

[语境] She feels equal to the task.

她认为能胜任该项工作。

He feels that they are his equals.

他觉得他们和他地位相等。

[考点] be equal to 等价于,和……平衡;on terms of equality with 和……平等相处

equip[4] [ɪˈkwɪp] *vt.* 装备,设备

[语境] The room is equipped with air conditioning.

这个房间装有空调设备。

He is equipped with much experience in teaching.

他具有丰富的教学经验。

equipment[8] [ɪˈkwɪpmənt] *n.* 设备,器材,装置;才能

[语境] The ship was provided with radar equipment.

那船装有雷达设备。

error[25] [ˈerə(r)] *n.* 错误,过失

[语境] The accident was caused by human error.

这一事故是人为错误造成的。

erupt [ɪˈrʌpt] *v.* 爆发

[巧记] e(出来) + rupt(破开)→破开发出来→爆发

[语境] Words of anger erupted from him.

他突然破口大骂。

escape[6] [ɪˈskeɪp] *n.* 逃跑,逃脱 *v.* 逃跑;避开,避免

[巧记] 同义词:evade, flee, get away

[语境] The soldier escaped from the enemy's prison.

这个士兵从敌人的监狱里逃了出来。

[考点] escape from 从……逃脱，幸免

especially [ɪˈspeʃəlɪ] *ad.* 特别，尤其，格外；专门地，主要地

[语境] It can be quite windy there, especially in spring.

那里有时容易刮风，特别在春季。

essential[10] [ɪˈsenʃəl] *a.* 必不可少的，必要的；本质的，实质的；基本的

[语境] In considering this problem, you should grasp its essentials.

在考虑这一问题时，你应当抓住实质。

Her most essential quality is kindness.

她最主要的品质是善良。

[考点] It is essential + that 句型，表示"……是非常必要的"

establish[20] [ɪˈstæblɪʃ] *v.* 建立，设立；安置，使定居

[语境] We have established diplomatic relations with the newly independent nations.

我们已与那几个新近独立的国家建立了外交关系。

establishment [ɪˈstæblɪʃmənt] *n.* 建立，设立，建立的机构（或组织）

[语境] They used their savings for the establishment of the business.

他们把积蓄花在创办生意上。

estimate[12] [ˈestɪmeɪt] *v./n.* 估计，估价，评价

[语境] They estimated the number of visitors at 10 million.

他们估计参观者人数为1 000万。

He is highly estimated among his colleagues.

他在同事中受到的评价很高。

[考点] at a rough estimate 大略估计，大略来说；make an estimate of 给……作一估计；评价

euro [ˈjuərəʊ] *n.* 欧元

[语境] Despite these problems, the euro will continue to exist for the foreseeable future.

尽管存在这些问题，在可预见的未来，欧元还将继续存在。

Europe[ˈjʊərəp] *n.* 欧洲

[语境]All Europe was then embroiled in war.
当时整个欧洲都被卷入了战争。

European[ˌjʊərəˈpɪən] *a.* 欧洲的 *n.* 欧洲人

[语境]I accompanied him on his European travel.
我陪他周游了欧洲。

evaluate[6] [ɪˈvæljʊeɪt] *vt.* 评价,评估

[语境] Let's evaluate the evidence.
让我们评定一下此证据的价值。

even[ˈiːvən] *ad.* 甚至(更) *a.* 均匀的;平的;相等的;偶数的

[语境]Her teeth were white and even.
她的牙齿洁白而整齐。
Even those who were once for him began to turn against him.
连那些原来支持他的人也开始反对他了。

evening [ˈiːvnɪŋ] *n.* 傍晚,晚上,黄昏

[语境]In the evening they smoked and talked.
晚上,他们一面抽烟一面聊天。

event[ɪˈvent] *n.* 大事,事件

[语境]The tragic event is sharply etched into my memory.
那起悲惨的事件深深地铭刻在我的记忆中。

ever [ˈevə(r)] *ad.* 曾经;永远;在任何时候;究竟

[语境]Has anybody ever seen any beings from outer space?
有人见到过外星人吗?

everybody[ˈevrɪbɒdɪ, -bədɪ] *pron.* 每人,人人

[语境]Not everybody can do it.
并不是人人全都能做。

everyday[ˈevrɪdeɪ] *a.* 每天的,日常的

[语境]After the everyday practice, I could go very fast by bicycle.
经过每天的练习,我可以骑得很快了。

everyone[ˈevrɪwʌn] *n.* 每个人 *pron.* 每人,人人

[语境]Everyone would sympathize with you.
每个人都会同情你的。

everything [ˈevrɪθɪŋ] *pron.* 每件事，一切

[语境] She bore down everything before her.

她克服了面前一切困难。

evidence[16] [ˈevɪdəns] *n.* 明显；显著；根据；证据；迹象

[语境] Evidence has now disproved that theory.

事实现已证明那种理论是不正确的。

[考点] in evidence 看得见，到场，处于明显的地位

考点集训

1. Louis Herman, at the University of Hawall, has _____ a series of new experiments in which some animals have learned to understand sentences.

   A. installed   B. equipped
   C. devised   D. formatted

2. There is a fully _____ health center on the ground floor of the main office building.

   A. installed   B. equipped
   C. provided   D. projected

3. It _____ you to at least 50% off the regular price of either frames or lenses when you buy both.

   A. presents   B. entitles
   C. credits   D. tips

4. These teachers try to be objective when they _____ the integrated ability of their students.

   A. justify   B. evaluate
   C. indicate   D. reckon

5. There has been a collision _____ a number of cars on the main road to town.

   A. composing   B. consisting
   C. involving   D. engaging

6. These overseas students show great _____ for learning a new language.

155

A. enthusiasm B. authority
C. convention D. faith

7. In the _____ of the project not being a success, the investors stand to lose up to $30 million.
   A. face B. time
   C. event D. course

8. On New Year's Eve, New York City holds an outdoor _____ which attracts a crowd of a million or more people.
   A. incident B. event
   C. case D. affair

9. A season ticket _____ the holder to make as many journeys as he wishes within the stated period of time.
   A. grants B. promises
   C. entitles D. presents

10. Everyone should be _____ to a decent standard of living and an opportunity to be educated.
    A. attributed B. entitled
    C. identified D. justified

11. The police are trying to find out the _____ of the woman killed in the traffic accident.
    A. evidence B. recognition
    C. status D. identity

12. This ticket _____ you to a free boat tour on the lake.
    A. entitles B. appoints
    C. grants D. credits

13. Everyone has faced the embarrassing _____ of deciding how much extra to give a waiter or taxi-driver.
    A. incident B. event
    C. dilemma D. menace

答案与解析

1. C 夏威夷大学的路易斯·何曼设计了一系列新的实验,在实

核心词汇精解

验中,一些动物已学会了理解句子的意思。A 安装;B 配备;C 设计,发明;D 使格式化,安排……的格局,设计……的版面。故选 C。

2. B 在办公主楼的一楼,有一个设备齐全的医疗中心。A 安装;B 配备;C 提供;D 投射,放映。故选 B。

3. B 如果你框架和镜片都买的话,每件均至少半价。entitle sb. to sth. 有权做某事。故选 B。

4. B 这些老师评定学生的综合能力时,尽量做到客观。A 证明……有理,为……辩护,对……作出解释;B 评价;C 表明;D 预算,估计。故选 B。

5. C 在通往镇里的主干道上,多辆小汽车发生碰撞。A 组成,构成;B 由……组成(+ of);C 包括;D 从事。故选 C。

6. A 根据题干中 show 和 for learning a new language,得知空格处应填入表示"热情"的词。enthusiasm 表示"狂热,积极性";authority 表示"权威,威信,权威人士";convention 表示"大会,协定,习俗,惯例";faith 表示"信任,信念,宗教信仰,忠实"。答案为 A。

7. C 倘若这个项目不成功的话,投资者就要损失 3 000 万美元。A 面对;B 时间;D 过程。故 C in the event of "倘若,如果"为正确答案。

8. B 新年前夜,纽约市举办了一场室外活动,吸引了 100 来万人。A 小事故;B 活动,大事件;C 案件,案例;D 事情。故 B 为正确答案。

9. C 季票的持有者在规定的时段内可以去他想去的地方。A 批准;B 许诺;C 使……能;D 呈现。故 C 为正确答案。

10. B 每个人都应该有权过上体面的生活,享有受教育的机会。A 归因于;B 使……有权做;C 识别;D 解释……有理,说明……有理。故 B 为正确答案。

11. D 警察尽力找出在这起交通事故中死者的身份。A 证据;B 认可;C 地位;D 身份。故选 D。

12. A 有了这张票,你可以在湖上免费游玩一次。A 给……权利;B 任命,委任;C 授予,允许;D 相信,信任,把……归功于。

故选 A。
13. C dilemma 困境；incident 事故,骚乱；event 事件,大事；menace 威胁。

Word List 17

evolve [ɪˈvɒlv] v. (使)进化,(使)演化；(使)发展,(使)演变
[语境] He has evolved a new theory after many years of research.
他经过多年的研究,逐渐总结出了新的理论。
The American constitution was planned, the British constitution evolved.
美国宪法是精心制定的,英国宪法是约定俗成的。
[考点] evolutionary processes 进化过程

exact[10] [ɪɡˈzækt] a. 确切的,正确的,精确的
[巧记] ex(外) + act(做)：做出来→做对→精确的
[语境] The exact date of his birth is not known.
他出生的确切日期无人知道。
[考点] be more exact 更精密些；确切地说

exam(ination)[10] [ɪɡˈzæm; ɪɡˌzæmɪˈneɪʃn] n. 考试,测验
[语境] Failing the exam was a hard dose to swallow.
考试不及格是一服难咽的苦药。

examine[20] [ɪɡˈzæmɪn] v. 检查,调查；对……进行考试
[语境] He examined the quality of the furniture critically.
他以挑剔的目光审视家具的质量。

example[46] [ɪɡˈzɑːmpəl] n. 例子,实例；范例,榜样
[语境] This church is a classic example of medieval architecture.
这座教堂是中世纪建筑风格的典型实例。
Many great men have risen from poverty—Lincoln, for example.
许多伟人从贫困中崛起,例如林肯。

excellent[4] [ˈeksələnt] a. 卓越的,极好的

[巧记] 同义词：fabulous, first-class

[语境] Their band has some excellent brass players.

他们乐队有几个出色的铜管乐器手。

except[32] [ɪkˈsept] *prep.* 除……之外 *v.* 除外；反对

[语境] He never drinks except on special occasions.

除非在特别场合，否则他从不喝酒。

[考点] except for 除……之外，只是；except that 除了，只是

excess [ˈekses] *a.* 过量的，额外的 [ɪkˈses] *n.* 过量；过剩；超额；无节制

[语境] An excess of rain caused severe floods.

雨水过量造成了严重的水灾。

[考点] go to excess 走极端；to excess 过度，过分

exchange[6] [ɪksˈtʃeɪndʒ] *vt./n.* 交流，交换；调换，兑换 *n.* 交换台，交易所

[语境] He gave me an apple in exchange of an orange.

他给我一个苹果，交换一个橙子。

We exchanged our opinions about the event at the meeting.

在会上，我们就此事交换了意见。

[考点] exchange…for sth. 以……交换……；exchange…with sb. 和某人交换某物；in exchange 交换

excite [ɪkˈsaɪt] *v.* 刺激，使激动；激发，激励

[巧记] 派生词：excitement *n.* 刺激，兴奋，激动

[语境] The professor's lecture on Shakespeare excited our interest.

那位教授关于莎士比亚的讲座引起了我们的兴趣。

excited [ɪkˈsaɪtɪd] *a.* 兴奋的

[巧记] 神情很兴奋(excited)的人肯定遇到了令人兴奋的(exciting)事。

[语境] He was getting excited just thinking about the trip.

一想到那次旅行他就兴奋。

excuse [ɪkˈskjuːz] *v.* 原谅，宽恕，免除 *n.* 借口，辩解

[语境] She excused herself for coming late.

她因来晚而请求原谅。

[考点] in excuse of 为……辩解

execute [ˈeksɪkjuːt] v. **执行,实行,完成;处死,处决**

[巧记] execution n. 执行,实行;executive a. 执行的;管理的

[语境] Never once did I doubt that I would be able to execute my plan.

我从未怀疑过我能执行自己的计划。

He was executed as a deserter.

他被作为叛逃者处决。

exercise [ˈeksəsaɪz] n. **练习,习题;训练,锻炼** v. **训练,锻炼;行使**

[语境] Plenty of exercise will help you keep in shape.

充分的运动将帮助你保持健康。

[考点] bring…into exercise(充分)运用,应用;发挥 do one's exercise 做功课;take exercise 做体操,做健身活动

exhibition [ˌeksɪˈbɪʃən] n. **展览,显示;展览会**

[巧记] exhibit(v. 展览)

[语境] They went to an exhibition of modern art yesterday.

昨天,他们参观了现代美术展览。

exist[17] [ɪɡˈzɪst] v. **存在;生存;生活**

[语境] Such laws exist only to conserve the privilege of this selfish minority.

这种法律的存在只会保护这一小部分自私自利者的特权。

[考点] exist in 存在于……中;exist on 靠……生活[生存]

existence[4] [ɪɡˈzɪstəns] n. **存在,生存**

[语境] The newspaper ceased to appear after an existence of three months.

该报发行3个月后停刊了。

The family lived a precarious existence.

这家人过着朝不保夕的生活。

expand[13] [ɪkˈspænd] v. **扩大,扩张,膨胀**

[巧记] expansion n. 扩大,增加;expansionism n. 扩张主义,扩展政策

[语境] Foreign trade has expanded during recent years.

近年来我们的对外贸易有所扩大。

The petals of many flowers expand in the sunshine.

许多花的花瓣在阳光中绽放。

expect[33] [ɪkˈspekt] *vt.* **期待,盼望;料想,预期**

[语境] The journey was not as nice as we had expected.

旅途不像我们预想的那样好。

I will do what is expected of me.

我会尽本分的。

expense[4] [ɪkˈspens] *n.* **开销,花费;(*pl.*)费用**

[语境] It's too much of an expense for me to own a car.

对我来说,拥有一辆汽车的花费太大。

He finished the job at the expenses of his health.

他以牺牲健康为代价完成了这项工作。

expensive[9] [ɪkˈspensɪv] *a.* **花费的,昂贵的**

[巧记] expensively *ad.* 昂贵地,高价地

[语境] It is often less expensive to see a doctor in a clinic than in a hospital.

通常去诊所看病比去医院看病便宜。

experience[49] [ɪkˈspɪərɪəns] *v.* **经验,经历** *n.* **经验,感受,体验;经历**

[语境] He experienced great difficulty in getting a visa to leave the country.

他申请出国签证经历了很大的困难。

I know from my own experience how difficult the work can be.

我从自己的经验中明白这项工作会有多难。

experiment[11] [ɪkˈsperɪmənt] *n.* /*vi.* **(on, with)实验,试验,尝试**

[语境] Finally he succeeded in his experiment.

他终于试验成功。

The scientists have already experimented at each other's test sites.

科学家已经在彼此的实验场所进行了实验。

[考点] experiment on/ with 在……身上做实验/用……做实验

expert [ˈekspɜːt] *n.* **专家,能手** *a.* **专家的,内行的**

[语境] According to experts' opinions, they gave up the experiment immediately.

根据专家们的意见,他们马上放弃了这项实验。

He is an well-known expert in finance.

他是知名的金融专家。

[考点] be expert in/at...在……方面是专家

explain[20] [ɪksˈpleɪn] *vt.* 解释,说明

[语境] That explains why she is not here.

那就说明了她不在这里的原因。

The lawyer explained the new law to us.

律师向我们解释了新法律。

explanation[8] [ˌekspləˈneɪʃən] *n.* 解释,说明

[语境] There may be a physical explanation for these strange happenings.

这些奇怪现象也许有符合自然法则的解释。

[考点] in explanation of 解释

explode [ɪkˈspləʊd] *v.* (使)爆炸,(使)爆发

[巧记] 同义词: blow up, burst, erupt

[语境] The city's population has exploded in the last few years.

在最近几年里这个城市的人口急剧增加。

explore[5] [ɪkˈsplɔː(r)] *vt.* 探险;探索,探究;勘探

[语境] He had an itch to get away and explore.

他等不及要动身去探险。

Can you explore the market possibility for us?

您能为我们考察一下市场前景吗?

export [ˈekspɔːt] *v./n.* 输出,出口 *n.* 出口商品

[巧记] exportable *a.* 可出口的,可输出的

[语境] Rubber is the country's principal export.

橡胶是该国主要出口物。

express[30] [ɪkˈspres] *v.* 表达,表示 *a.* 特快的,快速的 *n.* 快车,快运

[语境] He expressed the hope that we would keep in touch with his firm.

他表示希望我们与他的公司保持联系。

[考点] express oneself 表达自己的思想[感情、意见]

expression[12] [ɪkˈspreʃən] n. 表达;表情;声调;腔调;榨出;措辞;式;符号

[巧记] expressional a. 表现的,表情的

[语境] He had a dissatisfied expression on his face.
他脸上流露出不满的神色。

[考点] beyond expression 无法形容,难以表达; give expression to 表达,反映,表现,叙述; without expression 毫无表情地

extend[5] [ɪkˈstend] vt. 伸,延伸,扩大;致,给予

[语境] The hot weather extended into October.
炎热天气一直持续到十月。

My garden extends as far as the river.
我的花园一直延伸到河边。

external [ɪkˈstɜːnl] n. 外部 a. 外部的,外用的,客观的,表面的

extra[15] [ˈekstrə] n. 附加物,额外的东西 a. 额外的,附加的 ad. 特别地

[语境] There were so many people that the company put on extra buses.
人数太多,公司加开了公共汽车。

This dress is of extra fine quality.
这件衣服的质地特别好。

extraordinary [ɪkˈstrɔːdɪnərɪ] a. 非常的;格外的;意外的;离奇的;临时的

[巧记] 超出(extra)普通(ordinary)的:非凡的

[语境] She smiled with an extraordinary niceness.
她笑得异常甜美。

extreme[10] [ɪkˈstriːm] n. 极端 a. 极端的,极度的;尽头的,末端的

[语境] She's been generous in the extreme.
她一直非常慷慨。

The capital is in the extreme south of the country.
首都在这个国家的最南端。

[考点] go to extreme 走极端；in the extreme 极端地，极度地

eye[aɪ] *n.* 眼睛

[语境] He has a good eye for detail and notices almost everything.
他明察秋毫，几乎一切事情都注意到了。

考点集训

1. In order to show his boss what a careful worker he was, he took _____ trouble over the figures.
   A. extensive   B. spare
   C. extra   D. supreme

2. My oldest son had just finished an _____ holiday stay prior to moving to a new state, a new job, and the next chapter in his life.
   A. enlarged   B. expanded
   C. extended   D. increased

3. The older New England villages have changed relatively little _____ a gas station or two in recent decades.
   A. except   B. besides
   C. in addition to   D. except for

4. Being ignorant of the law is not accepted as an _____ for breaking the law.
   A. excuse   B. intention
   C. option   D. approval

5. _____ quantities of water are being used nowadays with the rapid development of industry and agriculture.
   A. Excessive   B. Extensive
   C. Extreme   D. Exclusive

6. Local government _____ could be obtained through a local income tax and/or a local sales tax.
   A. budget   B. expense
   C. finance   D. revenue

7. The Huntington Library has an _____ collection of rare books and manuscripts of British and American history and literature.

A. intensive B. intentional
C. extensive D. extensional

8. They are trying to _____ the waste discharged by the factory for profit.
   A. expose B. exhaust
   C. exhibit D. exploit

9. The board of the company has decided to _____ its operations to include all aspects of the clothing business.
   A. multiply B. lengthen
   C. expand D. stretch

10. His business was very successful, but it was at the _____ of his family life.
    A. consumption B. credit
    C. exhaustion D. expense

11. _____ the few who have failed in their examination, all the other students in the hall are in very high spirits.
    A. In spite that B. But for
    C. Apart from D. For the sake of

答案与解析

1. C 为了向他的老板证明他工作认真,他承担了额外的工作。A 广泛的;B 抽出的,多余的;C 额外的,另外的;D 最高的,最多的。故 C 为正确答案。

2. C extend 指时空上的延展;increase 指某事物数量或强度的增长;expand 是范围的扩张;enlarge 是扩大物体的尺寸。故选 C。

3. D 在最近几十年,古老的新英格兰村庄,除了一个或两个加油站,变化相对不大。A 除……以外;B 除……还有;C 除了;D 除了,从总体……除去一部分。故 D 为正确答案。

4. A 根据题干,再结合四个选项——excuse 表示"借口";intention 表示"企图";option 表示"选择";approval 表示"同意",可知,只有 excuse 符合题意,答案为 A。

5. A 根据题干中 water being used 和 with the rapid development of

industry and agriculture,得知空格处应填入表示"大量"的词。excessive 表示"过多的,过分的";extensive 表示"广大的,广阔的,广泛的";extreme 表示"极端的,极度的";exclusive 表示"排外的,独占的,唯一的"。只有 excessive 符合题意,答案为 A。

6. B 地方政府的花费可以通过地方所得税或地方销售税获得。budget 表示"预算";expense 表示"费用,开支";finance 表示"金融,财务";revenue 表示"收入"。

7. C extensive 大量的,广泛的;intensive 强烈的,精深的;intentional 故意的;extensional 外延的。故选 C。

8. D 他们正尽力利用工厂丢弃掉的垃圾以盈利。A 暴露;B 使……筋疲力尽;C 展览;D 开采,利用。故选 D。

9. C 公司董事会决定拓展业务范围,涵盖了布料行业的方方面面。A 繁殖,乘以,增加;B 延长;C 拓展;D 伸展,延伸。故选 C。

10. D 他经商很成功,但是那是以他家庭生活为代价的。A 消费;B 信用,分数;C 筋疲力尽,枯竭;D 费用。at the expense of 以……为代价的,故选 D。

11. C 除了几个在考试中失利的人,其他在大厅的学生情绪高昂。故 C 为正确答案。

Word List 18

fabric[ˈfæbrɪk] *n.* 织物,布,结构
[语境]The jacket is comfortable because the fabric breathes.
这件短上衣穿着很舒适,因为这种织物透气。
We are really in the fiber, the fabric of life.
我们的确是在纤维构造的世界中。

face [feɪs] *n.* 脸,面貌,表情;正面 *v.* 面对着;朝,面向
[语境] Her face lighted up at the good news.
她听到这好消息脸上露出了喜色。
[考点] lose one's face 丢脸,失面子;make a face 做鬼脸或怪

相；face up to 勇敢面对

facility [fəˈsɪləti] *n.* 设施,设备

[语境] It describes completely the facility and its safety basis.

它完整地描述了设备和它的安全基础。

fact [fækt] *n.* 实际,事实

[语境] Her argument is grounded on fact.

她的论点是基于事实的。

[考点] as a matter of fact 事实上,其实；in fact 实际上,其实

fail[21] [feɪl] *v.* 失败,不及格；衰退,减弱

[语境] She failed to unlock the safe in spite of all her exertions.

她虽然费尽力气,仍未能将那保险箱的锁打开。

[考点] without fail 必定, 务必；fail of 缺乏……能力；不能达到；fail to 没有(做某事)；疏忽；忘记(做某事)

failure[6] [ˈfeɪljə(r)] *n.* 失败,不及格；失败者；没做到；失灵

[语境] The play was a dead failure.

这场戏完全失败了。

I shall have another chance in the event of failure.

如果失败,我还有另一个机会。

fair [feə(r)] *n.* 定期集市,交易会,博览会 *a.* 公平的,合理的；相当的,尚好的；晴朗的；美丽的,金发的

[语境] It's not fair to kick another player in football.

足球比赛中不允许踢另一位球员。

His knowledge of the language is fair.

他对这种语言的了解相当不错。

fairly [ˈfeəli] *ad.* 公正地,正当地；相当,还算

[巧记] 反义词：partially, unjustly

[语境] We're not rich but we're fairly comfortable.

我们并不富有,但生活还较宽裕。

faith [feɪθ] *n.* 信任,信用；信念,信心；信仰

[语境] He has great talent, but he has lost his faith.

他很有天赋,但是他已经丧失了信心。

She signed the letter in good faith, not realizing its implications.

她真心实意地在信上签了字,没意识到其中另有含义。

fall [fɔːl] v. 跌倒;下降;减弱;坠落;变成,陷于 n. 秋季

[语境] Her necklace fell off because the clasp had broken.

她的项链掉了下来,因为钩环坏了。

false [fɔːls] a. 假的;人造的,假造的;虚伪的

[语境] Your answer to this question is false.

你对这个问题的回答是错误的。

They lulled me into a false sense of security.

他们哄骗我,让我产生了一种虚假的安全感。

familiar [fəˈmɪliə(r)] a. 熟悉的,通晓的;亲密的,交情好的

[语境] This nursery rhyme is very familiar to me.

我对这首摇篮曲很熟悉。

He yearned for a sight of the old familiar faces.

他渴望见一下那些熟悉的老面孔。

[考点] be familiar to 为……所熟悉; be familiar with 熟悉,通晓,精通

family [ˈfæməli] n. 家庭,家;氏族,家族;系,族,属

[语境] She talked at us about her family life.

她对我们滔滔不绝地讲她的家庭生活。

She married into a prominent family.

她嫁到一个显赫的家族。

famous [ˈfeɪməs] a. 著名的

[语境] The famous actress is now appearing at the Capital Theatre.

目前这位著名女演员正在首都剧场演出。

[考点] be famous for 因……而著名

fan [fæn] n. 扇子,风扇;(影、球等)迷 v. 扇,扇动,激起

[语境] Gossiping about her neighbors fanned them into resentment.

背后议论她的邻居激起了他们的愤恨。

fancy [ˈfænsi] n. 想象(力);爱好,迷恋 a. 别致的;异想天开的 v. 想象,幻想;想要,喜欢;相信,猜想

[语境] Fancy her saying a thing like that!

想不到她竟然说出这种话来!

I fancy I have met you before.
我想我以前或许见过你。

[考点] have fancy for 喜欢,想要;take a fancy to 爱上,喜欢;take/catch the fancy of 引起……喜爱;fancy oneself 自以为是

far [fɑː(r)] *a./ad.* **远,久远,遥远** *ad.* **到……程度,……得多**

[语境] He often works far into the night.
他常常工作到深夜。

[考点] as far as 远到;到……为止;至于;就……而言;in so far as (表示程度、范围)就……而言;尽……;至于;so far 到目前为止

fare [feə(r)] *n.* **车费,船费**

[语境] I think I fared quite well in the interview.
我觉得我这次面试表现不错。

I've nowhere near enough for the fare.
我的钱肯定不够买车票的。

farm [fɑːm] *n.* **农场,农田,牧场** *v.* **耕作,经营作物**

[语境] They keep cattle on their farm.
他们在农场上养牛。

How can you farm if the profits will be theirs?
如果收益都是他们的,你怎么会去种田?

farmer [ˈfɑːmə(r)] *n.* **农夫,农场主**

[语境] The farmer milks the cows twice a day.
那农夫一天挤两次母牛的奶。

farther [ˈfɑːðə(r)] *a./ad.* **更远(的),进一步(的)**

[语境] I can throw the ball farther than you can.
这个球我能扔得比你远。

fashion[9] [ˈfæʃən] *n.* **样子,方式;流行,风尚,时髦**

[语境] Fashions have changed a lot since I was a little girl.
现在的时装和我孩提时代流行的样子很不一样了。

Many influences help to fashion our children's characters.
各种各样的影响有助于塑造我们孩子们的性格。

[考点] after the fashion 时髦的,流行的; be all fashion 很时兴;be

in(out of)fashion 流行(过时)

fast [fɑ:st] *a.* 快的,迅速的;坚固的 *ad.* 紧紧地;迅速地

[语境]A fast highway is being built.

一条高速公路正在修建。

Hold fast to this rope, and I will pull you up.

抓紧绳子,我把你拉上来。

fat [fæt] *a.* 多脂肪的,肥胖的;丰厚的 *n.* 脂肪,肥肉

[语境]The doctor told him to stay away from fat foods.

医生要他不要吃油腻的食品。

father [ˈfɑ:ðə(r)] *n.* 父亲

[语境]She took one of the parcels from her father to lighten his load.

她从父亲那儿拿过一个包以减轻他的负担。

favo(u)r[4] [ˈfeɪvə(r)] *n.* 好感,喜爱;恩惠;帮助,支持 *vt.* 赞成,支持

[语境] In their discussion, I was in favor of Mr. Li.

在他们的争论中,我支持李先生。

Would you do me a favor?

你能帮我一个忙吗?

[考点] ask a favor of sb. 要人帮忙,求人做事;do a favor for sb. 给某人帮忙,给某人做事;in favor of 赞成,主张;in one's favor 对……有利

favo(u)rable[6] [ˈfeɪvərəbl] *a.* 赞许的,有利的,讨人喜欢的

[巧记] 反义词:adverse, unfavorable

[语境] You made a favourable impression on the examiners.

你给主考留下了很好的印象。

favo(u)rite [ˈfeɪvərɪt] *a.* 最喜爱的 *n.* 最喜爱的人/物

[语境] Spain is our favorite holiday spot.

西班牙是我们最喜欢的度假地点。

What's your favorite food?

你最喜欢的食物是什么?

fear[20] [fɪə(r)] *n.* 害怕,恐惧;危险 *vt.* 畏惧,害怕,担心

[语境] Military observers fear that the US could get entangled in another Vietnam.

军事观察家们担心美国有可能陷入另一次越南战争中。

feasible [ˈfiːzəbl] *a.* 可行的,可能的

[语境] We all think this proposal feasible.

大家认为这个建议是可行的。

feature[7] [ˈfiːtʃə(r)] *n.* 特征;容貌;特色;特写 *v.* 以……为特色

[语境] A characteristic feature of this area is the detached pillars of rock that stand in the sea.

这一区域的特色是耸立在海中的孤立的石柱。

[考点] make a feature of 以……为特色;以……为号召

February [ˈfebruərɪ] *n.* 二月

[语境] But from February through July, Joy sat around with nothing to do.

但是从二月到七月,乔伊又无事可做了。

fee [fiː] *n.* 酬金;手续费;学费

[巧记] fee 发音接近"费"

[语境] You pay one fee and then get all you want.

你付一次费用就可以得到所有你想要的。

feed [fiːd] *v.* (on, with) 喂养,饲养;(with) 向……供给

[语境] She crumbed the bread before feeding it to the birds.

她把面包弄碎,然后喂给鸟吃。

[考点] feed up 供给食物[营养];养肥;使吃饱

feel [fiːl] *v.* 触;认为 *vi.* 摸上去有……感觉;摸索;觉得

[语境] Silk feels soft and smooth.

丝织品摸起来柔软而光滑。

[考点] feel at home 感觉舒适

feeling [ˈfiːlɪŋ] *n.* 感情;心情;知觉;同情

[语境] I found it hard to convey my feelings in words.

我觉得难以用言语表达我的感情。

female [ˈfiːmeɪl] *n.* 女性;女人;雌兽 *a.* 女性的;雌的;柔弱的

[巧记] 同义词: feminine, ladylike, womanly;反义词: male

[语境] Sewing is considered a female occupation.

缝纫被认为是女性的职业。

festival ['festɪvəl] *a.* 节日的,喜庆的,快乐的 *n.* 节日,庆祝及祭祀,欢宴

[语境] They are gathering flowers for the festival.

他们正在采集节日用花。

[考点] spring festival 春节

fetch [fetʃ] *n.* 取得 *v.* 接来,取来,带来

[语境] Fetch me my hat please.

请把我的帽子取来。

fever ['fiːvə(r)] *n.* 发热,狂热

[语境] A fever is a symptom of illness.

发烧是生病的症状。

few [fjuː] *a.* [表肯定]有些,几个;[表否定]几乎没有的

[语境] Only a few of my friends were informed about it.

这件事只有我的几个朋友知道。

[考点] a few 少数,几个; only a few 仅仅少数,一点点

field [fiːld] *n.* 田野;运动场;(电或磁)场;领域,范围

[语境] We passed through wheat fields and golden plots of sunflowers.

我们穿过小麦地和金黄色的向日葵地块。

fierce ['fɪəs] *a.* 凶猛的,凶恶的;猛烈的,强烈的

[巧记] fiercely *ad.* 猛烈地,厉害地

[语境] Because there is so much unemployment, the competition for jobs is fierce.

因为失业严重,求职的竞争十分激烈。

The little baby was frightened by the fierce dog.

那个小孩被恶狗吓坏了。

fifteen [fɪfˈtiːn] *num.* 十五

[语境] The ages of the students of our class range from fifteen to eighteen.

我班同学的年龄在十五岁到十八岁之间。

fifth [fɪfθ] *num.* 第五

[语境]The clever boy jumped the fifth grade in school.
那个聪明的男孩跳过了小学五年级。

fifty [ˈfɪftɪ] *num.* 五十

[语境]He can not be more than fifty.
他不可能超过五十岁。

fight [faɪt] *v./n.* 打(仗),搏斗,斗争,战斗

[语境] The fight against inflation has been going on for almost two years.
抑制通货膨胀的战斗已开展了近两年了。

figure[15] [ˈfɪɡə(r)] *n.* 外形,轮廓,体形;图形,图表;数字,数值;形象,人物

[语境] They figured it was better to stay where they were.
他们断定还是待在原地好。

Mahatma Gandhi was both a political and a religious figure in Indian history.
甘地在印度历史上是政治和宗教要人。

fill [fɪl] *v.* (with)填满,充满

[巧记]反义词：drain , empty

[语境] Her eyes filled with tears.
她热泪盈眶。

[考点] be filled with 充满着; fill in 填写,填上; fill out 填满,填好

film [fɪlm] *n.* 电影;胶卷 *v.* 把……拍成电影

[语境]The director expresses his sorrow in his film.
导演在影片中表达出他的悲哀。

He had filmed her life story.
他把她一生的经历拍成了电影。

[考点] film, movie, picture 辨析:这些名词均有"电影"之意。film:指电影、影片,普通用词。movie:美国英语中的口语用词。picture:从原义指银幕或电视屏幕上的图像,引申指影片

final [ˈfaɪnəl] *a.* 最后的,最终的;决定性的

[语境] The game is now in its final stages.

这场比赛现在处于最后阶段。

He is expected to get through to the finals.

我们期待他进入决赛。

[考点] prepare for the finals 准备参加期终考试

finally [ˈfaɪnəlɪ] *ad.* 最后,终于

[语境] The word was finally given for us to get on board.

终于通知我们登乘了。

finance[7] [ˈfaɪnæns] *n.* 财政,金融 *vt.* 提供资金,接济

[巧记] 派生词:financial *a.* 财政的,金融的

[语境] Unless we can get more finance, we'll have to close the store.

除非我们能得到更多的资金,否则我们将不得不关闭这家商店。

The politician was appointed as the Minister of Finance.

这位政治家被任命为财政部长。

financial[9] [faɪˈnænʃəl] *a.* 财政的,金融的

[语境] They offer financial aid with no strings attached.

他们无条件提供财务援助。

find [faɪnd] *v.* 找到;发现;发觉;感到

[语境] Newton found that all masses attract each other.

牛顿发现所有的物质都相互吸引。

[考点] find out 发现,找出;猜着,想出;揭发(坏人等);find in 供给,供应(某人衣、食、费用等)

finding[24] [ˈfaɪndɪŋ] *n.* 发现,发现物;(*pl.*) 调查(研究)的结果

[语境] The finding appears in the journal *Science*.

这项发现发表在《科学》期刊上。

We hope that manufacturers will take note of the findings and improve their products accordingly.

我们希望制造商能注意到这些结果,并对它们的产品作出相应的改进。

fine [faɪn] *vt./n.* 罚款 *a.* 美好的,优良的;优秀的,晴朗的,明朗的;纤细的;精细的,精致的

[语境] It poured all morning, but turned fine later.

下了一上午的瓢泼大雨,后来才转晴。

You are making very fine distinctions.

你做的区分非常精细。

finger [ˈfɪŋɡə(r)] *n.* 手指,指针

[语境] He would not stir a finger to help you.

他不会动一根指头来帮助你的。

finish [ˈfɪnɪʃ] *n.* 完成;结束;磨光 *v.* 完成;结束;用完;毁掉

[语境] We hope to finish the work next week, but the schedule's very tight.

我们希望在下周做完这工作,但日程安排很紧。

[考点] finish up 完成,吃光;用尽;finish up with 以……结束;finish with 完成;结束;与……断绝关系

fire [ˈfaɪə(r)] *n.* 火;火灾,失火;炉火 *vi.* 开火 *vt.* 放(枪)

[语境] They made a fire to prepare for supper.

他们生火做晚饭。

We fired our guns at the enemy.

我们向敌人开炮。

[考点] catch fire 着火;cease fire 停火

fit[6] [fɪt] *v.* 合适,试穿,安装 *a.* 合适的,适宜的;恰当的,正当的,得体的

[语境] We must fit the action to the word.

我们必须言行一致。

He is not fit to be a lawyer.

他不适合当律师。

考点集训

1. She keeps a supply of candles in the house in case of power _____.
   A. failure   B. lack

C. absence   D. drop

2. Last night he saw two dark _____ enter the building, and then there was the explosion.
   A. features   B. figures
   C. sketches   D. images

3. He wrote an article criticizing the Greek poet and won _____ and a scholarship.
   A. status   B. fame
   C. faith   D. courage

4. Owing to _____ competition among the airlines, travel expenses have been reduced considerably.
   A. fierce   B. strained
   C. eager   D. critical

5. The film provides a deep _____ into a wide range of human qualities and feelings.
   A. insight   B. imagination
   C. fancy   D. outlook

6. Urban crowdedness would be greatly relieved only if the _____ charged on public transport were more reasonable.
   A. fees   B. fares
   C. payments   D. costs

答案与解析

1. A 为预防停电,他房里放了好多蜡烛。A 失败,中断(电)等;B 缺少;C 缺席;D 丢掉,放下。故选 A。

2. B 昨晚他看见两个黑色的身影进了楼里,接着就发生了爆炸。A 特征,特点;B 人物;C 轮廓;D 肖像。故选 B。

3. B 他写了一篇批评希腊诗人的文章,这篇文章为他赢得了名声和奖学金。A 地位,身份;B 名声;C 信念;D 勇气。由此 B 为正确答案。

4. A 由于航空公司激烈的竞争,旅行费用降低了很多。A 激烈的;B 紧张的,担忧的;C 急切的;D 批评的。故 A 为正确答案。

5. A 这部电影深度挖掘了人类的各种品质和情感。A 洞察;B 想象;C 幻想;D 世界观。故 A 为正确答案。
6. B 只要公共交通费用更加合情合理,城市拥堵现象会得到很大缓解。A 费用;B 付款;C 车费,船费;D 成本,花费。故选 B。

Word List 19

firm[fɜːm] *a.* 坚定的,坚固的,结实的;坚决的,坚强的 *n.* 商行,公司

[语境] At the age of 50 he still had a firm chin and a smooth neck.
他 50 岁时还有结实的下巴和光滑的脖子。

My firm was office in the city.
我的公司在市里设有办公室。

[考点] be on firm ground(尤指讨论中)理直气壮

first[fɜːst] *ad.* 首先,第一,优先 *a.* 第一的

[语境] You have first to motivate the children and then to teach them.
你首先得激发孩子们的学习兴趣,然后再去教他们。

first-rate[ˌfɜːstˈreɪt] *a.* 第一流的,极好的

[语境] The electronics products were first-rate and eagerly embraced.
人们急切地想拥有这些第一流的电子产品。

fish[fɪʃ] *n.* 鱼 *v.* 捕鱼,钓鱼

[语境] This pan smells of fish.
这个盘子有股鱼腥味。

They fish every spring and early summer before visiting relatives can get in the way.
他们会在每年春天和初夏的时候,赶在亲戚们登门打扰之前,去钓鱼。

fitness[ˈfɪtnɪs] *n.* 适当,恰当,合理;健康

[语境] At another time, your attention might be concentrated on overhauling your diet and changing your fitness habits.

另一些时候,你的注意力可能会集中在饮食大调整和改变健康习惯上。

five [faɪv] *num.* 五(个)

[语境] We work from nine to five.

我们从九点工作到五点。

fix [fɪks] *v.* (使)固定;修理;安装;决定;注视 *n.* 困境

[语境] She fixed her eyes on the picture.

她凝视着那幅画。

[考点] fix over 修理

flag [flæg] *n.* 旗

[语境] The brave soldier tore down the enemy's flag.

那位勇敢的士兵扯下了敌人的旗子。

flat [flæt] *n.* 一套房间,公寓套房 *a.* 平坦的,扁平的;平淡的,乏味的;单调的

[语境] After the excitement was over, she felt flat.

令人兴奋的事过后,她感到平淡无味。

flexible[7] [ˈfleksɪbəl] *a.* 柔软的,易弯曲的;灵活的,可变通的

[语境] We need a foreign policy that is more flexible.

我们需要一个更为灵活的外交政策。

[考点] flexible 表示根据形式的变化、要求而变化

flood[6] [flʌd] *n.* 洪水,水灾 *v.* 泛滥,淹没

[语境] The town was destroyed by the floods after the storm.

暴风雨后的洪水冲毁了这座城镇。

Applications flooded into the office.

申请书像潮水般涌进办公室。

[考点] in flood 泛滥; flood in 大量地涌入; flood out 淹没

floor [flɔː(r)] *n.* 地板,楼层,底部

[语境] She clinked down on the floor.

她啪的一声倒在地板上。

flow [fləʊ] *vi./n.* 流,流动;漂浮,飘扬 *n.* 流动,流量,流速

[语境] The flow of melted snow cascaded down the mountainside

and into the river.

融化的雪水如瀑布般沿着山崖边泻入河里。

They divided the house into flats.

他们把那栋房屋分成许多套住房。

[考点] flow away 流走；流逝；flow down 流下；flow from 从……产生；是……的结果；flow into 流入

flower[8] [ˈflaʊə(r)] *n.* 花,花卉 *vi.* 开花

[巧记] 面粉(flour)散发着一种鲜花(flower)的味道

[语境] It is a flower common in the field.

这是一种田野里常见的花。

flu [fluː] *n.* 流行性感冒

[语境] Most of my colleagues have gone down with flu.

我的大多数同事因流感而病倒了。

fly [flaɪ] *n.* 飞行；苍蝇 *v.* 飞行；飘扬

[语境] The Red Cross flew to the area of the floods, ready to dole out supplies of food and medicine.

红十字会飞往洪涝地区,准备发放食物与药品。

focus[20] [ˈfəʊkəs] *n.* 中心,焦点,焦距 *v.* 聚焦,集中

[语境] He always wants to be the focus of attention.

他总想成为注意力的焦点。

You should focus your attention on your work.

你应该把注意力放到工作上。

[考点] concentrate, focus 辨析：这两个动词均有"集中,聚集"之意。concentrate 指把人或物集中在一起,也可指把精力或注意力集中于某一事物上。focus 侧重指把光、热、射线等集中于一点,也可指把思想或精力等集中于某人或某事情上

follow [ˈfɒləʊ] *vt.* 跟随,追随,追求；顺……走；听众,遵循；理解,听清楚

[语境] I didn't quite follow, could you explain it again?

我不太明白,你能再解释一下吗？

The police are following a murderer who's in hiding.

警察正在追赶藏匿起来的杀人犯。

following [ˈfɒləʊɪŋ] *a.* 下列的，其次的

[语境] You should see the following screen.
您应该看下面的屏幕。

fond [fɒnd] *a.* (of)喜爱的，爱好的

[巧记] 派生词：fondly *ad.* 亲爱地，深情地；fondness *n.* 喜欢，爱好

[语境] He was very fond of writing and reciting poetry.
他很喜欢写诗、背诗。

food [fuːd] *n.* 食物，粮食；养料

[语境] This food disagrees with her.
这种食物对她有害。

foolish [ˈfuːlɪʃ] *a.* 愚蠢的

[语境] Let me disabuse you of that foolish idea.
让我纠正你那种愚蠢的想法。

foot [fʊt] *n.* 足，底部；英尺；最下部，底部

[语境] Can you balance on one foot?
你能独脚站着保持平衡吗？

[考点] on foot 步行

football [ˈfʊtbɔːl] *n.* 足球 *n.* 橄榄球

[巧记] foot(脚) + ball(球)→用脚踢的球→足球

[语境] Our school defeated that school at/in football.
我校在足球比赛中打败了那个学校。

for [fə(r), fɔː(r)] *prep.* 为了；给；代替；向；支持 *conj.* 因为

[语境] Prices for consumer goods are going up.
消费品价格在上涨。

forbid[4] [fəˈbɪd] *vt.* 禁止，不准，不许

[语境] I forbid you to tell anyone.
我不许你告诉任何人。

Lack of time forbids any further discussion at the point.
由于时间不够，现在不能深入讨论这个问题。

force[18] [fɔːs] *vt.* 强迫，迫使 *n.* 力，力量，力气；暴力，武力；(*pl.*) 军队，部队

[语境] The force of the explosion broke all the windows in the building.

爆炸的力量震碎了这座建筑上的所有窗户。

The rider forced his horse on through the storm.

骑士迫使他的马在暴风雨中前进。

foreign ['fɒrən] *a.* **外国的,(to)无关的;外来的;异质的**

[巧记] 同义词：alien, external；反义词：domestic, home, interior

[语境] Foreign affairs are his strong point.

外交事务是他的特长。

foreigner ['fɒrɪnə(r)] *n.* **外国人**

[语境] He sounds like a foreigner.

他的发音像个外国人。

forest ['fɒrɪst] *n.* **森林,森林地带**

[语境] A path winds through the forest.

一条小路蜿蜒穿过森林。

forever [fər'evə(r)] *ad.* **永远,总是**

[巧记] for ever（永远）

[语境] His words will be forever imprinted on my mind.

他的话将永远铭刻在我心中。

forget [fə'get] *v.* **忘记,遗忘**

[语境] We'll never forget the cruelties of the invaders.

我们永远不会忘记入侵者的暴行。

forgive [fə'gɪv] *vt.* **原谅,宽恕,饶恕**

[语境] He is not a man who forgives easily.

他不是一个肯轻易宽恕人的人。

I'll never forgive you!

我永远都不会饶恕你！

[考点] forgive and forget 宽大为怀；不念旧恶

form[21] [fɔːm] *n.* **形状,形式;表格** *v.* **组成,构成;形成**

[语境] She formed a strong attachment for him.

她对他产生了强烈的爱慕之情。

[考点] form from 由……组成,用……构成；form into 组

成……,编成……

formal[8] [ˈfɔːməl] *a.* 正式的;礼仪上的;形式的

[语境] Business letters must always be formal, but we should write in a natural way to friends.

商业信函必须是正式的,但是写信给朋友应写得自然一些。

There is only a formal likeness between the two brothers, for their natures are very different.

这两兄弟仅外表相似,本性却很不一样。

former[7] [ˈfɔːmə(r)] *a.* 在前的,以前的 *n.* 前者

[语境] Mr. Heath is the former Prime Minister of Britain.

希思先生是英国前任首相。

Of these two men, the former is dead but the latter is still alive.

这两个人中,前者已死,而后者仍然活着。

forth [fɔːθ] *ad.* 向前;向外,往外

[语境] I had expected much from his speech, but nothing new came forth.

我曾对他的演讲抱有很大希望,但实际上没有什么新鲜东西。

[考点] and (so on and) so forth 等等

fortunate [ˈfɔːtʃənət] *a.* 幸运的,侥幸的

[巧记] 同义词:auspicious, lucky;反义词:unfortunate

[语境] A fortunate encounter brought us together.

一次幸运的邂逅让我们相识了。

fortunately [ˈfɔːtʃənətlɪ] *ad.* 幸亏

[语境] Fortunately, you have the power to change all that.

幸运的是,你还有能力去改变所有这一切。

fortune[6] [ˈfɔːtʃən] *n.* 财富,财产;命运,运气

[语境] These two brothers decided to go to America to try their fortunes.

这兄弟俩决定去美国碰碰运气。

Everyone is the architect of his own fortune.

每个人都是自己命运的创造者。

[考点] a small fortune 一大笔钱;make a fortune 发财;seek one's fortune 外出找出路;try one's fortune 碰运气

forty[ˈfɔːtɪ] *num.* 四十

[语境] She can't be more than forty.

她不可能超过四十岁。

foundation[7] [faʊnˈdeɪʃən] *n.* **基础,根本,建立,创立;地基,基金,基金会**

[语境] The foundation of the university took place over 400 years ago.

该大学于四百多年前创办。

[考点] lay the foundation for 给……打下基础,为……奠定基础

four[fɔː(r)] *num.* 四(个)

[语境] The department offers four specialities.

这个系有四个专业。

fourteen[ˌfɔːˈtiːn] *num.* 十四

[语境] In the next twenty years it went through fourteen editions.

在后来的二十年里,该书再版了十四次。

framework[ˈfreɪmwɜːk] *n.* **构架;框架;结构;组织;机构**

[语境] You should adhere to a basic framework when writing it.

在书写这类信函时,您应参照一个基本的结构。

free[25] [friː] *a.* **自由的;免费的;免税的;空闲的** *vt.* **释放**

[语境] Abraham Lincoln freed the slaves.

亚伯拉罕·林肯解放了奴隶。

freedom[12] [ˈfriːdəm] *n.* **自由,自主,免除,特权**

[巧记] 反义词: constrain, repression

[语境] The freedom of speech should not be abridged.

言论自由不应受限制。

[考点] with freedom 自由地;随便地,无拘束地

freely[ˈfriːlɪ] *ad.* 自由地,随意地

[语境] The value of this exercise is that it challenges the students to express themselves freely.

这项练习的价值在于它能促使学生自由地表达自己的思想。

freeze [fri:z] *v.* 使结冰,使凝固
[语境] Water freezes at zero degrees Centigrade.
水在零摄氏度结冰。

French [frentʃ] *a.* 法国(人)的,法语的 *n.* 法国人,法语
[语境] The word derives from French.
这个词来自法语。

fresh [freʃ] *a.* 新的,新鲜的;有生气的,健壮的;清新的,凉爽的
[语境] It's a bit fresh this morning, isn't it?
今天早晨有点儿凉,是吗?
I feel really fresh after my holiday.
我真觉得度假之后精神饱满了。

Friday ['fraɪdɪ] *n.* 星期五
[语境] I'll hand your dictionary back to you on Friday.
我星期五把你的词典还给你。

friend [frend] *n.* 朋友,友人
[语境] I enjoy a chat with a friend.
我喜欢与朋友在一起聊天。
[考点] make a friend with somebody 与某人交朋友

friendly ['frendlɪ] *a.* 友好的,友谊的
[巧记] 反义词:inimical, unfriendly
[语境] The manager is friendly with his inferiors.
经理对他的部属很友好。

frighten ['fraɪtən] *vt.* 吓唬,使惊恐
[语境] He frightened the old man into giving him all the money.
他恐吓那位老人把所有的钱都给了他。
The children's shouts frightened off the birds.
孩子们的喊声把鸟儿吓飞了。

from [frəm, frɒm] *prep.* 从,自从;由于;离;根据,按;去除
[语境] From the hill top we could see the plains below.
从山顶上我们可以看到山下的大平原。

front [frʌnt] *a.* 前面的,前部的 *n.* 正面;前线,战线 *v.* 面对
[语境] The front of the car was damaged and we had to get out by

the rear door.

车身前部受损,我们只得从后门出来。

Seeing her son returning from the front she was climbing the wall.

见到儿子从前线归来,她欣喜若狂。

fruit[fruːt] *n.* 水果

[语境]Those children have finished off the fruit.

那些孩子们把水果都吃光了。

frustrate[frʌ'streɪt] *v.* 挫败,击败,破坏 *a.* 无益的,挫败的,挫折的

[巧记] frustration *n.* 挫折

[语境]The standard of embellishment can frustrate the honest.

修饰的标准可以使诚实的人感到挫败。

He left the company in a frustrate mood.

他怀着挫败的心情离开了公司。

fuel [fjuːəl]*n.* 燃料 *vt.* 加燃料,供给燃料

[语境] The newspaper article provided him with fuel for his speech.

报纸上的这篇文章为他的演讲带来了启发。

All aircraft must fuel before a long flight.

所有飞机均须先加油方能长途飞行。

fulfil(l) [fulˈfɪl]*vt.* 完成;履行;达到

[巧记] 派生词:fulfillment *n.* 完成,结束

[语境] Does your job fulfill your expectations?

你的工作符合你的期望吗?

You must fulfill your promise.

你必须履行诺言。

full [ful]*a.* (of)满的,充满的 *n./ad.* 完全,充分

[语境]The full moon has a circular shape.

满月呈圆形。

fun [fʌn]*n.* 玩笑,娱乐;有趣的人(或事物)

[语境] All work and no play is no fun.

只工作而不娱乐不会使人开心。

[考点] for fun 开玩笑,不是认真的

function[20] [ˈfʌŋkʃən] *n.* 机能,官能,功能;职务,职责;函数 *vi.* 活动,运行,起作用

[语境] The minister has to attend all kinds of functions.
部长必须参加各种活动。
The function of an adjective is to describe or add to the meaning of a noun.
形容词的作用是描述或增加名词的意思。

fund [fʌnd] *n.* (*pl.*) 资金;基金,专款;储备

[语境] They clubbed a fund of money for poor children.
他们为贫穷的孩子们募集了一笔资金。
They have subscribed large sums to the fund.
他们向基金会捐了巨款。

funny [ˈfʌnɪ] *a.* 滑稽的,可笑的

[巧记] 反义词:serious

[语境] The clown tickled the audience with his funny actions.
小丑用滑稽动作逗观众发笑。

furnish [ˈfɜːnɪʃ] *v.* 供应,提供;陈设,布置

[语境] The shop furnishes everything that is needed for camping.
这家商店供应各种野营用品。
They are renting a furnished flat.
他们正在租一套带有家具的公寓房子。

[考点] furnish sth. to sb. 提供某物给某人;furnish sb./sth. with 供给某人[某物]……

furniture[8] [ˈfɜːnɪtʃə(r)] *n.* 家具

[语境] He dusted down the furniture.
他掸掉家具上的灰尘。

further[12] [ˈfɜːðə(r)] *ad./a.* 更远,更往前;进一步 *v.* 促进,增进

[语境] Our object is to further cement trade relations.
我们的目标是进一步加强贸易关系。

furthermore[5] [fɜːðəˈmɔː(r)] *ad.* 而且,此外

[语境] The house isn't big enough for me, and furthermore, it's too far from the town.

这栋房子不够我们住,而且,它离市区太远。

Furthermore, he informs Elizabeth, Wickham had been carrying on an intrigue with Darcy's sister Georgiana.

而且,他还告诉伊丽莎白,韦翰过去一直同他妹妹乔治亚娜有私通关系。

future[23] [ˈfjuːtʃə(r)] *n.* 将来,未来;前途,前景 *a.* 将来的,未来的

[语境] His future seemed filled with gloom.

他的前程似乎黯淡无光。

[考点] in the future 将来,未来

考点集训

1. The machine looked like a large, _____, old-fashioned typewriter.
   A. forceful   B. clumsy
   C. intense   D. tricky

2. The other day, Mum and I went to St. James's Hospital, and they did lots and lots of tests on me, most of them _____ and frightening.
   A. cheerful   B. horrible
   C. hostile   D. friendly

3. All her energies are _____ upon her children and she seems to have little time for anything else.
   A. guided   B. aimed
   C. directed   D. focused

4. His wife is constantly finding _____ with him, which makes him very angry.
   A. errors   B. shortcomings
   C. fault   D. flaw

5. In Africa, educational costs are very low for those who are _____ enough to get into universities.
   A. ambitious   B. fortunate
   C. aggressive   D. substantial

6. Finding a job can be _____ and disappointing, and therefore it

is important that you are prepared.

A. exploiting　　　　　B. frustrating
C. profiting　　　　　　D. misleading

7. We have arranged to go to the cinema on Friday, but we can be _____ and go another day.

A. reliable　　　　　　B. probable
C. feasible　　　　　　D. flexible

答案与解析

1. B　这台打字机看起来庞大、臃肿、过时。A 强有力的；B 臃肿的；C 紧张的，强烈的；D 棘手的，狡猾的。故选 B。
2. B　前几天妈妈和我去圣詹姆斯医院,医生们给我做了很多项检查,大多数检查很恐怖。A 高兴的；B 恐怖的；C 怀有敌意的；D 友好的。故选 B。
3. D　她把所有的精力都集中在她女儿身上,似乎没有时间干其他的事了。A 引导；B 对准；C 指导；D 聚焦。故 D 为正确答案。
4. C　他的妻子不断地挑他的毛病,这让他很生气。固定搭配,find fault with sb. 找茬,挑某人的错,故选 C。
5. B　在非洲,教育成本对有幸进入大学的人而言很低。A 有雄心的；B 幸运的；C 侵略性的；D 大量的。故选 B。
6. B　找工作可能会令人很沮丧,很失望,因此做好准备是十分重要的。A 开采；B 令人沮丧的；C 盈利；D 误导的。故选 B。
7. D　根据题干中 go another day,再结合四个选项——reliable 表示"可靠的"；probable 表示"很可能的"；feasible 表示"可行的"；flexible 表示"灵活的",可知只有 flexible 符合题意,答案为 D。

Word List 20

gain[12] [geɪn] *v.* 获得,赢得；增加,增进；(钟表)走快 *n.* 赢利；(*pl.*) 收益,利润；增加,增进,获利

[巧记] 派生词:gainable *a.* 可得到的, 可赢得的;gainless *a.* 无利益的

[语境] He has gained rich experience in these years.

这些年来,他取得了丰富的经验。

After swimming for an hour,he finally gained the shore.

他游了一小时以后,终于到达岸边。

[考点] No pain,no gain. 一分耕耘,一分收获。

game[ɡeɪm] *n.* 游戏

[语境] I dived in when the game started.

游戏开始时我就进去了。

garage[6]['ɡærɑːʒ,-rɪdʒ] *n.* 车库,汽车修理厂

[语境] The garage floor was swilled down by father.

爸爸用水把车库地面冲洗干净了。

garden['ɡɑːdn] *n.* 花园,果园,菜园

[语境] She came to the garden.

她来到了这个花园。

garlic['ɡɑːlɪk] *n.* 大蒜

[语境] This salad tastes of garlic.

这色拉有大蒜味。

gas[ɡæs] *n.* 煤气,气体,汽油

[语境] Gas has hardly any weight.

气体几乎没有重量。

[考点] gas leak 煤气泄漏

gather[6]['ɡæðə(r)] *v.* 聚集,聚拢;推测,推断

[巧记] 派生词:gatherable *a.* 可收集的,可计[测]量的,可推测的

[语境] A rolling stone gathers no moss.

滚石不生苔。

gene[6][dʒiːn] *n.* 基因

[语境] They have one abnormal gene from that parent and one normal gene from the other parent.

他们具有来自父母一方的一个异常基因和来自父母另一方

的一个正常基因。

general[28] [ˈdʒenərəl] *a.* 普通的,通用的;总的,大体的 *n.* 将军;一般,概括

[语境] Please give me a general idea of the work.

请告诉我这项工作的梗概。

Napoleon was a great general.

拿破仑是一位伟大的将领。

generally[10] [ˈdʒenərəlɪ] *ad.* 一般地,通常,大体上,广泛地,普遍地

[语境] The new prime minister is generally acknowledged as a far-sighted statesman.

新首相是一位公认的有远见的政治家。

generation[11] [dʒenəˈreɪʃən] *n.* 产生,发生;代,世代

[巧记] 派生词:generational *a.* 生殖的,生育的;一代的

[语境] My generation behaves differently from my father's and grandfather's.

我这一代人和我父辈及祖辈表现不同。

gentle [ˈdʒentəl] *a.* 和蔼的,文雅的,有礼貌的;轻柔的,徐缓的;坡度小的

[语境] My new teacher is a very gentle person.

我的新老师是一个温文尔雅的人。

Gentle persuasion is more effective than force.

温和的说服胜于强迫。

gentleman [ˈdʒentlmən] *n.* 绅士,先生

[巧记] gentle(温柔的,彬彬有礼的) + man(人)→绅士

[语境] He demeaned himself like a gentleman.

他举止颇有些绅士风度。

geography [dʒɪˈɒɡrəfɪ] *n.* 地理

[巧记] geo(地球) + graphy(画)→画地球→地理

[语境] The question is one of psychology rather than geography.

这是一个心理层面的问题,而非地理问题。

German [ˈdʒɜːmən] *a.* 德国(人)的,德语的 *n.* 德国人,德语

[语境]Half of the books are in German.

这些书有一半是德语的。

He is German.

他是德国人。

get [get] *v.* **获得,得到;使,使得;变得,成为;到达**

[语境] It's much easier to get into debt than to get out of debt.

借债容易还债难。

[考点] get along 过日子,过活;相处;进展[步];get at 得到;get away from(使)摆脱,(使)离开;get by 维持生活;走动,通过;get down to 开始认真考虑;着手办理(某事);get in 进站;到达,回来;get off 下来;下车;起飞;(动身)离开;get out 下车,走出,离开;摆脱;get over 复原,痊愈;完成;走完;get through 完成;到达,通过;get to 到达;get together 收集,积累

girl [gɜːl] *n.* **女孩,少女,姑娘**

[语境]I must emphasize the fact that she is only a little girl.

我必须强调这样一个事实,这就是她只不过个小女孩。

give[84] [gɪv] *v.* **给,授予;供给;献出,让步;捐赠;发表**

[语境] Give my respects to your parents.

代我向你的父母亲致意。

[考点] give in 屈服,投降,退让; give up 放弃,停[中]止

glad [glæd] *a.* **高兴的,快活的;乐意的,情愿的**

[语境] The prisoner was glad to get his discharge.

因犯获准释放,感到很高兴。

glance [glɑːns] *n.* **一瞥,闪光,一滑** *v.* **瞥闪,瞥见,反光**

[语境]I saw my wife glance up at me.

我看到我的妻子瞥了我一眼。

[考点] glance at 浏览

glass [glɑːs] *n.* **玻璃;玻璃杯;镜子;(*pl.*)眼镜**

[语境]He took a glass of beer and relaxed after a day's work.

一天工作下来,他喝杯啤酒轻松一下。

global[6] [ˈgləʊbəl] *a.* **球形的;全球的,全世界的;全面的**

[巧记] 派生词:globality *n.* 全球性

[语境] Obesity became a global issue.

肥胖已经成为一个全球性的问题。

glory [ˈɡlɔːrɪ] *n.* 光荣,荣誉

[语境] His brave deeds in the battle earned him everlasting glory.

他在那场战斗中的英勇事迹为他赢得了永恒的荣誉。

No road of flowers lead to glory.

没有一条通往光荣的道路是铺满鲜花的。

[考点] win glory for our motherland 为国争光;be in one's glory 处于全盛时期

go [ɡəʊ] *v.* 去,离开;走;放置;变成;运转

[语境] He goes to the gymnasium every afternoon to sweat off some weight.

他每天下午去健身房以减轻一点体重。

[考点] go away 离去,带走,拐逃;(with)go back 回去;追溯到(to),回顾;go through 通过(考试等);经过

goal[36] [ɡəʊl] *n.* 终点,球门;目标,目的;进球得分

[语境] He has achieved his goal.

他已经实现了他的目标。

If we lose sight of the goal, we cease to be Communists.

如果忘记了这个目标,我们就不再是共产党员了。

[考点] aim at goal 瞄准目标

gold[ɡəʊld] *n.* 金,黄金;金币;金黄色 *a.* 金的,金制的

[语境] The gold glinted in the sunlight.

金子在阳光下闪闪发光。

She held up two pairs of shoes, one blue, one gold.

她双手举着两双鞋:一双蓝色的和一双金色的。

good [ɡʊd] *a.* 好的;善良的;擅长的;乖的 *n.* 好处;利益

[语境] His good intentions were repaid by good results.

他的善意得到了善报。

[考点] a good deal 许多,大量

goodby(e) [ˌɡʊdˈbaɪ] *int.* 再见

[语境] I have to say goodbye now.

我现在不得不说再见啦。

[考点] say goodbye to somebody 向某人告别

goods [gudz] *n. (pl.)* 货物,商品

[语境] He buys and sells leather goods.

他买卖皮货。

government[40] [ˈɡʌvənmənt, -vəm-] *n.* 政府,内阁;管理,支配;政治,政体

[巧记] govern(管理) + ment(名词后缀)→管理,支配

[语境] She was a woman of high position in the government.

她曾是个在政府中占有重要地位的女人。

There are different regulatory compliances for different industrial sectors mandated by the government.

政府管辖的不同行业部门,遵从不同的法规。

gradual [ˈɡrædʒuəl] *a.* 逐渐的,逐步的

[巧记] 派生词:gradually *ad.* 逐渐地;gradualness *n.* 循序性

[语境] There has been a gradual increase in the number of people owning cars.

拥有汽车的人数一直在逐渐上升。

graduate[13] [ˈɡrædʒuət] *n.* 毕业生;研究生 *vi.* 毕业 *a.* 毕了业的,研究生的

[语境] He graduated as an M.D. at Edinburgh.

他毕业于爱丁堡大学,获得医学博士学位。

He is a graduate in medicine.

他是医科毕业生。

[考点] graduate from 从……毕业

grandfather [ˈɡræn(d)fɑːðə(r)] *n.* (外)祖父

[巧记] grand(大) + father(父亲)→大父亲→(外)祖父

[语境] My grandfather's eyesight is going.

我祖父的视力在减退。

grandmother [ˈɡræn(d)mʌðə(r)] *n.* (外)祖母

[语境] My father often speaks of my grandmother.

我爸爸常常提起我的祖母。

grass [grɑːs] *n.* 草,牧草

[语境] She spread our lunch on the grass.

她在草地上摆好了我们的午饭。

grateful ['greɪtfʊl] *a.* 感激的,感谢的

[语境] I can't express how grateful I am.

我说不出我有多么感激。

I am heartily grateful to your help.

我衷心地感激你的帮助。

[考点] be grateful to sb. for sth. 为某事而感谢某人

gray = **grey** *a.* 灰色的;灰白头发的;阴暗的;(指脸因恐惧、生病等)苍白的

[语境] The blue shirt and gray tie are a good match.

蓝衬衫与灰领带很协调。

great [greɪt] *a.* 伟大的;重要的;大量的;很好的;美好的

[语境] Great heat melts iron.

高温使铁熔化。

greedy ['griːdɪ] *a.* 贪吃的,嘴馋的;贪婪的;渴望的

[语境] He looked at the shop window with greedy eyes.

他用贪婪的眼光看着商店的橱窗。

The greedy little boy ate all the candy at the party.

那个贪吃的小男孩把宴会上所有的糖果都吃光了。

[考点] greedy for sth./to have sth. 贪图……;greedy to do 急于干某事情

Greek [griːk] *n.* 希腊人,希腊语 *a.* 希腊(人)的,希腊语的

[语境] So he steals her away from the Greek guy.

于是他从希腊人手中偷走她。

They all read it in Greek.

他们读的是希腊语的。

green [griːn] *a.* 绿色的 *n.* 绿色

[语境] I shall paint the gate green.

我将把大门油成绿色。

greenhouse ['griːnhaʊs] *n.* 温室

[语境]Our greenhouse is nothing compared with yours.

我们这个温室比起你们那个简直是小巫见大巫。

greeting[ˈɡriːtɪŋ] *n.* 问候,招呼

[语境]He drawled a greeting to her.

他慢吞吞地对她说声问候。

grey[ɡreɪ] *a./n.* 灰色(的)

[语境]He often interchanges his black hat with his grey hat.

他经常交换着戴他的黑帽子与他的灰帽子。

grocery[ˈɡrəʊsərɪ] *n.* (*pl.*)食品(店),杂货(店)

[语境]He shut his grocery.

他关闭了他的杂货店。

ground[8][ɡraʊnd] *n.* 地,地面,土地;场地,场所;理由,根据

[语境] He refused the request on moral grounds.

基于道德上的考虑,他拒绝了这个请求。

[考点] on the ground(s) that 因为,以……为理由

group[33][ɡruːp] *n.* 群,组 *v.* 分组

[语境] There appeared a group of aeroplanes in the sky.

天空中出现了机群。

[考点] a group of 一群,一组,一批

grow[11][ɡrəʊ] *v.* 生长,成长;渐渐变成;栽培,种植;发展

[语境] As he grew older, his appreciation of art grew.

随着年龄的增长,他对艺术的鉴赏力也提高了。

[考点] grow in 增加;在……方面成长;grow into 成长为;变得成熟有经验

grown-up[ˌɡrəʊnˈʌp] *a.* 成长的,成熟的,成人的 *n.* 成年人

growth[17][ɡrəʊθ] *n.* 生长,增长,发展

[语境]The soil is adaptable to the growth of peanuts.

这土壤适宜于花生的生长。

[考点]mushroom growth 雨后春笋般的增长,迅速发展

guarantee[6][ˌɡærənˈtiː] *vt.* 保证,担保 *n.* 保证,保证书

[语境] South winds in winter are a guarantee of rain in these parts.

在这一带,冬天刮南风是下雨的迹象。

This radio has a two-year guarantee.

这台收音机保修两年。

[考点] guarantee 经常指的是对产品的质量、服务实施或尽职之许诺。

guard[7] [gɑːd] v./n. 保卫,守卫,提防 n. 哨兵,警卫,看守

[语境] The guard was punished for deserting his post.

卫兵因擅离职守而受到处罚。

[考点] be off one's guard 疏忽, 大意; guard against 提防, 预防

guess [ges] v./n. 猜测,推测;以为;猜想

[巧记] 同义词:surmise

[语境] My guess was the furthest from the correct answer.

我的猜测与正确的答案相差极远。

[考点] wild guess 乱猜, 瞎猜

guest [gest] n. 客人,宾客,旅客

[语境] He saw the guest out and took up his work again.

他把客人送出去以后又接着做他的工作。

guide[8] [gaɪd] n. 领路人;指南,导游 v. 领路;指导;支配;管理

[语境] The guide showed us the old home of former President Theodore Roosevelt.

导游带我们看了前总统西奥多·罗斯福的故居。

guilty[7] ['gɪltɪ] a. 犯罪的,有罪的;自觉有罪的,负疚的

[语境] It was apparent to all that he was guilty.

众所周知,他是有罪的。

The jury brought in a verdict of guilty.

陪审团作出有罪的裁决。

[考点] be guilty of a crime 犯了罪

guitar [gɪ'tɑː(r)] n. 吉他

[语境] He strummed his guitar when he talked to me.

他和我说话时把吉他拨弄响了。

gun [gʌn] n. 枪,炮

[语境] He stooped and put down his gun.

他弯下腰放下了他的枪。

考点集训

1. He has _____ rich experience in these years.
   A. acquired   B. obtained
   C. gained   D. gaited
2. There is a generation _____ between my parents and I.
   A. gape   B. gap
   C. garb   D. garage
3. She turned her head away, feeling too ashamed to meet his _____.
   A. glare   B. stare
   C. glance   D. gaze
4. The accident _____ a lot of public interest in the nuclear power issue.
   A. brought   B. generated
   C. engendered   D. generalized
5. It is rare to find such a _____ nowadays.
   A. genie   B. genesis
   C. genuine   D. genius
6. What a _____ of a tree!
   A. big   B. great
   C. king-size   D. giant
7. He has a _____ for music.
   A. gift   B. present
   C. grant   D. tip
8. The young heir was so _____ that he gave all his money away in a couple of years.
   A. handsome   B. genuine
   C. talented   D. generous
9. The glasses _____ and twinkled in the firelight.
   A. gazed   B. glared
   C. glanced   D. glimpsed

· 197 ·

10. The bright moonlight showed the Taj Mahal in all its _____.
    A. honour   B. glory
    C. glorifier   D. shame
11. You'd better set a(n) _____ before you start the drill.
    A. goal   B. objective
    C. object   D. end
12. They demand the right to _____ themselves.
    A. control   B. govern
    C. reign   D. rule
13. The Car Club couldn't _____ to meet the demands of all its members.
    A. ensure   B. guarantee
    C. assume   D. confirm
14. Extensive reporting on television has helped to _____ interest in a wide variety of sports and activities.
    A. gather   B. generate
    C. assemble   D. yield
15. We are quite sure that we can _____ our present difficulties and finish the task according to schedule.
    A. get across   B. get over
    C. get away   D. get off

答案与解析

1. C 这些年来,他取得了丰富的经验。acquire 通过自己的工作、技艺、行动而获得;obtain 通过自己或别人努力或请求而获得;gain 通过努力获得自己想要得到的。

2. B 父母和我之间有代沟。gape 哈欠,张口;garb 制服,装束;garage 车库。

3. D 因为害羞而不敢和他凝视的目光相遇,她把头扭开了。glare 怒视某人或某物;stare 凝视某人或某物;glance 一瞥,粗略地看。

4. B 这次事故引起了人们对核能力的广泛关注。bring 带来;engender 突然产生某种想法;generalize 概括地说,笼统地表达。

5. D 这样的天才现在很少见。genie 妖怪;genesis 起源;genuine *a.* 真正的。

6. D 多高大的树!great 表示某一方面给人留下深刻的印象;king-size 商业用语,尺寸比普通的大些;big 面积、体积和范围大。

7. A 他有音乐天赋。present 礼物;grant 给予个人或团体一笔钱或礼物,为了达到某种目的;gift 还可以作天赋理解,常和 for 连用。

8. D 那个年轻的继承人如此的慷慨,在两年内把他所有的钱都捐赠了出去。handsome 帅气的,长相好看的;talented 天才的;genuine 真正的,纯正的。

9. C 杯子在炉火照耀下闪闪发亮。gaze 凝视着,盯着看;glare 怒视,瞪眼;glimpse 一瞥,粗略地看。

10. B 泰吉·玛哈尔陵在明亮的月光下显得光彩夺目。honor 和 glory 含义相同,但 glory 还有壮丽的意思;glorifier 是名词,赞美者;shame 是 glory 的反义词。

11. A 练习开始前,你最好设定一个目标。objective 尤其指的是军事目标;object 物质;end 结束,结果,最终实现的目标。

12. B 他们要求拥有自治权。control 控制;reign 君主统治;rule 着重指有指定法律、发号施令以及强使服从最高或绝对的权利。

13. B 汽车俱乐部不能保证满足所有成员的要求。A 确使,确保;B 保证;C 承担,认为;D 证实。故 B 为正确答案。

14. B 电视媒体的广泛报道助推了人们对很多不同的运动和活动的兴趣。A 收集;B 使……产生;C 组装;D 收获,大喊。故 B 为正确答案。

15. B 词组搭配题。根据题干中 present difficulties 和 finish the task according to schedule,得知空格处应填入表示"克服"的词。get across 表示"(使)越过,通过,被理解";get over 表示"爬过,克服,熬过";get away 表示"逃脱,离开,把……送走";get off 表示"下来,脱下,出发"。答案为 B。

Word List 21

habit [ˈhæbɪt] *n.* 习惯,习性,脾性

[语境] His idle habits bode ill for his future.
他那懒散的习惯预示着他不会有好的前途。

[考点] be in a habit of 惯于,有某种习惯; break off the habit of 改掉……的习惯

hair [heə(r)] *n.* 头发

[语境] Fear caused his hair to rise.
恐惧使他的毛发竖立起来。

haircut [ˈheəkʌt] *n.* 理发,剪发的方式

[语境] He had his haircut once a month.
他每个月理发一次。

half [hɑːf] *a.* 一半的,不完全的 *ad.* 一半地 *n.* 半,一半

[语境] Divide it in half.
把它分成两半。

hand[50] [hænd] *n.* 手,人手,雇员 *v.* 支持,搀扶,交给

[语境] He handed me a knife with a keen edge.
他递给我一把锋利的刀。

[考点] at first hand 第一手地,直接地; at no hand 无论如何也不,决不; at second hand 第二手地; 间接的

handle[14] [ˈhændəl] *vt.* 触,摸,抚弄;操纵;处理,应付 *n.* 手柄,把手,拉手

[语境] We don't handle that sort of book.
我们不经销那一类书。

Gelignite is dangerous stuff to handle.
葛里炸药是不可随便触碰的危险材料。

[考点] fly off the handle 十分激怒,大怒

handwriting [ˈhændraɪtɪŋ] *n.* 笔迹,书法

[巧记] hand(手) + writing(写的东西)→笔迹,书法

[语境]She astonished me with her beautiful handwriting.

她以其秀丽的书法而使我惊异。

hang[6] [hæŋ] *v.* **悬挂,垂吊;吊死,绞死**

[语境] Hang your overcoat in the closet.

把你的大衣挂在衣橱里。

[考点] hang about/round 聚集在……附近;徘徊,闲荡

happen[22] ['hæpən] *v.* **(偶然)发生;碰巧,恰好**

[语境] It happened even as he had expected.

事情正如他所料的那样发生了。

[考点] as it happens 碰巧来到,恰好出现;be likely to happen 可能要发生

happy ['hæpɪ] *a.* **快乐的,幸福的;乐意的;令人满意的**

[语境]Her happy smile was only a disguise for her sadness.

她喜悦的微笑仅仅是为了掩饰她的忧伤。

The children's faces beamed with happy smiles.

孩子们的脸上充溢着幸福的笑容。

hard[54] [hɑːd] *a.* **坚硬的;结实的;困难的;难忍的;严厉的**

[语境] Hard work is the gateway to success.

勤奋乃成功之母。

hardly[12] ['hɑːdlɪ] *ad.* **几乎不,简直不;仅仅**

[语境] She hardly eats enough to keep body and soul together.

她没有足够的食物来维持生命。

harm[25] [hɑːm] *n./vt.* **损害,伤害,危害**

[语境] It wouldn't do him any harm to work a bit harder.

工作努力一点对他没什么害处。

His failures did his reputation a lot of harm.

他屡次失败使他的声誉受到很大损害。

[考点] come to harm 受到损害;遭到不幸;do no harm 无害;do sb./sth. harm 对……有害

harvest[8] ['hɑːvɪst] *n./vt.* **收获,收割**

[语境] We have a plenteous harvest this year.

我们今年取得了大丰收。

The bad harvest led to severe food shortage.

歉收引起食物严重短缺。

[考点] harvest festival 收获感恩节；harvest moon 秋分后的满月

hate [heɪt] *v.* 恨，憎恨；不愿，不喜欢 *n.* 恨，憎恶

[语境] A competitive person loves to win and hates to lose.

竞争心强的人喜欢赢，讨厌输。

[考点] dislike, hate, disgust 辨析：这些动词均含有"不喜欢"之意。dislike 是普通用词，指任何程度的憎恶，但永远指正面的憎恶和反对。hate 指因对某人或某事强烈不满或反感，或因利害关系等而产生憎恨。disgust 指对令人不快、生厌或坏的东西或行为怀有强烈的憎恶

have [hæv; həv] *v.* 有，具有；体会，经受；从事；使；吃，喝

[语境] She has had enough of her alcoholic husband.

她对酒鬼丈夫再也无法容忍了。

[考点] have had it 受够了，忍无可忍了

he [hɪ; hiː] *pron.* 他

[语境] He found someone on him.

他发现有人在跟踪他。

head [hed] *n.* 头，头脑，领袖 *v.* 为首，朝向，前进

[语境] His head rested on my shoulder.

他的头靠在我的肩上。

Turn the page on this chapter of your life and head for the future!

将章节翻到自己的生活这一面，向未来出发！

headache ['hedeɪk] *n.* 头痛

[巧记] head(头) + ache(疼痛) → 头痛

[语境] He was constantly tormented with headache.

他经常受到头痛的折磨。

heal [hiːl] *v.* 治愈，愈合

[语境] Time heals most troubles.

时间会消除痛苦。

The holy man healed them of their sickness.

那位神职人员治好了他们的疾病。

[考点] heal over 愈合,称合; heal up 彻底愈合

health[63] [helθ] *n.* 健康,卫生
　[语境] Fresh air and exercise are good for the health.
　　新鲜空气和运动有益于健康。
　　It is believed that health is above wealth.
　　一般人都认为健康重于财富。

healthy[9] [ˈhelθɪ] *a.* 健康的,健壮的;有益健康的,卫生的
　[巧记] 派生词:healthily *ad.* 健康地
　[语境] His cheeks have healthy glow.
　　他的双颊有着健康的红晕。

hear [hɪə(r)] *v.* 听见;审讯;(from) 收到……的信/电话;听说
　[语境] We heard sounds of laughter from the next room.
　　我们听到隔壁房间传来的阵阵笑声。
　[考点] hear about 听到(关于)

heart [hɑːt] *n.* 心,中心,要点
　[语境] Her words warmed his heart.
　　她的话温暖了他的心。
　　The heart of the teacher's talk was that she was there to help us.
　　老师讲话的要点是她随时愿意帮助我们。
　[考点] heart and soul 全心全意;learn by heart 记住,背下;lose heart 失去信心

heat [hiːt] *n.* 热,热度,高潮 *v.* 加热,激昂
　[语境] Heat will melt iron.
　　热将使铁熔化。
　　The two materials will bond if you heat them.
　　如果你加热两种材料,它们会黏合起来。

heavy [ˈhevɪ] *a.* 重的,沉重的,繁重的;大量的;猛烈的
　[语境] Don't go so heavy on the sauce!
　　沙司不要加得太多!
　　My car is rather heavy on petrol.
　　我的汽车很费油。

height [haɪt] *n.* 高,高度,身高;高处,高地;顶点

[语境] His height makes him stand out in the crowd.

他身材高大,因此在人群中很突出。

What's the height of that wall?

那堵墙有多高?

help [help] *v.* 帮(援)助;有助于;[呼救]救命 *n.* 帮助(手)

[语境] Advertisement helps to sell goods.

广告有助于推销商品。

[考点] by the help of 得到……的帮助;cannot help (doing) 不禁,忍不住,不得不;help oneself to[口]随意取用[取食]

helpful ['helpful] *a.* 有帮助的;有益的

[语境] It's often helpful during an illness to talk to other sufferers.

通常,病中与同病者聊天是有益的。

I hired a car the day after landing and bought a comprehensive book of maps, which I found most helpful in crossing the country.

着陆后的当天,我租了一辆汽车并买了一本内容详细的地图册。我觉得在穿越村的旅途中,这本地图是很有帮助的。

her [hɜː(r);hə(r)] *pron.* [宾格]她;[所有格]她的

[语境] What should I talk to her?

我该对她说什么呢?

here [hɪə(r)] *ad.* 在(到,向)这里;这时;在这一点上

[语境] The damp climate here disagrees with my mother.

这儿潮湿的气候不适合我母亲。

hero ['hɪərəʊ] *n.* 英雄,勇士;男主角,男主人公

[巧记] heroine (*n.* 女英雄,女豪杰)

[语境] A reporter interviewed the combat hero.

记者访问了这位战斗英雄。

In romance novels, the heroine learns about the secret inner life of the hero.

在浪漫小说中,女主角会去了解男主角内心生活的秘密。

hers [hɜːz] *pron.* 她的

[语境] He compared my paper with hers.

他拿我的作业与她的相比较。

核心词汇精解

herself [hɜːˈself, ə-] *pron.* 她自己

[语境] She cares only for herself.
她只关心她自己。

hesitate[4] [ˈhezɪteɪt] *vi.* 犹豫，踌躇；含糊，支吾

[语境] He hesitated before replying.
她犹豫了一下才回答。

[考点] hesitate 指的是不能果断地作出决定或不能立即采取行动而踌躇

hi/hey *int.* 嗨

[语境] Hi, why you look so down?
嗨，你为什么看起来这么低沉啊？

hide [haɪd] *v.* 隐藏，躲藏；隐瞒

[语境] She hid the key under the door mat.
她将钥匙藏在擦鞋垫下。

high [haɪ] *a.* 高的，高度的，高级的，高尚的 *ad.* 高高地

[语境] The high cost of the machine prohibits its widespread use.
这机器价格昂贵，很难普及使用。

highlight[4] [ˈhaɪlaɪt] *n.* 最重要的部分，最精彩的场面 *vt.* 使显著，使突出

[语境] The highlights of the match will be shown on TV tonight.
比赛的最精彩场面将在今晚的电视节目中播放。

The highlight of our tour was seeing the palace.
我们旅游中最有意思的活动就是参观宫殿。

考点集训

1. The truck _____ only at the edge of the cliff.
   A. desisted   B. quited
   C. ceased   D. halted

2. It was a difficult situation and he _____ it very well.
   A. handled   B. tackled
   C. treated   D. managed

3. We were _____ put to find a replacement for our assistant.

205

A. hard B. harbour
C. harm D. harp

4. Using extremely different decorating schemes in adjoining rooms may result in _____ and lack of unity in style.

   A. conflict B. confrontation
   C. disturbance D. disharmony

5. From the incident they have learned a lesson: _____ decisions often lead to bitter regrets.

   A. urgent B. hasty
   C. instant D. prompt

答案与解析

1. D 汽车到了悬崖边停住了。quit 含有自动辞职的意思,还表示退出程序;desist 由于反对势力的阻断而停止;cease 指的是完成。

2. A 这是一种很困难的局势,但是他控制得很好。tackle 对付比较棘手的事情;treat 对待;manage 管理。

3. A 我们很难找到一个人来代替我们的助手。harbour 港口;harp 竖琴;harm 伤害。

4. D 使用极其不同的装饰形式来搭配房间会使房间缺少统一的风格和和谐性。conflict 冲突;disturbance 打扰。

5. B 通过这一事件,他们吸取了一个教训:仓促的决定会导致痛苦的后悔。urgent 紧急的,迫切的;instant 立刻的,紧急的;prompt 迅速的,果断的。

Word List 22

highly[ˈhaɪlɪ] *ad.* 高度地,很,非常

[语境]That would be highly unwise.

这将是非常不明智的。

核心词汇精解

high-tech[ˌhaɪˈtek] *n.* 高科技
　[语境]Not all pay toilets are high-tech, like this one in India.
　　并不是所有的付费厕所都是高科技的,比如在印度。

hill[hɪl] *n.* 小山
　[语境]My bike spanked down the hill.
　　我的自行车疾驶滑下了山坡。

him[hɪm] *pron.* [宾格]他
　[语境]I thanked him for his help.
　　我感谢他的帮助。

himself[hɪmˈself] *pron.* 他自己;他亲自
　[语境]He barred himself in.
　　他把自己关在里面。

hire [ˈhaɪə(r)] *v./n.* 雇用,租借
　[语境] We hired an advertising company for help to sell our products.
　　我们雇用了一家广告公司来推销我们的产品。
　　Hire a car for the day.
　　白天租用一辆汽车。

his[hɪz] *pron.* 他的;他的(东西)
　[语境]That should be his mother.
　　那大概是他的母亲。

history[25] [ˈhɪstərɪ] *n.* 历史,历史学;来历,经历
　[语境] A Survey of World History is one of the courses offered this semester.
　　世界史概论是本学期开的课程之一。
　[考点] go down to history 载入史册; make history 创造历史,做出永垂史册的事业

hit [hɪt] *v.* 打,击;碰撞 *n.* 击中;成功而风行一时的事物
　[语境] To hit a weaker person is a sign of cruelty.
　　殴打弱者是残忍的表现。

hobby [ˈhɒbɪ] *n.* 业余爱好,嗜好,兴趣
　[语境] My hobby is stamp-collecting/collecting stamps.
　　我爱好集邮。

207

My hobby is a good safety-valve for the tension that builds up at work.

我用业余爱好来消除工作中产生的紧张情绪。

hold[24] [həʊld] *v.* 拿着；保有；托住；举行；继续 *n.* 握住；船舱

[语境] We held a party to celebrate our success.

我们举行宴会庆祝我们的成功。

holiday[4] ['hɒlədeɪ] *n.* 假期，假日

[语境] He works all the year round without a holiday.

他一年到头工作，没有假日。

[考点] bank holiday 银行假期；公共假期

home [həʊm] *a.* 家(乡)的 *ad.* 回家，在家 *n.* 家

[语境] Last night they stayed at home and watched TV.

昨晚他们待在家里看电视。

Hi, Mom, I'm home!

嘿，妈妈，我回家了！

[考点] at home and abroad 国内外

hometown ['həʊm'taʊn] *n.* 故乡，家乡

[巧记] 家(home)所在的那个镇(town)就是我的故乡(hometown)

[语境] The houses in my hometown were chiefly composed of wood.

过去我家乡的房子多由木料制成。

homework ['həʊmwɜːk] *n.* 家庭作业

[巧记] home(家) + work(作业)→学生回到家做的作业→家庭作业

[语境] The teacher insisted on all the homework being handed in on Monday.

老师坚持要求所有作业都要在星期一交上来。

honest ['ɒnɪst] *a.* 诚实的，正直的，老实的

[巧记] 派生词：honestly *ad.*

[语境] Honest students despise cheating.

诚实的学生鄙视作弊。

honesty ['ɒnɪstɪ] *n.* 诚实，正直，坦诚

[语境] "Honesty is the best policy" was his creed in all his business dealings.

"以诚为本"是他做生意的信条。

[考点] Honesty is the best policy. [谚] 诚实是上策

hono(u)r[4] [ˈɒnə(r)] *n.* 荣誉,光荣,敬意 *vt.* 尊敬,给以荣誉

[语境] I promise I'll pay you back, on my honour.

我以人格担保,一定将钱还给你。

May I have the honour of this dance?

可以赏光和我跳这个舞吗?

[考点] do honour to 表示敬意,纪念; have a honour of 有幸地,荣幸地; in honour of 为了纪念

honourable [ˈɒnərəbl] *a.* 诚实的,正直的;光荣的,荣誉的;可尊敬的

[巧记] honour(敬意) + able(可以的) → 可尊敬的

[语境] I believe he was an honourable man, dedicated to the people and his union.

我认为他是个品行高洁的人,一心奉献于人民和工会的事业。

An honourable death is better than a disgraceful life.

宁为玉碎,不为瓦全。

hope[14] [həʊp] *n.* 希望,期望;希望的人或事 *v.* 希望,期望

[巧记] 派生词:hopeless *a.* 绝望的,办不到的,毫无办法的

[语境] Hope for the best, but prepare for the worst.

抱最好的愿望,做最坏的准备。

hopeful [ˈhəʊpfʊl] *a.* 给人希望的,抱有希望的

[语境] He was hopeful that he would win.

他抱有胜利的希望。

horse [hɔːs] *n.* 马

[语境] He bet on that horse.

他把赌注下在那匹马上。

hospital [ˈhɒspɪtl] *n.* 医院

[语境] We rushed him to the hospital.

我们急忙把他送往医院。

[考点] be in hospital 住院

host [həʊst] *n.* 主人,旅店老板;节目主持人

[语境] At the end of the party, we thanked our host and went away.
宴会结束时,我们谢了主人后便回家去了。
Which country will be the host country for the next Olympic Games?
哪个国家将是下届奥运会的主办国?

hostess [ˈhəʊstɪs] *n.* 女主人

[巧记] host(*n.* 男主人)

[语境] One of the hostess's duties is to mingle with the guests.
女主人的任务之一就是和客人周旋交际。

hot [hɒt] *a.* (炎)热的;辣的;急躁的;激动的;热衷的

[语境] Hot weather multiplied the bacteria in the food rapidly.
炎热的天气使食品中的细菌迅速繁殖。

hotel [həʊˈtel] *n.* 旅馆,宾馆,酒店,饭店

[语境] The hotel is now open to guests.
这个旅馆现在已向客人开放。

hour [ˈaʊə(r)] *n.* 小时

[语境] I pay them by the hour.
我按小时付给他们钱。

house [haʊs] *n.* 房子,住宅

[语境] He ordered us out of the house.
他命令我们离开这所房子。

how [haʊ] *ad.* (表示方法、手段、状态)怎样;如何

[语境] How did you earn your daily bread when you were there?
你在那里的时候以什么为生?

however [haʊˈevə(r)] *ad.* 然而,可是,不过,无论如何 *conj.* 无论

[语境] However he tries, he never seems able to work satisfactorily.
不管他怎么努力,他好像总不能令人满意地工作。

huge [hjuːdʒ] *a.* 庞大的,巨大的

[语境] The musical evening was voted a huge success by everyone.

人人都认为这次音乐晚会是一次巨大的成功。

human [ˈhjuːmən] a. 人的,人类的 n. 人

[巧记]派生词:humankind n. 人类(总称)

[语境] Humans may be able to live in the depths of the ocean some day.

有朝一日人类也许能在海洋深处生活。

humid [ˈhjuːmɪd] a. 湿的,湿气重的

[巧记] humidity n. (空气中的)湿度;潮湿,高温潮湿;湿热

[语境] Outside, the sun beats mercilessly down in the humid air.

外面,太阳无情地照射在潮湿的空气中。

humo(u)r [ˈhjuːmə(r)] n. 幽默,诙谐

[语境] Jack was late and was in a bad humor.

杰克迟到了,心情不好。

She had a lively sense of humor.

她幽默感很强。

[考点] sense of humour 幽默感;in a good humour 情绪好;out of humour 心情不好

hundred [ˈhʌndrəd] n. 百,百个东西 a. 百的,百个的

[语境] He came in third in the hundred-meter dash.

在百米竞赛中他跑了第三名。

hunger [ˈhʌŋɡə(r)] n. 饥饿;渴望

[语境] People in this area were ground down by hunger and poverty.

这个地区的人们受着饥饿和贫穷的折磨。

The beggar fell down in a swoon from sheer hunger.

那个乞丐饿得晕倒了。

hungry [ˈhʌŋɡrɪ] a. 饥饿的,渴望的

[语境] The hungry child asked for a piece of bread.

饥饿的孩子要一块面包吃。

[考点] go hungry 挨饿

hunt [hʌnt] v./n. 打猎,狩猎;寻找,搜索

[语境] Winter is the best time for hunting in mountain areas.

冬季是山区狩猎的最佳时间。
The hunt is on for the culprit.
正在搜捕该罪犯。

hurry [ˈhʌrɪ] *vi.* 匆忙 *vt.* 催促；急运（派） *n.* 急（匆）忙
[语境] She hurried away in the opposite direction.
她朝相反的方向匆匆离去。
[考点] in a hurry 匆忙地；hurry up 快点，赶紧

hurt[8] [hɜːt] *vi.* 感到疼痛，有坏处 *n.* 损害，伤害 *vt.* 伤害，刺痛；伤……感情；损害
[巧记] 反义词：cure, heal
[语境] It was a severe hurt to her pride.
这严重地伤害了她的自尊心。
The experience left me with a feeling of deep hurt.
这段经历给我心灵上留下了严重的创伤。

husband [ˈhʌzbənd] *n.* 丈夫
[语境] She had a boy by her first husband.
她与她的第一个丈夫有一男孩。

考点集训

1. The medicine and rest will soon _____ your wound.
   A. treat　　　B. cure　　　C. mend　　　D. heal

2. I _____ about taking his side until I knew the whole story.
   A. hesitated　　　　　B. faltered
   C. vacillated　　　　　D. wavered

3. I thought they'd never go—some people just can't take a(n) _____!
   A. suggestion　　　　B. hint
   C. intimation　　　　D. innuendo

4. Christmas is a holiday usually celebrated on December 25th _____ the birth of Jesus Christ.
   A. in accordance with　　B. in terms of
   C. in favor of　　　　　　D. in honor of

核心词汇精解

5. Though tired, he pretended he was a strip-cartoon hero to _____ the children.
   A. humour   B. coddle
   C. indulge   D. spoil

6. There was a big hole in the road which _____ the traffic.
   A. set back   B. stood back
   C. held up   D. kept down

7. The old paper mill has been _____ to make way for a new shopping centre.
   A. abandoned   B. decorated
   C. dissolved   D. held down

答案与解析

1. D　药物治疗和休息会使你的伤口很快愈合。treat 对病人或受伤者进行治疗；cure 把疾病治疗好了；mend 把破损的部分缝合或结合起来治愈创伤。

2. A　我在完全了解事实真相后，才打消顾虑，支持他。falter 犹豫，失去勇气而犹豫；vacillate 在两者之间作选择而犹豫；waver 在两者之间作选择而犹豫，但暗示不能坚持。

3. B　我以为他们是永远也不会走的——有些人根本就不明白别人的暗示。suggestion 指的是更直接的暗示；intimation 用方法将事情一点点地点出；innuendo 对某事影射的批评。

4. D　圣诞节是为了纪念耶稣的诞辰而定于12月25日的。in favor of 支持；in terms of 从……方面而言；in accordance with 和……一致。

5. A　尽管他累了，还是假装做连环画英雄的样子来哄孩子玩。coddle 溺爱；indulge 放任，纵容；spoil 纵容，宠坏，惯坏；humour 作动词，表示"迁就，迎合"。

6. C　路上有一个很大的洞，阻碍了交通。A 推迟，延误；B 退后；C 阻碍；D 压缩，缩减，控制，压制。因此正确答案为 C。

7. A　根据题干中 to make way for a new shopping centre，得知空格处应填入表示"废弃"的词。abandon 表示"放弃，遗弃"；decorate

213

表示"装饰";dissolve 表示"溶解";hold down 表示"压制,抑制"。

Word List 23

ice [aɪs] *n.* 冰;冰冻甜食 *vt.* 冰冻,使成冰
[语境] Ice is water in a solid state.
冰是水的固体状态。
The hostess iced a bottle of beer.
女主人冰了瓶啤酒。

idea [aɪˈdɪə] *n.* 想法,念头;概念,观念;意见,主意
[语境] Feudal ideas were stamped on her mind.
封建思想在她头脑中根深蒂固。

identify[17] [aɪˈdentɪfaɪ] *vt.* 认出,鉴定;等同,打成一片
[语境] Can you identify your umbrella among this lot?
你能在这些伞中认出你自己的伞吗?
She identified that the man was her attacker.
她认出那个男人就是袭击过她的人。
[考点] identify with...把……和……联系起来;identify oneself with 和……联系,支持

if [ɪf] *conj.* (用于连接宾语从句)是否;是不是
[语境] If there is going to be a volleyball team, please don't forget to add me in.
要是成立排球队,请别忘了算我在内。
I will see if he wants to talk to you.
我去了解一下他是否想和你谈话。

ignorance [ˈɪɡnərəns] *n.* 无知,愚昧;不知道
[语境] We are in complete ignorance of his plans.
我们对他的计划一无所知。

ignorant [ˈɪɡnərənt] *a.* 无知的,愚昧的;不知道的

[巧记] 派生词：ignorantly ad.

[语境] He is ignorant of what happened.

他不知道发生了什么事。

[考点] ignorant, illiterate 辨析：这两个形容词均可表示"无知的"之意。ignorant 指一般的无知或指不知道某个具体的事。illiterate 指不识字的人或没有文化的人

ignore[6] [ɪɡˈnɔː(r)] vt. 不理，不顾，忽视

[语境] I said hello to her, but she ignored me completely!

我向她打招呼，可她根本不理我！

He's his own man, but he doesn't ignore advice.

他虽然自有主张，但并不轻视别人的意见。

The wisest course would be to ignore it.

上上策是不予理睬。

ill [ɪl] a. 有病的；坏的；恶意的 ad. 坏地；不利地

[巧记] 反义词：good, healthy, well

[语境] She never speaks ill of anyone in his or her absence.

她从不趁人不在时说别人的坏话。

illegal [ɪˈliːɡəl] a. 不合法的，非法的

[巧记] i(否定) + l + legal(a. 合法的)：非法的

[语境] Abortion is illegal in some states.

堕胎在某些州是非法的。

illness [ˈɪlnɪs] n. 病，疾病

[巧记] 反义词：health

[语境] Her illness was induced by overwork.

她的病是由过度工作引起的。

image[15] [ˈɪmɪdʒ] n. 像，肖像，形象；影像，图像

[语境] I have this image of you as always being cheerful.

在我的心目中，你总是兴高采烈的。

According to the *Bible*, God created man in his image.

据《圣经》所述，上帝按自己的形象创造了人。

[考点] public image 群众心目中的形象

imaginary [ɪˈmædʒɪnəri] a. 想象的，虚构的

[巧记] 反义词：actual, real

[语境] All the characters in this book are imaginary.

这本书中的人物都是虚构的。

imagination[7] [ɪˌmædʒɪˈneɪʃən] *n*. **想象(力)；空想，幻觉；想象出来的事物**

[语境] It took a lot of imagination to come up with such an ingenious plan.

设计出如此巧妙的方案需有极大的想象力。

[考点] imagination, fancy, fantasy 辨析：这些名词均含有"想象，幻想"之意。imagination 含义广，一般不含贬义。可指认真、带有启发性的想象，也可指凭记忆的想象或凭空想象事物的能力。fancy 指脱离实际的幻想或幻想力，常暗含所想象的东西近乎怪诞的意味。fantasy 指与现实完全脱节、荒诞离谱、稀奇古怪的想象。

imagine[10] [ɪˈmædʒɪn] *vt*. **想象，设想；料想**

[语境] I imagined she was quite surprised when she heard the truth.

我想她听说真相后一定很惊讶。

He imagines that people don't like him, but they do.

他以为人们不喜欢他，但他们是喜欢他的。

imitate [ˈɪmɪteɪt] *vt*. **模仿，仿效；仿造，伪造**

[语境] The stage was designed to imitate a prison cell.

舞台设计成牢房的样子。

[考点] imitate 有意识地效仿，效法，模仿某人的举止、外表、语言、动作等。

immediate[11] [ɪˈmiːdɪət] *a*. **立即的，即时的；直接的，最接近的**

[巧记] immediateness *n*. 直接，立刻

[语境] There must be immediate action if chaos is to be averted.

要避免混乱就必须立即采取行动。

immigrant [ˈɪmɪɡrənt] *n*. **移民，侨民**

[巧记] im(向内) + migrant(移动的人)→向内移动的人→移民，侨民

[语境] And like me, she is an immigrant, so we have at least that in common.

同我一样,她也是位移民,所以我们至少有这个共同点。

impact[13] [ˈɪmpækt] *n.* **影响,冲击,碰撞**

[语境] Her speech made a tremendous impact on everyone.

她的演说对大家震动很大。

It's difficult to assess the impact of the President's speech.

总统讲话的影响力很难估计。

impatient[4] [ɪmˈpeɪʃənt] *a.* **不耐烦的,急躁的**

[巧记] im(否定) + patient(耐心的)→没有耐心的→急躁的

[语境] He was so impatient that I could hardly hold him back.

他是那样急躁,我简直拉不住他。

imply[7] [ɪmˈplaɪ] *vt.* **意指,暗示**

[语境] I think freedom does imply responsibility.

我认为自由一定包含着责任。

I don't wish to imply that you are wrong.

我无意暗示你错了。

import [ɪmˈpɔːt] *n.* **进口** *v.* **进口,输入**

[巧记] im(向内) + port(港口)→向港口内运→进口,输入

[语境] We must produce more food for ourselves and import less.

我们必须增产食品,减少进口。

Britain last year spent nearly £5,000 million more on importing food than selling abroad.

去年英国的进口食品支出比其出口食品收入多出近50亿英镑。

importance[20] [ɪmˈpɔːtəns] *n.* **重要,重要性**

[语境] Here I would stress the importance of mathematics to the whole of science.

这里我要强调数学对整个科学的重要性。

[考点] attach/put importance to sth. 认为某事物重要

important[64] [ɪmˈpɔːtənt] *a.* **重要的,重大的;有地位的,有权力的**

[巧记] 派生词:importantly *ad.*

［语境］It is important to make a study of abnormal psychology.

研究变态心理学是重要的。

impossible [ɪmˈpɒsəbəl] *a.* **不可能的；难以忍受的，很难对付的**

［语境］It is almost impossible to skirt the knotty problem.

想回避这个棘手的问题几乎是不可能的。

impress [ɪmˈpres] *vt.* **使感动；印入脑海，留下印象**

［语境］My father impressed me with the importance of hard work.

我父亲使我明白了努力工作的重要性。

I had a chance to impress her with my efficiency and I muffed it up.

我本来有机会使她了解我的办事效率，但是我错过了这个机会。

［考点］impress on/upon/with 压印，盖印，对……有印象

impression[15] [ɪmˈpreʃən] *n.* **印象，感想；盖印，压痕**

［语境］My advice seemed to make little impression on him.

我的忠告似乎对他不起作用。

［考点］make an impression on sb. 给某人留下印象；给人……以影响；be under the impression that...以为，认为

impressive [ɪmˈpresɪv] *a.* **给人深刻印象的，感人的**

［巧记］impress(*v.* 留有，印象) + ive：印象深刻的

［语境］This is the most impressive architecture I've seen on this trip.

这是我此次旅行见到的最令人难忘的建筑。

improve[31] [ɪmˈpruːv] *vt.* **改善，改进** *vi.* **好转，进步**

［语境］I want to improve my English.

我想提高我的英语水平。

I hope the weather will improve before Friday.

我希望星期五之前天气会好转。

［考点］improve on/upon 改善，改进，改良

improvement[8] [ɪmˈpruːvmənt] *n.* **改进，进步；增进；改进措施**

［巧记］反义词：deterioration

［语境］Housing improvement was the speaker's text.

改善住房是那位演讲人的题目。

[考点] make an improvement 改进

in [ɪn] *prep.* 在……里(内,上);用……(表示) *ad.* 进,入

[语境] A case in point of this is the steady increase in crime in New York City.

这方面很好的例子就是纽约市的犯罪率在不断地上升。

incentive [ɪnˈsentɪv] *n.* 刺激;动力;鼓励;诱因;动机

[语境] The child has no incentive to study harder because his parents cannot afford to send him to college.

这孩子没有努力学习的动力,因为他父母供不起他上大学。

inch [ɪntʃ] *n.* 英寸 *v.* 慢慢前进,慢慢移动

[语境] It has been taken up an inch.

已经将它收短了一英寸。

The worm inched along.

这条虫子向前慢慢移动着。

include[19] [ɪnˈkluːd] *vt.* 包含,包括,计入

[语境] My job doesn't include making coffee for the boss!

为老板煮咖啡不是我分内的事!

The graphic arts include calligraphy and lithography.

平面造型艺术包括书法和平版印刷术。

income[25] [ˈɪnkʌm] *n.* 收入,所得

[巧记] in(向内)+come(来)→向内来的钱→收入,所得

[语境] His way of life conforms to his income.

他的生活方式与他的收入是相符的。

考点集训

1. Most broadcasters maintain that TV has been unfairly criticized and argue that the power of the medium is _____.

   A. granted   B. implied

   C. exaggerated   D. remedied

2. At yesterday's party, Elizabeth's boyfriend amused us by _____ Charlie Chaplin.

A. copying B. following
C. imitating D. modeling
3. Some research workers completely _____ all those facts as though they never existed.
   A. ignore B. leave
   C. refuse D. miss
4. The new airport terminal is sure to _____ the development of tourism.
   A. imitate B. fascinate
   C. impose D. facilitate

答案与解析

1. C 大多数广播员认为电视得到了不公正的批评，而且争辩媒体的力量被夸大了。A 授予，批准；B 暗示；C 夸大；D 修正，更改。故正确答案为 C。
2. C 昨天的派对上，伊丽莎白的男朋友模仿卓别林，把我们逗乐了。A 复印，抄写；B 跟踪，追随；C 模仿；D 做模型。故选 C。
3. A 某些研究人员完全忽略了所有的这些事实，好像它们不存在似的。A 忽略，忽视；B 离开，留下；C 拒绝；D 错过。故选 A。
4. D facilitate 使容易；imitate 模仿；fascinate 着迷；impose 征税，强加。故选 D。

Word List 24

increase[60] [inˈkriːs] v. /[ˈɪnkriːs] n. 增加，增长，增进
[巧记] 派生词：increased a. 增加的，增强的
[语境] Travel increases one's knowledge of the world.
旅游增进了人们对世界的了解。
[考点] on the increase 不断增加，有增无减；increase with 随……而增长

220

incredible [ɪnˈkredəbl] *a.* <口> 难以置信的

[巧记] in(否定) + credible(可信的)→难以置信的

[语境] It sounded incredible in common.

乍一听来,简直不可思议。

indeed [ɪnˈdiːd] *ad.* 确实,实在;真正地,多么

[巧记] 在行为(deed)事实里(in)即确实

[语境] A friend in need is a friend indeed.

患难之交才是真正的朋友。

independent[^5] [ˌɪndɪˈpendənt] *a.* 独立的,自立的,自主的

[巧记] in(否定) + depend(依靠) + ent(形缀):不需要依靠的→独立的

[语境] She is so independent that she refused all pecuniary aid.

她如此独立以至于拒绝一切金钱上的资助。

The former colonial possessions are now independent states.

以前的许多殖民地现已成为独立的国家。

[考点] be independent of 与……无关;不依赖;不取决于;不受……限制[制约]

India [ˈɪndjə] *n.* 印度

[语境] Burma borders on India.

缅甸与印度毗邻。

Indian [ˈɪndjən] *a.* 印度人的,印第安人的 *n.* 印度人,印第安人

[语境] It will prove I am an Indian.

它将证明我是一个印度人。

Farmers occasionally plow up old Indian relics.

农民偶尔能用犁翻出古老的印第安人的遗物。

indicate[^5] [ˈɪndɪkeɪt] *vt.* 指示,表示;暗示

[语境] Don't forget to indicate before turning.

拐弯之前别忘记指示车行方向。

indirect [ˌɪndəˈrekt] *a.* 间接的,迂回的

[语境] He gave only an indirect answer.

他只作了间接的回答。

individual[^43] [ˌɪndɪˈvɪdʒuəl] *a.* 个别的,单独的;独特的 *n.* 个人,个体

[巧记] in(不) + divide(划分) + ual(的):不能再分开的→个人的,个体的

[语境] She has her own individual way of walking.

她有自己独特的走路姿势。

A teacher can't give individual attention to each pupil if his class is large.

如果班上的人数多,老师就不能给予个别辅导了。

industrial[11] [ɪnˈdʌstriəl] *a.* **工业的,产业的**

[巧记] 派生词:industrially *ad.* 企业[工业]地;industrialism *n.* 产业主义;industrialist *n.* 工业主义者;实业家

[语境] Industrial wastes have poisoned the river.

工业废弃物污染了这条河。

industry[ˈɪndəstrɪ] *n.* **工业,产业;勤勉,刻苦**

[语境] The conference underscored the importance of modern industry.

会议强调了现代工业的重要性。

Industry is fortune's right hand, and frugality her left.

勤勉是幸运的右手,节俭是幸运的左手。

inevitable [ɪnˈevɪtəbəl] *a.* **必然的,不可避免的**

[巧记] in(否定) + evitable(可避免的):不可避免的

[语境] An argument was inevitable because they disliked each other so much.

他们争论是不可避免的,因为他们非常厌恶彼此。

Positions surrendered to our troops earlier in the day had now to be prepared against the inevitable counter-attack.

那天早些时候,敌人投降的军事要点需要布置起来,对付那必然的反攻。

infant[ˈɪnfənt] *a.* **婴儿的,幼稚的,初期的** *n.* **婴儿,幼儿**

[语境] What is it like to look at the world like an infant?

像婴幼儿那样看世界是一个什么样子?

infect [ɪnˈfekt] *vt.* **传染,感染**

[语境] The young teacher infected the whole class with her enthusiasm.

这位年轻的老师以她的热情感染了全班。

The open wound soon became infected.

裸露的伤口很快就感染了。

[考点] be infected with 感染,沾染上

infer[16] [ɪnˈfɜː(r)] *vt.* **推论,推断**

[巧记] in 里面, fer 带来→带来内部的意义→推断;推测

[语境] It is possible to infer two completely opposite conclusions from this set of facts.

从这些事实中可能推断出两种截然相反的结论。

Can I infer that you think I'm not telling the truth?

看来你认为我没说实话?

influence[18] [ˈɪnfluəns] *vt./n.* **影响,感化** *n.* **势力,权势**

[语境] He is a man of some influence in the government circles.

他是个在政府内有一定势力的人。

Don't let me influence your decision.

不要让我影响你的决定。

[考点] have influence on/upon 对……产生影响;under the influence of 受……影响

influential [ˌɪnfluˈenʃəl] *a.* **有影响的;有权势的**

[巧记] 派生词:influentially *ad.* 有影响地,有力地

[语境] Influential friends helped him to get a good job.

有权势的朋友们帮他弄到一份美差。

influenza [ˌɪnfluˈenzə] *n.* **流行性感冒**

[语境] They all come down with influenza.

他们都得了感冒。

inform [ɪnˈfɔːm] *vt.* **通知,告诉,报告;告发,告密**

[语境] Could you please inform me how to go about contacting a lawyer?

请您告诉我怎样去联系律师?

Our only resort is to inform the police.

我们唯一的办法就是向警方报案。

[考点] inform sb. of sth./that 报告某人……,告诉某人……; inform against/on sb. 告发某人,告密

information[58] [ˌɪnfəˈmeɪʃən] *n.* **通知,报告;情报,资料,消息;信息**

[巧记] 派生词:informational *a.* 报告的,情报的

[语境] He compiled enough information on his tour of South American capitals to write a book.

他在南美各国首都旅游时收集了不少资料,足够写本书。

injure [ˈɪndʒə(r)] *vt.* **损害,损伤,伤害**

[巧记] 反义词: cure, heal

[语境] She was injured badly in the accident.

她在那次事故中受了重伤。

Don't injure yourself with that tool.

不要让工具伤害到你。

injury [ˈɪndʒərɪ] *n.* **伤害,损害**

[语境] The driver received internal injuries in the accident.

司机在事故中受了内伤。

[考点] be an injury to 伤害……,危害……,对……有害;do sb. an injury 伤害某人

innocent [ˈɪnəsənt] *a.* **无罪的,清白的;无害的;天真的,单纯的**

[语境] Don't be so innocent as to believe everything you hear.

不要头脑太简单而相信你所听到的每一件事。

She asserted that he was innocent.

她断言,他是无罪的。

[考点] be innocent of 无罪的,清白的

innovate [ˈɪnəveɪt] *v.* **创新,改革**

[语境] This forces you to innovate.

这就迫使你去创新。

innovation [ˌɪnəˈveɪʃən] *n.* **改革,革新;新观念,新方法,新发明**

[巧记] in(强调) + novation(用新事物替代旧的) → 革命

[语境] The innovation of air travel during this century has made the world seem smaller.

本世纪空中旅行的革新使世界看起来变小了。

input [ˈɪnpʊt] *n./v.* **输入**

[语境] The output should be proportional to the input.

产出应和输入成比例。

insect[4] [ˈɪnsekt] *n.* **昆虫**

[巧记] in(里面) + sect(切)→里面像被切断了(截肢类动物)→昆虫

[语境] The insect can take on the color of its surroundings.

这种昆虫能随环境而变色。

inside [ˈɪnsaɪd] *a.* **里面的** *ad.* **在里面** *n.* **内部** *prep.* **在……里**

[语境] He did not see the inside of the house before he bought it.

他买这栋房子前也没进去看看里面是什么样的。

I keep my wallet in an inside pocket.

我把钱包放在里面的口袋里。

Two minutes later we were inside the taxi.

两分钟以后我们已经坐在出租车里面了。

insist[5] [ɪnˈsɪst] *vt.* **坚持,坚决主张,坚决认为** *vi.* (on/upon) **坚持,坚持主张,坚决认为**

[语境] He insisted that he had done right.

他坚决认为自己做对了。

Since you insist, I must amend the letter of credit.

既然你坚持,那我只好修改证明信。

[考点] insist on/upon 坚持,坚持要求

inspect[4] [ɪnˈspekt] *vt.* **检查,调查,视察**

[语境] It was strange that nobody inspected my ticket before I got on the train.

很奇怪,我上火车前,竟然没有人查看我的车票。

The stewards will inspect the course to see if racing is possible.

那些干事将检视赛马场,看它是否适宜比赛。

[考点] inspect 指仔细查看,重点放在事物的优质标准或是否符合标准以及不足之处

inspiration [ˌɪnspəˈreɪʃən] *n.* **灵感;鼓舞,激励**

[巧记] 反义词: expiration

[语境] After a good night's sleep, he had a brilliant inspiration.
他美美睡了一夜后想到一个绝妙的主意。

[考点] get/draw inspiration from 从……得到启示；give (the) inspiration to 启发；鼓舞

考点集训

1. The same factors push wages and prices up together, the one _____ the other.
   A. emphasizing   B. reinforcing
   C. multiplying   D. increasing

2. Their products are frequently overpriced and _____ in quality.
   A. influential   B. inferior
   C. superior   D. subordinate

3. Mr. Smith was the only witness who said that the fire was _____.
   A. mature   B. deliberate
   C. meaningful   D. innocent

4. First published in 1927, the charts remain an _____ source for researchers.
   A. identical   B. indispensable
   C. intelligent   D. inevitable

5. He never arrives on time and my _____ is that he feels the meetings are useless.
   A. preference   B. conference
   C. inference   D. reference

答案与解析

1. B 工资和物价得以上涨是相同因素作用的结果,一方面的上涨使另一方面也上涨。A 强调;B 强化;C 乘以,繁殖;D 增加,上涨。故 B 为正确答案。

2. B 他们的产品常常是价格高、质量差。A 有影响力的;B 低等的,次等的;C 高等的,优越的;D 从属的。故 B 为正确答案。

3. B 史密斯先生是这场火灾的唯一目击者,说火灾是有人故意放的。A 成熟的;B 故意的;C 有意义的;D 无辜的。故选 B。
4. B 这份图表在 1927 年首次出版,对现今的研究人员而言,仍是一份必不可少的资料。A 相同的;B 必不可少的;C 智力的;D 不可避免的。故选 B。
5. C 他总是迟到,我想他感觉这会议没什么意义。A 偏爱,喜爱;B 会议;C 推断,推测;D 参考。故选 C。

Word List 25

instead [ɪnˈsted] *ad.* **代替,顶替;反而,却**

[语境] I gave him advice instead of money.
我给了他忠告,而不是钱。
We've no coffee. Would you like tea instead?
我们没有咖啡了,改喝茶好吗?

[考点] instead of 代替;而不是;不……而……

instinct [ˈɪnstɪŋkt] *n.* **本能,直觉;天性**

[巧记] 派生词:instinctive (*a.* 凭本能的, 天生的, 直觉的)

[语境] When I saw the flames I acted on instinct and threw a blanket over them.
我看见火焰时便本能地把一张毯子扑在火焰上。
Instinct is not always a good guide.
凭本能行事不一定都对。

[考点] by instinct 出于本能;have an instinct for 生来就有……的本能;instinct with 充满,受……的鼓舞

instrument [ˈɪnstrəmənt] *n.* **乐器,工具,仪器,器械**

[语境] This instrument is highly sensitive.
这架仪器很灵敏。

[考点] instrument, device, equipment, tool, facilities 辨析:这些名词均有"仪器,设备,器械,器具"之意。instrument:通常指

227

能使人们完成某一精确动作或测量的一种小型仪器,尤指电工仪表、测量装置、航海或航空用的控制装置。device:多指为某一特殊用途或解决某一特定机械问题而设计或改装的精巧的仪器或装置。equipment:多指成套的或重型的设备或装备。通常用作不可数名词。tool:一般指进行特种工作的手工工具,也可指人造使用动力的工具,还可作引申用。facilities:常用复数形式,指可供使用的设备或设施

insult[4] ['ɪnsʌlt] *vt./n.* **侮辱,凌辱**

[巧记] 反义词:esteem, honor, respect

[语境] He shouted insults at the boy who had kicked him.
他大声辱骂那个踢了他的男孩。

insurance[5] [ɪn'ʃʊərəns] *n.* **保险,保险费,保险业**

[语境] Insurance is one of Britain's most profitable invisible exports.
保险业是英国获益最大的无形出口之一。

[考点] an insurance company 保险公司;insurance policy 保险单

insure [ɪn'ʃʊə(r)] *vt.* **保险**

[巧记] 要想心里面(in)有把握(sure),就应该买保险

[语境] "Did you insure the jewels before they were stolen?" "No, more's the pity!"
"你那些被窃的珠宝买保险了吗?""没有,真倒霉!"
I am insured for all risks.
我给自己保了综合险。

[考点] insure against 投保……险;使免受

intelligence[7] [ɪn'telɪdʒəns] *n.* **智力,理解力;情报,消息,报道**

[语境] Intelligence has/have reported that the enemy is planning a new attack.
情报人员报告说,敌军正在策划发动新进攻。
His intelligence is rather limited.
他的智力相当有限。

[考点] intelligence 指处理或对付问题或情况的特殊才智;也指运用、展示智慧的能力。

intelligent[7] [ɪnˈtelɪdʒənt] *a.* 聪明的,明智的,理智的

[巧记] 派生词:intelligently (*ad.* 聪明地)

[语境] Is there any other intelligent life elsewhere in the cosmos?

在宇宙的其他星球上还存在别的有智慧的生物吗?

intend[9] [ɪnˈtend] *vt.* 想要,打算,企图

[巧记] intending *a.* 预期的;未来的

[语境] He intends his son to manage the company.

他打算让他儿子经营该公司。

[考点] it is intended that 企图,意图是;intend for 打算供……使用;打算使……成为

interact[11] [ˌɪntərˈækt] *v.* 互相作用,互相影响

[巧记] inter(在……之间) + act(作用)→相互作用

[语境] Mother and baby interact in a very complex way.

母亲与婴儿以非常复杂的方式相互影响。

[考点] interact on 作用,影响,制约,配合;interact with 与……相合

interest[11] [ˈɪntrəst] *n.* (in)兴趣,重要性;利益 *v.* (in)使发生兴趣

[语境] The linguists' main interest has been to analyze and describe languages.

语言学家的主要兴趣一直在于分析并描述语言。

[考点] be interested in 对……感兴趣[关心]

interesting[10] [ˈɪntrəstɪŋ] *a.* 有趣的,引人入胜的

[语境] I think these interesting old customs should be preserved.

我认为这些有趣的旧习俗应该保持下去。

interfere [ˌɪntəˈfɪə(r)] *vi.* (in/with)干涉,干扰,妨碍

[语境] He tries not to let(his)business interfere with his home life.

他尽量不让日常工作妨碍他的家庭生活。

Don't interfere with my business.

不要干涉我的事情。

[考点] interfere in 干涉,干预;interfere with 妨碍;乱动;干涉,干扰

internal [ɪnˈtɜːnəl] *a.* 内部的,内的;国内的,内政的

· 229 ·

[巧记] 里面(inter) + 形容词后缀(nal)→内部的
[语境] The driver received internal injuries in the accident.
司机在事故中受了内伤。

international [ˌɪntəˈnæʃənəl] *a.* 国际的，世界(性)的，跨国的
[巧记] 派生词：internationally (*ad.* 国际性地，在国际上)
[语境] An international meeting between each minister and his opposite member will be held next month.
下月将举行部长级的国际会议。

Internet[35] [ˈɪntənet] *n.* 因特网
[语境] He wrote off for information on Internet.
他写信要有关互联网的资料。

interpret [ɪnˈtɜːprɪt] *vt.* 解释，说明；口译
[巧记] 派生词：interpretable (*a.* 能说明的，能翻译的)
[语境] We have to interpret his words in a modern light.
我们必须以现代的观点来解释他的话。

interrupt [ˌɪntəˈrʌpt] *vt.* 打断，打扰；断绝，中断
[语境] Don't interrupt me, children.
孩子们，别打断我的话。
Don't interrupt the speaker now; he will answer questions later.
现在不要打断他的话，他稍后再回答问题。

interview [ˈɪntəvjuː] *n.* 面谈，访问，接见 *v.* 接见，会谈
[巧记] inter(互相) + view(看)→面谈，面试
[语境] The television interview will be aired to all parts of the country.
这个电视采访节目将向全国各地播放。
The manager will interview the candidates in order of arrival.
经理将按(到达)先后次序接见这些应聘者。

into [ˈɪntʊ, ˈɪntə] *prep.* 到……里面，进入；成为(表示变化)
[语境] They packed into the bus after much trouble.
他们费了好大劲才挤进公共汽车。

introduce[9] [ˌɪntrəˈdjuːs] *vt.* 介绍；引进，传入；提出
[语境] The next programme is introduced by Mary Davidson.
下一个节目由玛丽·戴维森主持。

The company is introducing a new family saloon this year.

公司准备今年推出一种新型家庭轿车。

[考点] introduce into 把……引进, 传入

intuition [ˌɪntjuˈɪʃən] *n.* **直觉, 直觉的知识**

[语境] This is what we call grammar intuition.

这就是我们所说的语法直觉。

[考点] by intuition 凭直觉

invade [ɪnˈveɪd] *v.* **侵入, 拥入**

[巧记] invasion (*n.* 入侵); invasive (*a.* 侵袭的, 扩散的)

[语境] Germs invade the organism.

病菌会侵入机体。

invent [ɪnˈvent] *v.* **发明, 创造; 捏造, 虚构**

[语境] We must invent an excuse for being late.

我们必须为迟到编一个借口。

inventive [ɪnˈventɪv] *a.* **发明的, 有发明才能的**

[语境] He has an inventive genius.

他有发明的天才。

invest[30] [ɪnˈvest] *v.* **投资, 投入**

[语境] I won't invest my money in his company.

我不会把我的钱投资到他的公司。

Everyone should invest some time in community service.

每个人都应该花些时间在社区服务上。

[考点] invest with 授予; invest in 在……上投资, 在……投入(时间、精力等)

investigate[5] [ɪnˈvestɪɡeɪt] *vt.* **调查, 调研**

[语境] The police are investigating the murder.

警察正在调查这件谋杀案。

Applicants for government posts are always thoroughly investigated before being appointed.

申请担任政府公职人员总要经过彻底审查才能受到委任。

investment[13] [ɪnˈvestmənt] *n.* **投资, 投资额**

[语境] He made a large investment in the business enterprise.

他对那个企业做了大量投资。

invitation [ˌɪnvɪˈteɪʃən] *n.* **邀请，招待；请柬**

[巧记] 派生词：invitational *a.* 邀请的，恳愿的

[语境] She received an invitation to the party.
她接到参加聚会的邀请。

invite[5] [ɪnˈvaɪt] *vt.* **邀请，招待**

[语境] We invited all our relatives to the wedding.
我们邀请了所有的亲戚来参加婚礼。

You are just inviting trouble if you do that.
你那么做就是在自找麻烦。

involve[27] [ɪnˈvɒlv] *vt.* **卷入，陷入，连累；包含，含有**

[语境] Painting the room involved moving out the piano.
粉刷房间就要把钢琴搬出去。

How should we involve ourselves in school life?
我们应该怎样投入学校生活？

[考点] involve in 使卷入，使陷入；involve with 和……混在一起，和……有密切联系；be/become/get involved in sth. / with sb. 和某事[某人]有关联

iron [ˈaɪən] *a.* **刚强的** *n.* **铁，熨斗** *v.* **熨，烫，熨衣服**

[语境] He is a man of cast-iron will.
他是一个意志刚强的人。

Heat will melt iron.
热将使铁熔化。

I must iron my shirt.
我必须熨自己的衬衫。

irony [ˈaɪrəni] *n.* **反讽，讽刺，讽刺之事**

[巧记] 近义词：satire, sarcasm *n.* 讽刺

[语境] This brings us back to the irony of the question.
这将我们带回到了这个问题的讽刺性。

Islam [ˈɪzlɑːm, ɪzˈlɑːm] *n.* **伊斯兰教**

[语境] The established religion of Egypt is Islam.
埃及的国教是伊斯兰教。

isolate[7] [ˈaɪsəleɪt] *vt.* 隔离,孤立

[语境] When a person has an infectious disease, he is usually isolated (from other people).

人患传染病时通常要(与他人)隔离。

Scientists have isolated the virus causing the epidemic.

科学家们已分离出引起这种流行病的病毒。

[考点] isolate from 使孤立,使脱离

issue[13] [ˈɪʃuː, ˈɪsjuː] *vt.* 发行,发布 *n.* 问题,论点,争端;发行,发行物

[语境] Banknotes of this design were first issued 10 years ago.

这种图案的钞票是十年前首次发行的。

Parliament will debate the nationalization issue next week.

下周议会将辩论国有化议题。

[考点] at issue 在争论中;不一致, 有分歧;issue out/forth/from 出来,流出;join/take issue with sb. on/about sth. 和某人争吵

it [ɪt] *pron.* 它

[语境] It is a table.

这是一张桌子。

Italian [ɪˈtæljən] *a.* 意大利人/语的 *n.* 意大利人/语

[语境] Her beauty is of the Italian type.

她的美是意大利型的。

Then I fell in love with an Italian.

后来,我与一个意大利人坠入了爱河。

item [ˈaɪtəm] *n.* 项目,条款

[语境] He pricked down each item.

她记下了每一项。

its [ɪts] *pron.* 它的

[语境] He emphasized its importance to me.

他向我强调它的重要性。

itself [ɪtˈself] *pron.* 它自己,它本身

[语境] The battery recharges itself.

电池自行再充电。

233

考点集训

1. As one of the world's highest paid models, she had her face _____ for five million dollars.
   A. deposited   B. assured
   C. measured   D. insured

2. I had just posted the letter when I remembered that I hadn't _____ the cheque.
   A. imposed   B. involved
   C. enclosed   D. contained

3. The university has launched a research center to develop new ways of _____ bacteria which have become resistant to drug treatments.
   A. regulating   B. halting
   C. interrupting   D. combating

4. Mr. Smith asked his secretary to _____ a new paragraph in the annual report she was typing.
   A. inject   B. install
   C. invade   D. insert

5. Most laboratory and field studies of human behavior _____ taking a situational photograph at a given time and in a given place.
   A. involve   B. compose
   C. enclose   D. attach

6. Putting in a new window will _____ cutting away part of the roof.
   A. include   B. involve
   C. contain   D. comprise

答案与解析

1. D 作为世界上薪水最高的模特之一,她花500万美元给自己的脸上了保险。A 储存,存款;B 保证;C 测量;D 上保险。故选 D。

2. C 刚把信寄出去,这时我想起没有附上支票。A 强制实行;B 包括;C 附上;D 包含。故选 C。

3. D 学校成立了一个研究中心,该中心负责开发抗击细菌的新方法,因为细菌具有了抗药性。A 管理;B 停止;C 打断;D 打击。故选 D。

4. D 根据题干中 a new paragraph in the annual report she was typing,再结合四个选项——inject 表示"注射";install 表示"安装,安置";invade 表示"侵略,侵袭";insert 表示"插入,嵌入",可知只有 insert 符合题意,答案为 D。

5. A 根据题干中 taking a situational photograph at a given time and in a given place,再结合四个选项——involve 表示"包括";compose 表示"组成,写作";enclose 表示"放入封套,装入";attach 表示"缚上,系上,贴上",可知只有 involve 符合题意,答案为 A。

6. B 要把这个新窗户装进去,就得拆去一部分房顶。A 包括在内,多用于列举;B 包括;C 包含[容纳];D 由……组成。故 B 为正确答案。

Word List 26

jealous ['dʒeləs] *a.* 嫉妒的
[巧记]派生词:jealousness(*n.* 嫉妒,吃醋,猜忌);jealousy(*n.* 妒忌,羡慕,猜忌)
[语境] Don't let her make mischief between you, she's only jealous.
别让她在你们之间挑拨——她就是太妒忌了。
[考点] be jealous of 嫉妒

job [dʒɒb] *n.* 工作,职业,零活 *v.* 做零工;假公济私;做股票经纪;代客买卖;承包;批发
[语境] It's the job of the church to help people lead better lives.
帮助人们生活得好些是教会的责任。

join [dʒɔɪn] *v.* 结合,接合,连接;参加,加入
[语境] He joined us in the discussion yesterday.
他昨天参加了我们的讨论。

· 235 ·

Can you see the join in the coat?

你能看到衣服上的接缝吗?

[考点] join battle 交战;join hands 握手,携手;join in 参加

joke [dʒəuk] *n.* 笑话,玩笑 *vi.* 说笑话,开玩笑

[巧记] 同根词:joker(*n.* 爱开玩笑的人);jokey(*adj.* 好开玩笑的,滑稽的);joking(*adj.* 开玩笑的)

[语境] You must be joking.

你一定是在开玩笑吧。

Can't you take a joke?

跟你开个玩笑你都受不了吗?

[考点] make/play joke on sb. 开某人的玩笑

journal [ˈdʒɜːnəl] *n.* 日报,期刊;日志,日记

[巧记] 派生词:journalist(*n.* 新闻工作者);journalism(*n.* 新闻业;报章杂志);同义词:diary(*n.* 日记),newspaper(*n.* 报纸)

[语境] In our school, each teacher books a kind of journal.

在我们学校,每一个老师都订了一种杂志。

The journal is published monthly.

那本杂志是月刊。

journey [ˈdʒɜːnɪ] *n.* 旅行,旅程 *vi.* 旅行

[语境] Jack and Mary described their journey in vivid detail.

杰克和玛丽以生动的细节叙述了他们的旅行。

He journeyed on foot.

他徒步旅行。

[考点] journey, tour, travel, trip, voyage 辨析:这些名词均含"旅行"之意。journey:最普通用词,侧重指时间较长、距离较远的单程陆上旅行,也指水上或空中的旅行。tour:指最后返回出发地,旅途中有停留游览点,距离可长可短,目的各异的周游或巡行。travel:泛指旅行的行为而不指某次具体的旅行,多指到远方做长期旅行,不强调直接目的地,单、复数均可用。trip:普通用词,口语多用,常指为公务或游玩做的较短暂的旅行。voyage:指在水上旅行,尤指海上旅行,也可指空中旅行

joy [dʒɔɪ] *n.* 欢乐,喜悦;乐事,乐趣

[巧记] 派生词:joyful(*adj.* 欢喜的,令人高兴的,高兴的);joyfulness(*n.* 高兴,快乐);joyless(*adj.* 令人不愉快的,哀愁的);joyous(*a.* 快乐的);反义词:sorrow(*n.* 悲伤,不幸,哀惜 *v.* 悲伤,遗憾,懊悔);grief(*n.* 悲痛;不幸;伤心事)

[语境] I saw the joy in her smiling face.
从她的笑脸上我看到欢欣。
They complained about the bad service, but got no joy from the manager.
他们反映服务质量差,但经理并未理会。

judge [dʒʌdʒ] *n.* 审判员,法官;评判员,裁判 *vt.* 评价,鉴定;认为,断定,判断;审判,裁判,裁决

[巧记] 派生词:judgement(*n.* 审判,判断,判决)

[语境] We judge that he is the best candidate.
我们认为他是最佳人选。
I judge him to be about 40.
我断定他有40来岁。

[考点] judge by 由……判断

July [dʒu'laɪ] *n.* 七月

[语境] The swimming pool was opened to the public on July 1st.
游泳池于七月一日对外开放。

jump [dʒʌmp] *v./n.* 跳跃,跳动,跳过;暴涨,猛增

[语境] I couldn't understand his lecture because he kept jumping from one topic to the next.
我听不懂他的演讲,他总是从一项内容跳到另一项内容。

June [dʒuːn] *n.* 六月

[语境] London is full of visitors during May and June.
五六月间伦敦挤满了游客。

keen [kiːn] *a.* 锋利,尖锐;敏捷,敏锐;(on)热心,渴望

[巧记] 派生词:keenly(*ad.* 敏锐地,锐利地;热心地;强烈地);keenness(*n.* 敏锐,锐利;热心;强烈);同义词:sharp(*adj.* 锐利的,明显的,锋利的)

[语境] That is a keen football match.

那是一场激烈的足球比赛。

Mrs Hill is keen on Tom's marrying Susan.

希尔太太很希望汤姆能和苏珊结婚。

[考点] 常用的同义搭配：be eager to, be enthusiastic about, be intent on

keep [kiːp] *v.* 保持，保存，遵守，经营，看守，拘留，维持

[语境] Keep straight on until you get to the church.

一直朝前走就走到教堂了。

key [kiː] *n.* 钥匙；答案，解答；键，琴键；方法，关键 *a.* 主要的，关键的

[语境] She reached for her coat and car keys.

她伸手拿外套和汽车钥匙。

Diet and relaxation are two important keys to good health.

限制饮食和放松身心是保持健康的两个要诀。

He is expected to be the key witness at the trial.

他将成为审判的关键证人。

[考点] key point 要点；key industry 基础工业

kick [kɪk] *n./v.* 踢

[语境] My shirt is kicking around on the floor somewhere.

我的衬衫在地板上的某个地方。

kid [kɪd] *n.* 小孩，儿童 *vi.* 戏弄

[语境] All the kids in my class could read.

我们班所有的孩子都能阅读。

Are you sure you're not kidding me?

你确定不是在和我开玩笑吗？

kill [kɪl] *vt.* 杀死，消灭；破坏，毁灭；消磨（时间）

[语境] His wife was killed in a car accident.

他的妻子在车祸中丧生。

kind [kaɪnd] *a.* 仁慈的，友好的，亲切的，和蔼的 *n.* 种类

[语境] People had told me she was very pleasant but she's nothing of the kind.

人们告诉我她很可爱,可是她根本不是那样。

kindness ['kaɪndnɪs] *n.* 仁慈,亲切;好意;友好行为

[语境] Your kindness is grateful.

你的友善令人感激。

king [kɪŋ] *n.* 国王

[语境] After the old king died, his son ruled over the kingdom.

老国王死后,他儿子统治这个王国。

kiss [kɪs] *n./v.* 吻,接吻

[语境] He remembered her parting kiss in the following years.

在以后的岁月中,他一直记着她临别时的一吻。

kitchen ['kɪtʃɪn] *n.* 厨房

[语境] Two families share in the use of the kitchen.

两户人家合用这间厨房。

[考点] kitchen maid 厨房女仆;kitchen car 炊事汽车

knife [naɪf] *n.* 刀,餐刀 *vt.* 用刀切,用匕首刺

[语境] The knife is so dull that it will not cut.

刀子太钝了,割不开东西。

She was knifed in the back six times.

她的背部中了6刀。

knock [nɒk] *n./v.* 敲,敲打;碰撞

[语境] He knocked a big hole in the wall.

他把墙撞出了一个大洞。

Did you hear the knocks at the door?

你听到敲门声了吗?

[考点] knock someone cold 打晕(倒)某人;knock something on the head 阻止……的实现;knock the bottom out of 使失去基础

know [nəʊ] *vt.* 知道,了解;认识;识别 *vi.* 知道,了解

[语境] I know London as the place where I spent my childhood.

我熟悉伦敦,那是我度过童年的地方。

knowledge ['nɒlɪdʒ] *n.* 知识,常识;知道,了解

[语境] They did it without my knowledge.

他们是背着我做这件事的。

My knowledge of Japanese is rather poor.

我的日语相当差。

[考点] be common knowledge 人所共知的事情；bring to the knowledge of 让知道……；to one's knowledge 据……所知；without the knowledge of 在不知道……的情况下

lab = laboratory

labo(u)r[ˈleɪbə(r)] *n.* 工作，劳动；劳力 *v.* 劳动，苦干

[语境] Farming is productive labor.

耕作是有生产价值的劳动。

[考点] Labor Day 劳动节

laboratory[ləˈbɒrətərɪ] *n.* 实验室，研究室

[语境] She has donated money to establish a pharmaceutical laboratory.

她捐款成立了一个药剂实验室。

lack[27][læk] *n./v.* 缺乏，没有，缺少

[巧记] 派生词：lacking (*adj.* 缺乏的；不足的)

[语境] Lack of enough water, many animals die in the area.

由于缺少足够的水，这一地区的许多动物都死了。

[考点] be lacking 欠缺……，缺……；be lacking in 缺乏某种(特征、气质)，不够……；lack for 缺……

lady[ˈleɪdɪ] *n.* 夫人，小姐，女士

[语境] The old lady engaged herself in making clothes for her children.

这位老太太忙着为孩子们做衣服。

lake[leɪk] *n.* 湖

[语境] They can go fishing in the lake.

他们可以在湖里钓鱼。

lamp[læmp] *n.* 灯

[语境] The desk lamp fell to the floor with a crash.

台灯哗啦一声掉到地上。

land[lænd] *n.* 陆地，土地，国家 *v.* (使)靠岸(登陆，降落)

[语境] New buildings appreciates the value of land.

新建筑物提高了土地的价值。

landing [ˈlændɪŋ] *n.* **登陆,着陆;楼梯平台**

[巧记] land(*v.* 登陆) + ing(动名词后缀)→登陆,着陆(*n.*)

[语境] Owing to engine trouble, the plane had to make a forced landing.

由于发动机出了毛病,飞机迫降了。

I ran out onto the landing.

我冲出去到了楼梯口。

landlord [ˈlændlɔːd] *n.* **房东,地主**

[巧记] land(*n.* 土地) + lord(*n.* 统治者,君主)→地主

[语境] The landlord is doing my apartment over.

房东正在翻修我的房子。

language [ˈlæŋɡwɪdʒ] *n.* **语言**

[语境] Language is the most important mental creation of man.

语言是人类头脑最重要的产物。

large [lɑːdʒ] *a.* **大的,广大的,大规模的**

[语境] He has a large number of reference books at his disposal.

他有大量的参考书可供使用。

largely [ˈlɑːdʒlɪ] *ad.* **大部分,基本上;大规模地**

[巧记] 近义词:mainly, mostly 主要地

[语境] The achievement of one's purpose depends largely on one's perseverance.

一个人的志愿的实现大部分靠他的毅力。

Because we were largely working within the RUP framework, this worked well for us.

因为我们在 RUP 中完成大量的工作,这将使我们工作得很好。

last [lɑːst; læst] *a.* **最后的,刚过去的** *ad.* **最后** *n.* **最后** *v.* **持续**

[语境] Ten years ago this dress was considered the last word in elegance.

十年前这种连衣裙还算是最高雅的款式呢。

late [leɪt] *a.* **迟的,晚的,晚期的;已故的** *ad.* **迟,晚**

[语境]The train was 10 minutes late.

火车晚点了10分钟。

lately [ˈleɪtlɪ] *ad.* 最近,不久前

[语境] That kind of bird has become more numerous around here lately.

近来附近一带那种鸟越来越多了。

later [ˈleɪtə(r)] *ad.* 后来,过一会儿

[语境]A butterfly emerged in its full splendour a week later.

一周后蝴蝶破茧而出,绚丽夺目。

laugh [lɑːf; læf] *v.* 笑;(on) 讥笑 *n.* 笑,笑声

[语境]Someone in the audience began to laugh.

观众中有人开始笑起来。

launch [lɔːntʃ] *vt.* 发射;下水;开始,发起 *n.* 发射;下水

[巧记]同义词:fire(*v.* 点燃,开枪,着火,射击)

[语境] A new ship is being launched today.

一艘新船今天下水了。

The ship launched in the direction of Japan.

船起航前往日本。

[考点] launch an attack 发起进攻,也可以用 deliver/make an attack。常用词组:launch into 开始

law [lɔː] *n.* 法律,法规,法学,规律,定律

[语境]All government should be government under the law and by the law.

凡政府都该是受法律控制,依法而治的政府。

lay[9] [leɪ] *vt.* 放,搁;下(蛋);铺设,敷设;设置,布置

[语境]Don't lay your watch on the bed.

不要把你的手表放到床上。

These hens are laying well.

这些母鸡产蛋很多。

They are laying sewers.

他们在铺设下水道。

The butler always laid the table.

每次都是男管家把餐具摆好。

[考点]lay out 安排;设计;陈列

lazy ['leɪzɪ] *a.* 懒惰的,懒散的

[语境] A lazy youth, a lousy age.

【谚】少壮不努力,老大徒悲伤。

lead [li:d] *v.* 领导;领先;通向,导致 *n.* 带领,引导;铅

[巧记]派生词:leader(*n.* 领袖,指挥者,领导者);leadership(*n.* 领导能力;领导阶层)

[语境] The police are investigating an important new lead.

警方正在调查一条重要的新线索。

Our scientists are leading the way in space research.

我们的科学家在宇宙探索方面处于领先地位。

[考点] lead management(*n.* 主管,大的组织或公司的主要管理);lead the way(带路;示范)

leader ['li:də(r)] *n.* 领袖,领导者

[巧记]lead(*v.* 带领) + er(人)→领袖,领导者

[语境]As the leader of this office, she can work with everyone.

作为办公室的领导,她和每个人都合作得很好。

lean[4] [li:n] *v.* 倾斜,屈身;倚,靠,依赖 *a.* 瘦的,无脂肪的

[巧记]派生词:leaning(*n.* 倾斜,性癖,倾向);leanness(*n.* 瘦;缺乏;贫瘠);反义词:fat

[语境] They came to Pisa and saw the leaning tower.

他们来到了比萨也看到了斜塔。

The farmer tried to fatten the lean cattle for market.

农夫试图把瘦牛养肥以上市。

[考点] 常用词组:lean on 依赖,依靠

least [li:st] *a.* 最小的;最少的 *ad.* 最小;最少

[语境] Who knows most says least.

懂得最多的人,说得最少。

He was in fact worth at least three-quarters of a million pounds.

他至少拥有75万英镑的财产。

[考点] 常用词组:least of all 最不;at least 最低限度;至少

英语 词汇分频速记

leave[25] [liːv] *v.* 离开;留下,忘带;让,听任;交付 *n.* 许可;假期
[语境] I like to leave the best bits till last.
　　我喜欢把最好的留到最后。

lecture ['lektʃə(r)] *n./v.* 演讲,讲课
[语境] She ran over her notes before giving the lecture.
　　她讲课前把讲稿匆匆看了一遍。

left [left] *n.* 左面,左方 *a.* 左边的,左面的;在左方的
[语境] His left arm was broken.
　　他的左臂断了。

考点集训

1. It is obvious that the sports games are no longer amateur affairs; they have become professionally _____.
   A. laid off　　　　　　　B. laid out
   C. put off　　　　　　　D. put out

2. The discussion was so prolonged and exhausting that _____ the speaker stopped for refreshments.
   A. at large　　　　　　　B. at intervals
   C. at ease　　　　　　　D. at random

3. Everybody _____ in the hall where they were welcomed by the secretary.
   A. assembled　　　　　　B. accumulated
   C. piled　　　　　　　　D. joined

4. My grandfather had always taken a _____ interest in my work, and I had an equal admiration for the stories of his time.
   A. splendid　　　　　　　B. weighty
   C. vague　　　　　　　　D. keen

244

答案与解析

1. B lay out 陈设,展开;lay off 停止工作(活动);put off 延期;put out 扑灭,出版,发行。

2. B 讨论延长了很长时间,让人感到筋疲力尽,发言人时不时停下来喘口气。A 详细地;B 时不时地;C 放心;D 随机地。故 B 为正确答案。

3. A 大家在大厅集合,在那里,秘书向大家表示了欢迎。A 集合;B 积累,聚集;C 堆起,堆叠,放置,装入;D 联合,联结。故 A 为正确答案。

4. D 根据题干中 interest 和 and I had an equal admiration for the stories of his time,再结合四个选项——splendid 表示"壮丽的,辉煌的";weighty 表示"重的";vague 表示"含糊的,不清楚的";keen 表示"热烈的,热情的,锋利的,敏锐的",可知只有 keen 能修饰 interest,符合题意,故答案为 D。

Word List 27

leg [leg] *n.* 腿,腿脚

[语境]The dog struck at my leg.
那条狗咬伤了我的腿。

legal ['liːgəl] *a.* 合法的,正当的;法律的

[巧记] 反义词:illegal(*a.* 违法的;不合规定的)

[语境] We should use legal methods to deal with the problem.
我们应该使用合法的手段去处理这一问题。

[考点] legal aid 法律援助;legal adviser 法律顾问

leisure ['leʒə(r)] *n.* 空闲,闲暇

[语境]She spends at least half of her leisure in reading.
她的空闲时间至少有一半花在阅读上。

[考点] at leisure 闲着的;at one's leisure 有空时

lend [lend] *vt.* 借给,贷(款)

[巧记]反义词:borrow(v. 借)

[语境] Would you please lend me your pencil?

请把铅笔借给我用用好吗?

He used to lend money at an extremely high rate of interest.

他过去经常放高利贷。

[考点]词语辨析:borrow sth. from sb. 从某人借入某物; lend sb. sth. 借给某人某物

length [leŋθ] *n.* 长,长度;一段,一节,程度,范围

[语境]You spend a ridiculous length of time in the bath.

你洗澡用那么长时间,真不像话。

less [les] *a./ad.* 更少的(地),更小的(地)

[语境]It rains less in London than in Manchester.

伦敦的降雨量比曼彻斯特少。

lesson ['lesən] *n.* (功)课;[*pl.*] 课程;教训

[语境]I missed a lesson yesterday.

昨天我误了一节课。

let [let] *v.* 让,允许,听任;设,假设;出租,租给

[语境]Let me see:Where did I leave my hat?

让我想想——我把帽子落在哪儿了?

letter ['letə(r)] *n.* 信,函件;字母

[语境]I had received a letter from a very close friend.

我收到一个很要好的朋友的来信。

He sponged a wrong letter off with a rubber.

他用橡皮擦掉了一个错误的字母。

level ['levəl] *n.* 水平;水准,等级 *vt.* 弄平,铺平 *a.* 水平的

[语境] A football field should be level.

足球场地应该平坦。

The bombing raid practically leveled the town.

空袭几乎把这座城镇夷为平地。

[考点] level-headed 头脑冷静的,稳健的;reach level 达到某一水平;level up 平整

liar ['laɪə(r)] *n.* 说谎的人

[考点]lie v. 撒谎 lie to sb. 对某人撒谎
[语境]I know you for a thief and a liar!
我算认识你了,一个又偷又骗的家伙!

liberty [ˈlɪbətɪ] n. **自由,许可**
[巧记]派生词:libertarian(n. 自由意志主义者,行动自由者)
[语境]I am afraid that I am not at liberty to discuss this matter.
对不起,我无权讨论这个问题。
I took the liberty of borrowing your lawn-mower while you were away.
你不在的时候我擅自借用了你的刈草机。
[考点]be at liberty 可以随意(做某事),有权;take the liberty of 擅自

library [ˈlaɪbrərɪ] n. **图书馆;丛书,文库**
[语境]I ran across her in the public library yesterday.
我昨天在公共图书馆碰巧遇见了她。

lie[14] [laɪ] vi. **躺,平放;处于;位于** v. **说谎** n. **谎话**
[语境]And then it has no choice but to lie down and sleep.
于是,别无选择,它只好躺下睡觉。
Many women lie about their ages.
许多妇女常在自己的年龄上说谎。
[考点]常用词组:lie down 躺下休息

life [laɪf] n. **生命,生存;一生,寿命;生活;生物**
[语境]Children are always so full of life.
儿童总是那么的朝气蓬勃。

lifestyle [ˈlaɪfstaɪl] n. **生活方式**
[语境]They enjoyed an income and lifestyle that many people would envy.
他们的收入和生活方式会令很多人都羡慕不已。

lift [lɪft] v. **升起,举起,消散** n. **电梯,上升,免费搭车**
[巧记]同义词:raise(v. 举起,抬起)
[语境]I lifted the child down from the tree.
我把孩子从树上抱了下来。

I entered the lift and pressed the button on the fifth floor.

我走进电梯，按了按五楼的按钮。

He gave me a lift to the station.

他让我搭便车去车站。

[考点] 常用词组：lift off 起飞，发射；lift up 举起；吊起

light [laɪt] *n.* **光；灯** *v.* **点燃；照亮** *a.* **轻(快)；淡；明亮**

[巧记] 派生词：lighten(*v.* 使光明，照亮；使愉快；使轻松；变轻；变得愉快；变得轻松)

[语境] She was reading by the light of a candle.

她在蜡烛光下读书。

The room is brilliantly lighted up and full of guests.

房间里灯火辉煌，宾客济济。

Let's see a light film for a change.

咱们看部轻松的影片调剂一下。

[考点] 常用词组：light up 点燃；照亮

like [laɪk] *v.* **喜欢** *prep.* **像；比如** *a.* **相像的** *n.* **像……一样**

[语境] If you like, we could go out this evening.

你要是愿意的话，咱们今天晚上出去。

likely ['laɪklɪ] *a.* **可能的，有希望的** *ad.* **大概，多半**

[巧记] likely 是形容词，表示可能的；派生词：likable(*adj.* 可爱的，可喜的)；liking(*n.* 喜爱，喜好)

[语境] Earthquake is likely to occur according to the strange things.

根据这些奇怪的事情，有可能要发生地震。

[考点] 1. 很可能的 likely + to + do；2. 适当的，正合要求的 likely + for

limb [lɪm] *n.* **肢，翼，大树枝**

[巧记] 派生词：limbed(*adj.* 有肢的)；limbic(*a.* 边的；缘的)；同义词：arm branch

[语境] The workers saw off a limb from the tree.

工人从树上锯下了一根大树枝。

limit[34] ['lɪmɪt] *n.* **界线，限度；**(*pl.*) **范围** *vt.* **限制，限定**

[巧记]派生词:limitation(n. 限制,限制因素;极限,限度;局限),limited(a. 有限制的,少的,有限的)

[语境]We must limit our spending.
我们必须限制我们的开支。
I'm willing to help, within limits.
我愿适当予以帮助。

[考点]to the limit 到达极限;without limit 无极限;within limit 在一定范围之内

line [laɪn] n. 线,线条;界线;行,行列;航线,交通线,通信线 v. 排队,排列

[语境]The pupil joined the two points by a straight line.
那个小学生用直线把两点连接起来。
We have to cross the railway line by the foot bridge.
我们不得不从人行桥上越过铁路线。
I had been standing in line for three hours.
我已经排了3个小时的队。

[考点]in line 成一直线;line up 排队

link [lɪŋk] v. 环,链环;联系 n. 连接,联系

[巧记]派生词:linked(a. 环形的;连锁的;连接的;联合的);同义词:connect(v. 连接,联结)

[语境]The road links all the new towns.
这条路把所有的新城镇连接起来了。
Television stations around the world are linked by satellite.
全世界的电视台通过卫星联系在一起。

[考点]辨析:line 站队,list 列出,unite 与……相联合

lion [ˈlaɪən] n. 狮子

[语境]The coin has a crowned lion on its reverse.
这枚硬币反面的图案是个戴皇冠的狮子。

liquid [ˈlɪkwɪd] n. 液体 a. 液体的,液态的;流动的;可兑换成现金的

[语境]You have added too much liquid to the mixture.
你给这混合物加进了过多的液体。

Fats are solid at room temperature, and oil is liquid at room temperature.

脂肪在室温下为固态,油在室温下为液态。

list [lɪst] *n.* 表,目录,名单 *v.* 把……编列成表,列入表内

[巧记]同义词:enumeration;inventory

[语境] Can you give me a price list with specifications?

你能否给我一份有规格说明的价目单吗?

These names are to be listed in the catalog.

这些名字将列入目录。

[考点] list price 定价;价目表所列价格

listen [ˈlɪsən] *vi.* 倾听(与介词 to 并用,方可置宾语)

[语境] She is listening to the radio.

她在听收音机。

little [ˈlɪtəl] *a.* 小的,幼小的;不多的 *ad./n.* 不多,几乎没有

[语境] It's in Chinese: I can make little of it.

这是中文——我一点儿都不懂。

live [lɪv] *v.* 活着,生活,居住 [laɪv] *a.* 活的,生动的,直播的

[语境] Chinese live on rice.

中国人以大米为主食。

We watched a live television show.

我们观看了一场电视现场直播。

[考点] live 在(或从)表演现场;以实况(转播)

living [ˈlɪvɪŋ] *a.* 活的,现存的 *n.* 生活,生计

[语境] I am an American living in Europe.

我是一个住在欧洲的美国人。

He earns his living doing all kinds of things.

他做各种各样的活计来谋生。

[考点] alive,live,living 辨析:这些形容词均有"活着的,活的"之意。alive:其反义词为 dead;指生命从奄奄一息到精力旺盛的各种状态。live:通常作定语;指活生生的、生气勃勃的;还可表示现场直播的。living:其反义词为 dead;指包括人和动植物的生命没有消失、仍然存在的状态

load [ləʊd] *v.* 装(货),装载 *n.* 装载(量),负荷(量);(一)担

[巧记] 反义词:unload *v.* 卸货

[语境] Don't forget to load your camera.
别忘了给你的相机装胶卷。
The load on that beam is more than it will bear.
那根梁上的载重超过了它所能承受的量。

loan [ləʊn] *n.* 贷款 *n./v.* 借出

[语境] She offered me the loan of her car.
她提出把汽车借给我用。
How much interest do they charge on loans?
他们贷款收多少利息?

[考点] make a loan of... 贷款达……

lock[7] [lɒk] *n.* 锁 *v.* 锁,锁上

[语境] The lock keeper closed the lock gate.
船闸管理员关上了闸门。

logic ['lɒdʒɪk] *n.* 逻辑,逻辑学

[巧记] 派生词:logical (*adj.* 有逻辑的,合乎逻辑的); logically (*adv.* 伦理上;逻辑上)

[语境] I didn't follow her logic.
我不理解她的逻辑。
There's no logic in spending money on things you don't need.
把钱花在不需要的东西上是没有道理的。

logical[7] ['lɒdʒɪkəl] *a.* 逻辑的,符合逻辑的

[语境] It is logical to assume that they will attend.
按理他们是会出席的。

[考点] a logical argument 合乎逻辑的推理

lonely ['ləʊnlɪ] *a.* 孤独的,寂寞的;荒凉的,人迹稀少的

[巧记] 派生词:loneness (*n.* 幽静;孤寂);同义词:alone (*a.* 单独的 *ad.* 独自地)

[语境] He has so few friends that his life is lonely.
他的朋友很少,因此他的生活非常孤单。
They live a lonely life in a lonely house in the hills.

他们在山中一栋孤零零的房子里过着寂寞的生活。

long [lɒŋ] *a.* 长的,长时间的,长期的 *ad.* 长久地,长期地

[语境]He no longer lives here.

他不再住在这里了。

look[55] [lʊk] *vi./n.* 看,注视 *v.* 好像,显得 *n.* 外表,脸色

[语境]Just look at this beautiful present.

快来看看这件漂亮的礼物吧。

loose [luːs] *a.* 松,宽,松散

[巧记]派生词:loosen(*v.* 松开,解开),looseness(*n.* 松弛;轻率;零散;散漫)

[语境] I daren't let Bill loose in the garden where he'd pull up all the flowers.

我不敢把比尔放到花园去——他会把花全都拔掉的。

The guard loosed the dogs when the burglar alarm went off.

防盗警报器一响,警卫就放出了警犬。

[考点]at loose ends 无聊,闲着没事干;on the loose 不受约束;loosen *v.* 放松,松开

lose[9] [luːz] *v.* 丢失,迷路,输掉,亏本,失败,走慢,使沉湎于

[语境] Carl's father lost his job last month.

卡尔的父亲上个月失业了。

We lost a lot of money on that deal.

我们在那笔交易上亏损了许多钱。

Your watch is losing.

你的表走慢了。

The boy soon lost himself in the book.

这男孩不久便专心地看起书来。

[考点] 常用词组:lose control of 失去控制;lose one's mind 失去理智

loss[11] [lɒs] *n.* 丢,丢失,丧失;失败,输;迷(路)

[巧记]派生词:loser(*n.* 遗失者;损失物;损害者;失败者),losing(*n.* 失败;损失)

[语境] Loss of independence was a high price to pay for peace.

以丧失独立来换取和平是极高的代价。

It was a great loss to us all.

这对我们所有人来说都是一个巨大的损失。

[考点] lose 是动词,而 loss 是名词,loss leader 是招揽客人的特价商品,亏本卖商品;at a loss 不知所措;to one's own loss 使……吃亏的是

lost[lɒst] *a.* **失去的;错过的,浪费掉的;无望的,迷路的**

[语境] I took a wrong turn and we got lost in the mountains.

我拐错了弯,我们便在山里迷了路。

My paper got lost.

我的论文丢了。

The advantage is lost.

错失优势。

[考点] get lost 迷路;lost generation 迷惘的一代

lot [lɒt] *n.* **许多,大量;签,抽签;命运;场地**

[语境] You have lots of time to finish the work.

你有充裕的时间来完成这项工作。

She was chosen by lot to represent us.

她抽中签当我们的代表。

I would not want to share his lot.

我可不愿和他同甘共苦。

[考点] 常用词组:a lot of;lots of

loud[5] [laʊd] *a.* **大声的,响亮的;吵闹的,喧嚣的**

[语境] The television is too loud; turn the volume down.

电视声音太响了,把音量调低点儿。

love [lʌv] *n.* **爱,爱情,喜欢** *vt.* **爱,热爱;爱好,喜欢**

[语境] I love my motherland.

我爱我的祖国。

lovely[ˈlʌvlɪ] *a.* **可爱的,秀丽的;令人愉快的,美好的**

[语境] I like that lovely doll.

我喜欢那只可爱的娃娃。

What a lovely surprise!

真是个惊喜！

[考点] beautiful, fair, handsome, lovely, pretty, fine 辨析：这些形容词均含"美丽的,漂亮的"之意。beautiful：普通用词,含义广泛,语气最强,指优美和谐,是一种几乎接近完美的美。指人时通常形容女人或小孩,很少用于描写男子。fair：正式用词,多用于文学中,形容女子和儿童,侧重外表的美。handsome：多用于描写男性的英俊潇洒。有时也形容女人,指其五官端正,体态秀丽。lovely：普通用词,描写人时,主要指女人和小孩的相貌,语气不如 beautiful 强。pretty：普通用词,语气比 beautiful 弱,多用于描写妇女、儿童以及小巧玲珑、精美可爱之物。fine：指在容貌、身材或风度等方面令人感到可爱。用于事物时,强调形式或内容的优美

low [ləʊ] *a.* 低矮的；低级的,下层的,卑贱的；数量少的；低声的

[语境] A man's voice is usually lower than a woman's.

男子的嗓音通常比女子的低。

I'm low on cash right now.

我眼下现金不足。

He is a man of low birth.

他出身低微。

[考点] low on 不足的,快枯竭的

lower [ˈləʊə(r)] *a.* 较低的；下级的；下游的 *vt.* 放低,降低

[语境] Speak to her? I'd never lower myself.

跟她说话？我可不自贬人格。

Don't lower yourself by asking him for help.

不要向他求助以免降低身份。

[考点] 由 low 派生来的,合成词：the lower class 下层

loyal [ˈlɔɪəl] *a.* 忠诚的,忠贞的

[巧记] 派生词：loyalist（*n.* 忠诚的人）

[语境] He remained loyal to me through thick and thin.

他历尽艰辛始终都忠实于我。

We are loyal to our motherland.

我们忠于祖国。

[考点] loyalty n. 忠诚;royal 常用 be royal to 结构,表示"对……忠诚"

loyalty [ˈlɔɪəltɪ] *n.* **忠诚,忠心**
[巧记] 反义词:disloyal
[语境] Don't allow personal loyalty to colour your judgement.
不要因讲义气而影响了你的判断。
All the men took a vow of loyalty to their leader.
所有士兵都发誓效忠他们的指挥官。

luck [lʌk] *n.* **运气;好运,侥幸**
[巧记] 派生词:lucky (*a.* 幸运的);luckless (*a.* 不幸运的);luckiness (*n.* 幸运);luckily (*ad.* 幸运地)
[语境] Passing the exam is a good luck for me.
通过了考试对我来说真是幸运。
He had wonderful luck in all his ventures.
他干任何事情运气都好。
[考点] 常用词组:be in luck,be out of luck,good luck

lucky [ˈlʌkɪ] *a.* **幸运的,侥幸的**
[巧记] 反义词:unlucky (*a.* 不幸运的)
[语境] You're very lucky to have a caring family.
你很幸运有一个温馨的家庭。

luggage [ˈlʌgɪdʒ] *n.* **行李**
[语境] I held your luggage together with mine.
我把你的行李和我的捆在一起了。

lunch [lʌntʃ] *n.* **午饭**
[语境] She spread our lunch on the grass.
她在草地上摆好了我们的午饭。

lung [lʌŋ] *n.* **肺**
[语境] They forced air into his lung.
他们把空气吹入他的肺里。

考点集训

1. Any donation you can give will help us _____ the suffering and i-

solation of the homeless this New Year.

 A. lift   B. patch
 C. comfort   D. ease

2. Salaries for _____ positions seem to be higher than for permanent ones.

 A. legal   B. optional
 C. voluntary   D. temporary

3. The little girl was so frightened that she just wouldn't _____ her grip on my arm.

 A. loosen   B. remove
 C. relieve   D. dismiss

4. Actually, information technology can _____ the gap between the poor and the rich.

 A. link   B. break
 C. ally   D. bridge

5. Laws and regulations in each country have to be made _____ the constitution of the country.

 A. in honor of   B. in memory of
 C. in return for   D. in line with

6. The bank refused to _____ him any money, so he had to postpone buying a house.

 A. credit   B. borrow
 C. loan   D. lease

7. It may be necessary to stop _____ in the learning process and go back to the difficult points in the lessons.

 A. at a distance   B. at intervals
 C. at case   D. at length

答案与解析

1. D 今年过年你的任何捐赠都会帮助无家可归的人减轻痛苦，缓解孤独感。A 提高；B 修补；C 安慰；D 减缓，减轻。故选 D。

2. D 临时工的工资看似比长期工的工资高很多。A 合法的；B 选择的；C 自愿的；D 临时的。故选 D。

3. A 小女孩很害怕，紧紧抓住我的手不放。A 放开，放松；B 去除；C 减轻；D 开出，解散。故选 A。

4. D 事实上，信息技术可以缩小贫富差距。bridge the gap，缩小差距，固定搭配，故选 D。

5. D in line with 跟……一致，符合；in honor of 为了向……表示敬意；in memory of 为了纪念；in return for 作为……的报答。

6. C 根据题干中 so he had to postpone buying a house，得知空格处应填入表示"贷款"的词。credit 表示"相信，信任，把……归给"；borrow 表示"借入"；loan 表示"贷款，借给"；lease 表示"出租，租出"。答案为 C。

7. B 根据题干中 stop 和 go back to the difficult points in the lessons，再结合四个选项——at a distance 表示"在远处"，at intervals 表示"不时"，at length 表示"最后，详细地"，没有 at case 这个词组，可知，只有 at intervals 符合题意，答案为 B。

Word List 28

mad [mæd] *a.* 发疯的；狂热的，着迷的；恼火的，生气的

[语境] He said the modern generation was money mad or pleasure mad.

他说如今的一代人是金钱迷和享乐迷。

Don't be mad at me.

不要对我大发脾气。

[考点] 常用词组：mad at sb. 对某人生气；mad with sth. 对……生气；mad about/on/for 对……痴迷

magazine [ˌmæɡəˈziːn] *n.* 杂志，期刊

[语境] This magazine will discontinue next week.

这份杂志将于下周停刊。

magic [ˈmædʒɪk] *n.* 魔术，魔（魅）力，巫术 *a.* 有魔力的，魔术的

[巧记]派生词:magical *adj.* 魔术的,不可思议的,有魔力的; magician *n.* 魔术家

[语境] The good fairy made Cinderella's coach come by magic.
善良的仙女使用魔力赶来了灰姑娘的马车。
The magic of her voice charmed the audience.
她那歌喉的魅力令观众陶醉。
He looked about but could not see any magic cloth at all.
他四处寻找,根本没有看见有什么魔布。

[考点] by magic 借助魔法

magical [ˈmædʒɪkl] *a.* 有魔力的,不可思议的
[语境] There is no magical formula to business—it takes hard work, determination and the drive to do something great.
生意场上并没有神奇的公式。我们需要努力工作,有决心、有动力去做伟大的事情。

mail [meɪl] *n.* 邮件 *v.* 邮寄
[语境] I opened my mail and was surprised to see a broken vase.
我打开了邮件,惊讶地发现了一个打碎的花瓶。
I went to the post office to mail the letters.
我去邮局寄信。

main [meɪn] *a.* 主要的,总的 *n.* 总管道;干线
[语境] Fishing is still the main industry there.
捕鱼业仍为那里的主要行业。
The main road was flooded so we had to go round by narrow country lanes.
公路干线遭水淹没,我们只得择乡间小径绕行。

mainly [ˈmeɪnlɪ] *ad.* 主要地,大体上
[语境] He lives mainly on his monthly income.
他主要靠自己的月收入生活。

maintain[19] [meɪnˈteɪn] *vt.* 保养,维修;维持,保持,继续;赡养,负担;坚持,主张
[巧记]同义词:keep 保持,维持
[语境] He is too poor to maintain his family.

他太穷了,无法养活家人。

The car has to be constantly maintained.

汽车必须经常保养。

[考点] maintain one's family 供养家庭

major[16] ['meɪdʒə(r)] *a.* 较大的,主要的 *vi.* (*in*) 主修 *n.* 主科;(某)专业学生;少校

[语境] We were broadcasting on all the major channels.

我们在全部主要频道播送节目。

English majors would be asked to explore the roots of language.

英语专业的学生会被要求探究语言的根源。

[考点] major in 主修

make [meɪk] *n.* (产品)来源,制法 *vt.* 制造,做成,准备

[语境] What make is your car?

你的汽车是什么型号?

I couldn't make my car start this morning.

今天早晨我的汽车发动不起来了。

male [meɪl] *n./a.* 男性(的),雄性(的)

[语境] The male and female genders are equal.

男性和女性是平等的。

man [mæn] *n.* 男人;人,人类

[语境] I have always regarded him as a man of integrity.

我一向认为他是个正直的人。

manage[27] ['mænɪdʒ] *v.* 管理,经营,处理;设法,对付

[巧记] 派生词:manager(*n.* 经理;管理器;管理人员)

[语境] I shall be able to manage (the job) (without help).

(没有帮助)我可以应付(这项工作)。

In spite of these insults, she managed not to get angry.

尽管受到这些侮辱,她还是忍着没发火。

[考点] manage sb. to do sth. 使某人做某事,manage sb. to one's own views 使某人跟自己的观点一致

manager[10] ['mænɪdʒə(r)] *n.* 经理,管理人

[语境] The manager had found him out and was going to sack him.

经理发觉了他的不轨行为,打算炒他鱿鱼。

manner[15] [ˈmænə(r)] *n.* **方式,方法;态度,举止;(*pl.*)礼貌,规矩**

[巧记] 同义词:character(*n.* 个性,天性,性情),method(*n.* 方法;秩序;条理)

[语境] We all respect the man in good manners.
我们都尊重有礼貌的人。
I don't like to talk with him;he has a very rude manner.
我不喜欢和他说话,他态度粗野。

[考点] all manners of 各种各样;in a manner 在一定程度上;in...manner 以……方式/样子;in ill/rough/bad/manner 没有礼貌的

many [ˈmenɪ] *a.* **许多的,多的** *pron.* **许多人或物,许多**

[语境] Many diseases are caused by bacteria.
许多疾病是由细菌引起的。

map [mæp] *n.* **图,地图**

[语境] He unfolded the map and set it on the floor.
他打开地图,放在了地板上。

March [mɑːtʃ] *n.* **三月**

[语境] I had counted on having it completed by March. 我曾指望在三月份以前完成这件事情。

march [mɑːtʃ] *vi./n.* **行进,行军;游行示威** *n.* **进行曲**

[语境] Many people marched in the street last week because of the poor life situation.
上个星期,因为贫困的生活环境人们都上街游行。

[考点] be on the march 在行进中;steal a march on 抢先一步取得优势;a forced march 强行军

mark [mɑːk] *n.* **记号,标记,痕迹;分数** *vt.* **记分,打分;作标记,标志**

[语境] Enemy left some marks, and we hit them according to it.
我们根据敌人留下的记号痛击了他们。

[考点] give one full marks 给某人满分;leave one's mark 难以忘怀;be marked for 命中注定;mark with 做记号,做暗号

market [ˈmɑːkɪt] *n.* **集市,市场;销路,需求** *vt.* **销售**

[语境]He sold boots on a market stall.

他在集市上摆摊卖靴子。

We need somebody to market our products to the local people.

我们需要有人为我们向当地人推销产品。

marriage[42] ['mærɪdʒ] *n.* 结婚,婚姻;结婚仪式

[语境] It was a pleasant surprise to learn of her marriage.

得知她结婚是件令人惊喜的事。

His marriage is full of happiness.

他的婚姻生活很幸福。

[考点]marry sb. 或 be married to sb. 和……结婚,另外 get married 表示动作,而 be married 表示状态

married[10] ['mærɪd] *a.* 已婚的,夫妇的;(to) 与……结婚的

[语境]Her married life was exceptionally happy.

她的婚后生活十分幸福。

marry[8] ['mærɪ] *v.* 结婚,嫁,娶

[巧记]派生词:marriage(*n.* 结婚,婚姻;结婚仪式),married(*a.* 已婚的,夫妇的)

[语境] He is going to marry Jane in May.

他打算五月和珍结婚。

[考点] sb. marry sb. 某人和某人结婚

Mars [mɑːz] *n.* 火星

[语境]He contended that there must be life on Mars.

他坚信火星上面一定有生物。

mass [mæs] *n.* 团,块,堆;(*pl.*) 群众,民众;众多,大量;质量

[语境] Mass of buildings were destroyed in the war.

大量的建筑物在战争中被毁坏。

Crowds massed along the road where the king would pass.

群众聚集在国王要经过的街道旁。

[考点] a mass of...大量的……

master ['mɑːstə(r)] *vt.* 掌握,精通 *n.* 主人,雇主;能手,名家,大师;硕士

[巧记] 反义词:servant(*n.* 仆人,雇工,佣人)

[语境] He is a Master of Science.

他是理学硕士。

The puppy was fawning on its master.

小狗朝着主人摇尾乞怜。

[考点] be master of 精通……；study without a master 无师自通

match [mætʃ] *n.* 火柴；比赛，竞赛；对手，敌手 *v.* 匹配，相配

[语境] The hat and shoes are a perfect match.

这顶帽子和鞋子完全相配。

The curtains don't match the paint.

窗帘和油漆不相配。

[考点] be no match for sb. 不是某人的敌手；meet one's match 遇上对手；match sb. in... 在某方面是某人对手

material [mə'tɪərɪəl] *n.* 材料，原料；资料；*a.* 物质的，实物的，具体的

[语境] They are collecting this material at the points of origin.

他们正在产地收集这种材料。

Every room must have been stuffed with material things.

每个房间肯定都塞满了东西。

mathematics [ˌmæθə'mætɪks] *n.* 数学

[语境] I'm going to take a course in applied mathematics this semester.

我这学期打算学习应用数学课程。

maths = mathematics

matter[23] ['mætə(r)] *n.* 物质，物体；毛病，麻烦；事情 *v.* 有关系，要紧

[巧记] 同义词：affair (*n.* 事件，事情；事态)，material (*n.* 材料；物资；原料)

[语境] This important matter brooks no delay. We must talk about it now.

这件要事不容耽搁，我们必须现在谈谈。

Matter exists in three states: solid, liquid and gas.

物质以三种形态存在，即固态、液态和气态。

All these things do not matter now.

核心词汇精解

所有这一切现在都无关紧要了。

[考点] affair, matter 辨析:affair 常用复数表示"事物",指较重大、较正式的事情;matter 一般指需考虑或处理的麻烦事

may [meɪ] *aux. v.* **可能,也许;可以,被允许;祝,愿**

[语境]That may be our taxi now!

那辆可能就是我们的计程车了!

May [meɪ] *n.* **五月**

[语境]University examinations are held in early May.

大学考试于5月初进行。

maybe ['meɪbi] *ad.* **可能;大概;也许**

[语境]Maybe these nutrients are helpful to your health.

或许这些营养品对你的健康有帮助。

mayor [meə(r)] *n.* **市长**

[巧记]串联记忆:五月初(May)市长(mayor)要出席重要会议

[语境]The new mayor said he would clean the city up.

新市长说,他要整顿本市。

me [mi:, mɪ] *pron.* **[宾格]我**

[语境]He often speaks ill of me behind my back.

他常在背后说我的坏话。

meal [mi:l] *n.* **一餐,一顿饭,膳食**

[语境]She sat next to him throughout the meal.

用餐时她一直坐在他身旁。

mean [mi:n] *n.* **平均值** *vt.* **意指,意味着;意欲,打算** *a.* **低劣的,平庸的;卑鄙的,吝啬的;平均的**

[语境] I'm sorry I hurt you;I didn't mean to.

对不起,我弄伤了你;我不是故意的。

Do you mean Miss Anne Smith or Miss Mary Smith?

你指的是安·史密斯小姐还是玛丽·史密斯小姐?

[考点] mean 做动词时,mean to do 表示打算做某事,而 mean doing 表示意味着做某事。

meaning ['mi:nɪŋ] *n.* **意思,意义,含义**

[语境]There is a negligible difference in meaning between these two words.

这两个词之间在意义上有极小的差别。

At last he knew the meaning of life.

终于,他知道了生命的意义。

means[46] [mi:nz] *n.* 方法,手段,工具

[语境] Please find alternative means of transport.

请另外找一个运输方法。

Radio and television are important means of communication.

无线电和电视是重要的通信手段。

[考点] by means of 依靠,依赖;by all means 无论如何;by no means 决不

measure[21] ['meʒə(r)] *n.* 度量,测量;(*pl.*)措施,办法 *vt.* 量,测量;有……长(宽/高等)

[巧记] 派生词:measuring(*n.* 测量),measurement(*n.* 测量法;尺寸;度量),measureless(*adj.* 无限的,不可量的)

[语境] He measured the length of the room.

他量了房间的长度。

His resignation is a measure of how angry he is.

从他辞职一事可见其气愤的程度。

[考点] beyond/above/out of measure 不可估量,极度;for good measure 加重分量;know no measure 无止境

meat [mi:t] *n.* 肉,食用肉类

[语境] The meat was condemned as unfit for human consumption.

这种肉已被宣布不适宜人们食用。

media ['mi:diə] *n.* 媒体;媒介;方法 *a.* 半生熟的,中的

[巧记] 词根:med = middle,表示"中间"

[语境] Newer media are obsoleting the book.

新的传播媒介正在逐步淘汰书籍。

medical[40] ['medɪkəl] *a.* 医学的,医疗的,医药的;内科的

[巧记] 同根词:medic (*n.* 医学院学生;卫生员)

[语境] Great strides have been made in medical research.

医学研究取得了很大的进展。

[考点] medical certificate 健康状况证明；诊断书

medicine ['meds(I)n,-dIs(I)n] *n.* **内服药,医药;医学,医术**

[语境] Medicine should not be kept where it is accessible to children.

药物不应放在容易被小孩拿到的地方。

He pursued a career in medicine.

他从事医学。

meet [mi:t] *n.* 会,集会 *v.* 遇见;会谈;迎接;满足;符合

[语境] A policeman could meet danger any minute of his working day.

警察在值勤时随时都可能碰到危险。

The two trains met at a small station.

两列火车在一个小站相遇(即错车)。

meeting ['mi:tɪŋ] *n.* **会议,集会**

[语境] Can we have a meeting to discuss that?

我们可以开会来讨论那件事吗？

member ['membə(r)] *n.* **成员,会员**

[语境] The cello is a member of the violin family.

大提琴是提琴家族的一员。

memory ['meməri] *n.* **记忆力,记忆;回忆;内存**

[语境] He founded the charity in memory of his late wife.

他兴办那项慈善事业以纪念他已故的妻子。

He has a good visual memory.

他有良好的视觉记忆力。

[考点] bring back to memory 想起,记起来；to the best of my memory 凭我所记住的；speak from memory 凭记忆讲述

men [men] *n.* (man 的复数)

[语境] In the hotel, the old men were drinking away as usual.

在旅馆里,这些老人和往常一样喝个不停。

mend [mend] *vt.* **修补,修理,缝补**

[巧记] 反义词:break 弄坏

[语境] The mends were almost invisible.

修补过的地方几乎看不出来。

In the end, things will mend.

【谚】车到山前必有路。

[考点] on the mend 康复中,改进中;mend one's fences 加强,改善关系

mental[21]['mentəl] *a.* **思想的,精神的;智力的,脑力的**

[巧记] 派生词:mentally(*ad.* 心理上;智力上;精神上);mentality(*n.* 精神力, 头脑作用, 智力)

[语境] Many mental work makes farmers at loss.

许多智力活让农民不知所措。

[考点] mental age 心理年龄;mental deficiency 心理缺陷;mental home/hospital 精神病医院

mention[17]['menʃən] *vt./n.* **提及,说起,讲述**

[语境] In his class, he often mentions the importance of memory.

在他的课堂上,他经常提及记忆的重要性。

[考点] not to mention 更不必说;be mentioned in the dispatches 在战报中受到表彰;make(no) mention of(没有)提及/提到

menu['menju:] *n.* **菜单**

[语境] They have picked out the best items on the menu.

他们从菜单上选出最好的菜。

mercy['mɜ:sɪ] *n.* **仁慈,怜悯,宽恕**

[巧记] 同义词:kindness(*n.* 仁慈;好意;和蔼;友好的行为);反义词:cruelty(*n.* 残酷, 残酷的行为, 野蛮)

[语境] The prisoner appealed to the judge for mercy.

囚犯恳求法官开恩。

[考点] beg for mercy

mercy['mɜ:sɪ] *n.* **仁慈,怜悯,宽恕**

[语境] Mercy to the enemies means cruelty to the people.

对敌人的仁慈就意味着对人民的残忍。

[考点] have mercy on sb. 可怜某人;at the mercy of 在……的支配下

mere[mɪə(r)] *a.* **纯粹的;仅仅,只不过**

[语境] Don't scold him; he is a mere child.

别责备他,他只不过是个孩子。

Ignorance is mere privation.

无知是一种纯粹的贫乏。

merely [ˈmɪəlɪ] *ad.* **仅仅,只不过**

[语境] Do you really want to go or are you merely being amiable?

你是真的想去呢,还是仅仅为了表示友好?

mess [mes] *n.* **混乱,混杂,脏乱**

[语境] This illness makes a mess of my holiday plans.

这场病把我的假期计划给打乱了。

[考点] mess about 闲逛

考点集训

1. There was no light on the way and for a second she hesitated, unable to _____ the dim figure awaiting her.
   A. set out   B. make out
   C. pick up   D. clear up

2. I didn't _____ to take a taxi but I had to as I was late.
   A. assume   B. suppose
   C. mean   D. hope

3. The _____ stuck on the envelope says "By Air".
   A. diagram   B. label
   C. signal   D. mark

4. This research has attracted wide _____ coverage and has featured on BBC television's *Tomorrow's World*.
   A. message   B. information
   C. media   D. data

5. The work was almost complete when we received orders to _____ no further with it.
   A. progress   B. proceed
   C. march   D. promote

6. The rapid development of communications technology is transforming

the _____ in which people communicate across time and space.

A. mood　　　　　　　　B. mission

C. manner　　　　　　　D. vision

7. Arriving home, the boy told his parents about all the _____ which occurred in his dormitory.

A. occasions　　　　　　B. matters

C. incidents　　　　　　D. issues

答案与解析

1. B　在路上没有灯光,有一小段时间,她犹豫了一下,因为她无法看清那个等她的朦胧的身影。set out"出发,启程";make out"填写,理解,辨认";pick up"捡起,恢复精神,加快";clear up"整理,清除,放晴"。从意思上看,只有 B 能与 figure 搭配。

2. C　我并没打算要坐出租车,但是我不得不坐下,因为我要迟到了。A 承担,假定,设想;B 认为;C 打算;D 希望。故 C 为正确答案。

3. B　贴在信封上面的标签是"空邮"。A 图表;B 标签;C 信号;D 符号。故 B 为正确答案。

4. C　这个研究吸引了广泛的媒体报道,还在 BBC 电视的《明日世界》节目作了专题报道。A 讯息;B 信息;C 媒体;D 数据。故 C 为正确答案。

5. B　收到不再进行这份工作的命令时,我们基本上快把这份工作做完了。A 前进,进展;B 进行;C 行进,前进;D 提升。故选 B。

6. C　交流技术的快速发展改变了人们跨越时空交流的方式。A 情绪,心情;B 任务;C 方式,方法;D 视野。故选 C。

7. C　到家后,男孩子把所有宿舍发生的事告诉了他的父母。A 场合,情况;B 事情;C 小事;D 事件。故选 C。

Word List 29

message [ˈmesɪdʒ] *n.* 消息，音信，文电，口信，便条；启示，要旨

[语境] I often send messages to my friend by Internet.
我经常通过因特网给我的朋友发信息。

[考点] give/pass sb. a message 给某人发信息；leave sb. a message 给某人留个口信

metal [ˈmetəl] *n.* 金属，金属制品

[语境] Various metals are used to make the parts of this machine.
这部机器的零件是用多种金属制造的。

There isn't much metal in the bodywork of this new car; it's mainly plastic.
这辆新汽车的车身没用多少金属材料，大部分是塑料的。

[考点] metal head 金属摇滚音乐迷

meter/-tre [ˈmiːtə(r)] *n.* 公尺，米；仪表

[语境] He walked away from all his competitors in the 3,000-meter race.
在3 000米赛跑中，他遥遥领先于他的对手们。

The amount of electricity used is recorded by a meter.
电表记录下耗电量。

method[16] [ˈmeθəd] *n.* 方法，办法

[巧记] 同义词：way

[语境] The book pursues a different method in its treatment of the problem.
该书在论述这一问题时采用了不同的方法。

[考点] 作方式、方法解，可以用作可数名词

middle [ˈmɪdəl] *n./a.* 中间(的)，当中(的)

[语境] There are 300 students or so in this middle school.
这所中学大约有300个学生。

· 269 ·

A beautiful stone fountain was set in the middle of the garden.

花园中央砌造了一个漂亮的石头喷水池。

might [maɪt] *aux. v.* **可能,也许** *n.* **力量,威力,权力**

[巧记] may 的过去式

[语境] That might be in your favor.

那可能对你有利。

To be frank, this mission is beyond my might.

说实话,这一使命非我能力所及。

[考点] 1. (may 的过去式)(表示可能、不确定、期望、许可等,相当于 may,但更带迟疑、婉转等色彩)可能;可以

2. (may 的过去式)(用于表示与事实相反情况的虚拟语气中)会,能

3. (may 的过去式)(表示请求或婉转的责备)请;应该

mild [maɪld] *a.* **温暖的,暖和的;温和的,温柔的;(烟、酒)味重的**

[巧记] 派生词:mildness(*n.* 温和;温暖;和善)

[语境] He has a mild nature.

他的性格温和。

The patient has a mild fever.

那个病人有些轻微的发烧。

[考点] as mild as a dove/may 非常温和地;draw it mild 说(做)得适度,不夸张

mile [maɪl] *n.* **英里**

[语境] Traffic backed up for a mile.

交通阻塞长达一英里。

military[4] ['mɪlɪtərɪ] *a.* **军事的,军用的,军队的**

[巧记] 词根:milit = soldier,表示"兵";military 军人的,军队的(milit + ary);同义词:army

[语境] They are making further efforts to decrease military spending.

他们正在做进一步的努力来缩减军费开支。

milk [mɪlk] *n.* **乳,牛奶** *v.* **挤奶**

[语境] She soaked bread in milk.

核心词汇精解

她把面包浸在牛奶里。

Farm-workers milked cows by hand.

农场工人用手挤牛奶。

million ['mɪljən] *n.* **百万**

[语境] The purchase price figures out at about two million dollars.

交易的价格计算在 200 万美元左右。

mind[20] [maɪnd] *n.* **精神,理智,意见,记忆力** *v.* **注意,介意,反对**

[巧记] 同义词: attend brain

[语境] Two days later he changed his mind.

两天后他改变主意了。

She minded very much that he had not come.

他没有来,她为此十分不悦。

[考点](用于否定句和疑问句中)介意,反对

minor ['maɪnə(r)] *a.* **较小的,较少的,较次要的** *n.* **辅修学科** *vi.* **辅修**

[巧记] mini, min = small, 表示"小"

[语境] I've made a few minor adjustments to the seating plan.

我对座次表作了小小的调整。

The plan was approved, with some minor modifications.

计划已批准,仅作了些许更改。

[考点] 反义词: major *a.* 主要的,较大的 *n.* 主修课程 *v.* 主修……

minute ['mɪnɪt] *n.* **分钟,片刻;(*pl.*)会议记录** *a.* **微小的**

[巧记] mini, min = small, 表示"小"; (min + ute)

[语境] Every minute counts.

每分钟都很重要。

The office is minute, with barely room for a desk and two chairs.

那间办公室极小,只有刚够摆一张写字台、两把椅子的空间。

miracle ['mɪrəkəl] *n.* **奇迹,令人惊奇的人(或事)**

[巧记] 派生词: miraculous (*a.* 奇迹的; 不可思议的)

[语境] This cathedral was regarded as a miracle in architectural history.

这座大教堂被认为是建筑史上的奇迹。

[考点] miracle, wonder, phenomenon 辨析: 这些名词均含"奇迹"

271

之意。miracle：一般指被认为是人力所办不到的奇异之事。wonder：通常指使人惊奇的事迹、人物或景观,主要指人创造的奇迹。phenomenon：指罕见的现象或奇人、奇事

mirror ['mɪrə(r)] *n.* 镜子;反映,反射 *v.* 反映,反射

[语境] A glance in the mirror reassured him that his tie wasn't crooked.

他照了一下镜子,领带确实没有戴歪。

The clear water mirrored the blue sky.

清澈的水面映出了碧蓝的天空。

[考点] mirror image 镜中人[物];镜像

miserable ['mɪzərəbəl] *a.* 痛苦的,悲惨的

[巧记] 词根 miser 表示"可怜的";同义词:pitiful (*adj.* 慈悲的,同情的,可怜的), poor

[语境] In the old days the peasants lived a miserable life.

在旧社会,农民过着凄惨的生活。

[考点] miserable failure 惨败

mislead [mɪs'liːd] *vt.* 把……带错路;使误入歧途;使误解

[巧记] mis(错误) + lead(带领) → 使误入歧途

[语境] The guide misled the tourists in the woods.

向导在森林里给旅游者带错了路。

Don't let his friendly words mislead you.

别让他那友好的言辞把你蒙混住。

miss[28] [mɪs] *n.* 女士;(M-) 小姐 *vt.* 没达到,未击中;未看到;没赶上;遗漏,省去;惦念

[语境] He arrived too late and missed the train.

他到得太晚,没赶上火车。

I miss you very much.

我非常想念你。

[考点] miss the boat(bus) 坐失良机;miss the mark 未达到预期的效果或目的;miss out 遗忘,删掉

missing ['mɪsɪŋ] *a.* 失去的,失踪的

[语境] He searched all the drawers for the missing paper.

他翻了所有的抽屉以找寻那个不见了的文件。

mistake [mɪ'steɪk] *n.* 错误,过失,误解

［巧记］词根 mis-表示"错误,坏"

［语境］You've made several grammatical mistakes in the composition.

你的作文中犯了几处语法错误。

［考点］by mistake 错误地,无意中做错了某事;make a mistake 犯错误

mix [mɪks] *v.* 使混合;混淆

［语境］In my job, I mix with all sorts of people.

我在工作中常和各种人打交道。

Let's mix concrete, sand and stones.

让我们把水泥、沙子和石子掺合在一起。

［考点］mix up 混淆;调好

mixture ['mɪkstʃə(r)] *n.* 混合物,混合

［巧记］词根 mix,表示"混淆";-ture 表名词

［语境］This is a mixture of the best tobacco.

这是由最好的烟叶配制成的。

Do you know the constituents of the mixture?

你知道这种混合物的成分吗?

［考点］be mixed up 糊涂,一团糟;be mixed up (in) 卷入……,与……有关;be mixed up with sb. 交往,往来(通常指与不该交往的人交往);mix *v.* 混合,使混合

model ['mɒdəl] *n.* 样式,型;模范,模型,原型;模特 *v.* 模仿

［巧记］同义词:copy (*v.* 模仿)

［语境］All this year's new models are displayed at the motor show.

汽车展览会上展出了今年所有的新型号。

She models herself after her mother.

她以自己母亲为榜样。

modernize/-ise ['mɒdənaɪz] *v.* 使现代化;现代化,近代化

［巧记］modern(现代的) + -ize(……化)→使现代化;派生词: modernization(*n.* 现代化;现代化的事物)

273

[语境] It inaugurated an effort to modernize Chinese culture and society.

人们开始致力于中国文化和社会现代化的事业。

moment [ˈməʊmənt] *n.* 片刻,瞬间,时刻

[巧记] 同义词:instant(*n.* 立即,瞬间 *a.* 立即的,即时的)

[语境] I'd like to speak to you for a moment.

我想和你谈一会儿。

[考点] all of a moment 突然之间;at any moment 随时;在任何时候;马上;at moments 时刻,常常

Monday [ˈmʌndɪ] *n.* 星期一

[语境] That magazine comes out every Monday.

那份杂志每星期一出版。

money [ˈmʌnɪ] *a.* 金融的,货币的

[语境] I'd like to deposit some money.

我想存点儿钱。

monitor [ˈmɒnɪtə(r)] *n.* 班长;监听器,监视器 *v.* 监控,监测

[巧记] 派生词:monitory(*a.* 训诫的 *n.* 告诫书)

[语境] The monitor handed the papers out to the classmates.

班长把试卷分发给同学们。

Philby was there to monitor any unforeseen developments on a daily basis.

菲尔比在那里每日不断地监视着那些预料不到的事态的发展。

monkey [ˈmʌŋkɪ] *n.* 猴子

[语境] The monkey made a long arm for the peach.

猴子伸臂去摘桃子。

month [mʌnθ] *n.* 月,月份

[语境] It will take a month to clear the backlog of work.

要花一个月的时间才能清理完积压的工作。

monthly [ˈmʌnθlɪ] *a.* 每月的 *ad.* 每月一次,按月 *n.* 月刊

[巧记] 同义词:each month, every month 每月

[语境] We will pay for houses by monthly instalments.

我们将按月分期付款买房。

Some magazines come out monthly.

有的杂志每月出一期。

mood[8] [mu:d] *n.* 心情,心境,情绪;语气

[巧记]派生词:moodily(*ad.* 喜怒无常地;闷闷不乐地)

[语境] He's in no mood for (telling) jokes/to tell jokes.

他没心情说笑话。

He's in a mood/in one of his moods today.

他今天闹情绪了。

[考点] mood 用作可数名词,前面通常用 in。in a merry mood 心情愉快;in the mood for 想……;a man of mood 一个喜怒无常的人

moon [mu:n] *n.* 月亮,月球,卫星

[语境] The moon finally peeped out from behind the clouds.

月亮终于从云层后面露了出来。

moral ['mɔrəl] *n.* 寓意,教育意义 *a.* 道德的,道义的,有道德的

[巧记]派生词:morality(*n.* 道德,品行,教训);反义词:immoral(*a.* 不道德的)

[语境] We should obey the common moral level.

我们应该遵循一般的道德标准。

Human beings are moral individuals.

人是有辨别是非能力的。

[考点] moral standards 道德标准;the moral sense 是非感;moral rights/obligations 道德上的权利/义务

more[43] [mɔ:(r)] *a.* 更多的 *n.* 更多的人(或东西) *ad.* 更,更多

[语境] It took more or less a whole day to paint the ceiling.

粉刷天花板用了将近一整天的时间。

He couldn't lift the table and no more could I.

他抬不动那张桌子,我也抬不动。

I am becoming more and more irritated by his selfish behaviour.

我现在对他那种自私的行为越来越恼火。

[考点] more or less 或多或少;more and more 越来越……

moreover [mɔː'rəʊvə(r)] *conj./ad.* 再者,加之,而且

[语境] I don't like skating, moreover, the ice is too thin.
我不喜欢滑冰,而且冰太薄。
The price is too high, and moreover, the house isn't in a suitable position.
房价太高,而且房屋的地点也不太合适。

morning ['mɔːnɪŋ] *n.* 早晨,上午

[语境] During the morning your guide will take you around the city.
导游上午会带你们游览全城。

mostly ['məʊstlɪ] *ad.* 主要地,多半,基本上都

[语境] They mostly live on the outskirts of a town.
他们大多住在近郊。
[考点] mainly, chiefly, greatly, largely, mostly 辨析:这些副词均可表示"主要地,大量地"之意。mainly:指主要部分,突出在一系列事物中的相对重要性。chiefly:侧重某人或某物在众多的人或物中占主要和显著地位。greatly:通常强调程度的高。largely:着重范围或分量大大超过别的成分。mostly:强调数量占多半,近乎全部

mother ['mʌðə(r)] *n.* 母亲,妈妈

[语境] The mother sat by the sick child all night long.
妈妈整夜守在生病的孩子身旁。

motivate ['məʊtɪveɪt] *vt.* 作为……的动机,促动;激励

[语境] We were all motivated by the great ambition.
我们被这宏伟的理想激励着。
[考点] motivate 只做及物动词,但说激发、促使某人做某事时,通常用 make 或 cause

motive ['məʊtɪv] *n.* 动机,目的;*a.* 发动的,运动的

[巧记] mot(运动) + tive(倾向……的)→倾向……运动的→动机,目的
[语境] Jealousy was assigned as motive for the crime.
我们把这一犯罪行为的动机归因于忌妒。

motor ['məʊtə(r)] *n.* 发动机,电动机

[语境]She got in and started the motor.

她坐上车,启动了发动机。

mountain[ˈmaʊntən] *n.* 山

[语境]The road passes over a steep mountain.

这条路翻越一架陡峭的高山。

mouth[maʊθ] *n.* 嘴,口

[语境]His mouth was full of peas.

他满嘴都是豌豆。

move [muːv] *v.* 移动,迁移;活动;感动 *n.* 移动,活动,行动

[语境] The government's announcement is seen as a move towards settling the strike.

政府的通告已视为迈向解决罢工问题的一步。

movement [ˈmuːvmənt] *n.* 运动,活动;移动

[巧记]move(运动) + ment(名词后缀)→移动,运动

[语境]They collect funds to finance the movement.

他们为这一运动筹募基金。

But he makes no movement towards the foods.

但他没有对这些食物有所动作。

movie[ˈmuːvɪ] *n.* 电影,电影院

[语境]She is the most famous of all American movie queens.

她是全美国最著名的影后。

much [mʌtʃ] *a.* 多的,大量的 *ad.* 十分,非常;到极大程度

[语境]The patient is much the same this morning.

今晨病人情况几无变化。

murder[27] [ˈmɜːdə(r)] *n./vt.* 谋杀,凶杀

[巧记] 派生词:murderous(*a.* 凶狠的, 致命的, 杀人的)

[语境] He was accused of murdering the little girl.

他被指控谋杀了这个小女孩。

[考点] murder will out 谋杀案必然要暴露;get away with murder 逍遥法外,为所欲为

museum[mjuːˈzɪəm] *n.* 博物馆,展览馆

[语境]A trip to the museum is programmed for next Tuesday.

已计划下星期二去参观博物馆。

music['mjuːzɪk] *n.* 音乐,乐曲

[语境]She tried to educate her son's taste in music.

她试图培养她儿子对音乐的爱好。

He played a piece of music of his own composition.

他演奏了一首自己创作的曲子。

must [məst, mʌst] *aux./v.* 必须;很可能;一定要 *n.* 必须做的事

[语境]Something must be done about it.

必须得想个办法。

my[maɪ] *pron.* 我的

[语境]John's my best friend.

约翰是我最好的朋友。

myself[maɪ'self, mə's-] *pron.* 我自己

[语境]I woke up to find myself in the hospital.

我醒来发现自己在医院里。

mysterious[4] [mɪ'stɪərɪəs] *a.* 神秘的,可疑的,难理解的

[巧记]mystery（神秘的事物）+ -ious（形容词后缀）→神秘的

[语境] There are many mysterious stories about the Egyptian pyramids.

关于埃及金字塔有许多神秘的故事。

[考点]词语辨析:mysterious 神秘的,有关神秘的;mystical 神秘主义的

myth[mɪθ] *n.* 神话

[语境]The story has points of resemblance to a Hebrew myth.

这个故事与某个希伯来神话有相似之处。

考点集训

1. There will be a fuss when the _____ get the hold of the story.
   A. media   B. medias
   C. medium   D. method

2. He could _____ nothing after he was hit on the head by a stranger.

A. memorial B. memory
C. memorize D. memorandum

3. Young MacDonald had better _____ his ways or he is going to end up in prison like his older brother.
   A. patch B. repair
   C. mend D. correct

4. He has made _____ of his life.
   A. a mess B. mess
   C. massed D. a mass

5. He has a very _____ manner with children but is much harder on adults.
   A. gentle B. mild
   C. soft D. moderate

6. His father received only a _____ share of the wealth from his grandfather.
   A. majority B. minor
   C. minority D. major

7. I don't want to miss _____ the film on television.
   A. seeing B. to see
   C. see D. seen

8. The young actress is very _____ about her success; she says it is as much the result of good luck as of her own talent.
   A. modern B. modest
   C. model D. moderate

9. The government had misjudged the _____ of the public and was not prepared for the storm of anger which greeted its new measures.
   A. temper B. mood
   C. humor D. vein

10. The government has a _____ on oil production in that country.
    A. monopoly B. monopolize
    C. monotonous D. monopolistic

11. She is still _____ for her dead daughter, five years after she was

killed in an accident.
A. mourning   B. weeping
C. moaning   D. wailing

12. There was still no news about her lost daughter after two days, and her anxieties _____.
    A. added up   B. added to
    C. multiplied   D. increased

13. I like her and I hope the feeling is _____.
    A. mature   B. mutual
    C. common   D. commune

14. The manager urged his staff not to _____ the splendid opportunity.
    A. drop   B. miss
    C. escape   D. slide

15. Mrs. Morris's daughter is pretty and _____, and many girls envy her.
    A. slender   B. light
    C. faint   D. minor

16. "This light is too _____ for me to read by. Don't we have a brighter bulb somewhere?" said the elderly man.
    A. mild   B. dim
    C. minute   D. slight

答案与解析

1. A 如果新闻媒介报道这一情况,事情就会弄大。medium在表示新闻媒介时,常作media,可以说 a media 或 the media, media 是 medium 的复数形式,后不能加 s。

2. C 他的头被陌生人猛击了一下就失去了记忆。memorial *a./n.* 纪念碑,纪念馆,纪念性的;memory *n.* 记忆;memorize *v.* 记住;memorandum *n.* 备忘录。

3. C 年轻的麦当劳最好改过自新,否则就会像他哥哥一样以坐牢而告终。patch 主要指修补;repair 指修理全部毁坏的东西;

correct 改正。

4. A 他把日子过得乱七八糟。make a mess of 把……弄得一团糟糕；mass 团，堆，块。

5. B 他对孩子的态度非常温和，而对成人的态度却生硬很多。gentle 温柔的，轻轻的；soft 软的，表示质地软；moderate 表示态度温和，稳健。

6. B 他的父亲只得到他祖父遗产的一小部分。minor 娇小的，其次的。

7. A 我不想错过在电视上看那部电影的机会。miss 后接动名词。

8. B 这位年轻的女演员对她的成功显得很谦虚，她说她的成功一半靠自己的天赋，一半也靠运气。modern 现代的；model 模特；moderate 温和的，适度的。

9. B 政府对公众的情绪判断错误，没料到它采取的新措施会遭到如此愤怒的反对。temper 性格，脾气；humor 幽默；vein 心情，意向，心思。

10. A 政府垄断了那个国家的石油生产。monopolize v. 垄断，专利；monotonous a. 单调的，千篇一律的；monopolistic a. 垄断的，独占的。

11. A 她还在为她死去的女儿伤心，五年前他女儿死于一场事故中。weep 哭泣，流泪；weep 呻吟；wail 痛哭，哭泣。

12. C 她的女儿失踪两天了，现在仍然没有找到，她更加焦急了。added up 把……加起来；added to……增加了；increase 增长。

13. B 我喜欢她，我也希望她能喜欢我。mature 成熟的；common 普通的，一般的；commune 福利社。

14. B 经理要求他的员工把握好的机会。A 丢掉；B 错过；C 逃跑；D 衰落。故选 B。

15. A 莫瑞斯夫人的女儿既苗条又漂亮，许多女孩很羡慕她。A 苗条的；B 轻的；C 软弱的，无勇气的；D 较小的，少数的。故选 A。

16. B 根据题干中 bright bulb，得知空格处应填入表示"暗"的词。mild 表示"温和的，温柔的，轻微的，适度的"；dim 表示"暗淡

281

的,模糊的,无光泽的";minute 表示"微小的,详细的";slight 表示"轻微的,微小的"。只有 dim 符合题意,答案为 B。

Word List 30

name[20] [neɪm] *n.* 名字,名称;名声,名望;名义;*vt.* 给……取名;列举;任命,提名

[语境] They changed the name of the street.

他们改了街道名称。

My mother insisted on naming me Horace.

我母亲坚持给我取名叫霍勒斯。

He had a name for good judgement.

他以判断准确而闻名。

namely ['neɪmlɪ] *ad.* 即,也就是

[语境] Only one boy was absent, namely Harry.

只有一个孩子缺席,就是哈利。

narrow ['næroʊ] *a.* 狭的,狭窄的;狭隘的

[巧记] 反义词:broad(*a.* 宽广的)

[语境] The street is too narrow to carry the big furniture in.

街道太窄了以致无法把这个大家具搬进去。

She has very narrow ideas about religion.

她对宗教的见解很狭隘。

[考点] a narrow escape 九死一生;narrow road 窄路;a narrow mind 心眼窄小;a narrow circle of friends 交际不广

nation[4] ['neɪʃən] *n.* 国家,民族

[语境] The President gave an address to the nation over the radio.

总统向全国发表广播演说。

national[22] ['næʃənəl] *a.* 民族的,国家的,国立的

[语境] A lot of work has been done in the recovery of national economy in the past few years.

在过去的几年中我们为了国民经济的恢复做了大量的工作。

[考点] national income 国民收入

native[8] [ˈneɪtɪv] *a.* **本地的,本国的;天生的** *n.* **本地人,本国人**

[巧记] 反义词:foreign(*n.* 外国人)

[语境] He has been away from his native Poland for three years.

他离开故土波兰已有三年了。

The kangaroo is a native of Australia.

袋鼠是产于澳洲的动物。

natural[27] [ˈnætʃərəl] *a.* **自然界的,天生的;天赋的,固有的**

[语境] Compared natural with artificial colour, you will find the difference of the cloth.

比较自然和人工的颜色,你就会发现布料的不同。

It is natural that such a hardworking student should pass the exam.

这么用功的学生考试及格是很自然的事。

[考点] by nature 天性地,天生地;naturally 当然,必然;nature 自然;naturalist 自然主义者

nature[18] [ˈneɪtʃə(r)] *n.* **自然界,大自然;性质,本性,天性**

[巧记] 派生词:naturalness(*n.* 自然性, 自然状态), naturally(*ad.* 自然地, 天生地, 以自然力)

[语境] Nature is at its best in spring.

春天里万物欣欣向荣。

Cats and dogs have quite different natures: dogs like company, cats are independent.

猫和狗的习性迥异——狗喜欢有伴,猫爱独来独往。

[考点] human nature 人性;人情

near [nɪə(r)] *a.* **近的,接近的;亲近的** *prep.* **靠近** *ad.* **接近**

[语境] The job is at last nearing completion.

这项工作终于快要完成了。

nearby [ˈnɪəbaɪ] *a./ad.* **附近**;*prep.* **在……附近**

[语境] From the reports of guns we knew that hunters must be nearby.

听枪声我们知道猎人必定在附近。

The firemen pulled down some nearby sheds to stop the fire spreading.

消防队员们把附近的一些棚子拉倒,以防火势蔓延。

nearly ['nɪəlɪ] *ad.* 差不多,几乎

[语境]The train was nearly full.

火车差不多满座了。

The matter concerns him nearly.

这事与他有密切关系。

[考点]not nearly 相差甚远

neat [niːt] *a.* 整洁的,干净的,优美的,精致的

[巧记]反义词:dirty(*a.* 肮脏的);untidy(*a.* 不整齐的,懒惰的)

[语境]She laid her dress on the bed to keep it neat.

她把连衣裙放在床上以保持平整。

Your new car is a neat little job, isn't it?

你这辆新汽车很精巧哇,是吧?

[考点]neat as a new pin 十分整洁的

necessary ['nesəsərɪ] *a.* 必需的,必要的;必然的

[语境] The necessary outcome of a war is a fall in production.

战争带来的必然结果就是生产力下降。

I feel it is absolutely necessary.

我觉得这是绝对必要的。

[考点] be in necessity 处于贫困的境地;bow to necessity 处于被迫;under the necessity of 不得不,被迫

neck[nek] *n.* 颈,脖子

[语境]The girl twined her arms about her mother's neck.

女孩搂住母亲的脖子。

need [niːd] *aux./v.* 需要;必须 *n.* 需要;贫困,困窘

[语境]I need to make a phone call.

我需要打个电话。

neglect[6] [nɪ'glekt] *vt.* 疏忽,忽视

[巧记]派生词:neglectful(*a.* 疏忽的,不注意的);同义词:ignore

(v. 不顾,不理会;驳回;忽视)

[语境] He often neglect to forget opening the window.

他经常忘记关窗户。

Don't neglect to lock the door when you leave.

你走时别忘了锁门。

[考点] neglect 后面经常跟动词不定式或动名词形式。

negotiate [nɪˈgəʊʃɪeɪt] *v.* **谈判,交涉,商议**

[语境] We've decided to negotiate a loan with them.

我们决定和他们商定贷款之事。

[考点] negotiate sth. with sb. 与某人商议某事

neighbo(u)r [ˈneɪbə(r)] *n.* **邻居**

[语境] I heard about it at first hand from my neighbor.

我是直接从我的邻居那里听来的。

neither [ˈnaɪðə(r), ˈniːðə(r)] *a.* **两者都不的** *pron.* **两者都不** *ad.* **也不**

[巧记] 反义词:either(*a.* 任一,两方的 *ad.* 也,而且;根本)

[语境] We are going to play neither basketball nor volleyball.

我们既不打篮球也不打排球。

A zero rate of inflation is neither a realistic goal nor necessarily desirable.

通货膨胀率为零,这既不是现实的目标,也不一定合乎需要。

[考点] neither...nor... 既不……也不……

nephew [ˈnefju] *n.* **侄儿,外甥**

[语境] I am planning a 25th birthday party for my nephew.

我在为侄子筹划他 25 岁的生日聚会。

nerve [nɜːv] *n.* **神经;勇气,胆量**

[语境] Perhaps his nerve is naturally too dull to admit of any excitation.

大概他的神经天生就很迟钝以至不容有任何刺激。

He never got up enough nerve to meet me.

他从来没有足够的胆量来见我。

[考点] get on sb.'s nerves 使某人心烦,使某人不安 lose one's

nerve 不知所措

nervous[4] [ˈnɜːvəs] *a.* 紧张的,不安的;神经的;神经过敏的

[巧记] 派生词:nervousness(*n.* 神经质,胆小,焦躁)

[语境] He was nervous before the plane trip.

乘飞机旅行前他紧张不安。

[考点] be nervous of/about…有点害怕;make one nervous 使人发愁,使人不耐烦

never [ˈnevə(r)] *ad.* 永不,从不,决不;从来没有;不,没有

[语境] I have never seen him before.

我从没见过他。

nevertheless [ˌnevəðəˈles] *conj.* 然而,不过 *ad.* 仍然,不过

[语境] The news may be unexpected;nevertheless,it's true.

这消息也许是出乎预料,但它是真的。

The experiment failed. It was,nevertheless,worth making.

试验没有成功,尽管如此,还是值得做的。

[考点] nevertheless 作副词,一般都用逗号隔开。

new [njuː] *a.* 新(近)的;新来的;不熟悉的;没经验的

[语境] I'll just sew up that tear, and the coat will be as good as new.

我把大衣的破处缝好,就会完好如新了。

news [njuːz] *n.* 新闻,消息;新闻报道,新闻广播

[语境] He spread the news around the town.

他在镇上到处传播这一消息。

[考点] news agency 通讯社;news flash 简讯

newspaper [ˈnjuːspeɪpə(r)] *n.* 报纸

[语境] He unfurled the newspaper and began to read.

他展开报纸开始阅读。

next [nekst] *a.* 紧接的,其次的;贴近的 *ad.* 其次;居后

[语境] May I bring my chair next to yours?

我可以把我的椅子移到你的旁边吗?

nice [naɪs] *a.* 美好的,令人愉快的;友好的,亲切的

[语境] It's nice meeting you.

很高兴认识你。

niece[niːs] *n.* **侄女,外甥女**

[语境]He adopts his niece as his heiress.

他指定他的侄女为继承人。

night[naɪt] *n.* **夜,夜晚**

[语境]They broke into our house under cloud of night.

他们趁黑闯进了我们的房子。

[考点]at night 在晚上;good night 晚安

nine[naɪn] *num.* **九**

[语境]The schoolmaster requested a meeting at nine o'clock in the morning.

校长要求早上九点钟开会。

nineteen[ˌnaɪnˈtiːn] *num.* **十九**

[语境]Perseverance is failing nineteen times and succeeding the twentieth.

十九次失败,直到第二十次才获成功,这就是坚持。

ninety [ˈnaɪntɪ] *num.* **九十,九十个**

[语境]Over ninety countries ratify an agreement to ban the use of these chemicals.

九十多个国家批准了一项禁止使用这些化学品的协议。

no[nəʊ] *a.* **没有;并非;不许;完全不是** *ad.* **不,不是,没有,毫不**

[语境]There is no access to the street through that door.

那个门不通向大街。

Yesterday no fewer than thirty climbers reached the summit.

昨天至少30名攀登者登上了顶峰。

noble [ˈnəʊbl] *a.* **高尚的;贵族的,高贵的** *n.* **贵族**

[巧记] 派生词:nobleness(*n.* 高贵, 高尚, 崇高);同义词:great, important

[语境] Her gestures and movements were distinguished by a noble and stately grace.

她的举动和姿势很出色,显示出一种高贵和端庄的魅力。

Marriage is a noble institution.

结婚是种庄严的仪式。

nobody [ˈnəubədɪ] *n.* 没有人,谁也不

[语境] Nobody was keen to take on such a thankless task.
没有人愿意承担这种费力不讨好的任务。

noise [nɔɪz] *n.* 喧闹声,噪声,吵嚷声

[巧记] 派生词:noisy(*a.* 喧闹的,嘈杂的),noiseless(*a.* 无声的;噪声小的)

[语境] The least noise would startle the timid child.
最小的响声也会吓着这个胆小的孩子的。

It was noised about that the foreign minister intended to resign.
外界传说外交部长打算辞职。

noisy [ˈnɔɪzɪ] *a.* 吵闹的

[巧记] 派生词:noise(*n.* 噪声),make a noise 吵闹,喧哗

[语境] His daughter was very active and noisy in the mornings.
他的女儿一到上午就很好动,吵吵闹闹的。

none [nʌn] *pron.* 没有任何人(东西);都不 *ad.* 一点也不

[语境] I wanted some string but there was none in the house.
我需要一些绳子,但家里一根也没有。

He is none the worse for it.
即使这样他也一点也不在乎。

For all his years, he is none the less vigorous and active.
他虽年老,但仍然生气勃勃、精神旺盛。

[考点] none but 只有;none other than 不是别的;正是……;none the less 仍然;none the worse 依然如故;并不更差

nonsense [ˈnɒnsəns] *n.* 胡说,废话

[巧记] non(否定) + sense(意义)→说没有意义的话→胡说,废话

[语境] Most orthodox doctors however dismiss this as complete nonsense.
但大多数传统的医生认为此说法完全是胡说八道。

noon [nu:n] *n.* 正午,中午

[语境] The Prime Minister is scheduled to arrive at noon.

首相定于中午到达。

[考点] at noon 在中午

nor [nɔː(r)] *conj./ad.* **也不,也没有**

[语境] At any rate, there is neither room nor claim for me.

不管怎么样,我是既没余地又没权利了。

The story is neither interesting nor instructive.

这个故事既不有趣,也没有教育意义。

[考点] (用在 neither 之后)也不;(用在 not, no, never 之后)也不;(用在句首,句子需倒装)也不

normal[11] [ˈnɔːməl] *a.* **正常的,标准的;正规的;精神健全的**

[语境] She refused to conform to the normal social conventions.

她拒绝遵从常规的社会习俗。

It was several days before the floodwater sank and life returned to normal.

过了几天,洪水才退,生活才恢复正常。

normally [ˈnɔːməlɪ] *ad.* **一般地;通常**

[语境] The abdominal aorta is normally smaller than the thoracic aorta.

腹主动脉一般比胸主动脉小。

I normally do all my shopping on Saturdays.

我通常在星期六买东西。

north [nɔːθ] *a./n.* **北,北方** *ad.* **向/自/在北方**

[语境] Birds usually migrate from north to south.

鸟类通常由北向南迁徙。

They were coming in to land on the north coast of Crete.

他们将从克里特岛北海岸登陆上岛。

nose [nəʊz] *n.* **鼻子**

[语境] The eyes, nose and mouth are parts of the face.

眼、鼻子、嘴都是脸的组成部分。

not [nɒt] *ad.* **不,没,不是**

[语境] You should not humiliate her in public.

你不应该在公共场合出她的丑。

notebook [ˈnəʊtbʊk] *n.* 笔记本；笔记本电脑

[巧记] note(笔记) + book(本)→记笔记的本→笔记本

[语境] Copy this page in your notebook.

把这一页抄到你的笔记本上。

nothing [ˈnʌθɪŋ] *pron.* 没有东西,什么也没有；无,小事 *n.* 微不足道的人或事

[语境] I've done nothing much since coffee time.

咖啡时间过后,我什么都没干。

She kept bursting into tears over nothing at work.

她老是为工作上微不足道的事儿哭鼻子。

notice [ˈnəʊtɪs] *n.* 通知,通告,布告；注意,认识 *v.* 注意到,注意

[巧记] not = know,表示"知道,注意"

[语境] A notice was nailed up on the church door.

一张布告被钉在教堂的门上。

Can you be ready at short notice?

你能一接到通知马上就准备好吗?

[考点] notice board 布告栏

novel [ˈnɒvl] *n.* 长篇小说

[语境] She spent a peaceful afternoon by the river, reading a novel.

她在河边看小说,度过了一个宁静的下午。

November [nə(ʊ)ˈvembə(r)] *n.* 十一月

[语境] It happened on November first.

这件事发生在 11 月 1 日。

now [naʊ] *ad.* 现在,当前,如今；这时候；现在就,马上；[用以改变口气,加强语气]

[语境] But we are now a much more fragmented society.

但我们现在所处的是一个更加四分五裂的社会。

I'm sorry, but I must go now.

很抱歉我得马上走了。

nowadays [ˈnaʊədeɪz] *ad.* 现今,现在

[语境] Nowadays it is very easy to earn a living.

现今谋生很容易。

nuclear[31] [ˈnjuːklɪə(r)] *a.* 核心的,中心的;原子核的,核能的

[巧记] 同义词:atomic

[语境] The most terrifying aspect of nuclear bombing is radiation.
核弹轰炸最可怕的一面是辐射。

This old man is a famous nuclear physicist.
这位老人是一位著名的核物理学家。

[考点] nuclear family 核心家庭;基本家庭;小家庭

number [ˈnʌmbə(r)] *n.* 数,数字,数量,号码,一群 *v.* 共计,编号

[语境] The number of your fingers is ten.
你双手手指的总数是10。

nurse [nɜːs] *n.* 护士,保姆,保育员

[语境] She had spent 29 years as a nurse.
她做了29年的护士。

考点集训

1. He has 3 sons, _____ , Tom, Jack and Sam.
   A. namely   B. such as
   C. for example   D. likely

2. There is no _____ to buy tickets in advance.
   A. necessary   B. necessity
   C. necessaries   D. necessitation

3. Hoping to calm our _____ , we decided to spend the afternoon at the lake.
   A. nerves   B. nerve
   C. mind   D. spirit

4. _____ countries refuse to be drawn into the cold war.
   A. Fair   B. Neutral
   C. Unprejudiced   D. Objective

5. I can't go. _____ , I appreciate the invitation.
   A. Nevertheless   B. But
   C. In spite of   D. Despite

6. His growth is _____ for the age.

  A. normal   B. natural
  C. ordinary   D. regular
7. The fireman had a _____ escape when a staircase collapsed beneath his feet.
  A. close   B. narrow
  C. hard   D. near

答案与解析

1. A　他有3个儿子,即汤姆、杰克和赛姆。such as 表示举例,不列出所有例子;for example 后面常跟句子;likely a. 可能的;namely 列出所有例子。

2. B　没有必要提前买票。There is no necessity 后一般接 to do 或 doing;necessity 表示必要的事;necessitation 指"被迫,迫使"。

3. A　为了使我们紧张的神经放松,我们决定在湖边度过一个下午。nerve 用复数形式表示神经过敏,神经紧张;nerve 作为不可数名词,表示勇气,精力。

4. B　中立的国家拒绝加入冷战。fair 公正的,公平的;unprejudiced 无偏见的;objective 客观的。

5. A　我不能去。不过,我感谢这一邀请。but 不能用逗号隔开,in spite of 后面要跟宾语,despite 后面也要跟名词或动名词作宾语。

6. A　按年龄来说,他的发育是正常的。natural 自然的;ordinary 普通的,一般的;regular 有规律的,合乎某项规则的。

7. B　虽然消防员脚下的楼梯坍塌,消防员却幸免于难。A 近的,亲密的;B 窄的,勉强的;C 艰难的,硬的;D 附近的。have a narrow escape 为固定搭配,故选 B。

核心词汇精解

Word List 31

o'clock [ə'klɒk] *ad.* ……点钟
[语境] Now it is 9 o'clock.
现在是9点钟。

object[28] ['ɒbdʒɪkt] *n.* 物体;对象;目的
[语境] Some people objected that the new tax law was unfair.
一些人反对说,新税法不公平。
Various objects were on the table.
桌子上摆着各种各样的物体。
[考点] no object 没有困难,不成问题

objective[13] [əb'dʒektɪv] *n.* 目标,目的 *a.* 客观的
[语境] We have succeeded in our main objectives.
我们已经成功地达到了主要目标。
All our objectives were gained.
我们要夺取的军事目标均已拿下。
[考点] be objective about 对……很客观

observation[4] [ˌɒbzə'veɪʃn] *n.* 观察,观测,监视;(*pl.*) 观察资料;观察力
[巧记] 词根:observe(观察) + ation(名词后缀)→观察
[语境] He was taken into hospital for observation.
他被送进医院观察。
[考点] observation post 观测站

observe[11] [əb'zɜːv] *vt.* 观察,注意到,看到,遵守,奉行,说,评论
[巧记] 派生词:observing(*a.* 观察力敏锐的;注意观察的)
[语境] The police have been observing his movements.
警方一直监视着他的一举一动。
We should observe the proprieties.
我们应该遵守礼节。
[考点] observe sb. do sth. 看到某人做某事

obtain[14] [əbˈteɪn] *vt.* 获得,得到; *vi.* 通行,通用;流行,存在

[巧记] 派生词:obtainable(*a.* 能得到的;可到手的),obtainment(*n.* 获得,得到)

[语境] Where can I obtain a copy of her latest book?
在哪里能买到她最新出版的书?
These conditions no longer obtain.
这些条件已不复存在了。

obvious [ˈɒbvɪəs] *a.* 明显的,显而易见的

[巧记] 反义词:obscure(*a.* 微暗的,含糊的,难解的);同义词:clear

[语境] The merits of the scheme are quite obvious.
该计划的可取之处是相当明显的。
The embassy is an obvious target for terrorist attacks.
大使馆是恐怖分子攻击的明显目标。

[考点] It is obvious that = Obviously 明显地

obviously [ˈɒbvɪəslɪ] *ad.* 明显地,显然

[语境] He obviously enjoyed his work.
很明显,他喜欢他的工作。

occasion[12] [əˈkeɪʒən] *n.* 场合,时节,时刻;时机,机会

[巧记] 派生词:occasional(*a.* 偶然的,备不时之需的,临时的),occasionally(*ad.* 偶尔,间或)

[语境] I've met her on several occasions recently.
我最近见到过她好几次。
He was impeccably dressed for the occasion.
他的穿着在那种场合非常得体。

[考点] dressed for the occasion 穿着得体

occasional [əˈkeɪʒənl] *a.* 偶然的,不时的

[语境] The weather was good except for an occasional shower.
除下了一阵大雨外,天气还是很好的。

[考点] occasional, uncommon, scarce, rare 辨析:这些形容词均含"稀罕的,很少发生"之意。occasional:指偶然、不时或间或发生的事,侧重无规律可循。uncommon:指一般不发生或

很少发生的事情,故显得独特、异常与例外。scarce:指暂时不易发现、不存在或数量不足、供不应求的东西。rare:指难得发生的事或难遇见的人或事,侧重特殊性

occupation[ˌɒkjʊˈpeɪʃən] *n.* 占领;职业,工作

[语境] Prii had become fluent in German during the Wehrmacht's occupation of Estonia in 1942.
在1942年德军侵占爱沙尼亚期间,普里学得了一口流利的德语。
I haven't entered up your name and occupation yet.
我尚未记下你的名字和职业。

occupy[ˈɒkjʊpaɪ] *vt.* 占领,占据;使忙碌,使从事

[巧记] 派生词:occupied(*a.* 已占用的;无空闲的;在使用的)
[语境] Many problems occupied his mind.
他脑子里装着许多问题。
The striking office workers have occupied the whole building.
罢工的办公室人员占据了整座建筑物。
[考点] be occupied with/in doing sth. 忙于做某事

occur[21] [əˈkɜː(r)] *vi.* 发生,出现;(to) 想起,想到

[巧记] 同义词:come about, happen
[语境] Didn't it occur to you that he was lying?
你当时没想到他在撒谎吗?
That plane crash occurred only minutes after take-off.
飞机在起飞几分钟后就发生了空难。
[考点] occur to 想到,被想起

ocean[ˈəʊʃən] *n.* 海洋

[语境] The Indian Ocean is on the south of Asia.
印度洋位于亚洲南部。

October[ɒkˈtəʊbə(r)] *n.* 十月

[语境] The number of tourists starts to tail off in October.
游客在十月份开始逐渐减少。

of [ɒv, əv] *prep.* ……的;在……之中;用……制的;关于……的

[语境] I'm under a lot of pressure.

我的压力很大。

off [ɒf] *ad.* 离开;在远处;脱开 *prep.* 从,从……离开

[语境]We went to the station to see her off.

我们去车站为她送行。

offence/-se [əˈfens] *n.* 犯罪,犯规,过错;冒犯,触怒

[语境]Because it was his first offence, the punishment wasn't too severe.

由于他是初犯,惩罚较轻。

We have had our differences and I'm sorry if it has caused offence.

我们有过一些分歧,如有得罪我很抱歉。

offend [əˈfend] *vt.* 冒犯,触犯,得罪;使不快,使恼火

[巧记]派生词:offending(*a.* 惹是生非的,烦扰的,引起问题的;犯罪的),offender(*n.* 罪犯,得罪人的人,无礼的人)

[语境] She was offended at his remarks.

她被他的话惹恼了。

[考点] offend sb. 冒犯某人;be offended with/by sb. for sth. 因某事对某人生气;offend the ear 违反习惯

offensive [əˈfensɪv] *a.* 冒犯的,攻击的 *n.* 攻势,进攻

[巧记]词根:fend,fens = strike,表示"打击"

[语境] You will find it difficult to explain away your use of offensive language.

你使用这样无礼的语言是很难说得过去的。

In early March the Pathet Lao were ready to take the offensive.

三月初,Pathet Lao 准备发动攻势。

offer[8] [ˈɒfə(r)] *v.* 提出,提供;愿意做;奉献

[语境] I'll offer you 10 pounds for this book.

我出10英镑买你这本书。

Ask her about it when a suitable moment offers itself.

这个问题你在适当的时候问问她吧。

[考点] on offer 出售的; under offer 已经有人出价了

office [ˈɒfɪs] *n.* 办公室,办事处;职务,公职;部,局,处

[语境] He keeps his office neat and tidy.

他保持办公室清洁整齐。

officer [ˈɒfɪsə(r)] *n.* 工作人员,公务员;军官

[巧记] office(办公室) + er(人)→在办公室工作的人→公务员

[语境] The company's welfare officer deals with employee's personal problems.

公司负责福利的工作人员处理雇员的个人问题。

He pulled out the pistol and aimed at the enemy officer.

他拔出手枪,瞄准敌军官。

official [əˈfɪʃəl] *a.* 官方的,正式的 *n.* 官员,行政官员

[巧记] 词根:office(办公室,部,局,处) + ial

[语境] He is a pompous official.

他是个自命不凡的官员。

I happen to have the official statistics with me.

我碰巧身边有官方的统计数字。

[考点] official language 官方语言

often [ˈɒfən] *ad.* 常常,经常,通常

[语境] American girls are often very pretty.

美国女孩通常很漂亮。

How often do you go there?

你多长时间去一次那里?

oh [əʊ] *int.* 哦

[语境] Oh, I'm so glad you're here.

哦,你在这儿我太高兴了。

oil [ɔɪl] *n.* 油,石油;*vt.* 涂油,上油

[语境] The company buys and sells about 600,000 barrels of oil a day.

该公司每天买卖约60万桶石油。

The leather may need to be oiled every two to three weeks in order to retain its suppleness.

为了保持皮革的柔韧性,可能两三周就要上一次油。

okay/okey/OK/O.K. *a./ad.* 可以,不错,很好 *int.* 对,好,行 *n.* 同意

[语境]Is it okay if I come by myself?

我一个人来行吗?

We are ready to start flying to Britain as soon as we get the okay.

一旦获得批准,我们就随即启程飞往英国。

old [əuld] *a.* 年老的;……岁的;长时间的,老的;过去的

[语境]How old are you?

你多大了?

Don't play old tricks!

别玩老一套的把戏了!

omit [ə'mɪt] *vt.* 省略,省去;遗漏,忽略

[巧记]同义词:miss *v.* 遗漏

[语境] He omitted to state his reasons.

他没有叙述自己的理由。

Don't omit locking the door.

别忘了锁门。

[考点]omit to do/doing sth. 忘了做某事

on [ɒn] *a.* 连接上 *prep.* 在……上;靠近 *ad.* 向前,继续

[语境]The doctor put me on these tablets.

医生让我服用这些药片。

The strike has been on now for six weeks.

罢工至今已进行六个星期了。

once [wʌns] *ad.* 一次,曾经 *conj.* 一(旦)……就…… *n.* 一次

[语境]Be pleasant to each other just this once.

彼此要和睦些——就只为这一次吧。

The film is at once humorous and moving.

这部电影既幽默又动人。

one [wʌn] *num.* 一,一个 *pron.* 一个人;任何人 *a.* 一个的;某一……的;同一……的

[语境]They had three sons and one daughter.

他们有3个儿子,1个女儿。

It seems that the fifth man is one John Cairncross.

第五位好像是一个名叫约翰·凯恩克罗斯的人。

oneself [wʌn'self] *pron.* 自己,自身;亲自

[语境]To work one must have time to oneself.

一个人要工作就必须有属于自己的时间。

It is a very rewarding exercise to work this out oneself.

独自解决这个问题是一次受益匪浅的锻炼。

online [ˌɒn'laɪn] *a.* 联机;在线

[语境]We planned to build an online database.

我们计划建一个联机数据库。

You can chat to other people who are online.

你可以和其他在线的人聊天。

only ['əʊnlɪ] *ad.* 仅仅,只不过 *a.* 唯一的 *conj.* 可是,不过

[语境]The book is likely to be useful, only it's rather expensive.

这本书可能有用,只是相当贵。

open ['əʊpən] *n.* 公开,户外 *a.* 开的,开放的 *v.* 开

[语境]Another supermarket opened last week.

上星期又有一家超级市场开张了。

I'm not convinced your idea will work, but I'll keep an open mind for the moment.

我还没想通是否你的意见可行,不过我先考虑一下。

openly ['əʊpənlɪ] *ad.* 公然地,公开地;直率地,坦白地

[巧记]同义词:frankly,freely (*ad.* 公开地,坦率地)

[语境]He speaks more and more openly about his problem.

他越来越公开地谈他的问题了。

Talking to children openly will also help them overcome fears.

请坦率地与儿童沟通交流,这样可帮助他们战胜恐慌。

operate ['ɒpəreɪt] *v.* 操作,运转,开动,起作用,动手术

[巧记]operating(*a.* 操作的;业务上的;营运的;外科手术的);同义词:act

[语境] The new law operates to destroy our advantages.

这项新法律损害我们的利益。

The surgeon operated on her for appendicitis.

外科医生为她做阑尾切除手术。

operation [ˌɒpəˈreɪʃən] *n.* 运转,开动,操作,手术,运算,经营

[巧记] 词根:operate + ion

[语境] The surgeon has performed the operation.
外科医生做了手术。
The gown a surgeon wears during an operation is usually green.
外科医生在做手术时穿的手术服通常是绿色的。

opinion [əˈpɪnɪən] *n.* 意见,主张,看法

[语境] What's your opinion of the new President?
你对新总统有什么看法?
What's your opinion of the motion?
你认为这项提议怎样?

[考点] be of the opinion that... 主张……,认为……;in one's opinion 在某人看来;have a good/bad/high/low opinion 对某人有好/坏/高/低的评价

opportunity[5] [ˌɒpəˈtjuːnətɪ] *n.* 机会

[巧记] 同义词:chance

[语境] Showoffs never miss an opportunity to draw attention to themselves by some outrageous novelty.
爱显示自己的人遇事总喜欢标新立异。
There may be an opportunity for you to see the chairman of the board tomorrow.
明天你也许有机会见到董事长。

[考点] + of/for; + to do ……机会;……良机

oppose[5] [əˈpəʊz] *v.* 反对,使对立,使对抗,使相对

[巧记] 派生词:opposed(*a.* 反对的,对抗的,敌对的);反义词:agree

[语境] The rabbles met on the square to oppose their new mayor.
平民们在广场上集会反对他们的新市长。
Quakers strongly oppose violence and war.
教友派信徒们强烈反对暴力和战争。

opposite [ˈɒpəzɪt] *a.* 对面的,对立的;相反的 *n.* 对立物,对立面 *prep.* 在……对面

[巧记] 派生词：opposition（n. 反对，相反，敌对），oppositional（adj. 反对的；对抗的）

[语境] I sat opposite to him during the meal.
吃饭的时候我坐他的对面。
Have you seen the house opposite the railway station?
你看到火车站对面的房子了吗？
We have opposite views on this.
我们对此有相反的看法。
In fact, he's absolutely, to me, the opposite of arrogant.
其实，对我而言，他绝对是（站在）自大的对立面。

[考点] be opposite to 与……正好相反

optimistic[4] [ˌɒptɪˈmɪstɪk] *a.* 乐观（主义）的

[语境] But this could also be too optimistic.
但是，这样也可能过于乐观。

[考点] be optimistic about 对……持乐观态度

or [ə(r), ɔː(r)] *conj.* 或，或者（表示选择）；即，大约；否则

[语境] I don't care whether I get it or not.
我不在乎我是否可以得到它。

oral [ˈɔːrəl] *a.* 口头的，口的

[语境] He lucked out on the oral examination.
他侥幸通过了口语考试。

orange [ˈɒrɪndʒ] *n.* 橙，橘

[语境] The orange skin squirted in my eye.
橘皮汁喷进了我的眼睛。

orbit [ˈɔːbɪt] *n.* 轨道；*v.* 做轨道运行

[语境] They successfully lofted a spaceship into orbit.
他们成功地将一艘宇宙飞船射入轨道。
This is a satellite in orbit round the Earth.
这是一绕地球轨道运行的人造卫星。

[考点] into orbit（非正式）进入表演（或行动的）最佳状态；勃然大怒；万分激动

order [ˈɔːdə(r)] *n.* 命令；次序；整齐；订货单；等级 *v.* 定制，订购

[巧记]ordered(a.有条理的,整齐的),orderliness(n.整洁;规律;整齐)

[语境] The chairman ordered silence.

主席要求大家安静。

The social order of ants is very interesting.

蚂蚁的社会结构非常有趣。

[考点] order for 订购;订货

ordinary [ˈɔːdənəri] *a.* **平常,普通;平凡,平淡**

[巧记] 派生词:ordinarily(*ad.* 通常,大概,普通)

[语境] Now electrical appliances have entered into ordinary families.

现在家用电器已经步入普通家庭。

At that time they could not produce ordinary garments, not to speak of high-grade ones.

那时他们连普通衣服都不能生产,更不要说高级的了。

organization/-sation[18] [ˌɔːɡənaɪˈzeɪʃən] *n.* **组织,体制;团体,机构**

[语境]They posted this organization as corrupt.

他们公开谴责该组织腐败。

The charitable organization parted food among claimants.

慈善机构把食品分配给每个要求者。

organize/-ise[11] [ˈɔːɡənaɪz] *v.* **组织,编组**

[巧记] 派生词:organized(*a.*有组织的),organizer(*n.*组织者)

[语境] He has so organized his life that his wife suspects nothing.

他把生活安排得井井有条,为的是不让妻子有任何怀疑。

The department was badly organized until she took charge (of it).

这个部门在她负责以前组织工作做得很差。

[考点]arrange 指排成合意的或正确的顺序;organize 是指整理成便于工作的次序;plan 是指勾画出一地方或工程等的图样

origin[17] [ˈɔrɪdʒɪn] *n.* **起源,由来;出身,血统**

[巧记] 同义词:birth

[语境] He is a Dane by origin.

他原籍丹麦。

The social unrest has its origins in economic problems.

社会动荡是经济问题引起的。

[考点] original *a.* 起源的,由来的

The original picture is in the British Museum.

这幅画的原作在大英博物馆内。

other [ˈʌðə(r)] *a.* **另外的,其他的** *n./pron.* **另一个人(或事)**

[语境] The other students in my class are from Italy.

我班其余同学都是意大利人。

She is more clever than the other girls in her class.

她比班上其他任何女孩子都聪明。

otherwise [ˈʌðəwaɪz] *ad.* **另样,用别的方法;在其他方面** *conj.* **要不然**

[巧记] 词根:other 另外的

[语境] Seize the chance, otherwise you'll regret it.

抓住这个机会,否则你会后悔的。

You'd better give me my book, otherwise I'll fail my test.

你最好把我的书给我,否则我的测验将要不及格了。

[考点] otherwise 用作连词,意思为"否则;要不然",相当于 or,or else 或 if not;otherwise 用作副词,意为"另外;别样";意为"相反地;要不然;否则",相当于 in the other way 或 on the contrary

ought to 应该,应当;本应,本当

[语境] I think I ought to cut in on what they are doing.

我认为对他们现在干的事我应当进行干预。

our [aʊə(r)] *pron.* **我们的**

[语境] She spread our lunch on the grass.

她在草地上摆好了我们的午饭。

ours [aʊəz] *pron.* **我们的(东西)**

[语境] His opinion jarred with ours.

他的意见与我们的不一致。

ourselves [ˌaʊəˈselvz] *pron.* **我们自己**

[语境]We must rely on ourselves.

我们必须依靠自己。

out [aʊt] *ad.* **出去;离家;突出来** *a.* **外面的,往外去的**

[语境]The fire has gone out.

火已熄灭。

His book came out last month.

他的书上个月出版了。

outdoor [ˈaʊtdɔː(r)] *a.* **室外的,野外的**

[巧记]out(外面的) + door(门口) = 室外的,野外的

[语境]I never imagined that an outdoor life could do so much for a man! It's taken years off him.

我从未想到户外生活对一个人能起这么大的作用！这种生活使他年轻多了。

I'm very keen on outdoor sports.

我非常喜欢室外运动。

[考点]outdoor sports 室外运动

outdoors [ˌaʊtˈdɔːz] *ad.* **室外的,野外的**

[巧记]out(外面的) + doors(门口) = 室外地,野外地

[语境]She's outdoors gardening every afternoon.

她每天下午都在户外搞园艺。

Children of all ages should be outdoors several hours a day.

各个年龄段的孩子每天都应户外活动几个小时。

outer [ˈaʊtə(r)] *a.* **外部的,外层的,外表的**

[语境]Imagine that you and I go in outer space.

设想一下你和我将到外太空去。

outline[1] [ˈaʊtlaɪn] *n.* **轮廓,略图;大纲,梗概** *v.* **概述,略述**

[巧记] out + line 线条→画出线条→大纲

[语境] She drew the outline with a sure hand.

她笔力雄健地画出了轮廓。

Draw an outline before you fill in the details.

先画轮廓,再画细部。

[考点] give an outline of 概要说明；描绘……的轮廓；make an

outline of 为……拟出提纲

output [ˈaʊtpʊt] *n.* **产量,输出(量)**

[巧记] 同义词:harvest(*n.* 收获;收成,产量)

[语境] This country ranks last in industrial output.

这个国家的工业生产排名排在最后。

Due to low investment, our industrial output has remained stagnant.

由于投资少,我们的工业生产一直停滞不前。

outside [ˌaʊtˈsaɪd,'--] *a./n.* **外面,外部** *ad.* **向外,在外** *prep.* **在……外**

[语境] National policies should not be determined by outside influence.

国家政策的制定不该受外部影响。

Don't stay outside in the damp.

别待在外面的潮湿空气中。

outstanding [ˌaʊtˈstændɪŋ] *a.* **突出的,显著的,杰出的**

[巧记] out-出 + stand 站 + -ing……的:站出来的→ 突出的

[语境] He has many outstanding gifts.

他多才多艺。

Several clubs have already staked a/their claim to this outstanding young footballer.

有几个足球俱乐部均表示这个年轻的足球健将是他们的人。

[考点] balance outstanding 结余

over [ˈəʊvə(r)] *ad.* **在上方;遍及地** *prep.* **在……上方** *a.* **结束的**

[语境] He sprinkled sugar over his cereal.

他在麦片粥里撒上了糖。

By the time we arrived the meeting was over.

我们到达时,会议已结束了。

Take these letters over to the post office.

把这些信送到对面邮局去。

overall⁴ [ˌəʊvərˈɔːl] *a.* **全面的,综合的** *n.* **(*pl.*)(套头)工作服**

[巧记] over + all

[语境] Overall, the tone of the book is satirical/the book is satirical in tone.

总的说来,这本书是带讽刺性的。

The overall composition of the picture is good but some of the detail is distracting.

这幅画的构图不错,但有些细微处稍显喧宾夺主。

overcome[6] [ˌəʊvəˈkʌm] v. 战胜,克服

[巧记] over 在……上 + come 来

[语境] There are many obstacles to overcome.

有很多障碍需要克服。

[考点] overcome difficulties 战胜困难;overcome one's shortcomings 克服缺点

overlook [ˌəʊvəˈlʊk] v./n. 看漏,忽略;俯瞰,眺望;宽容,放任

[巧记] over-上 + look 看→由上往下看

[语境] It was a slight overlook on my part.

这是我的小疏忽。

My room overlooked the garden.

我的房间俯瞰花园。

overseas[9] [ˌəʊvəˈsiːz] a. 外国的,海外的 ad. 在海外

[巧记] 同义词:abroad(海外的)

[语境] The firm is working on a new product in combination with several overseas partners.

公司正在联合几家海外合伙人制造新产品。

Over the years, hundreds of overseas students have studied at that university.

几年来,几百个留学生在那所大学学习过。

overthrow [ˌəʊvəˈθrəʊ] vt. 推翻,颠覆

[巧记] over(侧,倾) + throw(扔出,抛出)→推翻,颠覆

[语境] The tyrant was overthrown.

暴君被打倒了。

owe [əʊ] v. 欠(债等),应向……付出,归功于,得感谢

[巧记] 派生词:owing(a. 由于;未付的;该付的);同义词:pay

(n. 薪水；工资 v. 付，支付)

[语境] He owes his success more to luck than to ability.
他认为他的成功是靠运气而不是因为自己有能力。
I owe a lot to my wife and children.
我很感激我的妻子和孩子。

[考点] owe it to oneself 认为自己有必要[不得不]，认为自己有责任；owe sth. to 把……归功于；为……而应感谢

own[55] [əʊn] a. (用在所有格后面，加强语气) 自己的

[巧记] 同义词：have

[语境] Nobody owned up to the theft.
这件偷窃事没有人承认是自己干的。
Although her father is in the firm she got the job on her own.
尽管她父亲也在公司里工作，但她那份工作却是靠自己得到的。

[考点] own to 承认，坦白地承认

owner [ˈəʊnə(r)] n. 物主，所有者

[语境] He denied doing any harm to the owner.
他否认坑害过物主。

考点集训

1. Though she began her _____ by singing in a local pop group, she is now a famous Hollywood movie star.
   A. employment   B. career
   C. occupation   D. profession

2. He is _____ about his chances of winning a gold medal in the Olympics next year.
   A. optimistic   B. optional
   C. outstanding   D. obvious

3. Petrol is refined from the _____ oil we take out of the ground.
   A. fresh   B. original
   C. rude   D. crude

4. You would be _____ a risk to let your child go to school by him-

self.

A. omitting B. attaching
C. affording D. running

5. He didn't have time to read the report word for word; he just _____ it.

A. skimmed B. observed
C. overlooked D. glanced

6. The _____ goal of the book is to help bridge the gap between research and teaching, particularly between researchers and teachers.

A. intensive B. concise
C. joint D. overall

7. Thomas Jefferson and John Adams died on July 4,1826,the fiftieth _____ of American Independence.

A. ceremony B. occasion
C. occurrence D. anniversary

答案与解析

1. B 尽管起初她只在当地的一流行乐队唱歌，但是她现在已是一位著名的好莱坞电影明星了。A employment：指受雇于他人，领取工资以谋生计，有较固定工作的职业。B career：指经过专门训练，终身愿意从事的职业。C occupation：泛指任何一种职业，既不分什么行业，也不管是脑力还是体力劳动。D profession：以前常指要受过高等教育（尤指法律、医学和神学）才能获得的职业，现在一般指为谋生的职业，尤指从事脑力劳动和受过专门训练，具有某种专业知识的职业。故选 B。

2. A 他对在明年的奥林匹克运动会赢金牌一事很乐观。A 乐观的，积极的；B 选择的；C 突出的，杰出的；D 明显的，显而易见的。因此，A 为正确答案。

3. D 汽油是从原油中提炼出来的，而原油是我们从地底下挖掘出来的。A 新鲜的，清新的；B 原本的；C 粗鲁的；D 天然的，未加加工的。故 D 为正确答案。

4. D 让孩子自己去上学是很冒险的举动。A 省略；B 附属；C 支付;run a risk 冒险。故选 D。

5. A 他没时间一字一字地读报告,他只是浏览了一下。A 浏览; B 观察;C 忽略;D 一瞥。故 A 为正确答案。

6. D 这本书的总体目标是架设研究和教学的桥梁,特别是研究人员和老师之间的桥梁。A 激烈的;B 精确的;C 连接的;D 总体的,全面的。故 D 为正确答案。

7. D 根据题干中 July 4 和 American Independence,再结合历史常识,得知空格处应填入表示"周年"的词。ceremony 表示"典礼,仪式";occasion 表示"场合";occurrence 表示"发生,出现,事件";anniversary 表示"周年纪念"。答案为 D。

Word List 32

pace[4] [peɪs] *n.* 步,步伐,步调,速度 *v.* 踱步,用步测

[巧记]派生词:pacemaking(*n.* 定步速;当标兵),pacesetter(*n.* 定步速者;带步人;标兵)

[语境] She works so fast that I can't keep pace with her.
她工作得很快,我跟不上她的速度。
The lion paced the floor of his cage restlessly.
狮子烦躁地在兽笼里走来走去。

[考点] at a foot's pace 用平常步走;at a good pace 相当快地;keep pace with sb./sth. 与某人[某物]齐步前进,跟上某人[某物];make the pace 为别人定速度[步调];树榜样

pack [pæk] *v.* 捆扎,打包;塞满,挤满 *n.* 包裹,背包,一群/副

[巧记]同义词:box;反义词:unpack[*vt. &vi.* 从(包裹等)中取出(所装的东西),打开行李取出]

[语境] The wind packed the snow against the wall.
风把雪吹得堆积在墙边。
The bus was packed with noisy schoolchildren.
这辆公共汽车里挤满了吵吵嚷嚷的小学生。

page[peɪdʒ] *n.* 页
  [语境]She wrote away all day, filling page after page.
    她写了一页又一页,整整写了一天。

pain [peɪn]*n.* 痛,痛苦;(*pl.*)努力,劳苦 *vt.* 使痛苦
  [巧记]派生词:painkiller(*n.* 止痛药),pained(*a.* 痛苦的;自尊心受到伤害的)
  [语境]She's been complaining again. She's a real pain!
    她又发牢骚了——真烦人!
    It pains me to have to tell you that…
    我以沉痛的心情告诉你……
  [考点]be at (the) pains 尽力设法,努力 be in pains 疼痛;在苦恼中

painful ['peɪnful]*a.* 疼痛的,使痛苦的,费力[心]的,棘手的
  [巧记]词根:pain + -ful 形容词后缀,充满的
  [语境]Teaching him Greek was a painful process.
    教他学希腊文是件很吃力的事。
    The sting of a jellyfish is very painful.
    让水母刺住是很痛的。
  [考点]painful tooth 牙疼;be painful to sb. 对某人是痛苦的;a painful duty 艰苦的任务

paint [peɪnt]*n.* 油漆,颜料 *v.* 油漆;涂,涂漆;画;描绘,描述
  [巧记]派生词:paintbox(*n.* 颜料盒),paintbrush(*n.* 画笔,画刷,漆刷)
  [语境]They painted a coat of paint to prevent the oxidation of the ship by seawater.
    他们刷了一层油漆以防止船只被海水氧化。
    The wall requires a new coat of paint.
    这墙需要再涂一层新油漆。
  [考点](as) fresh as (new) paint 精神焕发的,精力充沛的;as handsome as paint 非常漂亮;paint sth. out 用漆[颜料]涂去(某物)

painting['peɪntɪŋ] *n.* (一幅)油画,绘画;画法;(上)油漆

[语境]Someone stole a painting from the museum.

有人从博物馆盗走了一幅画。

Older boys put them up to painting the statue red.

大孩子唆使他们把塑像漆成红色。

pair [peə(r)] *n.* 一对,一双;一副;夫妇 *v.* 配对,成对

[语境]This pair of shoes is durable.

这双鞋很耐磨。

I found a couple of socks in the bedroom, but they don't make a pair.

我在卧室里发现两只袜子,但不成对。

[考点]a pair of 一双,一对……

palm [pɑ:m] *n.* 手掌

[语境]A bird settled on his palm.

一只鸟停落在他的手掌上。

[考点]have(或hold) someone in the palm of one's hand 把某人置于完全控制之下

panic ['pænɪk] *n.* 惊慌,恐慌 *a.* 恐慌的,惊慌的

[语境]There was a panic when the building caught fire.

大楼起火时,人们一片惊慌。

The first was her colleague in a panic, looking for an answer to an urgent question.

第一封是一位恐慌的同事发过来的,向她救助一个非常紧急的问题。

[考点]alarm, fear, fright, horror, panic, terror, dread 辨析:这些名词均含"恐惧,惧怕,惊恐"之意。alarm:强调突然意识到有危险而产生的恐惧心理。fear:普通用词,侧重指面临危险或灾祸时内心所引起的恐惧心情。fright:通常指一阵突然的、令人震惊的短暂恐惧,有时含夸张意味。horror:侧重指因看到令人讨厌或危险的东西或情景而引起的厌恶情绪、极度恐惧心情或战栗的动作。panic:常指因突如其来的外界威胁使人群出现惊慌、恐惧或混乱。terror:指极大的恐惧和惊骇,语气最强。dread:可与 fear 换用,着重害怕的心理,但 dread

常指胆怯和丧失勇气

pants [pænts] *n.* 裤子,衬裤

[语境] He rushed out in pants.

他穿着短裤就冲出来了。

paper [ˈpeɪpə(r)] *n.* 纸;纸制品;报纸;(*pl.*)文件;试卷;论文

[语境] It's a fine scheme on paper, but will it work in practice?

那计划不错,不过在实践上是否可行呢?

She papered the room green.

她把房间糊成绿色。

paragraph [ˈpærəɡrɑːf] *n.* 段,节

[语境] The length of a paragraph depends on the information it conveys.

段落的长度取决于它所传达的信息。

parallel [ˈpærəlel] *a.* 平行的,相同的,类似的 *n.* 平行线,类似,对比

[巧记] 派生词:parallel(l)ed(*a.* 平行的),parallel(l)ing(*n.* 并联[列,行])

[语境] The gymnast swung on the parallel bars.

体操运动员在双杠上摆动身子。

The painting is without parallel of the greatest artistic level.

这幅图画有无与伦比的艺术价值。

[考点] parallel A with B 把A和B相比;draw a parallel between…在……之间作比较;in parallel with 与……平行,与……同时

parcel [ˈpɑːsəl] *n.* 包裹,邮包,部分 *v.* 打包,捆扎,分配

[语境] He snipped the string and untied the parcel.

他剪断绳子,解开包裹。

He tied the parcel with twine.

他用细绳来捆扎包裹。

[考点] part and parcel of 不可缺少的一部分,……的重要部分,……的组成部分;parcel out 分给,分配;parcel up 包起来

parent [ˈpeərənt] *n.* 父母

[语境] No parent can duck out of his duty to his children.

没有一个父母可以逃避自己对孩子应尽的责任。

park [pɑːk] *n.* 公园;停车场;运动场 *v.* 停放(汽车等),寄放

[语境] Park yourself in that chair while I make you a cup of tea.
你坐在那张椅子上,我给你沏茶去。
My car is parked over there.
我的汽车停放在那儿了。

part [pɑːt] *n.* 部分,角色,一方,零件,地区,部,篇 *v.* 使分开

[语境] I want no part in this sordid business.
我不想和这一肮脏勾当有任何瓜葛。
I'm afraid I have to part company with you there.
恐怕在这一点上我不敢苟同。

[考点] play a part in (在……中)扮演角色;(在……中)起作用

participate[4] [pɑːˈtɪsɪpeɪt] *v.* (in) 参与,参加;分享,分担;含有,带有

[巧记] 同义词:take part(参加)

[语境] I don't want to participate in the English party.
我不想参加英语晚会。
A delegate sent to observe and report on the proceedings of an assembly or a meeting but not vote or otherwise participate.
一个代表团被派去观察并报告集会或会议进展,但不投票或参与其他活动。

particular[28] [pəˈtɪkjʊlə(r)] *a.* 特殊的,苛求的,个别的 *n.* 详情,细节,特色

[语境] He gave full particulars of the stolen property.
他详细列出全部被盗的财物。
This work should be done correctly in all particulars.
这项工作每一点都必须做到正确无误。

[考点] be particular about/of 讲究;in particular 特别地;详细地;
词语辨析:particular *a.* 特殊的,个别的;partly *ad.* 部分地,在一定程度上

particularly [pəˈtɪkjʊləlɪ] *ad.* 特别地,尤其地

[语境] Watch your step; the boss is in a particularly bad mood.

你要小心点,老板今天情绪特别不好。

partly[10] ['pɑ:tlɪ] *ad.* 部分地,不完全地,在一定程度上

[巧记] 词根:part 部分 + -ly……地;同义词:particular(*a.* 特殊的)

[语境] The scheme is partly financed by a government grant.

此计划有一部分是政府资助的。

His attitudes were shaped partly by early experiences.

他的想法在一定程度上是由他早期的经历决定的。

partner ['pɑ:tnə(r)] *n.* 合作者,合伙人,合股人;伙伴;舞伴;配偶

[巧记] 词根:part + ner 人

[语境] It's your call, partner.

伙伴,该你叫牌了。

He has a practical partner who organizes everything for him.

他有个很能干的伙伴,能替他把一切弄得井井有条。

[考点] trade partner 贸易伙伴

party ['pɑ:tɪ] *n.* 聚会,政党,当事人 *v.* 举行(参加)社交聚会

[语境] Most teenagers like to go to parties.

大多数青少年喜欢参加派对。

[考点] enter [join] the Party 入党;be a party to sth. 与某事发生关系,参与某事

pass [pɑ:s] *v.* 经/通/穿/度过;传递 *n.* 通行证;考试及格

[语境] Pass the salt, please.

请递给我盐瓶。

Six months had passed, and we still had no news of them.

六个月过去了,我们仍然没有他们的消息。

passage ['pæsɪdʒ] *n.* 通过,经过;通路,走廊;(一)段落,(一)节

[巧记] pass(经过) + -age;派生词:passenger(*n.* 乘客,旅客)

[语境] This passage may be given several interpretations.

这段文字可以有不同的解释。

This is our room, and yours is down the passage.

这是我们的房间,你们的在走廊的那一头。

passenger ['pæsɪndʒə(r)] *n.* 乘客,旅客

[语境] I sat in the passenger seat.

我坐在乘客座位上。

passion[4] [ˈpæʃən] *n.* **热情,激情;酷爱**

[语境] He spoke with great passion.

他发表了热情洋溢的讲话。

She had a passion for gardening.

她酷爱园艺。

[考点] with passion 热情洋溢地;have a passion for 酷爱……

passport [ˈpɑːspɔːt] *n.* **护照**

[语境] A passport that is out of date is invalid.

护照过期是无效的。

past [pɑːst; pæst] *a.* **过去的** *ad.* 经过,过 *n.* 过去,昔日 *prep.* (经)过

[语境] I've been there many times in the past.

我从前去过那儿很多次。

He hurried past me without stopping.

他匆忙从我身边走过,连停都没停。

path [pɑːθ] *n.* **小路,路线,途径**

[语境] He went up the garden path to knock on the door.

他穿过花园小径去敲门。

patience [ˈpeɪʃəns] *n.* **耐心,忍耐**

[巧记] 反义词:impatient 不耐烦

[语境] Her endless patience made her the best nurse in the hospital.

无限的耐心使她成为这个医院最好的护士。

Learning to walk again after his accident required great patience.

他出事后重新学习走路要有极大的毅力。

[考点] be out of patience with 对……忍无可忍;have no patience with 对……不能容忍;对……没有耐性。词语辨析:patience 指"容忍痛苦、困难等的能力";endurance 指"忍受较长期、较严重痛苦、困难等的能力";fortitude 指"在痛苦、危险、困难等前表现出的坚忍或刚毅"

patient[33] [ˈpeɪʃənt] *a.* 有耐心的,能忍耐的 *n.* 病人,患者

[语境] A patient throng was waiting in silence.

一大群人耐心地静候着。

The patient took no nourishment all day until dinner.

这个病人晚饭前什么东西都没吃。

pattern[11] [ˈpætən] *n.* **模式,式样;图案,图样** *v.* **仿制,模仿**

[语境] The wallpaper in our bedroom has a pattern of orchids.

我们卧室的壁纸是兰花图案的。

The curtains had an elaborate pattern of flowers.

窗帘上绘有精美的花卉图案。

[考点] pattern oneself after 模仿(某人的)样子;pattern sth. upon 仿照……式样制造某物

pause [pɔːz] *v./n.* **中止,暂停**

[巧记] pauseful(*a.*),pausefully(*ad.*),pauseless(*a.*)

[语境] There was a pregnant pause before she answered my question.

她耐人寻味地停顿了一下才回答我的问题。

His words were followed by a pregnant pause.

他说完话,接着是一段意味深长的停顿。

[考点] at/in pause 停止,踌躇,沉默;give pause to sb. 使某人踌躇不前;make a pause 中止,暂停

pay[17] [peɪ] *v.* **付款,付出代价,给予注意** *n.* **工资,薪金**

[语境] He gets his pay each Friday.

他每星期五领工资。

The manager wouldn't pay him his wages.

经理不肯付工资给他。

payment [ˈpeɪmənt] *n.* **支付,付款额**

[巧记] 词根:pay(支付)+ment(名词后缀)→付款额

[语境] They were involved in a long legal wrangle over payment.

他们在付款问题上陷入长期纠纷。

The payment of the goods is payable in instalments.

货款可以分期支付。

[考点] payment on account 分期偿还;suspend payment 无力支付,宣布破产

peace [piːs] *n.* 和平;平静,安宁

[巧记] 派生词:peaceloving(*a.* 爱好和平的),peacemaker(*n.* 调解人,和事佬)

[语境] His rage was soon calmed down by the rustic peace.
乡村的宁静很快就使他的怒气平静下来。
There is an atmosphere of peace and calm in the country, quite different from the atmosphere of a big city.
在乡间有一种和平宁静的气氛,和大城市的气氛截然不同。

[考点] at peace 处于平静状态,处于和平状态;keep one's peace 保持沉默;maintain peace 维护和平

peaceful [ˈpiːsfəl] *a.* 和平的,平静的,安宁的,爱好和平的

[巧记] 词根:peace + ful;派生词:peacefully *ad.* peacefulness *n.*

[语境] We hope there will be a peaceful transition to the new system.
我们希望能够和平过渡到新的制度。
His ending was peaceful.
他去世时很安详。

peculiar [pɪˈkjuːlɪə(r)] *a.* 古怪的,异常的;特殊的,特有的

[巧记] 同义词:odd(*a.* 古怪的)

[语境] There was this peculiar man sitting opposite me in the train.
在火车上有个挺特别的男人坐在我对面。
The Mid-Autumn Festival is peculiar to China.
中秋节是中国所独有的节日。

[考点] peculiar sound 独特的声音;peculiar way 特有的风味

pen [pen] *n.* 钢笔

[语境] Students are required to write their exercises in pen.
学生们被要求用钢笔做练习。

pencil [ˈpensl] *n.* 铅笔

[语境] He had written her a note in pencil.
他用铅笔给她写了个便条。

people [ˈpiːpəl] *n.* 人们,人;[the-] 人民;一国人民,民族

[语境] People do not know the value of health till they lose it.

直到失去健康,人们才知道健康的可贵。

She's spending Christmas with her people.

她与亲人一起过圣诞节。

per[13] [pə(r)] *prep.* 每;经,由

[语境] We were bowling along (the motorway) at seventy miles per hour.

我们以每小时七十英里的速度(在高速公路上)飞驰。

The vessel tax of anchorage is 5,000 dollars per year.

这艘船的停泊税一年是五千美元。

[考点] per day [month, year] 每天[月,年];as per usual 照常,一如往常

perceive [pəˈsiːv] *v.* 察觉,感知;理解,领悟

[巧记] 同义词:feel

[语境] I perceived his comment as a challenge.

我认为他的批评是对我的激励。

The patient was perceived to have difficulty in standing and walking.

据观察所见,病人站立和行走都有困难。

percent [pəˈsent] *n.* 百分之……

[语境] About 80 percent of the graduates advanced to senior high schools.

约有80%的毕业生升入了高中。

percentage [pəˈsentɪdʒ] *n.* 百分数,百分率,百分比

[巧记] 词根:percent 百分之几

[语境] Whisky contains a large percentage of alcohol.

威士忌所含酒精的百分比很高。

Of all the fibers now used by man, a very large percentage is man-made.

现在人类所使用的所有纤维之中,有很大的比例是人造的。

[考点] a percentage of 5 百分之五;no percentage 没利益

核心词汇精解

perfect[9] [ˈpɜːfɪkt] *a.* 完善的;完全的;(语法)完成的 *v.* 使完美

[巧记] fect 来自拉丁语词根 fact 做,制造;per- 完全,彻底

[语境] No one expects you to be perfect, but we do expect you to do your best always.

没人指望你完美无缺,但是我们盼望你总是尽最大的努力。

He flattered himself that he spoke French with a perfect accent.

他自以为他说法语的腔调很完美。

[考点] letter perfect 尽善尽美的;一字不漏的;熟记(台词、功课等);perfect oneself in 完全掌握;熟练;精通

perform [pəˈfɔːm] *v.* 履行,执行;表演,演出;完成(事业)

[巧记] per- 彻底,完全 + form 形状。造成完全的形状即为完成,执行。派生词:performable(*a.* 可执行的,可完成的,可演出的),performer(*n.* 执行者,表演者,演奏者;能手,选手)

[语境] Lasers can be used to perform operations nowadays.

现在激光可以用来做手术。

That notary is authorised to perform the certain legal functions.

公证人被授权执行某些法律职能。

[考点] perform one's duties 尽责任;perform a play 演一出戏

performance[20] [pəˈfɔːməns] *n.* 履行,执行;表演,演出;性能,特性;成绩

[巧记] 词根:perform + -ance

[语境] He goes through the whole performance of checking the oil and water every time he drives the car.

他每次开汽车都总是不厌其烦地把油和水整个检查一遍。

The novel is considered a brilliant performance.

这部小说被认为是出色的佳作。

[考点] continuous performance 连续演出

perhaps [pəˈhæps] *ad.* 也许,大概,恐怕

[语境] Yes, perhaps I'm wrong there.

是的,在这点上也许我错了。

As she's been ill, perhaps she'll need some help.

她由于生病可能需要些帮助。

period [ˈpɪərɪəd] *n.* 时期,时代;学时;周期,一段时间;句点
[巧记] 派生词:periodic(*a.* 周期的,定期的);同义词:time(*n.* 时代)
[语境] Last year was a prolific period in the composer's life.
去年是作曲家一生中创作丰收的时期。
He was on his feet again after such a long period in hospital.
住院很长一段时间后他康复了。
[考点] at no period 从来没有;come to a period 结束

permit[4] [pɜːˈmɪt] *v.* 许可,允许 *n.* [ˈpɜːmɪt] 许可证,执照
[巧记] per-通过 + mittere 让走,原意是放开,后来转为允许,许可
[语境] You can't work here without a work permit.
你没有许可证就不能在这里工作。
I'll come after the meeting if time permits.
如果时间允许的话,我开完会就来。
[考点] permit of [常用于否定句] 容许

persist [pəˈsɪst] *v.* (in) 坚持,持续
[巧记] 派生词:persistence(*n.* 坚持;持续),persistency(*n.* 固执;持续;坚韧;永恒),persistent(*a.* 固执的,持续的,坚持的)
[语境] If you persist in breaking the law, you will go to prison.
如果你再继续违法的话,你会坐牢的。
The cold weather will persist for the rest of the week.
这种寒冷的天气将持续到本周末。
[考点] persist in sth. 坚持做某事;persist in doing sth. 坚持做某事;persist with 继续努力,坚持不懈

考点集训

1. Because of a _____ engagement, Lora couldn't attend my birthday party last Saturday.
   A. pioneer B. premature
   C. prior   D. past

2. Only a few people have _____ to the full facts of the incident.
   A. access   B. resort

C. contact D. path

3. _____ that he wasn't happy with the arrangements, I tried to book a different hotel.
   A. Perceiving B. Penetrating
   C. Puzzling D. Preserving

4. The group of technicians are engaged in a study which _____ all aspects of urban planning.
   A. inserts B. grips
   C. performs D. embraces

5. Many painters, rock singers, and street dancers have distinct hair style, _____ to their group.
   A. particular B. essential
   C. special D. peculiar

6. You will not be _____ about your food in time of great hunger.
   A. special B. particular
   C. peculiar D. specific

7. Crime is increasing worldwide, and there is every reason to believe the _____ will continue into the next decade.
   A. emergency B. trend
   C. pace D. schedule

答案与解析

1. C 因为一个事先的约会，罗拉上个星期六没法参加我的生日派对。A 先驱的；B 提前的；C 先前的，前面的；D 过去的。故选 C。

2. A 这个事件的真相只有几个人知道。A 权利，接近；B 度假胜地；C 联系；D 小路。故选 A。

3. A 了解到他对安排不满意，我尽力预订其他宾馆。A 认识到，了解到；B 深入；C 迷惑；D 保存，保留。故选 A。

4. D 技术员们正致力于一项涵盖城市规划方方面面的研究。A 插入；B 抓住；C 表演，进行；D 包括，拥抱。故选 D。

5. D 许多画家、摇滚歌手和街头歌手的发型很特别，为他们这群人所特有。A 特别的;B 重要的;C 特别的;D 特有的,独特的。故 D 为正确答案。

6. B　在非常饿的时候,你就不会挑食了。固定搭配,be particular about 对……挑剔。

7. B　全世界犯罪活动数量不断上涨,这使得我们有足够的理由相信,在未来几十年这种趋势还会继续。A 紧急事件;B 趋势;C 步调;D 日程。故选 B。

Word List 33

person ['pɜːsən] *n.* **人,喜欢(或适应)……的人;人物;人称**
[语境]Help arrived in the person of his father.
前来帮忙的是他的父亲。
The firm has an important asset in the person of the director of research.
公司有一巨大财富,就是研究部主任这个人。

personal[45] ['pɜːsənəl] *a.* **个人的,私人的;亲自的;身体的,人身的**
[巧记]词根:person(个人) + al(的)→私人的,个人的
[语境] Personal cleanliness is important to health as well as to appearance.
个人清洁对于健康和仪表同样重要。
I have something personal to discuss with you.
我有点私事和你商量。
[考点]become personal/get personal 变成对个人的议论,进行人身攻击

personality [ˌpɜːsəˈnælɪtɪ] *n.* **人格,个性**
[语境]She has such a kind, friendly personality.
她个性如此善良友好。
[考点]temper, character, nature, personality 辨析:这些名词均有"性格,气质,性情,习性"之意。temper:指从感情方面体现

出来,决定处理问题或应付形势的方式的性格或性情,这种性情可以是暂时的,也可以是长久的。character:指对个性或人格所作出的客观评价,常常与道德有关。nature:指天生的、不可改变的性格。personality:主要指一个人稳定的心理特征

perspective [pəˈspektɪv] *n.* **透视画法,透视图;远景,前途;观点,看法**

[巧记] per-通过 + spective 看;派生词:perspectivity [*n.* 透视(性),明晰度]

[语境] The painting provides us with one of the earliest examples of the use of perspective.
那幅画给我们提供了采用透视画法的最早的范例。
You must get the story in its right perspectives.
你必须正确地了解这件事。

[考点] in perspective 合乎透视法;比例正确;in the right perspective 正确地、客观地、全面地(观察事物);out of perspective 不按透视法的(地);不成比例的(地)

persuade [pəˈsweɪd] *v.* **说服,劝说;(of) 使相信**

[巧记] 派生词:persuader(*n.* 说服者,强制的工具)

[语境] Can you persuade her out of her foolish plans?
你能劝她放弃她那些愚蠢的计划吗?
How can I persuade you of my sincerity?
我如何能够让你相信我的诚意?

[考点] persuade sb. to do sth. 说服某人做某事

philosophy[4] [fɪˈlɒsəfɪ] *n.* **哲学;人生哲学,见解,观点**

[巧记] philo(爱) + sophy (智慧)→爱智慧→哲学

[语境] He studied philosophy and psychology at Cambridge.
他在剑桥大学学习哲学和心理学。
I can't sum up his whole philosophy in one sentence.
我无法用一句话来概括他的全部人生观。

phone [fəʊn] *n.* 电话 *vt.* **打电话**

[语境] Two minutes later the phone rang.
两分钟后电话响了。

He'll soon phone you up and tell you all about it.

他会很快打电话告诉你那件事的。

photo = photograph

photograph [ˈfəʊtəɡrɑːf] *n.* 照片,相片

[语境] He wants to take some photographs of the house.

他想给这幢房子拍一些照片。

physical[34] [ˈfɪzɪkəl] *a.* 物质的;肉体的,身体的;自然科学的,物理的

[巧记] 派生词:physicality(*n.* 肉体性)

[语境] Staying up late makes him at his worst in terms of physical situation.

熬夜使得他的体力特别糟糕。

We suggest that Smith be told about his physical condition as soon as possible.

我们主张应尽快告诉史密斯他的身体状况。

[考点] the physical world 物质世界; physical laws 自然法则

physician[8] [fɪˈzɪʃən] *n.* 内科医生

[语境] The physician made a prescription against sea-sickness for him.

医生给他开了个治晕船的药方。

physicist [ˈfɪzɪsɪst] *n.* 物理学家

[语境] He is a physicist of the first rank.

他是一流的物理学家。

physics[5] [ˈfɪzɪks] *n.* 物理学

[语境] They are digging at physics.

他们在钻研物理学。

pick [pɪk] *v.* 拾,采,摘;挑选,选择

[语境] The child has picked a hole in his new jumper.

孩子的新毛衣上钩了一个洞。

It was easy to pick holes in his argument.

在他的论据里不难找出漏洞。

picnic [ˈpɪknɪk] *n.* 郊游,野餐 *vi.* (去)野餐

[语境] Only bad weather can disturb our plans for the picnic.

只有坏天气才会打乱我们的野餐计划。
To picnic is to eat a meal out of doors.
野餐式地用餐就是在户外吃饭。

[考点] go for a picnic 去野餐

picture ['pɪktʃə(r)] *n.* 画,图片;影片;美景 *v.* 画,描述,想象

[语境] I can't picture the village without the old church.
我无法设想村子里没有那座旧教堂会是什么样子。
The book gives a good picture of everyday life in ancient Rome.
那部书对古罗马人的日常生活描写得很生动。

piece [piːs] *n.* (一)件/片/篇;碎片 *v.* (together) 拼合,拼凑

[语境] After the car accident, she seemed to go to pieces.
撞车事故后她好像精神崩溃了。
His house is over there a piece.
他的房子在那边,离这儿有一段距离。

[考点] a piece of 一片,一件

pierce [pɪəs] *vt.* 刺穿,刺破,穿透;突破,深深感动

[语境] He pierced the rubber ball with a needle.
他用针刺穿橡皮球。
Her words pierced the students.
她的话感动了学生。

pig [pɪg] *n.* 猪

[语境] The pig nosed the trough down.
猪把食槽拱翻了。

pink [pɪŋk] *n.* 粉红色

[语境] These pink dresses are moving slowly.
这些粉红色的衣服卖得不快。

pity ['pɪtɪ] *v.* (觉得)可怜,惋惜 *n.* 憾事,怜悯

[巧记] sympathy [*n.* 同情(心)]
[语境] He lay helpless in the street under the pitying gaze of the bystanders.
他孤零零地躺在路边,旁观的人都投以怜悯的目光。
We took pity on the homeless girl and took her into our house.

我们同情这个无家可归的女孩,让她住进了我们的屋子里。

[考点] have pity on sb. 可怜某人;in pity (of) 怜悯……;同情;What a pity! 多么可惜。词语辨析:pity 指"对弱者或不幸者的苦难、不幸、忧虑等所寄予的同情";compassion 指"除同情外,还要给予帮助";sympathy 指"因对忧虑和不幸有所理解而寄予同情"

place [pleɪs] *n.* 地方;名次;地位;寓所 *v.* 安排;放置;投(资)

[语境] She has a foreign accent that I can't quite place.
她有外国口音,但我听不出是哪儿的口音。
The stockbroker has placed the money in industrial stock.
证券经纪人已用那笔钱购入了工业股票。

plain [pleɪn] *n.* 平原 *a.* 平易的,易懂的;简单的,朴素的

[语境] Little mountain stream is dashing down to the plain.
小山涧奔腾而下,流向平原。
She always wears plain clothes to work.
她总是穿朴素的衣服去上班。

plan [plæn] *n.* 计划,规划;平面图,设计图 *v.* 计划

[语境] As far as I am concerned, I'm not against your plan.
就我而言,我并不反对你的计划。
What is your plan?
你的计划是什么?

planet [ˈplænɪt] *n.* 行星

[语境] They claimed to have discovered a new planet.
他们宣称发现了一颗新的行星。

plant [plɑːnt] *n.* 植物,作物;工厂;装置 *v.* 栽种,播种,栽培

[巧记] 派生词:plantation(*n.* 农园,大农场;人造林;造林地;殖民地)

[语境] His strange remarks planted doubts in our minds about his sanity.
他那些怪话使我们心中生疑,不知他精神是否正常。
The speaker's supporters were planted in the audience and applauded loudly.

听众中安插了演讲人的支持者,他们使劲给他鼓掌。

[考点] in plant 生长着,活着

platform ['plætfɔːm] *n.* 台,讲台,站台,月台;平台

[语境] The train was about to leave and I was not even on the platform.

火车就快开了,可我还没到站台。

play [pleɪ] *v.* 玩,做游戏;参加比赛 *n.* 游戏;玩耍;剧本

[语境] I think we should play Bill on the wing in the next match.

我认为下一场应当让比尔任边锋。

I could hear music playing on the radio.

我听到收音机里在放音乐。

playground ['pleɪɡraʊnd] *n.* 玩耍场地

[巧记] play(玩) + ground(地方)→玩耍的地方→玩耍场地

[语境] I like going to the playground with my friends because we are happy there.

我喜欢和朋友们一起去游乐场,因为在那里我们很开心。

pleasant ['plezənt] *a.* 令人愉快的 *vt.* 使高兴

[巧记] 词根:pleas(使愉快) + -ant(……的)→令人愉快的

[语境] We spent many hours in a pleasant conversation.

我们畅谈了好几个小时。

It was a pleasant surprise to learn of her marriage.

得知她结婚是件令人惊喜的事。

[考点] 词语辨析:pleasant 表示被修饰的对象由于具有令人高兴的外表或热切的气质而使人感到有一种自然的吸引力;pleasing 具有 pleasant 的含义,但另外多一层有意识地去讨人喜欢的含义

please [pliːz] *v.* 请;使愉快,使满意;喜欢,愿意

[语境] That child behaves just as he pleases.

那孩子想干什么就干什么。

Please come with me.

请跟我来。

pleasure ['pleʒə(r)] *n.* 愉快,快乐;乐事,乐趣

[巧记] please 使高兴 + -ure 抽象名词后缀

[语境] She took no pleasure in her work.

她觉得自己的工作毫无乐趣。

She seemed to take pleasure in our suffering.

她似乎对我们的痛苦幸灾乐祸。

[考点] ask sb.'s pleasure 问某人的意愿; do sb. the pleasure of 使某人欢喜,为某人效劳

plentiful ['plentɪful] *a.* **富裕的,丰富的**

[巧记] plenty 丰富 + -ful……的

[语境] Some years we have a plentiful harvest, others a very poor one, but you have to take the good with the bad.

有些年我们获得大丰收,有些年则收成很坏,但好坏你都得接受。

She had a plentiful store of provisions.

她贮存了大量的食物和饮料。

[考点] 词语辨析:plentiful 指"大量的""丰富的"; abundant 指"丰富的""充裕的",语气比 plentiful 强,数量比 plentiful 多; ample 指"充分的""足以满足需要的"

plenty ['plentɪ] *n.* **丰富,大量**

[语境] For tracksuits you need material with plenty of stretch.

做田径服需要用弹性强的料子。

As I had plenty of money I was able to help her.

我钱很宽裕,能帮助她。

[考点] in plenty 很多; plenty more 还有很多,大量的; plenty of 很多,大量

plunge [plʌndʒ] *v.* **跳入,(使)投入,(使)陷入;猛冲**

[语境] He ran to the edge of the lake and plunge in.

他跑到湖边,跳进水里。

I am deeply moved by people's ardor in the preparation, which makes me plunge into the process unconsciously.

我被人们积极的热情深深地打动了,而这也使我不知不觉地投入到这项活动中去。

[考点] plunge into 突然冲入，突然或仓促地开始某事

plus [plʌs] *n.* **塞子,插头** *v.* **堵,塞,插上,插栓**

[巧记] 反义词：minus(*n.* 负号，不足)

[语境] We paid 1,000 dollars for the shop, plus 200 dollars for goodwill.

我们花了1 000美元买下这家商店，另加二百美元买它的商誉。

He seems to have mistaken a plus for a minus.

他似乎把正号误作负号了。

[考点] the plus and minus factors 有利和不利因素

pocket [ˈpɒkɪt] *n.* **衣袋；*a.* 袖珍的**

[语境] The man stood with his hands in his pockets.

那个男人双手插在兜里站着。

This handy pocket dictionary is a boon to me.

这本灵便的袖珍词典对我很有用处。

poem [ˈpəʊɪm] *n.* **诗**

[语境] I can knock off a poem in half an hour.

半小时之内我就能作一首诗。

poet [ˈpəʊɪt] *n.* **诗人**

[语境] The poet expressed his burning passion for the woman he loved.

这位诗人表达了他对自己热恋女人的强烈情感。

point [pɔɪnt] *n.* **尖；点；条款；分数，得分；论点** *v.* **(at, to) 指**

[巧记] 同义词：aim *v.* 指

[语境] At one point I thought she was going to refuse, but in the end she agreed.

当时我以为她要拒绝，但最后她却同意了。

He missed the whole point of my speech.

他完全没抓住我讲话的要点。

poison [ˈpɔɪzn] *n.* **毒物,毒药** *v.* **放毒,毒害**

[语境] Mercury is a known poison.

水银是一种人人皆知的有毒物质。

The rumours that she had poisoned him could never be proved.

她曾下毒害他的谣言永远都无法得到证实。

police [pəˈliːs] *n.* **警察,警察局**

[语境] I noticed a police car shadowing us.

我注意到一辆警车尾随着我们。

policeman [pəˈliːsmən] *n.* **警察**

[语境] The policeman discharged his gun at the fleeing robbers.

警察向逃跑的强盗开了枪。

policy[5] [ˈpɔlɪsɪ] *n.* **政策,方针**

[巧记] 派生词:policeman(*n.* 警察)

[语境] The annual premium on my policy is 3,000 yuan.

我的保险单每年的保险费是 3 000 元。

Until we'd built up sufficient forces to drive the invaders back, we pursued a policy of containment.

我们对入侵之敌采取牵制的方针,以备组织好兵力将之击退。

polite[10] [pəˈlaɪt] *a.* **有礼貌的,客气的;有教养的,文雅的**

[语境] I've never seen such a polite clerk.

我从未见过这样有礼貌的店员。

[考点] be polite to sb. 对某人有礼貌;do the polite 硬装文雅

political[10] [pəˈlɪtɪkəl] *a.* **政治的**

[巧记] politics *n.* 政治学

[语境] She entered the political arena after her husband's death.

她丈夫死后,她进入了政界。

This department collects information on political extremists.

这个部门搜集了有关政治极端分子的情报。

[考点] political economy 政治经济学;political liberties 政治自由

politics [ˈpɔlɪtɪks] *n.* **政治;政见,政纲**

[巧记] political *a.* 政治的,政治上的

[语境] He quickly involved himself in local politics.

他很快涉足了地方政治事务。

poliute [pəˈluːt] *vt.* **污染,玷污**

[语境]Bicycling is a good exercise; moreover, it doesn't pollute the air.

骑自行车是很好的运动;而且还不污染环境。

pollution[pə'lu:ʃən] *n.* 污染

[语境]The new law will reduce pollution of the rivers.

这条新法律将会减轻河流污染。

poor [pɔː(r); pʊə(r)] *a.* 贫困的;可怜的;贫乏的;贫瘠的;低劣的

[巧记]派生词:poorly(*a.* 身体不舒服的,心情恶劣的 *ad.* 贫穷地,贫乏地,不充分地)

[语境]Some people may regard radio as the poor relation of broadcasting.

有些人可能认为无线电广播在广播事业中稍逊一等。

Sparkling white wine is the poor man's champagne.

白葡萄汽酒算是廉价的香槟。

[考点]in poor health 身体不佳

pop [pɒp] *n.* 流行音乐;*v.* 突然出现,发生 *a.* 流行的,通俗的

[语境]The pop music added to our enjoyment of the film.

片中的流行音乐使我们对这部电影更加喜爱。

The balloon will pop if you put a pin in it.

如果扎进一颗大头钉,气球就会突然爆开。

popular[31] ['pɒpjʊlə(r)] *a.* 流行的,通俗的,大众的;广受欢迎的

[语境] Her charm of manner made her very popular.

她风度优雅,备受欢迎。

He is very interested in what are called popular songs.

他对所谓的流行歌曲很感兴趣。

population[37] [ˌpɒpjʊ'leɪʃən] *n.* 人口,(全体)居民

[巧记]popul 人民→居民,-ation 名词词尾,全体居民,人口

[语境] We have a growing population and therefore we need more food.

我们的人口在增长,因此我们需要更多的食物。

The entire population was wiped out by the terrible disease.

所有的居民都被可怕的疾病夺去了生命。

[考点] active population (经济上)自立人口,职业人口,参加经济活动人口; adult population 成年人口

portrait [ˈpɔːtrɪt] *n.* 肖像,画像

[语境] There is a portrait of King Charles on the wall.
墙上挂着查尔斯国王的画像。

pose [pəuz] *n.* 姿势,姿态 *v.* 造成,提出,摆姿势,伴装

[语境] Heavy traffic poses a problem in many old towns.
交通拥挤是许多旧城镇的难题。

His concern for the poor is only a pose.
他对穷人的关心只不过是做做样子罢了。

position[25] [pəˈzɪʃən] *n.* 位置;职位;姿势,姿态;见解,立场,形势

[巧记] 词根:post 岗位

[语境] The runners got into position on the starting line.
赛跑运动员已进入起跑线上的位置。

The orchestra were all in position, waiting for the conductor.
管弦乐队队员都已各就各位,等待着指挥。

[考点] be in a position to 能够;有做……的机会;fall into the position of 陷于某种地位

positive[11] [ˈpɒzɪtɪv] *a.* 肯定的,积极的,绝对的,无疑的,正的

[巧记] 派生词:positiveness(*n.* 肯定;确信),positively(*ad.* 明确地,断然地);反义词:negative(*a.* 否定的,负的)

[语境] Her behaviour was a positive outrage.
她的行为残暴到了极点。

He was positive that he had seen it in the newspaper.
他肯定他在报纸上看见过它。

[考点] be positive about(of) 确信,确知

possibility [ˌpɒsɪˈbɪlɪtɪ] *n.* 可能,可能性;可能的事,希望

[巧记] possible 可能的 + ity 性

[语境] She saw the possibilities of the scheme from the beginning.
她从一开始就预见到这计划可能成功。

She thought of several possibilities.
她考虑了几种可能的情况。

[考点] by some possibility 或许

possible [ˈpɒsɪbəl] *a.* 可能的，做得到的；合理的；可允许的

[语境] It isn't remotely possible that you will be chosen to go.

挑选你去的可能性并非很小。

I regret to say it's not possible.

很抱歉，这是不可能的。

[考点] possible 表示"某件事在行为者（尤其是作为人的行为者）的力所能及的范围内"，也可以表示"某件事的可能性"；probable 在表示某人做某事，或事物的可能性时，具有"迹象"或推理的内涵；likely 所修饰的人或物应当具备这样的特点：已被断定、被提出或被坚持的可能性；习惯用语 as...as possible 尽可能……；do one's possible 尽力，竭力；if possible 如果可能的话

possibly [ˈpɒsɪblɪ] *ad.* 可能地，也许；无论如何

[巧记] 反义词：impossibly

[语境] I don't know how I can possibly thank you enough.

我不知道该怎样来感谢你才好。

I can't possibly lend you so much money.

我没有可能借给你这么多钱。

postcard [ˈpəʊstˌkɑːd] *n.* 明信片

[语境] I bought a postcard yesterday.

昨天我买了一张明信片。

postpone [pəʊstˈpəʊn] *v.* 推迟，延期

[巧记] 同义词：delay

[语境] We agree to postpone the shipping date, considering (that) there is no steamer recently.

由于（考虑到）最近无船，我们同意推迟装货期。

Our financial situation is still precarious if we postpone the release of the new products.

如果我们推迟发布新产品的话，我们的财政状况就会仍然岌岌可危。

[考点]（postpone + until, till, to, for）使延期，推迟，搁置（postpone + to) 把……放在次要地位

potato [pəˈteɪtəʊ] *n.* 马铃薯

[语境] He beat the potato into a mash before eating it.

他把马铃薯捣烂后再吃。

potential[18] [pəˈtenʃəl] *a.* 潜在的，可能的 *n.* 潜能，潜力

[语境] The most perceptive of the three, she was the first to realize the potential danger of their situation.

她在他们三人中最敏感，首先意识到他们处境的潜在危险。

He hasn't realized his full potential yet.

他还没有意识到他的全部潜能。

考点集训

1. She's at the _____ of her career.
   A. head   B. height
   C. point   D. peak
2. She has paid the _____ for her crimes with five years in prison.
   A. penalty   B. pain
   C. punishment   D. patient
3. We had already _____ how the temperature fluctuated.
   A. polish   B. purchase
   C. perceived   D. pursue
4. What _____ of the earth is covered by oceans?
   A. percentage   B. percent
   C. rate   D. ratio
5. The project is far from _____.
   A. shameful   B. perfect
   C. dangerous   D. individual
6. The surgeon has _____ the operation.
   A. posed   B. performed
   C. masqueraded   D. played
7. Do you have any _____ address?
   A. sufficient   B. transparent

C. universal D. permanent

8. Mobile telecommunications _____ is expected to double in Shanghai this year as a result of a contract signed between the two companies.
   A. capacity B. potential
   C. possession D. impact

9. The football game comes to you _____ from New York.
   A. lively B. alive
   C. live D. living

10. He gave a _____ to handle the affairs in a friendly manner.
    A. pledge B. mission
    C. plunge D. motion

答案与解析

1. D 她正处于事业的顶峰。height 高度；point 点；head 头，头顶。
2. A 她因犯罪受到惩罚，被判刑五年。
3. C 我们已注意到温度的波动情形。polish 抛光；purchase 购买；pursue 追求。
4. A 地球上百分之多少被海水覆盖着？ratio 比率；rate 价值或速度的比率。
5. B 这项企划很不完美。shameful 害羞的；dangerous 危险的；individual 个人的，私人的。
6. B 外科医生做了手术。masquerade 假装；pose 摆出姿势；perform 表演，表现。
7. D 你有固定地址吗？sufficient 充足的；transparent 透明的；universal 普遍的。
8. A 因为两家公司签署了一份合同，上海的移动通信能力今年有望翻一番。A 能力，容量；B 潜力；C 拥有物，占有；D 影响。因此 A 为正确答案。
9. C 这里是纽约足球比赛现场直播。A 活泼的；B 活着的；C 直播的；D 活着的。故 C 为正确答案。
10. D 他以友好的方式处理事务是有动机的。A 誓言，保证；B 任务;C 插入,投入;D 动机。故选 D。

Word List 34

pound [paʊnd] *n.* 磅;英镑 *v.* (连续)猛击,(猛烈)敲打,捣碎
[巧记] 同义词:hit
[语境] He pounded the table angrily.
他生气地猛拍桌子。
I lost several pounds last month.
我上个月瘦了好几磅。
[考点] pound away at 乱打;不断地炮击;抨击;拼命地工作;
pound out 连续猛击而产生

pour[5] [pɔː(r)] *v.* 灌注,倾泻,涌入,流,倾盆大雨
[语境] The fans poured out of the stadium cheering wildly.
体育爱好者们欣喜若狂地从体育场中蜂拥而出。
I've poured coffee into your cup by mistake.
我错把咖啡倒在你的杯子里了。
[考点] pour down 倾泻;pour forth 连续不断地流[发]出;pour in
(使)川流不息地涌入

poverty ['pɒvətɪ] *n.* 贫穷,贫困
[巧记] 派生词:impoverish(*v.* 使成赤贫)
[语境] Although she was poor, she was living in genteel poverty.
尽管她贫穷,但她总想装出上流社会阶层的样子。
The novel is a searing indictment of urban poverty.
这部小说是对城市贫困的震撼心灵的控诉。
[考点] abject poverty 赤贫,一贫如洗;poverty line 贫困线

power[32] ['paʊə(r)] *n.* 力,精力;功率,电力;(数学)幂;权力,势力
[巧记] 派生词:powerful(*a.* 有力的,强的,有权力的),powerless
(*a.* 无力的,无效能的,无权的)
[语境] The powers of the police need to be clearly defined.

必须对警方的权限作出明确的规定。
Sitting out here, you really can feel the power of the sun.
坐在这里,你可以感到太阳的力量。

[考点] do all in one's power 尽力,竭尽全力

powerful[5] [ˈpauəfl] *a.* 强大的,有力的,有权的

[巧记] power 力量 + -ful 有……的

[语境] She redeemed her reputation with a powerful speech to the party convention.
她由于向党代表大会做了有力的演说而挽回了自己的声誉。
This athlete has a powerful frame.
这位运动员有着魁梧的体格。

practical[17] [ˈpræktɪkəl] *a.* 实际的,实用的

[巧记] practic[e]实践 + -al 形容词后缀

[语境] The whole scheme began to take on a more practical aspect.
整个计划开始具有更切合实际的性质。
He has a practical partner who organizes everything for him.
他有个很能干的伙伴,替他把一切弄得井井有条。

[考点] a practical method 实用的方法,有效的方法;practical minds 讲实际的头脑;a practical teacher 有经验的教师

practically [ˈpræktɪkəlɪ] *ad.* 几乎;实际上

[巧记] 近义词:in effect 实际上;反义词:theoretically(理论上)

[语境] He'd known the old man practically all his life.
他几乎打记事起就认识这个老人。

practice/-ice[20] [ˈpræktɪs] *n.* 练习,实践,实际,业务,惯例,习惯

[巧记] 派生词:practitioner(*n.* 从业者,开业者),practiced(*adj.* 熟练的;精通的;有经验的;习得的,练成的)

[语境] He is practiced in the art of design. She is a practiced lecturer.
他精通艺术设计。她是个老练的演说者。

praise [preɪz] *v.* 赞扬,歌颂;表扬 *n.* 称赞,赞美;赞美的话

[巧记] 同义词:commend

[语境] Praise can be a fine tonic.

赞美有时真让人感到振奋。

This doctor received high praise from everyone.

这位医生受到所有人的高度赞扬。

The American president praised Turkey for its courage.

美国总统赞扬了土耳其的勇气。

He referred to your work in terms of high praise.

他对你的工作大加赞扬。

[考点] in praise of 颂扬……,赞美……;词语辨析:praise 系常用词,指"对某人或某物衷心地称赞或钦佩",commend 更正式,指"正式地称赞或嘉许"praise sb. for something 因某事表扬某人

precious ['preʃəs] *a.* 珍贵的,贵重的

[巧记] preciously(*ad.* 昂贵地;仔细地),preciousness(*n.* 珍贵;过分讲究,小题大做)

[语境] Pandas are precious creatures.

熊猫是珍贵的动物。

You should make good use of every precious minute to study.

你应该很好地利用每一分钟宝贵的时间去学习。

precise [prɪ'saɪs] *a.* 精确的,准确的

[巧记] 派生词:preciseness(*n.* 精确;古板;严谨),precisian(*n.* 严格遵守教规的人)

[语境] I am not clear about the precise bearing of the word in this passage.

我说不准这个字在这段文章里的确切意义是什么。

He knew the precise psychological moment when to say nothing.

他知道什么时候该不说话的那心理上精确的一息间。

[考点] to be precise 确切地讲;at that precise moment 恰恰在那个时刻

predict[17] [prɪ'dɪkt] *v.* 预言,预测,预告

[巧记] 派生词:predictability(*n.* 可预测性)

[语境] I can predict something with great accuracy.

我能很准确地预测某事。

The zodiac is used in astrology to predict the future.

十二宫图用于占星术中预测未来。

[考点]词语辨析:forecast 更注重有理由的,更客观;而 predict 更多用在个人主观预测的时候

prefer[13][prɪˈfɜː(r)] *v.* **宁可,宁愿;提出;更喜欢;提升,提拔**

[巧记]派生词:preferable(*a.* 较好的, 较喜爱的),preferably(*ad.* 更可取地;更好地)

[语境] I prefer tea to coffee.

我更喜欢茶,而不是咖啡。

I prefer fish to meat.

相对于肉,我较喜欢吃鱼。

[考点] prefer -ing to -ing 喜欢……而不喜欢……;prefer sb. for 提拔某人为……

pregnant [ˈpregnənt] *a.* **怀孕的;重要的,富有意义的;孕育的**

[语境]Helen aborted when she was three months pregnant.

海伦怀孕三个月时流产了。

There was a long, pregnant silence.

当时出现了长时间耐人寻味的沉默。

premier[ˈpremjə(r)] *n.* **首相,总理** *a.* **第一的;最初的**

[语境]He requested that the Premier grant him an interview.

他请求总理准许给他一次会面的机会。

The billboard will be funded by 100 sponsors, including 40 premier sponsors.

这个布告板将由 100 位赞助商赞助,包括 40 位最初的赞助商。

preparation [ˌprepəˈreɪʃən] *n.* **准备,预备;制剂,制备品**

[巧记]prepar[e]准备 + -ation 名词后缀

[语境] A preliminary draft or plan, as of a project or proposal.

初步的草案或计划,如工程或建议的草案。

There are a lot of preliminaries to be gone through before you can visit a foreign country.

在出访外国之前要做好许多准备工作。

[考点] be in preparation 在准备中,在编辑中; in preparation for 作为……的准备; make preparations for 为……做准备

prepare [prɪˈpeə(r)] *v.* **准备,预备**

[巧记] pre-前 + pare 整理

[语境] Early experiments with military rockets prepared the ground for space travel.
早年对军用火箭进行的实验为发展航天技术奠定了基础。
He is preparing his speech for the meeting tomorrow.
他正准备明天集会的演说。

[考点] be prepared for[to do]准备; prepare against 准备应付(不好的事情); prepare for 为……做准备

prescribe [prɪˈskraɪb] *v.* **开处方,开药,规定,指示**

[巧记] pre(前面) + scribe(写)→在病人面前写的资料→开处方

[语境] The doctor prescribed his patient who was down with fever.
医生给发烧病人开了药方。
The supervisor prescribed the steps in which orders must be filled out.
主管规定了完成订货的步骤。

presence [ˈprezəns] *n.* **出席,到场,存在,在**

[巧记] 同义词:appearance(*n.* 外表,出现,登台)

[语境] He advocated the withdrawal of the American presence in Lebanon.
他主张美国人应该从黎巴嫩撤走。
Since she joined the team last season she has made her presence felt.
自从上个赛季加入这个队以来,她就使人感到她是个举足轻重的队员。

[考点] in the presence of...面临着……,在……面前;(with) presence of mind 镇定,沉着,方寸不乱

present[26] [ˈprezənt] *a.* **出席的,现在的** *n.* **现在,礼物** *v.* **赠送,提出**

[语境] Falling interest rates present the firm with a new problem.
利息下降给公司带来了一个新的问题。

He would not be elected on present form.

鉴于他的现时表现,他不可能当选。

[考点] at the present time 在目前;现在;the present price 现价;at present 现在,目前;be present to 出现在……面前

presentation [ˌprezənˈteɪʃən] *n.* 介绍,陈述;表现形式

[语境] My presentation should clarify any questions that you might have.

我的陈述应该可以澄清你可能有的疑问。

For instance, the first presentation might be of four cards, each with a number on one side and a colour on the other.

举个例子,第一轮展示可能是四张卡片,每一张的一面都有一个数字,相对应的背面有一种颜色。

presenter [prɪˈzentə(r)] *n.* 主持人,报幕员;赠与者,提出者

[语境] In her new film, Victoria plays a prima donna television presenter.

维多利亚在她的新片里扮演一位妄自尊大的电视节目主持人。

They often played the roles of "question presenter" or "assistant".

他们经常扮演问题提出者、协助者的角色。

presently [ˈprezntlɪ] *ad.* 不久,一会儿;现在,目前

[语境] I'll go to see your uncle presently.

我一会儿就去看望你叔叔。

She is presently developing a number of projects.

她现在正着手开发多个项目。

preserve[4] [prɪˈzɜːv] *v.* 保护,维持;保存,保藏

[语境] In the summer, large crops of fruit may be preserved by freezing or bottling.

夏天收获的大量水果可冷藏或装瓶装罐加以保存。

Salt and spices help to preserve meat.

盐和调味品有助于保藏肉类。

[考点] poach on sb.'s preserves 侵犯某人的活动范围,侵犯某人

的利益

president[ˈprezɪdənt] *n.* 主席,总统,校长,会长;总裁;董事长

[巧记] pre(前面) + sident(坐着)→坐在最前面的人→主席,总统

[语境] The President gave an address to the nation over the radio.
总统向全国发表广播演说。

Research and marketing operations will be Mr. Furlaud's job as president of the new company.
作为新公司的总裁,弗劳德先生将负责调研和市场运作。

press[6][pres] *v.* 压;压榨;紧迫,催促 *n.* 报刊,通讯社;压榨机

[巧记] 派生词:pressroom(*n.* 印刷室;记者室),pressrun(*n.* 一次印刷量)

[语境] I'm very pressed for cash at the moment, can I pay you next week?
我现在手头很紧——下周再付给你行吗?

He took a copy of the newspaper as it came off the press.
报纸在印刷机上印出来后他拿了一份。

[考点] press agent 广告宣传者;out of press 绝版

pressure[16][ˈpreʃə(r)] *n.* 压力,紧张;强制;压强 *vt.* 迫使

[语境] Pressure varies directly with temperature and inversely with volume.
压力与温度呈正比例变化,与容积呈反比例变化。

He changed his mind under the pressure from others.
他在别人的逼迫之下改变了主意。

He will never pressure you to get married.
他永远不会强迫你结婚。

[考点] under pressure 在压力下

pretty[6][ˈprɪtɪ] *ad.* 相当,很 *a.* 漂亮的,俊俏的,标致的

[巧记] 派生词:prettyish(*a.* 有些[相当,颇]漂亮的);同义词:beautiful

[语境] Renovating that house will cost you a pretty penny.
整修那所房子,你得花很多钱。

His good looks won him the election but he has still to prove that he's not just a pretty face.

他由于仪表堂堂而当选,但他还需要证明他绝非徒有其表。

[考点] pretty up 打扮,美化;pretty nearly 几乎

prevail [prɪ'veɪl] *v.* (over, against) **取胜,占优势;流行,盛行**

[语境] Sadness prevailed in our mind.

我们的心中充满悲痛。

Misty weather prevails in this part of the country.

该国的这一地区天气多雾。

[考点] prevail over /against 压倒,战胜;prevail upon/on/with 劝说好;说服;诱使

prevent[14] [prɪ'vent] *v.* (from) **预防,防止,阻止,制止,妨碍**

[巧记] prae-前 + venire 来,来到前面,先来者占强,后来者受阻;派生词:preventability(*n.* 可预防性,可制止性)

[语境] The government tried to prevent the diminution of resources.

政府试图阻止资源减少。

Props were used to prevent the roof collapsing.

用了一些支柱以防止屋顶塌落。

[考点] prevent...from 使……不做某事,阻止……做某事

previous[11] ['priːvɪəs] *a.* **先前的,以前的**

[语境] Have you had previous career experience?

你过去有过工作经验吗?

Previous to the conference we had discussed the matter among ourselves.

在会议之前,我们讨论了这个问题。

price [praɪs] *n.* **价格,价钱;代价,标价**

[语境] He knew it was dangerous to be seen—there was a price on his head.

他知道被人发现是很危险的——正在悬赏要他的脑袋呢。

I don't know enough about porcelain to be able to price these plates.

我不太懂得瓷器,估计不出这些盘子的价钱。

pride [praɪd] *n.* 自豪；自满；引以为自豪的东西 *v.* 使自豪

[巧记] 派生词：prideful(*a.* 自傲的；高傲的)

[语境] He prides himself on remaining calm in an emergency.
他在紧急关头十分镇静，为此他感到骄傲。
She takes great pride in her children's success.
她为自己的孩子取得的成绩感到无比骄傲。

[考点] take a pride in one's work 以工作自豪；national pride 民族自豪感；in the pride of 于全盛时期；pride oneself on [upon] 以……而得意

prince [prɪns] *n.* 王子，亲王

[语境] The Prince won warm applause for his ideas.
王子的想法赢得了热烈的掌声。

princess [prɪn'ses, '--] *n.* 公主，王妃

[语境] The youngest princess is only 13 years old.
最小的公主才十三岁。

principal ['prɪnsɪpəl] *a.* 最重要的，主要的 *n.* 负责人，校长；资本，本金

[巧记] prin 主要的 + cipal；同义词：chief

[语境] The agent spoke on behalf of his principal.
代理人代表他的委托人说话。
How much interest will there be on a principal of ＄5,000?
5 000 美元本金的利息是多少？

[考点] principal food 主食；the principal points 要点

principle ['prɪnsɪpəl] *n.* 原理，原则；主义，信念

[巧记] princeps 首先 + le；派生词：principled (*a.* 有原则的；有操守的)

[语境] They have agreed to the proposal in principle but we still have to negotiate the terms.
他们基本上同意了那项提议，但我们仍须商定条件。
The system works on the principle that heat rises.
该项装置是按照热力上升的原理运转的。

[考点] by principle 按照原则，根据原则；in principles 基本上，

原则上

print [prɪnt] *n.* 印刷,印刷品,字体 *v.* 印刷,出版;洗印

[语境] The print is too small for me to read without glasses.

印刷字体太小,我不戴眼镜就看不清。

Her first novel is out of print now but you may find a second-hand copy.

她的第一部小说现已绝版,不过你可以找到二手复制品。

prison [ˈprɪzn] *n.* 监狱

[语境] He was sentenced to life in prison.

他被判处终身监禁。

prisoner [ˈprɪzənə(r)] *n.* 囚徒

[语境] The police tried to break down the prisoner's opposition.

警察设法制住了那个囚犯的反抗。

private [ˈpraɪvɪt] *a.* 私人的,个人的,秘密的,私下的

[巧记] 派生词:privately(*ad.* 私下地,秘密地)

[语境] He's a rather private person.

他不太喜欢和别人交流思想感情。

The public is fascinated by the private lives of public figures.

公众对社会名流的私生活具有浓厚的兴趣。

[考点] in private 秘密地[的],私下地[的]

prize [praɪz] *n.* 奖赏,奖金,奖品 *v.* 珍视,珍惜

[巧记] 派生词:prized(*a.* 被看作最重要的,被看作最有价值的)

[语境] The portrait of her mother was her most prized possession.

她母亲的这张肖像是她最珍爱的物品。

She always makes a mess of things; she's a prize idiot.

她总是把事情弄糟;她是个不折不扣的大笨蛋。

probable [ˈprɔbəbəl] *a.* 很可能的,大概的;有希望的,可能的

[巧记] 词根 prob 尝试,证明;probable 可以证明的

[语境] Certainly they must know the probable result of such speeches.

无疑,他们一定知道这样讲话可能产生的后果。

The probable outcome of the talks is a compromise.

会谈的结果很可能是妥协。

[考点] It is probable that... 也许,恐怕

probably ['prɒbəblɪ] *ad.* **大概,或许**

[巧记] 词根 prob 尝试,证明;probable 可以证明的

[语境] It's probably not as bad as she says—she does tend to pile it on.

可能没有她说的那么糟——她确实有意夸大事实。

That hotel probably costs no less than 20 dollars a night.

那间旅馆的住宿费不低于 20 美元一晚。

problem ['prɒbləm] *n.* **问题,疑难问题;思考题,讨论题**

[语境] The problem is when to get the money we need.

问题是什么时候能得到我们所需要的钱。

That's your problem.

那是你的问题。

[考点] sleep on [upon, over] a problem 把问题留到第二天解决

process[18] ['prəʊses] *n.* **过程,进程;工序,制作法;工艺** *v.* **加工,处理**

[巧记] 派生词:processive(*a.* 前进的,进步的)

[语境] I started moving the china ornaments but dropped a vase in the process.

我动手搬那些瓷制饰物,但在移动时摔了一只花瓶。

It may take a few weeks for your application to be processed.

审查你的申请书也许要等几个星期。

考点集训

1. It gave me a strange feeling of excitement to see my name in _____.

   A. prospect   B. print

   C. process   D. press

2. Every culture has developed _____ for certain kinds of food and drink, and equally strong negative attitudes toward others.

   A. preferences   B. expectations

   C. fantasies   D. fashions

3. So far, _____ winds and currents have kept the thick patch of oil southeast of the Atlantic coast.
   A. governing
   B. blowing
   C. prevailing
   D. ruling
4. The _____ at the military academy is so rigid that students can hardly bear it.
   A. convention
   B. confinement
   C. principle
   D. discipline
5. I was so _____ in today's history lesson. I didn't understand a thing.
   A. amazed
   B. neglected
   C. confused
   D. amuse
6. Deserts and high mountains have always been a _____ to the movement of people from place to place.
   A. barrier
   B. fence
   C. prevention
   D. jam
7. It was the first time that such a _____ had to be taken at a British nuclear power station.
   A. presentation
   B. precaution
   C. preparation
   D. prediction
8. Unemployment seems to be the _____ social problem in this area and may undermine social stability.
   A. prevalent
   B. primitive
   C. previous
   D. premature
9. Many people, when ill, see their doctors and ask them to _____ something that will make them feel better.
   A. describe
   B. prescribe
   C. revise
   D. devise
10. I didn't know the word. I had to _____ a dictionary.
    A. look out
    B. make out
    C. refer to
    D. go over
11. A dark suit is _____ to a light one for evening wear.

A. favourable　　　　　　B. suitable
C. preferable　　　　　　D. proper

答案与解析

1. B　看见打印了我的名字,我有一种莫名其妙的激动。in print 打印,印刷。故选 B。
2. A　每一种文化都有偏好的特定食品和饮品,也有反感的食品和饮品。A 偏好;B 期望;C 幻想;D 时尚。故选 A。
3. C　到目前为止,盛行风和洋流把厚厚的油层吹向了大西洋海岸的东南方向。固定搭配,故选 C。
4. D　军事学院的纪律太严了,学生们都难以忍受。A 会议;B 拘束;C 原则;D 纪律。故选 D。
5. C　今天的历史课我很困惑,什么也听不懂。A 吃惊的,惊奇的;B 被忽视的;C 困惑的;D 被逗笑的,愉快的。故选 C。
6. A　沙漠和高山阻碍了人类的迁移。A 障碍;B 栅栏;C 阻止;D 果酱。故选 A。
7. B　英国核武器基地首次采取这样的预防措施。A 演讲;B 预防措施;C 准备;D 预测。故选 B。
8. A　prevalent 普遍的,根据题意选出 A。
9. B　prescribe 开处方,开药与题意相符。
10. C　我不懂这个单词,我不得不查阅词典。A 当心;B 理解,假装,辨认出,填写[表格];C 查阅,查看;D 重温。故选 C。
11. C　黑色西装比浅色西装更适合晚上穿。A 有利的;B 适合的;C 比……更好;D 合适的。be preferable to 比……更适合,故 C 为正确答案。

Word List 35

produce[32] [prəˈdjuːs] *v.* 生产,制造,显示,演出,导致 *n.* 产品
[巧记]派生词:product(*n.* 产品,产物),production(*n.* 生产,产

品,作品)

[语境] His announcement produced gasps of amazement.
他宣布的消息引起了一片惊叹声。

He hopes to find the money to produce a film about Japan.
他希望筹集到资金以便拍一部关于日本的影片。

[考点] 词语辨析:product:表示"产物,产品",多指工业产品,亦可指任何体力劳动或脑力劳动所生产的东西或发源于其他事物的东西,为可数名词;produce:是"农产品"或"自然产品"的总称,为不可数名词;production:表示"生产,制造",指生产的行为,也可指"产量",为不可数名词

product[6] [ˈprɒdʌkt] *n.* **产品,产物;乘积**

[语境] If our product is properly marketed, it should sell very well.
如果我们的产品适当加以推销,销路应该很好。

The gross national product had increased 5 percent last year.
去年的国民生产总值提高了百分之五。

[考点] 词语辨析:product:表示"产物,产品",多指工业产品,亦可指任何体力劳动或脑力劳动所生产的东西或发源于其他事物的东西,为可数名词;produce:是"农产品"或"自然产品"的总称,为不可数名词;production:表示"生产,制造",指生产的行为,也可指"产量",为不可数名词

production[21] [prəˈdʌkʃən] *n.* **生产,产品,作品,(研究)成果,总产量**

[巧记] 派生词:production-scale(*n.* 生产规模),production-level(*n.* 生产水平)

[语境] We must increase production levels.
我们必须提高生产水平。

The necessary outcome of a war is a fall in production.
战争带来的必然结果就是生产力下降。

[考点] 词语辨析:product:表示"产物,产品",多指工业产品,亦可指任何体力劳动或脑力劳动所生产的东西或发源于其他事物的东西,为可数名词;produce:是"农产品"或"自然产品"的总称,为不可数名词;production:表示"生产,制造",指生产的行为,也可指"产量",为不可数名词

productive [prəˈdʌktɪv] *a.* 生产(性)的,能产的,多产的

[巧记] 派生词:productively(*ad.* 有结果地;有成果地);productiveness(*n.* 多产;丰饶)

[语境] She was elected a productive worker.

她被选为劳动能手。

I spent a very productive hour in the library.

我在图书馆里的这一小时收获很大。

[考点] be productive of 有出现……的倾向,可能产生……的结果

profession [prəˈfeʃən] *n.* 职业,专业,表白,宣布

[巧记] 派生词:professional(*n.* 专业人才 *a.* 专业的,职业的),professor(*n.* 教授)

[语境] He has achieved eminence in his profession.

他在职业上出类拔萃。

Nursing is a vocation as well as a profession.

护理工作既是职业又是使命。

[考点] by profession 就职业来说;在职业上

professor [prəˈfesə(r)] *n.* 教授

[语境] She breathed in every word the professor was saying.

她全神贯注地聆听教授所说的每个字。

profit[23] [ˈprɒfɪt] *n.* 利润,收益 *v.* (by,from)得利,获益;有利于

[巧记] 派生词:profitability(*n.* 收益性;利益率)

[语境] It will profit you nothing to do that.

你做那件事没有什么好处。

You can profit by my mistakes and avoid them yourself.

你可以从我的错误中得到教训,避免犯同样错误。

[考点] profit and loss 盈亏账目;do sth. to one's profit [with profit] 做某事而得益于

progress[14] [ˈprəʊgres] *v./n.* 进步,进展;前进

[巧记] pro-前向 + 拉丁词根 gress 步,走;由"向前走"而引申为进步;同义词:advance

[语境] The student is showing rapid progress in his studies.

这个学生学习上进步很快。

The ship made slow progress through the rough sea.

船只在汹涌的大海中缓慢前进。

[考点] in progress 在进行中，在举行；make progress 取得进展，进步；make progress in 在……方面取得进步；make progress towards 朝着……（目标）前进

project[32]['prɒdʒekt] *n.* **方案，工程，项目** *v.* **投射，放映；设计，规划**

[语境] The class are doing a project on the Roman occupation of Britain.

这个班在进行一项关于古罗马人占领不列颠的研究。

Their project to establish a new national park will be completed next year.

他们建造一个新的国家公园的工程将于明年完工。

[考点] project oneself 突出自己，表现自己；project sth. onto sb. 设想某人怀有和自己一样的想法（或感情）；以己之心度人之腹

promise[6]['prɒmɪs] *v.* **允许，答应；有……可能** *n.* **承诺；希望，出息**

[巧记] promittere = pro-前 + mittere 送，交；派生词：promiseful（*a.* 有希望的，有前途的）

[语境] I don't trust his promise to come for a visit.

我相信他不会如约前来访问。

I promise to return your bicycle on good condition.

我答应一定完好无损地还你的自行车。

[考点] be promised to（指女方）与……订婚，被许配给……；break one's promise 违背诺言，违约；keep one's promise 遵守诺言，守约

promising ['prɒmɪsɪŋ] *a.* **有希望的，有前途的**

[巧记] promise + ing 变成形容词

[语境] But I distinctly remember you promising to phone me!

可我记得清清楚楚你是答应了要给我打电话的！

After a promising start, the project soon fizzled out.

这项计划开始时很有希望，但不久就失败了。

[考点] in a promising state [way] 有希望的

promote[8] [prəˈməut] v. 促进,发扬;提升,提拔;增进,助长

[巧记] 派生词:promotion(n. 晋级,增进,筹办); promoter(n. 促进者,助长者)

[语境] The government decided to promote public welfare.
政府决定发展公共福利。
He likes to read biographies of great men to promote himself.
他喜欢读伟人传记来提升自己。

promotion [prəˈməuʃən] n. 升级,晋级;宣传,推广

[语境] The teacher conferred with the principal about Dick's promotion.
教师与校长商谈了迪克的升级问题。
During 1984, Remington spent a lot of money on advertising and promotion.
1984年,雷明顿公司在广告和促销方面花费了大量的资金。

proof [pru:f] n. 证据,证明;校样,样张

[巧记] prove 的名词形式

[语境] Have you got any proof that you own this bike?
你有什么证据证明这辆自行车是你的?
A soldier's courage is put to the proof in battle.
士兵的勇气在战斗中得到考验。

[考点] give proof of 证明,提供……的证明;in proof of 作……的证据

proper[15] [ˈprɒpə(r)] a. 适合的;合乎体统的;固有的;有礼貌的

[巧记] 派生词:properly(ad. 恰当地;有礼貌地;正确地;体面地)

[语境] She hadn't had a proper holiday for years.
多年来她都没有过真正的假期。
His mother has trained him to be a very proper young man.
他的母亲已经把他训练成循规蹈矩的人了。

[考点] at a proper time 在适当的时候

property[5] [ˈprɒpətɪ] n. 财产,资产,地产,房地产,所有物;性质,

特性

[语境] A fence divides the two properties.

有一道栅栏隔着这两处房地产。

The city is developing rapidly and property in the center is becoming more expensive.

这个城市在飞速发展,市中心的房地产价格越来越高。

[考点] public property 公共财产

proposal[5] [prəˈpəuzəl] *n.* 提议,建议;求婚

[巧记] pro-(在……前) + poser(放)→提议

[语境] Her resistance to the proposal has crumpled.

她对这个建议的抵触情绪已化为乌有了。

We will discuss the proposal at the meeting.

我们将在会议上讨论这项提议。

[考点] offer proposals for[of] 提出……建议

propose[11] [prəˈpəuz] *v.* 提议,建议;提名,推荐;求婚

[巧记] pro-在……前 + poser 放,引申为建议;派生词:proposed (*a.* 被提议的;所推荐的), proposition (*n.* 提议,建议)

[语境] I wish to propose a toast to our friendship.

我提议为我们的友谊干杯。

He proposed that a change should be made.

他建议做一些改变。

[考点] propose sb. for 提名某人(任某职),推荐某人; propose to sb. 向某人求婚

prose [prəuz] *n.* 散文

[语境] His writings include poetry and prose.

他的作品包括诗和散文。

prospect [ˈprɒspekt] *n.* 景色;前景,前途,展望

[巧记] pro 向前 + spect→向前看→展望;派生词:prospection (*n.* 展望;勘察)

[语境] I see little prospect of an improvement in his condition.

我看他的情况没有什么改进的希望。

A rich harvest is in prospect.

丰收在望。

[考点] in prospect 可期待；有……希望；在考虑中；open up prospects (for) 为……开辟前景

protect[26] [prə'tekt] v. **保护，防护；为……保险；备款以支付**

[巧记] 派生词：protected(a. 受保护的)；protection(n. 保护，保护制度，防卫)

[语境] These gallant soldiers will protect our country.
这些勇敢的士兵会保卫我们的国家的。
The knights rushed into the palace to protect their king.
骑士们冲向宫殿去保护国王。

protection[10] [prə'tekʃən] n. **保护，保护制度，防卫**

[巧记] protect 保护 + -ion 名词后缀；派生词：protectionism(n. 保护贸易主义，保护政策，保护贸易论)

[语境] We subscribe to an animal protection society.
我们定期捐款给一个动物保护基金会。
The young in our society need care and protection.
我们社会的年轻人需要受到关怀和爱护。

[考点] under the protection of 在……保护之下

protective [prə'tektɪv] a. **给予保护的，保护的**

[巧记] 派生词：protectively(ad. 保护地；防护地)，protectiveness(n. 保护；防护)

[语境] The armadillo has a protective shell of bony plates.
犰狳有角质鳞片的护甲。
He put his arm round her in a protective gesture.
他用一只手臂环住她做出保护的姿势。

protein ['prəʊtiːn] n. **蛋白质**

[语境] Rice contains protein and fat.
大米含蛋白质和脂肪。

protest ['prəʊtest; prə'test] v./n. **主张，断言，抗议，反对**

[巧记] pro-test；派生词：protestation(n. 声明，断言，主张)

[语境] She protested that she had never seen the accused man before.

她坚持说她以前从未见过这个被指控的男子。

His protests on human rights sound hollow.

他就人权问题提出的抗议听来很空洞。

[考点] enter a protest 提出抗议；under protest 被迫地；持异议地；抗议地；without protest 乖乖地；心甘情愿地；毫无反对地

proud [praʊd] *a.* (of) 自豪的；引以为自豪的；妄自尊大的

[巧记] 派生词：proudly (*ad.* 自豪地)；反义词：arrogant (*a.* 傲慢的；自负的；自大的)

[语境] It was a proud day for us when we won the trophy.

我们夺得奖杯那一天是值得我们骄傲的日子。

He is too proud now to be seen with his former friends.

他现在忘乎所以了，觉得跟以前的朋友在一起有失他的脸面。

[考点] be proud of 以……为荣；以……自豪

do oneself proud 养尊处优，自奉优厚

do sb. proud 给某人面子，使某人感到荣幸；慷慨地款待某人；丰盛地招待某人

prove [pruːv] *v.* 证明，证实；检验；考验；鉴定；结果是，表明是

[巧记] 派生词 proven (*a.* 被证明的)；同义词：certify (*v.* 证明，证实；保证；担保)

[语境] She claimed that money had been wasted and our financial difficulties seemed to prove her point.

她断定那笔钱用得不是地方，而我们在经济上遇到的困难却也似乎说明她言之有理。

The old methods proved best after all.

老方法结果被证明是最好的方法。

[考点] prove (oneself) to be 证明（自己）是

prove up 具备……条件；探明

prove up to the hilt 充分证明

provide[35] [prəˈvaɪd] *v.* 供应，供给，准备，预防，规定

[巧记] 派生词 provided *conj.* 以……为条件；假如；同义词：furnish(v. 供应;装备;提供)

[语境] The possibility of the book being translated is provided for in your contract.

在你们的合同中已确定有可能要翻译这本书。

These books will provide us with all the information we need.

这本书将为我们提供所需要的全部信息。

[考点] provide against 为……做好准备,预防(灾荒、困难)

provide for 提供生活费;养活

provide with 给……提供;以……装备

psychology[5] [saɪˈkɒlədʒɪ] *n.* 心理学,心理

[巧记] psych(心理,精神) + ology(学)→心理学

[语境] She has a background in child psychology.

她受过儿童心理学的教育。

public[46] [ˈpʌblɪk] *a.* 公共的,公用的;公开的,公然的 *n.* 公众,民众

[巧记] 派生词:publication (*n.* 出版物)

[语境] The pension fund owns shares in several major public companies.

该养老基金在几家主要出售股份给公众的公司中均有股份。

The town has its own public library and public gardens.

那城市有自己的公用图书馆和公园。

publication[4] [ˌpʌblɪˈkeɪʃən] *n.* 出版物;出版,发行;公布,发表

[语境] Her last novel ran into three reprints in its first year of publication.

她最近的一部小说在出版当年就重印了三次。

A publication usually issued daily or weekly, contains current news, editorials, feature articles, and usually advertising.

刊物通常是每日或每周发行的出版物,内容包括时事、社评、人物传记和广告。

publicity [pʌbˈlɪsɪtɪ] *n.* 公开,宣传,广告,推销

[巧记] 派生词:publicize(*v.* 宣传;广告;公布),publicly (*adv.* 公开地,公然地)

[语境] Reply to Publicity Department, FREEPOST, Oxford University Press, Oxford.

回信免费邮寄至牛津牛津大学出版社宣传部。

The new publicity manager is really on the ball.

新的宣传部主任确实很内行。

[考点] the publicity department 宣传部; avoid [shun] publicity 避免惹人注意; give publicity to sth. (= give sth. publicity) 宣扬某事,公布某事

publish ['pʌblɪʃ] v. 出版,刊印;公布,发布

[巧记] 派生词:publishable(a. 可出版的;可发表的;可发行的), publisher(n. 出版者,发行人)

[语境] Only in 1687 did he at last publish his new theory.

终于在1687年他发表了他的新理论。

Her book was published last year.

她的书去年发表了。

pull [pʊl] v. 拉,拖 n. 拉,拖;拉力,牵引力

[巧记] 反义词:push(v. 推)

[语境] Her remark pulled me up short.

我听到她的话后一下子愣住了。

He has a lot of pull with the managing director.

他对总经理有很大的影响力。

[考点] pull down 拆毁;摧毁;推翻;pull in(火车)进站,到站,停站;pull off a plan 努力实现计划;pull through 使克服困难、渡过难关

punish ['pʌnɪʃ] v. 惩罚,处罚

[巧记] 派生词:punishable(a. 该罚的;可罚的), punishment(n. 处罚,惩罚,刑罚);反义词:forgive(v. 原谅,免除,宽恕)

[语境] The teacher warned them that she would punish anyone who stepped out of line.

老师警告他们说谁要不守规矩就罚谁。

The great thieves punish the little ones.

【谚】大贼罚小贼;大鱼吃小鱼。

[考点] punish sb. for his crime 处罚某人;punish sb. with [by]

death 处某人以死刑

pupil [ˈpjuːpl] *n.* 学生,小学生;瞳孔

[语境] The pupil joined the two points by a straight line.
那个小学生用直线把两点连接起来。

pure [pjʊə(r)] *a.* 纯的,纯洁的;纯理论的,抽象的;完全的

[巧记] 派生词 puree *n.* 煮烂过滤或制浆的食物;浓汤;反义词: applied(*a.* 实用的;应用的)

[语境] Water can be made pure by distilling it.
水可以通过蒸馏而提纯。

She has pure gypsy blood in her veins.
她血管里流的是纯吉普赛人的血液。

[考点] the pure in [of] heart 心地纯洁的人们
pure and simple 纯粹的,不折不扣的

purpose[23] [ˈpɜːpəs] *n.* 目的,意图;用途,效果

[巧记] 派生词:purposeful *a.* 有目的的;重大的;意味深长的;有决心的;同义词: aim(*n.* 瞄准;目标,目的;瞄准的方向 *v.* 瞄准;对准;意欲,旨在,致力于)

[语境] He purposed to visit South America.
他计划去参观南美。

Did you come to London for the purpose of seeing your family, or for business purposes?
你到伦敦来的目的是要看望家人还是为了公事?

[考点] on purpose 故意地;为了;特地

I came here on purpose to see you.
我特地来这里看你。

pursue [pəˈsjuː] *v.* 追赶,追踪;继续,从事

[巧记] 派生词:pursuer (*n.* 追赶者;追求者;追捕者;从事者);同义词: chaser(*n.* 猎人,驱逐舰)

[语境] She is pursuing her studies at the university.
她在大学继续深造。

The government is pursuing a policy of non-intervention.
政府正奉行不干预政策。

[考点] a fox that was pursued by hounds 被猎狗追捕的狐狸
pursue lofty political goals 追求崇高的政治目标

push [puʃ] v. 推；催逼，逼迫 n. 推，推力；促进，推进

[巧记] 派生词：pushed a. 处于窘境的，为难的；同义词：coax (v. 用好话劝，哄诱；耐心地处理，慢慢将……弄好；哄得，诱得；劝诱，哄骗)

[语境] He pushed his way to the front of the crowd.
他挤到了人群的前面。
He pushed her into making a decision.
他催促她做出决定。

put [put] vt. 放，搁，置；表达；使处于……状态，记下

[语境] He put his hands in his pockets.
他把手放在口袋里。
It's time to put the baby to bed.
该让那婴儿上床睡觉了。

[考点] put up to 鼓动；唆使……做……
Who put you up to this trick?
是谁唆使你玩这种把戏的？
put up with
忍受；忍耐；受苦

puzzle ['pʌzəl] n. 难题，谜，迷惑 v. (使)迷惑，(使)为难

[巧记] 派生词：puzzled (a. 困惑的，茫然的，搞糊涂的)；同义词：confusion (n. 混乱，无秩序，混淆)

[语境] Her reply puzzled me.
她的回答把我弄糊涂了。
He stood there watching with puzzled despair.
他束手无策地站在那儿看着。

考点集训

1. Facing growing costs and shrinking tax _____, the government is now threatening to cut funding for environmental protection programs.

A. budget B. collection
   C. profit D. revenue
2. The money I got from teaching on the side was a useful _____ to my ordinary income.
   A. profit B. supplement
   C. subsidy D. replacement
3. In Disneyland every year, some 800,000 plants are replaced because Disney refused to _____ signs asking his "guests" not to step on them.
   A. put down B. put out
   C. put up D. put off
4. Purchasing the new production line will be a _____ deal for the company.
   A. profitable B. tremendous
   C. forceful D. favorite
5. The leader of the expedition _____ everyone to follow his example.
   A. promoted B. reinforced
   C. sparked D. inspired
6. The _____ of finding gold in California attracted a lot of people to settle down there.
   A. prospects B. speculations
   C. stakes D. provisions
7. The British government often says that furnishing children with _____ to the information superhighway is a top priority.
   A. procedure B. protection
   C. allowance D. access

答案与解析

1. D 固定短语搭配。tax revenue 表示税收的意思。
2. B 我在外面捞的外快(the money)对我的普通收入(ordinary income)是一个补充吧！A 利益；B 补充；C 补贴；D 取代。故 B 为正确答案。
3. C 每年迪士尼乐园要补植大约 80 万棵树,因为它不同意竖起让游客勿踩的标志物。A 镇压;B 扑灭;C 竖起;D 推迟。故 C 为正确答案。
4. A 购买新的生产线对公司而言是一笔很合算的买卖。A 有利益;B 巨大的;C 强有力的;D 最喜爱的。故 A 为最佳选项。
5. D 远征队的队长激励大家效仿他。A 提升;B 强化;C 产生火花;D 激励,激发。故 D 为正确答案。
6. A 加利福尼亚的寻金热吸引了很多人在那里定居。A 前景,希望;B 投机;C 股份,在公司的重大利益;D 规定。故选 A。
7. D 英国政府经常说让孩子们接触信息高速公路是首要之事。A 步骤,程序;B 保护;C 津贴,补贴,零用钱;D 权利,接近。故选 D。

Word List 36

qualify[13] [ˈkwɔlɪfaɪ] *v.* **取得资格,使合格,使胜任**

[巧记] 派生词:qualifier (*n.* 已取得资格的人;修饰语;合格者);
同义词:characterise

[语境] The training course qualifies you to be/as a driving instructor.
参加了训练课程就有资格成为驾驶教练。
After three years here you'll qualify for a rise.
你在这里三年就可获加薪。

[考点] 类似的动词:amplify 放大,simplify 简化

quality[23] [ˈkwɔlɪtɪ] *n.* **质,质量;品质,特性**

[巧记] -ties 品质;性质(a watch of good quality 品质好的手表);
同义词:characteristic(*n.* 特性,特色,特征 *a.* 特有的;典型的;表示特性的)

[语境] It was a bad year for films, in terms of both quantity and quality.

今年的电影无论从数量上还是质量上都说不上好。

A large quantity of air-conditioners has been sold since the temperature is high.

因为气温很高,大量空调售出。

[考点]相关词:qualitative a. 定性的,性质的

quantity [ˈkwɒntɪtɪ] n. 数量,量;大量

[巧记]同义词:amount(n. 总额,数量 v. 总计;等于)

[语境]The long noses on these dogs are an inbred characteristic.

这些狗的长鼻子是同系交配的特点。

Her predominant characteristic is honesty.

她最为突出的特点是诚实。

[考点]a quantity of 一些;a known quantity【数】已知数[量];a negligible quantity【数】可忽略的量,无足轻重的人;微不足道的事

quarrel [ˈkwɒrəl] v./n. 争吵,吵架

[巧记]派生词 quarreler n. 争吵者;吵闹者;同义词:altercate(v. 争论,口角)

[语境] I can't help them to resolve their quarrel, they must fight it out between them.

我无法帮助他们解决争论,他们得打出个结果来。

I would rather be laughed at than quarrel with him.

我宁愿被嘲笑,也不愿和他吵架。

[考点]词组:pick a quarrel 寻衅

quarter [ˈkwɔːtə(r)] n. 四分之一;一刻钟;季,季度;(pl.)住处;地区,区域

[语境]The clothes should soak for a quarter before washing.

洗这些衣服之前应浸泡一刻钟。

She pays her rent by the quarter.

她按季度付房租。

Javert watched the quarter for more than a month.

沙威观察了那地区有一个多月。

核心词汇精解

queen [kwiːn] *n.* 女王,皇后,王后

[语境] They cringed before the queen.
他们在女王面前卑躬屈膝。

question [ˈkwestʃən] *n.* 问题;询问 *v.* 询问;怀疑,对……表示疑问

[巧记] 派生词:questioning *n.* 审问,讯问;同义词:ask(*v.* 问;请求;询问;要求)

[语境] A new bicycle is out of the question—we can't afford it.
买新自行车的事谈不到——我们买不起。

She is so talented that her success can only be a question of time.
她才华横溢,事业成功只是时间问题。

[考点] a loaded question 另有用意的问题;含义隐晦的问题;抱有偏见的问题;a previous question (议会中的)先决问题[动议];a question of questions 首要问题

quick [kwɪk] *a.* 快的;灵敏的,伶俐的;敏锐的 *ad.* 快,迅速地

[语境] Everyone is trying to get rich quick nowadays.
现在每个人都想要尽快发财致富。

He gave a quick answer to the teacher's question.
他对老师的提问作出了迅速的回答。

[考点] cut (a person) to the quick 伤害某人的感情

quiet [ˈkwaɪət] *n.* 安静 *v.* 使安静,平静

[巧记] 派生词:quieten (*v.* 使安静;抚慰;变安静);同义词:calm(*n.* 平稳, 风平浪静 *v.* 使镇定;使平静;镇定下来;平静下来 *a.* 平静的, 冷静的)

[语境] His health has turned all the better for him after a quiet holiday abroad.
在国外度过了一个宁静的假期后,他的身体状况有所好转。

The quiet contentment of a well-fed child satisfied the tired mother.
孩子喂饱后不哭不闹的满足状态使疲惫的母亲很满意。

[考点] on the quiet 私下;秘密地;暗地里

quit [kwɪt] *v.* 离开,退出;停止,放弃,辞职

[巧记]同义词：abandon(n. 放纵，放任；狂热 v. 丢弃；中止，放弃；遗弃，抛弃；使放纵)

[语境] He quit in disgrace over the bribe.
他因受贿而不光彩地辞职了。
You cannot quit smoking too soon.
你越早戒烟越好。

[考点]quit 还可以用来指计算机的程序中的退出操作；be quit of 摆脱，脱离，免除；quit it [美俚]死

quite [kwaɪt] *ad.* 十分，完全；相当，颇；的确，真正

[巧记]同义词：absolutely(ad. 绝对地，完全地；一点不错；正是如此)

[语境]It was quite wonderful.
那可太妙了。

[考点]quite a 相当……的；很有点……的；quite other 完全不同的

quotation [kwəʊˈteɪʃən] *n.* 引语，语录

[语境]We attributed this quotation to Shakespeare.
我们把这句引用语归于莎士比亚。

quote [kwəʊt] *vt.* 引用，援引

[巧记]派生词：quoter(n. 引用者；报价者；估价者)

[语境] He quotes the *Bible* to support his beliefs.
他引用《圣经》来支持他的信仰。
It was quoted 5 dollars.
这在市面上开价 5 美元。

[考点]quote 是重复别人的话作为证人或权威；(与 from 连用)举例引证，引述；(与 as 连用)引以为证；(常与 at 连用)开价；报价

radio [ˈreɪdɪəʊ] *n.* 收音机；无线电报，无线电话 *v.* 无线电通信

[巧记]同义词：broadcast(n. 广播)

[语境]The people next door play their radio from morning till night.
邻居从早到晚开着收音机。
I must get the radio fixed.

核心词汇精解

我必须找人把收音机修理好。

railway ['reɪlweɪ] *n.* 铁路

[巧记] rail(铁轨) + way(道路)→用铁轨建成的路→铁路

[语境] This railway has been splayed for 60 miles.

这条铁路已延长了60英里。

rain [reɪn] *n.* 雨 *vi.* 下雨

[巧记] rainy *a.* 多雨的;下雨的

[语境] Rain drips from the umbrella.

雨水从伞上滴下来。

It is going to rain; I think we best go tomorrow.

天快下雨了,我想我们最好明天去。

raise [reɪz] *vt.* 举起,提高

[巧记] 派生词:raised(*a.* 浮雕的;升高的;凸起的;发酵起泡的);raiser (*n.* 举起者,升起者,提出者,养育者,募集者,解除者);合成词:cattle-raiser 养牛者;curtain-raiser 开台戏;fire-raiser 放火者,纵火者

[语境] It's difficult raising a family on a small income.

依靠微薄的收入是很难养家的。

I was raised by my aunt on a farm.

我是在农场由姨妈抚养大的。

[考点] raise money 筹钱;raise an eyebrow 引起怀疑;竖起眉毛;raise from the dead 使某人起死回生

range[10] [reɪndʒ] *n.* 范围,距离,领域;排列,连续

[语境] The children's ages range from 8 to 15.

这些孩子们的年龄在8~15岁。

Our conversation ranged over many topics.

我们的谈话涉及很多话题。

[考点] at close range 接近地;in range 在射程内;out of range 在射程外

rank [ræŋk] *n.* 排,行列;等级,地位 *vt.* 评价,分等,归类;等级高于

[巧记] 派生词:rankly(*ad.* 繁茂地;恶臭地), ranking(*n.* 等级,顺序)

365

[语境]A general ranks a captain.

将军的级别比上尉高。

I rank her among the country's best writers.

我认为她可属全国最优秀作家之列。

[考点]rank 也可以用作动词,表示派名

rapid [ˈræpɪd] *a.* 快的,急速的

[语境]He made rapid progress in his studies.

他学习上进步很快。

Childhood is a period of rapid growth.

幼年是生长迅速的时期。

rare[11] [reə(r)] *a.* 稀有的,难得的,珍奇的;稀薄的,稀疏的

[语境] A collector of rare insects will show us some of his latest discoveries.

一位稀有昆虫采集家将给我们看一些他的最新发现。

It is rare to find such a genius nowadays.

这样的天才现在很少见。

[考点]派生词:rarity (*n.* 罕有;稀薄), rareness (*n.* 罕有;稀薄)

rarely [ˈreəlɪ] *ad.* 很少,难得,非常

[巧记]rare(稀少的) + -ly(副词后缀)→很少,难得

[语境] The country's car industry is so strongly protected that foreign cars are rarely seen there.

该国对汽车工业严加保护,在那很少可以看到外国汽车。

The leader rarely shows herself in public.

这位领导很少在公众场合露面。

[考点]a rare bird 珍禽;rare metals 稀有金属

rate [reɪt] *n.* 速率,比率;等级;价格,费 *vt.* 评级,评价

[语境] He is generally rated as one of the best modern writers.

他被公认为现代最杰出的作家之一。

They drove at a steady rate.

他们以平稳的速度开车。

[考点] rate of interest 利率;rate of exchange 货币兑换率

rather [ˈrɑːðə] *ad.* 相当,有些;宁可,宁愿

[语境] I would rather fail than cheat in the examination.

我宁愿考不及格,也不愿意考试作弊。

Poultry is rather cheap now.

现在的禽肉相当便宜。

[考点][常与 would 或 had 连用]宁愿,宁可;稍微;相当;[可与 or 连用]更确切,更恰当;更接近;[口]当然,确实如此,相反地,倒不如说……更……;[与连词 than 配合使用]与其……不如……;宁可……也不……

ratio [ˈreɪʃɪəʊ] *n.* 比率,比

[语境] The ratio of schoolboys to schoolgirls is 2 to 1.

男学生和女学生的比例是2∶1。

Men outnumber women here in the ratio of three to one.

此地男子数量以3∶1超过女子。

[考点] in direct ratio 按正比例;in inverse ratio 按反比例

rational[18] [ˈræʃənl] *a.* 理性的;合理的

[语境] But there are perfectly rational explanations for all of this.

其实,所有这一切都有完全合理的解释。

[考点] rational,reasonable,sensible 辨析:这些形容词均有"明智的,合情合理的"之意。rational:指有理性的,有思维推理能力,而不是凭感觉冲动从事。reasonable:表示合乎情理、公正或务实。sensible:一般指合乎常情、切合实际的行为与思想,侧重明白事理

raw [rɔː] *a.* 生的,未煮熟的;未加工过的

[语境] We imported raw rubber from Malaysia.

我们从马来西亚进口生胶。

The factory is in frequent scarcity of raw materials.

这家工厂经常原料不足。

[考点] in the raw 不加粉饰的,未加工的;touch sb. on the raw 碰到某人痛处

reach [riːtʃ] *vt.* 伸手,够到,触到;到,到达 *vi.* 达到,延伸;伸出手 *n.* 能达到的范围

[语境] I can just about reach the apples on the top branch.

我只差一点就能够着最上边树枝上的苹果了。

react[4] [rɪˈækt] *vi.* 反应,起作用

[巧记] 同根词:reaction *n.* 反应;reactor *n.* 反应者

[语境] How did they react to your suggestion?
他们对你的建议有什么反应?
She reacted to the insult by turning her back on him.
她受辱之后就不再理睬他了。

read [riːd] *v.* 朗读;阅读 *vt.* 辨认,观察 *vi.* 读到,获悉

[语境] The teacher read the poem to the class.
老师给全班同学朗诵这首诗歌。

reader [ˈriːdə(r)] *n.* 读者;读物,读本

[语境] The magazine she gave me is *Reader's Digest*.
她给我的杂志是《读者文摘》。
Your course reader will have most of the required articles and book chapters.
你的课程读物包含大部分的必读文章和书的章节。

readily [ˈredɪlɪ] *ad.* 容易地,乐意地

[巧记] ready *a.* 乐意的,情愿的

[语境] These data are not readily available.
这些资料不是轻易能得到的。

reading [ˈriːdɪŋ] *n.* 阅读,读书;读物,选读;读数

[语境] The students developed their reading skills further during this term.
本学期学生们进一步提高了阅读技巧。
A spate of English reading materials began to pour off the presses.
大量英语读物开始泛滥发行。

ready [ˈredɪ] *a.* (for)准备好的,现成的;甘心的

[语境] The troops were ready for anything.
部队已做好了一切准备。
She is always ready to help others.
她总是乐于助人。

[考点] 固定搭配 be ready to do sth.

real [rɪəl] *a.* 真的,真实的;实际的,现实的

[语境] Bottled lemon juice is no good—you must use the real thing.

瓶装柠檬汁可不行——你得用真货。

What was the real reason for your absence?

你缺席的真正原因是什么?

[考点] 词语辨析:real 所表示的"真实的"实际上指的是"客观存在";true(名词为 truth)有两层基本的含义:"真的",此意义指符合一定标准的、符合一定模式的;另一层的含义是"真实的",此意义主要是指符合真实情况

reality [rɪˈælɪtɪ] *n.* 现实,实际;真实

[语境] If we redouble our efforts, our dream will translate into reality.

如果我们加倍努力,我们的梦想就会变成现实。

In this case, how do we even define reality?

在这样的状态中,我们又如何定义"真实"?

realize/-ise[15] [ˈrɪəlaɪz] *v.* 认识到,体会到;实现

[巧记] 词根:real(现实的) + -ize(使……)→实现

[语境] Do you realize that all of these shirts are half off?

你知道这些衬衫都卖半价了吗?

Only after you lose your health will you realize the importance of health.

唯有在失去健康之后,你才能了解健康的重要性。

[考点] realize, understand 这两个词是近义词,在一起比较的一般含义是"意识到""弄明白",常常可以互换使用。但 realize 可以表示"实现",understand 可以表示"听懂""理解"

really [ˈrɪəlɪ] *ad.* 确实,实在,真正地,果然

[语境] After the shock of their electoral defeat, the party really began to pull together.

该党在受到选举失败的打击之后,才真正地团结起来。

He's quite a nice boy, really.

他真是个好孩子,一点不假。

reason [ˈriːzən] n. **原因,理性,理智** v. **推理,说服,辩论,讨论**

[语境] It stands to reason that nobody will work without pay.
做工作不能白做,这是明摆着的事。
He was excused by reason of his age.
他因为年龄的关系而得到宽恕。

[考点] for reasons of 因为;have reason for[to do] sth. 有做某事的理由[根据]

reasonable[8] [ˈriːzənəbəl] a. **合理的,有道理的;通情达理的;适度的**

[巧记] 词根:reason 理由 + able 能……的

[语境] The management took all reasonable safety precautions.
管理部门采取了一切合理的安全措施。
I think that's not reasonable.
我认为这是没有道理的。

recall[4] [rɪˈkɔːl] v. **回忆,回想;撤销,收回**

[巧记] re-(又、再) + call(喊,唤)→唤回来→回忆

[语境] I can't recall how long it has been.
我回忆不起来多长时间了。
I can recall the men's features.
我回忆得起这个人的容貌。

[考点] 再认(recognition)和回忆(recall)。recognition 指当感知过的事物重新出现在眼前时,仍能识别出来;recall 是指对不在眼前的过去经历过的事物能够重新在脑中出现映像的过程

receive [rɪˈsiːv] vt. **收到,接到;接待,接见;受到,蒙受**

[巧记] re-回来 + 拉丁词根 ceive 拿,取;把……拿回来,也就是收到,接受

[语境] His speech was favorably received.
他的演讲很受欢迎。
The boat received a heavy load.
这船负有重载。

[考点] receive 只表示收到了某物,并不表示接受,而 accept 则表

示接受。如：I don't accept his invitation。我不接受他的邀请

recent ['ri:sənt] *a.* 新近的，近来的

[巧记] 派生词：recently(*ad.* 最近，近来，新近)；反义词：ancient (*a.* 古代的，古老的)

[语境] The government's control over the newspapers has loosened in recent years.
近年来政府已放松了对报纸的控制。
The minister has put a different gloss on recent developments.
部长就局势的最新发展作了另一番解释。

recently ['ri:sntlɪ] *ad.* 最近，近来，新近

[语境] Her books have been in popularity recently.
她的书近来大受欢迎。
A ban on the importation of drugs had been issued recently.
最近已经发布了禁止进口毒品的法令。

reckon ['rekən] *v.* 数，计算；想，料想

[语境] Did you reckon in the time needed for unloading the cargo?
你把卸货所需的时间计算进去了吗？
I reckon we'll go next month.
我想我们下个月去。

[考点] reckon as 认为（看作）

recognition [ˌrekəg'nɪʃən] *n.* 认出，辨认；承认

[巧记] re(又) + cogno(知道)→又知道某个人→认出

[语境] After 25 years the town centre had changed beyond (all) recognition.
25年过去了，市中心变得认不出来了。
The photo has faded beyond recognition.
相片已经模糊，不能辨认。

[考点] out of recognition 完全改了模样，面目全非

recognize/-ise[5] ['rekəgnaɪz] *vt.* 认出，识别；承认

[巧记] 同根词：recognition *n.* 公认，认出，认识；recognized (*adj.* 公认的，经过验证的)

[语境] She could hardly recognize her son through the mist of tears that filled her eyes.

她泪眼蒙蒙,几乎不能认出自己的儿子。

He walked along in the shadows hoping no one would recognize him.

他走在暗处,希望没有人能认出他来。

recommend[11] [ˌrekəˈmend] *vt.* **劝告,建议;介绍,推荐**

[巧记] 同义词:advise *vt.* 劝告,建议

[语境] I wouldn't recommend you to go there alone.

我劝你不要孤身一人到那里去。

Can you recommend to me a good dictionary?

你能为我推荐一本好词典吗?

[考点] recommend sb./sth. to sb. 向某人推荐某人或某物

record [ˈrekɔːd] *n.* **记录;最高纪录;履历;唱片** *v.* **记录,录音**

[语境] Just for the record, the minister's statement is wrong on two points.

必须明确指出,部长的言论有两点是错误的。

My voice records quite well.

我的声音录下来很好听。

[考点] a record run 打破纪录的赛跑;keep a record (of) 记下来,记录

recover [rɪˈkʌvə(r)] *vi.* **恢复,痊愈** *vt.* **收回,挽回;重新获得,重新找回**

[语境] The police recovered the stolen jewellery.

警察找回了被盗的珠宝。

He's now fully recovered from his stroke.

他的中风病现在已经完全康复了。

[考点] recover sth. from sb./sth. 又获得(金钱、时间或地位)

recreation [ˌrekrɪˈeɪʃən] *n.* **娱乐,消遣**

[巧记] recreate *v.* 娱乐,消遣 recreative *a.* 消遣的

[语境] But you should have better recreation than TV.

但是你应该有比看电视还要好的消遣。

recycle [riːˈsaɪkl] *v.* **使再循环,反复利用**

[巧记] re(返回) + cycle(圆)→回到某过程的起点→使再循环

[语境] Developing countries all over the world already recycle materials.

全世界的发展中国家已经开始循环利用原材料。

red [red] *a.* 红色的 *n.* 红色

[语境] The machine sprang into operation when I touched the red button.

我一按那个红按钮,那部机器就突然开动起来了。

reduce[30] [rɪ'djuːs] *vt.* 缩小,减小,减低;使成为;简化;还原

[巧记] re 回 + duce→往回引→减少

[语境] He is reduced almost to a skeleton.

他瘦得几乎变成了一个骨头架子。

Taking extra vitamins may reduce your liability to colds.

多吃一些维生素会减少你得感冒的可能性。

[考点] reduce...to 使变为(更小,更少……)

refer[44] [rɪ'fɜː(r)] *vi.* (to) 参考,查阅,查询;(to) 提到,引用,指 *vt.* 叫(人)去……(以便得到消息、援助等);把……归因于

[语境] For further particulars, please refer to Chapter Ten.

详情请查阅第 10 章。

The matter was referred to the United Nations.

此事被提交给联合国。

[考点] refer sth. back to sb. 把文件等退回给某人;refer to sb./sth. 提到,说到,涉及某人或某物

reflect[16] [rɪ'flekt] *vt.* 反射;反映,表现 *vi* 反射,映出;思考,仔细考虑

[巧记] 派生词:reflectibility(*n.* 反射); reflectible(*a.* 可反射的,可映出的)

[语境] The results reflect the greatest credit upon all concerned.

这些成绩带给所有有关人员最大的荣誉。

The sunlight was reflected in the water.

日光由水面反射出来。

[考点] reflect on[upon] 仔细想,考虑,反省

reform [rɪ'fɔːm] *vt.* 改革,改良;改造;重新组成 *n.* 改革,改良;改过

373

自新

[巧记] re 再次 + form→再形成→改造

[语境] Our reform made an inexorable march of progress.

我们的改革取得了势不可当的进展。

They made a clamor for reform.

他们强烈要求改革。

[考点] reform 一般指改掉缺点、弊病使之更加完美,常用在社会或政治改革上;transform 是改变形态,也引申为改变性格、特点。There are signs that he's reforming. 有迹象表明他在变好

refrigerator[riˈfridʒəreitə]/fridge[fridʒ] *n.* **冰箱,冷冻机,冷藏库**

[语境] Take the beef out of the refrigerator to defrost.

把牛肉从冰箱里拿出来解冻。

考点集训

1. For more than 20 years, we've been supporting educational programs that _____ from kindergartens to colleges.
   A. move   B. shift
   C. range   D. spread

2. His temper and personality show that he can become a soldier of the top _____.
   A. circle   B. rank
   C. category   D. grade

3. That he brought the company big profits wouldn't _____ putting the company's money into his own pockets.
   A. justify   B. clarify
   C. testify   D. amplify

4. Eye contact is important because wrong contact may create a communication _____.
   A. tragedy   B. vacuum
   C. question   D. barrier

5. Though _____ in a big city, Peter always prefers to paint the

primitive scenes of country life.

A. grown B. raised
C. tended D. cultivated

6. The shop assistant was dismissed as she was _____ of cheating customers.

A. accused B. charged
C. scolded D. cursed

7. It was in the United States that I made the _____ of professor Jones.

A. acknowledgement B. acquaintance
C. recognition D. association

8. What is happening is a survival-of-the-fittest struggle affecting _____ smaller factories in relatively low-tech, labor-intensive industries.

A. primarily B. rationally
C. primitively D. respectively

9. A large _____ of the sunlight never reaches the earth while infrared heat given off by the earth is allowed to escape freely.

A. ratio B. proportion
C. rate D. fraction

答案与解析

1. C 这20多年来,我们一直在支持包括从幼儿园到大学的教育项目。A 移动;B 变化;C 延伸,变化;D 散开,蔓延。故选 C。

2. B 他的脾气秉性和个性,表明他能成为最优秀的士兵。A 圆圈;B 等级,军衔;C 分类;D 阶级,班级。故选 B。

3. A 他为这个公司挣了很多钱,但这不能成为他私吞公司钱财的理由。A 解释,说明;B 澄清,弄清楚;C 证明;D 放大,扩大。故 A 为正确答案。

4. D 眼神交流很重要的,因为眼神交流不正确,会导致交流障碍的出现。A 悲剧;B 真空,空虚;C 问题;D 障碍。因此 D 为正确答案。

5. B 尽管在大城市长大,皮特还是总喜欢画些乡村生活的原始画面。A 生长;B 抚养;C 照料,照顾;D 培养。结合语法知识可知 B 为正确答案。

6. A 售货员被开除了,因为她被指控欺骗客人。A 被控告;B 指控;C 责备;D 诅咒。故 A 为正确答案。

7. C 在美国时,我结识了琼斯教授。固定搭配,make the recognition of 结识,故选 C。

8. A primarily 主要地,rationally 理性,primitively 最初地,respectively 分别地。故选 A。

9. B 固定用法,表示"一部分",故选 B。

Word List 37

refuse [rɪˈfjuːz] *v.* 拒绝,谢绝 *n.* 废物,垃圾
[巧记] re 回 + fuse→向回流→拒绝
[语境] His selfishness caused him to refuse my solicitation.
他的自私让他拒绝了我的请求。
I refuse to be dictated to by you.
我不愿被你呼来唤去的。
[考点] refuse sb. 拒绝某人

region [ˈriːdʒən] *n.* 地区,地带,行政区,(科学等)领域
[巧记] 派生词:regional(*adj.* 地方的,地域性的),regionalism(*n.* 行政区域划分,地方主义)
[语境] The region near the erupting volcano was evacuated rapidly.
火山爆发处附近已迅速撤空。
These small spiced cakes are a peculiarity of the region.
这些别有风味的小蛋糕是该地的特产。
[考点] in the region (on) 在……附近;在……左右(指数字)

register [ˈredʒɪstə(r)] *vi.* 登记,注册 *vt.* 登记,注册,挂号 *n.* 登记,注册;登记簿,注册簿

[语境] Each class has a register of 50 students.

每班有50名学员注册。

[考点] register sb. as sth. , register at/for/with sth. 登记

regret [rɪˈgret] v./n. **遗憾,懊悔,抱歉**

[巧记] 同义词:be sorry for

[语境] We informed her with regret of our decision.

我们遗憾地通知她我们的决定。

She immediately regretted her decision.

她作出决定后立即感到后悔。

regular[11] [ˈregjʊlə(r)] a. **有规律的;整齐的,匀称的,正规的,正式的**

[巧记] regularize (v. 使有规则, 调整, 使有秩序)

[语境] His pulse is not very regular.

他的脉搏不很规律。

I am a regular reader of this newspaper.

我是这份报纸的长期读者。

reject[10] [rɪˈdʒekt] vt. **拒绝,谢绝,驳回;舍弃,排斥,退掉**

[巧记] re(回) + ject(投掷,扔) → 扔回来 → 拒绝

[语境] The supermarket rejected all spotted apples.

超级市场丢弃了所有的烂苹果。

The factory sells some of its better rejects cheaply, but it throws most of the rejects away.

这家公司廉价出售略好一些的次品,但将大多数次品丢弃。

relate [rɪˈleɪt] v. **叙述,讲述;使互相关联**

[语境] It is difficult to relate cause and effect in this case.

这个案件中的动机与效果很难联系起来。

These two events were related to each other.

这两个事件相互有联系。

[考点]相关, 关系到(+ to) ;符合(+ with)

relation[37] [rɪˈleɪʃən] n. **关系,联系;亲属,亲戚**

[巧记] relat[e] + -ion

[语境] Relation between the two countries has reached a crisis

· 377 ·

point.

两国关系已达到出现危机的地步。

A relation of mine is coming to stay.

我有个亲戚要来此暂住。

[考点] have relations with/to 和……有(某种)关系; in[with] relation to 关于……,就……而论

relationship[24] [rɪˈleɪʃənʃɪp] *n.* 关系,联系

[语境] She's seeing (i. e. having a relationship with) a married man.

她现在总和一个结了婚的男子在一起。

In view of our long-standing relationship, we agree to allow you a discount.

考虑到我们长期的关系,我方同意给你方折扣。

relative [ˈrelətɪv] *a.* 相对的,比较的 *n.* 亲属,亲戚

[巧记] relativeness(*n.* 亲戚关系)

[语境] The relative items in this report will be submitted to the committee for discussion.

这份报告中的有关事项将会提交到委员会讨论。

He showed such concern that people took him to be a relative.

他很关心别人,因而大家都把他当作亲人。

[考点] relative to sth. 与……相对应、成比例的

Supply is relative to demand.

供给和需求应保持一定比例。

The teacher asked me some questions relative to my paper.

老师问了我一些和我的论文有关的问题。

relax [rɪˈlæks] *vt.* 使放松,使休息;缓和,放宽 *vi.* 放松,休息;松弛

[巧记] 派生词:relaxation(*n.* 松弛;缓和;放宽)

[语境] His muscles relaxed.

他的肌肉松弛了。

The music will help to relax you.

音乐会使你感到轻松。

[考点] relax one's attention 放松注意力,疏忽; relax one's pace 放

慢步伐

release[6] [rɪˈliːs] *vt.* **释放,放出;发布,发行;放开,松开**

[语境] The new film will be released next month.
这部新的电影下个月发行。
He secured the release of the hostages.
他已经设法使人质获释。

[考点] release 释放,解除,指的是从某种束缚或某种痛苦中解除出来;relieve 不含有从根本上解除的含义

reliable [rɪˈlaɪəbl] *a.* **可靠的**

[语境] It is difficult to obtain reliable evidence.
很难获得可靠的证据。

relief[4] [rɪˈliːf] *n.* **缓解,消除;救济,援救**

[语境] It was a great relief to find that my family was all safe.
看到我的家人安然无恙,我感到极大的欣慰。
Relief was quickly sent to the sufferers from the great fire.
救济品很快被送到遭受火灾的灾民手中。

[考点] bring into relief 把某物烘托出来;使突出,使鲜明;go on relief 靠救济金生活

relieve [rɪˈliːv] *v.* **减轻,解除,援救,救济,换班**

[巧记] re(再) + lieve(欣然)→再高兴起来→减轻

[语境] The government acted quickly to relieve the widespread distress caused by the earthquake.
地震给广大地区造成了灾难,政府迅速采取行动赈济灾民。
The route was designed to relieve traffic congestion.
这条路是为缓解交通拥挤而开辟的。

[考点] relieve sb. of 解除某人的(负担等),减轻某人的(痛苦等),免除(职务)

religion [rɪˈlɪdʒən] *n.* **宗教,信仰**

[巧记] religious (*adj.* 宗教性的)

[语境] Jesus was the founder of the Christian religion.
耶稣是基督教的创始人。
I am unconcerned with questions of religion or morality.

我对宗教问题和道德问题不感兴趣。

religious [rɪˈlɪdʒəs] *a.* **宗教的,信教的,虔诚的**

[语境] She is very religious and goes to church three times a week.

她非常虔诚,每周去教堂三次。

These two countries had three religious wars in twenty years.

这两个国家在20年里发生过三次宗教上的冲突。

rely [rɪˈlaɪ] *v.* (on) **依赖,依靠;信赖,信任**

[语境] They have to rely on the river for their water.

他们用水只好依靠这条河。

I think I can come, but don't rely on it.

我想我能来,但还说不定。

[考点] rely on 依赖,依靠;信任

remain [rɪˈmeɪn] *vi.* **留下,余留;留待,尚需;仍然是,依旧是** *n.* (*pl.*) **余,残余,遗迹;遗体**

[语境] He remained poor all his life.

他终生贫穷。

[考点] remain(留下,剩下)和 stay 可以互换,指他人离开后继续留下,或指其他物遭到毁坏后仍留下的东西

remarkable [rɪˈmɑːkəbəl] *a.* **不平常的,显著的,值得注意的**

[巧记] re(再) + mark(记号) + able(可以的)→再做记号的→值得注意的

[语境] The Tang Dynasty is a period remarkable for its liberality.

唐朝是一段以开明著称的时期。

Remarkable economic results have been achieved.

取得了显著的经济效益。

remedy [ˈremɪdɪ] *n.* **药品;治疗措施,补救办法** *vt.* **纠正,补救;医疗,治疗**

[巧记] 同根词:remedial *a.* 作表语,治疗的,医治的

[语境] Your faults of pronunciation can be remedied.

你的发音毛病是可以纠正的。

Is there a sovereign remedy for this condition?

在这种情况下有没有万全之策?

核心词汇精解

[考点] There is no remedy but... 除……外,别无他法

remember [rɪ'membə(r)] v. 记住;(to) 转达问候,代……致意,代……问好

[巧记] re(回来) + member(成员)→返回成员那边的话→代……问好

[语境] I remember his objecting to the scheme.
我记得他曾经反对该计划。
I remember seeing him once.
我记得见过他一次。

[考点] remember of 记得……,想起……;remember one to sb. 代向某人致意[问候]

remind[4] [rɪ'maɪnd] vt. 提醒,使想起

[巧记] re + mind[= ment]→再次思考→提醒

[语境] Please remind me to write to my mother tomorrow.
请提醒我明天给我母亲写信。
He reminds me of his brother.
他使我想起了他的弟弟。

[考点] remind sb. of sth. 使某人想起某事

remove [rɪ'muːv] vt. 排除,消除,去掉;搬迁,移动,运走

[巧记] re(再) + move(移开)→去掉,消除

[语境] Our office has removed to Shanghai from Beijing.
我们的办公室已从北京迁到上海。

[考点] remove sb./sth. from sth. 将某物/某人从某物移到别处

rent [rent] v. 租,租赁 n. 租金

[语境] The lessor can evict the lessee for failure to pay rent.
出租人可驱逐不付租金的承租人。
They let the house to me at a rent of 100 dollars a month.
他们把房子租给我,每月租金一百美元。

[考点] 租用,把……租给某人(to);向……租入(from)

repair [rɪ'peə(r)] n. 修理,修补 v. 补救,纠正;修理

[巧记] re(再) + pair→重新准备好→修理

[语境] She turned the chair on its side to repair it.

381

她把椅子翻转过来修理。

The brickwork in this house is in need of repair.

这所房子的砖造部分需要修理。

repeat [rɪˈpiːt] *n.* 重复 *v.* 重复,重说,重做;背,背诵

[语境] Repeat the oath after me.

请跟着我宣誓。

He repeated several times that he was busy.

他一再说他很忙。

[考点] repeat after sb. 跟某人朗读;repeat itself 会再发生,会重演;repeat oneself 反复说,反复做

replace[19] [rɪˈpleɪs] *vt.* 放回;替换,取代

[巧记] re(重新) + place→重新放,引申为"代替"

[语境] He replaced the book in the shelf.

他把书放回到书架上。

We've replaced the old adding machine with a computer.

我们用电脑取代了老式的加法计算器。

[考点] replace sb./sth. (with sb./sth.)(用某人/某物)更换、替换别人

reply [rɪˈplaɪ] *v./n.* 回答,答复

[语境] He gave me no chance to reply to his question.

他没有给我回答他问题的机会。

I had no reply to my letter.

我没收到回信。

[考点] reply for 为某人作答;reply to sb./sth. 做答,回答;reply 也可以用作名词

report [rɪˈpɔːt] *n./v.* 报告,汇报;传说,传阅

[语境] You should have reported them to the police.

你应当向警方控告他们的。

He is reading a report of the state of the roads.

他正在看一篇关于道路状况的报告。

reporter [rɪˈpɔːtə(r)] *n.* 记者,报道者,通讯员

[语境] The reporter took the speech down with a recorder.

记者用录音机录下了那篇讲演。

represent[13] [ˌreprɪˈzent] *vt.* 表示,阐明,说明;描写,表现,象征;代理,代表

[语境] This essay represents a considerable improvement on your recent work.

这篇论文说明你最近的工作取得了相当大的改进。

[考点] represent sth. to sb. 向某人说明……

representative [ˌreprɪˈzentətɪv] *n.* 代表,代理人 *a.* (of) 典型的,有代表性的

[巧记] represent 动词,代表

[语境] The union representative was accused of being a puppet of the management.

那名工会代表受到了指责,说他是资方的傀儡。

He seemed to have constituted himself our representative.

他俨然自封为我们的代表。

[考点] sole representative 独家代理(人)

reproduce [ˌriːprəˈdjuːs] *v.* 生殖;翻版;繁殖;复制,仿造

[巧记] re(再) + produce 再生产,引申为"繁殖"

[语境] The photograph of the painting reproduces the colors of the original extremely well.

这幅画的照片绝妙地再现了原作的色彩。

Most fish reproduce themselves by laying eggs.

大多数鱼产卵繁殖。

republic [rɪˈpʌblɪk] *n.* 共和国,共和政体

[语境] The republic abuts on the lake.

该共和国紧靠大湖。

republican [rɪˈpʌblɪkən] *a.* 共和政体的 *n.* 共和党人

[语境] But he is in fact not only alive but still a force in Republican politics.

但是实际上他不仅活着,而且仍是共和党政治力量中的一员。

reputation[7] [ˌrepjʊˈteɪʃən] *n.* 名望,名声

[巧记] reput[e] + -ation；派生词：repute v.

[语境] This store has an excellent reputation for fair dealing.

这家商店因公平交易而获得好名声。

He spotted his reputation by lying repeatedly.

他因反复说谎而败坏了自己的名声。

[考点] be reputed as/to be 当作是某人或某物；have a good [bad] reputation 名誉好[坏]

request [rɪ'kwest] v./n. **请求，要求**

[巧记] re(再) + quest 询问，寻求

[语境] By popular request, the chairman was re-elected.

徇众要求，主席获重选连任。

Your presence is requested at the meeting.

请你务必出席会议。

[考点] at sb.'s request[at the request of sb.] 应某人要求；as requested 依照请求；request sth. from sb. 向某人要求某物

require[28] [rɪ'kwaɪə(r)] v. **需要；(of) 要求，命令**

[巧记] re(再) + quire[= ask]；同义词：order(v. 命令)

[语境] Is that all that you require, sir?

先生，您还要别的吗？

All passengers are required to show their tickets.

所有乘客都必须出示车票。

[考点] It requires that… 有……的必要；require sth. of sb. 对某人有……的要求；require sb. to do sth. 要求某人做某事

rescue[5] ['reskju:] vt./n. **营救，救援**

[语境] The government has rescued the firm from bankruptcy by giving them a grant.

政府拨款给这家公司使其免于破产。

rescue ['reskju:] vt./n. **营救，救出**

[巧记] 派生词：rescuer(n. 援救者；救助者；救星)；同义词：save

[语境] Then they all came to his rescues.

这时他们都来救援他。

[考点] rescue, ransom, save 的辨析：除 save 外，另外两个词还可

核心词汇精解

以用作含义相同的名词。rescue 的内涵是不失时机地以强有力的措施进行搭救;ransom 所表示的营救是向捕获者提供一定量的赎金而使受困者得到解脱;save 是通用词,但是这个词不仅有使受难者获释的意思,还具有使获释者继续生存、享受幸福的内涵

research[59] [rɪˈsɜːtʃ] *v./n.* (into, on) 研究,调查

[巧记] 派生词:researchful (*a.* 好探讨的; 好问的); researcher (*n.* 研究员; 调查者)

[语境] Research indicates that men find it easier to give up smoking than women.

研究表明,男人比女人更容易戒烟。

The book was the result of ten years of assiduous research.

那本书是十年苦心钻研的成果。

[考点] research into 研究, 探讨;make scientific researches on 进行……的科学研究

考点集训

1. Many in the credit industry expect that credit cards will eventually _____ paper money for almost every purchase.
   A. exchange   B. reduce
   C. replace   D. trade

2. All their attempts to _____ the child from the burning building were in vain.
   A. regain   B. recover
   C. rescue   D. reserve

3. Within two weeks of arrival, all foreigners had to _____ with the local police.
   A. inquire   B. consult
   C. register   D. resolve

4. A word processor is much better than a typewriter in that it enables you to enter and _____ your text more easily.
   A. register   B. edit

C. propose D. discharge

5. The world economic recession put an _____ end to the steel market upturn that began in 2002.
    A. irregular B. illegal
    C. abrupt D. absurd

6. It is said that the math teacher seems _____ towards bright students.
    A. partial B. beneficial
    C. preferable D. liable

7. To our _____, Geoffrey's illness proved not to be as serious as we had feared.
    A. anxiety B. relief
    C. view D. judgment

8. The energy _____ by the chain reaction is transformed into heat.
    A. transferred B. released
    C. delivered D. conveyed

9. We should concentrate on sharply reducing interest rates to pull the economy out of _____.
    A. rejection B. restriction
    C. retreat D. recession

答案与解析

1. C 从事信用行业的许多人希望信用卡会最终取代纸质钱币，用来交易。A 交流，交换；B 减少；C 取代；D 交易，贸易。故选 C。

2. C 把这个孩子从熊熊大火的大厦中救出来的所有努力都是徒劳的。rescue from 拯救，固定搭配，故选 C。

3. C 所有的外籍人士必须在入境两周内到当地公安局注册。A 询问；B 咨询；C 注册；D 解决。故选 C。

4. B 文字处理器比打字机要好得多，因为打开和编辑文本更加容易。A 注册；B 编辑；C 提议；D 排除，排放。故选 B。

5. C 这道题应选什么？应该是 abrupt，它表示唐突的，或者是突然的结束,所以答案是 C。

6. A 据说,数学老师偏爱聪明的孩子。A 偏爱的,不公平的;B 有益的,有好处的;C 较……更喜欢……的;D 有责任的,应受(罚)的,有……倾向的。故 A 为正确答案。

7. B 让我们感到欣慰的是,Geoffrey 的病并不像我们想得那么严重。A 焦急;B 宽慰;C 观点;D 判断。故 B 为正确答案。

8. B 这种链式反应所释放的能量转化成了热量。A 转移;B 释放;C 发送;D 传递。故选 B。

9. D 我们应该迅速降低利率,促使经济实现复苏。A 拒绝;B 限制;C 后退;D 衰退。故 D 为正确答案。

Word List 38

reserve[12] [rɪˈzɜːv] *vt.* **保留;储备;预定** *n.* **储备品,储备金,储备;保留地;节制,谨慎**

[巧记] re(再) + serve→再留住→预定;派生词:reserved(*a.* 留作专用的;储备的;预订的;沉默寡言的);reservist(*n.* 后备军人,在乡军人)

[语境] He still reserved his opinion on some points.
在一些问题上,他仍然保留自己的意见。
Please reserve a seat for me.
请为我预定一个座位。

[考点] reserve sth. for sb./sth. 保留或储备某物

resident[5] [ˈrezɪdənt] *n.* **居民,常住者** *a.* **居住的,住校的,住院的**

[巧记] re(再) + sid(坐) + ent(人;……的)→再次坐下的地方→居住的;居民

[语境] More than 10 percent of Munich residents live below the poverty line.
超过 10%的慕尼黑居民生活在贫困线以下。
They engaged a resident tutor.

他们聘用了一名住家的家庭教师。

[考点] resident area 常驻区

residential [ˌrezɪˈdenʃəl] *a.* 住宅的;与居住有关的

[语境] Fontbonne is a liberal arts college, located in a residential suburb of St. Louis.

芳邦大学是一所文科大学,位于圣路易斯市郊的居民区。

resign [rɪˈzaɪn] *vi.* 辞职 *vt.* 辞去,辞职,放弃

[巧记] 派生词:resignation(*n.* 辞职;辞呈;放弃;听任,顺从)

[语境] She resigned her children to the care of a neighbor.

她委托邻居照顾她的孩子。

Have you heard of her intention to resign?

你听到她打算辞职的传闻了吗?

[考点] resign oneself to sth./doing 听任,顺从

resist[19] [rɪˈzɪst] *vt.* 抵抗,反抗;忍住,抵制

[巧记] 派生词:resistance(*n.* 抵抗,反抗;抗性;抵抗力;耐性);resistant(*a.* 抵抗的;防……的;抗……的)

[语境] I can never resist an ice cream.

我一见到冰淇淋就忍不住想吃。

They are determined to resist invasion.

他们决定抵抗入侵。

resolve [rɪˈzɒlv] *n.* 决心,决意 *vt.* 解决(问题等);决定,下决心;决议;分解

[巧记] re(再) + solve(解决)→解决

[语境] He kept his resolve to do better.

他决心干得更出色。

Intensive efforts are being made to resolve the dispute.

现正全力以赴来解决这场纠纷。

[考点] resolve sth. into sth. 分解或解析某物

The discussion resolved itself into a pleasant chat.

讨论变成了愉快的闲聊。

resource[12] [rɪˈsɔːs] *n.* (*pl.*) 资源,财力;谋略,应付办法

[巧记] 派生词:resourcefully(*ad.* 机智地); resourcefulness(*n.* 足

智多谋)

[语境] Resources management is an important business skill.
资源管理是一项重要的经营技能。
He has no inner resources and hates being alone.
他没有内在的精神寄托,因而害怕孤独。

[考点] inner resources 内在的才力,智力;leave sb. to his own resources 让某人独自解决困难,不给某人以任何协助

respect [rɪˈspekt] *n./v.* **尊敬,尊重** *n.* **敬意,问候,关系,方面**

[巧记] re(回) + spect(看)→回过头看→尊重

[语境] Some people have no respect for the speed limit and consequently are punished.
有些人全然不顾限速规定,结果受到处罚。
Give my respects to your parents.
代我向你的父母亲致意。

[考点] give one's respects to 向……问候;have respect for 尊敬[重],重视;have respect to 牵涉到,关系到,注意到,考虑到

respond [rɪˈspɒnd] *vi.* **回答,答复;响应,起反应**

[语境] I invited her to dinner but she did not respond.
我请她吃晚饭,但她未作回答。

response[19] [rɪˈspɒns] *n.* **回答,响应,反应**

[巧记] re(回) + spond(答复)→反应;派生词:responder(*n.* 回答者,响应者;响应器;应答机)

[语境] His cool response suggested that he didn't like the idea.
他反应冷淡表明他并不喜欢这个主意。
Millions of people gave freely in response to the famine appeal.
千百万人响应救灾呼吁而慷慨解囊。

responsibility[8] [rɪˌspɒnsɪˈbɪlɪtɪ] *n.* **责任,责任心;职责,任务**

[语境] The captain is absolved from all blame and responsibility for the shipwreck.
那位船长未受到因船只失事而招致的非难和罪责。
You can't retreat from the responsibility in this affair.
你不能回避在这一事件中的责任。

389

[考点] bear responsibility for 对……负有责任;take full responsibility for 对……负完全责任

responsible[10] [rɪˈspɒnsɪbəl] *a.* **应负责的,有责任的;可靠的,认真的,负责的;责任重大的,重要的**
[语境] She holds a very responsible position in the firm.
她在公司里身居要职。
Our teacher is a very responsible person.
我们的老师是一个非常可靠的人。
[考点] hold sb. responsible for 使某人负……的责任;make oneself responsible for 负起……的责任;responsible for 为……负责;是造成……的原因

rest [rest] *n.* **休息;剩余部分** *v.* **休息;睡;放,靠,搁**
[语境] Ensure that our traditional markets are looked after; for the rest, I am not much concerned.
一定要满足我们传统市场的需要,其他方面倒无所谓。
We'll eat some of the bread and keep the rest for breakfast.
我们将吃一点面包,剩下的留到早饭时吃。

restaurant [ˈrestərɒnt,-rɒn] *n.* **餐馆,饭店**
[语境] The police ran down the thief in a restaurant.
警方在一个饭馆里抓到了这个小偷。

restore [rɪˈstɔː(r)] *vt.* **恢复,使回复;归还,交还;修复,重建**
[巧记] 同义词:mend(*vt. vi.* 修理,修补)
[语境] The military government promised to restore democracy within one year.
军人政府答应在一年内重新建立民主体制。
Drastic measures will have to be taken to restore order.
为恢复秩序必须采取严厉措施。
[考点] restore sb. to life 使某人苏醒过来;restore sb. to his old post 使某人复职

restrict[12] [rɪˈstrɪkt] *vt.* **限制,约束**
[巧记] 派生词:restriction(*n.* 限制;约束)
[语境] Fog restricted visibility.

雾天能见度很低。

Recent laws have tended to restrict the freedom of the press.

新法律有限制新闻自由的趋势。

[考点] restrict sb./sth. to sth. 限制或约束某人(某物)

result[52] [rɪ'zʌlt] *n.* 结果,成绩

[语境] These problems are the result of years of bad management.

这些问题是由于多年管理不善而造成的。

If this football team doesn't get a result tonight, they will be put down into a lower division.

如果今晚这支足球队不能赢球,他们将会被降级。

[考点] as a result 因此;结果

resume [rɪ'z(j)uːm] *v.* 重新开始,继续;恢复

[语境] There is also concern that North Korea will resume selling nuclear technology abroad.

也有人担心朝鲜将重新开始在国外出售核技术。

It symptomatizes that they will resume their relations.

这表明他们将恢复关系。

résumé ['rezjuːme,-zjʊm] *n.* 简历

[语境] Update your résumé, and remind yourself of your skills and strengths.

更新你的履历,回忆你所拥有的技能和长处。

retail ['riːteɪl] *n./v.* 零售 *a.* 零售的

[巧记] retailer *n.* 零售商;反义词:wholesale *a.* 批发的

[语境] These shoes retail at(or for) 80 dollars a pair.

这种鞋零售价为每双80美元。

He does wholesale business, while his brother is engaged in retail business.

他经营批发生意,他弟弟则经营零售生意。

retain [rɪ'teɪn] *vt.* 保持,保留

[巧记] re(回) + tain→拿回来→保留

[语境] He retained the best lawyer in the state to defend his case.

他为他的案子聘了该州最好的律师。

Her memory retains everything she reads.

她过目不忘。

[考点]派生词:retainer n. 聘用订金,订金

retire[25] [rɪˈtaɪə(r)] v. 退休;引退;退却,撤退;就寝

[语境] The boxer retired from the contest with eye injuries.

该拳击手因眼部受伤而退出比赛。

Our forces retired to prepared positions.

我们的部队撤退到既设阵地上。

return [rɪˈtɜːn] v./n. 返回,回来;归还,送还;回答

[语境]Our investment accounts return a high rate of interest.

我们的投资项目利润回报很高。

We look forward to the return of spring.

我们期待着春天的到来。

reunion [riːˈjuːnjən] n. 团圆,重聚

[巧记]re(再) + union(聚合)→再次走到一起→团聚

[语境]There was a sense of a grand reunion in the midst of this historic event.

在这个具有历史意义的事件中,有一种场面隆重团聚的感觉。

reveal[6] [rɪˈviːl] vt. 提示,揭露,展现;告诉,泄露

[巧记]派生词:revealer(n. 展示者;启示者),revealingly(ad. 透露真情地;露体地,袒胸露肩地;启发人地)

[语境] I promise never to reveal his secret.

我答应绝不泄露他的秘密。

These plans reveal a complete failure of imagination.

这些计划显得毫无想象力。

[考点] reveal sth. to sb. 透露,泄露,揭露

review[23] [rɪˈvjuː] vt./n. 复习;复查,审核;回顾;评论

[巧记]re(回,再) + view(看)

[语境]The play was very well reviewed.

这出戏得到很好的评价。

reward[9] [rɪˈwɔːd] n. 酬谢,报酬,奖金 vt. 酬谢,报答,奖酬

[语境] They rewarded the winners with gifts of fruits and flowers.

他们奖给优胜者一些水果和鲜花。

He got a reward for helping them.

他因帮助他们而拿到一笔酬金。

[考点] as a reward for 作为(对某事的)报酬；in reward of 为酬答……；作为奖励；reward sb. for sth. 为某事报答某人

rice [raɪs] *n.* 稻,米

[语境] Dropping ears of rice promise another good harvest.

沉甸甸的稻穗预示着又一个丰收。

rich [rɪtʃ] *a.* 富的,有钱的；富饶的；(in) 充足的,丰富的

[语境] Her rich experience gave her an advantage over other applicants for the job.

她丰富的经验使她比其他求职者具有有利条件。

The rich man left his son nothing in the will.

那位富翁在遗嘱中什么都没给他儿子留下。

rid [rɪd] *vt.* 使摆脱，解除……的负担，从……中清除

[语境] Let's get rid of this moldy old furniture.

咱们把这件老掉牙的旧家具扔掉吧。

We have an extractor fan in the kitchen to get rid of the smell of cooking.

我们的厨房里有台排气扇,用来消除油烟。

[考点] rid oneself of debt 还清债务；get [be] rid of 摆脱；除掉,拔除(眼中钉)；rid oneself [sb., sth.] of 摆脱；驱除；除去；解除

ride [raɪd] *v./n.* 骑,乘

[语境] She hasn't been out riding since the accident.

她自从出了事故以后,一直没有骑马外出过。

The luxury model gives a smoother ride.

坐这种豪华型汽车感觉很平稳。

ridiculous [rɪˈdɪkjʊləs] *a.* 荒谬,可笑

[语境] She broke in with a ridiculous objection.

她突然插嘴提了个可笑的异议。

right [raɪt] *a.* 右的,正确的 *n.* 右,权利 *ad.* 在右边,正确地

[语境] The Normans ruled England by right of conquest.

诺曼人征服了英格兰成了统治者。

It took me ages to put things to right after the workmen had finished.

工人干完活儿后,我用了很长时间才收拾好。

ring [rɪŋ] *n.* 戒指;环;铃声;(打)电话 *v.* 按(铃),敲(钟);包围

[语境] A high fence ringed the prison camp.

有一道高高的铁丝网围着战俘营。

The playground rang with children's shouts.

操场上到处都是儿童的喊叫声。

riot ['raɪət] *n./v.* 骚扰,闹事

[语境] The government succeeded in quenching the riot.

政府成功平息了暴乱。

ripe [raɪp] *a.* 熟的,成熟的;(for)时机成熟的

[巧记] 反义词:raw(*a.* 生的)

[语境] Most tomatoes are red when ripe, but some kinds are yellow.

大多数西红柿成熟时是红色的,但有些品种是黄色的。

I like the luscious taste of ripe peaches.

我喜欢熟桃的香甜味。

[考点] be ripe for...时机成熟;准备就绪;即可……;适于……

rise [raɪz] *v.* 升起;起立;上涨;起义 *n.* 上涨,增高;起源

[语境] She rose above her difficulties and became a tremendous success.

她战胜了重重困难,取得了巨大的成功。

Christians believe that Jesus rose from the dead on Easter Sunday.

基督徒相信耶稣在那个星期日(后定为复活节)里复活了。

[考点] at rise of sun 太阳升起的时候;be on the rise 上涨,上升;变得更有价值

risk[28] [rɪsk] *n.* 风险 *vt.* 冒风险

[语境] Anyone swimming in this lake does so at his own risk.

任何人在此湖中冒险游泳，后果自负。

He saved my life at the risk of his own.

他冒着自己的生命危险挽救了我的生命。

[考点] at all risk 无论如何，无论冒什么危险；at one's own risk 由自己负责；run a risk 冒险

risky[ˈrɪskɪ] *a.* 危险的；冒险的

[语境] That is highly risky if they take their entire client base away from one medium.

如果他们把整个客户群从某个媒介带走，那将是非常危险的。

river[ˈrɪvə(r)] *n.* 江，河

[语境] They were canoeing in the river.

他们在河中划独木舟。

road[rəʊd] *n.* 路，道路，途径

[语境] Did you come by the nearest road?

你是由最近的路来的吗？

roar [rɔː(r)] *n.*/*v.* 吼叫，怒号；轰鸣，咆哮

[语境] The roar of the train reverberated in the tunnel.

火车的轰隆声在隧道里回荡。

They drove away from the city centre, the roar of the traffic still dinning in their ears.

他们驶出了市中心，但车来人往的喧嚣声仍在耳中回响。

[考点] roar sb. down 大声喊叫得使某人停止讲话；轰下台

roast [rəʊst] *v.* 烤，炙，烘

[巧记] 派生词：roaster(*n.* 炙烤的人，红烧烤炉，烘烤器) roasting (*n.* 烧烤；烘焙；干炒；严厉批评；非难)

[语境] We suppered on cold roast beef.

我们晚饭吃的是凉的烤牛肉。

We had fish for the first course, followed by roast fowl and fresh vegetables.

我们吃的第一道菜是鱼，接着上的菜是烤禽肉和新鲜蔬菜。

[考点]donkey roast 盛大的节日集会或庆祝会;rule the roast 做主人,当家

rob [rɔb] *v.* (of)抢劫,盗取;非法剥夺

[巧记]派生词:robber(*n.* 强盗,盗贼)

[语境]Not only do they rob you, they smash everything too.

他们不仅抢夺你的财物,还要把每样东西都捣毁。

Do not rob Peter to pay Paul.

【谚】不要挖肉补疮。

robot [ˈrəʊbɒt] *n.* 机器人

[语境]The robot can acquire the object.

机器人能捕获该物体。

rock [rɒk] *n.* 岩,岩石;*v.* 摇

[语境]The rock has weathered away into soil.

岩石经雨蚀风化而变成泥土。

He dislodged the rock and it rolled down the hill.

他摇动了那块岩石,岩石便从小山上滚了下去。

rocket [ˈrɒkɪt] *n.* 火箭

[语境]The satellite was launched in a rocket.

这颗卫星是装在火箭上发射的。

role [rəʊl] *n.* 角色,作用,任务,职责

[语境] His dual role as a composer and a conductor made him very busy.

他兼任作曲家和指挥家的双重身份使他非常繁忙。

He's a natural for the role of Lear.

他是李尔王这一角色的理想人选。

[考点] play an important role in 在……中起重要作用

roll [rəʊl] *v.* 滚动;使摇摆;卷,卷起 *n.* 卷,卷形物;名单

[语境] She rolled in for work twenty minutes late.

她懒懒散散地来上班,迟到了二十分钟。

The ship was rolling heavily to and fro.

那船晃来晃去很不平稳。

[考点] roll back 击退;使物价回跌;roll call 点名;点名时间;

点名号角;be rolling in 在……中打滚;富于;沉溺于

room [ruːm,rʊm] *n.* **房间,室;余地,空间**
[语境]He shoved me back out of the room.
他把我从房间里推了出来。
So they have little room to manoeuvre.
这样他们也没有多少回旋的余地了。

root [ruːt] *n.* **根,根部;根本,根源** *v.* **(使)生根,(使)扎根**
[巧记]反义词:branch(*n.* 树枝, 支流)
[语境] Who's been rooting about among my papers?
谁翻过我的文件了?
Unhappiness is the root cause of his illness.
不开心是他生病的根源。
[考点] at(the) root 根本上;by the roots 连根地;从根本上

rope [rəʊp] *n.* **绳,索**
[语境]He uncoiled the rope.
他把绳子解开。

rose [rəʊz] *n.* **玫瑰,蔷薇**
[语境]These naughty kids have pulled off all the rose buds.
这些淘气的孩子把所有玫瑰花蕾都摘掉了。

rotten ['rɒtn] *a.* **腐烂的,腐朽的**
[语境]Scoop out the rotten part of the pear.
把梨烂的地方剜掉。
[考点] feel rotten 感觉不舒服

rough [rʌf] *a.* **粗糙的;粗野的,粗鲁的;大致的,粗略的**
[巧记] 反义词:smooth(*a.* 平滑的, 光滑的)
[语境] Could you give me a rough idea when you'll be back?
你能告诉我你大概什么时候回来吗?
They complained rough handling by the police.
他们抱怨受到警察粗野的对待。
[考点] rough sth. out 拟订事物的草案或纲要;cut up rough 发脾气,暴跳如雷;in rough 不精确,大约

round [raʊnd] *a.* **圆的** *prep.* **围绕** *ad.* **在周围** *v.* **绕行** *n.* **(一)回合**

[语境] Let's have a good round of applause for the next performer.

咱们为下一个表演者热烈鼓掌吧。

The earth moves round the sun.

地球绕着太阳运转。

route [ruːt] *n.* **路线，路程**

[巧记] 同义词：circuit

[语境] The route was once much travelled but has fallen into disuse.

这条路线旅行的人以前常走，但是现在已不用了。

The bus route goes as far as that, so you'll need to take a taxi.

汽车路线到此为止了，你得叫辆的士。

[考点] route 的含义是"路线"，通常是迂回的，可以包括数条道路或街道，有时甚至包括小路、小巷；使用范围也较广。如：登山运动员所攀登的路线，实际上不是路；其他方面，如公共汽车所行经的"路线"，邮递员发送邮件的"路线"等

royal [ˈrɔiəl] *a.* **王室的，皇家的**

[语境] The papers are full of stories about the royals.

报纸上尽是些关于王室成员趣闻逸事的报道。

rub [rʌb] *n.* **摩擦，障碍，困难** *v.* **擦，摩擦，搓；擦破**

[语境] In his job he's rubbing shoulders with film stars all the time.

他在工作中一直与电影明星有来往。

Please give the table a good rub with this cloth.

请用这块布好好擦擦桌子。

[考点] rub away 擦掉；消除；rub in 用力擦入；反复讲；rub off 擦掉

rubber [ˈrʌbə(r)] *n.* **橡皮，橡胶；橡胶制品，胶鞋** *a.* **橡胶的**

[语境] Rubber is an elastic material.

橡胶是一种弹性材料。

It's just a bad actor in a rubber suit.

那只是个很烂的演员，穿着橡胶制成的外衣。

rubbish [ˈrʌbɪʃ] *n.* **垃圾；废话；废物；无聊的想法** *vt.* **把……说得一文不值**

[语境]The film was rubbished by the critics.

影评家把这部影片贬得一无是处。

The government's plan was rubbished by the opposition parties.

政府的计划被反对党批得一钱不值。

rude[10] [ruːd] *a.* 粗鲁,不礼貌;粗糙,粗陋

[语境]Don't be so rude to your parents!

别对你的父母这么没礼貌!

It's strange for her to be so rude.

真奇怪,她竟然会如此粗暴无礼。

[考点]in rude health 十分健壮的

ruin [ˈruːin] *v.* 毁坏,破坏 *n.* 毁灭,崩溃;(*pl.*)废墟,遗址

[巧记]派生词:ruination (*n.* 毁灭, 灭亡);同义词:destroy

[语境] The castle now lies in ruins.

那城堡现在已成一片废墟了。

He ruined his prospects by carelessness.

他因疏忽大意而断送了前途。

[考点]go to rack and ruin/in ruin 严重受损,破烂不堪

rule [ruːl] *v.* 统治;支配;裁定 *n.* 规章,条例;习惯;统治

[语境] The rule is that someone must be on duty at all times.

按照规定,任何时候均需有人值班。

As a rule, I'm home by six.

我通常六点在/到家。

[考点] rule of law 法规;rule out 排除

ruler[ˈruːlə(r)] *n.* 统治者,支配者;尺子,直尺

[巧记]rule(统治) + er(人)→统治人的人→统治者

[语境]At last he made himself the ruler of Rome.

最后他成了罗马的统治者。

Could I use your ruler?

我可以用你的尺子吗?

rumo(u)r[ˈruːmə(r)] *n.* 传闻,谣言

[语境]Rumor has it that her husband has gone over the hill.

谣传她丈夫到山那边去了。

The rumor has been traced back to a bad man.

那谣言经追查是坏人造的。

run [rʌn] *v.* 奔,跑;流,淌;蔓延,伸展;经营;运转

[语境] He started off at a run but soon tired and slowed to a walk.

他跑步出发,但很快就累得慢下来而成了步行。

It's a lovely sunny day; why don't we run down to the coast?

天气多好哇,咱们何不开车到海边玩玩?

rush [rʌʃ] *v.* (使)冲;奔 *n.* 冲,急速行进 *a.* (交通)繁忙的

[语境] The cat made little rushes to and fro after the ball.

猫追着球跑过来跑过去。

They rushed up the stairs.

他们冲到楼上。

[考点] rush hour 高峰时间

Russian [ˈrʌʃən] *a.* 俄罗斯(人/语)的;*n.* 俄语,俄罗斯(人)

[语境] She called the waiter over and whispered to him in Russian.

她把侍者叫过来,同他用俄语耳语了两句。

He had practically no physical contact with Russian.

他同俄国人实际上并没有直接接触。

rust [rʌst] *v.* 生锈

[语境] Oil it regularly to prevent rust.

经常擦油,以免生锈。

[考点] rust away 锈蚀;锈坏;锈烂

考点集训

1. Inflation will reach its highest in a decade across most of Asia this year, threatening to _____ recent productivity gains.
   A. reverse   B. reserve
   C. retrieve   D. revise

2. It is amusing that she _____ her father's bad temper as well as her mother's good looks.
   A. inherited   B. retained
   C. preserved   D. maintained

3. The western media was astonished to see that China's GDP _____ by almost 40% just in two years' time.
   A. flourished   B. floated
   C. soared   D. roared
4. Cancellation of the flight _____ many passengers to spend the night at the airport.
   A. resulted   B. obliged
   C. demanded   D. recommended
5. Our hopes _____ and fell in the same instant.
   A. aroused   B. arose
   C. raised   D. rose
6. Only a selected number of landladies in the neighbourhood have been allowed by the university to take in _____.
   A. residents   B. inhabitants
   C. lodgers   D. settlers
7. We'd like to _____ a table for five for dinner this evening.
   A. preserve   B. retain
   C. reserve   D. sustain
8. The _____ of airplane engines announced a coming air raid.
   A. roar   B. exclamation
   C. whistle   D. scream
9. You should try to _____ your ambition and be more realistic.
   A. reserve   B. restrain
   C. retain   D. replace
10. Ten days ago the young man informed his boss of his intention to _____.
    A. resign   B. reject
    C. retreat   D. replace
11. The most basic reason why dialects should be preserved is that language helps to _____ a culture.
    A. retain   B. relate
    C. remark   D. review

12. In the late seventies, the amount of fixed assets required to produce one vehicle in Japan was _____ equivalent to that in the United States.

   A. rudely
   B. roughly
   C. readily
   D. coarsely

答案与解析

1. A reverse 使倒退,使逆转;reserve 储备,预留;retrieve 恢复;revise 校正,修订。

2. A 她遗传了她父亲的臭脾气和她母亲的好长相,这令人很惊奇。可以选出 A。

3. C 表示 GDP 的上升只能用 soared,其他均无此意。

4. B 因为航班的取消,许多乘客不得不在机场过夜。A 使……有……的结果;B 使得;C 命令,要求;D 推荐。故 B 为正确答案。

5. D 在那一刻我们有了希望,而又在同一刻希望破灭了。A 唤起;B 出现;C 提高;D 升起。由此可知 D 为正确答案。

6. C 在这附近,大学只允许少数的房东招揽寄宿者。A 居民;B 居民,居住者;C 寄宿者;D 定居者。故 C 为正确答案。

7. C 我们想为今晚预订一个五人座位的桌子。A 保留;B 保持;C 预订;D 支撑,支持。故选 C。

8. A 飞机发动机的轰鸣声预示了空袭的到来。A 轰鸣声;B 感叹,惊叫;C 口哨声;D 尖叫。故选 A。

9. B 你应该尽量抑制自己的野心,更现实一点。A 储存,预订;B 抑制,限制;C 保持,保留;D 取代。故选 B。

10. A 十天前年轻人告知他的老板他要辞职。A 辞职;B 拒绝;C 后退;D 取代。故选 A。

11. A 保留方言的最基本原因在于,语言有助于文化的留存。A 保留,保持;B 联系;C 评论,谈论;D 评论。故选 A。

12. B 70 年代末,日本制造一台机动车所需要的固定资产和美国 ____ 等价。A 侧重指态度"粗"鲁;B 大概,大致;C 乐意地,欣然;D 侧重指质感"粗"糙。故选 B。

Word List 39

sad [sæd] *a.* 悲哀的,忧愁的

[语境] The exclusion of women from the temple made them feel sad.

妇女被排斥于寺院之外使得她们很难过。

He was much affected by the sad news.

这个悲惨的消息使他非常难过。

safe [seɪf] *a.* 安全的,牢靠的;谨慎的,可靠的 *n.* 保险箱

[语境] The rescuers brought the climbers back safe and sound.

救援人员把登山的人都平安地救了回来。

The train is a safe means of transportation.

火车是一种安全的交通工具。

safety ['seɪftɪ] *n.* 安全

[语境] The safety of the ship is the captain's responsibility.

确保船只的安全是船长的责任。

The new aircraft is undergoing safety tests.

这种新飞机正在接受安全性能检验。

[考点] in safety 安全;with safety 安全地,可靠地,保险地;safety measure 保险措施;safety first 安全第一

sail [seɪl] *n.* 帆,航行 *v.* 航行

[巧记] 派生词:sailing(*n.* 航海, 航行;航海术;起航;水运班);同义词:coast(*n.* 海岸;滑坡 *v.* 沿岸航行;毫不费力地前进, 顺利进展;滑行;沿……岸航行)

[语境] He never actually tells lies, but he often sails pretty close to the wind.

他实际上从不撒谎,但说的话常几近撒谎。

She sailed through her finals.

她顺利通过期末考试。

salad ['sæləd] *n.* 色拉,凉拌菜

[语境]This salad tastes of garlic.

这色拉有大蒜味。

salary[ˈsælərɪ] *n.* 薪金,薪俸

[语境]He would not accept this office for such a small salary.

因为薪金低,他不愿担任这个职务。

sale [seɪl] *n.* 销售(额);廉价出售

[语境] The law forbids the sale of alcohol to people under 18.

法律禁止向18岁以下的人出售含有酒精的饮料。

The latest model of this washer is now on sale in your shops.

这种最新型号的洗衣机目前正在你们的商店中出售。

[考点] on sale 降价出售;出售的,上市的;for sale 待售

salesman[ˈseɪlzmən] *n.* 售货员,推销员

[巧记]sales(销售)+man(人)→搞销售的人→售货员,推销员

[语境]She was duped by the dishonest salesman.

她被不诚实的推销员骗了。

salt[sɔːlt] *n.* 盐,盐类;*vt.* 盐渍,给(食物)加盐

[语境]Mix up the salt with the pepper.

把盐和胡椒粉混合在一起。

Salt the stock to your taste and leave it simmering very gently.

根据自己的口味给原汤加点盐,然后用文火慢炖。

same [seɪm] *a.* 相同的 *pron.* 相同的人(或物) *ad.* 同样地

[语境]He praised my work and in the same breath told me I would have to leave.

他称赞我工作好,刚说完这话就让我离职。

I resigned on Friday and left that same day.

我星期五辞职后当天就离开了。

sample [ˈsɑːmpəl] *n.* 样品,标本 *vt.* 从……抽样

[巧记]派生词:sampler (*n.* 样品检查员;取样员);同义词:experiment(*n.* 实验,尝试,试验 *v.* 实验,尝试)

[语境] We sampled the stuff and found it satisfactory.

我们抽验了这批材料,认为满意。

What I need is nothing but a sample.

我需要的不过是一件样品而已。

[考点]派生词:sampler n. 品尝者,品尝家

sand [sænd] n. **沙;(pl.) 沙滩**

[语境]Dry sand absorbs water.

干沙吸收水分。

sandwich ['sænwɪdʒ,-tʃ] n. **三明治,夹肉面包**

[语境]He ordered a cheese sandwich, three bottles of beer and beered up.

他要了一份乳酪三明治和三瓶啤酒狂饮起来。

satellite ['sætəlaɪt] n. **卫星,人造卫星**

[语境]The satellite will be thrown into space.

这颗卫星将被发射到太空。

satisfaction[7] [ˌsætɪsˈfækʃən] n. **满足,满意;乐事,愉快**

[巧记]派生词:satisfactorily (ad. 令人满意地);反义词:discontent(n. 不满)

[语境] She gets a perverse satisfaction from making other people embarrassed.

她有一种不正常的心态,以使别人难堪来取乐。

Looking at a beautiful painting always gives one satisfaction.

观赏一幅美丽的图画使人心满意足。

[考点] entry of satisfaction【律】偿清登记; feel satisfaction at 对……感到满意

satisfactory [ˌsætɪsˈfæktərɪ] a. **令人满意的**

[巧记]反义词:unsatisfactory(a. 令人不满意的, 不得人心的, 不能解决问题的)

[语境] The answer was not quite satisfactory to him.

这个答复不能使他完全满意。

Everything was turning out most satisfactory.

一切都非常称心如意。

[考点]to the satisfactory of 使……满足; give satisfaction 使满足; with/in satisfaction 满意地; feel great satisfaction over sth. 对某事非常满意; satisfy the people's need 满足人民的需要; be satisfied with 对……满意;be satisfied of…确信……

satisfied[4] [ˈsætɪsfaɪd] *a.* 感到满意的

[巧记]派生词:satisfying (*a.* 令人满足的;令人满意的),satisfactory (*a.* 赎罪的, 满意的)

[语境] I satisfied my thirst with a glass of water.
我喝了一杯水解渴。
I am not at all satisfied with the present situation.
我对目前的状况根本不满意。

satisfy [ˈsætɪsfaɪ] *v.* 满意,使满意,使相信,说服

[巧记] 同义词:appease(*v.* 平息; 抚慰; 缓和; 绥靖, 姑息)

[语境] It is by no means easy to satisfy everyone.
要满足每一个人绝非易事。
My assurances don't satisfy him; he's still sceptical.
我保证的话他都不信:他仍存疑虑。

Saturday[ˈsætədɪ] *n.* 星期六

[语境] We often go out to cinema on Saturday.
我们常在星期六外出看电影。

sauce[sɔːs] *n.* 酱油,调味汁

[语境] We eat them with sauce.
我们就着酱汁吃。

save[17] [seɪv] *v.* 救,拯救;储蓄,贮存;节省;除了

[语境] Save your strength for the hard work you'll have to do later.
留着点儿劲儿,你一会儿还得干重活儿呢。
All the guests have gone save one.
除了一个人外,所有客人都走了。

saving[ˈseɪvɪŋ] *n.* 储蓄;(*pl.*) 储蓄金,存款

[语境] She drew all her savings from the bank.
她把所有的存款都从银行里取出来了。

say [seɪ] *vt.* 说, 讲;说明;比如说 *vi* 说,发表意见

[语境] Just what is the artist trying to say in her work?
那艺术家在她的作品中究竟想表达什么?
Don't interrupt her; let her have her say.

别打断她的话;让她把意见说出来。

saying[11] ['seɪɪŋ] *n.* 说话,发表言论;格言,谚语,警句;话,言论

[巧记] say(说) + ing(名词化后缀)→说的话→言论

[语境] What you're saying now is not consistent with what you said last week.

你现在说的话与上星期你说的不相符。

I could hear what he was saying on the phone through the partition.

我能隔着墙听见他在电话里说了些什么。

scale [skeɪl] *n.* 标度,刻度;(*pl.*) 天平,天平盘;标尺,比例尺;音阶

[语境] Scale the fish before cooking them.

烧鱼之前先去掉鱼鳞。

We are seeing unemployment on an unprecedented scale.

我们现在正经历规模空前的失业。

[考点] on a large (small) scale 大规模地/小规模地;out of scale 不合规定比例;turn the scale 扭转局面

scarce[5] [skeəs] *a.* 稀少的,罕见的;缺乏的,不足的

[巧记] 派生词:scarcely(*ad.* 几乎不;简直没有)

[语境] Good fruit is scarce in winter and costs a lot.

好的水果冬天难得见到,而且价格昂贵。

[考点] scarcely ever 几乎从不

scarcely ['skeəslɪ] *ad.* 几乎不;勉强

[语境] I can scarcely hear.

我几乎什么也听不见。

[考点] hardly, scarcely, barely 辨析:这些副词均含"几乎不"之意。hardly:指接近最低限度,差不多没有多余,强调困难和程度。scarcely:指不太充分,不太够,不足,不能令人满意,强调数量。barely:指仅仅够,一点不多,强调没有多余

scare ['skeə(r)] *vt.* 惊吓,受惊 *n.* 惊慌,惊恐

[巧记] 派生词:scaremonger (*n.* 散布骇人听闻消息的人), scarer (*n.* 吓人的人[物])

[语境] You did give me a scare.

你真吓了我一跳。

The child was scared of the fierce looking dog.

这孩子害怕那条外表凶恶的狗。

[考点] be scared of 害怕;scare away(off)吓跑;scare into(out of) doing 吓得(不敢)做某事;throw a scare into sb. 吓坏某人;scare sb. out of his wits 吓蒙了,吓坏了

scatter [ˈskætə(r)] vi. 分散,消散 vt. 撒,驱散,散开;散布,散播

[巧记] 派生词:scattering (n. 分散;散落),scatter site(a. 分散的网站)

[语境] When the tree falls, the monkeys scatter.

树倒猢狲散。

[考点] be scattered with 到处扔着;scatter about 四处逃跑,到处扔;scatter...with 这儿那儿掺杂……

scene [si:n] n. 景色,景象,舞台;(戏)一场

[巧记] 派生词:scenery(n. 风景,景色;舞台布景)

[语境] Reporters were soon on the scene after the accident.

那事故发生后不久记者就都赶到了现场。

His arrival set the scene for another argument.

他一来就要另有一场争论了。

[考点] behind the scenes 在后台;[喻]在幕后;在幕后活动的;知道内情的;scene of action 发生事情的地点,现场;come on the scene 出现;on the scene 在现场,到现场;set the scenes 准备了条件

scenery [ˈsi:nəri] n. 风景,景色;舞台布景

[语境] We passed through some beautiful scenery on our journey through this district.

我们在穿越这个地区的旅途中,看到了不少美丽的景色。

The scenery was beautiful beyond expression.

那风景美丽得无法形容。

[考点] a piece of scenery 一幅布景;natural scenery 自然风景;behind the scenes 在后台,在幕后

scent[8] [sent] n. 气味,香味,香水,线索,嗅觉 v. 嗅,发觉

[巧记] scented(a. 有气味的；洒有香水的；有嗅觉的), scentless(a. 无气味的；无嗅觉的；遗臭已消失的)

[语境] They walked through the forest breathing the scent of pines.
他们步行穿过森林，呼吸着松树的芳香。

If we're upwind of the animal it may smell our scent.
要是我们处于那动物的上风位置，它就能闻到我们的气味。

schedule ['ʃedjuːl] *n.* 时间表；进度表；一览表 *vt.* 安排；排定，预定

[语境] We've already finished the work anterior to the schedule.
我们已经提前完成了工作。

He was bidden to finish the work on schedule.
他被要求按时完成工作。

[考点] according to schedule 按照进度；ahead of schedule 提前进度；on schedule 准时，按进度；behind schedule 落后于进度

scholar ['skɒlə(r)] *n.* 学者

[语境] The library attracts thousands of scholars and researchers.
那个图书馆吸引了成千上万的学者和研究人员。

scholarship ['skɒləʃɪp] *n.* 奖学金；学问，学识

[语境] The student decides to lay down the scholarship.
这个学生决定放弃奖学金。

It was certainly an act of scholarship and of scientific insight.
这绝对是深具学识及科学洞察力的行为。

school [skuːl] *n.* 学校，学院；学派，流派

[语境] He gave his books to the school.
他把他的藏书捐赠给了学校。

He epitomized the thought of this school.
他是这一学派思想的集大成者。

science ['saɪəns] *n.* 科学；学科

[语境] She specializes in computer science.
她专攻计算机科学。

scientific[26] [ˌsaɪən'tɪfɪk] *a.* 科学的

[巧记] 派生词：science (*n.* 科学)

[语境] We all support his scientific research.

409

我们都支持他的科学研究。

She has a very scientific method of dealing with political problems.

她处理政治问题的方法很科学。

[考点] scientific method 科学方法;scientific farming 科学种田

scientist ['saɪəntɪst] *n.* 科学家

[巧记] scien(科学) + tist(人)→搞科学的人→科学家

[语境] The scientist thirsts after an achievement.

这名科学家渴望取得成就。

scold[4] [skəʊld] *v.* 训斥,责骂

[巧记] 派生词:scolding(*n.* 责骂;斥责)

[语境] If I walk in with muddy boots, Dad always scolds(me).

我的靴子上要是有泥,一进屋爸爸就骂(我)。

Don't scold him, he is a mere child.

别责备他,他只不过是个孩子。

[考点] scold sb. for sth. 为某事而责备某人

scope[6] [skəʊp] *n.* 范围,视野;余地,机会

[语境] Your question is beyond the scope of this book.

你所问的问题已超出了这本书的范围。

It is within my scope.

那是在我的范围之内。

[考点] in the scope of 在……范围以内;give/seek scope for 给予/寻求发展的机会;of wide scope 广泛的,广大的;within the scope of 在……范围内

scratch [skrætʃ] *n.* 搔,抓,抓痕 *v.* 搔,抓,扒;勾销,删除

[巧记] 记忆方法:sc(四川) + rat(老鼠) + ch(吃)→四川人抓老鼠吃

[语境] The recording was spoiled by scratches.

录音被沙沙声破坏了。

Somebody has scratched his name off the list.

有人已经把他的名字从名单上划去了。

[考点] start from/at/on scratch 白手起家;scratch out 把……划

掉;scratch the surface 讲了(了解)一点点皮毛;without a scratch 毫发未损

scream [skri:m] *n.* 尖叫声,喊叫声 *v.* 尖叫,尖啸,大笑;尖叫着说,大叫大嚷着要求

[巧记]派生词:screamy[*a.* 尖亮的(声音);尖声怪气的]

[语境] I pressed the accelerator until the engine screamed.
我猛踩油门踏板,发动机发出了尖厉的声音。
She screamed herself hoarse.
她把嗓子喊哑了。

[考点] scream with laughter 高声大笑

sculpture [ˈskʌlptʃə(r)] *n.* 雕刻,雕塑

[语境] He is skilled in sculpture.
他精于雕刻。

sea [si:] *n.* 海,海洋

[语境] This creek mouths into the sea.
这条小河注入大海。

seaman [ˈsi:mən] *n.* 海员,水手

[语境] Cook learnt fast and quickly became a skilled seaman.
库克学得很快,不久便成了一名技术熟练的水手。

seaport [ˈsi:pɔ:t] *n.* 海港,港口

[巧记] sea(海洋) + port(港口)→海港

[语境] The seaport cities supplied most of the leaders.
港口城市产生了许多领袖人物。

search [sɜ:tʃ] *v./n.* 搜索,寻找,探查

[语境] Scientists are still searching for a cure to the common cold.
科学家仍在寻求治疗感冒的方法。
I want to search out an old school friend.
我想寻找我的一个老同学。

[考点] in search of 寻找,寻求;search after 找寻;search out 找到,找寻;search one's heart 扪心自问

season [ˈsi:zn] *n.* 季,季节,时节

[语境] This is not the season for peaches.

现在不是桃子上市的季节。

seat [siːt] *n.* 席位;座位;底座;所在地;*vt.* 使……就座

[语境] Are you comfortable in this seat?

你坐在这个座位上舒坦吗?

He waved towards a chair, and seated himself at the desk.

他挥手指了指一把椅子,自己在书桌旁坐了下来。

second [ˈsekənd] *num.* 第二 *a.* 次等的,二等的

[语境] He is second only to my own son in my affections.

我除了爱我的儿子,最爱他。

Her beautiful roses won second prize at the flower show.

她那些美丽的玫瑰在花展上得了二等奖。

secret [ˈsiːkrɪt] *a.* 秘密的,机密的 *n.* 秘密

[语境] His secret died with him, for he never told anyone.

他的秘密至死也不为人知,因为他从未告诉过别人。

All the people who know this secret represent a security risk.

凡是知道这个秘密的人都对安全造成危险。

[考点] a top secret 绝密;let out a secret 泄露秘密

secretary [ˈsekrətrɪ] *n.* 书记;秘书;部长,大臣

[语境] The county Party secretary has gone to stay in a village to gain first hand experience.

县委书记到一个乡村蹲点去了。

His secretary got it down.

他的秘书把它记了下来。

section [ˈsekʃən] *n.* 章节;部分;地区;截面,剖视图

[巧记] sect(切,割) + ion;派生词:sectional (*a.* 分项的,分节的);sectionalism (*n.* 地方主义)

[语境] First the surgeon performed the section of the blood vessel.

外科医生首先切开血管。

The last section sums up all the arguments on either side.

最后一部分总结了双方的全部论点。

[考点] build in sections 分段制造;right section 右段,右部

sector[8] [ˈsektə(r)] *n.* 部门,部分;防御地段,防区;扇形

[巧记] 派生词:sectorial(a. 扇形的;适于切割的)

[语境] Prices in most sectors are steady to slightly easier today.

今天多数部门的价格从坚稳渐趋疲软。

All sectors of the economy suffer from the fall in the exchange rate.

所有经济部门都遭受到这次汇率下跌带来的损失。

[考点] a sector of a sphere 扇形圆锥;sector scan 监视某一有限地区的雷达扫描

secure [sɪˈkjʊə(r)] a. 安全的,可靠的 vt. 得到,获得;防护,保卫

[巧记] se(离开) + cure(留心)→不用留有戒心的→安全的

[语境] Make the windows secure before leaving the house.

出门之前把窗户关严。

The little boy felt secure near his parents.

那小男孩在父母身边感到安心。

[考点] be secure of 对……有把握,确信;feel secure about 对……(觉得)放心

security[10] [sɪˈkjʊərɪtɪ] n. 安全,治安防卫;(pl.) 证券,债券

[语境] It's your duty to superintend the security affairs.

主管安全保卫工作是你的职责。

If you own more than one security, you have an investment portfolio.

如果您有多于一种的证券,那么您就有一个投资的组合。

see [siː] vt. 看见;会面;探望;知道,获悉;送行

[语境] If you shut your eyes, you can't see.

要是把眼睛闭上,你就什么也看不见了。

It was getting dark and I couldn't see to read.

天渐渐黑了,我看不见字,无法再阅读了。

seek [siːk] v. 寻找,探索;试图,企图

[语境] The flood started and we had to seek higher ground.

发大水了,我们得到高的地方去。

We sought her out to tell her of her success.

我们找到她,告诉她她成功了。

[考点] seek for 试图获得；play hide and seed 捉迷藏；seek out 找到，搜出

seem [siːm] *v.* 好像，似乎

[巧记] 派生词：seeming(*n.* 外观，外貌；表象 *a.* 表面上的；似乎真实的)

[语境] The children seem unaffected emotionally by their parent's divorce.
孩子在情绪上似乎未受到父母离婚的影响。
He seems to know everything.
他似乎什么都懂。

[考点] seem，look，appear 辨析：这三个词一般用作半系词，都可以汉译作"似乎"或"看上去"。seem 所表示的"似乎"或"看来"是以客观的迹象为依据的；look 所表示的"看来"是以视觉所接受的印象为依据的；appear 与上两个词的含义似乎没有多大差异，但是如果要表示某种判断是由被歪曲了的印象而得出的，最好用 appear。

seize [siːz] *vt.* 抓住；夺取；占领

[巧记] 派生词：seizin(*n.* 依法占有；依法占有之财产)；反义词：loose(*v.* 释放)

[语境] She seized on my suggestion and began work immediately.
她采纳了我的建议，马上干了起来。
Seize any opening you can.
只要有机会就要抓住。

[考点] seize control 夺取控制权；seize hold of 抓住，占领；seize with both hands 积极抓住（机会）

seldom [ˈseldəm] *ad.* 很少

[巧记] 反义词：often(*ad.* 经常)

[语境] I have seldom seen such brutality.
我很少见到这种暴行。
The island is seldom, if ever, visited by ships.
这个岛难得有船停靠。
The apple tree is seldom fruitful.

这棵苹果树很少结果。

[考点] seldom 放在句首的时候用倒装。Very seldom does he eat any breakfast. 他很少吃早餐。

select [sɪˈlekt] *vt.* **选择,挑选**

[巧记] 派生词:selection(*n.* 选择)

[语境] This is a very select area, you have to be rich to live here.
这是高级住宅区,你必须有钱才能住在这里。

Our shops select only the very best quality produce.
我们商店都是精选的质量最高的产品。

[考点] selection *n.* 选择,精选物;selective *a.* 精选的,选择的

selection [sɪˈlekʃən] *n.* **选择,挑选;被挑选出来的人,精选品**

[语境] This is an "adverse selection" problem.
这是一种"逆向选择"问题。

The shop has a fine selection of cheeses.
那家商店有各种精美乳酪可供选购。

[考点] choice, alternative, preference, option, selection, election 辨析:这些名词均含有"选择"之意。choice:侧重指自由选择的权利或特权。alternative:指在相互排斥的两者之间作严格的选择,也可指两者以上中进行选择。preference:侧重因偏见、爱好或判断等而进行选择。option:着重特别给予的选择权利或权力,所选物常常相互排斥。selection:指作广泛的选择,着重选择者的识别力或鉴赏力。election:强调目的和达到目的的判断能力。

self [self] *n.* **自我,自己,本身**

[语境] She was back to her old self again.
她又恢复了老样子。

考点集训

1. Nancy is only a sort of _____ of her husband's opinion and has no ideas of her own.

    A. sample   B. reproduction
    C. shadow   D. echo

415

2. There is a _____ of impatience in the tone of his voice.
   A. hint   B. notion
   C. dot   D. phrase
3. Because of his excellent administration, people lived in peace and _____ and all previously neglected matters were taken care of.
   A. conviction   B. contest
   C. consent   D. content
4. If this kind of fish becomes _____, future generations may never taste it at all.
   A. minimum   B. short
   C. seldom   D. scarce
5. According to the American federal government, residents of Hawaii have the longest life _____: 77.2 years.
   A. scope   B. rank
   C. span   D. scale
6. I would never have _____ a court of law if I hadn't been so desperate.
   A. sought for   B. accounted for
   C. turned up   D. resorted to

答案与解析

1. D 南希只会附和她丈夫的意见,没有自己的想法。A 样本,样品;B 再现,繁殖;C 影子,阴影,阴暗,荫,暗处;D 附和,模仿。故选 D。

2. A 他说话的语调流露出他不耐烦了。A 暗示,线索;B 观念,想法;C 点;D 短语。故选 A。

3. D 由于他的出色管理,人们生活平静富足,所有先前忽视的问题得到了处理。A 定罪,证明有罪,确信,信念[+(that)],说服力;B 比赛,竞赛;C 同意,赞成;D 满足。故选 D。

4. D 如果这鱼变得很罕见,后世子孙也许再也吃不上这种鱼。A 最小;B 短的;C 很少,难得;D 罕见的,缺乏的。故 D 为正确答案。

5. C 据美国联邦政府统计,夏威夷居民寿命最长,平均 77.2 岁。A 范围;B 排名;C life span 寿命,固定搭配;D 范围。故 C 为正确答案。

6. D 如果我不是这样绝望,我也不会求助法庭。A 寻求;B 解释;C 出现;D 诉诸,求助。故选 D。

Word List 40

sell [sel] *v.* **卖,出售**

[语境] Her name will help to sell the film.

有她的名字,这部影片就卖座。

It's a real sell: the food seems cheap but you pay extra for vegetables.

真骗人:饭食好像很便宜,可是吃菜还得另付钱呢。

semester [sɪˈmestər] *n.* **学期**

[语境] He had three minors this semester.

这学期他有三门副修科目。

send [send] (sent, sent) *v.* **打发;派遣;送;寄出**

[语境] He was sent down for ten years for armed robbery.

他因持械抢劫被判入狱十年。

Men who refused to strike were sent to coventry by their colleagues.

凡是不参加罢工的人,同事都不理睬他们。

sense[25] [sens] *n.* **感官;感觉;判断力;意义** *v.* **觉得,意识到**

[语境] I hope she soon sees sense and stops fighting a battle she cannot win.

我希望她能很快明白过来,别再打这场打不赢的仗了。

It would make sense to leave early.

早点离开是明智的。

[考点] have plenty of sense 富有见识;have the sense to (do) 因

417

有头脑而做某事

sensible ['sensɪbəl] *a.* 明理的,明智的

[巧记] sens[e](感觉) + -ible(形容词后缀)

[语境] It was a sensible idea, I felt.

我觉得这是切合实际的想法。

I don't think that's sensible.

我认为这是不实际的。

[考点] be sensible of 知道,觉察到

sensitive ['sensɪtɪv] *a.* 敏感的;灵敏的

[语境] This tooth is sensitive to cold.

这颗牙对冷过敏。

The substance is irritable to sensitive skin.

这种物质对敏感的皮肤有刺激性。

The stock exchange is sensitive to political changes.

证券交易所对政治变化很敏感。

[考点] sensitive to sth. 对……过敏

sentence ['sentəns] *n.* 句子;判决,宣判 *v.* 宣判,判决

[语境] I'm not satisfied with his interpretation of this sentence.

我不太满意他对这个句子的翻译。

The sentence of six months imprisonment was most unjust.

六个月监禁的判决极其不公。

separate ['sepərət] *a.* (from)分离的,分开的

[巧记] se(离开) + parare(安排)

[语境] The war separated many families.

战争使许多家庭妻离子散。

This word has three separate meanings.

这个词有三个不同的意思。

[考点] separate...from... 把……和……分开; separate sth. into several portions 把某物分成几份

September [səp'tembər, sep-, sɪp-] *n.* 九月

[语境] Her son, Jerome, was born in September.

她儿子杰尔姆生于9月。

sequence[12] [ˈsiːkwəns] *n.* 继续,连续;序列,数列;先后,次序,顺序

[巧记] 派生词:sequencing(*n.* 按顺序安排);sequent(*a.* 连续的,相连的)

[语境] A sequence of murders had prompted the police to actions.
一连串的谋杀迫使警方不得不采取行动。

We will deal with events in historical sequence.
我们将按照历史上的先后顺序研究这些事件。

[考点] in sequence 依次,逐一

series [ˈsɪəriːz] *n.* 一系列,一连串,序列;丛书

[语境] After a series of unsuccessful attempts, he has finally passed the driving test.
经过连续几次的失败,他最后终于通过了驾驶考试。

The theory is based on a series of wrong assumptions.
这一理论是以一系列错误的设想为依据的。

[考点] a series of 一连串的……;a series of questions 一系列的问题;in series 成串联的,串联电路的

serious [ˈsɪərɪəs] *a.* 严肃的,庄重的;严重的,危急的;认真的

[巧记] 派生词:serious-minded(热心的),seriousness(*n.* 严肃性;当真;认真;严重性)

[语境] This company was in serious financial difficulties.
这家公司陷入严重的财政困难。

That could cause serious injury.
那可能造成重伤。

[考点] 指的是对工作或重要事情都能认真思考、对待,也指态度严肃、认真。a serious warning 严重警告;serious illness 毛病

serve [sɜːv] *v.* 服务,尽责;招待;使用,适合;服役

[语境] She has served the family faithfully for thirty years.
她为这个家忠心耿耿地操劳了30年。

We are well served with gas in this town.
这个城镇煤气供应得很好。

[考点] serve for 充当,用……作;serve as 作为,用作;serve sb. right 活该,给应得的报应;serve the needs of 满足……需要;

419

serve the people 为人民服务

service ['sɜːvɪs] *n.* 服务;公共事业;服役,帮助;公共设施 *vi* 维护,保养

[巧记] serv + ice(名词后缀)

[语境] You may need the services of a lawyer.

你也许需要律师的帮助。

The food is good at this hotel, but the service is poor.

这家旅馆饭菜很好,但服务很差。

[考点] do…a service 帮一个忙;at sb.'s service 听某人的吩咐;be in sb.'s service 在某人家帮佣;be of service to 对……有用;enter the service 入伍

set [set] *n.* 一套,一副,装置 *v.* 提出,调整,日落

[语境] She admired the firm set of his shoulders.

她喜欢他那结实的肩膀。

I rely on you to set a good example.

我全靠你来树立个好榜样。

[考点] set back 使倒退,使受挫折;推迟,拨回(钟表的针);set by 把……搁在一旁;set free 释放;解放;set off 出发,动身使爆炸,点燃, 发射;set up 竖起;建起,安装,设立, 开办

setting ['setɪŋ] *n.* 安装,放置;周围,环境

[语境] It is a durable gem that can be placed in any setting.

这是一个持久的宝石,可以在任何环境下放置。

Rome is the perfect setting for romance.

罗马是最适合谈情说爱的地方。

settle ['setəl] *v.* 安定,安顿;停息;定居;解决,调停

[巧记] 派生词:settled(*a.* 固定的, 不变的, 决定的),settler(*n.* 移民者, 财产赠予者, 殖民者)

[语境] The thunderstorm may settle the weather.

这场雷暴过后天气可能反而好些。

They moved the local people and settle them in another place.

他们把当地人迁移到别处定居。

[考点] settle down 安顿下来;settle an account 结清账目;进行清

算;算账;settle in 迁入

seven ['sevn] *num.* 七

[语境]The church clock chimed seven.
教堂的钟敲响了七点。

seventeen [ˌsevn'tiːn] *num.* 十七

[语境]She had seventeen children and two of them died.
她有十七个孩子,其中两个夭折了。

seventy ['sevntɪ] *num.* 七十

[语境]When you get to seventy, you are not so active as you were at fifty.
在你七十岁时,你不可能有你五十岁时那样的活力。

several ['sevrəl] *a.* 几个,若干,数个;各个的,各自的

[语境] Children of all ages should be outdoors several hours a day.
各个年龄段的孩子每天都应户外活动几个小时。

My husband has several shirts of different colors.
我丈夫有好几件颜色不同的衬衫。

[考点] several times 好几次;each several part 各部分;in several 分别地, 各个地

severe [sɪ'vɪə(r)] *a.* 严厉的;剧烈的,严重的,严峻的,艰难的

[巧记]派生词:severely(*ad.* 严格地;激烈地), severeness(*n.* 严格;严重;严厉;严酷);同义词:strict(*a.* 严格的)

[语境] Nothing can warrant such severe punishment.
这样严厉的惩罚毫无根据。

We should inflict severe chastisement on criminals.
我们应该对罪犯施加严厉的惩罚。

[考点] be severe upon/upon sb. 对某人很严厉;severe competition 激烈的竞争

sex [seks] *n.* 性别,性

[语境]There's lots of straight sex in the film, but nothing kinky.
那部影片里有不少性行为镜头,但是没有变态的。

He's got a one-track mind—all he ever thinks about is sex!
他只有一个心思——想的都是性事!

shadow [ˈʃædəʊ] *n.* 影子,阴影;暗处,阴暗

[巧记] 词根:shade

[语境] He walked along in the shadows hoping no one would recognize him.

他走在暗处,希望没有人认出他来。

He felt he was being shadowed, but he couldn't see anyone behind him.

他感觉到有人在跟踪他,但他看不见身后的人。

[考点] 派生词:shadowy *a.* 阴暗的,阴凉的;a shadow of 一点点; afraid of one's shadow 胆子小得要命

shake[9] [ʃeɪk] *n./v.* 摇动,摇;颤抖,震动

[巧记] 派生词:shakily(*ad.* 颤抖地;虚弱不堪地;摇动地), shakefork(*n.* 长柄叉)

[语境] Give the bottle a couple of shakes before pouring the juice.

倒果汁前,先把瓶子摇几下。

His voice shook with fear.

他害怕得声音发抖。

[考点] shake hand 握手;shake down 摇落(果实);shake up 摇匀[动,醒]

shall [ʃæl, ʃəl] *aux./v.* (我,我们)将要,会;必须,应该

[语境] Shall we take our swim-suits?

我们带着游泳衣好不好?

That was a moment that I shall never forget.

那个时刻我永远不会忘记。

shallow [ˈʃæləʊ] *a.* 浅的,浅薄的 *n.* 浅滩,浅处

[巧记] 反义词:deep (*a.* 深的)

[语境] Our ship grounded in shallow water/on a sandbank.

我们的船在浅水中[在沙滩上]搁浅了。

The rain ran in shallow runnels alongside the path.

雨水流进路边的小河沟里。

[考点] a shallow mind 浅薄的头脑

shame [ʃeɪm] *n.* 羞愧,耻辱;可耻的人/物 *vt.* 使羞愧,玷辱

[巧记]派生词:shamefaced(a. 脸带愧色的;谦逊的;害羞的) shameful(a. 可耻的,丢脸的;猥亵的,下流的;不道德的,不体面的)

[语境] She was full of shame at her bad behavior.
她对自己的不良行为感到羞耻。
Such an act of cowardice by an officer shames his whole regiment.
一个军官做出如此胆怯的行为使整个团都蒙受羞辱。

[考点] for shame 可耻,真不害臊;put to shame 使难为情;what a shame 真遗憾,真不像话;feel shame at 因……害臊

shape [ʃeɪp] *n.* 形状,外形;情况,状态;种类 *v.* 成型,塑造

[巧记]派生词:shapely(a. 匀称的, 美观的; 样子好的)

[语境]I'm having trouble giving shape to my ideas in this essay.
我在这篇文章中表达不清自己的想法。
A huge shape loomed up out of the fog.
在雾中隐约出现一个巨大的影像。

[考点]in shape 在形状上, 在外形上;结构恰当地,保持固有形式地;处于良好状态,处于有准备状态;get [put] sth. into shape 使成一定形状,整顿;使具体化,条理化

share [ʃeə(r)] *vt.* 分享,分担;均分,分配 *vi.* (in) 分担 *n.* 部分,一份;分担;分子,份额,股份

[巧记]派生词:shareholder(n. 股东),shareout(n. 配给物)

[语境] If you want a share of the pay, you'll have to do your fair share of the work.
要是你想得到一份报酬,你就必须做好你该分担的那一份工作。
She's got all her money in stocks and shares.
她把所有的钱都投放到股票里去了。

[考点] share...with... 和……合用;share in 分享;share out 分配; share sth. among/between sb. 在……中分配;take one's share 尽自己的一份责任;fall to sb's share 由某人承担,归某人享有

sharp [ʃɑːp] *a.* 锋利的;轮廓分明的;急转的 *ad.* (指时刻)正

[巧记]派生词：sharpen(v. 使尖锐，加重，使敏捷；变尖)

[语境]Bring the object into focus if you want a sharp photograph.

要照出清晰的照片，就要把焦点对准物体。

That woman has a very sharp tongue.

那个女人说话非常尖刻。

[考点]as sharp as a needle 很有鉴别力的，异常精明的；非常机敏的；keep a sharp lookout 严密监视；take sb. up sharp 唐突地打断某人

sharply[ˈʃɑːplɪ] *ad.* **严厉地，苛刻地，厉害地**

[语境]Environmentalists were sharply critical of the policy for its failure to encourage conservation.

环境保护主义者对该政策未能促进自然环境的保护提出了强烈的批评。

shave [ʃeɪv] *n.* **修面，刮胡子，惊险的免脱** *v.* **修面，剃，掠过**

[巧记]派生词：shaven(*a.* 修过脸的；削发的；刮过脸的)，shaver(*n.* 理发师；骗子；刮胡须的用具；男孩子)

[语境]The lorry shaved the barrier, scraping its side.

那辆卡车掠过路障，刮坏了车身。

The ball narrowly shaved his off stump.

那个球紧贴着他的三柱门的外柱掠过。

[考点]clean shave 剃光胡子；shave off 削去，剃去，划去

she[ʃiː] *pron.* **她**

[语境]In a TV interview she hit back at her critics.

她在接受电视采访时，反驳了那些批评者的观点。

sheep[ʃiːp] *n.* **羊，绵羊**

[语境]The boy was driving the sheep down the hill.

这个男孩正把羊赶下山。

shelf[ʃelf] *n.* **架子**

[语境]He lifted the books down from the top shelf.

他把书从上边的架子上取下来。

[考点]on the shelf 在书架上

shelter[ˈʃeltə(r)] *n.* **躲避处，掩蔽部** *v./n.* **掩蔽，庇护**

[语境]We are at another shelter.

我们在另一个避难所。

But not everyone has even this most basic shelter.

但并不是每个人都有这个最基本的庇护。

shift[11] [ʃɪft] *v./n.* **转移,移动,转变**

[巧记] 同义词:alter, change(*v.* 改变)

[语境] A sudden shift in the wind warned of the coming storm.

风向的突然转变预示着暴风雨即将来临。

The tools shift around in the car boot every time we turn a corner.

我们每次转弯,汽车行李箱里的工具就来回动。

[考点] shift sth. (from/to)移动,从……移到……;shift for oneself 自谋出路;on the night shift 上夜班

shine [ʃaɪn] *n.* **光泽,阳光** *v.* **使发光,发亮**

[语境]I think that dog has taken a shine to me: it follows me everywhere.

我想这狗已经喜欢上我了:我走到哪儿它跟到哪儿。

Shine your torch into the drawer.

你用手电筒照一下这抽屉里面。

[考点]shine up to 百般讨好某人;make a shine 引起(大)风潮

ship [ʃɪp] *n.* **船,舰;太空船** *vt.* **航运,装运,运送**

[语境]This ship went between China and Japan.

这船往来于中国和日本之间。

Food is being shipped to drought-stricken Southern Africa.

食物正被运往遭受旱灾的非洲南部。

shirt [ʃɜːt] *n.* **衬衫**

[语境]Jack's plaid shirt didn't mix well with his striped trousers.

杰克的方格衬衫与条纹长裤不相配。

shock[5] [ʃɒk] *n.* **冲击,震动,震惊;休克;电击,触电** *v.* **使震动,使震惊**

[巧记] 派生词:shocked(*a.* 震惊的;震撼的),shocker(*n.* 令人震惊的事物;耸人听闻的故事)

425

[语境] Anyone touching that wire could get badly shocked.

任何人碰到那根电线都会遭到严重的电击。

His death was a great shock to us all.

他的死使我们大家大为震惊。

[考点] shocking a. 使人震惊的; shockingly ad. 使人震惊地

shoe [ʃu:] n. 鞋

[语境] This shoe does not seem to pair up with that one.

这只鞋似乎与那只不成对。

shoot [ʃu:t] v. 发射;掠过,疾驰而过 n. 嫩枝,苗,射击

[巧记] shootout (n. 交火,开枪决斗;起弧),shootable (a. 可射击的,适于射猎的)

[语境] Rose bushes shoot again after being cut back.

玫瑰丛修剪后还能再长出新枝。

The film was shot in black and white.

这部电影拍成了黑白片。

[考点] be on the shoot [美] 预备射击;备战;come on a straight shoot 直截了当地进行;shoot at 对准……射击,(把……)向……投去

shop [ʃɒp] n. 商店,店铺;工场,车间 vi. 购物

[语境] The shop takes stock every week on Friday mornings.

这家商店每星期五早晨盘点存货。

He always shopped at the Co-op.

他一直在合作社买东西。

shopping[19] [ˈʃɒpɪŋ] n. 买东西,购物

[语境] We put the shopping away.

我们把买回来的东西放好。

[考点] go shopping 去购物

shore [ʃɔ:(r), ʃɔə(r)] n. 岸;海滨,湖滨

[语境] They walked down to the shore.

他们走到了湖边。

short [ʃɔ:t] a. 短的,矮的;(of) 缺乏,不足 n. (pl.) 短裤

[巧记] 反义词:long (a. 长的);派生词:short-sighted [a. 近视

（眼）的,眼光短浅的]

[语境]All his observations were short and to the point.

他的观察报告都很简单扼要。

His achievements had fallen short of his hopes.

他的成就没有达到他期望的那么大。

[考点]short for 简易格式；……的简略形式；break short off 中断,突然停止；in short 简单地说,总之

shortage [ˈʃɔːtɪdʒ] *n.* 不足,缺少

[巧记]short(短) + age(表抽象名词)→不足,缺少

[语境]The bad harvest led to severe food shortage.

歉收引起食物严重短缺。

The lack of rain aggravated the already serious shortage of food.

干旱少雨使原本就很严重的粮食短缺问题更加严重。

[考点]fund shortage 资金不足,资金短缺

shortcoming [ˈʃɔːtkʌmɪŋ] *n.* 短处,缺点

[巧记]反义词：flaw,weakness（*n.* 缺点,不足）

[语境]Rudeness is his chief shortcoming.

粗鲁是他主要的缺点。

shortly [ˈʃɔːtlɪ] *ad.* 立即,马上

[语境]Their trial will shortly begin.

他们的审判很快就要开始了。

shot [ʃɒt] *n.* 射击,枪声；射门,投篮；弹丸,炮弹；*adj.* 用尽的；杂色的；闪光的；*v.* 射击

[语境]He won the golf match by two shots.

他以两杆的成绩赢得了这场高尔夫球赛。

His stories are shot through with a gentle sadness.

他的小说充满了淡淡的忧伤。

[考点]shot away 连续射击；shot up 迅速升起,快速成长

should [ʃəd, ʃʊd] *aux./v.* 应该；万一；可能,该；就；竟然会

[语境]It should cost roughly £10.

这大约 10 英镑。

We should improve what is called the quality of living.

我们应该改进所谓的生活品质。

shoulder [ˈʃəʊldə(r)] *n.* 肩,肩膀

[语境] He glanced over his shoulder and saw me watching him.

他扭头瞥了一眼,看见我正看他。

[考点] shoulder to shoulder 距离非常贴近地;肩并肩地;密切合作地

shout [ʃaʊt] *v.* 大声叫,喊,呼出 *n.* 呼喊,叫

[语境] The crowd shouted the speaker down.

群众高声喊叫把演讲人的声音压了下去。

The children on the sand were shouting with excitement.

沙滩上的孩子们兴奋得大喊大叫。

[考点] shout for/with joy 欢呼; shout for help 呼救; shout with laughter 大声笑

show [ʃəʊ] *n.* 显示,展览,表现 *v.* 显示,露出;演出;陈列,展出;放映;露面,显现

[语境] Her laziness showed in her exam results.

她平时懒惰从她的考试成绩可以看得出来。

All the new products were on show at the exhibition.

展览会上陈列着所有的新产品。

shower [ˈʃaʊə(r)] *vt.* 倾注 *n./vi.* (下)阵雨;(冲)淋浴;似阵雨般降落

[语境] Dates showered down when we shook the tree.

我们摇树时,枣子纷纷落下。

Scattered showers are expected this afternoon.

预料今天下午有零星阵雨。

[考点] showers down 像雨点落下; showers on(upon) 大量给予,大量而来; showers of letters 大批信件

shrink [ʃrɪŋk] *vi.* 起皱,收缩;退缩,畏缩

[巧记] 派生词:shrinkage (*n.* 收缩,减低,缩水);反义词:expand(*v.* 使膨胀;扩张)

[语境] Will this woolen sweater shrink when washed?

这件羊毛衫洗后会缩水吗?

The economy is shrinking instead of growing.

经济正在萎缩而不是在增长中。

[考点] shrink(back)from 退缩,往后退;shrink up(由于不好意思)退缩

shut [ʃʌt] *a.* 关闭的,合拢的,围绕的 *v.* 关上,闭起,幽禁

[巧记] 派生词:shutdown (*n.* 关门,停工,关机)

[语境] He shut his eyes to her faults.

他对她的缺点视而不见。

He shut himself away for a month to catch up on his academic work.

他与世隔绝一个月,力图把功课赶上去。

[考点] shut down 停工;关闭,机器关机;shut off 关掉;切断;shut up 住口;禁闭;关闭

shuttle ['ʃʌtl] *n.* 往返汽车、列车、飞机;航天飞机;梭子;穿梭 *v.* 穿梭往返

[语境] The shuttle Endeavour will be taking the astronauts to the Hubble.

"奋进"号航天飞机将把宇航员送上哈勃。

He and colleagues have shuttled back and forth between the three capitals.

他和同事们在这3个首都之间往来穿梭。

shy [ʃaɪ] *n.* 惊退,投掷;讥刺,抨击;尝试 *v.* 惊退;厌恶;畏缩,胆怯;回避;乱投,乱掷;投,扔

[语境] The colt shied at the fence and refused to jump over it.

这马驹到障碍物前害怕不敢跳过去。

We are still a little shy of our quota.

我们离完成定额还差一点点。

[考点] have a shy at 乱投(at)

sick [sɪk] *a.* 有病的;恶心的;不舒服的;厌恶的

[考点] 同义词:ill (*a.* 生病的);反义词:healthy (*a.* 健康的)

[语境] It makes me sick to see her being treated so badly.

我看到她受到这样的虐待非常愤怒。

She left her home reluctantly and sick at heart.
她依依不舍地离开了家,心情很沉重。

[考点] be sick about(at) 因为某事而不高兴,感到遗憾;be sick for 思念;be sick of 讨厌,厌烦;feel sick 想呕吐;sick with 患……病

考点集训

1. The continuous rain _____ the harvesting of the wheat crop by two weeks.
   A. set back   B. set off
   C. set out   D. set aside
2. Some plants are very _____ to light; they prefer the shade.
   A. sensible   B. flexible
   C. objective   D. sensitive
3. Mass advertising helped to _____ the emphasis from the production of goods to their consumption.
   A. vary   B. shift
   C. lay   D. moderate
4. We're _____ 50 new staff this year as business grows.
   A. taking over   B. taking in
   C. taking on   D. taking up
5. The advertisement says this material doesn't _____ in the wash, but it has.
   A. contract   B. shrink
   C. slim   D. dissolve

答案与解析

1. A 持续的雨水把小麦的收割推迟了两周时间。A 推迟,延误;B 出发,开始,使点燃;C 出发;D 搁置,放一边。故选 A。

2. D 有些植物对光敏感,他们喜欢阴凉处。be sensitive to 对……敏感,固定搭配,故选 D。

核心词汇精解

3. B　大众广告有助于实现由产品生产向产品消费的重要转变。shift sth. from…to…由……转向……,固定搭配,故选 B。
4. C　因为公司业务的增长,我们想雇用50名新员工。A 接管;B 吸收,纳入;C 呈现,雇用;D 拿起。故 C 为正确答案。
5. B　广告中说这种面料洗后不会收缩,但现在却缩水了。A 变小,变窄;B 收缩(由于水、热量等的作用);C 使……体重减轻,使……苗条;D 分解。故选 B。

Word List 41

side [saɪd] *n.* 旁边,方面,侧 *v.* 偏袒,支持,同意;赞助
　[语境] A square has four sides but a circle has no sides.
　　正方形有四条边,而圆形没有边。
　　She argued her side of the case well.
　　她有理有据地陈述了自己的意见。
　[考点] side-kick 伙伴;密友;side by side 肩并肩地;一起;side effect 副作用;side with 支持
　[考点] a sideways view 侧视

sight[22] [saɪt] *n.* 视力,视觉;望见,瞥见;情景,奇观;(*pl.*)风景,名胜
　[巧记] 派生词:sighted(*a.* 有视力的;有瞄准器的;有某种视力的)
　[语境] The train is still in sight.
　　火车仍在视线内。
　　We laughed at the sight of his strange clothes.
　　一看到他古怪的穿着,我们就笑了。
　[考点] at the sight of 看见;catch sight of 发现;in sight 在看得见的范围;lose sight of 看不见;out of sight 在看不见的地方;at first sight 一眼,乍一看;take sight 瞄准

sightseeing [ˈsaɪtsiːɪŋ] *n.* 观光,游览
　[巧记] sight(景象) + see(观看) + ing(名词后缀)→观看美好的

431

景象→观光,游览

[语境]The tourists went sightseeing in the suburbs of the city.

游客们游览了市郊。

sign[59] [saɪn] *n.* 记号,符号;招牌;标志;标牌;前兆 *v.* 签;签名于,签署;写下;签字,署名;做手势示意

[巧记]派生词:signboard(*n.* 招牌,广告牌),sign-language(*n.* 手势语)

[语境] Arsenal have just signed a new striker.

阿塞纳尔队刚雇用了一名新前锋。

The football team has signed two new players.

该足球队已签约聘用了两名新队员。

[考点] at the sign of 当有……迹象时;in sign of 作为……的记号[标志];make a sign to 对……作暗号[打手势];sign in 签到,签收

signal ['sɪgnəl] *n.* 信号,暗号 *v.* 签(名),签署

[巧记]sign(符号,记号) + -al(名词后缀);派生词:signal(*adj.* 暗号的,作信号用的,显著的,非常的,重大的)

[语境] The police signalled the traffic to move forward slowly.

警察向来往车辆打信号,示意缓慢前行。

I corrected my watch by the time signal.

我按报时信号校正我的表。

[考点] signal to sb./sth. 向某人或某物发信号

significance [sɪgˈnɪfɪkəns] *n.* 意义,含义;重要性

[巧记]sign + ific(带有) + ance→带有信号→[有]意义;派生词:significant(*a.* 有意义的,重要的)

[语境] Could you explain to me the significance of this part of the contract?

你能给我解释一下合同这一部分的含义吗?

This new discovery of oil is of great significance to this area's economy.

这次新发现的石油对这个地区的经济有着重大的意义。

[考点]difference with significance 显著差别

significant[6] [sɪgˈnɪfəkənt] *a.* 有意义的;重大的,重要的

[巧记]派生词:significance (*n.* 意义;重要性)

[语境] Share prices showed significant advances today.
今日股票价格大幅上涨。
Her appointment was a significant, (al)though/albeit temporary success.
她受聘虽说是临时性的,但却是一大成功。

[考点]a significant wink 意味深长的眼色

silence [ˈsaɪləns] *n.* 寂静,沉默 *vt.* 使寂静,使沉默

[巧记]派生词:silencer(*n.* 使沉默者,灭音器,消音器)

[语境] The enemy's guns were silenced by repeated bombings.
敌人的炮火因遭到轮番轰炸而沉寂了。
There was nothing but silence in the room.
这间屋内声息全无,一片寂静。

[考点] in silence 一言不发;keep silence 安静,保持沉默;break silence 开口说话,打破沉默

silent [ˈsaɪlənt] *a.* 寂静的,沉默的

[语境] He was silent for a moment, then began his answer.
他沉默了一会儿,然后开始回答。
He is the strong, silent type.
他是个坚强而沉默的人。

[考点] be silent about 对……保持缄默,对……只字不提;keep [be] silent 保持沉默;保持肃静

silly [ˈsɪlɪ] *a.* 傻的,糊涂的,愚蠢的

[语境]That silly child never does anything; he just fools about all day long.
那个傻孩子从来不做事,只是整天游手好闲。
She torments everyone with silly questions.
她用无聊的问题来烦扰大家。

[考点]Don't be silly! [口]别傻啦! be knocked silly 被打得失去知觉

silver[ˈsɪlvə(r)] *n.* 银,银器,银币

[语境]He beat the rugs and polished the silver.

他拍打去地毯上的灰尘,还擦拭了银器。

similar[22] [ˈsɪmɪlə(r)] *a.* (to)相似的,类似的

[巧记]派生词:similarity(*n.* 类似;相似点;相似;类似点),similarly(*ad.* 同样地;类似地)

[语境] The two buildings are similar on the whole.

从整体来看,这两幢楼是相似的。

I sympathize with you; I've had a similar unhappy experience myself.

我很同情你,我自己也有过类似的不幸遭遇。

[考点] be similar to 与……相似,类似于……

similarly[ˈsɪmɪləlɪ] *ad.* 同样地,类似地

[语境]The brothers dress similarly.

兄弟俩穿得差不多。

simple[17] [ˈsɪmpəl] *a.* 简单,朴素;单纯,直率;迟钝的,头脑简单的

[巧记]派生词:simple-minded(*a.* 率直的;心地善良的;单纯的;愚笨的)

[语境] She doesn't understand you. She's a bit simple.

她不明白你的意思。她有点笨。

My father was a simple farm-worker.

我父亲是个普通的农民。

[考点]simple 还有仅仅、只有的含义,如:He failed simply because he is lazy. 他的失败只不过是他的懒惰所致

simply[16] [ˈsɪmplɪ] *ad.* 简单地;完全,简直;仅仅,只不过

[巧记] 近义词:merely,just, only(*ad.* 仅仅,只)

[语境]The meat was so tough that I simply couldn't get it down.

这肉太老了,我简直咽不下去。

What we need is simply money, money and money.

我们所需的仅仅是钱而已。

since [sɪns] *prep.* 自从 *conj.* 自从;因为,既然

[语境]She moved to London last May and has since got a job on a newspaper.

她去年五月到伦敦,此后一直在报社工作。
It was the first time I'd won since I'd learnt to play chess.
自从我学会下国际象棋以来,这是我第一次赢。

sincere [sɪnˈsɪə(r)] *a.* 诚恳的,真诚的

[巧记] 派生词:sincerely(*ad.* 真诚地;由衷地;诚恳地),sincerity(*n.* 诚挚;真挚;真实)

[语境] Please give my sincere regards to all the members of your family.
请向你全家转达我真挚的问候。
Please accept our sincere apologies for the error in your bank statement.
为你的银行报表中的错误,请接受我们诚挚的道歉。

[考点] in sincere 在……是诚挚的;Sincerely yours 你诚挚的,你真诚的,你的朋友,最好的问候(信件的结束语)

sing [sɪŋ] *v.* 唱,演唱;鸡叫

[语境] She'll sing if we put the pressure on.
我们给她些压力,她就会讲出来。
She was singing a lullaby to her child.
她正在给孩子唱摇篮曲。

singer [ˈsɪŋə(r)] *n.* 歌手,歌唱家

[语境] The voice of the singer still rings in my ears.
歌唱家的声音仍萦绕在我耳边。

single [ˈsɪŋɡəl] *a.* 单人的;单身的;单一的,单个的

[巧记] 派生词:singleness(*n.* 单独;诚意;独身;专心),singleton(*n.* 一个,单独,独身)

[语境] The letter was written on a single sheet of paper.
这封信只用一张纸写成。
The tax threshold for a single pensioner is 450 dollars.
单身养老金领取者的征税起点是450美元。

[考点] single out 挑选出

sink [sɪŋk] *v.* (使)下沉;降低 *n.* (厨房中的)洗涤槽

[巧记] 派生词:sinking(*n.* 下沉;凹陷;降低;虚脱感)

[语境] It was several days before the floodwater sank and life returned to normal.

过了几天,洪水才退,生活恢复了正常。

My feet sank into the mud.

我的双脚陷到泥里去了。

[考点] sink in 陷下去;sink into 渗入,深深印入(脑中);heart sink 心灰意冷;sink to 堕落到

sir [sə(r), sɜː(r)] *n.* 先生;[S-](用于姓名前)……爵士

[语境] I'll just measure you up, sir, if I may?

先生,我这就给您量量衣服尺寸行吗?

Of all her admirers the most permanent was Sir John.

在她所有的爱慕者当中,约翰爵士最有恒心。

sister ['sɪstə(r)] *n.* 姐妹

[语境] His sister Sarah helped him.

他姐姐萨拉帮助了他。

sit [sɪt] *vi.* 坐,坐下;位于;栖息;孵卵 *vt.* 使就座

[语境] All the others ran away, but I sat tight.

别人都跑了,但我在原地没动。

I sat every day for a week until the painting was finished.

我每天那样坐着,一个星期才把我画好。

sitting-room *n.* 起居室

[巧记] sitting(坐) + room(房间)→坐下来会客的地方→起居室

[语境] She has renewed all the curtains in the sitting-room.

她把客厅的窗帘都换成新的了。

situated ['sɪtjueɪtɪd] *a.* 位于……,坐落于……

[语境] The pain was situated above and around the eyes.

眼睛的上方和四周都很疼。

situation[27] [ˌsɪtjuˈeɪʃən] *n.* 形势,处境,状况;位置,场所;职位,职务

[语境] He doesn't seem to understand the gravity of the situation.

他似乎没有意识到形势的严重性。

Our financial situation is still precarious if we postpone the release of the new product.

如果我们推迟发布新产品的话,我们的财政状况仍然岌岌可危。

[考点]be in /out of a situation 有/失去职业

six[sɪks] *num.* 六

[语境]There's an age difference of six years between them.

他们之间相差六岁。

sixteen[ˌsɪks'tiːn] *num.* 十六

[语境]He worked sixteen hours a day.

他每天工作 16 个小时。

sixty['sɪkstɪ] *num.* 六十

[语境]At the age of sixty he took up the study of Russian.

在 60 岁时他开始学习俄语。

size [saɪz] *n.* **大小,尺寸,规模;尺码**

[语境]The sizes of the apples varied.

那些苹果大小不同。

What size of collar is this shirt?

这衬衣领子的尺寸是多少?

[考点]for size 试尺寸;看是否合适;按不同尺码;of a size 大小一样的;尺码相同的

sketch[sketʃ] *n.* **素描,速写;略图;梗概,大意;***vt.* **速写,写生;概述,简述**

[语境]I made the sketch; he filled in the colours.

是我打的稿子,他上的色。

My sister often goes into the country to sketch.

我姐姐常到乡间去写生。

[考点]sketch out 草拟,概述

skil(l)ful ['skɪlfəl] *a.* **灵巧的,娴熟的**

[巧记]skill(技术) + ful(形容词化);

[语境] That actress is both skillful and beautiful.

那位女演员演技精湛且长得漂亮。

[考点] skillful at sth./doing sth. 有技巧的,熟练的

skill [skɪl] *n.* **技能,技巧,手艺;熟练**

[语境] The crisis put his courage and skill to the test.

这次危难是对他的勇气和技能的考验。

Match your skill against the experts in this quiz.

在这一测验中你与专家较量一下技巧吧。

[考点] diplomatic skill 外交手腕；exert one's utmost skill 运用最大技巧；have no skill in 没有……的技能

skilled[4] [skɪld] *a.* **有技能的，熟练的；需要技能的**

[语境] He has become a skilled worker.

他已经成为一名熟练的工人。

[考点] be skilled at 对……很熟练；擅长于

skin [skɪn] *n.* **皮，皮肤** *vt.* **剥皮**

[语境] This ointment can work in your skin.

这种药膏能渗入你的皮肤。

But because people want these precious furs they will sometimes skin them alive and that is an even crueler method.

但是人们为了想要这些珍贵的动物毛皮，他们将动物活生生剥皮，那是更残忍的方式。

skirt [skɜːt] *n.* **裙子；**(*pl.*) **边缘，郊区**

[语境] She held out her new skirt for us to see.

她把新裙子拿出来给我们看。

She made a neat row of stitches along the edge of her skirt.

在裙子上的边缘她缝了一排整齐的缝线。

sky [skaɪ] *n.* **天，天空**

[语境] A clear atmosphere intensifies the blue of the sky.

纯净的空气使天空变得更蓝。

[考点] in the sky 在天空中

sleep[32] [sliːp] *v.* (slept, slept) **睡** *n.* **睡眠**

[巧记] 派生词：sleepily (*ad.* 想睡地；疲倦地)，sleepiness (*n.* 睡意；瞌睡)

[语境] He'd been sleeping rough for a week, in ditches and haystacks.

他在沟里和草堆里露宿了一个星期。

I haven't had enough sleep lately.

最近我睡眠不够。

[考点] fall into a deep sleep 酣睡

sleepy ['sli:pɪ] *a.* **困乏的,欲睡的**

[语境] She was still tired and sleepy when he woke her.

他叫醒她的时候,她仍然又累又困。

slight[6] [slaɪt] *a.* **轻微的,细微的;纤细的,瘦弱的**

[巧记] 派生词:slightly(*ad.* 轻微地;微小地;稍微地;纤细地),slightness(*n.* 些微;少许;细长)

[语境] I haven't the slightest idea what you are talking about.

我一点也不明白你在说些什么。

Her slight frame was shaken by bouts of coughing.

她纤弱的身躯因阵阵咳嗽而发颤。

[考点] not in the slightest 毫不,一点也不

slip [slɪp] *v.* **滑,滑倒;滑掉;溜走** *n.* **疏忽,小错,口误,笔误**

[巧记] 同义词:slide

[语境] The ship slipped into the harbour at night.

那艘船夜里悄悄开进了港口。

He caught the ball, then it slipped through his fingers.

那球他已接住却又从手中滑脱了。

[考点] slip a cog 出错;slip up 跌倒,疏忽,遭到不幸

slippery ['slɪpərɪ] *a.* **滑的,滑溜的**

[巧记] 词根:slip

[语境] having a slippery or smooth quality

质地平滑的;滑或光滑的品质

A wet road is usually slippery.

潮湿的路往往是滑的。

[考点] as slippery as an eel 难于应付的,滑头的

slow [sləʊ] *a.* **慢的,不活跃的** *v.* **(使)放慢,减速**

[语境] This student is slow in learning English.

这个学生学英语很笨。

My watch is five minutes slow.

我的表慢五分钟。

small [smɔːl] *a.* 小的；年幼的；不重要的；小规模(经营)的

[语境]Our house is smaller than yours but I think the garden is bigger.

我们的房子比你们的小,但花园比你们的大。

The car cost me a small fortune.

这辆汽车花了我很多钱。

smart [smɑːt] *a.* 漂亮的；聪明的；巧妙的 *v.* 剧痛,刺疼

[巧记] 同义词：clever

[语境] This boy is very smart; he may be another Edison.

这男孩很聪明,他可能成为另一个爱迪生。

I gave a smart blow on the lid, and it flew open.

我朝盖子猛一击,就把它打开了。

[考点] at a smart pace 步伐轻快地；a smart few 相当多(的)

smell [smel] *n.* 气味；嗅觉

[语境]One smell of the rotten meat was enough!

这腐烂的肉闻一下就够受的了。

I smelt a rat when he started being so helpful!

他主动帮起忙来,我怀疑其中另有文章！

[考点] smell 系常用词,指"任何气味",特别强调"在嗅觉器官所产生的效果"；scent 指"气味",尤指"香味"；odour 为较典雅和正式的词,指"强烈的、容易辨别出的气味",强调"气味本身的本质",常用于科技文体中

smile[5] [smaɪl] *n.* 微笑,笑容 *vi.* 微笑,露出笑容

[语境] A smile often denotes pleasure and friendship.

微笑常常表示高兴和友善。

The woman in this painting has a pensive smile.

这幅画上的女人脸上露出忧郁的微笑。

[考点] smile at 看着……微笑；一笑置之

smoke [sməʊk] *n.* 烟,烟尘；吸烟,抽烟 *v.* 抽(烟)；冒烟,冒气

[语境] The smoke of the burning house could be seen many blocks away.

着火的房子冒出的烟在几个街区外都能看到。

Peter smokes several cigars every day.

彼得每天抽好几支雪茄。

[考点] end up in smoke 烟消云散；完全落空；终成泡影

smooth [smu:ð] *a.* **光滑的；顺利的；柔和的** *v.* **(over) 掩饰**

[巧记] 派生词：smooth-acting (*a.* 平滑动作的)

[语境] The birch has smooth bark and slender branches.

桦树有光滑的皮和细长的枝。

She smoothed out wrinkles out of the tablecloth.

她把桌布上的皱褶弄平。

[考点] make things smooth for sb. 为某人排除困难；smooth away differences 消除分歧；smooth the anger 平息怒气

snack [snæk] *n.* **快餐，小吃**

[语境] Lunch was a snack in the fields.

午饭是在野外吃的便餐。

snake [sneɪk] *n.* **蛇**

[语境] The little girl commenced to cry when she saw the snake.

这小女孩一看到蛇就开始哭了起来。

snatch [snætʃ] *vt./n.* **攫取，抢夺**

[语境] It is rude to snatch.

攫夺是不礼貌的。

snow [snəʊ] *n.* **雪** *vt.* **下雪**

[语境] They shoveled a path through the snow.

他们在雪中铲出一条小路。

I bet that it will snow tomorrow.

我敢说明天一定下雪。

so [səʊ] *ad.* **那么；非常；也；不错** *conj.* **因此；以便**

[语境] He disconnected the phone so as not to be disturbed.

他为了不受打扰，把电话线路关掉了。

How could you be so stupid as to believe him?

你怎么这么笨竟相信他的话？

so-called [ˌsəʊˈkɔːld] *a.* **所谓的，号称的**

[语境]But not everyone is happy at this so-called outsourcing of tutors.

但并不是每个人都满意这个所谓的"外包导师"。

social[59] [ˈsəʊʃəl] *a.* 社会的;社交的,交际的

[巧记] 派生词:socialism(*n.* 社会主义,社会主义运动)

[语境] She swindled £1,000 out of the Social Security.

她骗得了1 000英镑社会保险金。

We are invited to a small social gathering.

我们被邀请参加一个小型社交聚会。

Most bees and wasps are social insects.

大多数蜜蜂和黄蜂都是群居昆虫。

[考点] social services 社会福利事业;social security 社会保障

society[27] [səˈsaɪətɪ] *n.* 社会;社团,协会,社;社交界,上流社会

[语境]We subscribe to an animal protection society.

我们定期捐款给一个动物保护基金会。

In old society, the gentry lived in luxury.

在旧社会,贵族们生活奢侈。

[考点]avoid [seek] the society of 避免[追求]和……来往[相处];be quit of sb.'s society 和……断绝来往;go into society 进入交际界,常赴宴会

soft [sɒft] *a.* 软的;温柔的;细嫩的,光滑的;不含酒精的

[巧记] 反义词:hard

[语境] Don't be so soft there's nothing to be afraid of.

别这么窝囊,没什么可怕的嘛。

It's very comfortable to step on the soft ground in the spring.

春天的时候,踩在松软的地面上非常舒服。

soldier [ˈsəʊldʒə(r)] *n.* 士兵,军人

[语境]The soldier disobeyed an order.

这名士兵违抗了命令。

solid [ˈsɒlɪd] *n.* 固体 *a.* 固体的;实心的,结实的;稳固的

[语境] Water becomes solid when it freezes.

水结冰时便变成固体。

Ice is water in solid state.

冰是水的固体状态。

[考点] on solid ground 在稳固的基础上；solid learning 实在的学问

solution[18] [səˈluːʃən] *n.* **解决(方法)；溶液，溶解**

[巧记] solut(解决)+ion(名词化)→解决方法

[语境] What color is copper sulfate solution?

硫酸铜溶液是什么颜色？

It seems (to me) (to be) the best solution.

(依我看)这似乎是最好的解决办法。

[考点] in solution 在溶解状态中

solve[14] [sɔlv] *v.* **解决，解答**

[语境] Something is bound to happen one way or another to end the conflict or solve the problem.

事情一定以某种方式发生以结束冲突或解决难题。

I think I can solve the problem.

我想我能解决这问题。

考点集训

1. The computer revolution may well change society as _____ as did the Industrial Revolution.

   A. certainly   B. insignificantly
   C. fundamentally   D. comparatively

2. Though he was born and brought up in America, he can speak _____ Chinese.

   A. smooth   B. fluent
   C. fluid   D. flowing

3. There is no _____ evidence that people can control their dreams, at least in experimental situations in a lab.

   A. rigid   B. solid
   C. smooth   D. harsh

4. Can you give me even the _____ clue as to where her son might

be?

A. simplest   B. slightest
C. least   D. utmost

答案与解析

1. C 电脑革命可以彻底改变社会,就像工业革命彻底改变社会一样。A 当然地;B 不重要地;C 根本地;D 相对地。故 C 为正确答案。
2. B 尽管他生在美国,长在美国,但是他汉语说得很流利。A 顺利的;B 流利的;C 流畅的;D 流动的。故 B 为正确答案。
3. B 没有强有力的证据表明人能控制他们的梦,至少在实验室里没有。A 僵化的;B 强有力的;C 顺利的;D 粗糙的,刺耳的,严厉的,严格的,残酷的。故选 B。
4. B 你能提供些我儿子有可能去的地方的基本线索吗? A 最简单的;B 最轻微的;C 最少的;D 极度的,最大的,最远的。故选 B。

Word List 42

some [sʌm] *a.* 几个;一些;有些;某(人或物) *pron.* 一些

[语境]She won a competition in some newspaper or other.
她参加某报纸举办的比赛获胜。
If you save some money each week, we can go on holiday.
要是你每星期能存点儿钱,咱们就可以外出度假了。

somebody['sʌmbədɪ,-bɒdɪ] *pron.* 某人,有人

[语境]I heard somebody skirling.
我听见有人尖声高叫。

somehow ['sʌmhaʊ] *ad.* 以某种方式,用某种方法;不知怎么地

[语境]He could have finished it on schedule, but somehow he fell behind.

他原本能按预定进度做完这件事的,但不知怎地却落后了。

We'll get there somehow, by boat or otherwise.

我们总要设法去那里的,乘船也好,用其他办法也好。

[考点] somehow or other 不知是什么原因

someone [ˈsʌmwʌn] *pron.* 某人,有人

[语境] Someone called you just now.

刚才有人给你打过电话。

something [ˈsʌmθɪŋ] *n.* 某物,有事

[语境] Something is wrong there.

那里有东西出了差错。

sometime [ˈsʌmtaɪm] *ad.* 近期内;曾经,在某时候

[语境] Sometime the data volume grows beyond expectations.

有时,数据量的增长会超过预期。

sometimes [ˈsʌmtaɪmz] *ad.* 将来(或过去)某个时候 *a.* 以前的

[巧记] some(某) + time(时间)→某个时候

[语境] Good student as he is (= Though he is a good student), he sometimes makes mistakes.

虽然他是好学生,偶尔也会犯错。

Mr. Smith sometimes condescends to help his wife with the housework.

史密斯先生有时屈尊帮他的妻子做家务。

somewhat [ˈsʌmwɔt] *pron./ad.* 一点儿,几分

[巧记] some(某) + what(什么)

[语境] We are suffering somewhat from the heat.

我们因为酷热有些不好受。

The cake we made was somewhat of a failure.

我们做的蛋糕不大成功。

[考点] somewhat of [口]有点;相当

somewhere [ˈsʌmweə(r)] *ad.* 某地,在某处;在附近,前后,大约

[巧记] some(某) + where(处)→某地

[语境] A musical bell softly sounded somewhere in the passageway.

走廊的某处响起轻柔悦耳的铃声。

It was dawn, and I could hear a cock crowing somewhere.

天亮了,我听到从某处传来雄鸡的啼叫声。

[考点] go somewhere out of town 到城外某处去;somewhere about 在……附近,大约

son [sʌn] *n.* 儿子

[语境] She lost her son in the crowd.

她在人群中看不见她儿子了。

song [sɒŋ] *n.* 歌声;歌曲

[语境] She transposed the song into a different key.

她把这首歌变成另一种调子。

soon [suːn] *ad.* 不久,即刻;快,早

[语境] He left as soon as he heard the news.

他一听到这事儿就走了。

He didn't arrive as soon as we'd hoped.

他到达的时间比我们预期的要迟。

sore [sɔː(r)] *a.* 疼痛的,痛心的 *n.* 痛处,疮口

[语境] Her sore foot bothers her.

她的痛脚困扰着她。

This medicine will quell your sore throat.

这种药可减轻你的喉痛。

sorrow ['sɒrəʊ] *n.* 悲伤,忧愁

[语境] Life has many joys and sorrows.

人生有许多欢乐和悲伤。

It was more in sorrow than in anger that he criticized his former colleague.

他批评以前的同事,并非出于气愤而是为他惋惜。

[考点] convert sorrow into strength 化悲痛为力量;share the sorrows and joys 同甘共苦

sorry ['sɒrɪ] *a.* 对不起的,抱歉的;难过的,悔恨的;使人伤心的

[语境] He was sorry for her and tried to cheer her up.

他为她感到难过,并试图使她振作起来。

I was sorry to hear that your cat had died.

听说你的猫死了,我觉得很难过。

sort[7] [sɔːt] *n.* **种类,类别** *v.* **分类,整理**

[语境] I'll leave you to sort this problem out.
我把这个问题交给你来处理。
She's been out of sorts since the birth of her baby.
她生了孩子以后身体一直不好。

[考点] sort out 分出,分类,归类;in a sort 有些,稍微,有几分;of the sort 那样的;这类的……,诸如此类的……

soul [səʊl] *n.* **灵魂,心灵;人;精华,中心人物**

[语境] She sold her soul for money.
她为金钱而出卖灵魂。
Some of these simple pleasures are good for your mind, body and soul.
这些简单的快乐对你的大脑、身体和精神都非常有好处。

sound [saʊnd] *n.* **声音** *v.* **发声,响** *a.* **健全的,完好的;正当的**

[语境] He's always sounding off about how he would manage the firm.
他总是大言不惭地说他能把公司经营好。
I caught a curious sound in the neighboring room.
我听到隔壁房间里有奇怪的响声。

soup [suːp] *n.* **汤**

[语境] The cook pinches salt into the soup.
厨师在汤里放了一些盐。

sour ['saʊə(r)] *a.* **酸的,酸腐的;脾气坏的,刻薄的;** *vt.* **使变酸;使变坏**

[巧记] 派生词:souring (*n.* 变酸,能引起变酸的物质), sourish (*a.* 微酸的;略带酸味的)

[语境] The old man has been soured by poverty.
那老人因贫困而变得乖戾了。
The hot weather has soured the milk.
炎热的天气使牛奶变酸了。

[考点] 合成词:sour cream 酸奶油;sour dough *n.* 含酵母的面团;

sourpuss n. 坏脾气的人；sour...on...使对……产生反感

source[26][sɔːs] *n.* 源，源泉；来源，根源

[巧记] 同义词：origin(*n.* 起源；起因；由来；出身)

[语境] He cited many sources for his book.

他在书中引用了许多资料。

This account provides you with a ready source of income.

这个户头为你提供了一个现成的收入来源。

[考点] source 产生，形成某事物的地方，来源或根源，这种来源一般持续存在，不会突然消失

south[saʊθ] *n./a.* 南，南方 *ad.* 向/自/在南方

[语境] He saw action in the South Pacific.

他在南太平洋参加过战斗。

souvenir[ˌsuːvəˈnɪə(r)] *n.* 纪念品

[语境] I'll keep it for a souvenir.

我要将它保存下来作为纪念。

space [speɪs] *n.* 间隔；空地，余地；空间 *v.* 留间隔，隔开

[语境] Space your words when you write.

写字的时候要把字均匀地隔开。

There is plenty of space here to move about.

这里有很大的活动空间。

[考点] breathing space 松口气的时间，喘息的机会，活动空间；走动场所；for a space 暂时；短时间；一段时间；for the space of a mile 一英里的距离

spacecraft[ˈspeɪskrɑːft] *n.* 宇宙飞船

[语境] The Voyager spacecraft would visit all of these.

航行者宇宙飞船将会全部到访。

spaceship[ˈspeɪsʃɪp] *n.* 宇宙飞船

[巧记] space(太空) + ship(船)→在太空行驶的船→宇宙飞船

[语境] They successfully lofted a spaceship into orbit.

他们成功地将一艘宇宙飞船射入轨道。

Spanish[ˈspænɪʃ] *a.* 西班牙(人/语)的 *n.* 西班牙人/语

[语境] I can't talk a word of Spanish.

我一句西班牙语都不会讲。

spare [speə(r)] *a.* 业余的,备用的 *v.* 让给,抽出(时间);饶恕

[语境] It was a horrible accident—I'll spare you the details.
这是一次令人毛骨悚然的事故,我就不告诉你细节了。

[考点] spare sth. for sb./sth., spare sb. sth. 和某人分享某物;
spare sb.'s feelings 不要使人难过

speak [spi:k] *v.* 说话,讲话;演说,发言;(in)说某种语言

[语境] I'm quite capable of speaking for myself, thank you!
我还是有能力把话说清楚的,谢谢你!

Does anyone speak English here?
这儿有人会说英语吗?

speaker ['spi:kə(r)] *n.* 说话者,发言者;说某种语言者;扬声器

[语境] The crowd fired questions at the speaker for over an hour.
群众向演讲者一连提了一个多小时的问题。

This kind of speaker box was handcrafted.
这种音箱的箱体是手工制作的。

special[39] ['speʃəl] *a.* 专门的,特殊的;特别好的

[巧记] 派生词:specialist(*n.* 专科医师,专家)

[语境] She is a special friend of mine.
她是我一个特别亲密的朋友。

Take special care tonight because the road is icy.
路面结冰了,今晚要格外小心。

[考点] on special 以特价出售;special purpose 特殊目的

specialist ['speʃəlɪst] *n.* 专家,行家

[巧记] special(特殊的)+ist(人)→专家

[语境] The provision of specialist teachers is being increased.
配备专业教员的人数有所增加。

He is a specialist in the theory and practice of education.
他是教育理论和实践方面的专家。

specialize/-ise ['speʃəlaɪz] *vi.* 专攻,专门研究

[语境] He specializes in archaeology.
他专修考古学。

[考点] specialize in 专攻……

specially['speʃəlɪ] *ad.* **特别地,特地;格外地**

[语境] They were all specially ordered.
它们都是专门预约的。

species³³['spiːʃiːz] *n.* **(物)种,种类**

[语境] Darwin stated that the species originate by descent.
达尔文阐明了物种的起源。

specific⁸[spɪ'sɪfɪk] *a.* **具体的,明确的;特有的,特定的**

[巧记] 派生词:specification(*n.* 规格,详细说明书,详述),specificity(*n.* 具体性;明确性)

[语境] She says she'll come, but I can't nail her down to a specific time.
她说她会来,我却无法让她说出确切的时间。
He gave us very specific instructions.
他给我们做了非常明确的指示。

[考点] speci-词根,表示特性,具有特性。这类词语还有:specify *v.* 明确说出,专门提到;specially *adv.* 特别,专门;specification *n.* 明确,具体要求

specifically[spɪ'sɪfɪkəlɪ] *ad.* **说得具体些**

[语境] Death frightens me, specifically my own death.
死亡让我感到恐惧,确切地说,是我自己的死亡。

speculate['spekjʊleɪt] *vi.* **(on) 思索,推测;投机**

[语境] This is the method that we have been speculating about.
这正是我们一直在思考的方法。
Now such freedom to speculate is wreaking havoc on many economies.
如今,这种投机自由正给很多经济体带来浩劫。

[考点] speculate on something 思索某事

speech[spiːtʃ] *n.* **讲话,演说;言语,语言**

[语境] Her speech affronted all of us.
她的讲话冒犯了我们大家。
She is dashing along her speech.

她正在滔滔不绝地演讲。

[考点] give a speech 演讲

speed [spi:d] *n.* 速度,快 *v.* 迅速,前进,急行;加速,使加速

[巧记] 派生词:speeding(*n.* 超速行驶)

[语境] The train soon speeded up.

火车不久就加快了速度。

This plane can reach speeds in excess of 1,000 kilometers an hour.

这架飞机可以达到每小时 1 000 公里以上的速度。

[考点] at speed 飞快地

spell [spel] *v.* 拼写

[巧记] spelling(*n.* 拼字;拼法;拼写)

[语境] Could you spell that word out for me again?

那个字你再拼一遍好吗?

The Americans spell some words differently from the British.

美国人拼写某些单词不同于英国人。

[考点] spell out 把一个词的字母拼出来,详细解释,清楚地说;spell over 思考,考虑

spend [spend] *v.* 花费;消耗,用尽;度过,消磨

[语境] We spent many hours in a pleasant conversation.

我们畅谈了好几个小时。

Come and spend the weekend with us.

来和我们一起度周末吧。

[考点] 固定搭配:spend time on doing sth.

spin [spɪn] *v.* 旋转;纺纱;织网,吐丝

[巧记] 派生词:spinnery(*n.* 纱,纺纱厂;纺织厂),spinnability(*n.* 可纺性,拉丝性)

[语境] The collision sent the car spinning across the road.

汽车被撞得转着圈儿冲到路的另一边。

[考点] spin out 拉长,拖延,使勉强维持一段时间,消磨,度过;spin round 旋转

spirit ['spɪrɪt] *n.* 精神;志气;(*pl.*) 情绪,心情;(*pl.*) 酒精

［巧记］spirited(*a.* 有精神的，生气勃勃的，活泼的)

［语境］We need a spirit of enterprise if we are to overcome our difficulties.

如果我们要克服困难，我们就要有进取精神。

The priest says that the human spirit never dies.

牧师说，人的灵魂永远不死。

［考点］a man of spirit 精神饱满的人；the fighting spirit 斗志

spiritual[6] [ˈspɪrɪtʃuəl] *a.* 精神(上)的，心灵的

［语境］It increases your spiritual development and awakening.

它能加快你精神的发展和觉醒。

spit [spɪt] *v.* 唾，吐痰 *n.* 唾液

［语境］It's rude to spit in public.

在公共场合随便吐痰是不礼貌的。

spite [spaɪt] *n.* 恶意；怨恨；不顾

［巧记］派生词：spiteful(*a.* 怀恨的；有恶意的)

［语境］He failed to lift the rock in spite of all his exertions.

他虽竭尽全力，但仍然未能将那石头搬起来。

I'm sure he took my parking space just out of spite.

我认为他侵占我的停车位肯定是有意和我作对。

［考点］in spite of 不管，不顾；out of spite 为泄愤，为出气；cut off one's nose to spite one's face 损人不利己

splendid [ˈsplendɪd] *a.* 壮丽的，辉煌的；极好的

［巧记］派生词：splendidly(*ad.* 很好，令人满意地)

［语境］The royal couple appeared in splendid array.

王室伉俪身穿盛装出现。

You're all doing a splendid job; keep up the good work!

你们干得都很出色，要坚持下去！

［考点］a splendid scene 壮丽的景象；a splendid idea 极好的主意

split [splɪt] *v.* 劈开，裂开 *a.* 分裂的 *n.* 裂缝，裂口；分化，分裂

［巧记］"split"谐音"死不裂它"——胡编：往死里裂它

［语境］The children split(up) into groups.

孩子们分成了小组。

[考点]split up 分成小组;split with 和……分开(离婚);split on 告密;split away 脱落下来,分裂出去;split hairs 吹毛求疵;split second 不到一分钟,一眨眼的时间

spoil [spɔɪl] *vt.* 搞糟,损坏;宠坏,溺爱 *vi* 食物变坏
　[巧记]派生词:spoilable(*a.* 能够被损坏的),spoilage(*n.* 掠夺;损坏物;糟蹋;印坏的废纸)
　[语境] The child was spoilt by his grandfather.
　　这孩子被他的爷爷给惯坏了。
　　He had spoiled the soup by putting in too much salt.
　　他往汤里放盐太多,把汤给糟蹋了。

spoken [ˈspəʊkən] *a.* 口头的,口语的
　[语境] I think this is a convenient way to learn spoken English.
　　这是我们学习英语口语的一种很便捷的方式。

spokesman [ˈspəʊksmən] *n.* 发言人
　[巧记] spokes(说话)+man(人)→在公开场合说话的人→发言人
　[语境] The spokesman finally disclosed the facts to the press.
　　发言人最终向新闻界公开了事实真相。

sponsor [ˈspɒnsə(r)] *n.* 发起人,主办者;资助者 *vt.* 发起,主办
　[语境] Who is the sponsor of the Olympic Games?
　　谁是本届奥运会的主办者?
　　The meeting was sponsored by 16 countries.
　　此次会议是由16个国家发起召开的。

sport [spɔːt] *n.* (体育)运动 (*pl.*) 运动会 *vi.* 开玩笑;玩耍
　[语境] Baseball is more popular than any other sport in Japan.
　　在日本,棒球比其他任何运动都受人欢迎。
　　Wrestling is in a twilight zone between sport and entertainment.
　　摔跤是介于运动和娱乐两者之间的活动。

sportsman [ˈspɔːtsmən] *n.* 运动员
　[语境] We are like a sportsman, not a coach or a referee.
　　我们就像运动员,而不是教练或者裁判。

spot[6] [spɒt] *vt.* 认出,认清;玷污,弄脏 *n.* 地点,场所;点,斑点,污点

[巧记]派生词:spotless(a.无脏污的,无可挑剔的,无缺点的);spotlight(n.照明灯,聚光灯,车头灯 v.聚光照明;使突出醒目;使公众注意)

[语境] He spotted his reputation by lying repeatedly.

他因反复说谎而败坏了自己的名声。

She had chicken-pox and was covered in spots.

她得了水痘,出了一身丘疹。

[考点] in a spot 处境困难;on the spot 当场,在现场;weak spot 弱点;spot check 抽查

spread[25] [spred] v./n. **伸开,伸展;散布,传播**

[语境] The rapid spread of the disease is alarming the medical authorities.

这种疾病的迅速蔓延使医疗当局感到忧虑不安。

A wide stretch of land spread in front of us.

展现在我们面前的是一片广阔的土地。

[考点] spread oneself 舒展四肢,夸夸其谈,做得过分;spread out 展开;spread the word 传言,散布谣言,散播耳闻

spring [sprɪŋ] n. **春;跳;泉,源泉;弹簧,发条** v. **跳,跳跃**

[巧记]派生词:springboard(n.跳板,出发点);springiness(n.弹性;润湿;轻快)

[语境] Spring is here.

春天来了。

A suspicion sprang up in his mind.

他的脑中突然产生了一些疑问。

[考点] spring over 跳过

spy [spaɪ] n. **间谍**

[语境] They have tracked down the spy.

他们已经追捕到那个间谍。

square [skweə(r)] n. **正方形;广场** a. **正方形的** v. **使成方形**

[巧记]派生词:squared(a.成正方形的;有方格的);squareness (n.呈方形;一丝不苟;公正,诚实)

[语境] Can I leave you to square up with the waiter?

我把跟服务员结账的事交给你办行吗?

[考点]square up 付讫;结清;square meter 平方米;square shooter 公正的人

stable ['steɪbəl] *a.* **安定的,稳定的**

[巧记]派生词:stability *n.* 稳定性;instability *n.* 不稳定性;unstable *a.* 不稳定的,不能变化的

[语境] The patient's condition is stable.

病人的情况稳定。

He's about the most stable person I know.

我认识的人当中,数他最稳重。

staff° [stɑ:f] *n.* **全体职工;棍,棒;参谋部** *v.* **配备工作人员**

[语境] I have arranged that one of my staff will meet you at the airport.

我已经安排了一个职员到飞机场接你。

[考点] be on the staff 在职,在编人员;set up one's staff (of rest) 在某地定居下来,住下来

stage [steɪdʒ] *n.* **舞台,戏剧;阶段,时期**

[巧记]派生词:stagehand (*n.* 舞台管理)

[语境] The disease is still in its primary stage.

这疾病仍然在初发阶段。

Negotiations were at a crucial stage.

谈判正处于一个关键的阶段。

[考点] stage effect 舞台效果;at this stage 眼下;go on the stage 当演员;by stages 分阶段地,分期地;set the stage for 为……打好基础;为……创造条件

stair [steə(r)] *n.* (*pl.*) **楼梯;阶梯**

[语境]We walked up a flight of stairs.

我们上了一段楼梯。

stamp [stæmp] *n.* **邮票;印;跺脚;标志** *v.* **跺脚,顿足;盖章**

[语境]She stamped on the insect and killed it.

她踩死了一只虫子。

The stamp in your library book shows it must be returned tomorrow.

你从图书馆借的书上的戳记表明,这本书必须明天归还。

[考点]stamp on sth. 踩在某物上面,拒绝;否决;stamp out 踏灭(火),根绝,扑灭[镇压](暴动等),用印模冲压;stamp sb. as 标志某人是……;表示某人是;stamp sth. on 在……上盖印,留下印记;惩治;stamp with sth. 把某物盖印在……上面,在……上面铭刻某物

stand [stænd] *vi.* 站立;位于;经受 *n.* 台,座;货摊;立场

[语境] She took a firm stand on nuclear disarmament.

她在核裁军的问题上态度很坚决。

He kicked the ball to the stand.

他把球踢到看台上了。

[考点] take a stand on[over] 对……采取坚定的立场;stand aside 站开;袖手旁观;stand up 站起来,持久;stand with 同……一致;和……站在一起

standard[26] [ˈstændəd] *n.* 标准,规格

[巧记]stand(站) + ard←ort 地点

[语境] The teacher sets high standard for his pupils.

这位老师给他的学生们定下高标准。

This is one of the standard books on the subject.

这是有关这个问题的权威著作之一。

[考点] The living standard 生活水平;be up to the standard 合乎标准;the working standard 工作条件

star [stɑː(r)] *n.* 星,恒星;明星,名人 *vi.* 主演

[语境] The star seemed to twinkle hope to us.

这颗星星似乎向我们闪烁希望。

He plans to star in a movie next year, but he says he has no desire to be in a big budget film.

他计划明年在一部电影中担任主角,但他说不想演预算投入太大的电影。

start [stɑːt] *v.* 开始;动身;吃惊;开办,开动 *n.* 开端;惊起

[语境] She started at the sound of my voice.

她听到了我的声音,蓦地一惊。

The society was started in 1980.

该协会是1980年创建的。

[考点] start for 动身去;start up 突然出现;start after 开始追赶某人

starve [stɑːv] *v.* 饿死,饿得慌

[语境] Many people starved to death in the famine.

许多人饿死于此次饥荒。

[考点] be starved of sth. 严重缺乏,迫切需要

state [steɪt] *n.* 状态,情况;国,州 *v.* 陈述,说明

[巧记] 派生词:statable(*a.* 可以陈述的),statement(*n.* 陈述,声明,指令;发表声明,表达)

[语境] Should industry be controlled by the state?

工业应该由国家控制吗?

His general state of health is fairly satisfactory.

他总的健康状况相当令人满意。

[考点] the state of affairs 事态,情况,形势;state one's views 陈述某人的观点;in state 堂皇地,庄重地;正式地;郑重地

statement[49] [ˈsteɪtmənt] *n.* 声明,陈述

[语境] The purport of the statement is that the firm is bankrupt.

该项声明大意是说该商行已经破产。

[考点] issue a statement 发表一项声明

statesman [ˈsteɪtsmən] *n.* 政治家,国务活动家

[巧记] states(国家)+man(人)→为国家奔走的人→政治家

[语境] A statesman must display initiative.

政治家必须有开创精神。

station [ˈsteɪʃən] *n.* 车站;站,局,所;身份,地位;岗位,位置

[语境] We have to change for Paris at this station.

我们必须在这个车站换车去巴黎。

He was always neatly and quietly dressed in accordance with his age and station.

他的穿着总是整洁得体,与其年龄和地位非常相配。

statistic [stə'tɪstɪk] *n.* 统计量；统计数值 *a.* 统计的，统计学的

[巧记] statistical(*a.* 统计的；统计学的),statistician(*n.* 统计员；统计学家),statistics(*n.* 统计，统计资料；统计学)

[语境] I happen to have the official statistics with me.
我碰巧身边有官方的统计数字。

Have you any statistics that would enforce your argument?
你有任何统计资料可以加强你的论点吗？

status[6] ['steɪtəs] *n.* 身份，地位；情形，状况

[巧记] state 状态；status 指人在社会上的地位或事物所处的状态

[语境] He's very aware of his status.
他很在意自己的身份。

[考点] class status 阶级成分；social status 社会地位

考点集训

1. Many countries have conservation programs to prevent certain _____ of fish from becoming extinct.
   A. species   B. sources
   C. numbers   D. members

2. The clothes a person wears may express his _____ or social position.
   A. curiosity   B. status
   C. determination   D. significance

3. A house with a dangerous gas _____ can be broken into immediately.
   A. leak   B. split
   C. mess   D. crack

4. Politically these nations tend to be _____, with very high birth rates but poor education and very low levels of literacy.
   A. unstable   B. reluctant
   C. rational   D. unsteady

5. The more a nation's companies _____ factories abroad, the smaller that country's recorded exports will be.

A. lie B. spot
C. stand D. locate

6. It is said in some parts of the world, goats, rather than cows, serve as a vital _____ of milk.
   A. storage B. source
   C. reserve D. resource

7. The temperature in this area is low enough to allow falling snow to _____ and slowly transform into ice.
   A. preserve B. accumulate
   C. melt D. spread

8. He was such a _____ speaker that he held our attention every minute of the three-hour lecture.
   A. specific B. dynamic
   C. heroic D. diplomatic

9. His trousers _____ when he tried to jump over the fence.
   A. cracked B. split
   C. broke D. burst

10. As the old empires were broken up and new states were formed, new official tongues began to _____ at an increasing rate.
    A. bring up B. build up
    C. spring up D. strike up

11. In order to make things convenient for the people, the department is planning to set up some _____ shops in the residential area.
    A. flowing B. drifting
    C. mobile D. unstable

12. Computer power now allows automatic searches of fingerprint files to match a print at a crime _____.
    A. stage B. scene
    C. location D. occasion

13. The situation described in the report _____ terrible, but it may not happen.
    A. inclines B. maintains

C. sounds D. remains

14. Now in Britain, wines take up four times as much _____ in the storehouse as both beer and spirits.
    A. block B. land
    C. patch D. space

答案与解析

1. A 许多国家设了保护区,以阻止某些鱼种濒临灭绝。A 物种;B 原因,来源;C 数量;D 成员。故 A 为正确答案。

2. B 一个人穿的衣服显示了他的身份或社会地位。A 好奇心;B 身份,地位;C 决定;D 意义,重要性。故正确答案为 B。

3. A 充满易燃气体的房子容易爆炸。gas leak 煤气泄露,固定搭配,故选 A。

4. A 根据题干中 with very high birth rates but poor education and very low levels of literacy 可知,空格处应填入表示"不稳定的"的词。unstable 表示"不牢固的,不稳定的";reluctant 表示"不顾的,勉强的";rational 表示"理性的,合理的";unsteady 表示"不稳固的,平稳的"。只有 unstable 可以修饰 nation,答案为 A。

5. D 根据题干,再结合四个选项,即 lie 表示"躺,平放";spot 表示"玷污,弄脏,侦察";stand 表示"站,持久,经受";locate 表示"查找……的地点,使……坐落于,位于",可知只有 locate 符合题意,答案为 D。

6. B 根据题干中 goat 和 milk,得知空格处应填入表示"来源"的词。storage 表示"存储";reserve 表示"储备(物),储藏量,预备队";resource 表示"资源,财力";source 表示"来源"。答案为 B。

7. B 这个地区的温度很低,足以使降落的雪积累并慢慢结成冰。preserve"保护,保持";accumulate"积累";melt"融化";spread"展开"。既然温度低,雪当然不会融化,排除 C,只有 B 意思相符。

8. B 他精力很充沛,三个小时演讲中,他吸引了我们全部的注意力。A 具体的;B 精力充沛的;C 英雄的;D 外交的。故选 B。

9. B 就在他想跳跃过栅栏时,他的裤子破了。A 破裂;B 撕扯开,裂开;C 破坏;D 冲破,胀破。故选 B。

10. C 随着老帝国的分崩离析、新帝国的成立,官方言论如春笋般猛增起来。A 抚养;B 建立;C 增长;D 开始演奏,开始(交谈),建立起(友谊等)。故选 C。

11. C 为了让人们更方便,这个部门计划在居民区建一些活动的商店。A 流动的(水);B 漂流的;C 移动的;D 不稳定的。故选 C。

12. B 现在可以利用计算机指纹文件的自动搜索功能去比对一个犯罪现场的印迹。at a crime scene 在犯罪现场,固定搭配。故选 B。

13. C 报告中描述的形势很糟糕,但是可能不会发生。A 使倾向,使倾斜;B 维持,维修,保养,坚持,断言;C 听起来;D 保持,依然。故选 C。

14. D 现在在英国,葡萄酒占据了储藏室啤酒和烈酒之和 4 倍的空间。A 街区;B 土地;C 小片,补丁;D 空间。故选 D。

Word List 43

stay [steɪ] *vi.* 逗留;保持 *vt.* 停止,延缓 *n.* 逗留,停留

[语境] I don't think he's sufficiently dedicated to stay the course.
我认为他不够坚定,不会坚持到底的。
I stayed late at the party last night.
昨晚我在晚会上待到很晚。

steady[7] [ˈstedɪ] *v.* (使)稳定 *a.* 稳定的,不变的;稳固的;坚定的,扎实的

[巧记] stead(stead = stand) + -y(……的)
[语境] The hunter steadied his rifle and fired.
猎人端稳了猎枪,然后开了火。
Such fine work requires a steady hand and a steady eye.
做这样精细的工作,手要稳、眼要准。
[考点] steady 指人或物在一定的发展时期不受干扰,保持没有

461

大的变化

steal [sti:l] *v.* 偷,窃取;偷偷地做,巧取

[巧记] 派生词:stealing(*n.* 偷窃;偷得的东西),stealth(*n.* 秘密行动;偷窃;鬼鬼祟祟)

[语境] Despite fine acting by several well-known stars it was a young newcomer who stole the show.

尽管几位名角演出都很出色,却未曾想竟让一名新秀抢尽风头。

He stole a glance at the pretty girl across the table.

他偷偷地看了一眼桌子对面那个漂亮的女孩。

[考点] steal the show 抢出风头

steam [sti:m] *n.* (蒸)汽;*vi.* 发出蒸汽;行驶;*vt.* 蒸煮

[语境] When water boils it passes into steam.

水沸腾时变成蒸汽。

Steam the carrots until they are just beginning to be tender.

将胡萝卜蒸至刚好变软。

steamer ['sti:mə(r)] *n.* 汽船,轮船

[语境] The steamer touched at 3 ports.

这艘轮船曾停靠3个港口。

steel[5] [sti:l] *n.* 钢

[语境] He is a representative for a large steel company.

他是一家大型钢铁公司的代理人。

stem[31] [stem] *n.* 茎,干 *vt.* 堵住,挡住 *vi.* 起源于,由……造成

[语境] Our ship stemmed on against the current.

我们的船逆流而上。

She bought some roses with long stems.

她买了一些枝干很长的玫瑰花。

[考点] stem from 起源于;from stem to stern 从头到尾(尤其指船)。由 stem 联想到的词汇:seed 种子,leaf 树叶,flower 花,root 根,branch 树枝

step [step] *n.* 脚步,脚步声;台阶,梯级;步骤,措施 *vi.* 举步,走

[语境] I took a step towards him.

我朝他迈了一步。

I tried to step back, but he held my upper arms too tightly.

我试图往后退,但他将我的上臂抓得太紧了。

stereotype[13] ['steriətaip] *n.* 陈腔滥调,老套 *vt.* 套用老套,使一成不变

[语境] There's always been a stereotype about successful businessmen.

人们对于成功商人一直都有一种固定印象。

He was stereotyped by some as a rebel.

他被一些人认定为叛逆者。

stick[7] [stik] *n.* 棍,棒;手杖 *vt.* 刺,戳,扎;粘贴 *vi.* 黏着,附着

[语境] The old man could not walk without a stick.

这老人没有手杖就走不了路。

Someone has sticked a label on the crate.

有人在板条箱上贴了标签。

[考点] stick down 贴好,放下;stick up for 为……辩护,支持,保护

sticky ['stiki] *a.* 黏的,黏性的;棘手的;(道路)泥泞的

[语境] I like films where the villain comes to a sticky end!

我喜欢恶有恶报的影片!

Shall I tie the parcel or use sticky tape?

我把包裹捆上还是用胶带粘上?

[考点] sticky weather 湿热的天气

stiff [stif] *a.* 硬的,僵直的;拘谨的;呆板的;艰难的

[巧记] 反义词:limp(*a.* 柔软的,软弱的,无力的)

[语境] That was a shock—I need a stiff drink。

这可真吓人——我得喝点烈酒了。

I cannot play the piano like I used to—my fingers have gone stiff from lack of practice.

我弹钢琴不如以前了——我的手指由于缺乏练习都不灵活了。

[考点] be stiff with cold 冻僵;stiff drink 烈性酒

still [stɪl] *a.* 静止的,寂静的 *ad.* 还,仍然;更;安静地
  [语境] Although she felt ill, she still went to work.
  她虽然觉得身体不舒服,但仍然去上班了。
  The fish is still alive.
  这条鱼仍活着。

stir [stɜ:(r)] *vi.* 微动,活动微动,动静;搅动 *vt.* 动,移动;搅拌,搅动;激动,轰动
  [语境] There was a stir of excitement as she entered the theatre.
  她一走进剧院就引起了一阵兴奋。
  A gentle breeze stirred the leaves.
  微风吹动了树叶。
  [考点] stir up 惹起麻烦;stir in(into)搅进去,搅匀

stock [stɔk] *n.* 储备,备料,库存,现货,股票,公债;牲畜
  [语境] She is tired of her husband's stock jokes.
  她听厌了她丈夫那些陈腐的笑话。
  That shop does not stock stationery.
  那家商店不卖文具。
  [考点] stock exchange 证券交易所;stock up 进货;使(商店)储足货物;stock with 向(商店等)补充

stocking ['stɔkɪŋ] *n.* 长(筒)袜
  [语境] I ripped my stocking on a nail.
  一个钉子挂破了我的袜子。

stomach ['stʌmək] *n.* 胃
  [语境] The blow found his stomach.
  这一击打中了他的腹部。

stone [stəʊn] *n.* 石,石料
  [语境] The house was made out of stone.
  这座房子是用石头修建的。

stool [stu:l] *n.* 凳子
  [语境] She sat in the sofa with her legs propping on a small stool.
  她坐在沙发上,双腿搁在一张小凳上。

stop [stɔp] *v.* 停止;塞住;阻止,阻挠 *n.* 停车站;停止

[语境]I only just managed to stop myself from shouting at him.

我极力控制住自己,没对他喊叫起来。

store[stɔː(r)] *vt. /n.* 贮藏,贮存 *n.* 商店,店铺;贮存品,备用品

[语境]The squirrel makes a store of nuts for the winter.

松鼠贮藏坚果以备过冬。

He crooked a necklace from that department store.

他从那家百货商店里偷到一条项链。

storm[stɔːm] *n.* 暴风雨

[语境]Black clouds forebode a storm.

乌云预示着有暴风雨。

story ['stɔːrɪ] *n.* 故事,传说,小说;(= storey)楼层

[语境]Only when he read the newspaper did he know the story.

他看了报纸后才知道那则报道。

straight [streɪt] *a.* 直的;整齐的,端正的

[巧记]反义词:bent(*a.* 弯曲的)

[语境] Please put your desk straight before you leave the office.

请你先把办公桌收拾好再离开办公室。

Come straight away after school.

放学后直接回家。

[考点] a straight conduct 正直的行为;keep sb. straight 使某人端正自己的行为;go straight 笔直走;直接去

strange [streɪndʒ] *a.* 奇怪的,奇异的;陌生的,生疏的;外地的

[语境] Do you know why she is so strange to him?

你知道她为什么对他如此冷淡吗?

It's strange for her to be so rude.

真奇怪,她竟然会如此粗暴无礼。

stranger['streɪndʒə(r)] *n.* 陌生人,生客;外地人,外国人

[语境]The child made off when he saw a stranger.

那小孩看见生人便急忙跑掉了。

As a stranger, he lost his way in the street.

因为是外地人,他在街上迷路了。

strategic [strə'tiːdʒɪk] *a.* 战略的,战略上的

[巧记]同根词:stratagem(n. 战略,计谋);strategist(n. 战略家;军事家)

[语境]global strategic balance and stability
全球战略平衡和稳定
It has long been of strategic importance in the Middle East.
它长期以来在中东具有重要的战略性。

strategy[6] [ˈstrætɪdʒɪ] n. **战略,策略**

[巧记]派生词:strategic a. 战略上的;strategist n. 战略家,军事家

[语境] I think we should work out a strategy to deal with this situation.
我想我们应该制订出一项行动计划,来应对这种情况。
By careful strategy she negotiated a substantial pay rise.
精心策划后,她谈妥了大幅增加工资的事。

[考点] strategy 表示的是战略,tactics 指的是战术,具体的作战方针

stream[striːm] n. **小河,溪流**;vi. **流,流出**

[语境]A stream meandered towards the sea.
一条小溪蜿蜒流向大海。
Tears streamed down their faces.
泪水顺着他们的脸颊流下。

streamline[ˈstriːmlaɪn] vt. **使成流线型;使简化,使有效率;使现代化**

[巧记]stream(流)+line(线)→使成流线型

[语境]Can you streamline this kind of airship?
你能把这种飞艇设计成流线型吗?
They tried to streamline the main panel of TV.
他们尽力简化了电视机的主板。

street[striːt] n. **街道,马路**

[语境]I ride this street every day.
我每天骑自行车走过这条大街。

strength[11] [streŋθ] n. **力,力量;实力;长处,优点;人力;兵力**

[巧记]派生词:strengthless(a. 无力量的);strengthen(vt. 加强,

核心词汇精解

巩固)

[语境] Union is strength.

【谚】团结就是力量。

I have hardly enough strength left to move my feet.

我连移动双脚的力气都几乎没有了。

[考点] in full strength 全体动员; with all one's strength 尽力

strengthen[7] [ˈstreŋθən] *vt.* **加强,巩固**

[巧记] 反义词:weaken(*v.* 弱化)

[语境] The wind strengthened during the night.

风在夜间刮得更猛了。

The soldiers strengthened their defenses.

士兵们加强了他们的防御工事。

stress[16] [stres] *n.* **压力;紧迫;强调** *vt.* **强调,着重**

[语境] We led a hard life in times of stress.

在困难时期我们过着艰苦的生活。

I must stress that what I say is confidential.

我要强调我所说的话是保密的。

[考点] under stress of 在……的压力下; lay stress on 强调,把重点放在; in the stress of the moment 一时紧张

stretch[6] [stretʃ] *v./n.* **拉长,延,伸** *n.* **连续的一段时间;一大片**

[巧记] 派生词:stretchable(*a.* 能伸展的);stretchy(*a.* 伸长的;易延伸过长的;有弹性的)

[语境] The painter stretched the canvas on a frame.

画家把油画布紧绷在画框上。

[考点] stretch oneself out 直躺在; be full stretched/at full stretch 全力以赴; by a stretch of 放宽(规定)等

strict[23] [strɪkt] *a.* **严格的,严厉的;严谨的,精确的**

[巧记] 派生词:strictness(*n.* 严格;不折不扣;严谨;精确)

[语境] Our manager is very strict with us.

我们的经理对我们要求很严格。

The doctor put me on a very strict diet.

医生严格限制我的饮食。

467

[考点] in the strict sense of the word 严格地讲; be strict with sb. 对某人严厉

strike[6] [straɪk] *n.* 打击;空袭;攻击;罢工,罢市,罢课 *v.* 打,攻击,击;咬伤;抓伤;侵袭;抓,打击

[巧记] 同义词: hit (*v.* 打击)

[语境] Enemy troops struck just before dawn.
敌军在拂晓前发起了进攻。
Strike while the iron is hot.
趁热打铁。

[考点] be on strike 举行罢工; be struck with(by) 为……所袭击;为……所侵袭,为……所触动[感动]; It strikes me that 我觉得……;我的印象是……; strike of day 破晓

striking [ˈstraɪkɪŋ] *a.* 引人注目的,显著的

[巧记] strik[e] + -ing

[语境] I was attracted by the striking idea.
我被这个惊人的想法吸引住了。

strong [strɒŋ] *a.* 强壮的,强大的;强烈的,浓的

[语境] I was surprised to find that the strong man liked to eat conserves.
我很惊讶地发现这个强壮的男人喜欢吃蜜饯。
A healthy shoot should form a strong graft.
健康的嫩枝可以长成强壮的接穗。

structure [ˈstrʌktʃə(r)] *n.* 结构,构造;建筑物

[巧记] struct = build,表示"建立"

[语境] You need to structure your arguments more carefully.
你需要更为仔细地组织自己的论点。
The structure had keeled over in the high winds.
那座建筑物让大风给刮倒了。

[考点] the structure of society 社会结构; administration structure 行政机构

struggle[6] [ˈstrʌɡəl] *n./v.* 斗争,奋斗,努力

[巧记] 派生词: struggler (*n.* 斗争者;挣扎着的人;奋斗者);

struggling(*a.* 奋斗的;苦斗的;努力的);同义词:fight

[语境] Several people were hurt in the struggle.

在打斗中,有几个人受伤。

He struggled with his assailants and eventually drove them off.

他同攻击他的人进行搏斗,最后把他们赶走了。

[考点] struggle against/with 与……作斗争;struggle to one's feet 挣扎着站起来;struggle for 为……而斗争;struggle on 拼命活下去,竭力支持下去,继续努力

student[ˈstjuːdənt] *n.* 学生,学员

[语境] The student trotted out his knowledge.

这个学生炫耀他的知识。

studio[ˈstjuːdɪəʊ] *n.* 画室,工作室,播音室

[语境] I still have it in my studio.

我仍然把它留在画室里。

study [ˈstʌdɪ] *vt.* 学习;研究;细看 *vi* 读书 *n.* 学习;研究

[语境] Give yourself to diligent study and you will certainly succeed.

努力读书,你一定会成功。

He had devoted his whole life to the study of contemporary art.

他把他的一生都献给了当代艺术研究。

stuff [stʌf] *vt.* 填满,塞满 *n.* 物品;个人的所有物;原料,材料

[语境] He stuffed the apples into the bag.

他把苹果塞进袋子里。

Leave your stuff in the hall.

把你的东西放在门厅里。

[考点] 派生词:stuffy *a.* 不透气的,闷热的;stuffing *n.* 填塞物;注意区分 staff 全体职员。常用词汇:stuff with 把……塞满;know one's stuff 内行,精通业务;stuff up 塞住,堵住

stupid [ˈstjuːpɪd] *a.* 愚蠢的,迟钝的

[语境] Why grumble at me about your own stupid mistakes?

你自己犯了愚蠢的错误,为什么向我抱怨?

It's stupid to go to the expense of taking music lessons if you never practise.

花钱上音乐课而从不练习是很愚蠢的。

sturdy ['stɜːdɪ] *a.* **强健的;坚定的**

[语境] They strode on their sturdy legs down the street.

他们迈着强健的双腿在街上大步走。

When I took office, I was determined to set our relationship on a sturdy, principled footing.

当我上任时,我决心让我们的关系有一个坚定的、有原则的基础。

style [staɪl] *n.* **风格,文体;时尚,流行样式;种类,类型**

[考点] 派生词:styling(*n.* 款式,样式);stylish(*a.* 时髦的,流行的,漂亮的)

[语境] I wouldn't tell lies to you; that's not my style.

我不会跟你撒谎,那不是我的风格。

The dress is carefully styled for maximum comfort.

这件服装精心设计,力求达到最大限度的舒适。

[考点] in style 雅致的,精致的,不过时;out of style 过时,不合时宜

subject[18] ['sʌbdʒɪkt] *n.* **主题,题目;学科,科目;实验对象**

[语境] How many subjects are you studying this semester?

这学期你选了几门课程?

I am French by birth and a British subject by marriage.

按出生我是法国人,因结婚而成为英国公民。

[考点] be subject to 受……支配,易于……的,以……为条件,取决于……; subject sb./sth. to sth. 使……经历或遭受; change the subject 改变话题

subjective [səb'dʒektɪv] *a.* **主观的;个人的**

[语境] Try to avoid being subjective and one-sided when looking at problems.

看问题要避免主观片面。

考点集训

1. Techniques for _____ sleep would involve learning to control both mind and body so that sleep can occur.
   A. cultivating   B. promoting
   C. pushing   D. strengthening

2. The opening between the rocks was very narrow, but the boys managed to _____ through.
   A. press   B. squeeze
   C. stretch   D. leap

3. The _____ that exists among nations could certainly be lessened if misunderstanding and mistrust were removed.
   A. tension   B. strain
   C. stress   D. intensity

4. His hand shook a little as he _____ the key in the lock.
   A. squeezed   B. inserted
   C. stuffed   D. pierced

5. The new aircraft will be _____ to a test of temperatures of -65℃ and 120℃.
   A. suspended   B. suppressed
   C. summoned   D. subjected

6. A transplant operation is successful only if doctors can prevent the body from rejecting the _____ organ.
   A. borrowed   B. strange
   C. novel   D. foreign

7. He is always here; it's _____ you've never met him.
   A. unique   B. strange
   C. rare   D. peculiar

8. I was about to _____ a match when I remembered Tom's warning.
   A. rub   B. hit
   C. scrape   D. strike

· 471 ·

9. His essay is _____ with more than 120 full-color photographs that depict the national park in all seasons.
   A. contained   B. illustrated
   C. exposed   D. strengthened

答案与解析

1. B 促进睡眠的技术手段包括学会控制身心情况,然后就可以睡着了。A 培养;B 促进;C 推;D 加强。故选 B。

2. B 两块石头间的缝隙很窄,但是男孩子们能挤过去。A 压;B 挤压;C 伸展,张开;D 跳跃。故选 B。

3. A 如果国家间的误会和猜疑尽释,国家间的关系自然会缓和。A 紧张,紧张关系;C 压力,负担;D 强烈,强烈程度。故选 A。

4. B 他把钥匙插进锁里,晃动了一下。A 挤进;B 插入;C 塞满;D 刺穿,穿透,洞悉。故选 B。

5. D 选择的是一个被动语态结构,是遭受、经受住这样的温度测试,或者是经历了,或者是遭受了这样的温度测试。在这里翻译成经历比较好。所以答案是 D。

6. D 只要医生能够阻止身体对外来的器官产生抗拒作用,移植手术就可以成功。A 借来的;B 陌生的,奇怪的;C 小说,新颖的;D 外来的。故 D 为正确答案。

7. B 他一直都在这里,你从没见过他这很奇怪。A 独一无二的;B 奇怪的,陌生的;C 稀少的;D 特殊的,独特的。故选 B。

8. D 我正要划火柴,这时我想起了汤姆的警告。固定搭配,故选 D。

9. B 他的文章中插入了 120 张彩色照片,这些照片描述了不同季节的国家公园景色。contain"包含";illustrate"举例说明,加插图于";expose"揭露";strengthen"加强,巩固"。由于后面所讲的意思就是加插图,故选 B。

Word List 44

substance[8] ['sʌbstəns] *n.* 物质；实质，本质；要旨，大意

[语境]This substance will fly off.

这种物质会挥发掉。

These are the things that bring substance, fulfillment, and lasting joy to our lives.

这些事物为我们的生活带来了实质、满足感和恒久的快乐。

[考点]have substance 有道理的，有根据的；in substance 本质上，基本上，大体上

substitute[8] ['sʌbstɪtjuːt] *n.* 代用品，代替者 *vt.* 用……代替，代以

[语境] We substituted a red ball for blue to see if the baby would notice.

我们用红皮球换下了蓝皮球，看这婴儿会不会发觉。

The coach substituted Smith for Jones.

教练让史密斯上场，换下了琼斯。

[考点] substitute for 代替，替换

suburb['sʌbɜːb] *n.* (*pl.*) 郊外，近郊

[语境]Toward the suburb the houses begin to thin out.

靠近市郊的地方房屋渐渐稀少。

subway ['sʌbweɪ] *n.* 地铁；地下人行道

[巧记]sub(下)+way(道路)→位于地下的路→地下人行道

[语境]I can do anything on the subway.

我乘地铁的时候可以做任何事情。

succeed[8] [sək'siːd] *vi.* 成功；继承，接着发生 *vt.* 接替，接……之后

[语境] If you work hard you will succeed.

如果你努力工作，你就会成功。

Our plan succeeded, and soon we were in complete control.

我们的计划顺利完成了，很快就控制了局面。

[考点] succeed to 表示继承头衔、财产等；succeed in doing 成功

473

地做了……

success[41] [sək'ses] *n.* 成就,成功;成功的事物,有成就的人

[语境]Success and wealth transformed his character.

成功和财富改变了他的性格。

successful[18] [sək'sesfʊl] *a.* **成功的**

[语境] He aims to be a successful writer.

他的目标是成为一个成功的作家。

A successful businessman must be aggressive.

一个成功的商人必须有进取心。

such [sʌtʃ] *a.* 这样的;上述的 *ad.* 那么 *pron.* 这样的人/事物

[语境]Students now prefer vocational subjects such as e-commerce.

现在的学生偏爱职业化的学科,例如电子商务。

[考点]such as 例如,如(for example)

sudden ['sʌdən] *a.* 突然的,出乎意料的

[巧记]派生词:suddenly(*ad.* 突然地)

[语境]His sudden death upset everybody.

他的突然去世使大家深感悲伤。

All of a sudden, the tyre burst.

轮胎突然爆裂了。

[考点]all of sudden 突然

suddenly ['sʌdənlɪ] *ad.* **突然地**

[语境] He suddenly became wealthy, which changed his whole mode of life.

他突然致富,富有改变了他的整个生活方式。

suffer ['sʌfə(r)] *vt.* 忍受,承受;遭受 *vi.* 忍受痛苦;受损失

[语境] She couldn't suffer criticism.

她受不了批评。

How can you suffer such insolence?

你怎么能容忍这种蛮横的态度?

[考点] suffer from 受……之苦,患……疾病

suffering['sʌfərɪŋ] *n.* 受难;苦楚 *a.* 受苦的;患病的

[语境]I participate your suffering and joy.

我和你同甘共苦。

What can you do if you see an animal suffering?

如果你看到受苦的动物,那么你可以做些什么?

sufficient[5] [səˈfɪʃənt] *a.* **足够的,充分的**

[语境] Desertion is a ground (i. e. legally sufficient reason) for divorce.

被配偶遗弃是离婚的充足理由。

The money I have saved is sufficient for buying a car.

我所存的钱足以买一辆汽车。

[考点] be sufficient for sb./sth. 对某人或某物是足够的

sugar [ˈʃʊɡə(r)] *n.* **糖**

[语境] Both salt and sugar dissolve easily in water.

盐和糖都容易溶解于水。

suggest[34] [səˈdʒest] *vt.* **建议,提议;表明,暗示**

[语境] His pale face suggests bad health.

他面色苍白,说明他身体不好。

I suggested going for a walk.

我建议去散步。

[考点] 当 suggest 表示意味着或暗示的意思时,后面的从句就不再使用虚拟语气。如:His cool response suggested that he didn't like the idea. 他反应冷淡表明他并不喜欢这个主意

suggestion [səˈdʒestʃən] *n.* **建议,意见;细微的迹象;暗示,联想**

[语境] Could you enlarge your suggestion?

你能详细地谈谈你的建议吗?

suicide [ˈs(j)uːɪsaɪd] *n.* **自杀**

[语境] He cheated the law by suicide.

他以自杀逃避法律的制裁。

suit[26] [suːt, sjuːt] *v.* **合适,适合;相配,适应** *n.* **一套西服;诉讼**

[语境] I've found a job that suits me down to the ground.

我找到了一份工作,对我再合适不过了。

He is wearing a black suit.

他穿着一套黑西装。

suitable[6] ['sjuːtəbəl] *a.* (for)合适的,适宜的

[语境] The director is looking for a suitable locale for his new film.
导演在为新片物色合适的拍摄场地。

suitcase['s(j)uːtkeɪs] *n.* 小提箱

[语境] He carted a suitcase.
他提着一个衣箱。

sum [sʌm] *n.* 总数,总和;金额;算术 *v.* 总结,概括;估量,估计

[语境] The last section sums up all the arguments on either side.
最后一部分总结了双方的全部论点。

Is that the sum of what you've done in the last two years?
这就是你最近两年中完成的全部数量吗?

[考点] sum total 总和;sum up 总结,概括;in sum 总而言之

summarize/-ise ['sʌməraɪz] *vt.* 概括,总结

[语境] I'd like to ask Mr. Lee to summarize the situation.
我想请李先生概括一下形势。

summary['sʌmərɪ] *n.* 摘要,概要

[语境] His summary prosifies the poem.
他的摘要把诗散文化了。

summer['sʌmə(r)] *n.* 夏天,夏季

[语境] We tour by car every summer.
每年夏天我们都驾车出外旅行。

[考点] in summer 在夏季

sun[sʌn] *n.* 太阳,日

[语境] The hot sun soon melted the ice.
炎热的阳光很快使冰融化了。

Sunday['sʌndɪ] *n.* 星期日

[语境] We work every day except Sunday.
除了星期日,我们每天都上班。

[考点] on Sunday 在星期天

sunlight['sʌnlaɪt] *n.* 日光,阳光

[语境] Sunlight poured in through the windows.
阳光通过窗户映入屋内。

sunny ['sʌnɪ] *a.* 阳光充足的

[语境] We basked ourselves on the sunny beach.

我们在阳光充足的海滩上晒太阳。

sunrise ['sʌnraɪz] *n.* 日出

[语境] That day he was up before sunrise.

那天他在日出以前就起来了。

[考点] sunrise industry 朝阳产业

sunset ['sʌnset] *n.* 日落

[语境] The author tried to depict the splendor of the sunset.

作家试图摹写落日的光彩。

sunshine ['sʌnʃaɪn] *n.* 日光,日照

[语境] The countryside was bathed in brilliant sunshine.

乡间沐浴在灿烂的阳光下。

super ['suːpər, 'sjuːpər] *a.* 极好的,超级的

[语境] Then they spent a super week at the seaside.

然后他们在海边度过了极好的一周。

superb [s(j)uː'pɜːb] *a.* 极好的;高质量的

[语境] The best maple produces a superb stripe effect.

最好的枫树能产生极好的条纹效果。

supermarket ['suːpəmɑːkɪt, 'sjuː-] *n.* 超市

[巧记] super(超级的) + market(市场)→超级市场→超市

[语境] The street leads to the supermarket.

这条街通向超级市场。

supper ['sʌpə(r)] *n.* 晚饭

[语境] She rustled up a supper for us.

她急急忙忙给我们弄了一顿晚饭。

supply[12] [sə'plaɪ] *n.* 供应(量);供应(品) *vt.* 供应,供给

[语境] The camp has a plentiful supply of food.

营地有充足的食品供应。

Demand began to exceed supply.

开始供不应求。

[考点] supply sb. with sth. 为某人提供某物; supply the market

with sth. 向市场提供某物；supply and demand 供求关系

support[28] [sə'pɔːt] vt. 支持，支撑；鼓励；供养，资助 n. 支持，支撑；支持物；支援，生活费

[语境] He needs a high income to support such a large family.

他需要有高收入才能供养得起这样一个大家庭。

Her father supported her until she got married.

她父亲抚养她直到她结婚。

[考点] supporter n. 支持者；come to one's support 来支持某人；in support of 支持，支援，拥护

suppose[10] [sə'pəʊz] vt. 猜想，料想；假定，以为

[语境] Creation supposes a creator.

有了创造者，才能有创造。

I suppose you want to borrow money from me again?

我猜你又要找我借钱了吧？

[考点] be supposed to 理应，应该；not supposed to 不应当；supposing (that) 假使（引导状语）

sure [ʃʊə(r)，ʃɔː(r)] a. 肯定的；一定会……的；有信心的，有把握的

[语境] Be sure to make it clear and concise and avoid long-windedness.

注意简明扼要，不要长篇大论。

[考点] for sure 确切地；make sure 确保；to be sure 确实，当然

surface[11] ['sɜːfɪs] n. 表面，外表，水面 a. 表面的，肤浅的

[语境] A large proportion of the earth's surface is covered with water.

地球表面的大部分被水所覆盖。

[考点] on the surface 表面上

surgeon ['sɜːdʒən] n. 外科医生

[语境] As a surgeon, Philip was exceptionally gifted.

作为外科医生，菲利普才华出众。

surgery ['sɜːdʒəri] n. 外科，外科手术

[语境] The nurse prepared the patient for surgery.

护士为病人做好外科手术前的准备。

surname ['sɜːneɪm] *n.* 姓

[语境]Wang is a very common Chinese surname.

王是一个很常见的中国姓。

surprise [sə'praɪz] *n.* 诧异,惊奇 *vt.* 使诧异,使惊奇;突然袭击

[语境]His coming surprised me.

他的到来令我感诧异。

At the beginning of the match, we surprised the visiting team.

比赛刚一开始,我们就打了客队一个措手不及。

[考点] to one's surprise 使某人惊奇的是;居然;竟然

surprising [sə'praɪzɪŋ] *a.* 令人惊讶的

[语境]But that is not surprising, either.

但这一结果也不令人惊讶。

surround[6] [sə'raʊnd] *vt.* 包围,环绕 *n.* 环绕物

[语境] We are surrounded by dangers.

我们的处境危机四伏。

Trees surround the pond.

树木围绕着池塘。

surrounding[7] [sə'raʊndɪŋ] *a.* 周围的;附近的

[语境]Jolmo Lungman dominates over all surrounding mountains.

珠穆朗玛峰高耸于周围群山之上。

survey[14] ['sɜːveɪ] *vt.* 纵览,环视;调查,检查;测试,勘定 *n.* 调查,研究;概说,概观;测量

[语境] Follow-up survey shows that the reoccurrence rate is only 5%.

跟踪调查表明,复发率仅为5%。

This survey is the work of a real professional.

这份调查是真正内行人做的。

We stood on the top of the mountain and surveyed the countryside.

我们站在山顶上,眺望乡村。

[考点] make a survey of 对……做全面的调查

survive[6] [sə'vaɪv] *vi.* 活下来,幸存 *vt.* 从……中逃出,从(困境)中挺过来

[语境] These birds are able to survive the perils of the Arctic winter.

这些鸟能够战胜北极冬天的危险。

If the industry doesn't modernize it will not survive.

制造业若不现代化就不能继续存在。

[考点] 派生词:survival *n.* 幸存,生存;survivor *n.* 幸存者,活着的人;sur-表示 to live,所以 survive 联想到 to live longer

suspect[8] [sə'spekt] *v.* 猜想,对……表示怀疑 *a.* 可疑的 *n.* 可疑分子,嫌疑犯

[语境] She has more intelligence than we suspected her to possess.

她的智慧比我们猜想的要高。

Are political suspects kept under police observation in your country?

你们国家的政治嫌疑犯受警察监视吗?

[考点] suspect sb. of sth. 怀疑某人犯有过错;suspect sb. to be 怀疑某人是……,猜想某人是……

suspicious [sə'spɪʃəs] *a.* 可疑的,多疑的,疑心的

[语境] The fire is of suspicious origin.

这场火灾起因可疑。

[考点] be suspicious of sb. 怀疑某人

swear [sweə(r)] *v.* 诅咒,咒骂;宣誓,发誓

[语境] They swore an oath to carry out their duties faithfully.

他们发誓要忠实履行自己的职责。

I swore her to secrecy about what I had told her.

我要她起誓对我告诉她的事保守秘密。

[考点] swear off 保证戒掉,放弃;swear at sb. 咒骂某人;swear in 宣誓就职;swear by 对……发誓,极其信赖

sweat [swet] *n.* 汗 *v.* 出汗

[语境] Sweat soused him all over.

汗水浸透了他的全身。

sweater ['swetə(r)] *n.* 毛衣,绒衣

[语境]Somebody pinched my sweater.

有人偷了我的运动衫。

sweep [swi:p] *vi.* 快速移动,扫描 *vt.* 扫,打扫;(风)吹,(浪等)冲

[语境] She swept the floor clean.

她把地板打扫干净了。

This floor needs a good sweep.

这地板需要好好清扫一下。

[考点] sweep aside 放到一边,不予理会;sweep off 扫去,拂去;sweep over 席卷,卷走;make a clean sweep of 彻底清除,全部撤掉

sweet [swi:t] *a.* 甜的;可爱的,美好的 *n.* (常 *pl.*)糖果;甜食

[语境] I had a sweet sleep last night.

昨晚我美美地睡了一觉。

The dentist told the boy not to eat too many sweets.

牙医告诫这男孩不要吃太多糖果。

swell [swel] *n./v.* 肿胀;膨胀;增大;增加

[语境] Small extra costs all swell the total cost.

零星的额外费用积少成多使总数增大了。

swim [swɪm] *vi./n.* 游泳;浸,泡

[语境]Do you like swimming in the sea?

你喜欢在海里游泳吗?

Her eyes are swimming with warm tears.

她的眼中满含热泪。

switch[6] [swɪtʃ] *n.* 开关;突然转变 *v.* 改变,交换

[语境] Our glasses have been switched—this is mine.

咱们的玻璃杯对调了,这个是我的。

Long lectures really switch me off.

我觉得冗长的演讲很烦人。

[考点] switch from 变换,转移;switch on 打开;switch off 关上;switch through 接过来;switch to 转而讨论,转移话题、节目等

symbol ['sɪmbl] *n.* 象征,符号,标志

· 481 ·

[语境]The letter was the symbol of her calling.

那字母成了她响应号召的象征。

symbolic[sɪmˈbɒlɪk] *a.* 象征的,象征性的;符号的,记号的;象征主义的

[语境]But how do you find a fossil of a symbolic thought?

但你如何找到一块象征性思维的化石呢?

Thinking symbolically is the foundation of everything we do—we live in a symbolic world.

象征性思维是我们做一切的基础,我们生活在一个象征性的世界里。

sympathetic [ˌsɪmpəˈθetɪk] *a.* 有同情心的;赞同的 *n.* 交感神经

[语境] You've got to be firm, but at the same time you must be sympathetic.

你态度要强硬,但还必须有同情心。

sympathize/-ise [ˈsɪmpəθaɪz] *v.* 同情;共鸣,同感;赞成

[语境] I sympathize with you; I've had a similar unhappy experience myself.

我很同情你,我自己也有过类似的不幸遭遇。

sympathy [ˈsɪmpəθɪ] *n.* 同情,同情心;赞同,同感;慰问

[语境] A man in sorrow craves for sympathy.

一个悲伤的人渴望得到同情。

symptom[4] [ˈsɪmptəm] *n.* 症状,症候

[语境]She saw my essay as describing another symptom of that.

她认为我的文章是从另一个方面描述了这个症状。

system[28] [ˈsɪstəm] *n.* 系统,体系;制度,体制

[语境]Something just crashed the system.

某物刚刚使系统失灵了。

She tried to beat the system by helping people directly.

她企图通过直接帮助人们以抵消制度的影响。

systematic(al) [ˌsɪstəˈmætɪk(l)] *a.* 系统的;有计划的,有步骤的;有秩序的,有规则的

[语境]Investing, he said, should be systematic.

他表示，投资应该是系统的。

The way he works isn't very systematic.

他的工作不是很有条理。

考点集训

1. Doctors warned against chewing tobacco as a _____ for smoking.
   A. relief   B. revival
   C. substitute   D. succession

2. It is obvious that this new rule is applicable to everyone without _____.
   A. exception   B. exclusion
   C. modification   D. substitution

3. The President _____ his deputy to act for him while he was abroad.
   A. promoted   B. substituted
   C. authorized   D. displaced

4. The European Union countries were once worried that they would not have _____ supplies of petroleum.
   A. proficient   B. efficient
   C. potential   D. sufficient

5. Many people like white color as it is a _____ of purity.
   A. symbol   B. sign
   C. signal   D. symptom

6. Vitamins are complex _____ that the body requires in very small amounts.
   A. matters   B. materials
   C. particles   D. substances

7. The rest of the day was entirely at his _____ for reading or recreation.
   A. dismissal   B. survival
   C. disposal   D. arrival

8. Those governments will provide big food and fuel _____ according

to the Asian Development Bank.
A. substitutes B. substances
C. subsequences D. subsidies

答案与解析

1. C 医生警告咀嚼烟草替代抽烟不可取。A 减轻,放松;B 复活;C 替代;D 继承权,继位。故选 C。

2. A 显而易见,新规则适用于每一个人,没有例外。A 例外;B 排除;C 修改;D 替代,代替物。故选 A。

3. C 总统授权副总统在他出国这段时间代他处理事务。A 提高,提升;B 替代;C 授权;D 取代。故 C 为正确答案。

4. D 欧盟国家曾担心他们得不到足够的石油供应。A 精通的;B 高效的;C 有潜力的;D 足够的。故 D 为正确答案。

5. A 许多人喜欢白色,因为它象征纯洁。A 象征;B 信号,符号;C 信号;D 症状。故 A 为正确答案。

6. D 维生素是复杂的物质,身体对它的需求量很小。A 事物;B 材料,矿物;C 颗粒,微粒;D 物质。故选 D。

7. C 那天剩余的时间任他自由支配,不管是读书还是娱乐。at one's disposal 任某人处理,故选 C。

8. D subsidies 补助金,津贴; substitutes 代替品; substances 物质; subsequences 后继,随后。故选 D。

Word List 45

table[ˈteɪbl] *n.* 桌子;表格,目录

[语境]He spread out the newspaper on the table.
他把报纸铺开放在了桌子上。
Next, we have to create the inner table.
接下来,我们必须创建内部表格。

tablet [ˈtæblɪt] *n.* 平板电脑;药片;小块;碑

[语境]How do you use your tablet?

你是怎样使用你的平板电脑的?

Dissolve the tablet in warm water.

把药片放进温水中溶化。

take[teɪk] *vt.* **拿,取,握;拿走,带去;需要,花费;接收,获得;认为,当作;做(一次动作)**

[语境]Go and take some coffee cups.

去拿几个咖啡杯。

His design took the first prize.

他的设计得了头等奖。

Let's take a walk.

咱们散散步吧。

[考点] take place 发生,举行

talent['tælənt] *n.* **才能,天资;人才**

[语境]Fate blessed him with great talent.

命运之神赋予他伟大的天才。

The child has musical talent [a gift for music].

这孩子有音乐天才。

[考点]have a talent for 有……的天赋

talk[tɔːk] *vt.* **谈,讨论** *vi.* **讲话,谈话,交谈** *n.* **谈话,演讲,讲话**

[语境]They sat down and began to talk.

他们坐下来开始交谈。

He distracted her with talk.

他用谈话分散她的注意力。

[考点]talk about sth. 谈论某事

tall[tɔːl] *a.* **高的,身材高的**

[语境]A tall pine dominated the landscape.

一棵高耸的松树俯视全景。

target[12]['tɑːgɪt] *n.* **靶子,目标;(嘲笑、批评、轻蔑等的)对象,目标;达到总数指标**

[语境] He aimed the target, but it missed.

他瞄准了靶子,但是没有射中。

[考点] shot sb. as target 把……当作靶子

task[tɑːsk] *n.* **任务,工作**

[语境] She breezed through the task.
她轻快地完成了任务。

taste [teɪst] *n.* **滋味,味道;味觉;鉴赏力,审美力** *vt.* **尝,品尝;体验,领略**

[语境] This soup tastes of chicken.
这汤里有鸡肉的味道。
The medicine has a bitter taste.
这药有苦味。

[考点] 许多感官动词以主动来表示被动,如 feel,notice,look

tasty['teɪstɪ] *a.* **美味的**

[巧记] nasty *a.* 令人讨厌的,肮脏的。串联记忆:美味的(tasty)东西才不令人讨厌(nasty)

[语境] Healthy and tasty food is an important part of balanced living.
健康与美味的食物是平衡生活的重要的一部分。

tax[tæks] *vt.* **征税;** *n.* **税(款)**

[语境] The government taxed the rich and the poor alike.
政府对富人和穷人同样征税。
Father is trying to figure out his tax.
父亲在设法计算出他的税额。

[考点] impose tax on sb. 对某人征税

taxi['tæksɪ] *vi.* **乘出租车**

[语境] They taxied to the zoo.
他们乘出租车去动物园。

taxpayer['tækspeɪər] *n.* **纳税人**

[语境] So why should the taxpayer take them?
那凭什么要纳税人来承担呢?

tea[tiː] *n.* **茶叶,茶;茶点**

[语境] The tea has lost its flavour.
茶叶走味了。
They discussed the question over tea and cakes.

他们边吃茶点边讨论问题。

teach[43] [tiːtʃ] *v.* 教,教书;教训

[语境] He taught me how to swim.

他教我怎样游泳。

All this taught them how to cope with difficulties.

所有这些都教育了他们应如何克服困难。

teacher [ˈtiːtʃə(r)] *n.* 教师,教员

[语境] They all look up to their teacher.

他们都很钦佩他们的老师。

team [tiːm] *n.* 小队,小组

[语境] The team was crippled by his absence.

他的缺席使这支球队的实力削弱。

teamwork [ˈtiːmwɜːk] *n.* 团队精神;团队合作

[语境] I think if we have a better teamwork, it will be much better.

我想如果我们有一个很好的团队合作,就会好很多。

tear [tɪə(r)] *n.* (*pl.*)眼泪;*vt.* 撕,撕下

[语境] She stood there looking at me through her tear.

她站在那里,眼里浸着泪水望着我。

This material does not tear.

这种料子撕不破。

[考点] tear sth. into pieces 把……撕成碎片

technical[8] [ˈteknɪkəl] *a.* 技术(性)的,工艺的;专门性,专业性的

[语境] The engineer explained the plane's technical capabilities.

工程师讲解了该飞机的技术性能。

He continued to maintain his technical innocence of any indictable offence.

他仍然声称自己从严格的法律意义上说并未犯有任何可以起诉的罪行。

technology[56] [tekˈnɒlədʒɪ] *n.* 工业技术,应用科学

[语境] Large scale industry emerged only gradually as technology evolved.

大工业只是随着技术发展而逐渐开始存在的。

487

The government saw the introduction of new technology as vital.
政府认为引进新技术至关重要。

teenager [ˈtiːneɪdʒə(r)] *n.* (13~19岁的)青少年
[语境] When I became a teenager, I always had a few thousand dollars.
当我长成一个青少年的时候,我总是会有几千美元。

telephone/phone *n.* 电话 *vt.* 打电话
[语境] You can get me by telephone.
你可以通过电话与我联系。

television/TV/t. v. *n.* 电视,电视机
[语境] We should tout our wares on television.
我们应该在电视上兜售商品。
[考点] watch TV 看电视

tell [tel] *vt.* 告诉,讲述;告诫,劝告;吩咐,命令;辨别,区别
[语境] He has told me about the new colleague.
他已经向我告知新同事的情况。
You can only tell which the conclusion is by looking at the function played by the particular sentence.
你们只能通过它在句子中的作用来识别结论。
[考点] tell sb. to do sth. 让某人做某事

ten [ten] *num.* 十
[语境] He charged me ten something for the hat.
他用十几块钱换了我那顶帽子。

tend[60] [tend] *v.* 趋向,往往是;照料,看护
[语境] Exporting and importing countries tend to prefer to adopt different kinds of policies.
出口国和进口国的政策倾向不同。
The shepherd tends the sheep alone.
这个牧羊人独自照顾着羊群。

tender [ˈtendə(r)] *a.* 嫩的,柔软的;脆弱的,纤细的;温柔的,亲切的
[语境] He recovered soon under his wife's tender loving care.

在妻子体贴入微的关怀下,他很快就痊愈了。

He gave her a tender kiss.

他给了她一个温柔的吻。

[考点] a tender spot 痛处,使人不愉快的话题

term[9] [tɜːm] *n.* 学期;期,期限;词,措辞,术语;(*pl.*) 条件,条款 *vt.* 称为,叫作

[语境] I have to bat out a term paper before class.

我必须在上课前匆匆写出一篇学期论文。

The term of practice is tentatively fixed at half a year.

实习期限暂定半年。

[考点] in terms of 根据;用……的话;就……而言;以……为单位

terrible [ˈterəbəl] *a.* 很糟的;可怕的,骇人的;极度的,厉害的

[语境] He could not stand the terrible English climate.

他忍受不了英国糟糕的气候。

terror [ˈterə(r)] *n.* 恐怖,惊恐

[语境] Ann froze with terror as the door opened silently.

门一声不响地开了,把安吓呆了。

She recoiled from the gunman in terror.

她面对持枪歹徒吓得直往后缩。

[考点] have a terror of sth. 对某事感到恐怖

test [test] *v./n.* 测验,试验,检验

[语境] He has stood up to the test of his honesty.

他已经通过了这次对他是否诚实的考验。

[考点] test on sth./sb. 在……身上做实验

text [tekst] *n.* 课文;原文,文本,正文

[语境] This sentence fell from that textbook.

这话是从那本教科书中摘录下来的。

textbook [ˈtekstbʊk] *n.* 教科书,课本

[语境] She wrote a textbook on international law.

她写了本国际法教材。

than [ðən, ðæn] *conj.* 比

[语境]She speaks more English than she did last term.

她讲英语比上学期要多。

thank[θæŋk] *vt.* 感谢 *n.* (*pl.*)感谢

[语境]She thanked me for the present.

她对我送的礼物表示感谢。

that[ðət,ðæt] *pron./a.* 那,那个 *pron.* [引出定语从句]*conj.* [引出名词性从句]*ad.* 那样,那么

[语境]That tastes lovely.

那东西味道不错。

She telephoned me that she was ill.

她打电话告诉我说她病了。

the[ðə,ðɪ,ðiː] *art.* 这,那

[语境]How do you like the novel?

你觉得那本小说怎样?

their[ðeə(r),ðə(r)] *pron.* 他们的

[语境]Have you looked at their reports?

你看过他们的报告了吗?

theirs[ðeəz] *pron.* 他们的(所有物)

[语境]My books are interesting, so are theirs.

我的书很有趣,他们的书也很有趣。

them[ðəm,ðem] *pron.* 他/她/它们

[语境]It was very kind of them.

他们太客气了。

theme[θiːm] *n.* 主题,话题

[语境]The theme carried through all his writing.

这个主题贯彻在他所有的作品中。

themselves[ðəm'selvz] *pron.* 他/她/它们自己

[语境]They themselves made the decision.

他们自己做的决定。

then[ðen] *ad.* 在那时,当时;那么,因而;然后,于是

[语境]Then you must be my cousin.

那么你一定是我的远亲了。

I heaved him up and then put him down on the ground lightly.
我奋力把他举了起来,然后又把他轻轻地放到了地上。

theory [ˈθɪərɪ] *n.* 理论,原理;学说,见解,看法
  [语境] Not everyone can understand Einstein's Theory of Relativity.
  不是每个人都能读懂爱因斯坦的相对论。

there [ðeə(r), ðə(r)] *ad.* 在那里,往那里;在那一点上,在那方面;(与 be 连用,表示"有")
  [语境] They were all there except me.
  除了我以外他们都在那里。
  There is very little time.
  没剩下多少时间了。

therefore[18] [ˈðeəfɔː(r)] *ad.* 因此,所以 *conj.* 因此
  [语境] The lazy girl is dreaming of marrying a millionaire and therefore won't do any work.
  这个懒惰的女孩正梦想着嫁给一个百万富翁,从此不再工作。

these [ðiːz] *pron./a.* 这些
  [语境] Are these all yours?
  这些都是你的吗?

they [ðeɪ] *pron.* 他/她/它们
  [语境] They are my students.
  他们是我的学生。

thick [θɪk] *a.* 厚的,粗的,稠的,浓的 *ad.* 厚,浓,密
  [语境] He wore a thick overcoat as a protection against the bitter cold.
  他穿着厚实的大衣以抵御严寒。

thin [θɪn] *a.* 薄的,细的;稀薄的,淡的;瘦的 *v.* 变薄;变稀
  [语境] The air became even thinner when I climbed to the top of the mountain.
  我爬到山顶时,空气变得更加稀薄了。

thing [θɪŋ] *n.* 物,东西;事,事情,问题;(*pl.*)所有物,用品;(*pl.*)情况,事态

[语境]I will do anything to make you happy.

为了让你高兴我愿做任何事情。

They took a gloomy view about the whole thing.

他们对整个情况持暗淡的看法。

think [θɪŋk] *vt.* 以为,认为;想要,打算 *vi.* 想,思索

[语境]We all thought her charming.

我们都认为她长得媚人。

He thought to go home as soon as possible.

他打算尽快回家。

Think happy thoughts and you'll feel better.

想些开心事儿,你就会感到舒服一些。

[考点]think of 想起,想到;认为

thinking[23] [ˈθɪŋkɪŋ] *n.* 思想,思考,思索;意见,想法

[语境]My thinking always lags behind reality.

我的思想老落后于现实。

The manager talked us over to his way of thinking.

经理说服我们接受了他的想法。

third [θɜːd] *num.* 第三 *n.* 三分之一

[语境]The dispute was settled by mediation of the third country.

这场争端通过第三国的斡旋而得以解决。

thirst [θɜːst] *n.* 口渴;渴望

[语境]I satisfied my thirst with a glass of water.

我喝了一杯水解渴。

Many boys have a thirst for adventure.

许多男孩都渴望冒险。

thirsty [ˈθɜːstɪ] *a.* 口渴的;(for)渴望的,热望的

[巧记]thirst + -y(形容词后缀)

[语境]The fields are thirsty for rain.

田地干旱,需要雨水。

[考点] be thirsty for 渴望……

thirteen [ˌθɜːˈtiːn] *num.* 十三

[语境]Thirteen States formed the original Union.

（北美）十三州组成最初的美利坚合众国。

thirty [ˈθɜːtɪ] *num.* 三十

[语境] His words refreshed my memory that he remained a bachelor at the age of thirty.

他的话使我回想起他三十岁时还是个光棍。

this [ðɪs] *a.* 这 *pron.* 这,这个

[语境] This is all I have.

这就是我的全部家当。

thorough [ˈθʌrə] *a.* 彻底的,完全的;仔细周到的,精心的

[语境] She underwent a thorough examination at the hospital.

她在医院里接受了全面检查。

I gave the radio a thorough inspection before buying it.

我把收音机彻底检查了一遍才买了下来。

[考点] be thorough in one's work 工作认真

those [ðəʊz] *a.* 那些 *pron.* 那些,那些人

[语境] He dotted down those notes.

他匆匆记下了那些注解。

though [ðəʊ] *ad.* 可是,然而,不过 *conj.* 尽管,虽然

[语境] He still argues, though he knows he's wrong.

虽然他知道错了,可仍在争辩。

thought [θɔːt] *n.* 思想,思考,思维;意图,打算;想法 *v.* think 的过去式和过去分词

[语境] ancient Greek thought

古希腊观念

thousand [ˈθaʊznd] *num./n.* 一千 (*pl.*) 许许多多,成千上万

[语境] A thousand angels dance around you.

成千的天使围绕你跳舞。

threat[20] [θret] *n.* 恐吓,威胁;坏兆头,危险迹象

[语境] The financial crisis poses a grave threat to world peace.

金融危机对世界和平构成了严重的威胁。

threaten[9] [ˈθretən] *vt.* 威胁,恫吓;预示;逼近,危及

[语境] The black clouds threatened rain.

乌云密布预示着将要下雨。
While danger threatens, we must all be on guard.
危险逼近时,我们必须保持警惕。
[考点] threaten with 威胁着要……

three [θriː] *num.* 三

[语境] She is the youngest of us three.
她是我们三人中间最年轻的。

through [θruː] *prep./ad.* 穿过;自始至终;由,以 *a.* 直达的

[语境] climbed in through the window
从窗户爬进去
bought the antique vase through a dealer
通过一个商人买到这只古花瓶

throughout [θruːˈaʊt] *prep.* 贯穿,遍及 *ad.* 到处,始终,全部

[语境] He accompanied her throughout her stay there.
她在那儿逗留期间他一直陪着她。
These strategic themes run throughout our work.
这些战略主题贯穿我们的全部工作。

throw [θrəʊ] *vt.* 扔;使突然陷入;使困惑 *n.* 投掷(距离)

[语境] He quickly threw the ball to another player.
他迅速把球传给了另一名球员。

[考点] throw away 抛弃,扔掉; throw in 插入,加入; throw off 摆脱,排出; throw out 发出,射出; throw over 翻过来,放弃; throw up 呕吐,停止

Thursday [ˈθɜːzdɪ] *n.* 星期四

[语境] We have meetings every Thursday afternoon.
我们每个星期四下午开会。

thus [ðʌs] *ad.* 如此;像这样;于是;因此

[语境] Few of the nation's largest cities are state capitals; thus neither New York nor Chicago is the seat of its state's government.
很多国家最大的城市并非州首府;例如,纽约和芝加哥都不是本州政府的所在地。

ticket [ˈtɪkɪt] *n.* 票,门票,车票;票签,标签;(交通违章)罚款传票

[语境]He poked about in his bag for his ticket.

他翻包里的东西,寻找他的票。

He got a traffic ticket.

他得到了一张违反交通规则罚款单。

tidy ['taɪdɪ] *vt.* **整理,收拾,整洁,整齐**

[语境] He keeps his office neat and tidy.

他保持办公室清洁整齐。

He combed his horse's mane tidy.

他把马的鬃毛梳理整齐。

[考点] tidy 多指是通过精心的安排或照料而显得整齐的

考点集训

1. The girl seems to have a _____ for drawing.
   A. skill   B. talent
   C. authority   D. expert

2. The food _____ very good. We all like it.
   A. tastes   B. is tasted
   C. has been tasted   D. tasting

3. The hunter made a _____ shelter out of branches.
   A. continual   B. permanent
   C. temporary   D. lasting

4. He was _____ into making a false step.
   A. tended   B. tempted
   C. tempered   D. termed

5. In summer fruit _____ to decay.
   A. tends   B. tenses
   C. tests   D. tempts

6. The leaves in spring are green and _____.
   A. soft   B. smooth
   C. delicate   D. tender

7. The two countries began to discuss their _____ relations.
   A. nervous   B. tense

  C. tent   D. temple
8. He became a _____ to all who knew him.
  A. terrify   B. fear
  C. terror   D. alarm
9. He always has a _____ for knowledge.
  A. thin   B. thirst
  C. thirsty   D. third
10. She gave the house a _____ cleaning.
  A. perfect   B. complete
  C. though   D. thorough
11. He summed up the _____ in these words.
  A. notion   B. thought
  C. notice   D. idea
12. The rising water was a continual _____ to the city.
  A. thrill   B. warn
  C. risk   D. threat
13. All sorts of grain _____ very well because the soil here is fat.
  A. profit   B. thrive
  C. prosper   D. succeed
14. I pride myself on always having a _____ garden.
  A. tide   B. tidy
  C. tire   D. tie
15. She cooked the meat for a long time so as to make it _____ enough to eat.
  A. mild   B. slight
  C. light   D. tender
16. Within two days, the army fired more than two hundred rockets and missiles at military _____ in the coastal city.
  A. goals   B. aims
  C. targets   D. destinations
17. When carbon is added to iron in proper _____, the result is steel.

A. rates B. thicknesses
C. proportions D. densities

答案与解析

1. B 这个女孩似乎有绘画才能。skill 技巧；authority 权威，当局；expert 专家。

2. A 食物尝起来味道非常的好，我们都很喜欢。

3. C 猎人用树枝搭了一个临时的窝棚。continual 连续的；permanent 永久的；lasting 持续的。

4. B 他被引诱做了一件傻事。tend 倾向于；temper 使回火，锻炼；term 把……称为。

5. A 夏天水果容易腐烂。tense 时态；test 检测。

6. D 春天里，树叶长得又绿又嫩。soft 柔软的；smooth 光滑的；delicate 纤细的，易损的。

7. B 两国开始讨论他们之间的紧张关系。nervous 人处于某种环境中变得紧张；tent 帐篷；temple 庙宇。

8. C 他成了所有认识他的人都感到恐怖的人物。terrify 使恐怖；fear 使害怕；alarm 对突然出现的事故表现出的恐惧。

9. B 他总是对知识有强烈的渴望。thin 瘦小的；third 第三；thirsty 口渴的。

10. D 她彻底地打扫了房间。perfect 人或物完美无缺；complete 事物的各个部分都完备；though 虽然。

11. B 他用这几句话概括了这个思想。notion 模糊不清的概念，思想；notice 意识到；idea 想法。

12. D 水位不断上涨，对这个城市的威胁不断增大。thrill 令人愉快的事情；warn 警告；risk 危机。

13. B 这里的土壤肥沃，谷物生长茂盛。profit 受益；prosper 事业繁荣；succeed 成功。

14. B 我常为自己有个整洁的花园而感到自豪。tide 潮汐；tire 疲倦；tie 捆，系。

15. D 她肉煮了很长时间，直到软到能吃。A 温柔的，温暖的，轻微的；B 少量的，少许的；C 轻的，轻微的；D（肉等食品）软的，嫩的,易咀嚼的。故 D 为正确答案。

16. C 根据题干中 fire more than two hundred rockets and missiles 和 military,可知空格处应填入表示"目标"的词。goal,aims 和 target 都有"目标"的意思。但是,goal 侧重表示长远的目标;aim 侧重表示短期的目标;target 侧重表示靶子。destination 表示"目的地"。target 最合适,答案为 C。

17. C 把炭按照适当的比例添加到铁中,就能炼出钢。in proportions 按照……的比例。故选 C。

Word List 46

tie [taɪ] *n.* 领带;联系,关系,纽带;束缚 *v.* 扎,系,捆

[语境] Does this sash tie in front or at the back?

这腰带是在前面打结还是在后面?

[考点] tie down 限制;tie up 阻碍;tied in 系紧,拉紧的,系上的

tiger [ˈtaɪɡə(r)] *n.* 虎

[语境] Tiger hunts in the night.

老虎在夜间猎食。

tight [taɪt] *a.* 紧,紧身,贴身;密封的,紧密的 *ad.* 紧紧地

[巧记] 派生词:tightly(*ad.* 紧紧地,满满地),tighten(*v.* 使变紧,使绷紧;变紧,绷紧)

[语境] This drawer is too tight for me to open it.

这抽屉太紧了,我打不开。

The lovers held each other tight.

这一对情侣紧紧地搂抱着。

[考点] tight corner 紧要关头

till [tɪl] *prep.* 直到,直到……为止(与 until 意思相同)

[语境] The meeting adjourned till five o'clock.

会议延至五点召开。

time [taɪm] *n.* 时间,时刻;次,回;时代,时期;倍,乘

498

[语境]Only time will tell if you are right.

只有时间才能证明你是否正确。

tired[18] ['taɪəd] *a.* 疲劳的;厌倦的

[巧记]其发音为"太饿"→引申为疲劳,疲惫

[语境] I was too tired to walk any further.

我累得再也走不动了。

[考点]tired 系常用词,泛指"由于劳动过度、工作紧张、休息不足或其他原因而导致疲乏"

to [tʊ, tə] *prep.* (表示方向)到;向;(表示间接关系)给

[语境]This road leads to London.

这条路通向伦敦。

today [tə'deɪ, tʊ'd-] *ad./n.* 今天;现在,目前

[语境]How do you find yourself today?

今天你身体感觉如何?

But in order to realize these benefits, we need to recognize some of the hurdles found in most organizations today.

但是为了实现这些利益,我们需要认识到现今大多数组织上存在的障碍。

together [tə'geðə(r)] *ad.* 共同,一起;合起来,集拢地

[巧记]to(到) + gether(一起)

[语境]The man talked for hours together.

这个人一连讲了几个小时。

tomato [tə'mɑːtəʊ] *n.* 西红柿

[语境]He staked his tomato vines with bamboo.

他用竹竿支撑起西红柿秧。

tomorrow[tə'mɒrəʊ, tʊ'm-] *n.* 明天 *ad.* 明天,在明天

[语境]Whether we will go there tomorrow depends on the weather.

我们明天是否去那里取决于天气。

ton[tʌn] *n.* 吨

[语境]The raw coal was quoted at $15 per ton.

原煤报价为每吨15美元。

tone[təʊn] *n.* 音,音调,声调;腔调,语气;色调,气氛,调子

[语境]The musician can discriminate minute variations in tone.

乐师能辨别声调的各种细微变化。

You'd better modify your tone.

你最好缓和一下你的口气。

tongue[tʌŋ] *n.* 舌,舌头;语言

[语境]He protruded his tongue.

他伸出了舌头。

I know that his tongue wags.

我知道他一说话就喋喋不休。

tonight[tə'naɪt,tu'n-] *n./ad.* 今晚

[语境]We can hut on the mountain tonight.

今晚我们可以住在山上的棚屋里。

too [tuː]*ad.* 也,还;太,过于;很,非常

[语境]He plays the guitar and sings too.

他会弹吉他,也会唱歌。

tool[tuːl] *n.* 工具

[语境]He looked into the box to see if the tool was there.

他朝箱子里看,看看工具是否在里面。

tooth[tuːθ] *n.* 牙齿;齿,齿状物

[语境]I have a loose tooth.

我的一个牙齿松动了。

top [tɒp]*n.* 顶,顶端;首位;顶点 *a.* 最高的;顶上的

[语境]The green book is at the bottom of the pile and the red one is on top.

绿皮书在那一堆书的底下,红皮书在上边。

topic['tɒpɪk] *n.* 话题,论题,题目

[语境]No one touched on this topic.

没人谈及这个话题。

total ['təʊtl]*n.* 总数,合计 *a.* 总的,完全的 *v.* 合计,总计

[语境] Add this numbers together and give me the total.

把这些数字加起来,告诉我总数是多少。

We have debts totaling 5,000 dollars.

我们的债务总计为 5 000 美元。

touch [tʌtʃ] v. 触,碰,摸;感动;涉及 n. 触动,碰到;少许

[巧记] touchable(a. 可触的;可食用的),touch-and-go(危急的,一触即发的,危险的;简略的;不确定的;草率的)

[语境] He helped to keep us in touch with what was going on there.
他帮助我们了解那儿的情况。

[考点] get into touch with 和……取得联系

tough⁶ [tʌf] a. 坚韧的;难嚼烂的;结实的,能吃苦耐劳的;艰巨的,困难的,严厉的

[语境] We won the contract but only through a lot of tough negotiating.
我们虽然赢得了合同,但是却经过了多次不屈不挠的谈判。
The company faces tough competition.
这家公司面临着艰难的竞争。

[考点] as tough as old boots 非常硬,坚强

tour [tʊə(r)] v./n. 旅游,旅行

[语境] We tour by car every summer.
每年夏天我们都驾车出外旅行。

[考点] tour around 游历周边

tourism [ˈtʊərɪzəm] n. 旅游,观光;旅游业

[语境] In this resort you can enjoy all the comfort and convenience of modern tourism.
在此旅游胜地,您可尽享现代旅游的舒适便利。
Some countries obtain large sums of foreign exchange from tourism.
有些国家靠旅游业赚取大量外汇。

tourist [ˈtʊərɪst] n. 旅游者,观光者

[语境] Beijing has a multitude of attractions to beguile the foreign tourist.
北京有许多能迷住外国旅游者的景物。

toward [təˈwɔːd] prep. 朝,向;将近;对于;为了

[语境] The United Nations' work is toward peace.

联合国的工作是为了实现和平。

towards [tə'wɔːdz, tɔːdz] *prep.* 朝,向;将近;对于;为了

[语境] As you get older your attitude towards death changes.

人随着年龄的增长,对死亡的看法也会有所改变。

town [taʊn] *n.* 市镇;闹区,商业区

[语境] They march on the next town.

他们向下一个城镇进军。

toy [tɔɪ] *n.* 玩具

[语境] He was handling his toy all the morning.

整个上午他一直在玩着他的玩具。

trace [treɪs] *n.* 痕迹 *v.* 查找

[语境] I can't trace that letter you sent me.

我找不到你寄给我的那封信。

Did the police find any trace of the murderer?

警方找到凶手的行踪了吗?

[考点] trace back to…可以追溯到……

track[4] [træk] *n.* 跑道,路线,轨道;足迹,踪迹 *vt.* 跟踪,追踪

[语境] The wheel plays in a track.

轮子在轨道上转动。

What else should you track?

你还应该追踪什么?

[考点] keep track of 掌握最新情况,追踪

trade[11] [treɪd] *n.* 贸易,商业;职业,行业 *v.* 经商,交易

[巧记] 派生词:tradeable(*a.* 可做交易的;有销路的);trademark(*n.* 商标;标记,特征)

[语境] Britain does a lot of trade with America.

英国与美国进行大量的贸易。

[考点] foreign trade 对外贸易;trade in 做……生意,经营

tradition[42] [trə'dɪʃən] *n.* 传统,惯例

[巧记] 派生词:traditional(*a.* 传统的)

[语境] The story is based mainly on tradition.

这故事主要来自传说。

By tradition, people play practical jokes on 1 April.

按照传统风俗,4月1日可以开恶作剧的玩笑。

traffic[16] [ˈtræfɪk] *n.* 交通,交通量

[语境] The bridge is now open to traffic.

这座桥现在可以通行。

His left knee was hurt in a traffic accident.

他的左膝在一次交通事故中受伤了。

[考点] traffic accident 交通事故;traffic jam 交通拥塞

train [treɪn] *vt.* 培训,训练 *n.* 列车;一连串

[语境] We should train our students to speak English fluently and accurately.

我们应培养学生流利而准确地讲英语。

They made the station in time to catch the train.

他们及时到达车站,赶上了那班火车。

training [ˈtreɪnɪŋ] *n.* 训练,培训,培养

[语境] His training fits him for the job.

他受过的训练使他能胜任此项工作。

transfer[10] [trænsˈfɜː(r)] *vt./n.* 转移;转换;转让;过户;迁移;改乘

[巧记] trans(从一边到另一边)+fer(迁,搬)→转移

[语境] The company has transferred to an eastern location.

这家公司已搬到东部某地。

transform[7] [trænsˈfɔːm] *vt.* 转换,变形,变革,变化,变压

[巧记] trans(变)+form(形式)→变形;派生词:transformation (*n.* 改造,改变);transformer (*n.* 变压器)

[语境] In the situation, we must transform ourselves.

在这种情形下,我们只能改变我们自己。

[考点] transform into 把……转变成……

translate [trænsˈleɪt] *v.* 翻译,解释;转化

[巧记] trans(交换)+late→交换拿出→翻译

[语境] I need to translate it into English.

我必须把它译成英语。

[考点] translate...as 把……解释为……;translate...into 把……

译成……，把……转变成……；使……体现为……

translation[63] [trænsˈleɪʃən] *n.* 翻译；译文，译本

[巧记] translate + ion（名词化）

[语境] The teacher laid emphasis on the precision of the translation from the outset.
老师从一开始就强调翻译的准确性。

transmit[17] [trænzˈmɪt] *vt.* 传输/导；转送；发射 *vi.* 发射信号；发报

[巧记] trans（交换） + mit→交换过去→传；派生词：transmition（*n.* 传输，传送，传达）

[语境] All the signals must be transmitted by radio.
所有的信号必须通过电台来传输。

[考点] transmit to 把……传给

transport[15] [trænˈspɔːt] *v.* 运输，运送，搬运 *n.* 运输；运输系统，运载工具

[巧记] trans（通过） + port（港口）；派生词：transportation（*n.* 运输）

[语境] The role of the railways declined in the transport system.
在运输系统中，铁路的重要性逐渐下降。
Please find alternative means of transport.
请另外找一种运输方法。

[考点] transport to 把……运送到

travel [ˈtrævəl] *n.* 旅行 *v.* 旅行；行进，传播

[语境] Travel in the mountains can be slow and dangerous.
走山路又慢又危险。

[考点] 合成词：travel agency 旅行社；travel agent 旅行代理人；travel service 旅行社服务

treasure [ˈtreʒə(r)] *n.* 财宝，财富；珍宝 *vt.* 珍视，珍爱

[语境] We all treasure our good friendship.
我们都很珍惜我们良好的友谊。

[考点] treasure 作为名词，还有宝贝、珍宝的含义。
Her father treats her as the best treasure.
她爸爸把她当成心肝宝贝。

treat [tri:t] *v.* 对待,处理;治疗 *n.* 对待,请客

[语境] My mother always treats us like children.
妈妈总把我们当孩子看待。
This delicate glass must be treated with care.
精致的玻璃杯要小心放置。

[考点] treat as 把……当作,看作;treat of 论述,讨论;treat with 和……谈判

treatment ['tri:tmənt] *n.* 治疗,处置,待遇

[巧记] treat + ment

[语境] You should follow your treatment with plenty of rest in bed.
你应该在治疗之后好好卧床休息。

tree [tri:] *n.* 树

[语境] All the peaches rotted on the tree.
所有的桃子都在树上烂掉了。

tremble ['trembəl] *n.* 战栗,颤抖 *v.* 发抖,颤抖;摇动;焦虑

[巧记] 派生词:tremblingly(*ad.* 颤抖地;发抖地)

[语境] When listened to the news, he trembled without a word.
当听到这个消息时,他颤抖得说不出一句话。

[考点] in fear and trembling 震惊的,发抖的,十分担心的

trend[16] [trend] *n.* 倾向,趋势 *vi.* 伸向,倾向

[巧记] 派生词:trendy(*a.* 时髦的;流行的)

[语境] The trend of prices is still upwards.
物价仍有上涨趋势。

[考点] set the trend (在风尚、式样上)开个头,带个头

trial ['traɪəl] *n.* 讯问,审讯;试验;试用;尝试

[语境] He's on trial for his life.
他正在接受决定他生死的审判。
Her child is a trial to his teachers.
她的孩子让老师很伤脑筋。

[考点] be on trial 在受审;bring to trial 传讯

trick [trɪk] *vt.* 欺诈,哄骗 *n.* 诡计,花招;恶作剧;窍门

[巧记] 派生词:tricker(*n.* 欺骗者;恶作剧者);trickery(*n.* 欺骗;

奸计)

[语境] He played some clever magic tricks.

他表演了一些巧妙的魔术。

The police tricked him into making a confession.

警察哄骗他做了招认。

[考点] play a trick on 开……玩笑;trick into 诱使;trick out of 骗走

trip[trɪp] *n.* 旅行,远足

[语境]We assimilated many new experiences on our European trip.

我们从欧洲之行中吸收了许多新的经验。

[考点]go for a trip 去旅行

troop[truːp]*n.*(一)群,(一)队;(*pl.*)部队,军队

[语境]A troop of children gathered around the teacher.

一群孩童聚集在老师四周。

The troop trotted the hills and valleys.

这支部队快步翻山越谷。

trouble ['trʌbəl]*n.* 烦恼;动乱;疾病;故障;辛苦 *v.*(使)烦恼

[语境] I'm sorry to have to put you to so much trouble.

很抱歉,给您添了这么多麻烦。

trousers['traʊzəz] *n.* 裤子

[语境]I wear these old trousers for knocking about the garden.

我穿这条旧裤子是为了在花园里干粗活。

truck [trʌk] *n.* 卡车,载重汽车

[语境]They unloaded the books from the truck.

他们把书从卡车上卸下来。

true [truː]*a.* 真实的,不假的;忠实的,可靠的;正确无误的

[语境] She gave the true account of what had happened.

她如实地讲述了发生的事情。

truly['truːlɪ] *ad.* 正确地,事实上;真诚地

[巧记]近义词:actually 事实上,honestly 真诚地

[语境]I truly never minded caring for Rusty.

我真的从不介意照顾拉斯蒂。

He truly loved his children.
他由衷地爱他的孩子们。

trust [trʌst] vt. 信任;盼望;委托 n. (in)信任,依赖;委托

[语境] My husband trusts me and I don't intend to break that trust.
我的丈夫信任我,所以我不想失去这种信任。

[考点] trust sb. with sth. 把某事托付给某人去办

truth [truːθ] n. 真实,真相;真实性;真理

[巧记] true(真实的) + -th(名词后缀)

[语境] We shall find out the truth early or late.
我们迟早会查明事实真相。

try [traɪ] v. 尝试,试图;试验,试用;审讯 n. 尝试

[语境] I think I'll try my luck at roulette.
我想玩玩轮盘赌碰碰运气。

T-shirt ['tiːʃɜːt] n. T恤衫,圆领汗衫

[语境] There are a lot of new T-shirts out now.
现在这里有许多新T恤。

tube [tjuːb] n. 管,软管;电子管,显像管;地铁

[语境] With the words he handed Professor Wang a tube.
说着他交给王教授一个试管。
He travelled by tube.
他乘地铁旅行。

Tuesday ['tjuːzdɪ] n. 星期二

[语境] Try to fix the meeting for Tuesday.
设法把会议安排在星期二。

tune [tjuːn] n. 调子,曲调;和谐,协调 vt. 调音,调节,调整

[巧记] tuneable(a. 可合调的;音调美的), tunefulness(n. 音调优美,声音悦耳)

[语境] Stay tuned to us for the latest sports results.
请继续收听我们播放的最新比赛结果。

[考点] tune in 调整频率(至……),调整(收音机、电视);tune into 和……协调;tune to 调到……

turn [tɜːn] v./n. (使)转动;(使)旋转;(使)转变 n. 机会

[语境]The river turns north at this point.

这条河从这里转向北方。

TV = television

twelve[twelv] *num.* 十二

[语境]These regulations do not relate to children under the age of twelve.

这些规则不适用于十二岁以下儿童。

twenty[ˈtwentɪ] *num.* 二十

[语境]She can reproduce the call of over twenty birds.

她能模仿二十多种鸟叫的声音。

twice[twaɪs] *ad.* 两次，两倍

[语境]She does for us twice a week.

她每周两次来帮我们做家务。

The figure of seventy-million pounds was twice as big as expected.

7 000万英镑的金额是预期的两倍。

two[tuː] *num.* 二

[语境]They separated two months ago.

他们两个月前分居了。

type [taɪp] *n.* 型式，类型；印刷字体；活/铅字 *v.* 打字

[语境] A mammoth is a large hairy type of elephant in ancient times.

猛犸是古代一种身体庞大、长着长毛的大象。

typical[12][ˈtɪpɪkəl] *a.* 典型的，有代表性的；独有的，独特的

[巧记]type（类型）+cal（形容词化）→典型的，有代表性的

[语境] The play contains a number of typical Stoppard set pieces.

这出戏里有若干典型的斯托帕特式的场景。

This chair is typical of Anthony's way of designing furniture.

这把椅子是安东尼式家具设计的代表。

[考点] be typical of…是……的特点

考点集训

1. The lecture which lasted about three hours was so _____ that the audience couldn't help yawning.
   A. tedious   B. bored
   C. clumsy   D. tired

2. Chinese people are now enjoying better dental health, as shown by the declining _____ of tooth decay.
   A. treatment   B. incidence
   C. consequence   D. misfortune

3. In mild winters apple buds began to break soon after Christmas, leaving them _____ to frost damage.
   A. reluctant   B. tough
   C. hostile   D. vulnerable

4. Mr Tunick filed suit against the New York police department after city officials _____ his request.
   A. turned down   B. turned in
   C. turned off   D. turned out

5. Some diseases are _____ by certain water animals.
   A. transplanted   B. transformed
   C. transported   D. transmitted

6. A lot of ants are always invading my kitchen. They are a thorough _____.
   A. nuisance   B. trouble
   C. worry   D. anxiety

7. American football and baseball are becoming known to the British public through televised _____ from the United States.
   A. transfer   B. deliveries
   C. transportation   D. transmissions

8. The twentieth century has witnessed an enormous worldwide political, economic and cultural _____.
   A. tradition   B. transportation

· 509 ·

C. transmission D. transformation

9. To speed up the _____ of letters, the Post Office introduced automatic sorting.

    A. treatment B. delivery
    C. transmission D. departure

10. Jessica was _____ from the warehouse to the accounting office, which was considered a promotion.

    A. delivered B. exchanged
    C. transferred D. transformed

11. A traditional critic has the advantage of being able to _____ standards and values inherited from the past.

    A. turn up B. turn over
    C. turn to D. turn in

答案与解析

1. A 演讲持续了大约三个小时,枯燥无味,观众情不自禁打起了哈欠。A 枯燥的,乏味的;B 感到枯燥的;C 臃肿的;D 疲劳的,劳累的。故选 A。

2. B 现在中国人的牙齿健康怎么样? 更好了。所以我们可以通过最后一个单词 decay 来推理。这个单词叫作牙齿的蛀牙或者是腐败,这句话是说牙齿腐败的概率在下降。本题空前有一个形容词 declining,它表示下降,也就是说,中国的牙齿健康更好了。A 是治疗的意思,应该选择 B incidence,它表示小事儿,而且 incidence 实际上是一个抽象意义的单词。

3. D vulnerable 易受攻击的;reluctant 勉强的;tough 强硬的;hostile 敌对的。故选 D。

4. A 在市政官员拒绝了他的要求后,Tunick 先生向法院起诉了纽约警察局。A 拒绝;B 上交;C 关掉;D 证明,表明。故 A 为正确答案。

5. D 某些疾病是由特定的水生动物传播的。A 移植;B 改变;C 运输;D 传播。因此 D 为正确答案。

6. A 我厨房里有好多蚂蚁,它们很让人讨厌。A 令人讨厌的事物;B 麻烦;C 担心;D 焦急。故 A 为正确答案。

7. D 英国公众通过美国电视节目了解了美式足球和棒球。A 转移;B 传递;C 运输;D 传输,传播。故 D 为正确答案。

8. D 20 世纪目睹了世界范围内政治、经济、文化方面的巨大发展。A 传统;B 交通,运输;C 传播;D 改变,发展。因此 D 为正确答案。

9. B 根据题干中 speed up 和 post office,得知空格处应填入表示"送信"的词。treatment 表示"对待,处理,治疗";delivery 表示"递送,交付,分娩,交货";transmission 表示"播送,发射,传送,传输";departure 表示"出发,离开"。答案为 B。

10. C 根据题干中 from the warehouse to the accounting office 和 which was considered a promotion,得知空格处应填入表示"调任"的词。deliver 表示"递送";exchange 表示"交换,交流";transfer 表示"迁移,传递,转移,调任";transform 表示"转换,改变,改造,使……变形"。答案为 C。

11. B turn over (使)翻转,打翻,移交,交给;turn up 找到,出现;turn to 变成,致力于;turn in 上交。故选 B。

Word List 47

ugly [ˈʌglɪ] a. 丑的,丑陋的;讨厌的,邪恶的

[语境] No animal of the horoscope is considered dumb or ugly or evil.

天宫图上的动物没有一种被认为是愚笨的、丑陋的或邪恶的。

His face was covered in ugly red blotches.

他脸上有许多难看的红色大斑点。

[考点] an ugly face 难看的脸。反义词:beautiful。ugly 可用作很多引申意义,如:an ugly word 令人不快的话;an ugly wound 可怕的伤口;an ugly-tempered person 脾气不好的人

umbrella[ʌmˈbrelə] *n.* 伞

[语境]Harry held an umbrella over Dawn.

哈里为唐打着伞。

uncle[ˈʌŋkl] *n.* 伯父,叔父,舅父,姑父,姨夫

[语境]I expect to see my uncle.

我期望见到我的舅舅。

under [ˈʌndə(r)] *prep.* 在……下面,在……以下 *ad.* 在下面;少于

[语境]We study English under his direction.

我们在他的指导下学习英语。

undergraduate[ˌʌndəˈɡrædʒuɪt] *n.* 大学生,大学肄业生

[巧记]under(在……下) + graduate(毕业生)→大学生

[语境]Each year, I pose this question to my undergraduate students.

每一年,我都会向我的本科学生们提出这个问题。

understand[36] [ˌʌndəˈstænd] *v.* 懂,理解;获悉,听说,揣测,认为

[语境]A good teacher must understand children.

一个好的教师必须了解孩子。

understanding[9] [ˌʌndəˈstændɪŋ] *n.* 理解,理解力;谅解 *a.* 能体谅人的,宽容的

[语境]The other students admired his depth of understanding.

别的学生佩服他的理解力深刻。

Her boss, who was very understanding, gave her time off.

她的老板很通情达理,准了她的假。

unemployed[ˌʌnɪmˈplɔɪd] *a.* 失业的;未动用的

[巧记]un(不) + employed(被雇用的)→未被雇用的→失业的

[语境]There are now over four million unemployed workers in this country.

这个国家现有四百万失业人员。

unemployment[ˌʌnɪmˈplɔɪmənt] *n.* 失业,失业人数

[语境]The unemployment figures are not necessarily related to the rise in prices.

失业的数目同物价的上涨并没有必然的联系。

unfair [ˌʌnˈfeə(r)] *a.* 不公平的，不公正的；不正直的

[巧记] un(不) + fair(公平的)→不公正的

[语境] The referee made an unfair decision.

裁判作出不公正的判决。

unfortunately [ʌnˈfɔːtʃənɪtlɪ] *ad.* 恐怕，不幸的是

[巧记] un(否定) + fortunate(幸运的) + ly(副词后缀)→不幸运地

[语境] Unfortunately, the war broke out.

不幸的是，战争爆发了。

uniform [ˈjuːnɪfɔːm] *n.* 制服，军服 *a.* 相同的，一律的

[巧记] uni(统一) + form(形式) = 一律的，相同的

[语境] The new uniforms will arrive tomorrow.

新制服明天就到。

The earth turns around at a uniform rate.

地球以相同的速度旋转。

[考点] in full uniform 穿着一套军礼服；out of uniform 穿着便服

unique[14] [jʊˈniːk] *a.* 唯一的；独一无二的

[语境] He's caught the unique opportunity.

他抓住了那唯一的机会。

The elephant's trunk is a unique appendage.

象的鼻子是一种独特的附肢。

[考点] unique 含有绝对的意思，不能用比较级、最高级修饰；unique to... 只有……才有的

unite[30] [jʊˈnaɪt] *vi.* 联合，团结；统一，合并 *vt.* 使联合

[语境] The broken bones of a child unite easily.

儿童的断骨容易接合。

universal[6] [ˌjuːnɪˈvɜːsəl] *a.* 宇宙的，全世界的；普通的，一半的；通用的，万能的

[巧记] 派生词：universality(*n.* 普遍性；多方面性；一般性)

[语境] When was universal suffrage introduced in your country?

贵国是什么时候实行普选权的？

English is referred to as a universal language.

英语被称为世界语言。

[考点] general 也指普遍的,意思是普通人的、大众化的,一般指的是被看成一个整体的一群人

universe [ˈjuːnɪvɜːs] *n.* 宇宙,万物

[巧记] uni(一) + verse(多样)→一个物体由东西组成→宇宙,万物

[语境] We still don't know how many galaxies there are in the universe.

我们还不知道宇宙中有多少个星系。

university [ˌjuːnɪˈvɜːsɪtɪ] *n.* (综合性)大学

[语境] He is studying hard with a view to going to university.

他为了上大学正在努力学习。

unless [ʌnˈles] *conj.* 如果不,除非

[语境] I won't go to the party unless I'm invited.

除非被邀请,否则我不会去参加晚会的。

I sleep with the window open unless it's really cold.

我总是开着窗户睡觉,除非天气非常冷才关上窗户。

[考点] unless and until 直到……才……

unlike [ʌnˈlaɪk] *a.* 不同的,不相似的 *prep.* 不像……,和……不同

[语境] The two men are unlike in disposition.

这两个人的气质不同。

She was unlike him in every way except for her coal black eyes.

她除了那双乌黑的眼睛外,跟他没有一点儿相像。

until [ʌnˈtɪl] *conj./prep.* 直到……为止,在……以前;直到……

[语境] He lived in California until he was twenty.

他在加利福尼亚一直住到20岁。

unusual[1] [ʌnˈjuːʒl] *a.* 不平常的,稀有的;例外的;独特的

[巧记] un(不) + usual(平常的)

[语境] Snow is an unusual sight in this warm place.

下雪在这个温暖的地方是一种罕见的景象。

This bird is an unusual winter visitor to Britain.

这种鸟很少冬季到英国来。

up [ʌp] *ad.* 向上,……起来;……完;起床 *prep.* 向上
　[语境]Put the packet up on the top shelf.
　　把这个包放到架子顶格上去。

update [ʌpˈdeɪt] *v.* 更新,使最新 *n.* 最新资料,最新版
　[语境]He was back in the office, updating the work schedule on the computer.
　　他已回到办公室,正在电脑上更新工作日程。
　　She had heard the news-flash on a TV channel's news update.
　　她在一家电视台的新闻快讯中听到了这则简明新闻。

upon [əˈpɔn] *prep.* 在……上;在……旁[= on]
　[语境]Once upon a time, there was an old man living in a small village.
　　从前,在一个小村庄里住着一位老人。
　[考点]once upon a time 从前

upper[12] [ˈʌpə(r)] *a.* 上,上部的,较高的
　[语境]We sat in the upper tier at the stadium.
　　我们坐在体育场的上排。

upset [ˌʌpˈset] *vi.* 倾覆 *vt.* 弄翻,打翻;扰乱,打乱,使不安
　[语境] He has an upset stomach.
　　他胃不舒服。
　　The news quite upset him.
　　这消息使他心烦意乱。
　[考点]disturb 也有搅乱之意,表示紊乱,持久的心神不宁变成越来越厉害的不安

urban[4] [ˈɜːbən] *a.* 城市的,都市的
　[巧记]urbanization (*n.* 城市化),urbanize (*v.* 使城市化)
　[语境]More attention should be paid to urban development.
　　人们应该更多地关注城市发展。

urge [ɜːdʒ] *v.*/*n.* 强烈希望,竭力主张/鼓励,促进
　[语境] They urged on us the need for cooperation.
　　他们向我们强调合作的必要性。
　　They urged us to give our support.

515

他们敦促我们给予支持。

[考点] urge 后面的句子要使用虚拟语气

urgent [ˈɜːdʒənt] 紧迫的;催促的

[巧记] 派生词:urgency(n. 紧急;强求;紧急的事)

[语境] They've made an urgent request for international aid.

他们紧急请求国际援助。

I was prevented from going by urgent business.

我因急事不能去。

[考点] 在 it is urgent that…句型中,that 后面的宾语从句要使用虚拟语气

us [əs; ʌs] pron. [宾格]我们

[语境] None of us like to swim this weekend.

这周末我们都不想去游泳。

use [juːs] n. 使/应用;用法;途;益/用处 vt. 用;消耗

[语境] The present phone boxes will go out of use next year.

现有的公共电话亭明年就不再使用了。

used [juːst; jʊs(t)/juːs(t)] a. 旧的,用旧了的;(to) 习惯于……;过去惯常,过去经常

[语境] This store buys and sells used (and new) exercise equipment.

这个商店买卖二手的(和新的)运动装备。

She was used to having her orders instantly obeyed.

她习惯了让人即刻服从她的命令。

[巧记] get used to doing 习惯于做……

useful [ˈjuːsfl] a. 有用的,实用的;有益的,有帮助的

[巧记] use(用) + ful(形容词化)→有用的

[语境] It is a useful book and, what is more, not an expensive one.

这是本有用的书,更难得的是价格便宜。

useless [ˈjuːslɪs] a. 无用的,无价值的,无效的

[巧记] use(用) + less(否定形容词后缀)→无用的

[语境] It's useless to argue with them.

同他们争论是没有用的。

usual [ˈjuːʒʊəl] *a.* **通常的,平常的**

[语境] The vintage was later than usual.

那次葡萄采收期比平常年份晚。

usually [ˈjuːʒʊəlɪ] *ad.* **通常,平常**

[语境] I usually wake up early.

我通常醒得很早。

utilize/-ise[4] [ˈjuːtəlaɪz] *vt.* **利用,实用**

[巧记] 派生词:utilization(*n.* 利用;使用)

[语境] How can we utilize his knowledge and skill to our advantage?

我们如何利用他的知识和技术才对我们有利?

In order to utilize land more fully, they adopted close planting.

为了更充分地利用土地,他们采取了密植的办法。

[考点] use,utilize,employ 都可以指"利用":use 是最一般的用法;utilize 表示利用资源、方法、手段、途径等;employ 应用,雇用

utter [ˈʌtə(r)] *a.* **完全的,彻底的,绝对的** *vt.* **说,发出(声音);说出,说明,表达**

[语境] She is an utter stranger to me.

对我来说,她完全是一个陌生人。

I didn't know who first uttered the truth.

我不知道最先吐露真情的是谁。

考点集训

1. The students were asked to _____ all the new words in the passage and then look them up in the dictionaries.

   A. understand　　　　　　B. underline

   C. underlie　　　　　　　D. underestimate

2. Before we can pass you fit, you will have to _____ a number of medical tests.

   A. suffer　　　　　　　　B. endure

C. undergo   D. undertake
3. The album is _____ as it was the only one ever signed by the president.
   A. unusual   B. unique
   C. rare   D. singular
4. The commander asked his officers to put aside their differences of opinion and work together in _____ to win the battle.
   A. unity   B. settlement
   C. relation   D. neighbourhood
5. English is fast becoming _____ language as it is widely used in most of the international activities.
   A. an isolate   B. a national
   C. a universal   D. an European
6. In ancient China, there was no _____ currency until the reform of Empire Qing.
   A. personal   B. efficient
   C. uniform   D. consistent
7. _____ other blood cells, white cells have a nucleus that enables the cell to divide and reproduce.
   A. Unlike   B. Dislike
   C. Likely   D. Alike
8. You can arrive in Beijing earlier for the meeting, _____ you don't mind taking the night train.
   A. if   B. unless
   C. though   D. until
9. Tom belongs to the _____ class.
   A. up   B. upper
   C. above   D. high
10. It's a pleasure to do business with _____ man.
    A. a crooked   B. a dishonorable
    C. an untrustworthy   D. an upright
11. Paul was very _____ while working over the weekend.

A. upset　　　　　　　　　B. underhanded
C. uneven　　　　　　　　D. upraised

12. Linda doesn't like to live in the country. She prefers _____ life.
    A. subtle　　　　　　　　B. potent
    C. tropical　　　　　　　D. urban

13. The class is discussing a newspaper editorial that _____ citizens to help decrease the noise and air pollution in the city.
    A. ordered　　　　　　　B. demanded
    C. promised　　　　　　D. urged

14. From the incident they have learned a lesson：_____ decisions often lead to bitter regrets.
    A. urgent　　　　　　　 B. hasty
    C. instant　　　　　　　D. prompt

15. In the modern factory all the equipment was _____.
    A. up-to-date　　　　　 B. out of date
    C. dated　　　　　　　 D. no date

16. By law, when one makes a large purchase, he should have _____ opportunity to change his mind.
    A. accurate　　　　　　B. urgent
    C. excessive　　　　　 D. adequate

答案与解析

1. B 学生被要求在这篇文章中所有的生词下画线,并且在词典中找出来。underlie"成为……的基础";underestimate"低估";understand"理解"。

2. C 在我们判定你伤病以前,你要接受一些医学检查。suffer"遭受";endure"忍受";undertake"从事"。

3. B 这本相册独一无二,因为他是总统签名的唯一一本。unusual"非同寻常的";rare"稀少的,稀罕的";singular"单数的"。

4. A 指挥官要求军官们撇开分歧,为获得战争的胜利而一致努力。settlement"解决方法,定居";relation"联系";neighbourhood"社区"。

· 519 ·

5. C 随着英语在大部分国际活动中的广泛应用,它很快成为一门普遍通用的语言。isolate"孤立的";European"欧洲的";national"国家的,民族的"。

6. C 古代中国直到秦始皇改革才有了统一的货币。personal"个人的";efficient"高效的";consistent"持续的"。

7. A 白细胞不像其他血液细胞,它有一个细胞核,可以分裂和再生。dislike"不喜欢";likely"可能的";alike"相似"。

8. A 如果你不介意坐夜里的火车,你能够早些到达北京开会。

9. B 汤姆属于上流社会的人。

10. D 和诚实的人做生意真是令人愉快。crooked"狡诈的";dishonorable/untrustworthy"不诚实的"。

11. A 整个周末都在工作,这让保罗心烦意乱。uneven"不平,不稳定";underhanded"阴险的,狡诈的";upraised"提高的"。

12. D 林达不喜欢住在农村,她更喜欢城市的生活。subtle"微妙的";potent"烈性的";tropical"热带的"。

13. D 全班正在讨论报纸上一篇敦促市民帮助减少该市噪声和空气污染的社论。promise"许诺";demand"要求";order"命令"。

14. B 通过这一事件,他们吸取了一个教训:仓促的决定会导致痛苦的后悔。

15. A 在这个现代的工厂里,所有设备都是最新的。out of date "过时的";dated"不再使用的"。

16. D 依据法律的规定,一个人购买大批量的物品时,他享有足够的机会改变他的决定。A 准确的;B 紧急的;C 过分的;D 足够的,充分的。故选择 D。

Word List 48

vacation [vəˈkeɪʃən] *n.* 休假,假期;空出,腾出

[语境]Mary was on vacation when the accident happened.

事故发生的时候,玛丽正在度假。

vague[veɪɡ] *a.* **不明确的,含糊的**
  [巧记]派生词:vagueness (*n.* 含糊,不明确); vaguely (*ad.* 不明确地)
  [语境]She has only a vague idea of that incident.
  她对那件事只有模糊的印象。

valid [ˈvælɪd] *a.* **有效的;有根据的;正当的**
  [巧记]派生词:validate(*v.* 使有效,确认,使生效); validation (*n.* 批准;确认;合法授权)
  [语境] Oversleeping is not a valid excuse for being late for school.
  睡过头并不是上学迟到的正当理由。

valuable [ˈvæljuəbəl] *a.* **贵重的,有价值的** *n.* (*pl.*) **贵重物品,财宝**
  [巧记]value(价值) + -able
  [语境] She has put all her valuables in the bank.
  她已把她所有的贵重物品存进了银行。

value [ˈvælju:] *n.* **价值,实用性,重要性** *vt.* **评价,估计;尊重,重视**
  [巧记]派生词:valuable *a.* 有价值的,贵重的 *n. pl.* 贵重物品,财宝
  [语境] The value of that antique is inestimable.
  那件古董的价值无法估计。
  The value of most newspaper writing is only fugitive.
  大多新闻报道的价值都不长久。
  [考点] a rise in value 价格上涨; average value 平均值; value at 估(某物的)价格为……

van[væn] *n.* **有篷货车,搬运车**
  [语境]The bus and the van collided.
  公共汽车与运货车相撞了。

variety [vəˈraɪəti] *n.* **种种,多种多样;种类,品种**
  [巧记]词根:vary 使多样化
  [语境] This variety of dog is very useful for hunting.
  这种狗对狩猎很有用。
  [考点] in a variety of ways 用种种方法; a variety of 各种各样的,

品类繁多的

various[11] [ˈveərɪəs] *a.* **各种各样的,不同的;多方面的**
　[巧记] 派生词:variously(*ad.* 各种各样地;多方面地;不同地;各自地)
　[语境] The products we sell are many and various.
　　　　我们出售的产品是各式各样的。
　　　　For various reasons I'd prefer not to meet him.
　　　　由于各种原因,我不愿见他。

vary [ˈveərɪ] *v.* **变化,改变**
　[巧记] 派生词:various(*a.* 变化多样的);variety(*n.* 种类)
　[语境] The size of the apples varied.
　　　　那些苹果大小不同。
　　　　She varied her dress as fashion changes.
　　　　她的衣着随着潮流而变化。
　[考点] vary from...to... 从……到……不等,在……到……之间变动;vary with 随……而变化

vegetable [ˈvedʒɪtəbl] *n.* **植物,蔬菜**
　[语境] The land is cultivated with rice, cotton and vegetable.
　　　　地里种着水稻、棉花和蔬菜。

venture [ˈventʃə(r)] *v./n.* **冒险,拼,闯** *v.* **敢于,大胆表示** *n.* **冒险(事业)**
　[语境] Don't venture into the jungle without a guide.
　　　　没有向导,不要冒险进入丛林中。
　　　　Writers should venture at exploration and creation.
　　　　作家要勇于探索,敢于创新。
　[考点] venture to do sth. 冒险做某事

very [ˈverɪ] *ad.* **很,非常;完全** *a.* **正是的;真正的,真实的**
　[语境] This is a very exciting book.
　　　　这是一本非常扣人心弦的书。

veteran [ˈvetərən] *n.* **老手,老兵** *a.* **老练的**
　[语境] The baseball veteran loved to coach young players.
　　　　这位棒球老手喜欢指导年轻选手。

We asked two veteran nutritionists to help us identify seven great foods most of us skip.

我们邀请了两位富有经验的营养学家帮助我们识别7种被我们大多数人忽视的健康食品。

via [ˈvaɪə] *prep.* 经；通过；凭借

[语境] The flight is routed to Chicago via New York.

这个航班经纽约飞往芝加哥。

victim[9] [ˈvɪktɪm] *n.* 牺牲品，受害者

[语境] The victim was knifed in the chest.

受害者胸部被刺了一刀。

victory [ˈvɪktərɪ] *n.* 胜利，获胜

[语境] The man put up a valiant fight for victory.

这个人为了赢得胜利进行了英勇的斗争。

Our chances of victory are very faint now.

现在我们取胜的机会已经微乎其微了。

[考点] 形容词：victorious in sth. 在……成功的

video [ˈvɪdɪəʊ] *n.* 电视，视频，录像 *a.* 电视的，视频的；录像的

[语境] The children are addicted to video games.

孩子们醉心于电视游戏。

videophone [ˈvɪdɪəʊfəʊn] *n.* 视频电话

[语境] Your wristwatch videophone suddenly rings.

突然，你手表上的可视电话响了。

view [vjuː] *n.* 观察，视域，录像 *a.* 电视的，视频的；录像的

[语境] His view of life is different from yours.

他的人生观与你的不同。

The valley was hidden from view in the mist.

峡谷隐没在雾霭之中，看不见了。

viewer [ˈvjuːə(r)] *n.* 电视观众，观众

[语境] There was no rivalry then between the viewer and the reader.

在那个年代，观众和读者之间没有较量。

viewpoint [ˈvjuːpɔɪnt] *n.* 观点

[巧记] view(观察) + point(点) → 观点

[语境] He explained his viewpoint that taxes should be increased.
他解释了他认为应该增加税收的观点。

village [ˈvɪlɪdʒ] *n.* 村,村庄

[语境] The car slushed through the village.
汽车在泥泞中穿过了村庄。

violate [ˈvaɪəleɪt] *vt.* 违反,违背,违例

[巧记] 派生词:violation(*n.* 违反;违犯;违背;违反行为),violative(*a.* 违犯的;亵渎的;妨害的)

[语境] The country violated the international agreement.
这个国家违反了国际协议。

I'm committed not to violate the rules.
我有义务不违反规定。

[考点] violate a law 犯法;violate sleep 妨碍睡眠;violate sb.'s privacy 侵扰某人的安静;闯入私室

violence [ˈvaɪələns] *n.* 猛烈,强烈;暴力,暴行;强暴

[巧记] 词根:violent(*a.* 猛烈的,强烈的)

[语境] War is the most acute form of expression of violence.
战争是暴力所表现的最剧烈的形式。

[考点] use violence 用暴力;an act of violence 暴力行为;do violence to 损害,侮辱,侵[伤]害;违犯;歪曲事实

violent [ˈvaɪələnt] *a.* 猛烈的,强烈的,剧烈的;强暴的,由暴力引起的

[巧记] 派生词:violator(*n.* 违背者;侵犯者;亵渎者),violence(*n.* 暴力,暴行,暴虐)

[语境] They showed violent opposition to the oppressor.
他们对压迫者表现出强烈的不满。

One must deplore their violent behavior.
人人都会强烈反对他们的残暴行为。

[考点] violent storm 十一级风;暴风;violent acceleration 急剧加速

virtual [ˈvɜːtʃuəl] *a.* 虚的,虚拟的;实际上的

[巧记] virtu[e] + -al

[语境] A virtual state of war exists between the two countries.

这两国间实际上处于战争状态。

Our deputy manager is the virtual head of the business.

我们的副经理是公司的实际负责人。

virus ['vaɪərəs] *n.* 病毒

[语境] All of the software would be napooed by such a virus.

这种病毒能毁坏整个软件。

visa ['viːzə] *n.* 签证

[语境] The visa expires next month.

签证下月到期。

vision ['vɪʒən] *n.* 视觉,视力;幻想,幻影;眼力,想象力,远见

[巧记] 同义词:sight(*n.* 视觉)

[语境] How do you cope with the problem of poor vision?

你怎样解决视力不好这一难题呢?

It came within my range of vision.

它进入了我的视野。

[考点] the field of vision 视野;a person of broad vision 见解广阔的人;beyond one's vision 在视野之外,看不见的

visit ['vɪzɪt] *n.* 访问,参观 *v.* 访问,参观;视察;降临;闲谈

[语境] I'm going to visit my aunt for a few days.

我打算去姑妈家住几天。

visual[19] ['vɪzjuəl] *a.* 视觉的

[语境] The film is a visual art.

电影是一种视觉艺术

vital ['vaɪtəl] *a.* 极其重要的,致命的;生命的,有生机的

[巧记] 同源词:vitality(*n.* 活力,生动性,生命力)

[语境] She's a very vital sort of person.

她是个精力旺盛的人。

This matter is of vital importance to us.

这件事对我们来说至关重要。

[考点] vital force 生命力;活力;vital spark 精神

vitamin ['vɪtəmɪn] *n.* 维生素

[语境] Vitamin C is supposed to prevent colds.

维生素 C 可以预防感冒。

voice[vɔɪs] *n.* 嗓音,声音;发言权

[语境]There was a sound of loud voices from the kitchen.

厨房传来一阵喧闹声。

But your partners will have no voice in how you operate your company.

但是你的合伙人对你如何经营公司不会有发言权。

volunteer[19] [ˌvɒlənˈtɪə(r)] *n./v.* 志愿者(兵);志愿提供

[语境] The volunteers for community service are doing a good job.

社区服务的志愿者做得很出色。

vote [vəʊt] *n.* 选票,选票数 *v./n.* 选举,表决

[语境] The show was voted a success.

大家一致认为表演很成功。

UK nationals get the vote at 18.

英国国民 18 岁开始有选举权。

[考点] vote against 投票反对;vote for 投票赞成;vote on 对……进行表决;vote through 投票通过

voyage [ˈvɔɪɪdʒ] *n.* 航海,航程 *vt.* 海行

[语境] The ship went under on its first voyage.

那只船在首次航行时就沉没了。

[考点] voyage 一般专指海上和太空的旅行

考点集训

1. The neighborhood boys like to play basketball on that _____ lot.
   A. valid   B. vacant
   C. vain   D. vague
2. The hopes, goals, fears and desires _____ widely between men and women, between the rich and the poor.
   A. alter   B. shift
   C. transfer   D. vary
3. _____ recent developments we do not think your scheme is practical.

    A. In view of   B. In favor of
    C. In case of   D. In memory of

4. Since retiring, father has had a great deal of _____ time on his hand.

    A. occupied   B. booked up
    C. tenantless   D. vacant

5. Your reason for refusing to help are quite _____ ; I can't understand it clearly.

    A. obvious   B. typical
    C. vague   D. unreasonable

6. He thought the painting was of little _____ , so he let me have it only for ten pounds.

    A. cost   B. value
    C. price   D. expense

7. The kite went so high, it seemed to _____ in the clouds.

    A. dissolve   B. melt
    C. penetrate   D. vanish

8. During observations made over a fifty-year period the power output of the sun has _____ than a few tenths of one percent.

    A. varied by no more   B. varied no more by
    C. not varied more by   D. more varied by not

9. The x and y by Ayn Rand are two lengthy novels that serve as _____ her philosophy of objectivism.

    A. an escape from   B. vehicles for
    C. ends to   D. chapters in

10. He _____ to insist on certain changes.

    A. bets   B. ventures
    C. gambles   D. tries

11. Early in life she chose nursing as her _____ .

    A. future   B. hobby
    C. vocation   D. profession

12. The flood _____ were taken to the hospital in a neighboring

town.
   A. witnesses   B. victims
   C. patients   D. emigrates
13. The candidate's _____ at the poll is overwhelming.
   A. victory   B. defeat
   C. popularity   D. triumph

答案与解析

1. B 邻家的男孩子喜欢在那片空地上打篮球。A 有效的;B 空着的;C 徒劳的,无作用的;D 模糊的,不清楚的。故 B 为正确答案。

2. D 希望、目标、恐惧和欲望因性别和贫富的差别而有所不同。A 改变,变更;B 转变,变化;C 转移;D 不同,多样化。从意思上来看,D 为正确答案。

3. A 根据题干中 we do not think your scheme is practical,得知空格处应填入表示"依据"的词。in view of 表示"考虑到,依据,由于";in favor of 表示"赞同,有利于";in case of 表示"假设,万一";in memory of 表示"纪念,追念"。答案为 A。

4. D 退休后,父亲有了很多的空闲时间。occupied 占有的,占用的;booked up 预订的;tenantless 无人租用的。

5. C 你拒绝帮助的原因十分模糊,我弄不明白。obvious 明显的;typical 典型的;unreasonable 不合情理的。

6. B 他认为这幅画不值钱,所以只要 10 镑就卖给我了。cost 花费,成本;price 价格;expense 花销,花费;value 价值。

7. D 风筝飞得太高了,仿佛消失在云中一样。melt 融化;dissolve 驱散,散开;penetrate 突然不见,逐渐消失,消散。

8. A 经过为期 50 年的观察,太阳发出的能量差别不过千分之一。只有 A 中的 no more 可以和 by 组成一个词组,其他的不行。no more than 不超过。

9. B x 和 y 是 Ayn Rand 的两部表达她唯心主义哲学的长篇小说。an escape from 逃避;ends to……的终结;chapters in……的章节。

10. B 他大胆坚持要做某些改变。bet 打赌;gamble 赌博,孤注一掷。
11. C 在她生活的早期,她选择了护士作为职业。future 将来;hobby 爱好;profession 侧重指需要比较高的技术的专业。
12. B 水灾的受害者被送到邻镇的医院。witness 目击者;patients 病人;emigrates 移民。
13. A 候选人在选举中取得了压倒多数的胜利。defeat 击败;popularity 流行,受欢迎;triumph 巨大的成功。

Word List 49

wage [weɪdʒ] *n. (pl.)* 工资,报酬

[巧记]派生词:wage-earner(*n.* 拿工资者,挣钱的人,有工资的人)

[语境]We've decided to negotiate with the employers about our wage claim.
我们决定就工资问题与雇主谈判。
How do they manage to subsist on such a low wage?
他们这点工资怎么糊口?

[考点] salary 是其近义词;wage 是指一般的工资,包含月工资

wait [weɪt] *v.* (for)等待;(on)侍候 *n.* 等候,等待时间

[语境]He kept us waiting for ages while he packed his luggage.
他收拾行李,让我们等了好半天。

waiter [ˈweɪtə(r)] *n.* (男)侍者,(男)服务员

[巧记]wait(等待) + er(人)→在旁边等你点菜的人→服务员

[语境]He got work in a hotel as a waiter.
他在一家旅馆找到了当服务生的工作。

wake [weɪk] *v.* 醒来,唤醒;使觉醒,激发,引起

[语境] The incident woke memories of his past sufferings.
这件事唤起了他对过去苦难经历的回忆。

529

[考点] wake up 醒来；开始警觉

walk [wɔ:k] *v.* 走，步行，散步；走遍 *n.* 走，步行，散步

[语境] I missed the bus and had to walk home.

我没赶上公共汽车，只好走回家。

wall [wɔ:l] *n.* 墙壁，围墙

[语境] There are four windows and two doors in the wall.

墙上有四个窗户和两扇门。

want [wɒnt] *vt.* 想要；希望；需要；缺，缺少 *n.* 需要；短缺

[语境] I want to speak to her in the matter of my salary.

我想跟她谈谈我的薪水问题。

war [wɔ:(r)] *n.* 战争，战斗

[语境] The book gave a graphic description of the war.

这本书生动地描述了战争的情况。

warm [wɔ:m] *a.* 温暖的，热心的，热情的 *v.* (使)变暖

[语境] The room was furnished in warm reds and browns.

这个房间是用红色和棕色装饰的暖色调。

[考点] warm up 热身；变暖；重新加热；warm work 激烈冲突

warmth [wɔ:mθ] *n.* 暖和，温暖；热心，热情

[巧记] warm(温暖的)+th(名词后缀)→温暖

[语境] We felt the warmth of the sun.

我们感受到太阳的温暖。

warn [wɔ:n] *v.* 警告，告诫

[语境] I warned them that there might be snakes in the woods.

我提醒他们树林里可能有蛇。

He warned us against pickpockets.

他告诉我们要小心扒手。

[考点] warn sb. of... 警告某人……

warning ['wɔ:nɪŋ] *n.* 警告

[语境] Experts regarded it as a warning signal of an economic smashup.

专家们把它看作一场经济灾难的警告信号。

wash [wɒʃ] *n.* 洗；洗的衣物 *vt.* 冲刷，洗；冲出 *vi.* 洗澡

530

[语境]She has a large wash this week.

这星期她有大量衣服要洗。

waste [weɪst] *a.* 荒废的,没用的 *vt./n.* 浪费,消耗 *n.* 废物,废品

[语境] It's only a waste of time to speak to her.

和她说话纯粹是浪费时间。

All his efforts were wasted.

他的所有努力都白费了。

watch [wɒtʃ] *v.* 观看;看守;(for)窥伺,等待 *n.* 看管;表

[语境] He watched to see what would happen.

他观察着,看会发生什么情况。

watchful ['wɒtʃf(ʊ)l] *a.* 警惕的

[语境]It is important that health organizations remain watchful.

卫生组织保持警惕是极为重要的。

water ['wɔːtə(r)] *n.* 水 *vt.* 浇灌;给……饮水 *vi.* 流泪,加水

[语境]Water is changed into steam by heat and into ice by cold.

水加热则成为蒸汽,冷却则成为冰。

wave [weɪv] *n.* 波浪;(挥手)示意;飘扬 *v.* (挥手)示意,致意

[语境] The flag waved in the wind.

旗帜在风中飘扬。

He waved the servant out of his room.

他挥手叫仆人离开房间。

way [weɪ] *n.* 道路,路程;方法/式,手段;习惯;状态

[语境]She showed them the way to do it.

她向他们示范做这件事的方法。

we [wiː, wɪ] *pron.* 我们

[语境]We reminded them that the meeting had been postponed.

我们提醒他们会议已经延期。

weak [wiːk] *a.* 虚弱的,软弱的;不够标准的;淡薄的,稀的

[巧记]派生词:weak-headed(*a.* 易醉的;优柔寡断的;怯懦的;迟钝的)

[语境] Your argument is too weak to convince me.

你的论点太薄弱了,说服不了我。

weaken [ˈwiːkən] v. (使)变弱,虚弱
　[巧记]同根词:weak(a. 瘦弱的);weakness(n. 瘦弱/弱小);反义词:strengthen
　[语境] These internal disputes have weakened the Party's power.
　　这些内部纠纷削弱了这个政党的力量。
　　She weakened as the illness grew worse.
　　随着病情加重,她的身体日渐衰弱。

weakness [ˈwiːknɪs] n. 衰弱,软弱;弱点,缺点
　[语境] I have got over my weakness and fatigue.
　　我已从虚弱和疲劳中恢复过来了。
　　It is my great weakness now.
　　这是我现在极大的弱点。

wealth [welθ] a. 富,财产;丰富,大量
　[语境] It is believed that health is above wealth.
　　一般人都相信健康重于财富。
　　Health is better than wealth.
　　【谚】健康胜于财富。
　[考点]wealthy a. 有财富的,丰富的,富裕的

wealthy [ˈwelθɪ] a. 富裕的,富有的,富庶的
　[语境]He cheated her into believing him a wealthy man.
　　他骗得她相信他是一个富翁。

weapon [ˈwepən] n. 武器,兵器
　[语境]This weapon can kill at a range of 200 yards.
　　这种兵器在200码内有杀伤力。

wear [weə(r)] v. 穿着,戴着;磨损,用旧 n. 穿,戴;磨损
　[语境]Plain and simple clothes are appropriate for school wear.
　　朴素的服装适合在学校里穿。

weary [ˈwɪərɪ] a. (of) 疲倦的;令人厌烦的 vt. 使疲倦
　[语境]He managed a weary smile.
　　他勉强挤出了一丝疲倦的笑容。
　　He had wearied of teaching in state universities.
　　他已经厌烦了在州立大学教书。

[考点] weary of 厌烦了……

weather ['weðə(r)] *n.* 天气,气象

[语境] The weather was bad.
天气很糟。

web [web] *n.* 蜘蛛网;网状物

[语境] I found this on the web.
这是我在网上找到的。

website[5] ['websaɪt] *n.* 网址

[巧记] web(网) + site(地址)→网址

[语境] I created a bookmark for my favourite website.
我为自己最喜欢的网址创建了一个书签。

wedding ['wedɪŋ] *n.* 婚礼

[语境] Most Britons want a traditional wedding.
大多数英国人都想要传统的婚礼。

Wednesday ['wenzdɪ] *n.* 星期三

[语境] He undertook to finish the job by Wednesday.
他答应在星期三以前完成这项工作。

week [wiːk] *n.* 星期,周

[语境] Sunday is the first day of the week.
星期日是一周的第一天。

weekday ['wiːkdeɪ] *n.* 周日,工作日

[语境] We never see each other on weekday evenings because we both work.
我们从不在晚上见面,因为我们都有活干。

weekend [ˌwiːk'end] *n.* 周末

[语境] Is there any possibility that you'll be back by the weekend?
周末以前你有可能回来吗?

weekly ['wiːklɪ] *a.* 每星期的,一周的 *ad.* 每周一次 *n.* 周刊,周报

[巧记] week(一周) + ly(形容词后缀)→每星期的

[语境] He writes a weekly letter to his parents.
他每周给父母写一封信。

weep [wiːp] *vi.* 哭泣,流泪 *n.* 悲叹,哀悼,为……伤心

[语境]She wanted to laugh and weep all at once.
她哭笑不得。
[考点]weep about sb. 为某人哭泣

weigh [weɪ] *vi.* 重…… *vt.* 称,量;重,重达;考虑,权衡
[语境] It's been weighing on my mind for days whether to tell her or not.
我这几天心烦意乱,不知道应不应该告诉她。
He weighed in at several pounds below the limit.
他赛前量体重比规定限度少几磅。
[考点] weigh down 压下,使下垂;weigh on 使焦虑,使担忧;weigh sth. out 量出,称出

weight[weɪt] *n.* 重量,体重;砝码,秤砣;重压,负担;重要性,价值
[语境]He blinked at the weights of the players.
他对那些运动员的体重感到吃惊。
Another factor is the weight of the evidence.
其次是此次证据的重要性。

welcome [ˈwelkəm] *int.* 欢迎 *a.* 受欢迎的 *vt. /n.* 欢迎;迎接
[语境]Welcome to China!
欢迎到中国来!

well [wel] *ad.* 好,令人满意地;很 *int.* 哎呀,好啦,嗯
[语境] Read the document well before you sign it.
仔细审阅文件后方可签字。

well-known[ˌwelˈnəʊn] *a.* 知名的
[语境]The well-known professor espies the smallest slip I make.
我一有哪怕最小的差错,那位著名的教授都能看出来。

west[west] *n. /a.* 西,西部,西方 *ad.* 向/自/在西方
[语境]The window opens to the west.
这扇窗户是向西开的。

wet [wet] *a.* 湿的,潮湿的;有雨的,多雨的 *v.* 弄湿,沾湿
[语境]My overcoat is wet through.
我的大衣完全湿透了。

what [wɔt] *pron.* 什么 *a.* 多么,何等;什么;尽可能多的

核心词汇精解

[语境]What color is your dress?
你的衣服是什么颜色?

whatever [wɔt'evə(r)] *pron.* 无论什么 *a.* 无论什么样的

[语境] We will never give up working, whatever happens.
无论发生什么事,我们都不会放弃工作。

wheat[wi:t] *n.* 小麦

[语境]They are cropping wheat.
他们正在收割小麦。

wheel[wi:l] *n.* 轮,车轮

[语境]The mechanic has trued up a wheel.
机修工已经装准了一个轮子。

when [wen]*ad.* /*pron.* 何时;当时 *conj.* 那时;然后;而

[语境]How can they learn anything when they spend all their spare time watching television?
他们把所有的空闲时间都用来看电视了,还能学什么东西呢?

whenever [wen'evə(r)]*conj.* 无论何时,随时;每当

[语境]I'd like to see you whenever it's convenient.
在你方便的时候我想来看看你。

where [weə(r)]*ad.* 在哪/那里 *conj.*/*pron.* 哪里 *conj.* 然而

[语境]Where did she get the news?
她从哪儿得到这个消息的?

wherever[weər'evə(r)] *ad.* 无论(去)哪里;究竟在/到哪里 *conj.* 无论在/到哪里

[语境]Some people enjoy themselves wherever they are.
有些人能够随遇而安。

whether ['weðə(r)]*conj.* 是否,会不会;不管,无论

[语境] We pondered whether to tell her.
我们考虑是否要告诉她。

Little does he care whether we live or die.
他一点也不管我们是死是活。

[考点] whether 一般可以引导宾语从句

· 535 ·

which [wɪtʃ] *a./pron.* 哪个,哪些;什么样的;那个,那些
[语境]Here are the chairs. Tell me which are worth buying.
就是这些椅子。告诉我买哪几把好。

whichever [wɪtʃˈevə(r)] *pron./a.* 无论哪个,无论哪些
[语境]I have three cars, and you may have whichever you like.
我有三辆车,你可以挑一辆你喜欢的。

while/whilst [waɪl/waɪlst] *conj.* 当……的时候;而;虽然;尽管 *n.* 一会儿
[语境]While Mary was writing a letter, the children were playing outside.
玛丽写信时,孩子们在外面玩耍。

考点集训

1. As he has _____ our patience, we'll not wait for him any longer.
   A. torn   B. wasted
   C. exhausted   D. consumed

2. _____ elephants are different from wild elephants in many aspects, including their tempers.
   A. Cultivated   B. Regulated
   C. Civil   D. Tame

3. She was paid by the hour, and she managed to keep her family with her pitiful _____.
   A. salary   B. wages
   C. stipend   D. payment

4. A good student is eager to learn and does not need to be _____ for being absent too much.
   A. punished   B. belittled
   C. spanked   D. warned

5. Her coffee was too strong, so Sally _____ it with milk.
   A. flavored   B. soaked
   C. softened   D. weakened

6. Some people say that health is _____ because they consider good

health more valuable than money or material possessions.

   A. value B. strength
   C. significance D. wealth

7. He _____ the books he no longer needed.

   A. brought out D. brought about
   C. weeded out D. broke away

8. He lost control of his feelings and began to _____.

   A. itch B. burn
   C. suppurate D. weep

9. Both the advantages and disadvantages of using foreign faculty in teaching positions have to be _____.

   A. regulated B. weighed
   C. shielded D. screwed

10. She is in _____ work; she helps people who have no jobs, family problems, etc.

    A. pension B. subsidy
    C. prospect D. welfare

答案与解析

1. C 我们对他完全没有耐心了,我们不能再等他了。A 撕裂,撕碎;B 浪费;C 穷尽;D 消费。故选 C。

2. D 驯服的大象跟野生大象在许多方面存在不同,包括他们的脾气。A 培养,开发;B 被管理的;C 市民的,公民的;D 驯养的。故选 D。

3. B 她按小时取酬,以微薄的薪金养家。salary 指的是月薪;stipend 俸禄,薪金;payment 为常用词,为报酬,付款。

4. D 好学生总是热爱学习,不需要别人老是提醒不要逃课。punish 惩罚;belittle 蔑视,贬低;spank 用手掌打(一般指打小孩的屁股)。

5. D 萨利觉得她的咖啡太浓了,所以用牛奶冲淡了。flavor 给……调味,给……加味;soak 浸,泡;soften 使……变柔软。

6. D 有人说健康就是财富,因为他们认为身体的健康比钱财或物质财富更有价值。value 经济学中的价值,wealth 指本身就有一大笔的财富。

7. C　他把不需要的书清理出去。brought out 生产,出版;brought about 造成,带来;broke away 逃脱;weed out 清理,淘汰。

8. D　他控制不住感情,开始哭泣。itch 痒;burn 燃烧;suppurate 化脓。

9. B　用外籍员工担任教学职务的优缺点都要考虑到。regulate 调节;shield 保护;screw 拧紧。

10. D　她从事福利事业,她向失业者或有家庭问题等的各种人员提供帮助。pension 福利金,养老金;subsidy 补助金,津贴;prospect 前景,前途。

Word List 50

white[waɪt] *a.* 白的,白色的;苍白的;白种的 *n.* 白色;白种人
[语境]I saw his white car rolling along the highway.
我看见他的白色汽车沿公路驶去。
Moreover, it is not just a question of white supremacy.
此外,这不仅仅是白种人优越的问题了。

white-collar[ˌwaɪtˈkɒlə(r)] *a.* 白领阶层的;脑力劳动者的
[语境]I am a white-collar worker.
我是脑力劳动者。

who [huː] *pron.* 谁,什么人;……的人;他,她,他们
[语境]People who cannot speak can talk by using signs.
不会说话的人可以用手势沟通。

whoever [huːˈevə(r)] *pron.* [引导名词从句]谁;无论谁;究竟是谁
[语境]Whoever commits the crime shall be sentenced to ten years in prison.
任何人犯了此罪就要被判处十年徒刑。

whole [həʊl] *n.* 全部 *a.* 全体的;全部的;完整的;无缺的

[语境] The whole country was anxious for peace.

全国上下都渴望和平。

wholly [ˈhəʊlɪ] *ad.* 完全,一概

[语境] They contract work out wholly.

他们把工作全部包了出去。

whom [hu:m] *pron.* [宾格]谁

[语境] From whom shall I get comfort?

我从谁那儿能得到安慰呢?

whose [hu:z] *pron.* 谁的;哪个(人)的,哪些(人)的

[语境] Whose turn is it to treat next?

下次该谁请客了?

why [waɪ] *ad./conj.* 为什么;……的理由 *int.* 咳,哎呀

[语境] Why not let her do as she likes?

为什么不让她想怎么做就怎么做呢?

wide [waɪd] *a.* 宽阔的;睁大的;远离的 *ad.* 广阔地;偏差地

[巧记] 反义词: narrow(*adj.* 狭窄的)

[语境] He is a man of wide interests.

他兴趣广泛。

[考点] wide-eyed 天真的,吃惊的;wide awake 十分清醒的;机敏的

widespread[6] [ˈwaɪdspred] *a.* 普遍的,分布广的

[巧记] wide(广的) + spread(散布,散开)→分布广的

[语境] Widespread flooding is affecting large areas of Devon.

洪水泛滥,淹没了德文郡的广大地区。

The high cost prohibits the widespread use of the drug.

较高的成本影响了这种药的广泛使用。

wife [waɪf] *n.* 妻子,夫人,太太

[语境] I run the shop and my wife does the bookkeeping.

我经营商店,妻子记账。

wild [waɪld] *a.* 野性的,野生的;野蛮的;狂热的;荒芜的

[语境] In nature, all animals are wild and free.

在自然界,一切动物都是野生的、自由自在的。

[考点] wild about 热衷于;wild animal 野兽

wildlife[14] ['waɪldlaɪf] *n.* 野生动物

[巧记] wild(野生的) + life(生命)→野生的、有生命的生物→野生动物

[语境] This area was once a wildlife reserve.
该地区曾是一个野生动物保护区。

will [wɪl] *aux. v.* 将;会;愿意 *n.* 意志;决心;愿望

[语境] Free will makes us able to choose our way of life.
自由的意志使我们可以选择自己的生活方式。

win [wɪn] *vi.* 获胜,赢 *vt.* 赢得;在……中获胜 *n.* 胜利

[语境] A competitive person loves to win and hates to lose.
竞争心强的人喜欢赢,讨厌输。

wind [wɪnd] *n.* 风;气息 *v.* 转动;缠绕;上发条;蜿蜒而行

[语境] In northern countries, a north wind is colder than a south wind.
在北方各国,北风比南风冷。

window ['wɪndəʊ] *n.* 窗,窗户

[语境] They climbed out through the window.
他们从窗户爬出来。

wine [waɪn] *n.* (葡萄)酒,果酒

[语境] He filled the bottle with wine.
他用酒装满了那只瓶子。

winter ['wɪntə(r)] *n.* 冬天

[语境] He prophesied that there would be a bad winter.
他预言,将会有一个气候恶劣的冬天。

wipe [waɪp] *v./n.* 擦,揩,抹

[语境] She wiped her tears away.
她擦掉了眼泪。

[考点] wipe off 擦去;去除;wipe out 擦洗……的内部,洗雪,去除;wipe up 擦干净;消灭

wisdom ['wɪzdəm] *n.* 智慧,明智;名言,格言;古训

[巧记] 词根:wise *a.* 聪明的,明智的,博学的;反义词:folly, stupidity

[语境] According to conventional wisdom, voters usually make their choice on the basis of domestic issues.

根据传统的思想,选民常常着眼于国内问题来选择候选人。

She had acquired much wisdom during her long life.

她经年累月造就了很高的智慧。

[考点] wisdom tooth 智齿

wise [waɪz] *a.* 有智慧的,聪明的

[巧记]派生词:wiseacre(*n.* 自以为聪明者,自以为懂事的人);反义词:foolish

[语境] Learned men are not necessarily wise.

博学者未必都是聪明的。

wish [wɪʃ] *v.* 希望;但愿;祝 *n.* 愿望,希望;[*pl.*]祝愿

[语境] His colleagues wished him happiness on his retirement.

他退休时同事们祝他幸福。

[考点] get one's wish 达到愿望,如愿以偿;wish for 希望得到,渴望

with [wɪð] *prep.* 跟……一起;用;具有;关于;因;随着

[语境] I leave the baby with my mother every day.

我每天都把婴儿交给我母亲照料。

within [wɪˈðɪn] *prep.* 在……里面,在……以内 *ad.* 在内

[语境] We did the work within the time they had allotted to us.

我们在指定的时间内把工作做完了。

without [wɪˈðaʊt] *prep.* 无,没有 *n.* 外面,外部

[语境] I feel very lonely without my dog.

我的狗不在旁边我就很寂寞。

witness[5] [ˈwɪtnɪs] *n.* 目击者,见证人 *vt.* 目击,证明

[巧记] 派生词:witnessable (*adj.* 可目睹的)

[语境] Police have appealed for witnesses to come forward.

警方呼吁目击者挺身而出。

Did anyone witness the traffic accident?

有谁目击了这场交通事故?

541

wolf[wʊlf] *n.* 狼
　[语境]The hunter is following up a wolf.
　　那猎人正在追踪一条狼。
　[考点]复数:wolves

woman['wʊmən] *n.* 妇女,女人
　[语境]In the film she was cast as a hardworking upright middleaged woman.
　　她在这部影片中扮演了一个勤劳正直的中年妇女。

wonder ['wʌndə(r)] *n.* 惊奇,惊异;奇迹,奇事 *v.*(at)诧异;想知道
　[巧记]派生词:wonderful(*a.* 令人惊奇的,极好的,奇妙的), wondering(*a.* 觉得奇怪的;疑惑的)
　[语境] The Great Wall is one of the wonders of the world.
　　长城是世界奇观之一。
　[考点] the seven wonders of the world 世界七大奇观

wonderful['wʌndəf(ʊ)l] *a.* 惊人的,奇妙的,极好的
　[巧记]wonder(奇迹)+ful(充满……)→充满奇迹的→惊人的,奇妙的
　[语境]The audience rose to his wonderful performance.
　　他的精彩表演使观众情绪高涨。

wood[wʊd] *n.* 木头,木材;(*pl.*)小森林,树林
　[语境]I like working in the best wood.
　　我喜欢用最好的木料做活。
　　We tramped through the wood for over two hours until we arrived at a deep stream.
　　我们在树林中跋涉了两个多小时,到了一条深溪边。

word [wɜːd] *n.* 词,单词;言语,话;诺言,保证;音信,消息;文本文档
　[语境]How do you pronounce this word?
　　这个单词怎么发音?
　　Attend to my word.
　　注意听我的话。
　　I will hold me to my word.

我一定会遵守诺言的。

work [wɜːk] *n.* 工作(量);作品;(*pl.*) 工厂 *v.* 工作;运转

[语境] He's got a lot more work to do on the book.

这本书他还有许多工作要做。

worker [ˈwɜːkə(r)] *n.* 工人,工作者

[语境] The worker was labelled as a revolutionary.

这个工人被说成是一名革命者。

workshop [ˈwɜːkʃɒp] *n.* 工场,车间;研讨会,讲习班

[巧记] work(工作) + shop(工厂) → 车间

[语境] The workers parted gold from silver in the workshop.

在车间里工人们把金子从银子中提炼出来。

If you have all this information before you conduct a portal workshop, then you are ahead of the game.

如果在召开门户研讨会之前获取了所有这些信息,则您有了一个良好的开头。

world [wɜːld] *n.* 世界,地球;……界,领域;世间,人间;全世界,世人

[语境] Our world is but a small part of the cosmos.

我们的世界仅仅是宇宙的一小部分而已。

Now he hopes to take those lessons to the business world.

现在他希望能把这些课程应用到商业领域。

worldwide [ˌwɜːldˈwaɪd] *a.* 世界范围的,遍及地球的

[巧记] world(世界) + wide(宽广的) → 如同世界一样宽广的 → 遍及地球的

[语境] The wine is in high repute worldwide.

这酒在世界上享有盛名。

worried[ˈwʌrɪd] *a.* 焦虑的,烦恼的,担忧的

[语境] The mother is worried about her son's safety.

这位母亲担心她儿子的安全。

worry [ˈwʌrɪ] *v.* 烦恼;(about) 对……感到烦恼 *n.* 烦恼,焦虑

[语境] Don't worry how much you spend on the trip.

别担心花多少钱用于旅行。

worse [wɜːs] *a./ad.* 更坏,更差

[语境] His praise would only cart me worse.

他的表扬只会让我处境更糟。

worst [wɜːst] *a./ad.* 最坏,最差

[语境] This is her worst film.

这是她最糟糕的电影。

worth [wɜːθ] *prep.* 值……,值得……的 *n.* 价值

[语境] The book is worth reading.

这本书值得读。

The book is worth 5 yuan.

这本书值五元钱。

Whatever is worth doing at all is worth doing well.

任何值得做的事就值得做好。

[考点] worth 后面可以直接跟名词,或动名词

worthwhile [wɜːθˈwaɪl] *a.* 值得(做)的

[语境] That's worthwhile.

那是值得的。

Thank you for making my visit so worthwhile. I shall treasure your friendship and kind hospitality you have given me.

感谢你们使我的访问如此有价值。我将珍惜我们之间的友谊及你们给予我的盛情款待。

[考点] worthwhile 表示的是值得做的事

would [wəd, wʊd] *aux./v.* 将;可能;将会;总是,总会;宁愿

[语境] He prophesied that war would break out.

他预言说战争将要爆发。

wound [wuːnd] *n.* 创伤,伤口 *vt.* 受伤,伤害

[语境] Blood started out of his wound.

血从他的伤口涌了出来。

"Did you get wounded, Uncle Rhett?"

"您受过伤吗,瑞德伯伯?"

[考点] get wounded 受伤

wrap [ræp] *v.* 裹,缠,卷,包 *n.* 披肩,围巾

[巧记] 派生词: wrapped (*a.* 在恋爱中的; 谦恭顺从的; 狂热发昏的), wrapper (*n.* 包装材料, 书皮, 包装纸)

[语境] You'd better wrap it with a piece of clean cloth.
你最好用一块干净的布把它包起来。
Mind you wrap up well if you go out.
你出外的话要围好围巾。

[考点] wrap around 卷绕的, 环绕的, 抱合的; be wrapped up in 包在……里, 被……掩蔽, 被……笼罩; wrap up *n.* 总结, 报告的最后总结; 新闻摘要 *v.* 收拾好, 打好包, 盖好; 结束, 处理最后的细节

wretched ['retʃɪd] *a.* 不幸的, 可怜的; 卑鄙的, 无耻的

[语境] The pay has always been wretched.
薪水总是少得可怜。
Clearly, it is my sacred duty to smite these wretched abominations.
很明显, 彻底击垮这些卑鄙可憎的东西是我神圣的职责。

write [raɪt] *v.* 写, 书写, 写字; 写作; 写信(给), 函告

[语境] I've been writing for three hours.
我已经写了三个小时了。

writer ['raɪtə(r)] *n.* 作者, 作家

[语境] He is not so much a journalist as a writer.
与其说他是个新闻工作者, 不如说他是个作家。

writing ['raɪtɪŋ] *n.* 写, 写作; 文章, 著作, 作品; 笔迹, 字迹

[语境] She had begun to be a little bored with novel writing.
她开始对写小说有些厌倦了。
It was a little difficult to read your writing.
你写的字有点不好认。

wrong [rɒŋ] *a.* 错的 *ad.* 错误地, 不正确地 *n.* 错误 *v.* 委屈

[巧记] 反义词: right (*a.* 正确的)

[语境] There is something wrong with the car.
这车有点毛病。

X-ray ['eksreɪ] *n.* X 射线, X 光

[语境]She was advised to have an abdominal X-ray.

她被建议拍一张腹部的 X 光片。

yeah[jeə] *ad.* 是

[语境]Yeah. I made all of these books.

是的。这些书都是我制作的。

year [jɪə(r),jɜː(r)] *n.* 年,年度,学年 *a./ad.* 每年,一年一次

[语境]He is 16 years old.

他 16 岁了。

I've known her for years.

我认识她好几年了。

yearly[ˈjɪəlɪ] *a.* 每年的,一年一度 *ad.* 每年,一年一次地

[巧记]同义词:annually(*ad.* 一年一次,每年)

[语境]A periodical published yearly; a yearbook.

年鉴为每年出版一次的期刊;年刊

Many Greek cities had to send yearly tribute to Athens.

许多希腊城市不得不每年向雅典进贡。

yellow[ˈjeləʊ] *n./a.* 黄色

[语境]We papered the room (in) yellow.

我们用黄色墙纸裱糊房间。

yes[jes] *ad.* 是的

[语境]Yes, I know. I'd studied it up in a book.

是的,我知道,我在一本书里专门查阅过。

yesterday[ˈjestədɪ,-deɪ] *n./ad.* 昨天

[语境]I fell in upon her yesterday.

我昨天意外地遇到了她。

yet [jet] *conj.* 然而,可是 *ad.* 还,仍然;更;到目前为止

[语境] He hasn't done much yet.

他做得还不很多。

She is vain and foolish, and yet people like her.

她自负而愚蠢,然而人们喜欢她。

[考点] yet 表示转折时,语气要比 but 弱

you[juː,jʊ,jə] *pron.* 你,你们

young [jʌŋ] *a.* 年轻的,幼小的;没经验的 *n.* 青年人

[语境] I can't bear young people casting away their youth.

我无法忍受年轻人虚掷青春。

I spent my youth in the country.

我在乡间度过了青少年时代

your [jɔː(r);jə(r)] *pron.* 你的,你们的

[语境] You have your choice between the two.

在这两个之中,你有选择权。

yours [jɔːz,jʊəz] *pron.* [所有格]你的,你们的

[语境] His poem compares poorly with yours.

他的诗做得不如你的好。

yourself [jɔːˈself] *pron.* 你(们)自己,你(们)本身

[语境] Your bad behaviour reflects only on yourself.

你的恶劣行为只对你自己不利。

zero [ˈzɪərəʊ] *num.* 零 *n.* 零点,零度

[语境] The thermometer fell to zero last night.

寒暑表昨夜降至零度。

zone [zəʊn] *n.* 地带,区域

[语境] Germany, however, is not the whole zone.

然而德国并不能代表整个地区。

zoo [zuː] *n.* 动物园

[语境] How far does zoo's land go down?

动物园的地盘有多大?

考点集训

1. In the Mediterranean seaweed is so abundant and so easily harvested that it is never of great _____.

    A. fare   B. payment

    C. worth   D. expense

2. Mr. Smith says:"The media are very good at sensing a mood and then _____ it."

    A. overtaking   B. enlarging

547

C. widening D. exaggerating
3. We take our skin for granted until it is burned _____ repair.
   A. beyond B. for
   C. without D. under
4. The defense lawyer was questioning the old man who was one of the _____ of the murder committed last month.
   A. observers B. witnesses
   C. audiences D. viewers

答案与解析

1. C　地中海里海藻丰富，收获起来很容易，却从来价值不高。of great worth"价值很高的"，故选 C。

2. D　史密斯先生说："媒体擅长嗅出人类的情绪，然后夸大它。"A 追上，赶上；B 拉大，扩大；C 拓宽；D 夸大。故选 D。

3. A　我们把皮肤想成理所当然的，直到烧到难以修复为止。A 超过；B 因为；C 没有；D 在……下面。故 A 为正确答案。

4. B　根据题干中 questioning 和 murder，得知空格处应填入表示"证人"的词。observer 表示"观测者，观察员，遵守者"；witness 表示"证人，目击者"；audience 表示"听众，观众"；viewer 表示"电视观众，阅读器"。答案为 B。

认知词汇扫描

A

abnormal[4] [æb'nɔːml] a. 反常的,不正常的,不规则的
abolish [ə'bɒlɪʃ] v. 废止,革除
abortion [ə'bɔːʃən] n. 流产,堕胎
abrupt [ə'brʌpt] a. 突然的,唐突的
absurd [əb'sɜːd] a. 荒唐的
abundance [ə'bʌndəns] n. 充裕,丰富
abundant [ə'bʌndənt] a. 丰富的,充裕的
abuse [ə'bjuːs] n. 滥用,恶习 v. 滥用,辱骂,虐待
academic[8] [ˌækə'demɪk] a. 学院的,理论的,学术性的
accelerate[5] [ək'seləreɪt] vt. 使加快;使增速 vi. 加速;促进;增加
acceptance [ək'septəns] n. 接受,接纳,承认
accessory [ək'sesərɪ] n. 附件,配件;附加物件
accommodate [ə'kɒmədeɪt] vt. 为……提供膳宿;使适应
accompany [ə'kʌmpənɪ] v. 陪伴,伴随;伴奏
accomplish[4] [ə'kʌmplɪʃ] v. 完成,实现,达到
accord [ə'kɔːd] vt. 使一致;给予
accountable [ə'kaʊntəbl] a. 有责任的;有解释义务的;可解释的
accountant [ə'kaʊntənt] n. 会计
accounting [ə'kaʊntɪŋ] n. 会计,会计学
accumulate[5] [ə'kjuːmjəleɪt] vi. 积累;积聚 vt. 堆积
accuracy ['ækjərəsɪ] n. 准确(性),精确度

achievement [əˈtʃiːvmənt] n. 成就,成绩,完成,达到
acknowledge [əkˈnɒlɪdʒ] vt. (公开)承认;感谢,答谢
acquaint [əˈkweɪnt] vt. (with) 使认识;使熟悉
acquisition[7] [ˌækwɪˈzɪʃən] n. 获得,所获之物
activate [ˈæktɪveɪt] v. 刺激,使……活动,创设
acupuncture [ˈækjupʌŋktʃə(r)] n. 针刺疗法;针刺
acute [əˈkjuːt] a. 敏锐的,激烈的,尖锐的
addict [ˈædɪkt] v. 使……耽溺,使……上瘾 n. 耽溺者,上瘾者
addicted [əˈdɪktɪd] a. 沉溺于某种(尤其是不良的)嗜好的;入了迷的,上了瘾的
adequate [ˈædɪkwət] a. 足够的,充分的
adhere [ədˈhɪə(r)] v. 黏附,附着,坚持,支持
       adhere to 黏附,依附,坚持
adjective [ˈædʒɪktɪv] n. 形容词
admission [ədˈmɪʃən] n. 承认;进入许可;录用;入场费
adolescence [ˌædəˈlesns] n. 青春期
adolescent [ˌædəˈlesnt] a. 青春期的;未成熟的 n. 青少年
adore [əˈdɔː(r)] vt. 爱慕;崇拜;喜爱;[口]极喜欢
advancement [ədˈvɑːnsmənt] n. 前进,进步;提升
adverb [ˈædvɜːb] n. 副词
adverse[4] [ˈædvɜːs] a. 不利的;相反的;敌对的
advisable [ədˈvaɪzəbl] a. 明智的,可取的
advocate[4] [ˈædvəkeɪt] vt. 提倡,主张;拥护
aerial [ˈeərɪəl] a. 空气的;空中的 n. 天线
aerospace [ˈeərəuspeɪs] n. 航空宇宙;航空航天空间
aesthetic [iːsˈθetɪk] a. 美学的,审美的,有美感
aesthetics [iːsˈθetɪks] n. 美学
affection[7] [əˈfekʃən] n. 慈爱,爱,感情,作用,影响
affiliate [əˈfɪlieɪt] vt. (with) 接纳;使附属
affirm [əˈfɜːm] vt. 断言;肯定
affix [əˈfɪks] n. 词缀;附加物
affordable [əˈfɔːdəbl] a. 负担得起的

afterward(s) ['ɑːftəwədz] *ad.* 后来,以后

aggravate ['ægrəveɪt] *vt.* 加重;使恶化

aggregate ['ægrɪgət] *vi./vt.* 聚集;集合;合计

aggressive [ə'gresɪv] *a.* 侵犯的,攻击性的,有进取心的

agony ['ægəni] *n.* (极度的)痛苦,创痛

agriculture[7] ['ægrɪkʌltʃə(r)] *n.* 农业

air-conditioning [eə(r)kən'dɪʃənɪŋ] *n.* 空调,空调系统,空调机

aircraft ['eəkrɑːft] *n.* 飞机

aisle [aɪl] *n.* 走道;侧廊

alarm [ə'lɑːm] *n.* 警报,惊慌,警告,报警器 *v.* 使……惊慌,警告

album ['ælbəm] *n.* 集邮本,照相簿,唱片簿

alert[11] [ə'lɜːt] *a.* 警觉的,提防的 *vt.* (to) 使警觉 *n.* 警惕,警报

alien ['eɪliən] *n.* 外侨;外星人 *a.* 外国的,相异的

allege [ə'ledʒ] *v.* 断言,宣称

alleged [ə'ledʒd] *a.* 所谓的;声称的;被断言的

allergic [ə'lɜːdʒɪk] *a.* 对……过敏的

alleviate [ə'liːvieɪt] *vt.* 减轻,缓和

alliance[5] [ə'laɪəns] *n.* 结盟,联盟,联姻

allocate ['æləkeɪt] *vt.* 派给;分配;拨出

allowance [ə'laʊəns] *n.* 限额,定量 *n.* 津贴,零用钱

ally [ə'laɪ] *n.* 盟友,同盟国 *v.* 联盟,联合,与……有关系

aloft [ə'lɒft] *ad.* 在高处;在上面;在空中 *a.* 在上面的;在空中;在高处的

alphabet ['ælfəbet] *n.* 字母表

altar ['ɔːltə(r)] *n.* 祭坛;圣坛

alter ['ɔːltə(r)] *vt.* 改变,变更

alternate ['ɔːltəneɪt] *a.* 交替的,轮流的 *v.* 交替,轮流

alternative[5] [ɔːl'tɜːnətɪv] *a.* 两者选一的,可供选择的 *n.* 选择,替换物

altitude ['æltɪtjuːd] *n.* 高度,海拔

alumin(i)um [ˌæljʊ'mɪniəm] *n.* 铝

amass [ə'mæs] *vt.* 积聚,积累

amateur [ˈæmətə(r), -tʃə(r)] a. 业余的 n. 业余爱好者
amaze [əˈmeɪz] v. 使吃惊
　　　　　　be amazed at (by) 对……大为惊奇
amazon [ˈæməzən] n. 亚马逊
ambiguity [ˌæmbɪˈɡjuːɪtɪ] n. 含糊,不明确;暧昧
ambiguous [æmˈbɪɡjʊəs] a. 模棱两可的
amend [əˈmend] vt. 改善,改进;修改 vi. 改正,改善;改过自新
amid [əˈmɪd] prep. 在其间,在其中
ammunition [ˌæmjʊˈnɪʃən] n. 军火,弹药
ample [ˈæmpl] a. 充足的,丰富的
amplify [ˈæmplɪfaɪ] v. 扩大,详述,使……增幅
analogy [əˈnælədʒɪ] n. 类似;类推;类比
ancestor [ˈænsestə(r)] n. 祖宗,祖先
anchor[4] [ˈæŋkə(r)] n. 铁锚 v. 停泊,抛锚,用锚系住 v. 担任(广播、电视新闻节目)的主持人
anemia [əˈniːmɪə] n. 贫血;贫血症
angel [ˈeɪndʒəl] n. 天使
angle [ˈæŋɡl] n. 角,角度;观点
animate [ˈænɪmeɪt] vt. 使有生气;使活泼 a. 有生命的
ankle [ˈæŋkl] n. 踝,踝关节
anniversary [ˌænɪˈvɜːsərɪ] n. 周年纪念(日)
announce [əˈnaʊns] v. 发表,广播(电台节目),通告,正式宣布
anonymous [əˈnɒnɪməs] a. 匿名的,无名的
ant [ænt] n. 蚂蚁
antarctic [æntˈɑːktɪk] a. 南极(区)的 n. (the A-) 南极洲,南极圈
antique [ænˈtiːk] a. 古代的 n. 古物,古董
apart [əˈpɑːt] ad. 分离,隔开;相距,相隔
apparent [əˈpærənt] a. 明显的;表面的
appeal[7] [əˈpiːl] vi. (to) 请求;呼吁;吸引;上诉;求助 n. 呼吁;吸引力;上诉
appearance [əˈpɪərəns] n. 外表,出现,出场
　　　　　　at first appearance 乍看起来

in appearance 表面上,外表上

applaud [ə'plɔːd] vt. 向……喝彩;赞同;称赞 vi. 喝彩;鼓掌欢迎

appliance [ə'plaɪəns] n. 器具,器械,装置

applicant ['æplɪkənt] n. 申请者

application[5] [ˌæplɪ'keɪʃən] n. 申请 n. 应用软件程序

applied [ə'plaɪd] a. 实用的;应用的

appraise [ə'preɪz] vt. 评价,鉴定;估价

appropriate[8] [ə'prəʊprɪət] a. 适当的,恰当的

approve[9] [ə'pruːv] v. (of) 赞成,赞许,同意;批准,审议,通过

approximate [ə'prɒksɪmət] a. 大致的,近似的

apt [æpt] a. 恰当的,合适的;倾向于,易于

  be apt for 适合

  be apt to 易于;有可能

arbitrary ['ɑːbɪtrərɪ] a. 任意的;武断的;专制的

archaeology [ˌɑːkɪ'ɒlədʒɪ] n. 考古学

architect ['ɑːkɪtekt] n. 建筑师

architecture ['ɑːkɪtektʃə(r)] n. 建筑学,建筑业,[总称]建筑物,
  建筑风格

arctic ['ɑːktɪk] a. 北极的 n. (the A-) 北极

ardent ['ɑːdnt] a. 热烈的,激动的;热心的,热切的;燃烧的,炽
  热的

arena [ə'riːnə] n. 竞技场

arithmetic[8] [ə'rɪθmətɪk] n. 算术

armo(u)r ['ɑːmə(r)] n. 装甲;盔甲

army ['ɑːmɪ] n. 军队,陆军

array [ə'reɪ] n. 数组,排列,陈列,大批,一系列 v. 排列,部署,打扮

arrival [ə'raɪvəl] n. 到来,到达;到达物

arrow ['ærəʊ] n. 箭 v. 箭(头),射箭

art[7] [ɑːt] a. 美术(品)的,艺术(品)的 n. 艺术

artist ['ɑːtɪst] n. 艺术家,美术家

artistic(al) [ɑː'tɪstɪk] a. 艺术(家)的,美术(家)的

artwork ['ɑːtˌwɜːk] n. 艺术品;美术品;插图

ascend [ə'send] v. 上升,攀登

ascend to 升至;追溯(到……时间)

ascertain [ˌæsə'teɪn] v. 确定,探知

ascribe [ə'skraɪb] vt. (to) 归因于;归咎于

ash [æʃ] n. 灰,灰烬

ashore [ə'ʃɔː(r)] ad. 在岸上,上岸

aspiration [ˌæspə'reɪʃən] n. 渴望;抱负

assassinate [ə'sæsɪneɪt] vt. 暗杀;行刺

assault [ə'sɔːlt] n. 攻击,突袭;袭击

assemble [ə'sembəl] vt. 集合,集会;装配,组装 vi. 集会,聚集

assembly [ə'semblɪ] n. 集合,集会,装配

assert [ə'sɜːt] v. 主张,声明,断言

assess [ə'ses] vt. 估计,估算;评估,评价,评定

asset ['æset] n. 资产,有用的东西,优点,长处

assign[7] [ə'saɪn] vt. 派给,分配;选定,指定(时间、地点等)

assimilate [ə'sɪmɪleɪt] v. 使……同化,比较,比拟

assistant [ə'sɪstənt] a. 助理的;辅助的 n. 助手,助理;助教,店员

assumption [ə'sʌmpʃən] n. 假定,设想

astronomy [ə'strɒnəmɪ, -trɑ-] n. 天文学

athlete ['æθliːt] n. 运动员

atlantic [ət'læntɪk] a. 大西洋的 n. [the A-] 大西洋

atlas ['ætləs] n. 地图集

atomic [ə'tɒmɪk] a. 原子的,原子能的

attach[5] [ə'tætʃ] vt. (to) 贴上,系上,附上;使依附

attain[5] [ə'teɪn] vt. 达到,实现;获得 vi. 达到,获得

attorney [ə'tɜːnɪ] n. 律师

attraction [ə'trækʃən] a. 有吸引力的 n. 吸引,吸引力

attribute[4] [ə'trɪbjuːt] vt. (to) 把……归因于 n. 属性,特征

auction ['ɔːkʃən] n. 拍卖

authentic [ɔː'θentɪk] a. 可靠的,可信的,真的,真正的

authoritative [ɔː'θɒrətətɪv] a. 有权威的;可相信的

authority[4] [ɔː'θɒrətɪ] n. 权力,权威;权威人士,(pl.) 当局

automate ['ɔːtəmeɪt] vt. 使自动化,使自动操作 vi. 自动化,自动操作

automatic [ˌɔːtə'mætɪk] n. 自动的机器 a. 自动的,无意识的

autonomous [ɔː'tɒnəməs] a. 自治的;自主的

autonomy [ɔː'tɒnəmi] n. 自治

auxiliary [ɔːg'zɪljəri, -əl-, -ɡːɪ-] n. 帮助者,辅助物,助动词 a. 附加的,辅助的

avail [ə'veɪl] vt. (of) 有利,有用

avenue ['ævənuː, -njuː] n. 林荫道,大街

avert [ə'vɜːt] vt. 避免,防止;转移

aviation [ˌeɪvi'eɪʃən] n. 航空,飞机制造业

await [ə'weɪt] v. 等候,准备……以待

awake [ə'weɪk] a. 醒着的;意识到的 vt. 唤醒,唤起 vi. 醒来,醒悟,觉悟

awesome ['ɔːsəm] a. 可怕的,引起敬畏的

ax(e) [æks] n. 斧子

axis ['æksɪs] n. 轴

B

bachelor ['bætʃələ(r)] n. 单身汉,学士

backup ['bækʌp] n. 后援 v. 把……做备份

backward(s) ['bækwəd(z)] a. 向后的,相反的;落后的 ad. 向后地,倒,逆

bacon ['beɪkən] n. 咸肉;熏肉

bacteria [bæk'tɪəriə] n. (pl.) 细菌

badge [bædʒ] n. 徽章;标记;证章

bakery ['beɪkəri] n. 面包店

balcony ['bælkəni] n. 阳台;包厢;戏院楼厅

ballet ['bæleɪ] n. 芭蕾舞

balloon [bə'luːn] n. 气球 v. 如气球般膨胀

bamboo[4] [bæm'buː] a. 用竹子制的 n. 竹

ban[5] [bæn] vt. 禁止;取缔,查禁 n. 禁止,禁令

bandage ['bændɪdʒ] n. 绷带

bang [bæŋ] n. 重击,突然巨响 v. 发巨响,重击

bankrupt ['bæŋkrʌpt] a. 破产的 n. 破产者 v. 使破产
　　　　　　　　　　go bankrupt 破产

banner ['bænə(r)] n. 旗帜,横幅

banquet ['bæŋkwɪt] n. 宴会

barber ['bɑːbə(r)] n. 理发师

barely ['beəlɪ] ad. 几乎没有;仅仅

bargain ['bɑːgɪn] v. 讨价还价 n. 便宜货;交易

bark [bɑːk] vi. 吠;叫骂 n. 树皮;吠声

barn [bɑːn] n. 谷仓,牲口棚

barrel ['bærəl] n. 枪管,炮管,桶 vi. 快速移动 vt. 把……装桶

barren ['bærən] a. 不育的,贫瘠的

barrier[11] ['bærɪə(r)] n. 栅栏;障碍,屏障

baseball ['beɪsbɔːl] n. 棒球

basement ['beɪsmənt] n. 地下室

basin ['beɪsn] n. 盆,脸盆,盆地

basis ['beɪsɪs] n. 基础,基底;基准,根据

basket ['bɑːskɪt] n. 篮子

bat [bæt] n. 蝙蝠,球棒

battery[4] ['bætərɪ] n. 电池

bay [beɪ] n. 海湾

beam [biːm] n. 光线,电波,横梁,容光焕发 v. 微笑,闪亮

bean [biːn] n. 豆

beard [bɪəd] n. 胡须

beast [biːst] n. 畜生

beauty ['bjuːtɪ] n. 美,美丽,美人,美的东西

beforehand [bɪ'fɔːhænd] ad. 预先,事先

beg [beg] v. 乞讨;请求,恳求

beggar ['begə(r)] n. 乞丐 vt. 使贫穷

being ['biːɪŋ] n. 人,生物 art. 在,有,是

bell [bel] *n.* 钟,铃

belly ['belɪ] *n.* 腹部

belongings [bɪ'lɔːŋɪŋz] *n.* 财产,所有物

beloved [bɪ'lʌvd, bɪ'lʌvɪd] *a.* 心爱的

belt [belt] *n.* 带,腰带

bench [bentʃ] *n.* 长凳,工作台

bend [bend] *n.* 弯曲,曲折处 *vt.* 折弯;使屈服

beneficial [ˌbenɪ'fɪʃəl] *a.* 有益的,有利的

bet [bet] *n.* 打赌,赌注 *v.* 打赌

betray [bɪ'treɪ] *vt.* 背叛,辜负,暴露

beverage ['bevərɪdʒ] *n.* 饮料

bewilder [bɪ'wɪldə(r)] *v.* 使……不知所措

beyond[6] [bɪ'jɒnd] *prep.* 在……那边,在……以外;超出,超过 *ad.* 在那边,在远处

bias ['baɪəs] *n.* 偏见;斜纹;偏爱

bible ['baɪbl] *n.* 圣经

bid [bɪd] *n.* 出价 *v.* 命令,吩咐,投标

billion ['bɪljən] *num.* / *n.* 十亿

billionaire [ˌbɪljə'neə(r)] *n.* 亿万富翁

biochemistry [ˌbaɪəʊ'kemɪstrɪ] *n.* 生物化学

biography [baɪ'ɒɡrəfɪ] *n.* 传记

biology [baɪ'ɒlədʒɪ] *n.* 生物学

biomedical [baɪəʊ'medɪk(ə)l] *a.* 生物医学的

birthright ['bɜːθraɪt] *n.* 与生俱来的权利

biscuit ['bɪskɪt] *n.* 饼干

bite [baɪt] *v.* / *n.* 咬,叮 *n.* 一口

bizarre [bɪ'zɑː(r)] *a.* 奇异的(指态度、容貌、款式等)

blackboard ['blækbɔːd] *n.* 黑板

blade [bleɪd] *n.* 刀锋,刀口

blank [blæŋk] *a.* 空白的 *n.* 空白(处)

blanket ['blæŋkɪt] *n.* 毛毯

blast [blɑːst] *n.* 爆破,冲击波,一阵,汽笛声 *v.* 爆破,炸掉

blaze [bleɪz] *n.* 火焰,烈火 *v.* 燃烧
blend [blend] *v.* 混合 *n.* 混合物
bless [bles] *vt.* 祝福;保佑;赞美
blink [blɪŋk] *vt.* 眨眼;使闪烁 *vi.* 眨眼;闪烁 *n.* 闪光;眨眼;瞬间
blog[4] [blɒg] *n.* 博客,网络日志
bloodshed ['blʌdʃed] *n.* 流血;杀戮
bloody ['blʌdɪ] *a.* 血腥的,嗜杀的,非常的
bloom [bluːm] *n.* 花 *v.* 开花
blossom ['blɒsəm] *vi.* 开花,兴旺 *n.* 花;开花期;兴旺期
blouse [blaʊz] *n.* 女衬衫
blue-collar [ˌbluː'kɒlə(r)] *a.* 蓝领阶级的,体力劳动者
blueprint ['bluːprɪnt] *n.* 蓝图,设计图,(周详的)计划 *v.* 制成蓝图,计划
blunder ['blʌndə(r)] *n.* 大错,大失策 *v.* 失策,绊倒,弄糟
blur [blɜː(r)] *n.* 模糊,模糊之物 *v.* 使……模糊
blush [blʌʃ] *vi.* 脸红;感到惭愧
boiler ['bɔɪlə(r)] *n.* 锅炉
bolt [bəʊlt] *n.* 门闩,突发,螺钉
bond [bɒnd] *n.* 契约,公债,债券;联结,联系
bonus ['bəʊnəs] *n.* 红利,奖金
booklet ['bʊklɪt] *n.* 小册子
bookmark ['bʊkmɑːk] *n.* 书签
boost[6] [buːst] *vt./n.* 举起;提高,促进
booth [buːð, buːθ] *n.* 电话亭,货摊
bore [bɔː(r)] *vt.* 令人厌烦 *n.* 令人讨厌的人或事物,麻烦
botany ['bɒtənɪ] *n.* 植物学
bounce [baʊns] *n.* 跳,反跃,弹力 *v.* 弹跳,使……跳
bound[4] [baʊnd] *a.* 必定,注定;受约束的;开往
boundary ['baʊndərɪ] *n.* 界线,边界
bow [baʊ] *n.* 弓,弓形 *vi./n.* 鞠躬,点头
boycott ['bɔɪkɒt] *v.* 抵制(贸易),拒绝参加
brake [breɪk] *n.* 制动器;闸;刹车

brand⁶ [brænd] n. 商标,牌子,烙印 v. 打烙印,铭刻

brass [brɑːs] n. 黄铜,铜管(乐器)

breach [briːtʃ] n. 裂口,违背

bread [bred] n. 面包

breadth [bredθ] n. 宽度

breast [brest] n. 胸脯,乳房

breathe [briːð] v. 吸入,呼吸

breed⁹ [briːd] vt. 生殖,繁殖;生产,饲养 n. 品种,种类

breeze [briːz] n. 微风,轻而易举的事

bribe [braɪb] vt./n. 贿赂,(向……)行贿

brick [brɪk] a. 似砖的 n. 砖

bride [braɪd] n. 新娘

bridge [brɪdʒ] n. 桥,桥梁;桥牌

briefcase ['briːfkeɪs] n. 公文包

brighten ['braɪtn] v. 变亮,使……生辉

brilliant ['brɪljənt] a. 灿烂的,有才气的,杰出的

brink [brɪŋk] n. 边缘

brisk [brɪsk] a. 敏锐的,活泼的,轻快的 vi. 活跃起来;变得轻快 vt. 使活泼;使轻快

broadband ['brɔːdbænd] n. 宽频;宽波段 a. 宽波段的;宽频带的

broadcast⁷ ['brɔːdkɑːst] n./v. 广播,播音

broaden ['brɔːdn] vi. 变宽,加宽;变阔 vt. 使变宽

brochure ['brəʊʃə(r)] n. 手册,小册子

broken ['brəʊkən] a. 坏掉的;破碎的

broker ['brəʊkə(r)] n. 经纪人

bronze [brɒnz] a. 青铜色的 n. 青铜

brood [bruːd] n. 窝 v. 孵,沉思

broom [bruːm, -ʊm] n. 扫帚

brow [braʊ] n. 眉毛,额

browse [braʊz] v. 浏览,吃草

browser ['braʊzə(r)] n. 浏览器

bruise [bruːz] n. 瘀伤,擦伤 v. 受伤,擦伤

559

brunch [brʌntʃ] n. [口] 早午餐
brutal ['bruːtl] a. 野蛮的
bubble ['bʌbl] n. 泡沫
bucket ['bʌkɪt] n. 水桶
bud [bʌd] n. 芽,花蕾 v. 发芽,萌芽
budget[5] ['bʌdʒɪt] n. 预算 v. 编预算,为……做预算
bug [bʌg] n. 小虫,臭虫
bulb [bʌlb] n. 电灯泡,球状物
bulk [bʌlk] n. 大部分,大多数,大块,大批,容积,体积
bull [bʊl] n. 公牛
bullet ['bʊlɪt] n. 子弹
bulletin ['bʊlətɪn] n. 公报 vt. 发表
bully ['bʊlɪ] n. 欺凌弱小者,土霸,开球 v. 威胁,恐吓,欺负
bump [bʌmp] n. 撞击,隆起物 v. 碰撞,颠簸而行
bunch [bʌntʃ] n. 一束,一串
bundle ['bʌndl] n. 捆,包,束
bureau ['bjʊərəʊ] n. 局,办公处
bureaucracy [bjʊə'rɒkrəsɪ] n. 官僚政治
bureaucrat ['bjʊərəkræt] n. 官僚主义者;官僚
burial ['berɪəl] n. 埋葬;葬礼
burst [bɜːst] vi./n. 破裂,爆炸 vi. (into) 突然发生,突然发作
bush [bʊʃ] n. 灌木,灌木丛
business[58] ['bɪznɪs] n. 生意,业务;事务,职责;公司,产业
bust [bʌst] n. 半身像,胸部,萧条,破产,不景气
butcher ['bʊtʃə(r)] n. 屠夫,肉商,小贩
butter ['bʌtə(r)] n. 黄油
butterfly ['bʌtəflaɪ] n. 蝴蝶
button ['bʌtn] n. 纽扣,按钮 v. 扣住
buzz [bʌz] n. 嗡嗡声 v. 发出嗡嗡声
bypass ['baɪpɑːs] vt. 忽视;绕开;设旁路;迂回 n. 旁路;支路
bystander ['baɪstændə(r)] n. 旁观者;看热闹的人
bye [baɪ] int. 再见

C

cab [kæb] *n.* 出租汽车
cabbage [ˈkæbɪdʒ] *n.* 卷心菜,洋白菜
cabin [ˈkæbɪn] *n.* 船舱,机舱,小木屋
cabinet [ˈkæbɪnət] *n.* 橱柜,内阁
cable[6] [ˈkeɪbl] *n.* 电缆,海底电报
café [ˈkæfeɪ] *n.* 咖啡馆
cafeteria [ˌkæfɪˈtɪərɪə] *n.* 自助餐厅
cage [keɪdʒ] *n.* 笼子 *v.* 关入笼中
calcium [ˈkælsɪəm] *n.* 钙
calculator [ˈkælkjʊleɪtə(r)] *n.* 计算器
calendar [ˈkælɪndə(r)] *n.* 日历,月历,日程表
calorie [ˈkælərɪ] *n.* 卡(热量单位)
camcorder [ˈkæmkɔːdə] *n.* 摄录像机
camel [ˈkæməl] *n.* 骆驼
campaign [kæmˈpeɪn] *n.* 战役;运动
canal [kəˈnæl] *n.* 运河,沟渠
cancer[12] [ˈkænsə(r)] *n.* 癌,巨蟹座
candidate[6] [ˈkændɪdɪt] *n.* 候选人,求职者
candle [ˈkændl] *n.* 蜡烛
candy [ˈkændɪ] *n.* 糖果
cannon [ˈkænən] *n.* 大炮 *vi.* 开炮
canvas [ˈkænvəs] *n.* 帆布
capability [ˌkeɪpəˈbɪlətɪ] *n.* 能力,才能;性能,容量
capacity [kəˈpæsɪtɪ] *n.* 容量,容积;能量;能力;接受力
capsule [ˈkæpsjuːl] *n.* 胶囊,太空舱
captive [ˈkæptɪv] *n.* 俘房,迷恋者 *a.* 被俘的,被迷住的
carbon[12] [ˈkɑːbən] *n.* 碳,复写纸
cardiac [ˈkɑːdɪæk] *a.* 心脏的,心脏病的

career[18] [kəˈrɪə(r)] n. 生涯,职业,事业

carefree [ˈkeəfriː] a. 无忧无虑的;不负责的

cargo [ˈkɑːgəʊ] n. 船货,货物

caring [ˈkeərɪŋ] a. 有同情心的;表示或感到关怀或关心的

carpenter [ˈkɑːpɪntə(r)] n. 木匠 v. 做木工活

carpet [ˈkɑːpɪt] n. 地毯,毛毯 v. 铺以地毯,铺盖

carriage [ˈkærɪdʒ] n. 四轮马车,车厢

carrier [ˈkærɪə(r)] n. 运送者,媒介物,带菌者

carrot [ˈkærət] n. 胡萝卜

cart [kɑːt] n. 手推车;两轮运货马车

cartoon [kɑːˈtuːn] n. 动画片 vt. 为……画漫画

carve [kɑːv] v. 雕刻,切

cashier [ˈkæʃɪə(r)] n. 出纳员,收银员

cassette [kəˈset] n. 盒式录音带

cast [kɑːst] n. 演员阵容,投掷 v. 投,掷,抛

castle [ˈkɑːsl] n. 城堡

casualty [ˈkæʒuəltɪ] n. 变故,伤亡者,伤亡人数

catalog(ue) [ˈkætəlɒg] n. 目录,总目 v. 编入目录

catastrophe [kəˈtæstrəfɪ] n. 大灾难;大祸;惨败

category [ˈkætəgərɪ] n. 种类,别,[逻]范畴

cater [ˈkeɪtər] vi. (for)满足需要;投合,迎合;提供饮食及服务

cathedral [kəˈθiːdrəl] n. 大教堂

Catholic [ˈkæθəlɪk] a. 天主教的 n. 天主教徒

caution [ˈkɔːʃən] n./vt. 警告;小心;告诫

cautious [ˈkɔːʃəs] a. 十分小心的,谨慎的

cave [keɪv] n. 山洞

cease [siːs] v. 停止,中止

ceiling [ˈsiːlɪŋ] n. 天花板

celebrity [səˈlebrətɪ] n. 名人,著名,著名人士,名声,名誉,社会名流

cell [sel] n. 细胞,电池,单人牢房,蜂房

cellar [ˈselə(r)] n. 地窖;地下室

celsius ['selsɪəs] *a.* 摄氏的

cement [sɪ'ment] *n.* 水泥,接合剂

cemetery ['semɪtrɪ] *n.* 公墓,墓地

censorship ['sensəʃɪp] *n.* 审查机构;审查制度

census ['sensəs] *n.* 户口普查 *v.* 实施统计调查

centigrade ['sentɪgreɪd] *a.* 分为百度的,摄氏的

centimeter/-tre ['sentɪmiːtə(r)] *n.* 厘米

cereal ['sɪərɪəl] *n.* 谷类制食物;谷物

certificate [sə'tɪfɪkɪt] *n.* 证(明)书,执照 *vt.* 批准

certify ['sɜːtɪfaɪ] *vt.* 证明;保证

chalk [tʃɔːk] *n.* 粉笔

chamber ['tʃeɪmbə(r)] *n.* 室;议院

champagne [ʃæm'peɪn] *n.* 香槟酒;香槟酒色

champion ['tʃæmpɪən] *n.* 冠军,优胜者

chaos ['keɪɒs] *n.* 混乱

chap [tʃæp] *n.* 小伙子;家伙

characterize/-ise ['kærɪktəraɪz] *v.* 表示……的特色,赋予……特色

charity ['tʃærɪtɪ] *a.* 仁慈的,宽厚的 *n.* 慈善机构(团体),仁慈,宽厚

charm [tʃɑːm] *n.* 吸引力,魔力,魅力 *v.* 迷人,使……迷醉,用符咒

chart[4] [tʃɑːt] *n.* 图表 *v.* 制成图表

charter ['tʃɑːtə(r)] *n.* 特许状,执照,宪章 *v.* 特许,发给特许执照

chat [tʃæt] *n.* 聊天,闲谈 *v.* 谈天,闲谈

checkpoint ['tʃekpɔɪnt] *n.* 检查站,关卡

cheek [tʃiːk] *n.* 面颊

cheer [tʃɪə(r)] *v./n.* 喝彩,欢呼 *vt.* 使高兴,使振作

cheerful ['tʃɪəfl] *a.* 快乐的,高兴的

cheese [tʃiːz] *n.* 乳酪,干酪

chemist ['kemɪst] *n.* 化学家,药剂师

chemistry ['kemɪstrɪ] *n.* 化学

chess [tʃes] n. 国际象棋

chest [tʃest] n. 胸腔,胸部

chew [tʃuː] v. 咀嚼,嚼碎,细想

childish ['tʃaɪldɪʃ] a. 幼稚的,孩子气的

childlike ['tʃaɪldlaɪk] a. 天真烂漫的,孩子似的

chill [tʃɪl] n. 寒冷,寒意,失意 a. 寒冷的,冷漠的

chimney ['tʃɪmnɪ] n. 烟囱

chin [tʃɪn] n. 下巴,颏

china ['tʃaɪnə] n. 瓷器

chip [tʃɪp] n. 薄片,芯片

chocolate[4] ['tʃɒkəlɪt] n. 巧克力

choke [tʃəʊk] v. 窒息,阻塞

chop [tʃɒp] n. 厚肉片,排骨 v. 剁碎,砍,切

Christ [kraɪst] int. 天啊 n. 基督

Christian ['krɪstʃən] n. 基督教徒 a. 基督教(徒)的

Christmas[4] ['krɪsməs] n. 圣诞节

chronic[4] ['krɒnɪk] a. 长期的,慢性的

chronicle ['krɒnɪkl] n. 编年史,年代记

chunk [tʃʌŋk] n. 大块

church [tʃɜːtʃ] n. 教堂

cigar [sɪ'gɑː(r)] n. 雪茄烟

cigarette(te) [sɪgə'ret] n. 香烟

cinema ['sɪnɪmə] n. 电影院

circuit ['sɜːkɪt] n. 电路,一圈,巡回

circular ['sɜːkjʊlə(r)] a. 圆形的;循环的

circulate ['sɜːkjʊleɪt] v. 流通,循环,传播

circus ['sɜːkəs] n. 马戏团

cite [saɪt] vt. 引用;引证

citizen ['sɪtɪzn] n. 公民,市民

civic ['sɪvɪk] a. 公民的,市民的,市的

civil ['sɪvl, 'sɪvɪl] a. 市民的,公民的,国民的;民间的;民事的,根据民法的;文职的;有礼貌的

civilian [sɪˈvɪljən] *a.* 平民的 *n.* 平民

civilization/-isation[9] [ˌsɪvɪlaɪˈzeɪʃən] *n.* 文明,文化

civilize/-ise[4] [ˈsɪvɪlaɪz] *v.* 使……开化

clan [klæn] *n.* 宗族;部落;集团

clap [klæp] *n.* 拍手,拍手声 *v.* 鼓掌,轻敲

clarify [ˈklærɪfaɪ] *vt.* 澄清,阐明 *vt.* 使明晰

clash [klæʃ] *n.* 冲突,撞击声,抵触 *v.* 冲突,抵触,使……发出撞击声

classical [ˈklæsɪkl] *a.* 古典的

classic [ˈklæsɪk] *a.* 经典的,古典的

classification [ˌklæsɪfɪˈkeɪʃən] *n.* 分类,分级

classify [ˈklæsɪfaɪ] *v.* 分类,归类,分等

clause [klɔːz] *n.* 分句,从句,条款,款项

claw [klɔː] *n.* 爪 *v.* (用爪)抓,撕

clay [kleɪ] *n.* 黏土,泥土

clerk [klɑːk] *n.* 职员,办事员

click [klɪk] *n.* 点击,滴答声,拍打声

cliff [klɪf] *n.* 悬崖,峭壁

climax [ˈklaɪmæks] *n.* 高潮,极点,层次法

cling [klɪŋ] *vi.* (to) 黏着;缠着;坚持

clinical [ˈklɪnɪkl] *a.* 门诊的,临床的

clip [klɪp] *n.* 夹子,别针,回形针,修剪,剪下来的东西 *v.* 修剪,剪报,痛打

clockwise [ˈklɒkwaɪz] *ad./a.* 顺时针方向地/的

clone[5] [kləʊn] *n.* 无性繁殖系(的个体),克隆

closet [ˈklɒzɪt] *n.* 壁橱,小室 *a.* 秘密的,空论的

clothing [ˈkləʊðɪŋ] *n.* (总称)衣服

cloudy [ˈklaʊdɪ] *a.* 多云的

clue[9] [kluː] *n.* 线索 *v.* 提示

clumsy [ˈklʌmzi] *a.* 笨拙的

coach [kəʊtʃ] *n.* 长途汽车,(火车)客车车厢,教练 *v.* 训练,指导

coalition [ˌkəʊəˈlɪʃən] *n.* 结合,合并,联合

coarse [kɔːs] *a.* 粗,粗糙,粗劣;粗鲁,粗俗

coast [kəʊst] *n.* 海岸,海滨

Coca-Cola [ˌkəʊkəˈkəʊlə] *n.* 可口可乐(美国饮料公司)

cocaine [kəʊˈkeɪn, kɒˈk-] *n.* 可卡因

cocktail [ˈkɒkteɪl] *a.* 鸡尾酒的 *n.* 鸡尾酒

code[5] [kəʊd] *n.* 码,密码,法规 *v.* 把……编码,制成法典

cognitive [ˈkɒgnɪtɪv] *a.* 认知的,认识的,有认识力的

coherent [kəʊˈhɪərənt] *a.* 连贯的,一致的

cohesion [kəʊˈhiːʒən] *n.* 聚合;结合

coin [kɔɪn] *n.* 硬币,金钱,货币 *v.* 制造钱币

coincide [ˌkəʊɪnˈsaɪd] *vi.* (with)一致,符合;同时发生

collaborate [kəˈlæbəreɪt] *vt.* 合作

collapse [kəˈlæps] *vi./n.* 倒塌;崩溃

collar [ˈkɒlə(r)] *n.* 衣领

colleage[9] [ˈkɒliːg] *n.* 同事

collection[5] [kəˈlekʃən] *n.* 收藏品,收集物

collective[5] [kəˈlektɪv] *a.* 集体的,共同的 *n.* 集体

collide [kəˈlaɪd] *vi.* (with)碰撞,抵触

collision [kəˈlɪʒən] *n.* 碰撞,冲突,抵触

colony [ˈkɒlənɪ] *n.* 殖民地;聚居地

colorful [ˈkʌləfəl] *a.* 多色的;丰富多彩的

column [ˈkɒləm] *n.* 柱,圆柱;柱形物,专栏

comb [kəʊm] *n.* 头梳,鸡冠 *v.* 梳头发,梳毛

combat [ˈkɒmbæt, kəmˈbæt] *n.* 争斗,战斗 *v.* 奋斗,争斗

combination [ˌkɒmbɪˈneɪʃən] *n.* 结合,联合

comedy [ˈkɒmɪdɪ] *n.* 喜剧

comet [ˈkɒmɪt] *n.* 彗星

comic[4] [ˈkɒmɪk] *n.* 连环图画,杂耍滑稽演员 *a.* 滑稽的,有趣的,喜剧的

commander [kəˈmɑːndə(r)] *n.* 司令官,指挥官

commemorate [kəˈmeməreɪt] *vt.* 庆祝,纪念;成为……的纪念

commentary [ˈkɒmənˌtərɪ] *n.* 注释,评论,批评

commerce [ˈkɒmɜːs] n. 商业,贸易

commercial[6] [kəˈmɜːʃəl] a. 商业的 n. 商业广告

commission[5] [kəˈmɪʃən] n. 委员会,调查团;佣金,酬劳金;(权限、任务等的)委任,委托

committee [kəˈmɪtɪ] n. 委员会,全体委员

commodity [kəˈmɒdɪtɪ] n. (pl.)日用品;商品;农/矿产品;有用的东西

commonplace [ˈkɒmənpleɪs] n. 老生常谈;司空见惯的事;普通的东西 a. 平凡的;陈腐的

commonsense [kɒmənˈsens] a. 具有常识的

commonwealth [ˈkɒmənwelθ] n. 共和国,联邦

communication[38] [kəˌmjuːnɪˈkeɪʃən] n. 沟通,交通

communism [ˈkɒmjʊnɪzəm] n. 共产主义

communist [ˈkɒmjʊnɪst] a. 共产主义的 n. 共产主义者

commute [kəˈmjuːt] vi. 乘公交车上下班 n. 上下班交通

compact [kəmˈpækt] a. 紧凑的,紧密的,简洁的 v. 使装满,使简洁

companion [kəmˈpænjən] n. 同伴,同事

comparable [ˈkɒmpərəbl] a. 可比较的,比得上的

comparative [kəmˈpærətɪv] a. 比较的,相当的

compartment [kəmˈpɑːtmənt] n. 隔间;卧车上的隔间

compass [ˈkʌmpəs] n. 指南针

compel [kəmˈpel] vt. 强迫,迫使

compensate [ˈkɒmpenseɪt] vt. (for)给……补偿,酬报;给……付工钱;赔偿

competence [ˈkɒmpɪtəns] n. 能力

competent [ˈkɒmpɪtənt] a. 有能力的,胜任的

competitive [kəmˈpetɪtɪv] a. 比赛的;竞争的

competitor [kəmˈpetɪtə(r)] n. 竞争者

compile [kəmˈpaɪl] vt. 编译;编辑;汇编;编制

complement [ˈkɒmplɪmənt] n. 补语;补足物 vt. 补足,补助

complementary [ˌkɒmplɪˈmentərɪ] a. 补足的,补充的

complex[9] [ˈkɒmpleks] a. 复杂的,复合的

complexity [kəm'pleksətɪ] n. 复杂(性),复杂的事物

complicated[4] ['kɒmplɪkeɪtɪd] a. 错综复杂的,难懂的

compose[5] [kəm'pəʊz] vt. 写作,作曲;(of) 由……组成

composer [kəm'pəʊzə(r)] n. 作曲家

composition[41] [ˌkɒmpə'zɪʃən] n. 作文,著作,组织,合成物,成分

comprehension[55] [ˌkɒmprɪ'henʃən] n. 理解(力),领悟

comprehensive [ˌkɒmprɪ'hensɪv] a. 综合的;有理解力的

compress [kəm'pres] v. 压缩,压榨

comprise [kəm'praɪz] vt. 包含;由……组成

comrade ['kɒmreɪd] n. 同志

concede [kən'siːd] v. 承认,让步,退让

conceive [kən'siːv] vt. 构思;持有;以为;怀孕 vi. 怀孕;(of) 设想,考虑

concentration [ˌkɒnsən'treɪʃən] n. 集中,专心,浓度

concerning[9] [kən'sɜːnɪŋ] prep. 关于;就……而言

concession [kən'seʃən] n. 让步,妥协

concise [kən'saɪs] a. 简明的,简要的

concrete[5] ['kɒŋkriːt] n. 水泥,混凝土 a. 具体的,实在的,水泥的

condemn [kən'dem] v. 判刑,责备,处刑

condense [kən'dens] v. 浓缩,摘要,缩短

conduction [kən'dʌkʃən] n. 传导

conference ['kɒnfərəns] n. 会议

confess [kən'fes] vt. 承认;坦白;供认 vi. 承认;坦白;供认

confidence[11] ['kɒnfɪdəns] n. 信心;信任

confidential [ˌkɒnfɪ'denʃəl] a. 机密的,获他人信赖的,易于信任他人的

configuration [kənˌfɪɡə'reɪʃən] n. 结构;外形;配置

confine [kən'faɪn] n. 界限,边界 vt. 限制;禁闭

conform [kən'fɔːm] vi. (to) 遵照,遵从;与……一致

Confucian [kən'fjuːʃən] a. 孔子的,儒家的;儒家学说的 n. 儒家,儒家学者

confusion [kən'fjuːʒən] n. 混淆,搞乱

congratulation(s) [kəngrætju'leɪʃn] n. 祝贺,恭喜
congress ['kɒŋgres] n. 代表大会,国会,议会
conjunction [kən'dʒʌŋkʃən] n. 连接词,联合,关联
connection⁴ [kə'nekʃən] n. 联系,关系,连接
conquest ['kɒŋkwest] n. 征服;克服;攻取
conscience ['kɒnʃəns] n. 良心,道德心
consensus [kən'sensəs] n. 一致,合意,交感
consent [kən'sent] vi. 同意;答应;赞成 n. 同意;赞成;(意见等的)一致
consequence⁶ ['kɒnsɪkwəns] n. (in)结果;后果;重要,重大
consequent ['kɒnsɪkwənt] a. 作为结果的,随之发生的
consequently ['kɒnsɪkwəntlɪ] ad. 所以,因此
conservation¹⁹ [ˌkɒnsə'veɪʃn] n. 保存,保护
conserve [kən'sɜːv] n. 蜜饯,果酱 v. 保存,保全
considerable [kən'sɪdərəbl] a. 值得考虑的;相当的,客观的
considerate [kən'sɪdərɪt] a. 考虑周到的,体谅的
consideration [kənˌsɪdə'reɪʃn] n. 考虑;要考虑的事;体贴,关心
consistency [kən'sɪstənsɪ] n. 一致性;稠度;相容性
consistent [kən'sɪstənt] a. 始终如一的,一致的,坚持的
console [kən'səʊl] v. 安慰,慰藉 n. 控制台,操纵台
consolidate [kən'sɒlɪdeɪt] v. 巩固,联合,统一
conspicuous [kən'spɪkjʊəs] a. 显著的;显而易见的
constituency [kən'stɪtjʊənsɪ] n. 选举区;选举区全体选民
constitute ['kɒnstɪtjuːt] vt. 构成,组成
constitution [ˌkɒnstɪ'tjuːʃn] n. 组织,宪法,体格
constrain [kən'streɪn] vt. 强迫;束缚;驱使
constrict [kən'strɪkt] vt. 压缩;束紧
construct [kən'strʌkt] vt. 建设,建造
consultant [kən'sʌltənt] n. 顾问
consume⁹ [kən'sjuːm] vt. 消费,消耗
consumer³⁴ [kən'sjuːmə(r)] n. 消费者,用户
consumption¹⁵ [kən'sʌmpʃən] n. 消费

contain[14] [kən'tein] vt. 包含,容纳;克制,抑制

container [kən'teɪnə(r)] n. 容器,集装箱

contaminate [kən'tæmɪneɪt] v. 弄脏,污染

contemplate ['kɒntempleɪt] vt. 沉思,注视;思忖;预期 vi. 冥思苦想;深思熟虑

contemporary [kən'tempərəri] a. 当代的;同时代的;属于同一时期的 n. 同时代的人;同时期的东西

contempt [kən'tempt] n. 轻视,轻蔑

contend [kən'tend] vi. 竞争;斗争;奋斗;争论 vt. 主张;为……斗争

content[5] ['kɒntent] n. (pl.) 内容,目录 a. 满足的,满意的

contest[20] ['kɒntest] n. 竞赛,争论 v. 竞赛,争取,争辩

contestant [kən'testənt] n. 竞争者;争辩者

continual [kən'tɪnjuəl] a. 不断的,频繁的

continuous [kən'tɪnjʊəs] a. 连续的,继续的,持续的

contradict [ˌkɒntrə'dɪkt] vt. 反驳;否定;与……矛盾;与……抵触 vi. 反驳;否认;发生矛盾

contradiction [ˌkɒntrə'dɪkʃən] n. 反驳,矛盾

convene [kən'viːn] vt. 召集,集合;传唤 vi. 聚集,集合

conventional [kən'venʃənl] a. 普通的,常见的;习惯的,常规的

convert [kən'vɜːt] vt. (to) 把……改变为,转换,兑换

convey[5] [kən'veɪ] vt. 传达;传送,运输

conviction [kən'vɪkʃən] n. 定罪,信服,坚信

coordinate [kəʊ'ɔːdɪneɪt] v. (使)协调,调整;(使)互相配合

cop [kɒp] n. [俚语] 警察

cope[12] [kəʊp] v. (with) 竞争,对抗,对付,妥善处理 vi. 对付,妥善处理

cope with 处理,应付

copper ['kɒpə(r)] a. (紫)铜色的,铜(制)的 n. 铜,铜币,铜制品

copyright ['kɒpɪraɪt] a. 版权(的) n. 版权,著作权

core [kɔː(r)] n. 果心,核心,要点

corn [kɔːn] n. (美)玉米;(英)小麦,谷物;(中)包裹

corner ['kɔːnə(r)] n. 角落,转角,窘境 v. 将……逼入困境,

使……陷入绝境,垄断

cornerstone ['kɔːnəstəʊn] *n.* 基础;柱石;地基

corporate ['kɔːpərɪt] *a.* 公司的;法人组织的;社团的;共同的;自治的

corps [kɔːz] *n.* 军团,队,团

corpse [kɔːps] *n.* 尸体

correlate ['kɒrɪleɪt] *n.* 有相互关系的东西,相关物 *v.* 使有相互关系,互相有关系

correspondent [ˌkɒrɪˈspɒndənt] *n.* 通讯记者,通信者

corresponding [ˌkɒrɪˈspɒndɪŋ] *a.* 相应的,相当的;符合的,一致的

corridor ['kɒrɪdɔː(r)] *n.* 走廊

cosmetic [kɒzˈmetɪk] *n.* 化妆品 *a.* 化妆用的

costume ['kɒstjuːm] *n.* 服装,剧装

cottage ['kɒtɪdʒ] *n.* 村舍,小屋

cotton ['kɒtn] *a.* 棉花的 *n.* 棉花

couch [kaʊtʃ] *n.* 长椅,睡椅,卧榻

council ['kaʊnsəl] *n.* 理事会,委员会

counsel ['kaʊnsəl] *n.* 商议,忠告,法律顾问

countdown ['kaʊntdaʊn] *n.* 倒数计秒

counterclockwise [ˌkaʊntəˈklɒkwaɪz] *a.* 反时针方向的 *ad.* 反时针方向

counterpart ['kaʊntəpɑːt] *n.* 与对方地位相当的人, 与另一方作用相当的物

county ['kaʊntɪ] *n.* 郡,县

coupon ['kuːpɒn] *n.* 试样(配给票,息票,附单)

courtesy[6] ['kɜːtəsɪ] *n.* 礼貌,好意,恩惠

courtyard ['kɔːtjɑːd] *n.* 庭院;院子

cow [kaʊ] *n.* 母牛,母兽

coward ['kaʊəd] *a.* 胆小的 *n.* 懦夫

cowboy ['kaʊbɔɪ] *n.* 牛仔,牧童

cozy/cosy ['kəʊzɪ] *a.* 舒适的

crack [kræk] *vi.* 使破裂,砸开;发爆裂声 *n.* 裂纹,龟裂;爆裂声

571

crackdown ['krækdaʊn] n. 镇压

craft [krɑːft] n. 工艺,手艺,航空器

crane [kreɪn] n. 鹤,起重机

crash [kræʃ] v./n. 摔坏,坠毁

crawl [krɔːl] n. 爬行,匍匐而行 v. 爬行

cream [kriːm] n. 乳酪,奶油,面霜,精华

credible ['kredəbl] a. 可信的,可靠的

creep [kriːp] n. 爬,徐行,蠕动 vi. 爬,蔓延,潜行

crew [kruː] n. 全体船员,全体乘务员 vi. 一起工作

criminal[7] ['krɪmɪnl] a. 犯罪的,刑事的 n. 罪犯

crisp [krɪsp] a. 脆的,易碎的 n. 油炸马铃薯片

criterion [kraɪ'tɪərɪən] n. 标准,准则

crossing ['krɒsɪŋ] n. 横越,横渡;交叉点,渡口

crossroad ['krɒsrəʊd] n. 十字路口;交叉路;岔道;重大的抉择关头

crown [kraʊn] n. 王冠,王权,顶点 v. 使……成王,加冕,居……之顶

crucial ['kruːʃəl] a. 决定性的;重要的;定局的;决断的

crude [kruːd] a. 粗鲁的,简陋的,天然的,未加工的 n. 原油

cruity ['kruəltɪ] n. 残忍,残酷行为

cruise [kruːz] n. 巡航,巡弋,漫游 v. 巡航,巡弋,漫游

crumble ['krʌmbl] vi. 崩溃,破碎,粉碎

crust [krʌst] n. 外壳,面包皮

crystal ['krɪstl] a. 清澈透明的,晶体的 n. 水晶

cube [kjuːb] n. 立方体;立方

cubic ['kjuːbɪk] a. 立方体的

cue [kjuː] n. 开端,线索,开始

culminate ['kʌlmɪneɪt] vi. 到绝顶;达到高潮;达到顶点 vt. 使结束;使达到高潮

cultivate[5] ['kʌltɪveɪt] vt. 培养;耕作;陶冶

cupboard ['kʌbəd] n. 碗橱

curb [kɜːb] n. 抑制;勒马绳;路边 vt. 勒住;控制

curfew ['kɜːfjuː] n. 宵禁;宵禁令

认知词汇扫描

curl [kɜːl] n. 卷曲,鬈发 vt. 弄卷 vi. 卷曲,弯曲
currency [ˈkʌrənsɪ] n. 货币
curriculum [kəˈrɪkjʊləm] n. 课程,全部课程[curricula(复数)]
curse [kɜːs] n./v. 诅咒,咒骂
curtain [ˈkɜːtn] n. 窗帘
curve [kɜːv] n. 曲线,弯曲,曲球 v. 弯,使……弯曲
cushion [ˈkʊʃən] n. 垫子,坐垫
cute [kjuːt] n. 聪明的;伶俐的
cyclist [ˈsaɪklɪst] n. 骑自行车的人
cylinder [ˈsɪlɪndə(r)] n. 气缸;圆筒;圆柱状物
cynical [ˈsɪnɪkl] a. 愤世嫉俗的

D

dairy [ˈdeərɪ] a. 牛奶的 n. 牛奶场,乳品店,乳制品
dam [dæm] n. 水坝
damn [dæm] v./n. 诅咒
damp [dæmp] n. 湿气 a. 潮湿的
daring [ˈdeərɪŋ] a. 大胆的,勇敢的
darling [ˈdɑːlɪŋ] n. [称呼]亲爱的;心爱的人
dash [dæʃ] n. 冲撞,破折号 v. 猛掷,泼溅,冲撞
database/-bank [ˈdeɪtəbeɪs] n. 数据库
date [deɪt] n. 日期,年代;约会 v. 注日期;约会
dawn [dɔːn] n. 破晓
      at dawn 拂晓,天一亮
daylight [ˈdeɪlaɪt] n. 白昼,日光
dazzle [ˈdæzl] v. 使……眼花
deadly [ˈdedlɪ] a. 致命的,致死的 ad. 非常地,如死一般地
deaf [def] a. 聋的;不愿听的,装聋的
decade [ˈdekeɪd, dɪˈkeɪd] n. 十年
decay [dɪˈkeɪ] vi./n. 腐败;衰落

decent ['di:snt] a. 有分寸的,得体的,相当好的

deception [dɪ'sepʃən] n. 欺骗,欺诈;骗术

decimal ['desɪməl] a. 十进位的,小数的

decisive [dɪ'saɪsɪv] a. 决定性的

deck [dek] n. 甲板,露台 v. 装饰

declaration [ˌdeklə'reɪʃən] n. 宣布,宣言

decorate ['dekəreɪt] vt. 装饰,装潢,布置

decree [dɪ'kri:] n. 法令;判决 vt. 颁布;命令;判决 vi. 发布命令;注定

dedicate ['dedɪkeɪt] vt. (to) 致力;现身;题献

deduce [dɪ'dju:s] vt. (from) 推论,推断;演绎出

deed [di:d] n. 事迹,行为

deer [dɪə(r)] n. 鹿

default [dɪ'fɔ:lt] n. 违约;缺乏;缺席;系统默认值 vi. 拖欠;不到场;不履行

defect ['di:fekt] n. 缺点

defendant [dɪ'fendənt] n. 被告

defiance [dɪ'faɪəns] n. 蔑视;挑战;反抗

deficiency [dɪ'fɪʃənsɪ] n. 缺乏,不足

deficient [dɪ'fɪʃənt] a. 不足的;有缺陷的;不充分的

deficit ['defɪsɪt] n. 赤字,不足,缺乏

define[7] [dɪ'faɪn] vt. 下定义,解释

definite ['defɪnɪt] a. 明确的,确定的,限定的

definitely ['defɪnətlɪ] ad. 明确地,一定地

definition [ˌdefɪ'nɪʃən] n. 定义,清晰度

defy [dɪ'faɪ] v. 藐视,挑衅

degenerate [dɪ'dʒenəreɪt] a. 堕落的 v. 退化,堕落

degrade [dɪ'greɪd] vt. 使……丢脸;使……降级;使……降解;贬低 vi. 退化;降级,降低

delegate ['delɪgət] n. 代表 vt. 派……为代表;委任

delete [dɪ'li:t] v. 删除

deliberate[5] [dɪ'lɪbərɪt] a. 故意的;从容的;深思熟虑的 vt. 仔细考

虑；商议

delicacy ['delɪkəsɪ] n. 细软，娇嫩；精致；脆弱；微妙

delivery[5] [dɪ'lɪvərɪ] n. 递送，交付，分娩

demanding [dɪ'mɑːndɪŋ] a. 要求高的；苛求的

democracy [dɪ'mɒkrəsɪ] n. 民主，民主制，民主国家

denial [dɪ'naɪəl] n. 否认，拒绝

denote [dɪ'nəʊt] vt. 表示，指示

denounce [dɪ'naʊns] v. 告发，公然抨击

density ['densətɪ] n. 密度

dental ['dentl] a. 牙齿的，牙科的

dentist ['dentɪst] n. 牙科医生

depart [dɪ'pɑːt] v. 离开，出发，放弃

departure [dɪ'pɑːtʃə(r)] n. 离开，出发

dependent[4] [dɪ'pendənt] a. (on/upon) 依靠的，依赖的；从属的

depict [dɪ'pɪkt] v. 描述

deplore [dɪ'plɔː(r)] vt. 悲悼；哀叹；谴责；对……深感遗憾

deploy [dɪ'plɔɪ] v. 展开，配置，部署

deposit [dɪ'pɒzɪt] n. 存款，定金，堆积物 vt. 存放，堆积

depress [dɪ'pres] vt. 压抑；降低

depression[9] [dɪ'preʃən] n. 沮丧，萧条

deprive [dɪ'praɪv] vt. (of) 使丧失，剥夺

deputy ['depjʊtɪ] a. 代理的，副的 n. 代表

derail [dɪ'reɪl] vt. 使出轨 vi. 出轨

derive[4] [dɪ'raɪv] v. 衍生；派生；引出

descendant [dɪ'sendənt] n. 子孙，后代

descent [dɪ'sent] n. 降落，家系，侵袭

describe[25] [dɪs'kraɪb] vt. 描写，形容；叙述

designate ['dezɪgneɪt] v. 指定，标示

desire[8] [dɪ'zaɪə] n. 愿望，希望 vt. 希望，渴望；要求

desperate[8] ['despərət] a. 不顾一切的，绝望的

despite[7] [dɪ'spaɪt] prep. 不管，不顾

dessert [dɪ'zɜːt] n. 甜食

575

destination [ˌdestɪ'neɪʃən] n. 目的地,终点

destined ['destɪnd] a. 命定的;注定的;(for) 去往……的

destiny ['destənɪ] n. 命运,定数,天命

destroy[6] [dɪs'trɔi] vt. 破坏,摧毁;消灭,扑灭;打破,粉碎

destruction [dɪ'strʌkʃən] n. 破坏,毁灭

detach [dɪ'tætʃ] vt. 分开;使分离

detain [dɪ'teɪn] v. 扣留,扣押

detention [dɪ'tenʃən] n. 拘留;挽留;延迟

deteriorate [dɪ'tɪərɪəˌreɪt] v. 恶化

determination[6] [dɪˌtɜːmɪ'neɪʃən] n. 决心,决定

device[8] [dɪ'vais] n. 装置,设备;策略,方法,设计

devil ['devl] n. 魔鬼,恶魔

diagnosis [ˌdaɪəɡ'nəʊsɪs] n. 诊断

diagram ['daɪəɡræm] n. 图解,图表 v. 用图解法表示

dial ['daɪəl] n. 刻度盘,针面,转盘 v. 拨

dialect ['daɪəlekt] n. 方言

diameter/-re [daɪ'æmɪtə(r)] n. 直径

diamond ['daɪəmənd] n. 钻石 方块牌

diary ['daɪərɪ] n. 日记,日记簿

dictate [dɪk'teɪt] v. 听写,口述,口授 n. 命令,指挥,指令

dictation [dɪk'teɪʃən] n. 听写

dictator [dɪk'teɪtə(r)] n. 独裁者

diet ['daɪət] n. 日常饮食

  be/go on a diet 节食

digest [dɪ'dʒest, daɪ-] v. 消化

digital[19] ['dɪdʒɪtl] a. 数字的

dignity ['dɪɡnɪtɪ] n. 尊严

dilemma [dɪ'lemə] n. 困境,进退两难

diligent ['dɪlɪdʒənt] a. 勤奋的,用功的

dilute [daɪ'luːt] v. 冲淡,稀释

dim [dɪm] a. 暗淡的,模糊的 vt. 使暗淡,使失去光泽

dimension [dɪ'menʃən, daɪ-] n. 维;尺寸

diminish[7] [dɪˈmɪnɪʃ] vt. 使减少；使变小 vi. 变小；减少，缩小

dine [daɪn] v. 用正餐，进餐

dioxide[14] [daɪˈɒksaɪd] n. 二氧化物

diploma [dɪˈpləʊmə] n. 文凭，证书

diplomat [ˈdɪpləmæt] n. 外交家

director[4] [dɪˈrektə(r), daɪ-] n. 董事，经理，主管，指导者，导演

dirt [dɜːt] n. 污垢，泥土

disagree [ˌdɪsəˈɡriː] vi. (with...on/about) 不一致；不适宜；不同意；争执

disapprove [ˌdɪsəˈpruːv] v. 不赞成

disarm [dɪsˈɑːm] vt. 解除武装；缓和；裁军 vi. 放下武器；裁减军备

disc/disk [dɪsk] n. 圆盘，盘状物；磁盘

discard [dɪsˈkɑːd] vt. 丢弃；抛弃；放弃 vi. 放弃

discharge [dɪsˈtʃɑːdʒ] v. 卸下，放出，解雇，放电，解除

discipline[5] [ˈdɪsɪplɪn] n. 训练，纪律，惩罚 v. 训练，惩罚

disclose [dɪsˈkləʊz] vt. 揭露；公开

disco [ˈdɪskəʊ] n. 迪斯科舞厅

discourage [dɪsˈkʌrɪdʒ] vt. 使失去信心，使泄气

discovery[9] [dɪˈskʌvərɪ] n. 发现

discreet [dɪˈskriːt] a. 小心的；谨慎的

discrepancy [dɪˈskrepənsɪ] n. 不符；相差；矛盾

discriminate [dɪˈskrɪmɪneɪt] vt./vi. 区别；辨别；歧视

disgraceful [dɪsˈɡreɪsfəl] a. 不名誉的，可耻的

disguise [dɪsˈɡaɪz] n. 假面目，假装 v. 假装

disgust [dɪsˈɡʌst] vt. 令人作呕，厌恶

dislike [dɪsˈlaɪk] v./n. 不喜欢，厌恶

dismay [dɪsˈmeɪ] n. 沮丧 v. 使……灰心，使……害怕

disorder[9] [dɪsˈɔːdə(r)] n. 紊乱，混乱；骚动，骚乱；疾病，失调

dispatch [dɪˈspætʃ] vt. 派遣，发送 n. 派遣；急件

dispense [dɪˈspens] vt. 分配，分发；执行；免除 vi. 免除，豁免

disperse [dɪˈspɜːs] v. 分散，传播，散开

displace [dɪsˈpleɪs] vt. 取代；置换；转移；把……免职
dispose [dɪˈspəʊz] vi. (of) 处理，解决，去掉，除掉
disregard [ˌdɪsrɪˈɡɑːd] vt. 忽视；不理；漠视；不顾 n. 忽视；不尊重
disrupt [dɪsˈrʌpt] a. 分裂的，分散的 v. 使……分裂，使……瓦解
dissolve [dɪˈzɒlv] v. 溶解，解散
distil(l) [dɪˈstɪl] vi. 蒸馏；提炼；渗出 vt. 蒸馏；提取……的精华；使渗出
distinction [dɪˈstɪŋkʃən] n. 差别，不同，对比，区分，辨别
distort [dɪˈstɔːt] v. 扭曲；曲解
distract[4] [dɪˈstrækt] v. 转移，分心
distress [dɪˈstres] n. 苦恼，贫困 v. 使……苦恼
disturbance [dɪˈstɜːbəns] n. 扰乱，骚动
ditch [dɪtʃ] n. 沟渠 v. 坠沟中
dive [daɪv] n./vi. 跳水，潜水；俯冲，扑
diversion [daɪˈvɜːʃən] n. 转移；消遣；分散注意力
divert [daɪˈvɜːt] vt. 转移；使……欢娱；使……转向 vi. 转移
dividend [ˈdɪvɪdend] n. 红利，股息，彩金，被除数
divine [dɪˈvaɪn] a. 神的，神圣的
division [dɪˈvɪʒən] n. 分，分割，分裂；除法
dizzy [ˈdɪzɪ] a. 眩晕的
DNA abbr. 脱氧核糖核酸
dock [dɒk] n. 码头，船坞 v. 靠码头，入坞
doctrine [ˈdɒktrɪn] n. 教义，主义，学说
dodge [dɒdʒ] vi. 躲避，避开 vt. 躲避，避开
dogma [ˈdɒɡmə] n. 教条，教理
doll [dɒl] n. 玩具娃娃
dolphin [ˈdɒlfɪn] n. 海豚
domain [də(ʊ)ˈmeɪn] n. 领域；域名
dome [dəʊm] n. 圆屋顶
domestic [dəˈmestɪk] a. 家里的，家庭的；国内的，国产的；驯养的
dominant [ˈdɒmɪnənt] a. 占优势的
dominate[4] [ˈdɒmɪneɪt] vt. 支配，统治，控制；在……中占首要位置

donate [dəʊ'neɪt] v. 捐赠

donation [dəʊ'neɪʃən] n. 捐款,捐赠物

donkey ['dɒŋkɪ] n. 驴

donor ['dəʊnə(r)] n. 捐赠人

doom [duːm] n. 命运,不幸,宣告判决 v. 命中注定,宣告

dorm(= dormitory) [dɔːm] n. 宿舍

dormitory ['dɔːmɪtərɪ] n. (集体)宿舍

dose [dəʊs] n. 剂量,服用量

dot [dɒt] n. 点,圆点,小孩子,小东西

doubtful ['daʊtfəl] a. 可疑的,疑心的,不确定的

downstairs [ˌdaʊn'steəz] a. 楼下的 ad. 在楼下 n. 楼下

downward ['daʊnwəd] a. 向下的 ad. 向下

draft/draught [drɑːft] n. 草稿,草图,汇票 v. 起草,征兵

dragon ['drægən] n. 龙

drastic[4] ['dræstɪk] a. 激烈的;猛烈的

draw[10] [drɔː] vt. 绘画;拖,拉;吸引;推断出 n. 平局,和局

drawback ['drɔːbæk] n. 缺点,不利条件

drawer [drɔː(r); 'drɒə/'drɔːə(r)] n. 抽屉

drawing ['drɔːɪŋ] n. 绘图,图画

dread [dred] vi. 惧怕;担心 vt. 惧怕;担心

dreadful ['dredfəl] a. 可怕的

dreamy ['driːmɪ] a. 梦想的;空幻的;轻柔的;恍惚的

drift[4] [drɪft] n. 漂移,漂流物,观望,漂流,吹积物,趋势 v. 漂移,漂流,吹积

drill [drɪl] n. 钻孔机,钻子,播种机 v. 训练,钻孔

drilling ['drɪlɪŋ] n. 演练;钻孔

drip [drɪp] n. 滴,点滴,乏味的人,水滴

dropout ['drɒpaʊt] n. 中途退学;缀学学生

drought[13] [draʊt] n. 干旱

drum [drʌm] n. 鼓,鼓声

drunk [drʌŋk] a. 喝醉了的

dryer ['draɪər] n. 干燥剂;烘干机

dual ['djuːəl] a. 双重的
dubious ['djuːbɪəs] a. 怀疑的,可疑的
duck [dʌk] n. 鸭子
due[6] [djuː] a. 预定的;应付的,到期的
dumb [dʌm] a. 无言的,哑的
duplicate ['djuːplɪkɪt] n. 副本,复本,复制品
durable ['djʊərəbl] a. 耐久的
dusk [dʌsk] n. 黄昏
dust [dʌst] n. 灰尘,尘埃
dustbin ['dʌstbɪn] n. 垃圾箱
dusty ['dʌstɪ] a. 落满灰尘的
dwarf [dwɔːf] n. 矮子,侏儒
dwell[5] [dwel] vi. 居住;存在于;(on) 细想某事
dweller ['dwelə(r)] n. 居民,居住者
dye [daɪ] n. 染料,染色
dynamic(al)[4] [daɪ'næmɪk(l)] a. 有活力的;动力的;动态的

E

eagle ['iːgl] n. 鹰
ear [ɪə(r)] n. 耳朵,听力
earnest ['ɜːnɪst] a. 认真的,热心的
earnings ['ɜːnɪŋz] n. 收入,收益
earthquake ['ɜːθkweɪk] n. 地震
ease[4] [iːz] n. 容易,轻易;安逸 v. 减轻,放松,缓和
Easter ['iːstə(r)] n. 复活节
eastern ['iːstən] a. 东部的,东方的
easy-going [ˌiːzɪ'gəʊɪŋ] a. 随和的,容易相处的
eccentric [ɪk'sentrɪk] n. 怪人 a. 古怪的,反常的
echo ['ekəʊ] n. 回声,回音,回波
eclipse [ɪ'klɪps] n. 日食,月食,衰落

economic[22] [ˌiːkəˈnɒmɪk] a. 经济的,经济学的
economical[4] [ˌiːkəˈnɒmɪkl] a. 节俭的,经济的,合算的
economics [ˌiːkəˈnɒmɪks] n. 经济学
ecosystem[5] [ˈiːkəʊsɪstəm] n. 生态系统
edge [edʒ] n. 刃;边缘 v. 侧身移动,挤进
edit [ˈedɪt] vt. 编辑,校订,剪辑
edition [ɪˈdɪʃən] n. 版,版本
editor [ˈedɪtə(r)] n. 编辑,编者
editorial [ˌedɪˈtɔːrɪəl] n. 社论 a. 编辑的
egg [eg] n. 蛋
eighth [eɪtθ] num. 第八
eject [ɪˈdʒekt] v. 逐放,放逐,驱逐
elaborate [ɪˈlæbərɪt] a. 精细的,详尽的,精心的
elastic [ɪˈlæstɪk] a. 有弹性的;易伸缩的;灵活的
elbow [ˈelbəʊ] n. 手肘,急弯,扶手
elderly [ˈeldəlɪ] a. 上了年纪的
electric[12] [ɪˈlektrɪk] a. 电的,带电的,电动的
electrical[5] [ɪˈlektrɪkl] a. 电的,电气科学的
electrician [ɪˌlekˈtrɪʃən] n. 电学家,电工
electron [ɪˈlektrɒn] n. 电子
electronic[18] [ɪˌlekˈtrɒnɪk] a. 电子的
elementary[4] [ˌelɪˈmentərɪ] a. 初级的,基本的
elevate [ˈelɪveɪt] v. 举起,提拔,鼓舞
elevator [ˈelɪveɪtə(r)] n. 电梯
eleventh [ɪˈlevnθ] num. 第十一
elicit [ɪˈlɪsɪt] vt. 抽出,引出
eligible [ˈelɪdʒəbl] a. 可以选的,有资格的,合格的 n. 有资格者,合格者,适任者
eliminate[9] [ɪˈlɪmɪneɪt] vt. 排除,消除
elite [eɪˈliːt, ɪ-] n. 精华,精锐,中坚分子
eloquent [ˈeləkwənt] a. 雄辩的,有口才的;有说服力的
elsewhere [ˌelsˈweə(r)] ad. 在别处,到别处

e-mail/e-mail [ˈiːmeɪl] n. 电子邮件

embargo [emˈbɑːɡəʊ] vt. 禁止出入港口；禁止或限制贸易 n. 封港令；禁令；禁止

embark [ɪmˈbɑːk] vi. 上船或飞机；从事，着手 vt. 使上船；使从事

embarrass [ɪmˈbærəs] vt. 使窘迫，使困惑，使为难

embassy [ˈembəsɪ] n. 大使馆

embed [ɪmˈbed] v. 使插入，使嵌入，深留

embody [ɪmˈbɒdɪ] v. 具体表达，使具体化

embrace [ɪmˈbreɪs] vt. 拥，拥抱；包括，包含；包围，环绕

emigrate [ˈemɪɡreɪt] v. 移居，移民

emission[14] [ɪˈmɪʃən] n. 发射，射出，发行

emperor [ˈempərə(r)] n. 皇帝

empire [ˈempaɪə(r)] n. 帝国

empirical [ɪmˈpɪrɪkl] a. 经验主义的

employee[20] [ɪmˈplɔɪiː] n. 雇员

employer[8] [ɪmˈplɔɪə(r)] n. 雇主

emulate [ˈemjʊleɪt] vt. 仿真；模仿；尽力赶上；同……竞争

enclose[4] [ɪnˈkləʊz] vt. 装入；放入封套

encounter[7] [ɪnˈkaʊntə(r)] vt./n. 遭遇，遇到

endanger[11] [ɪnˈdeɪndʒə(r)] v. 危及

endeavo(u)r [ɪnˈdevə] n. 努力；尽力 vi. 努力；尽力

ending [ˈendɪŋ] n. 结尾，结局

endless [ˈendlɪs] a. 无止境的，没完没了的

endorse [ɪnˈdɔːs] vt. 背书；签署；认可；赞同在背面签名

energetic [ˌenəˈdʒetɪk] a. 精力充沛的；积极的

enforce [ɪnˈfɔːs] vt. 实行，执行；强制，强迫

engagement [ɪnˈɡeɪdʒmənt] n. 约会；交战；婚约；诺言

engine [ˈendʒɪn] n. 发动机，引擎，机车，火车头

engineering[9] [ˌendʒɪˈnɪərɪŋ] n. 工程（学），工程技术

enhance [ɪnˈhɑːns] vt. 提高，增强

enlarge [ɪnˈlɑːdʒ] v. 扩大，增大

enlighten [ɪnˈlaɪtn] v. 授予……知识，启发，启蒙

enlist [ɪnˈlɪst] vi. 从军;应募;赞助;支持 vt. 征募;使入伍
enormous[6] [ɪˈnɔːməs] a. 庞大的,巨大的
enrich [ɪnˈrɪtʃ] vt. 使富足;使肥沃;装饰
enrol(l) [ɪnˈrəʊl] vt. 登记,编入,招收
enterprise [ˈentəpraɪz] n. 企业,事业
entertain [ˌentəˈteɪn] vt. 使欢乐,使娱乐;招待,款待
entity [ˈentətɪ] n. 存在,实体
entrepreneur [ˌɒntrəprəˈnɜː(r)] n. 企业家
entrust [ɪnˈtrʌst] vt. 委托,信托
entry [ˈentrɪ] n. 进入,入口,登记
envelope [ˈenvələʊp] n. 信封,信皮
epic [ˈepɪk] n. 史诗
epidemic [ˌepɪˈdemɪk] n. 传染病,流行病 a. 流行的,传染性的
episode [ˈepɪsəʊd] n. 插曲,插话,(作品的一段)情节,有趣的事件
equality [ɪˈkwɒlətɪ] n. 同等,平等,相等,等同性
equation [ɪˈkweɪʒn,-ʃən] n. 方程(式),等式
equator [ɪˈkweɪtə(r)] n. 赤道
era [ˈɪərə] n. 纪元,时代,年代
eradicate [ɪˈrædɪkeɪt] vt. 根除,根绝;消灭
erect [ɪˈrekt] a. 直立的,竖立的,笔直的 v. 竖立,使……直立,建筑
erode [ɪˈrəʊd] vt. 腐蚀,侵蚀 vi. 侵蚀;受腐蚀
erosion [ɪˈrəʊʒən] n. 腐蚀,侵蚀
essay [ˈeseɪ] n. 短文,散文
essence [ˈesns] n. 本质,实质;精华
estate [ɪˈsteɪt] n. 不动产,财产
esteem [ɪˈstiːm] n. 尊敬 v. 尊敬,尊重
eternal [ɪˈtɜːnl] a. 永久的,永恒的
evacuate [ɪˈvækjʊeɪt] v. 疏散,撤出,排泄
evade [ɪˈveɪd] vt. 逃避;规避;逃脱 vi. 逃避;规避;逃脱
evaporate [ɪˈvæpəreɪt] v. 蒸发,失去水分,消失

eve [iːv] n. 前夜,前夕 n. [圣]夏娃

eventually[9] [ɪˈventʃʊəlɪ] ad. 最后,终于

everlasting [ˌevəˈlɑːstɪŋ] a. 永恒的;连接不断的

every [ˈevrɪ] a. 每,每个;每隔……的

everywhere [ˈevrɪweə(r)] ad. 到处,处处

evident [ˈevɪdənt] a. 明显的,明白的

evidently [ˈevɪdəntlɪ] ad. 明显地,显而易见地

evil [ˈiːvl] a. 坏的,邪恶的 n. 邪恶,罪恶;祸害

evoke [ɪˈvəʊk] v. 唤起,引起

evolution [ˌiːvəˈluːʃən, ˌe-] n. 进化,发展,进展

exaggerate [ɪgˈzædʒəreɪt] v. 夸大,夸张

exceed [ɪkˈsiːd] vt. 超过,胜过

exception[11] [ɪkˈsepʃən] n. 例外

exceptional [ɪkˈsepʃənl] a. 例外的,异常的,特别的

excerpt [ˈeksɜːpt] n. 摘录 v. 摘录,摘要

excessive[4] [ɪkˈsesɪv] a. 过多的,过分的

excitement [ɪkˈsaɪtmənt] n. 激动,兴奋

exclaim [ɪkˈskleɪm] v. 大叫,呼喊,大声叫

exclude [ɪkˈskluːd] vt. 拒绝接纳,把……排除在外,排斥

execution[5] [ˌeksɪˈkjuːʃən] n. 执行,实行;完成;死刑

executive[11] [ɪgˈzekjʊtɪv] a. 执行的,实施的 n. 执行者,行政官;高级官员

exemplify [ɪgˈzemplɪfaɪ] vt. 示例;例证

exempt [ɪgˈzempt] vt. (from) 免除 a. (from) 被免除的

exhaust [ɪgˈzɔːst] n. 排气,排气装置 v. 用尽,耗尽,使……精疲力尽

exhibit [ɪgˈzɪbɪt] n. 展览,展品 vt. 展览,陈列;显示

exile [ˈeksaɪl] n. 放逐,流放,被放逐者 v. 放逐,流放

exit [ˈeksɪt] n. 出口,退场,离去

expansion [ɪkˈspænʃən] n. 扩大,膨胀

expedition[5] [ˌekspɪˈdɪʃən] n. 远征,探险队,迅速

expel [ɪkˈspel] v. 驱逐,逐出,开除

expenditure[5] [ɪkˈspendɪtʃə(r)] n. (时间、劳力、金钱等)支出,使用,消耗

experimental [ɪkˌsperɪˈmentl] a. 实验(性)的,试验(性)的

expertise [ˈeksp3ːtaɪz] n. 专家的意见,专门技术

expire [ɪkˈspaɪə(r)] v. 期满,失效,终止,断气

explicit [ɪkˈsplɪsɪt] a. 清楚的;明确的

exploit[5] [ˈeksplɔɪt] vt. 使用,利用;开采,开发

explosion[5] [ɪkˈspləʊʒən] n. 爆炸,爆发

explosive [ɪkˈspləʊsɪv] a. 爆炸(性)的 n. 炸药

expose [ɪkˈspəʊz] vt. (to) 暴露;揭露

exposure [ɪkˈspəʊʒə(r)] n. 暴露;揭露;曝光

expressway [ɪkˈspresweɪ] n. (美)高速公路

exquisite [ˈekskwɪzɪt, ɪkˈs-] a. 精致的,细腻的,敏锐的

extension [ɪkˈstenʃən] n. 延长,扩充,范围

extensive[5] [ɪkˈstensɪv] a. 广泛的,广阔的

extent[6] [ɪkˈstent] n. 广度,宽度,长度,大小,范围,程度

  to a certain extent 在一定程度上

  to a great/large extent 在很大程度上

  to some extent 在某种程度上

exterior [ɪkˈstɪərɪə(r)] n. 外部,表面,外形 a. 外部的,外在的,表面的

extinct[12] [ɪkˈstɪŋkt] a. 灭绝的,熄灭的 n. 消灭,熄灭

extinguish [ɪkˈstɪŋgwɪʃ] v. 熄灭,消减,偿清

extract [ɪkˈstrækt] vt. 提取,榨取;取出;摘录 n. 摘录;榨出物;汁;选粹

extravagant [ɪkˈstrævəgənt] a. 奢侈的;浪费的;过度的;放纵的

extremely[6] [ɪkˈstriːmlɪ] ad. 极,非常

eyesight [ˈaɪsaɪt] n. 视力

F

fable ['feɪbl] *n.* 寓言

fabricate ['fæbrɪkeɪt] *v.* 制造,建造,装配

fabulous ['fæbjʊləs] *a.* 难以置信的;极好的

facet ['fæsɪt] *n.* 面;方面

facial ['feɪʃəl] *a.* 面部的,表面的;脸的

facilitate[5] [fə'sɪlɪteɪt] *vt.* 促进;帮助;使容易

factor ['fæktə(r)] *n.* 因素,因子

factory ['fæktərɪ] *n.* 工厂

faculty ['fækəltɪ] *n.* 才能,能力,全体教员

fade [feɪd] *vi.* 褪色;凋谢;逐渐消失 *vt.* 使褪色

Fahrenheit ['færənhaɪt] *a.* 华氏的

faint [feɪnt] *vi.* 发晕,昏过去 *a.* 微弱的,模糊的

fairy ['feərɪ] *n.* 仙女,精灵

faithful ['feɪθf(ʊ)l] *a.* 忠诚的,忠实的

fake [feɪk] *n.* 假货,欺骗 *a.* 假的

fallacy ['fæləsɪ] *n.* 谬论,谬误

fame [feɪm] *n.* 名声,名望

famine ['fæmɪn] *n.* 饥荒

fantastic [fæn'tæstɪk] *a.* 极好的,难以相信的,奇异的,幻想的

fantasy ['fæntəsɪ] *n.* 幻想

farewell [ˌfeə'wel] *a.* 告别的 *int.* 再会,别了 *n.* 告别

farming ['fɑːmɪŋ] *n./a.* 农业(的)

fascinate ['fæsɪneɪt] *v.* (使)着迷,(使)神魂颠倒,极度迷人

fascinating ['fæsɪneɪtɪŋ] *a.* 迷人的

fashionable ['fæʃənəbl] *a.* 流行的,时髦的

fasten ['fɑːsn] *vt.* 扣紧,结牢,闩上

fatal[7] ['feɪtl] *a.* 致命的,毁灭性的

fate [feɪt] *n.* 命运

fatigue [fə'tiːg] *n.* 疲乏,疲劳

fault[6] [fɔːlt] n. 缺点,缺陷;过失,过错
faulty ['fɔːltɪ] a. 有错误的,有缺点的
fax [fæks] n. 传真 v. 传真
fearful ['fɪəfʊl] a. 担心的,可怕的
feasibility [ˌfiːzə'bɪlɪtɪ] n. 可行性,可能性
feasible[4] ['fiːzəbl] a. 可行的,可用的
feather ['feðə(r)] n. 羽毛
federal ['fedərəl] a. 联邦的 n. 同盟盟友
fee [fiː] n. 费用
feeble ['fiːbl] a. 虚弱的,无力的
feedback[8] ['fiːdbæk] n. 反馈
fellow ['feləʊ] n. 人,朋友,同事
fellowship ['feləʊʃɪp] n. 研究员资格(身份),奖学金,交情
feminine ['femənɪn] a. 女性的
fence [fens] n. 围墙,剑术
ferry ['ferɪ] n. 渡船,渡口
fertile ['fɜːtaɪl] a. 肥沃的,能繁殖的 n. 多产,肥沃
fertilizer ['fɜːtəlaɪzə(r)] n. 肥料
fiber/-bre ['faɪbə(r)] n. 纤维
fiction[6] ['fɪkʃən] n. 小说,虚构
fifteenth [fɪf'tiːnθ] num. 第十五
file [faɪl] n. 文件夹,卷宗;(计算机)文件 vt. 把……归档
fireman ['faɪəmən] n. 消防队员
firewall ['faɪəwɔːl] n. 防火墙
firm[4] [fɜːm] a. 坚固的,结实的,稳固的;坚定的,坚决的,坚强的 n. 公司,商号
fisherman ['fɪʃəmən] n. 渔夫
fixture ['fɪkstʃə(r)] n. 固定装置;设备
flame [fleɪm] n. 火焰,火舌,热情
flap [flæp] n. 拍打,拍打声
flash [flæʃ] n. 闪光,一闪,闪光灯 vi. 发闪光;闪现,闪过;飞驰,掠过

flatter [ˈflætə(r)] v. 过分夸赞,奉承,阿谀
flavo(u)r [ˈfleɪvə(r)] n. 香味 vt. 给……加味
flaw [flɔː] n. 瑕疵,裂纹;缺点
flee [fliː] vt. 逃避;逃跑,逃走
fleet [fliːt] n. 船队,舰队
flesh [fleʃ] n. 肉
flight [flaɪt] n. 飞行,飞机的航程,航班,逃跑
fling [flɪŋ] n. 投掷,急冲,嘲弄 v. 投,猛冲,嘲笑
float[11] [fləʊt] v. 浮动,漂浮
flock [flɒk] n. 群 v. 成群而行,聚集
flour [ˈflaʊə(r)] n. 面粉
flourish [ˈflʌrɪʃ] v. 繁荣,茂盛,活跃
fluctuate [ˈflʌktʃueɪt] vi. 变动,波动,涨落,动摇 vt. 使波动,使起伏,使动摇
fluent [ˈfluːənt] a. 流利的,流畅的
fluid [ˈfluːɪd] a. 流体的,流动的 n. 流体,液体
flush [flʌʃ] n. 激动;面红 vt. 使激动;用水冲洗 vi. 发红,脸红;被冲洗
foam [fəʊm] n. 泡沫,水沫 v. 起泡沫
fog [fɒg] n. 雾
foggy [ˈfɒgɪ] a. 有雾的
fold [fəʊld] v. 折叠,合拢 n. 褶,褶痕
folk [fəʊk] a. 民间的 n. 人们
folklore [ˈfəʊklɔː(r)] n. 民间传说
fool [fuːl] n. 笨蛋,傻瓜 vt. 玩弄,愚弄
footstep [ˈfʊtstep] n. 脚步(声),足迹
forecast [ˈfɔːkɑːst] n. 预测,预报
forehead [ˈfɒrɪd; ˈfɔːhed] n. 额,前额
forerunner [ˈfɔːrʌnə(r)] n. 先驱;先驱者;预兆
foresee [fɔːˈsiː] vt. 预知;预见
foresight [ˈfɔːsaɪt] n. 先见,远见;预见;深谋远虑
forge [fɔːdʒ] n. 熔炉,铁工厂 v. 打制,想出,伪造

fork [fɔːk] n. 叉
format ['fɔːmæt] n. 设计，版式
formidable ['fɔːmɪdəbl] a. 可怕的；令人敬畏的
formula ['fɔːmjʊlə] n. 公式，配方，规则；婴儿食品
formulate ['fɔːmjʊleɪt] vt. 用公式表示；系统地阐述或提出
fort [fɔːt] n. 堡垒，要塞
forthcoming [ˌfɔːθ'kʌmɪŋ] a. 即将来临的
fortitude ['fɔːtɪtjuːd] n. 坚忍，刚毅
fortnight ['fɔːtnaɪt] n. 两星期
forum ['fɔːrəm] n. 论坛，讨论会
forward ['fɔːwəd] a. 前部的，向前的；进步的，激进的 ad. 向前，前进；向将来 vt. 转交，转递
fossil[6] ['fɒsl] a. 化石的 n. 化石
found[58] [faʊnd] v. 建立，创立，创办
fountain ['faʊntɪn] n. 泉水；喷泉；源泉
fourth [fɔːθ] num. 第四 n. 四分之一
fox [fɒks] n. 狐狸，狡猾的人
fraction[5] ['frækʃən] n. 分数，小部分，破片
fragile ['frædʒaɪl] a. 易碎的，脆的
fragment ['frægmənt] n. 碎片，破片，断片
fragrant ['freɪgrənt] a. 芳香的
frame [freɪm] n. 框，结构，骨架 v. 构成，设计，陷害
franc [fræŋk] n. 法郎
frank [fræŋk] a. 坦白的，直率的
frantic ['fræntɪk] a. 疯狂的，狂乱的
fraud [frɔːd] n. 骗子，欺骗，诈欺
freeway ['friːweɪ] n. 高速公路
freezer ['friːzə(r)] n. 冷藏箱/库
freight [freɪt] n. 船货，运费，货运
frequency ['friːkwənsɪ] n. 频繁，频率
frequent ['friːkwənt] a. 频繁的
friction ['frɪkʃən] n. 摩擦，摩擦力

fridge(= refrigerator) [frɪdʒ] n. 电冰箱
friendship ['frendʃɪp] n. 友谊,友好
frog [frɒg] n. 蛙
frontier ['frʌntɪə(r)] n. 边界,边境
frost [frɒst] n. 霜,冰冻,冷漠
frown [fraʊn] v. (at/on/upon) 皱眉,蹙额;不赞成,反对
fruitful ['fruːtfʊl] a. 多产的,富有成效的
fry [fraɪ] vt. 油煎,油炸
fundamental[11] [ˌfʌndə'mentl] a. 基础的,根本的,重要的
funeral[5] ['fjuːnərəl] a. 葬礼的 n. 葬礼
fur [fɜː(r)] n. 毛皮,皮,皮子
fury ['fjʊərɪ] n. 愤怒,狂暴;狂怒的人
fuse [fjuːz] n. 保险丝
fusion ['fjuːʒən] n. 融合物;熔化;融合;熔接
fuss [fʌs] n. 大惊小怪,小题大做

G

gadget ['gædʒɪt] n. 小玩意;小器具
galaxy ['gæləksɪ] n. 银河,一群显赫之人
gallery ['gælərɪ] n. 美术馆,画廊
gallon ['gælən] n. 加仑
gamble ['gæmbl] n./v. 赌博,投机
gang [gæŋ] n. 队,群,帮
gap[17] [gæp] n. 间隙,缺口;隔阂,差距
gardener ['gɑːdnə(r)] n. 园丁,花匠,园艺家
garment ['gɑːmənt] n. 衣服
gasoline[9] ['gæsə(ʊ)liːn] n. 汽油
gate [geɪt] n. 大门
gauge [geɪdʒ] n. 标准度量,计量器
gaze [geɪz] v. 凝视,注视

gear [gɪə(r)] n. 齿轮,传动装置;用具,装备 v. 开动,连接
generate[4] ['dʒenəreɪt] vt. 产生,发生;引起,导致
generator ['dʒenəreɪtə(r)] n. 发电机,发生器
generous ['dʒenərəs] a. 慷慨,大方;丰盛,丰富;宽厚的
genetic[22] [dʒɪ'netɪk] a. 遗传的,起源的
genetics [dʒɪ'netɪks] n. 遗传学
genius ['dʒiːnɪəs] n. 天才
genuine[5] ['dʒenjʊɪn] a. 真正的,真实的,诚恳的
geology [dʒɪ'ɒlədʒɪ] n. 地质学
geometry [dʒɪ'ɒmətrɪ] n. 几何(学)
germ [dʒɜːm] n. 微生物,细菌
gesture ['dʒestʃə(r)] n. 手势,姿态
ghost [gəʊst] n. 鬼,幽灵
giant ['dʒaɪənt] a. 巨大的 n. 巨人
gift [gɪft] n. 礼物;天赋
gigantic [dʒaɪ'gæntɪk] a. 巨大的,庞大的
giraffe [dʒɪ'rɑːf] n. 长颈鹿
glamo(u)r ['glæmə(r)] n. 魅力(魔法) vt. 迷惑;使有魅力
glide [glaɪd] n. 滑动,滑过,流水 v. 滑动,滑翔,溜走
glimpse [glɪmps] n. 一瞥,一闪
globe [gləʊb] n. 地球,地球仪,球体
gloom [gluːm] n. 黑暗,忧郁
glorious ['glɔːrɪəs] a. 光荣的,辉煌的
glove [glʌv] n. 手套
glow [gləʊ] n. 炽热,光辉,热情
glue[15] [gluː] n. 胶,胶水 vt. (用胶水)粘贴
goat [gəʊt] n. 山羊
god [gɒd] n. 神,(G-)上帝
golden ['gəʊldən] a. 金色的;黄金的;金制的
golf [gɒlf] n. 高尔夫球
goodness ['gʊdnɪs] int. 天哪 n. 善良,美德
goose [guːs] n. 鹅

gorgeous ['gɔːdʒəs] *a.* 华丽的,灿烂的,好极了

gossip ['gɒsɪp] *n.* 闲聊,随笔 *v.* 说闲话

govern ['gʌvn] *vt.* 统治,管理;支配,影响

governor ['gʌvənə(r), -vn-] *n.* 统治者,管理者,理事

gown [gaʊn] *n.* 长袍,长外衣

grab [græb] *n.* 抓握,接应,掠夺 *v.* 抓取,抢去

graceful ['greɪsf(ʊ)l] *a.* 优美的,文雅的

grade [greɪd] *n.* 年级

grain [greɪn] *n.* 谷物,谷类,颗粒,细粒,纹理

gram(me) [græm] *n.* 克

grammar ['græmə(r)] *n.* 语法

grand [grænd] *a.* 重大的,主要的;宏大的,盛大的;伟大的,崇高的

grant [grɑːnt] *vt.* 同意,准予;给予,授予 *n.* 授予物,拨款

grape [greɪp] *n.* 葡萄

graph [grɑːf] *n.* 图表,曲线图

graphic ['græfɪk] *a.* 生动的,图表的

grasp [grɑːsp] *vt./n.* 掌握,理解;抓紧,抓住

gratitude ['grætɪtjuːd] *n.* 感激

grave [greɪv] *a.* 严肃的,庄重的,严重的 *n.* 坟墓

gravity ['grævətɪ] *n.* 地心引力,重力,严重,庄重,严肃

graze [greɪz] *n.* 放牧,擦伤

greet [griːt] *vt.* 致敬,敬意,迎接

grieve [griːv] *vt.* 使悲哀,使伤心

grim [grɪm] *a.* 冷酷的;残忍的;糟糕的

grin [grɪn] *n.* 露齿笑,裂口笑 *v.* 露齿而笑

grind [graɪnd] *vt.* 研,磨,碾

grip [grɪp] *n.* 紧握,手提包 *v.* 抓紧,抱住,吸住

groan [grəʊn] *n.* 呻吟

grocer ['grəʊsə(r)] *n.* 食品杂货商

grope [grəʊp] *vi.* (for) 摸索;探索

gross [grəʊs] *n.* 总数,总量 *a.* 总共的,未打折扣的,毛重的

guardian ['gɑːdjən] *n.* 保护人,监护人

guidance ['gaɪdns] n. 引导,指导
guideline ['gaɪdlaɪn] n. 指南,方针
gulf [gʌlf] n. 海湾
gum [gʌm] n. 树胶,橡皮,橡皮糖
guy [gaɪ] n. (男)人,家伙
gym(nasium) [dʒɪm('neɪzɪəm)] n. 健身房,体育馆
gymnastics [dʒɪm'næstɪks] n. 体育,体操

H

habitual [hə'bɪtjʊəl,-tʃʊ-] a. 惯常的,习惯的
hacker ['hækə(r)] n. 黑客
hail [heɪl] n. 冰雹 v. 致敬,招呼
hairdresser ['heədresə(r)] n. 美发师,理发师
hairy ['heərɪ] a. 多毛的;毛状的;长毛的
hall [hɔːl] n. 大厅,礼堂
halt [hɔːlt] n. 停止,立定,休息
ham [hæm] n. 火腿
hammer⁵ ['hæmə(r)] n. 锤,榔头 v. 锤击,敲打
handbag ['hæn(d)bæg] n. 手提包
handbook ['hæn(d)bʊk] n. 手册,指南
handicap⁴ ['hændɪkæp] n. 障碍 v. 妨碍
handicraft ['hændɪkrɑːft] n. 手工艺;手工艺品
handkerchief ['hæŋkətʃɪf] n. 手帕
handmade [ˌhænd'meɪd] a. 手工的;手制的
handsome ['hænsəm] a. 英俊的
handy ['hændɪ] a. 方便的,手边的
harass ['hærəs] v. 骚扰/(使)烦恼
harbo(u)r ['hɑːbə(r)] n. 海港 vt. 停泊
harden ['hɑːdn] vt. 硬化,变硬
hardship ['hɑːdʃɪp] n. 艰难,困苦

hardware ['hɑːdweə(r)] n. 五金器具 n. (计算机)硬件
hardy ['hɑːdɪ] a. 坚强的;能吃苦耐劳的;勇敢的
harmful[13] ['hɑːmf(ʊ)l] a. 有害的;能造成损害的
harmony ['hɑːmənɪ] n. 协调,和睦,调和
harness ['hɑːnɪs] vt. 控制,利用
harsh[4] [hɑːʃ] a. 粗糙的,刺耳的,严厉的
haste [heɪst] n. 急速,急忙 v. 匆忙,赶快
hasty ['heɪstɪ] a. 匆匆的,轻率的,急忙的
hatch [hætʃ] n. 孵化,舱口 v. 孵,孵出
hatred ['heɪtrɪd] n. 憎恶,憎恨,怨恨
haul [hɔːl] n. 用力拖拉,努力的结果 v. 拖,改变方向
haunt [hɔːnt] n. 常到的地方 v. 常到,出没,萦绕于心
hawk [hɔːk] n. 鹰,隼
hay [heɪ] n. 干草
hazard ['hæzəd] n. 冒险,危险,危害
heading[4] ['hedɪŋ] n. 标题
headline ['hedlaɪn] n. (pl.)新闻提要,大字标题
headmaster [ˌhed'mɑːstə(r)] n. 校长
headquarters [ˌhed'kwɔːtəz] n. 司令部,指挥部,总部
healthcare ['helθkeə] n. 医疗保健;卫生保健;健康护理,健康服务
heap [hiːp] n. 堆,许多,累积 v. 堆积
hearing ['hɪərɪŋ] n. 听力
heater ['hiːtə(r)] n. 加热器,发热器
heating ['hiːtɪŋ] n. 供暖;暖器装置
heaven ['hevn] n. 天堂;天空
hedge [hedʒ] n. 树篱
heel [hiːl] n. 脚后跟
heir [eə(r)] n. 继承人
helicopter ['helɪkɒptə(r)] n. 直升机
hell [hel] n. 地狱
hello [hə'ləʊ] int. (见面打招呼或打电话用语)喂,你好
helpless ['helplɪs] a. 无助的,无依靠的

hemisphere ['hemɪˌsfɪə(r)] n. 半球

hen [hen] n. 母鸡

hence [hens] ad. 因此；今后

herb [hɜːb] n. 药草，香草

herd [hɜːd] n. 兽群，人群，牧人

heritage ['herɪtɪdʒ] n. 遗产，继承物

heroic [həˈrəʊɪk] a. 英雄的，英勇的

heroine ['herəʊɪn] n. 女英雄；女主角，女主人公

heroism ['herəʊɪzəm] n. 英勇，英雄气概

hesitant ['hezɪtənt] a. 踌躇的；迟疑的；犹豫不定的

hibernate ['haɪbəneɪt] vi. （动物）冬眠

high-speed ['haɪ'spiːd] a. 高速的

highway ['haɪweɪ] n. 公路

hike [haɪk] n. 徒步旅行，远足，涨价

hinder ['hɪndə(r)] vi. 成为阻碍 vt. 阻碍；打扰

hinge [hɪndʒ] n. 铰链

hint [hɪnt] vt./n. 暗示，示意

hip [hɪp] n. 臀部，屋脊，忧郁

historian[5] [hɪˈstɔːrɪən] n. 历史学家

historic [hɪˈstɒrɪk] a. 有历史意义的

historical[8] [hɪˈstɒrɪkl] a. 历史的

hive [haɪv] n. 蜂房，蜂巢

hoist [hɔɪst] n. 升起，吊起；起重机 vi. 升起；吊起 vt. （用绳索、起重机等）使升起

hole [həʊl] n. 孔，洞，穴

hollow ['hɒləʊ] a. 空的，中空的；空洞的，空虚的

holy ['həʊlɪ] a. 神圣的，圣洁的

holiday ['hɒlədɪ, -deɪ] n. 假期，假日

homosexual [ˌhəʊmə(ʊ)ˈsekʃuəl] n. 同性恋者 a. 同性恋的

honey ['hʌnɪ] a. 蜂蜜似的 n. 蜂蜜，宝贝

honeymoon ['hʌnɪmuːn] n. 蜜月；蜜月假期 vi. 度蜜月

hook [hʊk] n. 钩，钩状物 vt. 钩住

hopeless ['həʊplɪs] *a.* 没有希望的,绝望的
horizon [hə'raɪzn] *n.* 地平线;眼界,见识
hormone⁴ ['hɔːməʊn] *n.* 荷尔蒙,激素
horn [hɔːn] *n.* 喇叭 *n.* (牛、羊等的)角,喇叭,触角
horrible ['hɒrəbl] *a.* 可怕的,令人毛骨悚然的,令人讨厌的
horror ['hɒrə(r)] *a.* (电影等)意在引起恐怖的 *n.* 恐怖,战栗
horsepower ['hɔːspaʊə(r)] *n.* 马力
hose [həʊz] *n.* 长筒袜;软管,水龙带
hospitality [ˌhɒspɪ'tælətɪ] *n.* 好客,殷勤
hostage ['hɒstɪdʒ] *n.* 人质
hostile⁵ ['hɒstaɪl] *a.* 怀敌意的,敌对的
  be hostile to 对……有敌意
hotdog ['hɒtdɒg] *n.* 热狗(面包)
hourly ['aʊəlɪ] *ad.* 每小时地 *a.* 每小时的,以钟点计算的
household⁷ ['haʊshəʊld] *a.* 家庭的 *n.* 家庭,户
housewife ['haʊswaɪf] *n.* 家庭主妇
housework ['haʊswɜːk] *n.* 家事,家务
housing ['haʊzɪŋ] *n.* 房屋(外壳,外套,外罩,住宅,卡箍,遮盖物)
hover ['hɒvə(r)] *v.* 盘旋,翱翔,徘徊
huddle ['hʌdl] *vi.* 挤作一团
hug [hʌg] *n.* 紧抱,拥抱 *v.* 紧抱,固执
hum [hʌm] *n.* 嗡嗡声;哼声
humane [hjuː'meɪn, hjʊ-] *a.* 仁慈的,人道的;高尚的
humanism ['hjuːmənɪzəm] *n.* 人文主义;人道主义
humanist ['hjuːmənɪst] *n.* 人文主义者;人道主义者 *a.* 人文主义的;
  人道主义的
humanitarian [hjuːˌmænɪ'teərɪən, hjʊ-] *n.* 人道主义者,博爱者,基督
  凡人论者 *a.* 人道主义的,博爱的,相信基督为凡
  人的
humanity [hjuː'mænɪtɪ, hjʊ-] *n.* 人类,人性;人道;慈爱
humble ['hʌmbl] *a.* 低下的,卑贱的;恭顺的,谦卑的
humidity [hjuː'mɪdətɪ] *n.* 湿度

humiliate [hjuːˈmɪlɪeɪt] vt. 使……丢脸；羞辱
humo(u)rous [ˈhjuːmərəs] a. 幽默的
hurricane [ˈhʌrɪkən,-k(e)ɪn] n. 飓风
hut [hʌt] n. 小屋，棚屋
hydrogen[7] [ˈhaɪdrədʒən] n. 氢
hypothesis [haɪˈpɒθɪsɪs] n. 假设
hysterical [hɪˈsterɪkl] a. 歇斯底里的，异常兴奋的

I

I [aɪ] pron. 我
iceberg [ˈaɪsbɜːg] n. 冰山
ice-cream [ˌaɪsˈkriːm] n. 冰淇淋
ideal[8] [aɪˈdɪəl] a. 理想的，称心如意的；唯心理论的 n. 理想
identical[9] [aɪˈdentɪkl] a. 相同的，同一的
identification [aɪˌdentɪfɪˈkeɪʃən] n. 身份的证明，确认
identity [(a)ɪˈdentɪtɪ] n. 身份
ideology [ˌ(a)ɪdɪˈɒlədʒɪ] n. 观念学，空论，意识形态
idiom [ˈɪdɪəm] n. 成语，惯用语
idiot [ˈɪdɪət] n. 白痴
idle [ˈaɪdl] a. 闲散的，闲置的；无用的，无效的 v. 空费，虚度
ignite [ɪgˈnaɪt] vt. 点燃；使燃烧
illicit [ɪˈlɪsɪt] a. 违法的；不正当的
illiterate [ɪˈlɪtərɪt] a. 文盲的 n. 文盲
illuminate [ɪˈluːmɪneɪt] v. 照明，阐释，说明
illusion [ɪˈluːʒən] n. 幻想
illustrate[4] [ˈɪləstreɪt] vt. 举例说明，图解
immense [ɪˈmens] a. 巨大的，广大的
immerse [ɪˈmɜːs] v. 浸，陷入
immigrate [ˈɪmɪgreɪt] vi. 移居（入境）
immigration [ˌɪmɪˈgreɪʃən] n. 移居，移民

immune [ɪˈmjuːn] a. (from) 被豁免的,免除的;免疫(性)的,有免疫力的;不受影响的

impair[15] [ɪmˈpeə(r)] vt. 损害;削弱

imperial [ɪmˈpɪərɪəl] a. 帝国的

imperialism [ɪmˈpɪərɪəlɪzəm] n. 帝国主义

imperialist [ɪmˈpɪərɪəlɪst] n. 帝国主义者 a. 帝国主义的

implement [ˈɪmplɪmənt] vt. 实现,使生效;实施

implication[4] [ˌɪmplɪˈkeɪʃən] n. 暗示,含义

implicit [ɪmˈplɪsɪt] a. 暗示的;盲从的;含蓄的

impose[5] [ɪmˈpəʊz] vt. (on) 征税,加强;以欺骗,利用,施影响

impractical [ɪmˈpræktɪkl] a. 不切实际的,不现实的;不能实行的

imprison [ɪmˈprɪzn] vt. 监禁;关押;使……下狱

impromptu [ɪmˈprɒmptjuː] ad. 即席地 a. 即席的

impulse [ˈɪmpʌls] n. 冲动 v. 推动

inaugurate [ɪnˈɔːgjʊreɪt] v. 开创,举行……开幕典礼

inborn [ˌɪnˈbɔːn] a. 天生的;先天的

incentive [ɪnˈsentɪv] n. 动机;刺激

incident [ˈɪnsɪdənt] n. 事件,政治事件,事变

incline [ɪnˈklaɪn] v. 使认为,使倾向;使倾斜,使偏向 n. 斜坡,斜面

inclusive [ɪnˈkluːsɪv] a. 包含……在内的

incompatible [ˌɪnkəmˈpætəbl] a. 矛盾的;不相容的

incorporate [ɪnˈkɔːpəreɪt] vt. 包含,吸收;体现 vi. 合并;组成一体

increasingly[5] [ɪnˈkriːsɪŋli] ad. 逐渐地,渐增地

incur [ɪnˈkɜː(r)] vt. 招致,引发;蒙受

independence [ˌɪndɪˈpendəns] n. 独立,自立,自主

index [ˈɪndeks] n. 索引;指标,指数

indication [ˌɪndɪˈkeɪʃən] n. 指示,表示;暗示

indifferent [ɪnˈdɪfərənt] a. 漠不关心的,无重要性的,中立的

indifference [ɪnˈdɪfərəns] n. 漠不关心;冷淡;不感兴趣

indignant [ɪnˈdɪgnənt] a. 愤慨的,愤愤不平的

indispensable [ˌɪndɪˈspensəbl] a. 不可缺少的;绝对必要的

indoor(s) [ˌɪnˈdɔː(z), -ˈdɒə(z)] a./ad. 室内的(地),户内的(地)

induce [ɪn'djuːs] vt. 引诱;感应

indulge [ɪn'dʌldʒ] v. 纵情于,放任,迁就

industrialization [ɪnˌdʌstrɪəlaɪ'zeɪʃn] n. 工业化

inertia [ɪ'nɜːʃjə] n. 惯性,惰性

infection [ɪn'fekʃən] n. 感染;传染;传染病

infectious [ɪn'fekʃəs] a. 传染的;易传染的

inference ['ɪnfərəns] n. 推论;推断;推理

inferior [ɪn'fɪərɪə(r)] a. 次等的,较低的,不如的

infinite ['ɪnfɪnɪt] a. 无限的,无穷的 n. 无限

inflation[8] [ɪn'fleɪʃən] n. 通货膨胀

ingredient[4] [ɪn'griːdjənt] n. 成分,因素

inhabit[4] [ɪn'hæbɪt] v. 居住于,占据,栖息

inhabitant [ɪn'hæbɪtənt] n. 居民

inherit[7] [ɪn'herɪt] vt. 继承

initial[8] [ɪ'nɪʃl] a. 最初的,开头的 n. 首字母

initiate[4] [ɪ'nɪʃɪeɪt] vt. 开始,创始;发起

initiative[5] [ɪ'nɪʃ(ɪ)ətɪv] n. 主动权;首创精神 a. 起始的;主动的;自发的

inject [ɪn'dʒekt] v. 注射

injection [ɪn'dʒekʃən] n. 注射

ink [ɪŋk] n. 墨水

inland ['ɪnlənd, 'ɪnlænd] a. 内陆的,国内的

inn [ɪn] n. 客栈,小旅店

inner ['ɪnə(r)] a. 内部的,里面的,内心的 n. 里面,内部

innocence ['ɪnəsəns] n. 无罪,无知,天真无邪

innumerable [ɪ'njuːmərəbl] a. 无数的,数不清的

inquire/enquire [ɪn'kwaɪə] v. (about/into) 询问,问明,查究

inquiry/enquiry [ɪn'kwaɪərɪ] n. (about/into) 质询,调查

insane [ɪn'seɪn] a. 疯狂的,精神错乱的

insert[7] [ɪn'sɜːt] vt. 插入

insight[7] ['ɪnsaɪt] n. 洞察力;洞悉

inspire [ɪn'spaɪə(r)] vt. 使产生灵感;鼓舞,感动

instal(l) [ɪnˈstɔːl] v. 安装,设置

installation [ˌɪnstəˈleɪʃən] n. 安装,装置

instal(l)ment [ɪnˈstɔːlmənt] n. 分期付款(安装,一期)

instance[7] [ˈɪnstəns] n. 例,例证,实例

instant[5] [ˈɪnstənt] a. 立刻的,立即的;紧急的,迫切的;(食品)速溶的,方便的 n. 瞬间,时刻

institute [ˈɪnstɪtjuːt] n. 学会,研究所,学院

institution[11] [ˌɪnstɪˈtjuːʃən] n. 公共机关,协会,学校;制度,习俗

institutional [ˌɪnstɪˈtjuːʃənəl] a. 制度的;制度上的

instruct[5] [ɪnˈstrʌkt] vt. 教,教授;指示,指令

instruction[4] [ɪnˈstrʌkʃən] n. (pl.)指令,指示,说明;教学,教导

insulate [ˈɪnsjʊleɪt] v. 使……绝缘,隔离

insurgent [ɪnˈsɜːdʒənt] a. 起义的,叛乱的 n. 叛乱者,起义者

intact [ɪnˈtækt] a. 完整的;原封不动的;未受损伤的

integral [ˈɪntɪɡrəl] a. 完整的,整体的

integrate [ˈɪntɪɡreɪt] vt. 使结合,使一体化 a. 完整的,综合的

integrity [ɪnˈteɡrɪtɪ] n. 正直,诚实;完整,完全,完整性

intellect [ˈɪntəlekt] n. 智力,思维逻辑领悟力,理解力,知识分子,才智超群的人

intellectual [ˌɪntɪˈlektjʊəl, -tʃʊ-] n. 有知识者,知识分子,凭理智做事者 a. 智力的,知性的,聪明的

intelligible [ɪnˈtelɪdʒəbl] a. 可理解的;明了的

intense [ɪnˈtens] a. 强烈地,激烈的,热烈的

intensify [ɪnˈtensɪfaɪ] vt. 加剧,加强,强化

intensity [ɪnˈtensətɪ] n. 激烈,强度,强烈,剧烈

intensive [ɪnˈtensɪv] a. 集中的,强化的,精细的,深入的

intention[8] [ɪnˈtenʃən] n. 意图,意向,目的

interaction[4] [ˌɪntərˈækʃən] n. 相互作用,相互影响

interior [ɪnˈtɪərɪə(r)] a. 内部的,内地的,国内的,在内的 n. 内部

interference [ˌɪntəˈfɪərəns] n. 冲突,干涉

interim [ˈɪntərɪm] a. 临时的,暂时的;中间的;间歇的 n. 过渡时期,中间时期

interior [ɪnˈtɪərɪə(r)] n. 内部,内地 a. 内部的,里面的;内地的
intermediate [ˌɪntəˈmiːdjət] a. 中间的,居中的 n. 中间体,媒介物
interpretation [ɪnˌtɜːprɪˈteɪʃən] n. 解释,演出,翻译,互动
interpreter [ɪnˈtɜːprɪtə(r)] n. 议员,口译者
interrogation [ɪnˌterəˈgeɪʃən] n. 审问;询问
interruption [ˌɪntəˈrʌpʃən] n. 打断,干扰;中断
interval [ˈɪntəvl] n. 间隔,间歇
intervene [ˌɪntəˈviːn] vi. 干涉;调停
intimate [ˈɪntɪmət] a. 亲密的,私人的,秘密的
intimidate [ɪnˈtɪmɪdeɪt] vt. 恐吓,威胁
intolerant [ɪnˈtɒlərənt] a. 无法忍受的
intricate [ˈɪntrɪkɪt] a. 复杂的;错综的
intrinsic [ɪnˈtrɪnsɪk] a. 本质的,固有的
introduction [ˌɪntrəˈdʌkʃən] n. 介绍,引进,传入;引论,导言,绪论;入门
invalid [ˈɪnvəliːd, -lɪd] a. 无效的,伤残的
invaluable [ɪnˈvæljʊəbl] a. 无价的;非常贵重的
invasion [ɪnˈveɪʒən] n. 侵入,侵略
invent[8] [ɪnˈvent] vt. 发明,创造;捏造,虚构
invention[4] [ɪnˈvenʃən] n. 发明,创造;捏造,虚构
inventory [ˈɪnvəntərɪ] n. 详细目录,存货清单
invert [ɪnˈvɜːt] a. 转化的 v. 反转,颠倒
invisible [ɪnˈvɪzəbl] a. 看不见的,无形的
invoice [ˈɪnvɔɪs] n. 发票;发货单
inward(s) [ˈɪnwəd(z)] a. 内心的,向内的
irrational [ɪˈræʃənəl] a. 无理性的;不合理的
irregular [ɪˈregjʊlə(r)] a. 不规则的,不整齐的,不合法的
irrigate [ˈɪrɪgeɪt] vi. 进行灌溉 vt. 灌溉
irritate [ˈɪrɪteɪt] v. 激怒,使……发怒
island [ˈaɪlənd] n. 岛
isle [aɪl] n. 岛,群岛
italic [ɪˈtælɪk] n. 斜体字(或字母、数码等) a. 斜体的

J

jacket ['dʒækɪt] n. 短上衣,夹克衫
jail/gaol [dʒeil] n. 监牢,监狱,拘留所
jam [dʒæm] n. 果酱,拥塞之物,堵塞
jar [dʒɑː(r)] n. 广口瓶,震动,刺耳声
jaw [dʒɔː] n. 颚,颌
jazz[7] [dʒæz] n. 爵士乐
jealousy ['dʒeləsɪ] n. 嫉妒;猜忌
jeans [dʒiːns] n. 牛仔裤
jeopardize/-ise ['dʒepədaɪz] v. 危害,使受困,使陷危地
jet [dʒet] n. 喷射,喷出,黑玉 v. 射出,进出,喷射
jetlag ['dʒetlæg] n. 时差综合征
jewel ['dʒuːəl] n. 宝石
jewel(l)ery ['dʒuːəlrɪ] n. [总称]珠宝;珠宝饰物
joint [dʒɔɪnt] n. 关节,骨节;接合处,接缝 a. 联合的,共同的,连接的
journalism ['dʒɜːnəlɪzəm] n. 新闻工作,新闻业
journalist ['dʒɜːnəlɪst] n. 记者,新闻工作者
judg(e)ment ['dʒʌdʒmənt] n. 审判,判决;判断力,识别力;意见,看法,判断
judicial [dʒuːˈdɪʃl] a. 法庭的,公正的,审判上的
juice [dʒuːs] n. 果汁
juicy ['dʒuːsɪ] a. 多汁的
jungle ['dʒʌŋgl] n. 丛林,密林
junior ['dʒuːnjə(r)] n. 年少者,地位较低者,大学三年级学生 a. 年少的,下级的,后进的
junk [dʒʌŋk] n. 垃圾,废物
Jupiter ['dʒuːpɪtə(r), 'dʒʊ-] n. 木星
jury ['dʒʊərɪ] n. 陪审团

just [dʒʌst] ad. 正好,恰好;刚刚,刚才;只是,仅仅是,只不过 a. 公正,公平
justice ['dʒʌstɪs] n. 公道,公平;审判,司法
justify ['dʒʌstɪfaɪ] vt. 认为有理,证明……正当
juvenile ['dʒuːvənaɪl] a. 青少年的 n. 青少年

K

kettle ['ketl] n. 水壶
keyboard ['kiːbɔːd] n. 键盘
kidnap ['kɪdnæp] v. 绑架,诱拐,拐骗
kidney ['kɪdnɪ] n. 肾,腰子
kilogram(me) ['kɪləgræm] n. 千克,公斤
kilometer/-tre ['kɪləmiːtə(r), kɪ'lɒmɪtə(r)] n. 公里
kilowatt ['kɪləwɒt] n. 千瓦
kindergarten ['kɪndəgɑːtn] n. 幼儿园
kingdom ['kɪŋdəm] n. 王国
kit [kɪt] n. 装备,工具箱
kite [kaɪt] n. 风筝
knee [niː] n. 膝,膝盖
kneel [niːl] vi. 跪,下跪
knit [nɪt] v. 编织,密接,结合
knob [nɒb] n. 把手,瘤
knot [nɒt] n. 结 v. 打结
knowledgeable ['nɒlɪdʒəbl] a. 有见识的;知识渊博的

L

label[5] ['leɪbl] n. 标签,标记 v. 贴标签,把……称为
lad [læd] n. 小伙子

ladder ['lædə(r)] n. 梯子

lag [læg] vi./n. 落后,滞后

lamb [læm] n. 羔羊,小羊,羔羊肉

lame [leɪm] a. 跛足的,僵痛的,不完全的

landscape ['lændskeɪp] n. 风景,山水,风景画

lane [leɪn] n. 小路,小巷,行车道

lap [læp] n. 膝盖,一周(圈)

laser ['leɪzə(r)] n. 激光

lateral ['lætərəl] a. 侧面的;旁边的 n. 旁边/侧面的东西

Latin[4] ['lætɪn] n. 拉丁文,拉丁语 a. 拉丁文的,拉丁语的

latter ['lætə(r)] a. 后者的;后一半的 n. 后者

laughter ['lɑːftə(r)] n. 笑,笑声

laundry ['lɔːndrɪ] n. 洗衣店,要洗的衣服,洗衣

lavatory ['lævətrɪ] n. 盥洗室,厕所

lawful ['lɔːf(ʊ)l] a. 法律许可的,守法的,合法的

lawn [lɔːn] n. 草地,草坪

lawsuit ['lɔːs(j)uːt] n. 诉讼;诉讼案件

lawyer ['lɔːjə(r)] n. 律师

layer ['le(ɪ)ə(r)] n. 层

layman ['leɪmən] n. 俗人,门外汉,凡人

layoff ['leɪɒf] n. 解雇;失业

layout ['leɪaʊt] n. 布局,安排,设计

leadership[4] ['liːdəʃɪp] n. 领导,领导才干

leading[5] ['liːdɪŋ] n. 领导,疏导,铅板 a. 领导的,主要的,在前的

leaf [liːf] n. 叶,树叶,花瓣

league [liːg] n. 联盟,社团

leak [liːk] n. 漏洞 v. 漏,泄漏

leap [liːp] n. 跳跃,剧增,急变 v. 跳跃,跃过,猛冲

learn [lɜːn] v. 学习,学会,记住;(of) 听说,获悉

learned[9] ['lɜːnɪd] a. 有学问的,博学的

learning[49] ['lɜːnɪŋ] n. 学习,学问,知识

lease [liːs] n. 租约,租期,租

leather ['leðə(r)] a. 皮革制的 n. 皮革
legend ['ledʒənd] n. 传说,传奇
legislation [ˌledʒɪs'leɪʃən] n. 立法,法律
legislative ['ledʒɪslətɪv] a. 立法的;有立法权的
legitimate [lɪ'dʒɪtɪmɪt] a. 合法的,正当的 v. 使合法
lemon ['lemən] n. 柠檬
lengthen ['leŋ(k)θən] vt. 伸长,延长
lengthy ['leŋ(k)θɪ] a. 漫长的,冗长的;啰唆的
lens [lenz] n. 镜头,透镜
lesbian ['lezbɪən] a. 女同性恋的 n. 女同性恋者
lest [lest] conj. 唯恐,以免 prep. 唯恐,以免
lever ['liːvə(r)] n. 杠杆,似杠杆之工具 v. 撬开,使用杠杆
liability [ˌlaɪə'bɪlɪtɪ] n. 责任,债务,倾向
liable[4] ['laɪəbl] a. 有义务的,应负责的,有……倾向的
  be liable for 负有……责任
  be liable to 易于……的
liaison [lɪ'eɪzn,-zɒn] n. 联络
liberal ['lɪbərəl] n. 自由主义者
liberate ['lɪbəreɪt] v. 解放,使获得自由,释出,放出
librarian [laɪ'breərɪən] n. 图书管理员
license/-ence ['laɪsəns] n. 执照,许可证,特许
lick [lɪk] n. 舔,少许,打 v. 舔,卷过,鞭打
lid [lɪd] n. 盖
lieutenant [le(f)'tenənt] n. 中尉;助理人员;副官
lifetime ['laɪftaɪm] n. 一生,终身
lighting ['laɪtɪŋ] n. 照明;照明设备;舞台灯光;点火
lightning ['laɪtnɪŋ] n. 闪电
likelihood ['laɪklɪhʊd] n. 可能性,可能
likewise[5] ['laɪkwaɪz] ad. 同样地,照样地;又,也
limitation [ˌlɪmɪ'teɪʃən] n. 限制
limited[20] ['lɪmɪtɪd] a. 有限的
limp [lɪmp] n. 跛行 a. 柔软的,无力的,软弱的

liner [ˈlaɪnə(r)] n. 班机,班轮

linger [ˈlɪŋɡə(r)] v. 逗留,消磨,徘徊

lip [lɪp] n. 嘴唇

liquor [ˈlɪkə(r)] n. 酒

liter/-tre [ˈliːtə(r)] n. 升(容量单位)

literacy [ˈlɪtərəsɪ] n. 读写能力,识字

literally [ˈlɪtərəlɪ] ad. 逐字地,按照字面上地,不夸张地

literary [ˈlɪtərərɪ] a. 文学的

literature [ˈlɪtərɪtʃə(r)] n. 文学,文献

litter [ˈlɪtə(r)] n. 垃圾,杂乱

livelihood [ˈlaɪvlɪhʊd] n. 生计,营生,生活

lively [ˈlaɪvlɪ] a. 活泼的,活跃的,栩栩如生的,真实的

liver [ˈlɪvə(r)] n. 肝脏

living-room n. 起居室

loaf [ləʊf] n. 条,块 v. 游手好闲,虚度光阴

lobby [ˈlɒbɪ] n. 大厅,门廊,门厅,休息室,游说议员者

local[25] [ˈləʊkl] a. 地方的,当地的;局部的

locate[4] [lə(ʊ)ˈkeɪt] vt. 找出,查出;设置在,位于

location[10] [lə(ʊ)ˈkeɪʃən] n. 地点,位置

lodge [lɒdʒ] n. 小屋,门房,支部 v. 临时住宿,安顿

lofty [ˈlɒftɪ] a. 崇高的

log [lɒɡ] n. 记录,圆木,日志

logo [ˈləʊɡəʊ, ˈlɒ-] n. 商标,徽标

longevity [lɒnˈdʒevɪtɪ] n. 长命,长寿;寿命

longitude [ˈlɒndʒɪtjuːd, -ŋɡɪ-] n. 经度

loom [luːm] vi. 朦胧地出现;隐约可见;可怕地出现

loop [luːp] n. 环,圈,弯曲部分 v. 使……成环,以圈联结,以环联结

loosen [ˈluːsn] v. 放松,松开,解除

lord [lɔːd] int. 主,天啊 n. 上帝,主

lorry [ˈlɒrɪ] n. 卡车

lottery [ˈlɒtərɪ] n. 彩票或奖券的发行,抽彩给奖法

lounge [laʊndʒ] n. 闲逛,休闲室,长沙发
lover ['lʌvə(r)] n. 爱好者,情人
lubricate ['luːbrɪkeɪt] v. 润滑,涂油
luminous ['luːmɪnəs] a. 发光的,发亮的
lump[15] [lʌmp] n. 块状,瘤,很多
lunar ['luːnə(r)] a. 月亮的
luncheon ['lʌntʃən] n. 午宴;正式的午餐会
lure [l(j)ʊə(r)] n. 饵,诱惑 v. 引诱,诱惑
lurk [lɜːk] vi. 潜伏,埋伏,潜藏 n. 埋伏;潜伏
luxury ['lʌkʃərɪ] n. 奢侈,豪华

M

machine [mə'ʃiːn] n. 机器,机械装置,机械般工作的人
machinery [mə'ʃiːnərɪ] n. (总称)机器,机械
madam/-ame ['mædəm] n. 夫人,女士
magistrate ['mædʒɪstreɪt,-trɪt] n. 地方法官
magnet ['mæɡnɪt] n. 磁体,磁铁
magnetic [mæɡ'netɪk] a. 有磁性的,有吸引力的,催眠术的
magnificent [mæɡ'nɪfɪsnt] a. 壮丽的,宏伟的
magnify ['mæɡnɪfaɪ] v. 放大
maid [meɪd] n. 女仆,侍女
mailbox ['meɪlbɒks] n. 邮筒,邮箱
mainland ['meɪnlənd,-lænd] n. 大陆,本土
mainstream ['meɪnstriːm] n. 主流
maintenance ['meɪntɪnəns,-tnəns] n. 维护,保持,维修,生活费用
majesty ['mædʒɪstɪ] n. 最高权威,威严,王权
majority[10] [mə'dʒɒrɪtɪ] n. 多数,过半数
makeup ['meɪkʌp] n. 化妆品
malicious [mə'lɪʃəs] a. 恶毒的;恶意的
mall [mɔːl,mæl] n. 商业街,购物商场

mammal ['mæml] n. 哺乳动物

management[12] ['mænɪdʒmənt] n. 管理,经营,处理

managerial [ˌmænɪ'dʒɪərɪəl] a. 经理的;管理的

mandate ['mændeɪt,-dɪt] n. 命令,指令;委托管理;授权 vt. 托管;
授权

maneuver/manoeuvre [mə'nʊvə] n. 演习,调遣,策略

manifest ['mænɪfest] vt. 证明,表明;显示 vi. 显示,出现 a. 明白的,
显然的

manipulate [mə'nɪpjʊleɪt] vt. 操作;操纵

mankind [mæn'kaɪnd] n. 人类

mansion ['mænʃən] n. 大厦;宅邸

manual ['mænjʊəl] a. 用手的,手工的;体力的 n. 手册,指南

manufacture[5] [ˌmænjʊ'fæktʃə(r)] vt. 制造,加工 n. 制造(业),产品

manufacturer [ˌmænjʊ'fæktʃərə(r)] n. 制造商

manuscript ['mænjʊskrɪpt] n. 手稿,原稿

marble ['mɑːbl] a. 大理石的,冷酷的 n. 大理石

margin ['mɑːdʒɪn] n. 页边空余,边缘

marginal ['mɑːdʒɪnl] a. 边缘的;末端的

marine [mə'riːn] n. (海军)士兵或军官 a. 海的,海生的;船舶的,
航海的

marketing ['mɑːkɪtɪŋ] n. 行销,买卖

marsh [mɑːʃ] n. 沼泽,湿地

marshal ['mɑːʃəl] n. (陆、空军)高级将官,典礼官,执法官

martyr ['mɑːtə(r)] n. 烈士;殉道者

marvel(l)ous ['mɑːvələs] a. 惊奇的

Marxism ['mɑːksɪzəm] n. 马克思主义

masculine ['mæskjʊlɪn] a. 阳性的;男性的

mask [mɑːsk] n. 口罩,假面具,掩饰

massacre ['mæsəkə(r)] n. 大屠杀 v. 大屠杀

massive ['mæsɪv] a. 巨大的

mastermind ['mɑːstəmaɪnd] vt. 策划

masterpiece ['mɑːstəpiːs] n. 杰作

mate [meɪt] n. 配偶,同事,助手

maternity [mə'tɜːnɪtɪ] n. 母性,母道

mathematical [ˌmæθɪ'mætɪkl] a. 数学的

mature [mə'tjʊə(r),-'tʃʊə(r)] a. 成熟的,考虑周到的 v. (使)成熟,长成

maturity [mə'tjʊərɪtɪ,-'tʃʊə-] n. 成熟

maximize ['mæksɪmaɪz] vt. 取得……最大值

maximum ['mæksɪməm] n. 极点,最大量,极大

meadow ['medəʊ] n. 草地

meantime [ˌmiːn'taɪm] n. 其间,其时 ad. 其间

meanwhile ['miːnwaɪl] n. 其时,其间 ad. 同时,当时

measurement ['meʒəmənt] n. 测量,衡量,尺寸,大小

mechanic [mɪ'kænɪk] n. 技工,机械工人

mechanical [mɪ'kænɪkl] a. 机械的,力学的,呆板的

mechanics [mɪ'kænɪks] n. 机械学,力学

mechanism[4] ['mekənɪzəm] n. 机械,机构,结构,机制,原理

medal ['medl] n. 奖章,勋章,纪念章

mediate ['miːdɪeɪt] vi. 调解,斡旋;居中 vt. 调停;传达

medieval [ˌmedɪ'iːvl] a. 中世纪的

Mediterranean [ˌmedɪtə'reɪnjən] n./a. 地中海(的)

medium ['miːdɪəm] n. 媒体,方法,媒介

melody ['melədɪ] n. 旋律,曲子,美的音乐,曲调

melt [melt] v. 熔化,融化

membership ['membəʃɪp] n. 成员资格,会员资格

memorandum [ˌmemə'rændəm] n. 备忘录

memorial [mə'mɔːrɪəl] n. 纪念碑(堂),纪念仪式

memorize/-ise ['meməraɪz] vt. 记住,背熟

menace ['menəs] n. 威胁,胁迫 v. 威吓,胁迫

merchant ['mɜːtʃənt] n. 商人,店主

mercury ['mɜːkjʊrɪ] n. 水银,水星

merge [mɜːdʒ] v. 合并,消失,吞没

merger ['mɜːdʒər] n. (企业等的)合并

merit ['merɪt] n. 功绩,价值,真相
merry ['merɪ] a. 欢乐的,兴高采烈的
messenger ['mesɪndʒə(r)] n. 报信者,先驱
metric ['metrɪk] a. 公制的,米制的 n. 度量标准
metropolitan [ˌmetrə'pɒlɪtən] n. 大都市的居民,大主教,母国的居民
Mexican ['meksɪkən] n./a. 墨西哥(的) n. 墨西哥(人)
microbe ['maɪkrəʊb] n. 微生物
microphone ['maɪkrəfəʊn] n. 麦克风,扩音器
microscope ['maɪkrəskəʊp] n. 显微镜
microwave ['maɪkrə(ʊ)weɪv] n. 微波
midday [mɪd'deɪ] n. 正午,中午
midnight ['mɪdnaɪt] n. 午夜
mid [mɪd] a. 中间的;中央的 prep. 在……之中
migrate [maɪ'greɪt] vi. 移动,移往;移植;随季节而移居,(鸟类的)迁徙 vt. 使移居,使移植
milestone ['maɪlstəʊn] n. 里程碑
militant ['mɪlɪtənt] a. 好战的 n. 富有战斗性的人;好斗者
militia [mɪ'lɪʃə] n. 义勇军,自卫队,国民军
mill [mɪl] n. 磨粉机,磨坊,制造厂
millimeter/-tre ['mɪlɪmiːtə(r)] n. 毫米
millionaire [ˌmɪljə'neə(r)] n. 百万富翁
mine [maɪn] n. 地雷,矿,矿山 pron. 我的
miner ['maɪnə(r)] n. 矿工
mineral ['mɪnərəl] a. 矿物的 n. 矿物,矿石
mingle ['mɪŋgl] v. 混合,联合,交际
miniature ['mɪnɪətʃə(r)] n. 缩图,小画像 a. 小规模的,纤小的
minimize/-ise ['mɪnɪmaɪz] vt. 使减到最少 vi. 最小化
minimum ['mɪnɪməm] n. 最小量,最低限度 a. 最低的,最小的
minister ['mɪnɪstə(r)] n. 部长,大臣
ministry ['mɪnɪstrɪ] n. (政府的)部
minority [maɪ'nɒrɪtɪ] n. 少数,少数民族

mint [mɪnt] *n.* 薄荷;造币厂

minus ['maɪnəs] *a.* 负的,减去的 *n.* 减号,负号 *prep.* 减去

miraculous [mɪ'rækjʊləs] *a.* 不可思议的,奇迹的

misconduct [ˌmɪs'kɒndʌkt] *n.* 行为不检

misery[4] ['mɪzərɪ] *n.* 痛苦,悲惨

misfortune [mɪs'fɔːtʃən] *n.* 不幸;灾祸,灾难

misguide [mɪs'gaɪd] *vt.* 误导;使误入歧途

missile ['mɪsaɪl] *n.* 导弹

mission[5] ['mɪʃən] *n.* 任务,代表团,使命

missionary ['mɪʃənərɪ] *n.* 传教士,负有任务者,工作人员

mist [mɪst] *n.* 薄雾

mistress ['mɪstrɪs] *n.* 主妇,女主人,情妇

misunderstand [ˌmɪsʌndə'stænd] *v.* 误解,误会

moan [məʊn] *n.* 呻吟声,悲叹声,抱怨声 *v.* 抱怨,呻吟

mobile[14] ['məʊbaɪl] *a.* 可移动的,易变的

mobilize/-ise ['məʊbɪlaɪz] *v.* 动员,赋予可动性,使流通

mock [mɒk] *n.* 嘲笑,戏弄,模仿 *v.* 嘲弄,模仿,轻视

mode [məʊd] *n.* 方式,样式

modem ['məʊdem] *n.* [计] 调制解调器

moderate ['mɒdərɪt] *a.* 中等的,适度的;温和的,稳健的

modern ['mɒdən] *a.* 现代的,近代的;新式的

modest ['mɒdɪst] *a.* 端庄的,朴素的;谦虚的,谦逊的;适度的

modesty ['mɒdɪstɪ] *n.* 谦逊

modify ['mɒdɪfaɪ] *vt.* 修改,修饰;更改 *vi.* 修改

module ['mɒdjuːl] *n.* 组件

moist [mɔɪst] *a.* 潮湿的,湿润的

moisture ['mɔɪstʃə(r)] *n.* 潮湿,湿气

molecule ['mɒlɪkjuːl] *n.* 分子

momentary ['məʊməntərɪ] *a.* 瞬间的;短暂的

monetary ['mʌnɪtərɪ] *a.* 货币的,金融的

monopoly [mə'nɒpəlɪ] *n.* 垄断,专利,独占,控制

monster ['mɒnstə(r)] *n.* 怪物,恶人,巨物

monument ['mɒnjʊmənt] n. 纪念碑
moon [muːn] n. 月亮
morality [məˈrælɪtɪ] n. 道德,美德
mortal ['mɔːtl] a. 人世间的,致命的,终有一死的 n. 凡人
mortgage ['mɔːgɪdʒ] n. / v. 抵押
Moslem ['mɒzləm] n. /a. 穆斯林,伊斯兰教徒
mosquito[23] [məˈskiːtəʊ] n. 蚊子
most [məʊst] a. 最多的,最大的 ad. 最,非常,极 n. 大多数,大部分
motel [məʊˈtel] n. 汽车旅馆
motion ['məʊʃən] n. 动,运动;提议,动议
motorbike ['məʊtəbaɪk] n. 摩托车
motorway ['məʊtəweɪ] n. 高速公路
mount [maʊnt] vt. 登上,爬上,骑上;装配,固定,镶嵌 n. 支架,底座,底板
mourn [mɔːn] v. 哀悼,忧伤,服丧
mouse [maʊs] n. 老鼠,鼠标
mud [mʌd] n. 泥,泥浆
muddy ['mʌdɪ] a. 泥泞的,污的,肮脏的
mug [mʌg] n. 杯
multicultural [ˌmʌltɪˈkʌltʃərəl] a. 多种文化的
multinational [ˌmʌltɪˈnæʃnl] a. 多国的,跨国公司的,多民族的 n. 跨国公司,多国公司
multiple ['mʌltɪpl] a. 多样的,多重的 n. 倍数
multiply ['mʌltɪplaɪ] v. 乘;增加;繁殖
multitude ['mʌltɪtjuːd] n. 众多,大量;群众;多数
municipal[6] [mjuːˈnɪsɪpl] a. 市的,市政的
murmur ['mɜːmə(r)] n. 低语;低语声;低声抱怨 vi. 低声说;私下抱怨
muscle ['mʌsl] n. 肌肉
mushroom ['mʌʃrʊm] n. 草,蘑菇,暴发户
musical ['mjuːzɪkl] a. 音乐的 n. 音乐片
musician [mjuːˈzɪʃən] n. 音乐家

mute [mju:t] n. 哑子,默音字母,弱音器 a. 哑的,无声的,沉默的
mutter ['mʌtə(r)] n. 喃喃低语 v. 喃喃自语,作低沉声,出怨言
mutual⁴ ['mju:tʃʊəl] a. 相互的;共同的
mysterious⁴ [mɪ'stɪərɪəs] a. 神秘的;不可思议的
mystery⁷ ['mɪstərɪ] n. 神秘,神秘的事;神秘小说,侦探小说

N

nail [neɪl] n. 钉子,指甲
naive [naɪ'i:v] a. 天真的,幼稚的
naked ['neɪkɪd] a. 裸体的;毫无遮掩的
narrate [nə'reɪt] vt. 叙述;给……作旁白 vi. 叙述;讲述
narrative ['nærətɪv] n. 叙述,故事 a. 叙述的,叙事的,故事体的
nasty ['nɑ:stɪ] a. 令人厌恶的;难弄的;恶劣的;污秽的
nationalist ['næʃənəlɪst] n. 国家主义者,民族主义者
nationality [ˌnæʃən'ælɪtɪ] n. 国籍,民族
naval ['neɪvl] a. 海军的,军舰的
navigation [ˌnævɪ'geɪʃən] n. 航行,航海
navy ['neɪvɪ] n. 海军
necessarily ['nesɪsərɪlɪ, ˌnesɪ'se-] ad. 必然,必定
necessity [nɪ'sesɪtɪ] n. 必要性,必然性;必需品
needle ['ni:dl] n. 针
negative ['negətɪv] a. 否定的,消极的,反面的;负的,阴性的
negligent ['neglɪdʒənt] a. 疏忽的;粗心大意的
negotiable [nɪ'gəʊʃɪəbl] a. 可通过谈判解决的;可协商的
neighbo(u)rhood ['neɪbəhʊd] n. 邻近(邻域)
Neptune ['neptju:n] n. 海王星
nest [nest] n. 巢,窝
net [net] n. 网,净利,实价 a. 净余的,纯粹的
network ['netwɜ:k] n. 网络
neutral⁴ ['nju:trəl] a. 中立的,中性的

neutralize ['njuːtrəˌlaɪz] vt. 抵消;使……中和;使……无效;使……中立 vi. 中和;中立化;变无效

nickel ['nɪkl] n. [化]镍;镍币;(美国和加拿大的)五分钱

nickname ['nɪkneɪm] n. 绰号,昵称

nightmare ['naɪtmeə(r)] n. 噩梦

ninth [naɪnθ] num. 第九 n. 九分之一

nitrogen ['naɪtrədʒən] n. 氮

nod [nɒd] v. 点头,打盹,使……摆动

nominate ['nɒmɪneɪt] v. 提名;任命

nonprofit [nɒn'prɒfɪt] a. 非营利的

noodle ['nuːdl] n. 面条;笨蛋

norm [nɔːm] n. 规范,基准

normalize/-ise ['nɔːməlaɪz] vt. 使规格化,使标准化;使正常化

northeast [ˌnɔːθ'iːst] n. 东北 a. 东北的,向东北的,来自东北的 ad. 向东北,来自东北

northern ['nɔːðən] a. 北部的,北方的

northwest [ˌnɔːθ'west] n. 西北,西北方 a. 西北的,在西北的,来自西北的 ad. 向西北

Norwegian [nɔː'wiːdʒən] a. 挪威(人)的 n. 挪威人/语

notable ['nəʊtəbl] a. 值得注意的,显著的

note [nəʊt] n. 笔记,记录;便条;名望;注意,注释,评论;钞票,纸币 vt. 记下,记录;注意

noteworthy ['nəʊtwɜːðɪ] a. 显著的;值得注意的

noticeable ['nəʊtɪsəbl] a. 显而易见的

notify ['nəʊtɪfaɪ] v. 通知,通告,报告

notion[7] ['nəʊʃən] n. 概念,意念;想法,见解

notorious [nə(ʊ)'tɔːrɪəs] a. 臭名昭著的

notwithstanding [ˌnɒtwɪθ'stændɪŋ] adv. 尽管,仍然 prep. 尽管,虽然

noun [naʊn] n. 名词

nourish ['nʌrɪʃ] v. 滋养,使……健壮,怀有

novelist ['nɒvəlɪst] n. 小说家

novelty ['nɒvltɪ] n. 新奇;新奇的事物;新颖小巧而廉价的物品

nowhere ['nəʊweə(r)] ad. 哪儿也不,什么地方都没有
nuisance ['njuːsns] n. 讨厌的东西,讨厌的人
numerical [njuːˈmerɪkl] a. 数字的;数值的
numerous ['njuːmərəs] a. 众多的,大批的,无数的
nursery ['nɜːsərɪ] n. 托儿所
nurture ['nɜːtʃə(r)] n. 营养物;养育,培育,教养 vt. 给……营养, 养育,培育,教养
nut [nʌt] n. 坚果,难对付的人(事)
nutrient[6] ['njuːtrɪənt] a. 营养的,滋养的 n. 营养物
nutrition [njuːˈtrɪʃən] n. 营养
nylon ['naɪlɒn] n. 尼龙

O

oak [əʊk] n. 橡树,橡木
oath [əʊθ] n. 誓言,誓约
obedience [ə(ʊ)ˈbiːdjəns] n. 顺从;服从;遵守
obedient [ə(ʊ)ˈbiːdjənt] a. 孝顺的;顺从的,服从的
obesity[4] [əʊˈbiːsɪtɪ] n. 肥大,肥胖
obey [əˈbeɪ] vt. 服从,顺从
objection [əbˈdʒekʃən] n. 反对,异议
obligation [ˌɒblɪˈgeɪʃən] n. 义务;职责;责任
oblige [əˈblaɪdʒ] v. 强制,赐,施恩惠
obscure [əbˈskjʊə(r)] a. 微暗的,难解的,不著名的
observer[4] [əbˈzɜːvə(r)] n. 观察者
obsession [əbˈseʃən] n. 痴迷;困扰
obstacle[9] ['ɒbstəkl] n. 障碍,干扰;妨害物
occurrence [əˈkʌrəns] n. 发生,事件,发现
Oceania [ˌəʊʃɪˈeɪnɪə] n. 大洋洲
odd [ɒd] a. 奇数的,单的;奇怪的,古怪的;临时的,不固定的;挂零的,剩余的

odo(u)r ['əʊdə(r)] n. 气味

offset ['ɒfset] n. 抵消,补偿 vt. 抵消;弥补

offspring[4] ['ɒfsprɪŋ] n. 子孙,后代,产物

olive ['ɒlɪv] n. 橄榄;橄榄色;橄榄树 a. 橄榄的;橄榄色的

Olympics [əʊ'limpiks] n. 奥林匹克运动会

omission [ə(ʊ)'mɪʃən] n. 省略;疏忽,遗漏

ongoing ['ɒngəʊɪŋ] a. 前进的,进行的 n. 前进,举止,行为

onion ['ʌnjən] n. 洋葱

onlooker ['ɒnlʊkə(r)] n. 旁观者

onset ['ɒnset] n. 开始;攻击;发作

onto ['ɒntu:] prep. 到……上

onward(s) ['ɒnwəd(z)] a. 向前的,前进的 ad. 向前,前进,在先

opening ['əʊpənɪŋ] n. 开始,口,揭幕,空缺的职务

opera ['ɒpərə] n. 歌剧

operational [ˌɒpə'reɪʃənl] a. 操作的,运作的

operator ['ɒpəreɪtə(r)] n. 操作员,话务员,报务员

opium ['əʊpjəm] n. 鸦片

opponent[8] [ə'pəʊnənt] n. 对手,敌手

oppress [ə'pres] vt. 压迫,压抑

opt [ɒpt] vi. 选择

optical ['ɒptɪkl] a. 眼睛的,视觉的,光学的

optimism ['ɒptɪmɪzəm] n. 乐观;乐观主义

optimum ['ɒptɪməm] n. 最适宜 a. 最适宜的

option[6] ['ɒpʃən] n. 选择,供选择的事物

optional[4] ['ɒpʃənl] a. 可以任选的,非强制的

oracle ['ɒrəkl] n. 神谕

orchestra ['ɔːkɪstrə] n. 管弦乐队

orderly ['ɔːdəlɪ] a. 有秩序的,整齐的 ad. 依次地,顺序地

ore [ɔː] n. 矿,矿石

organ ['ɔːgən] n. 器官;风琴;机构

organic[17] [ɔː'gænɪk] a. 器官的,有机的,根本的,接近自然的

organism[12] ['ɔːgənɪzəm] n. 生物体,有机体

oriental [ˌɔːrɪ'entl] a. 东方的;东方人的

orientation⁵ [ˌɔːrɪen'teɪʃən] n. 方向;定向;向东方;适应;情况介绍

original [ə'rɪdʒənəl] a. 最初的,原始的,有独创性的,原版的 n. 起源,原件,原稿

originality [əˌrɪdʒɪ'nælɪtɪ] n. 创意,新奇,原始

originate [ə'rɪdʒɪneɪt] v. 开始,发明,发起

ornament ['ɔːnəmənt] n. 装饰(物)

orphan ['ɔːfən] n. 孤儿

orthodox ['ɔːθədɒks] a. 正(传)统的

ouch [autʃ] int. 哎哟(突然疼痛时发出的声音)

ounce [auns] n. 盎司

outbreak ['autbreɪk] n. 爆发

outcome ['autkʌm] n. 结果,结局

outdate [ˌaut'deɪt] a. 过时的

outfit ['autfɪt] n. 用具,配备,机构

outgoing ['autgəuɪŋ] a. 即将离职的

outlet ['autlet] n. 出口,出路;销路,市场;批发商店;排水口,通风口;排遣,发泄

outlook ['autluk] n. 观点,见解,展望,前景

outrage ['autreɪdʒ] n. 暴行,侮辱,愤怒 v. 凌辱,虐待,触犯

outset ['autset] n. 开始,开端

outsider [ˌaut'saɪdə(r)] n. 外行(旁观者,没有关系的人)

outward(s) ['autwəd(z)] a. 向外的,表面的,外服的 ad. 向外,在外,表面

oval ['əuvl] a. 卵形的,椭圆的 n. 卵形,椭圆形

oven ['ʌvn] n. 烤炉,烤箱

overcoat ['əuvəkəut] n. 外套,大衣

overflow [ˌəuvə'fləu] n. 溢值,超值,泛滥 v. 泛滥,溢出,充溢

overhead [ˌəuvə'hed] n. 经常开支,普通用费 a. 在头上的,高架的 ad. 在头顶上,在空中,在高处

overhear [ˌəuvə'hɪə(r)] vt. 无意中听到,偷听

overlap [ˌəuvə'læp] n. 重叠;重复 vi. 部分重叠 vt. 与……重叠

overnight [ˌəʊvəˈnaɪt] n. 前晚 a. 通宵的,晚上的,前夜的 ad. 在前一夜,整夜,昨晚一晚上

overpass [ˌəʊvəpɑːs] vt. 胜过;超越;忽略

overt [ˈəʊvɜːt] a. 公开的,明显的,公然的

overtake [ˌəʊvəˈteɪk] vt. 追上,赶上,超过;突然袭击

overtime [ˈəʊvətaɪm] n. 加班时间(加班加点费)

overturn [ˌəʊvəˈtɜːn] vt. 推翻;倾覆;破坏 vi. 推翻;倾覆 n. 倾覆;破灭;周转

overwhelm [ˌəʊvəˈwelm] vt. 淹没,覆没;受打击;制服,压倒

owing [ˈəʊɪŋ] a. 欠着的,未付的

  owing to 由于

ownership[4] [ˈəʊnəʃɪp] n. 所有权

ox [ɒks] n. 公牛,牛

oxide [ˈɒksaɪd] n. 氧化物

oxygen [ˈɒksɪdʒən] n. 氧,氧气

ozone [ˈəʊzəʊn] n. 臭氧

P

Pacific [pəˈsɪfɪk] a. 太平洋的 n. [the ~] 太平洋

package [ˈpækɪdʒ] n. 包裹,套装软件,包

packet[8] [ˈpækɪt] n. 储存器,讯息封,小包

pact [pækt] n. 契约,协定,条约

pad [pæd] n. 填补,衬垫,印色盒,信笺簿

painter [ˈpeɪntə(r)] n. 画家

palace [ˈpælɪs] n. 宫殿

pale [peɪl] a. 苍白的;浅的,淡的

pamphlet [ˈpæmflɪt] n. 小册子

pan [pæn] n. 平底锅

panda [ˈpændə] n. 熊猫

panel [ˈpænl] n. 面板,嵌板,仪表盘,座谈小组

paperback ['peɪpəbæk] n. 平装本
paperwork ['peɪpəwɜːk] n. 文书工作
parachute ['pærəʃuːt] n. 降落伞
parade [pə'reɪd] n. 游行 v. 检阅,游行
paradise ['pærədaɪs] n. 天堂
paradox ['pærədɒks] n. 似是而非的隽语,自相矛盾的话
paralyze/-yse ['pærəlaɪz] vt. 使麻痹;使瘫痪
parameter [pə'ræmɪtə(r)] n. 参数;参量;系数
parasite ['pærəsaɪt] n. 寄生虫,食客
pardon ['pɑːdn] n. 原谅,请再说一遍 vt. 原谅,饶恕,豁免
parliament ['pɑːləmənt] n. 议会,国会
partial[7] ['pɑːʃəl] a. 部分的,偏袒的,偏爱的
participant [pɑː'tɪsɪpənt] n. 参加者,参与者
particle ['pɑːtɪkl] n. 粒子,点,极小量
passive ['pæsɪv] a. 被动的,消极的
password ['pɑːswɜːd] n. 口令
paste [peɪst] n. 糨糊 v. 贴,粘
pastime ['pɑːstaɪm] n. 消遣,娱乐
pasture ['pɑːstʃə(r)] n. 牧场
pat [pæt] n. 轻拍 v. 轻拍,拍
patch [pætʃ] n. 片,补丁,碎片
patent ['peɪtnt] n. 专利权,执照,专利品
pathetic [pə'θetɪk] a. 可怜的,悲哀的;感伤的
patriotic [ˌpeɪtrɪ'ɒtɪk] a. 爱国的
patriotism ['petrɪətɪzəm, 'peɪ-] n. 爱国心,爱国精神;爱国主义
patrol [pə'trəʊl] n. 巡逻,巡查
patron ['peɪtrən] n. 赞助人,保护人
pave [peɪv] v. 铺设,安排,为……铺路
   pave the way for 为……铺平道路
paw [pɔː] n. 手掌,手爪
pea [piː] n. 豌豆
peach [piːtʃ] n. 桃子

peak [piːk] n. 山顶,顶点,帽舌

peanut ['piːnʌt] n. 花生

pear [peə(r)] n. 梨

pearl [pɜːl] n. 珍珠

peasant ['peznt] n. 农民

pedal ['pedl] n. 踏板

pedestrian [pɪ'destrɪən] n. 行人

peel [piːl] n. 皮 v. 削……皮,剥落,脱皮

peer [pɪə(r)] v. 凝视,窥视

penalty[30] ['penltɪ] n. 处罚,惩罚

pendulum ['pendjʊləm] n. 钟摆

penetrate ['penɪtreɪt] v. 穿透,渗透,看穿

penguin ['peŋgwɪn] n. 企鹅

peninsula [pɪ'nɪnsjʊlə] n. 半岛

penny ['penɪ] n. 便士,一分

pension ['penʃən] n. 退休金,年金,抚恤金

pepper ['pepə(r)] n. 胡椒粉

perception[13] [pə'sepʃən] n. 认识,观念

perfection [pə'fekʃən] n. 完美,完善

perfume [pər'fjum] n. 香水,香气

periodic [ˌpɪərɪ'ɒdɪk] a. 周期的,定期的

periodical [ˌpɪərɪ'ɒdɪkl] a. 周期的,定期的 n. 期刊,杂志

perish ['perɪʃ] v. 毁灭,死亡

permanent ['pɜːmənənt] a. 永久的,持久的

permission [pə'mɪʃən] n. 许可,允许

perpetual [pə'petʃʊəl] a. 永久的

perplex [pə'pleks] v. 使……困惑,使……更复杂,使……为难

persecution [ˌpɜːsɪ'kjuːʃən] n. 迫害

personnel [ˌpɜːsə'nel] n. 人员,职员

persuasion [pə'sweɪʒən] n. 说服,说服力

persuasive [pə'sweɪsɪv] a. 劝诱的,劝说的;有说服力的

pervasive [pɜː'veɪsɪv] a. 普遍的;到处渗透的

pessimistic [ˌpesɪˈmɪstɪk] a. 悲观的

pest [pest] n. 害虫

pet [pet] n. 宠物

petition [pɪˈtɪʃən] n. 请愿,祈求,请愿书

petrochemical [ˌpetrəʊˈkemɪkl] a. 石化的

petrol[4] [ˈpetrəl] n. 汽油

petroleum [pəˈtrəʊlɪəm] n. 石油

petty [ˈpetɪ] a. 琐碎的,小规模的,小气的

pharmacy [ˈfɑːməsɪ] n. 药房,药剂学,配药业,制药业

phase [feɪz] n. 阶段,时期;相位

phenomenal [fɪˈnɒmɪnl] a. 现象的;能知觉的;异常的;杰出的,惊人的

phenomenon[8] [fɪˈnɒmɪnən] n. 现象

philosopher[7] [fɪˈlɒsəfə(r)] n. 哲学家

phoenix [ˈfiːnɪks] n. 凤凰

photocopy [ˈfəʊtəʊkɒpɪ] v./n. 影印,照相复印

photosynthesis [ˌfəʊtəʊˈsɪnθɪsɪs] n. 光合作用

phrase [freɪz] n. 短语,习语

physiology [ˌfɪzɪˈɒlədʒɪ] n. 生理学

pianist [ˈpɪənɪst, ˈpjɑːnɪst] n. 钢琴家;钢琴演奏者

piano [pɪˈænəʊ] n. 钢琴

pie [paɪ] n. 饼图

pierce [pɪəs] v. 刺穿,穿透,洞悉

pigeon [ˈpɪdʒɪn] n. 鸽子

pile [paɪl] n. 堆 v. 堆,迭,堆积

pilgrim [ˈpɪlgrɪm] n. 朝圣者

pill [pɪl] n. 药丸

pillar [ˈpɪlə(r)] n. 柱子,柱形物;栋梁

pillow [ˈpɪləʊ] n. 枕头

pilot [ˈpaɪlət] n. 飞行员,领航员,引航员

pin [pɪn] n. 大头针;别针;销,栓 vt. 钉住,别住

pinch [pɪntʃ] v./n. 拧,捏

pine [paɪn] n. 松树

pint [paɪnt] n. 品脱

pioneer⁵ [ˌpaɪəˈnɪə(r)] n. 先锋,拓荒者,开辟者

pipe [paɪp] n. 管,烟斗,笛

pistol [ˈpɪstl] n. 手枪

pit [pɪt] n. 深坑,核,矿井,陷阱

pitch [pɪtʃ] n. 程度,投掷,音高

pizza [ˈpiːtsə] n. 比萨饼

plague [pleɪɡ] n. 瘟疫;灾祸

plantation [plænˈteɪʃən, plɑːn-] n. 种植园

plastic [ˈplæstɪk] n. (pl.) 塑料 a. 塑料的,塑性的;可塑的

plate [pleɪt] n. 碟,盘,金属板,板块

plateau [ˈplætəʊ] n. 高原

plaza [ˈplɑːzə] n. 广场;市场,购物中心

plea [pliː] n. 恳求,请求;辩解,辩护

platform [ˈplætfɔːm] n. 平台,月台,讲台,坛

playground [ˈpleɪɡraʊnd] n. 操场

plead [pliːd] v. 辩护,恳求,托称

pleased [pliːzd] a. 高兴地;喜欢的;乐意做某事

pledge [pledʒ] n. 保证,誓言,抵押,抵押品 v. 保证,誓言,举杯祝……健康

plight [plaɪt] n. 困境;境况

plot [plɒt] n. 图,阴谋,情节

plow /plough [plaʊ] n. 犁,耕地,耕作

plug [plʌɡ] n. 塞子,消防栓,电插头

Pluto [ˈpluːtəʊ] n. 冥王星

poetry [ˈpəʊɪtrɪ] n. 诗歌

poisonous⁴ [ˈpɔɪzənəs] a. 有毒的

polar [ˈpəʊlə(r)] a. 两极的,南辕北辙的,极地的

pole [pəʊl] n. 极(点)

polish [ˈpɒlɪʃ] vi. 擦亮,变光滑 vt. 磨光,使发亮

politician [ˌpɒlɪˈtɪʃən] n. 政治家,政客

认知词汇扫描

poll [pəʊl] n. 投票,民意测验,选举人民意
pollutant [pəˈluːtnt] n. 污染物
polytechnic [ˌpɒlɪˈteknɪk] n. 工艺学校;理工专科学校
pond [pɒnd] n. 池塘
ponder [ˈpɒndə(r)] vt. 仔细考虑;衡量 vi. 沉思;考虑
pool [puːl] n. 水塘,池子,水潭 vt. 把……集中在一起
popcorn [ˈpɒpkɔːn] n. 爆米花,爆玉米花
pope [pəʊp] n. 罗马教皇
popularity [ˌpɒpjʊˈlærɪtɪ] n. 普及,流行
populate [ˈpɒpjʊleɪt] vt. 居住于
porch [pɔːtʃ] n. 门廊;走廊
pork [pɔːk] n. 猪肉
porridge [ˈpɒrɪdʒ] n. 粥,麦片粥
port [pɔːt] n. 港口
portable [ˈpɔːtəbl] a. 轻便的,手提式的
porter [ˈpɔːtə(r)] n. 搬运工人,守门人,门房
portion [ˈpɔːʃn] n. 部分,份
portray [pɔːˈtreɪ] v. 描写,描画……的肖像,逼真地描写
possess[6] [pəˈzes] vt. 拥有,占有
possession [pəˈzeʃn] n. (pl.) 所有物;拥有,占有
post [pəʊst] n. (支)柱;邮政;哨所;岗位,职位 vt. 贴出,宣布,公告;邮寄,投寄
postage [ˈpəʊstɪdʒ] n. 邮费,邮资
postcode [ˈpəʊstkəʊd] n. (英)邮政编码;邮区号
poster [ˈpəʊstə(r)] n. 海报,招贴,(布告、标语、海报等的)张贴者
postman [ˈpəʊstmən] n. 邮递员
posture [ˈpɒstʃə(r)] n. 姿势,态度,情形
pot [pɒt] n. 罐,壶
powder [ˈpaʊdə(r)] n. 粉,粉末
pray [preɪ] v. 祈祷,祈求;请求,恳求
prayer [preə(r)] n. 祈祷,祷告,祷文
precaution [prɪˈkɔːʃn] n. 预防,留心,警戒

precede [prɪˈsiːd] vt. 领先,在……之前;优于,高于 vi. 领先,在前面

precedent [ˈpresɪdənt] n. 先例;前例 a. 在前的;在先的

preceding [prɪˈsiːdɪŋ] a. 在前的,在先的

precision [prɪˈsɪʒən] n. 精确;精度,精密度

predecessor [ˈpriːdɪsesə(r)] n. 前辈,前任

predominant [prɪˈdɒmɪnənt] a. 卓越的;有力的;支配的

preface [ˈprefəs] n. 序文,绪言,前言

preferable [ˈprefərəbl] a. 更好的,更合意的

preference [ˈprefərəns] n. 偏爱,优先,喜爱物

prejudice[4] [ˈpredʒʊdɪs] n. 偏见,成见;损害,侵害

preliminary [prɪˈlɪmɪnərɪ] a. 预备的;初步的

premature [ˈpremətjʊə(r)] a. 比预期早的;不成熟的;早产的

premise [ˈpremɪs] n. 前提

premium [ˈpriːmjəm] n. 额外费用,奖金,保险费

preposition [ˌprepəˈzɪʃən] n. 介词,前置词

prescription [prɪˈskrɪpʃən] n. 药方

preservation [ˌprezəˈveɪʃən] n. 保存

prestige[6] [preˈstiːʒ] n. 威望,声望;声誉

presume [prɪˈzjuːm] vt. 假定;推测 vi. 相信

pretend [prɪˈtend] v. 假装,假托

prevalent [ˈprevələnt] a. 流行的;普遍的

prevention [prɪˈvenʃən] n. 预防,防止

priest [priːst] n. 教士,神父

primarily [ˈpraɪmerɪlɪ] ad. 首先,起初;主要地;根本上

primary [ˈpraɪməri] a. 首要的,主要的,基本的;最初的,初级的

prime [praɪm] a. 基本的;最好的;主要的 n. 全盛时期;初期;青年

primitive [ˈprɪmɪtɪv] a. 原始的 n. 原始人

printer [ˈprɪntə(r)] n. 打印机

prior [ˈpraɪə(r)] a. 优先的;在前的

priority [praɪˈɒrətɪ] n. 优先;优先权

privacy [ˈpraɪvəsɪ] n. 隐私,秘密;隐居

privilege ['prɪvɪlɪdʒ] n. 特权,特别恩典,基本人权
privileged ['prɪvɪlɪdʒd] a. 有特别恩典的;享有特权的
probability [ˌprɒbə'bɪlɪtɪ] n. 可能性,或然率,概率
probe [prəʊb] n. 探针,调查,探测针
procedure[6] [prə'siːdʒə(r)] n. 程序,手续,步骤
proceed [prə'siːd] vi. 继续进行
proceeding [prə'siːdɪŋ] n. 进行,行动,诉讼程序
proclaim [prə'kleɪm] v. 宣布,公告,宣言
productivity [ˌprɒdʌk'tɪvɪtɪ] n. 生产率,生产能力
professional[19] [prə'feʃənl] a. 职业的,专门的 n. 专业人员
proficiency [prə'fɪʃənsɪ] n. 熟练,精通
profitable ['prɒfɪtəbl] a. 有利可图的,有益的
profound [prə'faʊnd] a. 极深的,深奥的,深厚的
program(me)[51] ['prəʊgræm] n. 计划,规划,大纲;节目,节目单;程序 v. 编制程序
progressive [prə(ʊ)'gresɪv] a. 进步的,前进的
prohibit [prə'hɪbɪt] vt. 阻止,禁止
projector [prə'dʒektə(r)] n. 投影仪,放映机,幻灯机
prolong [prə'lɒŋ] v. 延长,拖延
prominent[5] ['prɒmɪnənt] a. 杰出的,显著的,突出的
prompt [prɒmpt] a. 敏捷的,迅速的,即刻的 vt. 促使,推动
prone [prəʊn] a. (to) 有……倾向的,易于……的
pronoun ['prəʊnaʊn] n. 代名词
pronounce [prə'naʊns] v. 发音
pronunciation [prəˌnʌnsɪ'eɪʃən] n. 发音
propaganda [ˌprɒpə'gændə] n. 宣传
propel [prə'pel] v. 推进,驱使
prophet ['prɒfɪt] n. 预言者,先知,提倡者
proportion [prə'pɔːʃən] n. 部分,份儿;比例,比重;均衡,相称
proportionate [prə'pɔːʃənət] a. (to) 成比例的;相称的;适当的
prosecute ['prɒsɪkjuːt] v. 进行,实行,起诉
prospector [prə'spektə(r)] n. 采矿者;探勘者

prosperity[6] [prɒˈsperɪtɪ] n. 繁荣,兴旺

prosperous [ˈprɒspərəs] a. 繁荣的,兴旺的

prototype [ˈprəʊtətaɪp] n. 原型

proverb [ˈprɒvɜːb] n. 谚语,格言

provided[9] [prəˈvaɪdɪd] conj. 假如,若是

province [ˈprɒvɪns] n. 省

provision [prəˈvɪʒən] n. 供应;(一批)供应品;预备,防备;条款,规定

provocative [prəˈvɒkətɪv] a. 刺激的,挑拨的

provoke [prəˈvəʊk] v. 激怒,惹起,驱使

prudent [ˈpruːdnt] a. 小心的,审慎的;精明的;节俭的

psychological[6] [ˌsaɪkəˈlɒdʒɪkl] a. 心理(学)的

psychologist [saɪˈkɒlədʒɪst] n. 心理学家

pub [pʌb] n. 酒吧,酒馆

publicize [ˈpʌblɪsaɪz] vt. 宣传;公布

publisher [ˈpʌblɪʃə(r)] n. 出版社;发行人

pudding [ˈpʊdɪŋ] n. 布丁

pulse [pʌls] n. 脉冲,脉波,脉搏

pump[4] [pʌmp] n. 泵 vt. 打气,泵送

pumpkin [ˈpʌmpkɪn] n. 南瓜

punch [pʌntʃ] n. 打洞器,钻孔机,殴打

punctual [ˈpʌŋktjʊəl] a. 准时的,正点的

punctuate [ˈpʌŋktjʊeɪt] vt. 不时打断;强调;加标点于 vi. 加标点

punishment[6] [ˈpʌnɪʃmənt] n. 惩罚

purchase[7] [ˈpɜːtʃəs] vt. 购买 n. 购买;购买的东西

purify [ˈpjʊərɪfaɪ] v. 纯净,净化,去除

purity [ˈpjʊərɪtɪ] n. 纯净;纯洁

purple [ˈpɜːpl] a. 紫色的 n. 紫色

purse [pɜːs] n. 钱包,资金,金钱,财富

pursuit [pəˈsjuːt] n. 追赶,追求

Q

quake [kweɪk] vi. 颤抖;震动 n. 地震;颤抖
qualification[7] [ˌkwɒlɪfɪˈkeɪʃən] n. 资格,条件,限制
qualitative [ˈkwɒlɪtətɪv] a. 定性的;质的,性质上的
quantitative [ˈkwɒntɪtətɪv] a. 定量的;量的,数量的
quarterly [ˈkwɔːtəlɪ] a. 季度的 ad. 每季一次
queer [kwɪə(r)] a. 奇怪的
quench [kwentʃ] v. 熄灭,结束,冷浸,解渴
questionnaire [ˌkwestʃəˈneə(r)] n. 调查表
queue [kjuː] n. 行列,长队 v. 排队
  queue up 排队
quiz [kwɪz] n. 小考,随堂测验,恶作剧
quota [ˈkwəʊtə] n. 配额,限额

R

rabbit [ˈræbɪt] n. 兔子
race [reɪs] n. 种族,赛跑
racial [ˈreɪʃəl] a. 种族的
rack [ræk] n. 架,行李架,拷问台
racket [ˈrækɪt] n. 球拍,喧闹纷乱
radar [ˈreɪdɑː(r)] n. 雷达
radiate [ˈreɪdɪeɪt] v. 放射,散发,辐射
radiation [ˌreɪdɪˈeɪʃən] n. 辐射
radical [ˈrædɪkl] a. 基本的,重要的;激进的,极端的
radioactive [ˌreɪdɪəʊˈæktɪv] a. 放射性的
radium [ˈreɪdjəm] n. 镭
radius [ˈreɪdjəs] n. 半径
rag [ræɡ] n. 破布,碎布

rage [reɪdʒ] n. 愤怒,情绪激动

raid [reɪd] n. 突然袭击,搜捕

rail [reɪl] n. 栏杆,铁轨,扶手

railroad ['reɪlrəʊd] n. 铁路

rainbow ['reɪnbəʊ] n. 彩虹

raincoat ['reɪnkəʊt] n. 雨衣

rainy ['reɪnɪ] a. 多雨的,下雨的

rally ['rælɪ] n. 集会,重整旗鼓,示威运动

random ['rændəm] a. 任意的;随机的

rape [reɪp] n./v. 抢夺,掠夺,强奸

rash [ræʃ] a. 轻率的,匆忙的,鲁莽的

rat [ræt] n. 鼠

rating ['reɪtɪŋ] n. 等级

ray [reɪ] n. 光线,射线

reaction[5] [rɪ'ækʃən] n. 反应

reactor [rɪ'æktə(r)] n. 反应堆

realistic[4] [ˌrɪə'lɪstɪk] a. 现实的,现实主义的

realization [ˌrɪəlaɪ'zeɪʃən] n. 实现,领悟,认识

realm [relm] n. 王国,领域

reap [riːp] v. 收获,获得

rear [rɪə(r)] n. 后面,背后

reassure [ˌriːə'ʃʊə(r)] v. 使……安心,再保证

rebel[4] ['rebl] n. 叛徒,反叛者 v. 反抗,谋反,抵抗

recede [rɪ'siːd] v. 向后退,退却,减弱

receipt [rɪ'siːt] n. 收据,收条;收到,接到

receiver [rɪ'siːvə(r)] n. 接收器,收款员,接待者

reception [rɪ'sepʃən] n. 接待,招待会,接收,欢迎,接受

receptionist [rɪ'sepʃənɪst] n. 接待员;招待员

recession [rɪ'seʃən] n. 后退,凹处,不景气

recipe[5] ['resɪpɪ] n. 食谱,处方,秘诀

reciprocal [rɪ'sɪprəkl] a. 相互的,互惠的

recite [rɪ'saɪt] v. 背诵,朗读,叙述

reckless ['reklɪs] a. 鲁莽的

recommendation[4] [ˌrekəmen'deɪʃən] n. 推荐,介绍

reconcile ['rekənsaɪl] vt. 使一致;使和解

recorder [rɪ'kɔːdə(r)] n. 录音机

recovery [rɪ'kʌvərɪ] n. 恢复,复原,痊愈

recruit [rɪ'kruːt] n. 新成员;新兵

rectangular [rek'tæŋgjʊlə(r)] n. 矩形

rectify ['rektɪfaɪ] vt. 改正

reduction [rɪ'dʌkʃən] n. 减少,缩小

redundant [rɪ'dʌndənt] a. 多余的,过剩的

referee [ˌrefə'riː] n. 仲裁人,调解人,裁判员

reference ['refərəns] n. 参考,出处,参照

refine [rɪ'faɪn] vt. 精练,精制,提纯;改善,改进

reflection [rɪ'flekʃən] n. 反映,沉思,映像

refresh [rɪ'freʃ] v. 提神,振作,(使)清新

refreshment [rɪ'freʃmənt] n. 点心,提神物,精神恢复

refugee [ˌrefjʊ'dʒiː] n. 难民

refund ['rɪ'fʌnd] n. 偿还 v. 付还,偿还借款,换回新公债

refusal [rɪ'fjuːzl] n. 拒绝,回绝

refute [rɪ'fjuːt] v. 驳斥,反驳

regard[17] [rɪ'gɑːd] vt. 看作,对待;考虑,认为;尊重;(pl.) 敬重,敬意,问候

regarding [rɪ'gɑːdɪŋ] prep. 关于,至于

regardless [rɪ'gɑːdlɪs] a. 不管的,不注意的,不顾的

regime [reɪ'ʒiːm] n. 政体,制度

regiment ['redʒɪmənt] n. 团,多数,管理

regulate[4] ['regjʊleɪt] vt. 管理,控制;调整,调节,校准

regulation[10] [ˌregjʊ'leɪʃən] n. 管理,控制;规章,规则

rehearsal [rɪ'hɜːsl] n. 排练,彩排

reign [reɪn] vi./n. 统治;支配

rein [reɪn] n. 缰绳;驾驭;统治 vt. 勒住;驾驭;控制

reinforce[7] [ˌriːɪn'fɔːs] vt. 增援,加强

relativity [ˌreləˈtɪvɪtɪ] n. 相对论
relay [ˌriːˈleɪ] n. 接力赛;中继转播(设备)vt. 传送,传达;中继转播
relentless [rɪˈlentlɪs] a. 无情的,残酷的;持续的,坚韧的
relevant[6] [ˈrelɪvənt] a. (to) 相关的,切题的;适当的,中肯的
reliance [rɪˈlaɪəns] n. 信赖,依靠
reluctant[9] [rɪˈlʌktənt] a. 不愿的,勉强的
remainder [rɪˈmeɪndə(r)] n. 余数,残余
remark[9] [rɪˈmɑːk] n. 评语,意见 vt. 说,评论 vi. (on) 议论,评论
remote[4] [rɪˈməʊt] a. 偏僻的,遥远的,远程的
removal [rɪˈmuːvl] n. 移动,移居,除去
Renaissance [rəˈneɪsəns] n. 文艺复兴
render [ˈrendə(r)] vt. 使得,致使;给予,提供;翻译
renew [rɪˈnjuː] v. 更新,复始,恢复
renowned [rɪˈnaʊnd] a. 著名的;有声望的
repay [rɪˈpeɪ] v. 偿还,报答
repeatedly [rɪˈpiːtɪdlɪ] ad. 重复地,再三地
repel [rɪˈpel] v. 逐退,使……厌恶,反驳
repetition [ˌrepɪˈtɪʃən] n. 重复,反复
replacement[5] [rɪˈpleɪsmənt] n. 交换,更换,代替者
representation [ˌreprɪzenˈteɪʃən] n. 表示法,表现,陈述,答辩
repressive [rɪˈpresɪv] a. 抑制的;镇压的;压抑的
requirement[7] [rɪˈkwaɪəmənt] n. 要求
resemble[5] [rɪˈzembl] vt. 相似,像……
reservation[8] [ˌrezəˈveɪʃən] n. 预定
resent[39] [rɪˈzent] vt. 怨恨;愤恨
reservoir [ˈrezəvwɑː(r)] n. 水库,蓄水池
residence [ˈrezɪdəns] n. 住处,住宅
resignation [ˌrezɪɡˈneɪʃən] n. 辞职,卸任;辞职书
resistance [rɪˈzɪstəns] n. (to) 抵抗,反抗;抵抗力,阻力;电阻
resistant[11] [rɪˈzɪstənt] a. 抵抗的,反抗的
  be resistant to 耐……的;对……有抵御能力的
resolution [ˌrezəˈluːʃn] n. 坚定,决心,决议,决定,果断

认知词汇扫描

resort[4] [rɪˈzɔːt] n. 度假胜地 vi. 诉诸,凭借
  resort to 诉诸,求助于
respectful [rɪˈspektfəl] a. 表示尊敬的,有礼貌的,谦恭的
respective [rɪˈspektɪv] a. 各自的,各个的
respectively [rɪˈspektɪvlɪ] ad. 各自地,分别地
responsive [rɪˈspɒnsɪv] a. (to) 应答的;回答的;响应的
restless [ˈrestlɪs] a. 不安宁的,焦虑的
restoration [ˌrestəˈreɪʃən] n. 恢复,归还,复位
restrain [rɪˈstreɪn] vt. 抑制,控制
retailer [ˈriːteɪlə(r)] n. 零售商
retell [riːˈtel] vt. 复述,再讲
retort [rɪˈtɔːt] vt. 驳斥
retreat [rɪˈtriːt] n. 休息寓所,撤退,隐居 v. 撤退,隐退,向后倾
retrieve[4] [rɪˈtriːv] v. 取回,恢复,补偿 n. 取回,恢复的希望
revelation [ˌrevəˈleɪʃən] n. 揭露,泄露,发觉
revenge[13] [rɪˈvendʒ] n./v. 报仇,复仇,报复
revenue [ˈrevɪnjuː] n. 财政收入,税收
reverse[4] [rɪˈvɜːs] v. 颠倒,反转;倒退,后退 n./a. 反面(的),颠倒(的),相反(的)
revise [rɪˈvaɪz] vt. 修订,修正
revival [rɪˈvaɪvl] n. 复活;复兴
revive [rɪˈvaɪv] v. 使……苏醒,复生,恢复精神
revolt [rɪˈvəʊlt] n. 叛乱,反抗,反感
revolution[15] [ˌrevəˈluːʃən] n. 革命;旋转,转数
revolutionary [ˌrevəˈluːʃənərɪ] a. 革命的 n. 革命者
revolve [rɪˈvɒlv] v. 旋转,考虑,循环
rhythm[4] [ˈrɪðəm] n. 节奏,韵律
rib [rɪb] n. 肋骨
ribbon [ˈrɪbən] n. 缎带,色带,带状物
riddle [ˈrɪdl] n. 谜,谜语;难解的问题,难理解的人、物或情况
ridge [rɪdʒ] n. 脊,山脊,山脉
rifle [ˈraɪfl] n. 步枪

· 631 ·

rightful ['raɪtfl] a. 正当的;合法的;正直的;公正的
rigid ['rɪdʒɪd] a. 坚硬的,刚性的,严格的
rigorous ['rɪɡərəs] a. 严厉的,严酷的,严格的
rip [rɪp] n. 裂痕,破绽,拉裂 v. 拉开,划开,裂开
ritual ['rɪtʃʊəl] n. 仪式,典礼,宗教仪式,固定程序
rival ['raɪvl] vt. 竞争,与……抗衡 a. 竞争的 n. 竞争对手
rivalry ['raɪvlrɪ] n. 竞争;竞赛;对抗
robbery ['rɒbərɪ] n. 抢劫
robust [rəʊ'bʌst] a. 强健的;健康的
rod [rɒd] n. 杆,棒
Roman ['rəʊmən] a. 罗马的,罗马数字的 n. 罗马人
romance [rəʊ'mæns] n. 冒险故事,浪漫史,传奇文学
romantic [rəʊ'mæntɪk] a. 浪漫的 n. 浪漫的人
roof [ruːf] n. 屋顶
rot [rɒt] v./n. 腐烂,腐朽
rotate [rəʊ'teɪt] v. (使)旋转
rouse [raʊz] n. 觉醒,奋起 v. 唤醒,鼓舞,激动
routine[25] [ruː'tiːn] a. 常规的,例行的 n. 例行公事,常规
row [rəʊ] n. (一)排,(一)行;争吵 v. 划船
rug [rʌɡ] n. 小地毯;围毯
rupture ['rʌptʃər] n. 破裂;决裂
rural[5] ['rʊərəl] a. 农村的

S

sack [sæk] n. 袋子
sacred ['seɪkrɪd] a. 神圣的
sacrifice ['sækrɪfaɪs] n. 牺牲,牺牲品;祭品,供物 v. 献祭,牺牲
safeguard ['seɪfɡɑːd] n. 保护;保卫;保护措施 vt. 保护,护卫
sailor ['seɪlə(r)] n. 海员,水手
saint [seɪnt] n. 圣人,圣徒

sake [seɪk] *n.* 缘故,理由
salute [sə'luːt] *v.* 行礼,致意,问候
salvation [sæl'veɪʃən] *n.* 得救,拯救
sanction ['sæŋkʃən] *n.* 核准,处罚,约束力
sarcasm ['sɑːkæzəm] *n.* 讽刺;挖苦;嘲笑
saturate ['sætʃəreɪt] *v.* 使渗透,浸,使饱和
saucer ['sɔːsə(r)] *n.* 茶托,碟子
sausage ['sɒsɪdʒ] *n.* 香肠,腊肠
savage ['sævɪdʒ] *a.* 野性的;凶猛的;粗鲁的;荒野的
saw [sɔː] *n.* 锯子
scan⁶ [skæn] *n.* 扫描,押韵,细查 *v.* 扫描
scandal ['skændl] *n.* 丑闻
scanner ['skænə(r)] *n.* 扫描机,扫描盘,光电子扫描装置
scar [skɑː(r)] *n.* 伤痕;创伤
scheme [skiːm] *n.* 方案,计划,阴谋
scissors ['sɪzəz] *n.* 剪刀
scorch [skɔːtʃ] *vt.* 把……烧焦/烤焦
score [skɔː(r)] *n.* 得分,刻痕,二十
scorn [skɔːn] *n.* 轻蔑;嘲笑 *vt.* 不屑做;轻蔑;藐视 *vi.* 轻蔑;鄙视
Scottish ['skɒtɪʃ] *a.* 苏格兰(人)的 *n.* 苏格兰(人);苏格兰语
scout [skaʊt] *n.* 童子军,侦察员 *v.* 侦察,搜索
scramble ['skræmbl] *v.* 攀登;扰乱
screen [skriːn] *vt.* 遮蔽,庇护;选拔,淘汰 *n.* 屏风,幕,屏幕
screw [skruː] *n.* 螺丝钉
script [skrɪpt] *n.* 原稿,手稿,手迹
scrub [skrʌb] *n./v.* 用力擦洗
scrutiny ['skruːtəni] *n.* 监视;详细审查;细看
seagull ['siːgʌl] *n.* 海鸥
seal [siːl] *n.* 印章,封条,海豹
seashell ['siːʃel] *n.* 海贝,贝壳
seaside ['siːsaɪd] *a.* 海边的,海滨的 *n.* 海边
seaweed ['siːwiːd] *n.* 海藻,海草

secondary [ˈsekəndrɪ] a. 中级的,中等的,次要的
second-hand [ˈsekənd ˈhænd] a. 旧的,用过的
secular [ˈsekjʊlə(r)] a. 世俗的;现世的
sedan [sɪˈdæn] n. 轿车
seed[19] [siːd] n. 种子
seemingly [ˈsiːmɪŋlɪ] ad. 表面上(看上去)
segment [ˈsegmənt] n. 部分
selfish [ˈselfɪʃ] a. 自私的,利己的
semiconductor [ˌsemɪkənˈdʌktə(r)] n. 半导体
seminar [ˈsemɪnɑː(r)] n. (大学的)研究班,研讨会
senate [ˈsenɪt] n. 参议院
senator [ˈsenətə(r)] n. 参议员
senior [ˈsiːnɪə(r)] a. 年长的,高级的,资深的
sensation [senˈseɪʃn] n. 感觉;轰动;感动
sensational [senˈseɪʃənl] a. 轰动的;使人感动的;耸人听闻的
sensitivity [ˌsensɪˈtɪvɪtɪ] n. 敏感,敏感性;过敏
sensor [ˈsensə(r)] n. 传感器
sensual [ˈsenʃʊəl] a. 感觉的;肉欲的
sentiment [ˈsentɪmənt] n. 感情,情绪;意见,观点
sergeant [ˈsɑːdʒənt] n. 警官
serial [ˈsɪərɪəl] a. 连续的;连载的 n. 连载小说;电视连续剧
servant [ˈsɜːvənt] n. 仆人
session [ˈseʃən] n. 会议,开庭期,市盘
setback [ˈsetbæk] n. 顿挫,挫折,退步
settlement [ˈsetlmənt] n. 解决,结算,居留地
seventh [ˈsevnθ] num. 第七
sew [səʊ] v. 缝纫,缝合
sexual [ˈsekʃʊəl] a. 性的;性别的
shade [ʃeɪd] n. 荫,阴影;遮光物,罩
shaky [ˈʃeɪkɪ] a. 摇晃的;不可靠的;不坚定的
shareholder [ˈʃeəhəʊldə(r)] n. 股东
shark [ʃɑːk] n. 鲨鱼

sharpen ['ʃɑːpən] v. 使……尖锐,变为锐利

shatter ['ʃætə(r)] n. 碎片

shed [ʃed] n. 车棚,小屋,脱落之物

sheer [ʃɪə(r)] a. 绝对的,全然的,峻峭的

sheet [ʃiːt] n. 床单,张,片

shell [ʃel] n. 贝壳,壳,外形

shepherd ['ʃepəd] n. 牧羊者,牧师,指导者

shield [ʃiːld] n. 盾,屏障 vt. 防护,保护

shiny ['ʃaɪnɪ] a. 有光泽的,擦亮的;晴朗的;闪耀的

shipment ['ʃɪpmənt] n. 装船,出货

shiver ['ʃɪvə(r)] vt. 颤动 n. 冷颤

shorts [ʃɔːts] n. 短裤

shrewd [ʃruːd] a. 精明的;机灵的

shrub [ʃrʌb] n. 灌木

shrug [ʃrʌg] n./v. 耸肩

shutter ['ʃʌtə(r)] n. 关闭物;百叶窗;快门

sidewalk ['saɪdwɔːk] n. 人行道

sideways ['saɪdweɪz] ad. 向侧面地;向一旁 a. 向侧面的;一旁的

siege [siːdʒ] n. 包围,围攻

sigh [saɪ] n. 叹息

signature ['sɪgnɪtʃə(r)] n. 签名,签署;画押

signify ['sɪgnɪfaɪ] v. 象征,预示

signpost ['saɪnpəʊst] n. 路标;指示牌

silicon ['sɪlɪkən] n. 硅

silk [sɪlk] n. 丝,绸

simplicity [sɪm'plɪsəti] n. 单纯,简朴

simplify ['sɪmplɪfaɪ] v. 简化,使单纯

simultaneous [ˌsɪml'teɪnɪəs] a. 同时的;同时发生的

sin [sɪn] n. 罪,罪孽

singular ['sɪŋgjʊlə(r)] a. 突出的

site [saɪt] n. 位置,场所

sixteenth [ˌsɪks'tiːnθ] num. 第十六

sixth [sɪksθ] *num.* 第六 *n.* 六分之一
sizable ['saɪzəbl] *a.* 相当大的
skate [skeɪt] *n.* 冰鞋 *vi.* 溜冰,滑冰
skeleton ['skelɪtn] *n.* (建筑物、计划的)骨架,纲要,骨骼
ski [skiː] *n.* 雪橇 *v.* 滑雪
skim [skɪm] *v.* 略读,掠过,滑过
skull [skʌl] *n.* 头骨
skyline ['skaɪlaɪn] *n.* 地平线;空中轮廓线
slack [slæk] *n.* 松弛部分 *v.* 使松弛,松弛
slam [slæm] *n.* 砰然声,猛然 *v.* 猛然关上,砰地关上
skyscraper ['skaɪskreɪpə(r)] *n.* 摩天大楼
slap [slæp] *n.* 掴,侮辱,拍击声 *v.* 拍击,侮辱,申斥
slaughter ['slɔːtə(r)] *n.* 残杀,屠杀,大量杀戮 *v.* 残杀,屠杀
slave [sleɪv] *n.* 奴隶,附件,卑鄙的人
slavery ['sleɪvərɪ] *n.* 奴隶制,奴役
sleeve [sliːv] *n.* 袖子
slender ['slendə(r)] *a.* 细长的,苗条的
slice [slaɪs] *n.* 薄的切片,一部分
slide [slaɪd] *vi./n.* 滑,滑动
slim [slɪm] *a.* 苗条的,细长的
slipper ['slɪpə(r)] *n.* 拖鞋
slogan ['sləʊɡən] *n.* 标语,口号
slope [sləʊp] *n.* 倾斜,斜坡
slot [slɒt] *n.* 狭槽;硬币投币口
slum [slʌm] *n.* 贫民窟
slump [slʌmp] *n.* 暴跌,意气消沉
smash [smæʃ] *n.* 破碎,大败,冲突 *v.* 粉碎,溃裂,使破产
snap [snæp] *n.* 啪地移动,突然断掉 *v.* 猛咬,咬断,谩骂,砰然关上
snapshot ['snæpʃɒt] *n.* 快照,快相
snowstorm ['snəʊstɔːm] *n.* 暴风雪
soak [səʊk] *n.* 浸;湿透;大雨
soap [səʊp] *n.* 肥皂

soar [sɔː(r)] vi. 高耸;高飞 n. 高飞;高涨

sober ['səubər] a. 冷静的,清醒的;未醉的

sob [sɒb] v./n. 哭泣,呜咽

soccer ['sɒkə(r)] n. 英式足球

socialism ['səuʃəlɪzəm] n. 社会主义

socialist ['səuʃəlɪst] n. 社会主义者

socialize ['səuʃəlaɪz] vi. 交际;参与社交

sociology [ˌsəusi'ɒlədʒɪ] n. 社会学

sock [sɒk] n. 短袜

soda ['səudə] n. 汽水,苏打

sodium ['səudiəm] n. 钠

sofa ['səufə] n. 沙发

software[6] ['sɒftweə(r)] n. 软件

soil [sɔɪl] n. 土地,土壤

solar ['səulə(r)] a. 太阳的,太阳能的

sole [səul] a. 单独的,唯一的

solemn ['sɒləm] a. 庄严的,严肃的;隆重的

solicitor [sə'lɪsɪtə(r)] n. 律师

solidarity [ˌsɒlɪ'dærɪtɪ] n. 团结

solo ['səuləu] n. 独奏,独唱 a. 单独的

soluble ['sɒljubl] a. 可溶解的

sonar ['səunɑːr] n. 声呐

sophisticated [sə'fɪstɪkeɪtɪd] a. 诡辩的,久经世故的

southeast [ˌsauθ'iːst] n./a. 东南(的),东南部(的)

southern ['sʌðən] a. 南部的,南方的

southwest [ˌsauθ'west] n./a. 西南(的),西南部(的)

sovereignty ['sɒvrəntɪ] n. 主权,独立国

sow [səu] v. 播种

spacious ['speɪʃəs] a. 宽敞的,广阔的

spade [speɪd] n. 铲子,铁锹

span [spæn] n. 跨度,跨距,范围

spark [spɑːk] n. 火花,火星 vi. 发火花,发电花

· 637 ·

sparrow ['spærəʊ] n. 麻雀
specialty ['speʃəlti]/speciality [speʃi'æləti] n. 专门,特别,特性
specification [ˌspesɪfɪ'keɪʃən] n. 规格,详述,详细说明书
specify ['spesɪfaɪ] vt. 指定,详细说明
specimen ['spesɪmɪn] n. 样本,标本
spectacle ['spektəkl] n. 值得看的东西,光景,眼镜
spectacular [spek'tækjʊlə(r)] a. 公开展示的,惊人的
spectator [spek'teɪtə(r)] n. 观众,旁观者
spectrum ['spektrəm] n. 光谱,(比喻)范围,系列
speculation [ˌspekjʊ'leɪʃən] n. 沉思,推测,投机
speculative ['spekjʊlətɪv] a. 推测的;思索性的
spelling ['spelɪŋ] n. 拼法,拼写
sphere [sfɪə(r)] n. 范围,领域,球,球体
spice [spaɪs] n. 药料,香料;情趣
spider ['spaɪdə(r)] n. 蜘蛛
spill [spɪl] n. 溢出,溅出 vt. 使溢出,使洒,使流出 vi. 溢出,涌流,充满
spine [spaɪn] n. 背骨,脊柱,尖刺
splash [splæʃ] n. 飞溅的水,污点,卖弄 v. 溅湿,溅开
sponge [spʌndʒ] n. 海绵,海绵状的东西
sponsorship ['spɒnsəʃɪp] n. 赞助者的身份/地位/任务
spontaneous [spɒn'teɪnɪəs] a. 自发的,自然产生的
spoon [spuːn] n. 匙,匙形的铲子
spouse[5] [spaʊs] n. 配偶
spray [spreɪ] n. 水沫,喷雾器 v. 喷雾,扫射,喷射
sprinkle ['sprɪŋkl] vi./n. 洒,撒
spur [spɜː(r)] n. 马刺 v. 刺激,激励
squeeze [skwiːz] n. 压榨,挤 v. 紧握,挤
stab [stæb] v./n. 刺,戳
stability [stə'bɪlətɪ] n. 稳定性
stack [stæk] n. 堆;堆叠
stadium ['steɪdɪəm] n. 体育场

stain [steɪn] *n.* 污染,污点 *vt.* 沾染,污染

stainless ['steɪnlɪs] *a.* 纯洁的;无瑕疵的;不锈的

staircase ['steəkeɪs] *n.* 楼梯

stake [steɪk] *n.* 木柱,赌注,奖金
  at stake 有危险

stale [steɪl] *a.* 不新鲜的,陈腐的

standby ['stændbaɪ] *a.* 备用的 *ad.* 待命地;备用地

standpoint ['stændpɔɪnt] *n.* 立场,观点

stare [steə(r)] *v.* 盯,凝视

starter ['stɑːtə(r)] *n.* (竞赛的)参加者

startle ['stɑːtl] *vt.* 使吓一跳;使惊奇 *vi.* 惊吓;惊跳;惊奇 *n.* 惊愕;惊恐

static ['stætɪk] *n.* 静电,静电干扰 *a.* 静态的,静电的

stationary ['steɪʃənərɪ] *a.* 不动的,稳定的

statistic [stə'tɪstɪk] *a.* 统计(学)的

statue ['stætjuː] *n.* 塑像,雕像

steak [steɪk] *n.* 牛排

steep [stiːp] *a.* 陡峭的,险峻的

steer [stɪə(r)] *vt.* 驾驶,掌舵

stern [stɜːn] *a.* 严厉的,坚决的 *n.* 尾部,船尾

stimulate ['stɪmjʊleɪt] *vt.* 刺激,使兴奋;激励

stimulus ['stɪmjʊləs] *n.* 刺激,激励,刺激品

sting [stɪŋ] *n.* 刺,刺痛,针刺 *v.* 刺,刺痛;刺激

stipulate ['stɪpjʊleɪt] *vt.* 规定;保证

stockholder ['stɒkhəʊldə(r)] *n.* 股东

stomachache ['stʌməkeɪk] *n.* 胃痛;腹痛,肚子痛

stoop [stuːp] *n.* 弯腰,屈背;屈服

storage ['stɔːrɪdʒ] *n.* 储存体,储藏,仓库

stove [stəʊv] *n.* 炉子,火炉窑;烘房

straightforward [ˌstreɪt'fɔːwəd] *a.* 简单的;坦率的;明确的;径直的
  ad. 坦率地;直截了当地

strain [streɪn] *n.* 紧张,拉紧,血统

strand [strænd] n. (线、绳、发的)股；缕

strap [stræp] n. 带,皮带 vt. 用带缚住,用带捆扎

straw [strɔː] n. 稻草,麦秆,吸管

stray [streɪ] v. 迷路,彷徨

stricken [ˈstrɪkən] a. 患病的；受挫折的；受……侵袭的；遭殃的

stride [straɪd] n. 步幅；大步 vi. 跨；跨过；大步行走

string [strɪŋ] n. 一串,一行,一列；弦,线,绳

strip[5] [strɪp] n. 窄条,长带 vt. 剥,剥去……衣服

strive [straɪv] v. 努力,奋斗,力争

stroke [strəʊk] n. 击,敲；(报时)钟声；抚摸；一划,一笔,一击；突然发作,中风；抚摸,抚爱

stroll [strəʊl] n./v. 闲逛,漫步

stubborn[4] [ˈstʌbən] a. 顽固的；难处理的；顽强的

stumble [ˈstʌmbl] v. 使绊倒,失策

stun [stʌn] v. 使晕倒,使惊吓

subdivide [ˌsʌbdɪˈvaɪd] vi. 细分,再分 vt. 把……再分,把……细分

submarine [ˈsʌbməriːn] a. 水底的,海底的 n. 潜水艇

submerge [səbˈmɜːdʒ] v. 使浸水,潜入水中,使陷入

submission [səbˈmɪʃən] n. 服从,柔和

submit [səbˈmɪt] v. (to) 屈服,服从,呈送,提交

subordinate [səˈbɔːdɪnət] a. 次要的；从属的 vt. 使……居下位；使……服从 n. 下属,下级；部属,属下

subscription [səbˈskrɪpʃən] n. 捐献,订金,订阅

subsequent[4] [ˈsʌbsɪkwənt] a. 随后的,后来的

subsidiary [səbˈsɪdɪərɪ] a. 辅助的,附属的 n. 子公司,附属机构

subsidy [ˈsʌbsɪdɪ] n. 津贴；补助金；补贴

subsistence [səbˈsɪstəns] n. 生存；存在；生活

substantial [səbˈstænʃl] a. 大量的,实质上的,有内容的

subtle [ˈsʌtl] a. 微妙的,敏感的,精细的,狡猾的

subtract [sʌbˈtrækt] vt. 减,减去

succession [səkˈseʃən] n. 连续,继承权,继位

successive [səkˈsesɪv] a. 连接的,连续的

successor [sək'sesə(r)] n. 继承人

suck [sʌk] v. 吸吮;吸取

sue [sjuː] v. 控告,起诉

suite [swiːt] n. 随员,套房,一组

sulfur/sulphur n. 硫黄

summit ['sʌmɪt] n. 顶点;最高官阶;最高级会议

superficial [ˌsuːpə'fɪʃəl, ˌsjuː-] a. 表面的

superintendent [ˌsuːpərɪn'tendənt, ˌsjuː-] n. 负责人;主管;监督人

superior [suː'pɪərɪə(r), sjuː-] n. 长者,高手 a. 上好的,出众的,高傲的

superman ['suːpəmæn, 'sjuː-] n. 超人

supersonic [ˌsuːpə'sɒnɪk, ˌsjuː-] a. 超声的

supervise ['suːpəvaɪz, 'sjuː-] v. 监督,管理,指导,监视

supervisor ['suːpəvaɪzə(r), 'sjuː-] n. 监督人,管理人,导师

supplement ['sʌplɪmənt] n. 补遗,补充;附录;增刊 v. 补充

supportive [sə'pɔːtɪv] a. 支持的

suppress [sə'pres] v. 镇压,使……止住,禁止

supreme [s(j)ʊ'priːm] a. 最高的

surf [sɜːf] n. 海浪

surge [sɜːdʒ] n. 巨浪,汹涌,澎湃 v. 汹涌,澎湃

surpass [sə'pɑːs] vt. 胜过,优于;超越

surplus ['sɜːpləs] a. 多余的,过剩的 n. 过剩,剩余物,盈余,顺差

surrender[8] [sə'rendə(r)] v. 投降,让与,屈服

survival[8] [sə'vaɪvəl] n. 生存

survivor [sə'vaɪvə(r)] n. 幸存者

suspend [sə'spend] vt. 吊,悬挂;延续

suspicion [sə'spɪʃən] n. 猜疑,怀疑

sustain [sə'steɪn] vt. 支撑,承担;维持;忍受;供养

sustainable [sə'steɪnəbl] a. 足可支撑的,可持续的

swallow ['swɒləʊ] n. 燕子;吞咽 vt. 咽;淹没,吞没 vi. 吞下,咽下

swamp [swɒmp] n. 沼泽,湿地

swan [swɒn] n. 天鹅

swap [swɒp] n./v. 交换
sway [sweɪ] n. 摇,影响力,支配 v. 使摇动,支配
swift [swɪft] a. 快的,迅速的
swing [swɪŋ] vi. 摇摆,摇荡;回转,转向 n. 秋千
Swiss [swɪs] a. 瑞士的 n. 瑞士人
sword [sɔːd] n. 剑,刀
symmetry ['sɪmətrɪ] n. 对称(性),匀称,整齐
symphony ['sɪmfənɪ] n. 交响乐
symposium [sɪm'pəʊzɪəm] n. 讨论会(论文集,酒会)
syndrome ['sɪndrəʊm] n. 综合征
synthesis ['sɪnθəsɪs] n. 综合,合成
synthetic [sɪn'θetɪk] a. 合成的,人造的 n. 人工制品

T

taboo [tə'buː] n. 禁忌;禁止
tackle ['tækl] vt. 解决,处理
tag [tæg] n. 标签,附属物,名称
tail [teɪl] n. 尾部,后部,辫子;跟踪者
tailor ['teɪlə(r)] vt. 裁制,剪裁 n. 裁缝
takeover ['teɪkəʊvə(r)] n. 接管
tale [teɪl] n. 传说,故事
tame [teɪm] vt. 驯养 a. 驯服的,易驾驭的
tank [tæŋk] n. 水槽,池塘,战车
tanker ['tæŋkə(r)] n. 油轮
tantalize ['tæntəlaɪz] vt. 逗弄;使干着急 vi. 逗弄人;令人干着急
tap [tæp] n. 旋塞,龙头,塞子 v. 轻叩,轻拍;开发,利用
tape [teɪp] n. 录像带,录音带,磁带,带子
tease [tiːz] v. 取消,戏弄
technician [tek'nɪʃn] n. 技术员,技师
technique[8] [tek'niːk] n. 技术

tedious ['tiːdiəs] a. 沉闷的，单调乏味的
teenage ['tiːneɪdʒ] a. 十几岁的
telecom ['telɪkɔm] n. 电信，电讯
telecommunications [ˌtelɪkəˌmjuːnɪ'keɪʃənz] n. 通信，电信
telegram ['telɪgræm] n. 电报
telegraph ['telɪgrɑːf] n. 电报，电报机
telescope ['telɪskəʊp] n. 望远镜
temper[4] ['tempə(r)] n. 脾气，情绪；怒气
  be in a good/bad temper 心情好/不好
  keep one's temper 忍住性子
  lose one's temper 发脾气
temperament ['tempərəmənt] n. 气质，性情，性格；急躁
temperature ['temprɪtʃə(r)] n. 温度
temple ['templ] n. 庙宇，寺院
temporary[12] ['tempərərɪ] a. 暂时的，临时的
tempt[16] [tempt] vt. 诱惑；吸引，使感兴趣
temptation [temp'teɪʃən] n. 诱惑，引诱
tendency[7] ['tendənsɪ] n. 趋向，趋势
tennis ['tenɪs] n. 网球
tense[5] [tens] a. 拉紧的，紧绷的；紧张的
tension[4] ['tenʃən] n. 紧张，张力，拉力
tent [tent] n. 帐篷 v. 住帐篷，宿营
tentative ['tentətɪv] a. 试验性的，暂定的
tenth [tenθ] num. 第十 n. 十分之一
terminal ['tɜːmɪnl] n. 终端机，终点，末端 a. 终点的，按期的，致死的
termination [ˌtɜːmɪ'neɪʃən] n. 结束，终止
terrific [tə'rɪfɪk] a. 极好的，非常的，极度的
terrify ['terɪfaɪ] v. 使恐怖
territory ['terɪtərɪ] n. 领土，版图，领域，范围
terrorism ['terərɪzəm] n. 恐怖统治，恐怖行动
terrorist ['terərɪst] n. 恐怖分子

testify [ˈtestɪfaɪ] v. 证明,作证

testimony [ˈtestɪmənɪ] n. 证言,证据

textile [ˈtekstaɪl] a. 纺织的 n. 纺织品

texture [ˈtekstʃə(r)] n. (材料等的)结构,质地

thanksgiving [ˈθæŋksgɪvɪŋ] n. 感恩节

theater/-tre [ˈθɪətə(r)] n. 戏院,电影院,剧场

theft [θeft] n. 偷窃

theoretical [ˌθɪəˈretɪkl] a. 理论的;理论上的

therapy [ˈθerəpɪ] n. 治疗,疗法

thereby [ˌðeəˈbaɪ] a. 从而,因此

thermal [ˈθɜːməl] a. 热的,热量的

thermometer/-tre [θəˈmɒmɪtə(r)] n. 温度计

thesis [ˈθiːsɪs] n. 论文

thief [θiːf] n. 贼,小偷

thoughtful [ˈθɔːtf(ʊ)l] a. 深思的,沉思的;体贴的,关心的

thread[5] [θred] n. 线;思路;线索

threshold [ˈθreʃhəʊld, ˈθreʃəʊld] n. 极限,门槛,入口,开端

thrill [θrɪl] n. 震颤,激动 v. 震颤,抖颤,激动

thriller [ˈθrɪlə(r)] n. 惊险小说

thrive [θraɪv] vi. 兴旺,繁荣

throat [θrəʊt] n. 喉咙

thrust [θrʌst] n. 推力,刺,力推

thumb [θʌm] n. 拇指

thunder [ˈθʌndə(r)] n. 雷电,雷声 v. 打雷,大声喊出

tick [tɪk] n. 记号,勾号;(钟表)嘀嗒声 vt. 发出嘀嗒声
  tick away/by (时间一分一秒地)过去

tide[11] [taɪd] n. 潮,趋势,潮流

timber [ˈtɪmbə(r)] n. 木材,木料

timely [ˈtaɪmlɪ] a. 及时的,适时的

timetable [ˈtaɪmteɪbl] n. 时间表,时刻表

timid [ˈtɪmɪd] a. 胆怯的,害羞的

tin [tɪn] n. 锡,马口铁,罐

tiny[5] ['taɪnɪ] a. 极小的,微小的

tip [tɪp] n. 尖,顶端;小费 v. 倾斜,倾倒;给小费

tire[43] ['taɪə(r)] vt. 使感到疲劳 n. 轮胎;头饰

tissue ['tɪsjuː, 'tɪʃuː] n. (动、植物的)组织,薄的纱织品;餐巾纸,手巾纸

title ['taɪtl] n. 头衔,名称,标题 v. 赋予头衔

toast [təʊst] n. 吐司面包,烤面包,干杯

tobacco [tə'bækəʊ] n. 烟草

toe [təʊ] n. 脚趾,足尖 vt. 趾触,趾踢

toilet ['tɔɪlɪt] n. 厕所,盥洗室

tolerance[4] ['tɒlərəns] n. 宽容,容忍

tolerant ['tɒlərənt] a. 宽容的,容忍的

tolerate[5] ['tɒləreɪt] v. 忍受,容忍,容许,宽恕

toll [təʊl] n. 通行费,代价,钟声

toothache ['tuːθeɪk] n. 牙痛

torch [tɔːtʃ] n. 火炬,火把,手电筒

torture ['tɔːtʃə(r)] n. 拷问,苦闷 v. 拷问,曲解

toss [tɒs] n. 投掷,震荡 v. 投掷,摇荡,辗转

towel ['taʊəl] n. 毛巾 v. 用毛巾擦

tower ['taʊə(r)] n. 塔,高楼,堡垒

toxic ['tɒksɪk] a. 有毒的

tractor ['træktə(r)] n. 牵引器,拖拉机

trademark ['treɪdmɑːk] n. 商标

tragedy ['trædʒɪdɪ] n. 悲剧,惨事,灾难

trail [treɪl] n. 踪迹,小径,尾

trainee [treɪ'niː] n. 练习生,新兵,训练中的动物

trait [treɪt] n. 特性,特点,品质

transaction [træn'zækʃən] n. 交易,处理,办理

transcend [træn'send] vt. 胜过,超越

transcendental [ˌtrænsen'dentl] a. 先验的;卓越的;超越的

transistor [træn'zɪstə(r)] n. 晶体管(收音机)

transition [træn'zɪʃən] n. 过渡,转变

transparent [træns'pærənt] a. 透明的

transplant [træns'plɑːnt] v. 移居,移植

transportation[9] [ˌtrænspɔː'teɪʃən] n. 运输,运输系统,运输工具

trap[7] [træp] n. 圈套,陷阱 v. 设圈套,设陷阱

trash [træʃ] n. 废物,垃圾

tray [treɪ] n. 盘,托盘,碟

treaty ['triːtɪ] n. 条约,协定

tremendous[4] [trɪ'mendəs] a. 巨大的,惊人的

triangle ['traɪæŋgl] n. 三角(形)

tribe[8] [traɪb] n. 部落

tribunal [traɪ'bjuːnl] n. 法庭;法官席

trifle ['traɪfl] n. 琐事,少量

trigger ['trɪgə(r)] vt. 触发;引发,引起 v. 触发器;扳机

trillion ['trɪljən] num./n. 万亿

trim [trɪm] n. 整齐,装饰,修剪 a. 整齐的 v. 整理,修剪

triple ['trɪpl] a. 三倍的 vi. 增至三倍 vt. 使成三倍

triumph ['traɪʌmf] n. 胜利,凯旋,欢欣 v. 得胜,成功

trivial ['trɪvɪəl] a. 不重要的,琐碎的

tropical ['trɒpɪkl] a. 热带的

trumpet ['trʌmpɪt] n. 喇叭,喇叭声 v. 吹喇叭,吹嘘

trunk [trʌŋk] n. 树干,躯干,(汽车后部)行李厢,象鼻

truthful ['truːθfl] a. 符合实际的,真的,诚实的

tuberculosis [tjuːˌbɜːkjʊ'ləʊsɪs] n. 肺结核;结核病

tuition [tjuː'ɪʃən] n. 学费

tunnel ['tʌnl] n. 隧道,地下道

turbulence ['tɜːbjələns] n. 骚乱,动荡;狂暴;湍流

turbulent ['tɜːbjələnt] a. 狂暴的,吵闹的

turkey ['tɜːkɪ] n. 火鸡,火鸡肉

turnout ['tɜːnaʊt] n. 出席者;产量;出动

tutor ['tjuːtə(r)] n. 家庭教师,指导教师 vt. 个别指导

tutorial [tjuː'tɔːrɪəl] a. 辅导的;家庭教师的,个别指导的 n. 个别

指导

twelfth [twelfθ] *num.* 第十二
twentieth ['twentiəθ] *num.* 第二十
twin [twɪn] *a.* 孪生的 *n.* 双胞胎之一
twist [twɪst] *v.* 搓,捻;拧,扭歪曲,曲解 *n.* 扭转,扭弯
typewriter ['taɪpraɪtə(r)] *n.* 打字机
typist ['taɪpɪst] *n.* 打字员
tyre [taɪə(r)] *n.* 轮胎

U

ultimate⁵ ['ʌltɪmɪt] *a.* 最后的,最终的 *n.* 终极,顶点
ultraviolet [ˌʌltrə'vaɪələt] *a.* 紫外线的
unanimous [ju'nænɪməs] *a.* 全体一致的,一致同意的
unbelievable [ˌʌnbɪ'liːvəbl] *a.* 难以置信的
uncertain [ʌn'sɜːtn] *a.* 不明确的,含糊的;无常的;靠不住的;迟疑不决的
uncomfortable [ʌn'kʌmfətəbl] *a.* 不舒服的;不自在的
unconditional [ˌʌnkən'dɪʃənl] *a.* 无条件的;绝对的
unconscious⁴ [ʌn'kɒnʃəs] *a.* 失去知觉的,不省人事的;无意识的,不知不觉的
uncover [ʌn'kʌvə(r)] *vt.* 揭开覆盖物;揭露;发现
underdeveloped [ˌʌndədɪ'veləpt] *a.* 不发达的
underestimate [ˌʌndər'estɪmeɪt] *vt.* 低估;看轻
undergo [ˌʌndə'gəʊ] *vt.* 遭受,经历
underground [ˌʌndə'graʊnd] *a.* 地下的,秘密的 *n.* 地铁 *ad.* 在地下,秘密地
underline³⁴ [ˌʌndə'laɪn] *v.* 在……下面画线
underneath [ˌʌndə'niːθ] *ad.* 在下面 *n.* 下部,底部 *prep.* 在……的下面
undertake⁴ [ˌʌndə'teɪk] *vt.* 接收,承担;约定,保证;着手,从事

underway [ˌʌndə'weɪ] a. 航行中的;进行中的

undo [ˌʌn'duː] vt. 解开,松开;取消,撤销

undoubtedly [ʌn'daʊtɪdlɪ] ad. 无疑,必定

uneasy [ʌn'iːzɪ] a. 不安的,担忧的

unexpected [ˌʌnɪk'spektɪd] a. 想不到的,意外的

unfold [ʌn'fəʊld] vt. 打开;呈现 vi. 展开;显露

unforgettable [ˌʌnfə'getəbl] a. 难忘的,不会忘记的

unify ['juːnɪfaɪ] vt. 统一;使相同

unintelligible [ˌʌnɪn'telɪdʒəbl] a. 无法了解的;莫名其妙的

union ['juːnjən] n. 结合,组合,联合;协会,工会,联盟

unit ['juːnɪt] n. 单位,单元

unity ['juːnɪtɪ] n. 个体,一致,结合

unknown [ʌn'nəʊn] a. 未知的,不知名的

unlikely [ʌn'laɪklɪ] a. 不太可能的;没希望的

unnecessary [ʌn'nesɪsərɪ] a. 不必要的;多余的,无用的

unpleasant [ʌn'plezənt] a. 使人不愉快的;讨厌的

unload [ʌn'ləʊd] vt. 卸;摆脱……之负担

unprecedented [ʌn'presɪdentɪd] a. 空前的

unquestionable [ʌn'kwestʃənəbl] a. 确实的;毫无疑问的

unveil [ʌn'veɪl] v. 揭开,揭幕

upcoming [ˌʌpkʌmɪŋ] a. 即将来临的

upgrade ['ʌpgreɪd] vt. 提升;使升级

uphold [ʌp'həʊld] v. 支撑,赞成,鼓励

upright ['ʌpraɪt] a. 直立的,竖立的;正直的,诚实的

upside-down [ˌʌpsaɪd'daʊn] a./ad. 颠倒的(地),倒置的(地)

upstairs [ˌʌp'steəz] a. 楼上的 ad. 在楼上,往楼上 n. 楼上

up-to-date [ˌʌptə'deɪt] a. 最新的,现代的

upward(s) ['ʌpwəd(z)] ad. 往上,向上

Uranus [jʊ'reɪnəs] n. 天王星

urgency ['ɜːdʒənsɪ] n. 紧急(的事)

usage ['juːsɪdʒ, -zɪ-] n. 惯用法,使用,用法

usher ['ʌʃə(r)] vi. (in) 引导,招待;迎接;开辟 n. 引座员,带位员

utility [juːˈtɪlətɪ] n. 公共设施,效用,公用程序,实用品,实用
utmost [ˈʌtməʊst] a. 极度的,最远的 n. 极限,最大可能
Utopia [juːˈtəʊpɪə] n. 乌托邦(理想中最美好的社会);理想国

V

vacancy [ˈveɪkənsɪ] n. 空缺;空位
vacant [ˈveɪkənt] a. 空的
vaccination [ˌvæksɪˈneɪʃən] n. 种痘;接种疫苗
vaccine [ˈvæksiːn] n. 疫苗;牛痘苗 a. 疫苗的;牛痘的
vacuum [ˈvækjʊəm] n. 真空,空间,真空吸尘器
vain[4] [veɪn] a. 徒劳的;虚荣的
validity [vəˈlɪdətɪ] n. 有效性,正确性
valley [ˈvælɪ] n. 山谷,溪谷
vanish[4] [ˈvænɪʃ] v. 消失,不见了
vapo(u)r [ˈveɪpə(r)] n. 蒸汽
variable [ˈveərɪəbl] a. 可变的,易变的 n. 变量
variation [ˌveərɪˈeɪʃn] n. 变化,变动,变种,变异
variety[7] [vəˈraɪətɪ] n. 多样;种类;杂耍;变化,多样化
vast[11] [vɑːst] a. 广阔的,巨大的
vehicle[8] [ˈviːəkl] n. 车辆,交通工具
veil [veɪl] n. 面纱,纱帐,幕
vein [veɪn] n. 静脉
vent [vent] n. 出口;通风孔
ventilate [ˈventɪleɪt] v. 使……空气流通
Venus [ˈviːnəs] n. 金星
verb [vɜːb] n. 动词
verbal [ˈvɜːbl] a. 动词的,口头的,用言辞的,用文字的
verdict [ˈvɜːdɪkt] n. 判决
verify [ˈverɪfaɪ] v. 查证,核实
versatile [ˈvɜːsətaɪl] a. 多才多艺的

verse [vɜːs] n. 诗,诗篇

version [ˈvɜːʃən] n. 版本;看法,说法;译文

versus [ˈvɜːsəs] a. 对抗,相对比 prep. 对……;与……相对

vertical [ˈvɜːtɪkl] a. 垂直的,竖的

vessel [ˈvesl] n. 船舶;容器,器皿;管,导管,血管

veto [ˈviːtəʊ] n. 否决权 v. 否决

vibrate [vaɪˈbreɪt] v. (使)振动,(使)摇摆

vice [vaɪs] n. 恶习,恶行,罪恶,缺陷,恶癖;老虎钳

vicious [ˈvɪʃəs] a. 恶毒的,恶意的,凶残的,剧烈的,严重的

victorious [vɪkˈtɔːrɪəs] a. 胜利的,得胜的

vigorous [ˈvɪɡərəs] a. 精力充沛的,元气旺盛的,有力的

vinegar [ˈvɪnɪɡə(r)] n. 醋

violet [ˈvaɪəlɪt] n. 紫罗兰 a. 紫罗兰色的

violin [ˌvaɪəˈlɪn] n. 小提琴

virgin [ˈvɜːdʒɪn] n. 处女 a. 纯洁的,原始的

virtually [ˈvɜːtʃʊəlɪ] ad. 实际上;几乎

virtue [ˈvɜːtʃuː] n. 美德;优点

virtuous [ˈvɜːtʃʊəs] a. 有道德的;贞洁的

visibility [ˌvɪzəˈbɪlətɪ] n. 能见度,可见性

visible [ˈvɪzəbl] a. 见的,有形的

visionary [ˈvɪʒənərɪ] a. 梦想的;幻影的 n. 空想家;梦想者

visitor [ˈvɪzɪtə(r)] n. 参观者,访问者

visual [ˈvɪʒʊəl] a. 视觉的

vitamin [ˈvɪtəmɪn] n. 维生素

vivid[4] [ˈvɪvɪd] a. 生动的,栩栩如生的,鲜艳的

vocabulary [vəˈkæbjələrɪ] n. 词汇(量/表)

vocal [ˈvəʊkl] a. 声音的

vocation [vəʊˈkeɪʃən] n. 职业,行业

volcano [vɒlˈkeɪnəʊ] n. 火山

volleyball [ˈvɒlɪbɔːl] n. 排球

volt [vəʊlt] n. 伏特

volume [ˈvɒljuːm] n. (一)卷,(一)册;体积,容积;音量,响度

voluntary[7] ['vɒləntərɪ] a. 自愿的,志愿的
vow [vaʊ] n. 誓约
vulgar ['vʌlgə(r)] a. 粗俗的
vulnerable[6] ['vʌlnərəbl] a. 易受伤害的,有弱点的

W

wag(g)on ['wægən] n. 牵引小车
waist [weɪst] n. 腰,腰部
waken ['weɪkən] vt. 唤醒;使觉醒 vi. 醒来;觉醒
wallet ['wɒlɪt] n. 皮夹,钱包
wander ['wɒndə(r)] vi. 徘徊,漫步;走神,恍惚;迷路,迷失;离开正道,离题
ward [wɔːrd] n. 守卫,监护,病房 vt. 避开
　ward off 避开,防止
wardrobe ['wɔːdrəʊb] n. 衣柜
warehouse ['weəhaʊs] n. 仓库
warfare ['wɔːfeə(r)] n. 战争;冲突
warrant ['wɒrənt] n. 正当理由,根据,委任状 v. 保证,辩解,担保
wasteland ['weɪstlænd] n. 荒地,不毛之地;未开垦地,荒漠
watchdog ['wɒtʃdɒg] n. 看门狗;监察人;忠实的看守人
watermelon ['wɔːtəˌmelən] n. 西瓜
waterproof[4] ['wɔːtəpruːf] n. 防水材料 a. 防水的 v. 使……能防水
watertight ['wɔːtətaɪt] a. 不漏水的;无懈可击的
watt [wɒt] n. 瓦特
wax [wæks] n. 蜡,蜡状物,震怒
wayside ['weɪsaɪd] n. 路旁
weave [wiːv] v. 编织
wedge [wedʒ] n. 楔子,楔形物
weed [wiːd] n. 杂草,烟草 v. 除草
weightlifting ['weɪtlɪftɪŋ] n. 举重

weird [wɪəd] *a.* 怪异的

weld [weld] *n.* 焊接,焊缝

welfare ['welfeə(r)] *n.* 福利

well-being [ˌwel'biːɪŋ] *n.* 幸福;康乐

well-off [ˌwel'ɒf] *a.* 富裕的;顺利的,走运的

western ['westən] *n.* 西方人,西部片,西部小说 *a.* 西方的,西洋的,西部的

westerner ['westənə(r)] *n.* 西方人

whale [weɪl] *n.* 鲸

whatsoever(= whatever) [ˌwɒtsəʊ'evə] *pron.* 无论什么,任何

whereas [weər'æz] *conj.* 鉴于;然而,但是,反之

whip [wɪp] *n.* 鞭子,车夫 *v.* 鞭打,抽打

whirl [wɜːl] *n.* 回旋,旋转,急走 *v.* 使……旋转,循环而行

whisper ['wɪspə(r)] *v./n.* 耳语,私语

whistle ['wɪsl] *v.* 吹口哨,鸣笛 *n.* 口哨声,汽笛声;哨子,汽笛

wholesale ['həʊlseɪl] *a.* 批发的;大规模的

wicked ['wɪkɪd] *a.* 邪恶的,恶劣的;淘气的,顽皮的

widen ['waɪdn] *v.* 弄宽

widow ['wɪdəʊ] *n.* 寡妇

width [wɪdθ] *n.* 宽度,幅;广阔,宽阔

willing ['wɪlɪŋ] *a.* 自愿的,心甘情愿的

windy ['wɪndɪ] *a.* 多风的,刮风的

wing [wɪŋ] *n.* 翅膀,翼

wire [waɪə(r)] *n.* 电线,电报,金属丝

wireless ['waɪəlɪs] *a.* 无线的 *n.* 无线电

wit [wɪt] *n.* 智力,才智

withdraw [wɪð'drɔː] *v.* 撤回,取回,撤退

withhold [wɪð'həʊld] *vt.* 保留,不给;抑制;隐瞒 *vi.* 忍住;克制

withstand [wɪð'stænd] *v.* 抵抗,对抗,经得起

wooden ['wʊdn] *a.* 木制的

wool [wʊl] *n.* 毛线,毛织品,羊毛

wool(l)en ['wʊlən] *n.* 毛织品 *a.* 羊毛制的

workforce ['wɜːkfɔːs] n. 劳动力, 工人总数, 职工总数
workman ['wɜːkmən] n. 工人, 工匠, 男工
workmate ['wɜːkmeɪt] n. 同事, 工友
workplace[8] ['wɜːkpleɪs] n. 工作场所
worm [wɜːm] n. 虫, 蠕虫
worship ['wɜːʃɪp] n. 礼拜, 礼拜仪式 v. 崇拜, 敬仰
worthless ['wɜːθlɪs] a. 无价值的, 无用的
worthy ['wɜːði] a. 有价值的, 可尊敬的, 值得的, 配得上的
wreck [rek] n. 失事, 残骸, 破坏, 健康受损的人
wreckage ['rekɪdʒ] n. (失事船或飞机等的)残骸
wrench [rentʃ] n. 扳手, 扳钳
wrinkle ['rɪŋkl] n. 皱纹 v. (使)起皱纹
wrist [rɪst] n. 腕, 腕关节

yacht [jɒt] n. 游艇, 快艇 vi. 驾快艇
yard [jɑːd] n. 庭院, 码
yawn [jɔːn] n. 哈欠 v. 打哈欠
yell [jel] v. 大叫
yield [jiːld] vt. 生产, 出产; 让步, 屈服 vi. 屈服, 服从 n. 产量, 收获量
yoga ['jəʊgə] n. 瑜伽
yoghurt ['jɒgət] n. 酸乳酪
youngster ['jʌŋstə(r)] n. 青年, 年轻人; 少年
youth [juːθ] n. 青春, 青(少)年时期; 男青年, 小伙子; [总称]青年, 青年人

Z

zebra [ˈziːbrə, ˈze-] *n.* 斑马；人行道
zigzag [ˈzɪgzæg] *a.* 锯齿形的；曲折的；之字形的
zinc [zɪŋk] *n.* 锌
zoology [zəʊˈɒlədʒɪ] *n.* 动物学

A

actually [ˈæktʃuəlɪ] *ad.* 事实上(积极词,略)

ad = advertisement(积极词,略)

aeroplane = airplane(积极词,略)

Africa [ˈæfrɪkə] *n.* 非洲(积极词,略)

African [ˈæfrɪkən] *a.* 非洲(人)的(积极词,略)

alleged [əˈledʒd] *a.* 所谓的;声称的;被断言的

   [巧记] allege *v.* 断言,声称;allegedly *ad.* 依其申述;据传

   [语境] Her alleged friends all disappeared when she was in trouble.

      她那些所谓的朋友,在她遇到麻烦时,都不见影踪。

altar [ˈɔːltə(r)] *n.* 祭坛;圣坛

   [巧记] alt(高) + ar(离出地面)→祭坛

   [语境] The priest bowed down before the altar.

      牧师在圣坛前行鞠躬礼。

Amazon [ˈæməzən] *n.* 亚马孙

   [语境] Some scientists hope to chart out that particular area of the Amazon.

      有些科学家希望对亚马孙河的那一特定区域进行勘察。

America [əˈmerɪkə] *n.* 美洲;美国(积极词,略)

American [əˈmerɪkən] *a.* 美洲(人)的;美国(人)的(积极词,略)

anemia [əˈniːmɪə] *n.* 贫血;贫血症

   [语境] The doctors analyzed the blood sample for anemia.

      医生们分析了贫血的血样。

Anemia is frequently seen in advanced disease.

贫血在进展期中最常见。

Antarctic [ænt'ɑːktɪk] *a.* 南极(区)的 *n.* (the A-)南极洲,南极圈

[语境] Antarctic exploration begins with Ptolemy.

南极的探险是由普特利姆首先进行的。

Antarctic Peninsula has the most moderate climate.

南极洲半岛气候最温和。

Antibiotic [ˌæntibaɪ'ɔtik] *n.* 抗生素 *a.* 抗生的

Arab ['ærəb] *n.* 阿拉伯人 *a.* 阿拉伯人的(积极词,略)

Arabian [ə'reɪbɪən] *a.* 阿拉伯人的,阿拉伯的(积极词,略)

archaeology [ˌɑːkɪ'ɒlədʒɪ] *n.* 考古学

[语境] He displayed interest in archaeology.

他对考古学有兴趣。

She teaches archaeology at the university.

她在大学里教考古学。

arctic ['ɑːktɪk] *a.* 北极的;极寒的 *n.* (the A-)北极

[语境] We can't stand this arctic weather.

我们受不了这种严寒的天气。

Wilderness forests give way to arctic tundra in the Far North.

原生森林一直延伸到极远的北方始由极地草原取代。

ardent ['ɑːdənt] *a.* 热烈的,激动的;热心的,热切的;燃烧的,炽热的

[巧记] ardently *ad.* 热心地,热烈地

[语境] The satisfaction derived from this act was all that the most ardent moralist could have desired.

这个行动使自己得到了连最热心的慈善家都希冀得到的满足。

An ardent outset may be followed by declension.

热情的开端可能继之以冷漠。

[考点] in an ardent manner 热情地

Asia ['eɪʃə, 'eɪʒə] *n.* 亚洲(积极词,略)

Asian ['eɪʃən, 'eɪʒən] *a.* 亚洲(人)的 *n.* 亚洲人(积极词,略)

astronaut ['æstrənɔːt, -nɑt] *n.* 宇航员,太空人(积极词,略)

大纲新增词汇

Atlantic [ət'læntɪk] *a.* 大西洋的 *n.* [the A-]大西洋

[语境]It took them several days to cross the Atlantic Ocean.

他们花了好几天的时间穿越大西洋。

A strong gale swept down on the Atlantic coast.

狂风突然猛袭大西洋海岸。

Australia [ɒ'streɪlɪə] *n.* 澳洲;澳大利亚(积极词,略)

Australian [ɒ'streɪlɪən] *a.* 澳洲的;澳大利亚的 *n.* 澳大利亚人(积极词,略)

B

banker ['bæŋkə(r)] *n.* 银行家(积极词,略)

bicycle ['baɪsɪkl] *n.* 自行车(积极词,略)

British ['brɪtɪʃ] *a.* (大)不列颠(人)的;英国(人)的 *n.* 英国人(积极词,略)

C

camcorder ['kæmkɔːdə] *n.* (便捷式)摄像机

[语境]One of the first steps in creating a movie is copying the video from your camcorder to your computer.

制作影片时的其中一个准备步骤是将视频从摄像机复制至电脑。

Canada ['kænədə] *n.* 加拿大(积极词,略)

Canadian [kə'neɪdɪən] *a.* 加拿大(人)的 *n.* 加拿大人(积极词,略)

capability [ˌkeɪpə'bɪlɪtɪ] *n.* 能力,才能;性能,容量

[巧记]capable *a.* 有能力的,能干的 be capable of 能干……

[语境]They both have the capability of winning.

他们都具备获胜的能力。

If you lose the capability, you lose it forever.

如果你一旦失去这个能力,你就将永远失去它。

cardiac[ˈkɑːdɪæk] *a.* **心脏的,心脏病的**

[巧记]cardi(心) + ac(的)→心脏的

[语境]Death is caused by cardiac failure.

心脏衰竭引起死亡。

This increased cardiac work load!

这个增加了心脏的工作负担!

Celsius[ˈselsjəs] *a.* **摄氏的**

[语境]The annual average temperature here is 24 degrees Celsius.

这里的年平均气温为24℃。

Centigrade Boiling point is 100 degrees Celsius.

百分度的沸点是100摄氏度。

China [ˈtʃaɪnə] *n.* **中国(积极词,略)**

Chinese[tʃaɪˈniːz] *a.* **中国(人/话)的** *n.* **中国人,汉语(积极词,略)**

collaborate [kəˈlæbəreɪt] *vi.* **合作**

[巧记]同义词:cooperate;join forces

[语境]The government and insurance industry have been urged to collaborate to calm public fears.

英国政府和保险业被迫合作平息公众的惊恐。

Teachers collaborate with each other from remote locations around the country on a common project.

教师们可以与国内边远地区的同行们就一共同项目彼此合作。

[考点]collaborate with 与……合作

colourful[ˈkʌləf(ʊ)l] *a.* **多色的;丰富多彩的**

[巧记]反义词:colourless(无色的)

[语境]The long-running children's educational show featuring colourful puppets is to have an Indian adaptation.

这个经久不衰的儿童教育节目以多彩的玩偶表演为特色。
它将会为印度儿童制作一个适合他们的版本。

commonsense[ˌkɒmənˈsens] *a.* **具有常识的**

[巧记]common(平常的) + sense(意识)→有常识的

[语境]I should have expected more commonsense from De Baudricourt. He is sending some cracked country lass here.

我没想到包椎古尔这么没有常识。他送来了一个乡下的疯丫头。

conditioner [kən'dɪʃənə(r)] *n.* 调节装置,空调(积极词,略)

conduction [kən'dʌkʃən] *n.* 传导

[巧记] conduct(*vi.* 进行,传导),conductive(*a.* 传导的;传导性的;有传导力的),conductor(导体;售票员;领导者;管理人);同义词:conductivity

[语境] The transfer of heat from one molecule to another is called conduction.

热量由一个分子传递给另一个分子的现象叫作传导。

However, unlike these other materials, all of the conduction occurs in a single layer of atoms in the sample.

不过,与这些其他材料所不同的是,传导过程发生在样本中一层单原子层。

consequently [ˈkɒnsɪkwəntlɪ] *ad.* 所以,因此

[巧记] 同义词:therefore, accordingly

[语境] Consequently I am able to show interest in him as a person.

结果是,我可以对作为一个人的他感到有了兴趣。

Consequently, they know very little but speak very well, albeit only in English.

因此,他们懂得很少,但话说得很漂亮,虽然只会用英语说。

constituency [kənˈstɪtjʊənsɪ] *n.* 选举区;选举区全体选民

[巧记] constituent *a.* 构成的;选举的 *n.* 成分;选民;委托人

[语境] He was deselected by his local constituency party because he didn't support the Prime Minister.

因为他不支持首相,所以他被地方选区政党取消了竞选资格。

They must demonstrate to a broad constituency—beyond their own employees and investors—that they do a useful job.

除了自己的员工和投资者,他们也必须向广大选民证明:自己做的是有用的工作。

crowded [ˈkraʊdɪd] *a.* 拥挤的(积极词,略)

D

definitely [ˈdefɪnɪtlɪ] *ad.* 明确地，一定地
 [巧记] definite (*a.* 一定的；确切的)
 [语境] It has not yet definitely settled.
　这事还没有明确解决。
　No, definitely not.
　不，绝对不会。

detailed [ˈdiːteɪld] *a.* 详细的（积极词，略）

directly [dɪˈrektlɪ, daɪ-] *ad.* 直接地，直截了当地；立即，马上（积极词，略）

diversity [daɪˈvɜːsɪtɪ] *n.* 多样化，差异，变化（积极词，略）

drilling [ˈdrɪlɪŋ] *n.* 演练；钻孔
 [巧记] drill (*v.* 钻孔；训练；条播)
 [语境] The soldiers were all out drilling.
　战士们正在努力训练。
　Instead, he told us to go drilling.
　相反，他告诉我们去钻探。
 [考点] drilling machine 钻孔机

E

earnings [ˈɜːnɪŋs] *n.* 收入，收益
 [巧记] 同近义词：income, proceeds, receipt
 [语境] He drinks half his earnings.
　他喝酒喝掉了一半收入。
　He is insured for damage to his property, but not for his loss of earnings.
　他正为他的财产损失投保，而不是为收入亏损投保。

大纲新增词汇

[考点]annual earnings 年收益

electronics [ɪˌlek'trɒnɪks] *a.* 电子学(积极词,略)

eleventh [ɪ'levnθ] *num.* 第十一

[语境]China is the host of The Eleventh Asian Olympic Games.

中国是第十一届亚洲奥林匹克运动会的主办国。

And Yang Linwei, an eleventh grader from China, says: "When I was young we couldn't use calculators."

来自中国十一年级的学生杨林伟说:"我年轻的时候,我们不能使用计算器。"

[考点]eleventh hour 最后一刻;危急之时

embargo [em'bɑːgəʊ] *vt.* 禁止出入港口;禁止或限制贸易 *n.* 封港令;禁令;禁止

[语境]The government embargoes the enemy ships.

该国政府禁止敌船出入其港口。

[考点]trade embargo 贸易禁运

England ['ɪŋglənd] *n.* 英格兰;英国(积极词,略)

English ['ɪŋglɪʃ] *a.* 英语的,英国(人)的 *n.* 英语,英国人(积极词,略)

epic ['epɪk] *n.* 史诗

[巧记]epical(*adj.* 英勇的;叙事诗的;有重大历史意义的)

[语境]That hunger for something epic is an important part of who I am and what I do.

渴望完成史诗般的事情是我所以是我以及我所做之事重要的一部分。

Having created this bond with the audience and taken them on an epic journey, he turned in on himself.

此前他与观众互动,并将他们领进了一段史诗般的旅程,而现在他开始转入自己的内心。

[考点]epic poetry 史诗

Europe ['jʊərəp] *n.* 欧洲(积极词,略)

European [ˌjʊərə'pɪən] *a.* 欧洲的 *n.* 欧洲人(积极词,略)

everlasting [ˌevə'lɑːstɪŋ] *a.* 永恒的;接连不断的

661

[巧记] ever(总是) + lasting(持续的) → 接连不断的

[语境] Once they were part of an everlasting love.

曾经,它们是永恒爱情的一部分。

Sinners may be damned to everlasting hellfire.

但愿罪人都被罚受永久的地狱之火。

every ['evrɪ] *a.* **每个,每;每隔……的**

[语境] They cocktailed once every week.

他们每星期喝一次鸡尾酒。

We go mushrooming every morning.

我们每天早上去采蘑菇。

[考点] every time 每次

evidently ['evɪdəntlɪ] *ad.* **明显地,显而易见地**

[巧记] evident(*a.* 明显的;明白的)、evidence(*n.* 证据,证明;迹象;明显)

[语境] They were evidently rationalizing.

他们显然是在给自己进行辩解。

In this world, evidently the vestibule of another, there are no fortunate.

这个世界显然是另一个世界的前厅,这儿没有幸福的人。

excited [ɪk'saɪtɪd] *a.* **兴奋的(积极词,略)**

extremely [ɪk'striːmlɪ] *ad.* **极,非常**

[巧记] 同近义词:badly, highly, greatly

[语境] I feel that that period in my life was extremely valuable.

我觉得,那段经历在我的人生中是非常宝贵的。

To be crude and careless is an extremely bad style of work.

粗枝大叶是一种极坏的作风。

F

Fahrenheit ['færənhaɪt] *a.* **华氏的**

[语境] How to get Celsius from Fahrenheit.

怎样从华氏温度获得摄氏温度。

If you existed in the world of Fahrenheit 451, which book would you want to memorize?

如果你生存在这个华氏451的世界,哪本书是你想要默记的?

fallacy [ˈfæləsɪ] *n.* 谬误,谬论

[巧记] fallacious (*a.* 谬误的;骗人的;靠不住的;不合理的)

[语境] Whether the age ratio is a prophecy or fallacy, the importance of pension activity to markets is clear.

无论年龄比例是预言还是谬论,退休金活动对于市场的重要性显而易见。

farming [ˈfɑːmɪŋ] *n.*/*a.* 农业(的)

[巧记] farm (*n.* 农场;农家;畜牧场),farmer (*n.* 农夫,农民)

[语境] He lives by farming.

他靠务农过活。

Ancient farming methods still survive in the Middle East.

在中东,古代的耕作方式依然存在。

fifteenth [fɪfˈtiːnθ] *num.* 第十五

[语境] In the fifteenth century, the British elevated the symbol by replacing iron with gold.

在15世纪,英国人用金子取代铁,使其象征意义更为珍贵。

first-rate [ˌfɜːstˈreɪt] *a.* 第一流的,极好的(积极词,略)

fitness [ˈfɪtnɪs] *n.* 适当,恰当,合理;健康(积极词,略)

flu [fluː] *n.* 流行性感冒(积极词,略)

fortitude [ˈfɔːtɪtjuːd] *n.* 坚忍,刚毅

[巧记] 近义词:backbone, grit, guts, pluck;反义词:cowardice

[语境] Fortitude and hard work are what is required.

坚忍的意志和努力工作是必要条件。

But fortitude, he argues, does not just happen. It depends on notions of civil harmony and responsibility, which governments have an important role in supporting.

他认为,不屈不挠的精神不会凭空而来,要依赖社会和谐和

公民责任,政府要起到重要的支持作用。

fortunately [ˈfɔːtʃnɪtlɪ] *ad.* 幸亏(积极词,略)

fourth [fɔːθ] *num.* 第四

[语境] She's barricaded herself into an office on the fourth floor.

她把自己关在四楼的办公室里。

freely [ˈfriːlɪ] *ad.* 自由地,随意地(积极词,略)

freezer [ˈfriːzə(r)] *n.* 冷藏箱/库

[巧记] freezing(*adj.* 冰冻的;严寒的;冷冻用的),freeze(*n.* 冻结;凝固 *vi.* 冻结;冷冻;僵硬 *vt.* 使……冻住;使……结冰)

[语境] I forgot to put them in the freezer.

我忘记把它们放进冰箱了。

French [frentʃ] *a.* 法国(人)的,法语的 *n.* 法国人,法语(积极词,略)

fridge = refrigerator

[语境] Then all three of you sign the contract and post in on the fridge.

然后你们三个人要都在协议上签名,并把它贴在冰箱上。

[考点] electric refrigerator *n.* 电冰箱

G

genetics [dʒɪˈnetɪks] *n.* 遗传学

[巧记] genic(基因) + tics(学) →遗传学

[语境] But genetics may not be the only explanation.

但是,遗传学也许不是唯一的解释。

Students are flocking to such fields as genetics and molecular biology.

大学生正在大量从事诸如遗传学和分子生物学等领域的研究。

German [ˈdʒɜːmən] *a.* 德国(人)的,德语的 *n.* 德国人,德语(积极词,略)

Greek [gri:k] *n.* 希腊人,希腊语 *a.* 希腊(人)的,希腊语的(积极词,略)

grey [greɪ] *a./n.* 灰色(的)(积极词,略)

grown-up [ˌɡrəʊnˈʌp] *a.* 成长的,成熟的,成人的 *n.* 成年人(积极词,略)

gymnastics [dʒɪmˈnæstɪks] *n.* 体育,体操

[语境] But I also like basketball and gymnastics.
但是我也喜欢篮球和体操。
As a cricketer, gymnastics is out of his domain.
他是个板球运动员,体操非其所长。

H

hairdresser [ˈheədresə(r)] *n.* 美发师,理发师

[语境] Hairdresser, how do you like it?
理发师,感觉怎么样?
Is he a hairdresser?
他是一个理发师吗?

harass [ˈhærəs] *v.* 骚扰/(使)烦恼

[巧记] 近义词: trouble

[语境] Some are just perverts—they rush to the stage and harass us.
有些人就是变态——他们冲到台上来骚扰我们。
He realized early that the best strategy was to harass the British.
他很早就认识到,最好的战略就是骚扰英国人。

heater [ˈhi:tə(r)] *n.* 加热器,发热器

[巧记] heat(加热) + er(物品) → 加热器

[语境] In addition, turn up, or off, the air conditioning or heater during the day.
补充一下,在白天开通或者关闭空调和加热器。
Then open the "hot out" valve at the electric water heater and turn the breaker on.

然后我们关闭热水器的电力加热器的开关并将断路器打开。

[考点] water heater 热水器

heating [ˈhiːtɪŋ] *n.* **加热,供暖;暖气装置**

[语境] Artificial heating hastens the growth of plants.

人工加热会加快植物的生长。

heroine [ˈherəʊɪn] *n.* **女英雄;女主角,女主人公**

[巧记] hero(英雄) + ine(女性) →女英雄

[语境] She became the heroine of France.

她成为法国的女英雄。

This story featured a plucky heroine.

这个故事描述了一个勇敢的女英雄。

high-tech [ˌhaɪˈtek] *n.* **高科技**(积极词,略)

hometown [ˌhəʊmˈtaʊn] *n.* **故乡,家乡**(积极词,略)

hostess [ˈhəʊstɪs] *n.* **女主人**(积极词,略)

humid [ˈhjuːmɪd] *a.* **湿的,湿气重的**(积极词,略)

humiliate [hjuːˈmɪlieɪt] *vt.* **使……丢脸;羞辱**

[巧记] 近义词:abase (*vt.* 降低……的地位)

[语境] She was humiliated because her children behaved so badly.

她为她的孩子表现不好而感到羞辱。

[考点] disgrace:侧重在别人,尤其在众人面前丢脸;humiliate:强调受辱者自尊心的损坏;shame:指由不光彩或不道德的行为引起的惭愧感或羞耻感;dishonor:有时可与 disgrace 换用,但前者是指因失去荣誉所致

I

immigrate [ˈɪmɪɡreɪt] *vi.* **移居(入境)**

[巧记] 派生词:immigrant (*a.* 移民的;迁入的;*n.* 移民,侨民), immigration (*n.* 移民人数;移居)

[语境] Many Jews immigrated into the United States.

许多犹太人移居美国。

Palestinians from around the world should have a right to immigrate, if they so choose, to a Palestinian state.

如果也这样选择的话,来自世界各地的巴勒斯坦人也有权利移居到一个巴勒斯坦国家。

[考点]immigrate into 移入

immigration[ˌɪmɪˈɡreɪʃən] *n.* **移居,移民**

[语境]But immigration should not be the only pathway for those seeking opportunities.

但移民对寻求机会的人来说不应该是唯一途径。

We should be treating this as an economic opportunity, not an immigration issue.

我们应当将此视为一个经济机遇,而不是移民问题。

India[ˈɪndjə] *n.* 印度(积极词,略)

Indian[ˈɪndjən] *a.* 印度人的,印第安人的 *n.* 印度人,印第安人(积极词,略)

indifferent[ɪnˈdɪfərənt] *a.* **不关心的;不在乎的;中立的;冷淡的**

[巧记]indifferently(*ad.* 冷淡地;漠不关心地;平庸地;相当差地),indifference(*n.* 冷淡,不关心)

[语境]He is indifferent to the result of the exam.

他对考试结果漠不关心。

She seems indifferent, but deep down she's very pleased.

她貌似无动于衷,其实心里非常高兴。

[考点]be indifferent to/towards 漠不关心;冷淡;不感兴趣

indirect[ˌɪndɪˈrekt] *a.* 间接的,迂回的(积极词,略)

industrialization[ɪnˌdʌstrɪəlaɪˈzeɪʃn] *n.* **工业化**

[语境]And, at this point, traces of industrialization can only be found in sediments in Europe.

而在这一点上,工业化的痕迹只在欧洲的沉积物中找到。

With the industrialization of food production and the globalization of its marketing, efforts to ensure food safety likewise take on an international dimension.

随着食品生产的工业化及其销售的全球化,努力确保食品安全的工作也同样具有了国际意义。

[考点]product industrialization 产品工业化

influenza[ˌɪnfluˈenzə] *n.* 流行性感冒(积极词,略)

innovate[ˈɪnə(ʊ)veɪt] *n.* 创新,改革(积极词,略)

interruption[ˌɪntəˈrʌpʃən] *n.* 打断,干扰;中断

[巧记]interrupted(*adj.* 中断的;被打断的;不规则的), interrupt(*vt.* 打断;中断)

[语境]Any small interruption is likely to throw me off in my calculations.

一点小小的干扰都有可能使我在计算上出错。

She has kept up physical training for several years without interruption.

她坚持锻炼,几年来从未间断。

[考点]power interruption 供电中断,电源中断

inventive [ɪnˈventɪv] *a.* 发明的,有发明才能的(积极词,略)

invoice[ˈɪnvɔɪs] *n.* 发票;发货单

[语境]The merchandise does not check with invoice.

这批货与发货单不符。

You then choose an invoice to view and print.

然后您可以选择查看和打印一个发票。

[考点]invoice amount 发票额

Islam [ˈɪzlɑːm, ɪzˈlɑːm] *n.* 伊斯兰教(积极词,略)

Italian[ɪˈtæljən] *a.* 意大利人/语的 *n.* 意大利人/语(积极词,略)

J

Japanese[ˌdʒæpəˈniːz] *a.* 日本(人/语)的 *n.* 日本人,日语(积极词,略)

jewelry [ˈdʒuːəlrɪ] *n.* [总称]珠宝;珠宝饰物

[语境]Purchased products:grains, food stuff, oil, diamond, jewelry, watches.

采购产品有:谷物,食品,油,钻石,珠宝,手表。
They were dressed in an array of silk and jewelry.
她们穿戴着精美的丝绸衣服和珠宝。

Jupiter [ˈdʒuːpɪtə(r), ˈdʒʊ-] *n.* 木星

[语境] The scientist could not calculate when the spaceship would reach the Jupiter.
那位科学家没有算出那艘宇宙飞船什么时候会到达木星。
The astronomers were taking an observation of Jupiter.
天文学家们正在观测木星。

K

key [kiː] *n.* 钥匙;答案,解答;键,琴键;方法,关键 *a.* 主要的,关键的(积极词,略)

L

Lab = laboratory(积极词,略)

legislation [ˌledʒɪsˈleɪʃən] *n.* 立法,法律的规定(或通过)

[巧记] 派生词:legislator (*n.* 立法者),legislative (*a.* 立法的),legislate (*v.* 立法;制定法律)

[语境] Expect that legislation will authorize value-based land tax.
期望立法能批准基于价值的土地税。
Such legislation is virtually per se unconstitutional.
该立法实质上其本身就是违宪的。

[考点] antitrust legislation 反托拉斯立法

landing [ˈlændɪŋ] *n.* 登陆,着陆;楼梯平台(积极词,略)

largely [ˈlɑːdʒli] *ad.* 大部分,基本上;大规模地(积极词,略)

lateral [ˈlætərəl] *a.* 侧面的;旁边的 *n.* 旁边/侧面的东西

[语境] To provide lateral stiffness to the building, a system of bracing

may be designed to resist lateral forces due to wind or earthquake.
为了保持建筑物的侧向刚度,可以设计一个支撑系统来抵抗由于风或地震引起的侧向力。

[考点] lateral thinking 涉及方方面面的考虑,多方考虑,周密的考虑

lengthen ['leŋ(k)θən] *vt.* 伸长,延长

[巧记] 反义词:shorten(*v.* 缩短)

[语境] To save time is to lengthen life.
节约时间就是延长生命。
As winter gave way to spring, the days began to lengthen.
冬去春来时,白天开始长了起来。

[考点] extend 指时间或空间的延长,也可指影响和使用范围等的扩大;lengthen 指把长度或期限拉长或延长,其反义词是 shorten;stretch 指长度的延伸以及宽度的增加;prolong 通常指时间上延长得超过了一般或正常的限度

lifestyle ['laɪfstaɪl] *n.* 生活方式(积极词,略)

lighting ['laɪtɪŋ] *n.* 光,光亮,光线;灯,灯光 *vt.* 点,点燃;照亮,照耀 *a.* 轻的;轻捷的,轻快地;淡(色)的;明亮的

[巧记] 同义词:ignition, inflammation;反义词:darkness

[语境] The stage lighting gives the effect of a moonlit scene.
舞台灯光产生月夜景色的效果。

[考点] lighting circuit 照明电路

longevity [lɒn'dʒevɪtɪ] *n.* 长命,长寿;寿命

[巧记] long(长的) + evity(抽象名词后缀)→长命

[语境] They symbolize immortality and longevity.
它们象征着不朽和长寿。
The longevity flower is a rare kind of flower found only in heaven. Whoever from the human world eats it will remain young forever.
长寿花,乃是天宫的宝物,谁能吃到它谁就长生不老。

lost [lɒst] *a.* 失去的;错过的;浪费掉的;无望的,迷路的(积极词,略)

lottery ['lɒtərɪ] *n.* 彩票或奖券的发行,抽彩给奖法

[语境] The smileage from winning the lottery shall last until the money is gone.

中了大奖的喜悦会持续到钱花光为止。

I guess my only chance of being a fat cat is to win ＄10m in the lottery.

我想我要成为一个有钱人的唯一机会就是中一张一千万美元的彩票。

lurk[lɜːk] *vi.* **潜伏;埋伏;潜藏** *n.* **埋伏;潜伏**

[语境] A fox was sneaking on the lurk.

一只狐狸正在偷偷摸摸地潜行窥探。

We cannot, we will not, succumb to the dark impulses that lurk in the far regions of the soul everywhere.

我们不能也不会屈服于这种隐藏在灵魂深处的黑暗本能。

M

magical['mædʒɪkl] *a.* **有魔力的,不可思议的(积极词,略)**
mainly['meɪnlɪ] *ad.* **主要地,大体上(积极词,略)**
mammal['mæml] *n.* **哺乳动物**

[语境] The function of a mammal's fur is to insulate the body.

哺乳动物皮毛的功能在于使身体保温。

A whale is a kind of mammal.

鲸是一种哺乳动物。

mandate['mændeɪt,-dɪt] *n.* **命令,指令;委托管理;授权** *vt.* **托管;授权**

[语境] He'd been mandated by the West African Economic Community to go in and to enforce a ceasefire.

他受西非经济共同体的委托介入并执行停火协定。

The elections are mandated by a peace accord signed by the government last May.

选举是在去年5月政府签署的和平协议的授权下进行的。

marketing[ˈmɑːkɪtɪŋ] n. 行销,买卖
　[巧记]market (v. 营销 n. 市场)
　[语境]The advertising manager is the mastermind of our new marketing policy.
　　广告制作商是我们新市场政策的策划人。
　　They are developing marketing network.
　　他们正在发展销售网络。
　[考点]go marketing 去市场做生意

Mars[mɑːz] n. 火星(积极词,略)

Marxism[ˈmɑːksɪzəm] n. 马克思主义
　[语境]Marxism possesses the theoretical character of keeping pace with the times.
　　马克思主义具有与时俱进的理论品格。

Mediterranean[ˌmedɪtəˈreɪnjən] n./a. 地中海(的)
　[语境]An American naval force is showing the flag in various Mediterranean ports.
　　美国的海军力量在地中海的多个港口炫耀武力。

men[men] n. (man 的复数)(积极词,略)

merely[ˈmɪəlɪ] ad. 仅仅,只不过(积极词,略)

Mexican[ˈmeksɪkən] a. 墨西哥的;墨西哥人的 n. 墨西哥人
　[语境]I read that the new director is a Mexican.
　　我获悉新董事是墨西哥人。

microbe[ˈmaɪkrəub] n. 微生物
　[语境]The probe is sensitive enough to detect the presence of a single microbe.
　　这个探针的灵敏度很高,足以测出任何微生物的存在。
　　The food microbe poisoning often come from the course of food production.
　　食品微生物中毒通常来源于食品加工的过程。

mid[mɪd] a. 中间的
　[语境]Our mid term exam is pending.
　　我们就要期中考试了。

大纲新增词汇

miner [ˈmaɪnə(r)] *n.* 矿工

[巧记] mine *n.* 矿,矿藏;矿山,矿井;地雷,水雷;mineral 矿物;(英)矿泉水;无机物;苏打水(常用复数表示)

[语境] He was a miner all his working life.
他一辈子都是矿工。
I am a coal miner.
我是煤矿工。

miraculous [mɪˈrækjʊləs] *a.* 不可思议的,奇迹的

[巧记] miracle(*n.* 奇迹,奇迹般的人或物;惊人的事例)

[语境] This is a miraculous thing.
这真是奇怪的事。
The wounded man made a miraculous recovery.
伤员奇迹般地痊愈了。

misconduct [ˌmɪsˈkɒndʌkt] *n.* 行为不检

[语境] The boy's misconduct cost his mother many sleepless nights.
这男孩的不轨行为,使他的母亲许多夜不得安眠。
His misconduct let in a host of troubles.
他的不端行为招致不少麻烦。

month [mʌnθ] *n.* 月,月份(积极词,略)

Moslem [ˈmɒzləm] *n. / a.* 穆斯林(的),伊斯兰教徒(的)

[语境] He is a Moslem.
他是一个伊斯兰教徒。
He later turned Moslem.
他后来改信了伊斯兰教。

N

narrate [nəˈreɪt] *vt.* 叙述;给……做旁白 *vi.* 叙述;讲述

[巧记] narrative(*a.* 叙事的,叙述的;叙事体的),narrator(*n.* 叙述者;解说员),narration(*n.* 叙述,讲述;故事)

[语境] He narrated to us the story of the two men's armed robbery.

673

他向我们讲述了那两个人持枪抢劫的经过。

to narrate a film

给一部电影作解说

negligent [ˈneglɪdʒənt] *a.* 疏忽的;粗心大意的

[巧记] neglected (*a.* 被忽视的;未被好好照管的), negligently (*ad.* 疏忽地;粗心大意地)

[语境] Yet both he and the team are hampered by corrupt, negligent and antagonistic officials.

然而他和小组的工作都被腐败、疏忽、敌对的官员们所阻挠。

Nor have the people yet turned with a vengeance on incompetent politicians or negligent regulators.

人们也没有去报复那些不称职的政客或疏忽的监管机构。

nephew [ˈnevjuː, ˈnef-] *n.* 侄儿,外甥(积极词,略)

Neptune [ˈneptjuːn] *n.* 海王星

[语境] Jupiter, Uranus, and Neptune also have rings, but Saturn's are by far the largest and most spectacular.

木星、天王星和海王星也有环,但土星的环是迄今为止规模最大、最为壮观的。

normally [ˈnɔːməlɪ] *ad.* 一般地;通常

[巧记] normal (*n.* 正常;标准;常态 *a.* 正常的,标准的), normalization (*n.* 正常化;标准化;正规化;常态化)

[语境] The patient began to breathe normally.

病人开始正常呼吸了。

He began to breathe in and out normally.

他开始正常呼气和吸气。

Norwegian [nɔːˈwiːdʒən] *a.* 挪威(人)的 *n.* 挪威人/语

[语境] But this year the focus should be on the wilds of the Norwegian countryside.

但今年我们不妨将目光转向挪威的乡村自然美景。

nutrient [ˈnjuːtrɪənt] *a.* 营养的,滋养的 *n.* 营养物

[语境] Each individual has a physiological requirement for each nutrient.

每个人对每种营养成分都有一种生理上的需要。

The roots transmit moisture and nutrient to the trunk and branches.
根将水分和养料输送到干和枝。

O

obviously [ˈɒbvɪəslɪ] *ad.* 明显地,显然(积极词,略)

Oceania [ˌəʊʃɪˈɑnɪə] *n.* 大洋洲

[语境] The Mummies of The World Exhibition brings together a collection of mummies and related artifacts from South America, Europe, Asia, Oceania and Egypt.
全球干尸展览汇集了来自南美、欧洲、亚洲、大洋洲和埃及的一系列干尸和艺术品。

oh [əʊ] *int.* 哦(积极词,略)

Olympics [əʊˈlimpiks] *n.* 奥林匹克运动会

[语境] What do you like about the Olympics?
你喜欢奥运会的什么呢?
What item do you like best in the Olympics?
你最喜欢的奥运会项目是什么?

[考点] the green Olympics 绿色奥运

onlooker [ˈɒnlʊkə(r)] *n.* 旁观者

[巧记] on(在……) + look(看) + er(人)→在旁边看的人→旁观者

[语境] One onlooker flew in with a friend Thursday from New York.
一位观众在周四和一位朋友从纽约飞过来。
By the time the ambulance arrived, a crowd of onlookers had gathered.
救护车赶到时,围观的人已经很多了。

openly [ˈəʊpənlɪ] *ad.* 公然地,公开地;直率地,坦白地(积极词,略)

opt [ɒpt] *vi.* 选择

[巧记] option(*n.* 选择), optional(*a.* 可选择的)

[语境] Or, you can opt to lick up her back.

或者你可以选择去舔她的香背。

These are the clothes which you can opt for.

这些是可供你选择的衣服。

[考点] opt for 选择

orphan [ˈɔːfən] *n.* 孤儿

[语境] They adopted an orphan as an heir.

他们立一个孤儿为继承人。

We may keep an orphan or adopt it out.

我们可以领养一个孤儿，或将孩子给人收养。

P

Pacific [pəˈsɪfɪk] *a.* 太平洋的 *n.* [the Pacific] 太平洋

[语境] He is serving on a warship in the Pacific.

他在太平洋海域的一般军舰上服役。

He beachcombed on a South Pacific island.

他在南太平洋一个岛屿海滨流浪。

particularly [pəˈtɪkjʊləlɪ] *ad.* 特别地，尤其地（积极词，略）

pavement [ˈpeɪvmənt] *n.* 人行道

[语境] He stopped his bike just off the pavement.

他把自行车就停在人行道旁边。

Inertia carried the car to the pavement.

惯性使汽车驶到了人行道上。

[考点] on the pavement 没住处；徘徊街头；被遗弃

personality [ˌpɜːsəˈnælɪtɪ] *n.* 人格，个性（积极词，略）

pharmacy [ˈfɑːməsɪ] *n.* 药房，药剂学，配药业，制药业

[语境] You can get some at the pharmacy across the street.

你可以在对面那条街的药店买到一些这种药。

Yes, probably at the pharmacy or in the shop in your hotel.

是的，在那家药店或者在你旅馆的商店里有可能买到。

大纲新增词汇

phenomenal [fɪˈnɒmɪnl] *a.* 现象的;能知觉的;异常的;杰出的,惊人的

[巧记] phenomenally (*ad.* 现象上地;明白地;从感官认识到),phenomenon (*n.* 现象;奇迹;杰出的人才)

[语境] If you make it the focus of your career, that would be phenomenal.

如果你让这个事情成为你职业生涯的中心,那将会是十分了不起的。

Both local and foreign banks want to find a way to attach themselves to this phenomenal growth story.

本土银行和外资银行都希望找到一种方式,将自己与这种显著的增长连在一起。

phenomenology [fɪˌnɒmɪˈnɒlədʒɪ] 现象学;现象论

[语境] If one begins with the phenomenology of consciousness one must give an account of the origin of material objects as they arise in conscious experience.

如果一个人以意识的现象学开始,那么当他们从意识经验中出现的时候他一定会考虑到这些客观事物的起源。

photosynthesis [ˌfəʊtəʊˈsɪnθɪsɪs] *n.* 光合作用

[语境] It has at least one gene necessary for photosynthesis—so far it's the only animal known with this ability.

它有至少一个基因是光合作用所必需的——到目前为止这是唯一被发现具有此项能力的动物。

plentiful [ˈplentɪf(ʊ)l] *a.* 富裕的,丰富的

Pluto [ˈpluːtəʊ] *n.* 冥王星

[语境] The next breath you take could have come from beyond Pluto.

你吸入的下一口空气有可能来自比冥王星更遥远的地方。

popcorn [ˈpɒpkɔːn] *n.* 爆米花,爆玉米花

[语境] a paper cone full of popcorn.

装满爆米花的锥形纸筒。

That one next to the one that look like popcorn.

那朵看起来像爆米花的旁边的那朵。

practically [ˈpræktɪkəlɪ] *ad.* 几乎;实际上(积极词,略)

presenter [prɪˈzentə(r)] *n.* 主持人,报幕员;赠与者,提出者(积极词,略)

presently [ˈprezntlɪ] *ad.* 不久,一会儿;现在,目前(积极词,略)

prevention [prɪˈvenʃən] *n.* 预防,防止

[巧记] preventive(*a.* 预防的,防止的),preventable(*a.* 可预防的;可阻止的;可防止的),prevent(*v.* 预防,防止;阻止)

[语境] But the prevention of these diseases begins in childhood.
但是这些疾病的预防应该从童年开始。

Herbs for the prevention of encephalitis can be found everywhere in this area.
预防脑炎的草药在这一地区俯拾皆是。

primarily [ˈpraɪmərɪlɪ] *ad.* 首先,起初;主要地;根本上

[巧记] primary(*a.* 主要的,根本的)

[语境] The debate, however, is not primarily over what he said, but his right to say it.
然而,这场辩论主要不是针对他所说的内容,而是他说这些话的权利。

However, we will only have one plug-in for this exercise, primarily to limit the scope of this article.
然而,我们将只能拥有这一运用的唯一插件,从根本上限制了这篇文章的作用域。

projector [prəˈdʒektə(r)] *n.* 投影仪,放映机,幻灯机

[巧记] project(投射) + or(事物) →投影仪

[语境] We have a projector.
我们有一个投影仪。

How to connect the projector to the computer?
怎样把投影仪连接到电脑上?

promotion [prəˈməʊʃən] *n.* 升级,晋级;宣传,推广(积极词,略)

proportionate [prəˈpɔːʃ(ə)nɪt] *a.* (to)成比例的;相称的;适当的

[巧记] proportion(*n.* 比例,部分),proportional(*a.* 成比例的)

[语境] The cost of the ticket is proportionate to the distance you travel.

票价和旅行的距离是成比例的。

The extra field cultivated meant a proportionate increase in work.

额外开发工地意味着工作量相应增加。

[考点] be proportionate to 与……成比例

prospector [prəˈspektə(r)] *n.* 采矿者;勘探者

[巧记] pro(向前) + spect(寻找,发现) + or(人)→向身体前方挖→寻找矿物的人→采矿者

[语境] The prospector staked his claim to the mine he discovered.

那个勘探者立桩标出他所发现的矿区地以示归己所有。

The book is 100% nicely narrated by Prospector Brann Bronzebeard.

本书是勘探者布莱恩·铜须百分之百细致地描述的。

proverb [ˈprɒvɜːb] *n.* 谚语,格言

[语境] An old Arab proverb says, "The enemy of my enemy is my friend."

一句古老的阿拉伯谚语说:"敌人的敌人是朋友。"

You should know the old proverb, "Call a maid by a married name."

你该知道"张冠李戴"这句古语。

prudent [ˈpruːdnt] *a.* 小心的,审慎的;精明的;节俭的

[巧记] 同义词:cautious, careful

[语境] Be modest and prudent, never lag behind!

谦虚谨慎,永不落后!

A prudent builder should forecast how long the stuff is likely to last.

一个精明的建筑师应是先考虑到工程可能持续多长时间。

psychologist [saɪˈkɒlədʒɪst] *n.* 心理学家

[巧记] psychology(*n.* 心理学), psychological(*a.* 心理学的)

[语境] He practises as a clinical psychologist.

他是一名临床心理医生。

Dr. Sinclair is a child psychologist.

辛克莱博士是一位儿童心理学家。

publisher[ˈpʌblɪʃə(r)] *n.* **出版社;发行人**

[语境]He's writing a history of the town for a local publisher.

他正为当地的一家出版社撰写该镇的历史。

The publisher is looking for a Chinese translator for her novel.

出版商正在为她的小说找一位中文翻译。

R

reactor[rɪˈæktə(r)] *n.* **反应堆**

[巧记]re(回)+act(运动)+or(物)→对……做出反应的事物→反应堆

[语境]An ageing nuclear reactor is an accident waiting to happen.

老化的核反应堆早晚会出事故。

A nuclear reactor is the apparatus in which atoms are split.

核反应堆是分裂原子的装置。

readily[ˈredɪlɪ] *ad.* **容易地,乐意地**

[巧记]近义词:easily, lightly(*ad.* 容易地;乐意地;无困难地)

[语境]Although fatigue shows readily on Carter, he bounces back quickly.

卡特虽然容易显出疲劳的样子,但他很快就恢复了。

Young people are readily pervious to new ideas.

青年人乐意接受新思想。

[考点]readily, accessible 易接近的;易达到的;可存取的

relentless[rɪˈlentlɪs] *a.* **无情的,残酷的;持续的,坚韧的**

[考点]relentlessly(*ad.* 残酷地,无情地)

[语境]We will be relentless in defense of our citizens and our friends and allies.

我们将不懈地保卫我们的国民以及我们的盟友的生命安全。

Government knows this, and hence its accumulation of weaponry and relentless propaganda.

政府知道这一点,所以正积累武器装备并不懈地宣传。

résumé [ˈrezjuːme, -zjʊm] *n.* 简历

[语境]Do you have a résumé with you?
你带个人简历了吗?
I enclosed my résumé in my letter.
我在信里附上了我的简历。

revival [rɪˈvaɪvl] *n.* 复活;复兴

[巧记]re(再) + viv(有生命) + al(名词后缀) →再一次获得生命→复活

[语境]This method is now undergoing a slow revival.
目前这种方法正在慢慢复兴。
The causes of this revival were many and complex.
这次复兴的原因是复杂多样的。

[考点]business revival 经济复兴

riddle [ˈrɪdl] *n.* 谜语,谜;难解的问题,难理解的人、物或情况

[语境]That painting is still a riddle to us.
那幅画对我们仍然是个谜。
He could not solve the riddle.
他不能解决这个难题。

[考点]puzzle:语气较强,指复杂令人费解的情况或问题;mystery:指常人难以认识其起因或性质的奥秘,或指有意不让人理解的奥妙;riddle:指供人猜的谜语游戏,也可指终究会有解答的难题;problem:指有待探讨的疑难问题,也可指令人困惑的情况

rightful [ˈraɪtf(ʊ)l] *a.* 正当的;合法的;正直的;公正的

[巧记]近义词:apt 恰当的,fair 公平的

[语境]What he said is a rightful claim.
他所说的是正当的要求。
This was a rightful but a hard demand.
这是一个正当但严格的要求。

Roman [ˈrəʊmən] *a.* 罗马的,罗马人的 *n.* 罗马人

[语境]Archaeologists have traced many Roman roads in Britain.

考古学家在英国发现了许多古罗马的道路。

Here is a book about Roman history.

这是一本关于古罗马历史的书。

Russian [ˈrʌʃən] *a.* 俄罗斯(人/语)的 *n.* 俄语,俄罗斯(人)(积极词,略)

S

scorch [skɔːtʃ] *vt.* 把……烧焦/烤焦

[语境] She scorched the cake.

她把蛋糕烤焦了。

Her arm that was scorched last week is better now.

她上星期被烧伤的胳臂现在好多了。

Scottish [ˈskɒtɪʃ] *a.* 苏格兰(人)的 *n.* 苏格兰(人);苏格兰语

[语境] This Scottish plant was a gift from my cousin.

这棵苏格兰植物是我的一个表亲给我的礼物。

My husband and I are Scottish.

我和我丈夫是苏格兰人。

seaport [ˈsiːpɔːt] *n.* 海港,港口(积极词,略)

sedan [sɪˈdæn] *n.* 轿车;轿子

[语境] This luxury sedan loses 84% of its purchase price.

这辆豪华小轿车损失了它买入价的84%。

Officers always went out in sedan chairs in Qing Dynasty.

清朝官员出行通常乘坐轿子。

sensor [ˈsensə(r)] *n.* 传感器

[语境] He plugged the sensor into an outlet.

他把传感器插进电源插座。

The scientists use a separate sensor to record each direction of movement.

科学家利用一个单独的传感器来记录运动的每个方向。

seventh [ˈsevnθ] *num.* 第七

[语境]He was laid out in the seventh round.

他在第七回合中被打倒了。

It has just entered the seventh edition.

它刚出版了第七版。

sharply [ˈʃɑːplɪ] *ad.* 严厉地,苛刻地,厉害地(积极词,略)

similarly [ˈsɪmɪləlɪ] *ad.* 同样地,类似于(积极词,略)

singer [ˈsɪŋə(r)] *n.* 歌手,歌唱家(积极词,略)

sitting-room *n.* 起居室(积极词,略)

situated [ˈsɪtjʊeɪtɪd] *a.* 位于……,坐落于……(积极词,略)

sixteenth [ˌsɪksˈtiːnθ] *num.* 第十六 *n.* 十六分之一

[语境]His name is the sixteenth on the list.

他的名字在名单上排第十六名。

Only one sixteenth of her was black, and that sixteenth did not show.

她只有十六分之一的黑人血统,而那十六分之一表面上又看不出来。

sixth [sɪksθ] *num.* 第六 *n.* 六分之一

[语境]He lifted the cup for the sixth time this year.

他今年第六次赢得优胜杯。

The company yesterday shed a sixth of its workforce.

这家公司昨天裁掉了1/6的员工。

skyscraper [ˈskaɪskreɪpə(r)] *n.* 摩天大楼

[语境]A skyscraper has been erected.

一栋摩天大楼拔地而起。

The skyscraper towers into the clouds.

那幢摩天大楼高耸入云。

sleepy [ˈsliːpɪ] *a.* 困乏的,欲睡的(积极词,略)

slipper [ˈslɪpə(r)] *n.* 拖鞋

[语境]I rescued the remains of my slipper from the dog's mouth.

我从那狗的口中夺回了我拖鞋的残留部分。

a soft leather slipper traditionally worn by native Americans

一种传统上由美洲土著人穿的软皮拖鞋

snowstorm [ˈsnəʊstɔːm] *n.* 暴风雪

[巧记] snow(雪) + storm(风暴)→暴风雪

[语境] All communications with the north have been stopped by snowstorm.

北部的一切通信均为暴风雪所阻。

After several weeks of travel, snowstorm hit us first.

我们旅行了几个星期,初次碰上暴风雪。

sob [sɒb] *v./n.* 哭泣,呜咽

[语境] She nodded with a sob.

她哭泣着点了点头。

She began to sob again, burying her face in the pillow.

她把脸埋在枕头里,又开始呜咽起来。

sodium [ˈsəʊdjəm] *n.* 钠

[语境] Common salt is a compound of sodium and chlorine.

食盐是钠和氯的复合物。

Out over the town the sodium lights were lit.

在外面,全城的钠光灯都亮了。

sonar [ˈsəʊnɑːr] *n.* 声呐

[语境] We picked up two submarines on sonar.

我们用声呐系统观察到两条潜水艇。

I'm getting a strong response on the sonar.

我在声呐上测得强力反应。

souvenir [ˌsuːvəˈnɪə(r)] *n.* 纪念品

Spanish [ˈspænɪʃ] *a.* 西班牙(人/语)的 *n.* 西班牙人/语(积极词,略)

specially [ˈspeʃəlɪ] *ad.* 特别地,特地;格外地(积极词,略)

specifically [spɪˈsɪfɪkəlɪ] *ad.* 说得具体些(积极词,略)

spoken [ˈspəʊkən] *a.* 口头的,口语的(积极词,略)

sponsorship [ˈspɒnsəʃɪp] *n.* 赞助者的身份/地位/任务

[巧记] sponsor(赞助人) + ship(抽象名词后缀)→赞助者的身份/地位/任务

[语境] Why do we need a total ban on advertising, promotion and sponsorship for tobacco?

为什么我们需要全面禁止烟草广告、促销和赞助?

Once you have your sponsors, make sure the logos go on the website in proportion and order to the level of sponsorship.

一旦有你的赞助商到场,必须确保网站上的标志必须按照赞助商的级别进行有序地排列。

starter [ˈstɑːtə(r)] *n.* (竞赛的)参加者

[语境] Of the 10 starters, four were eliminated or retired.

10 名参赛者中有 4 名被淘汰或自行退出了。

[考点] for starters (非正式)首先;一开始,开始时

stool [stuːl] *n.* 凳子(积极词,略)

surname [ˈsɜːneɪm] *n.* 姓(积极词,略)

surprising [səˈpraɪzɪŋ] *a.* 令人惊讶的(积极词,略)

suspicion [səˈspɪʃən] *n.* 猜疑,怀疑

[巧记] suspicious(*a.* 怀疑的,可疑的),suspect(*v.* 怀疑)

[语境] He was examined on (the) suspicion of being an enemy agent.

他因有敌特嫌疑而受审查。

He managed to avert suspicion.

他设法避嫌。

[考点] under suspicion 受到怀疑的

swan [swɒn] *n.* 天鹅

[语境] The stately swan glides gracefully on the pond.

高贵的天鹅在池面上优美地游动。

A young swan is called a cygnet.

小天鹅叫作"cygnet"。

Swiss [swɪs] *a.* 瑞士的 *n.* 瑞士人

[语境] The company has gone into partnership with Swiss Bank Corporation.

这家公司已经和瑞士银行公司建立合作关系。

The Swiss economy is a case apart; unlike any other.

瑞士经济是个独特的例子,不同于其他的经济形式。

T

takeover[ˈteɪkəʊvə(r)] *n.* 接管

[巧记]take over 接管

[语境]A German firm launched a takeover bid for the company.

一家德国公司试图收购这家公司。

The company saw off the threat of a takeover.

公司经受住了被收购的威胁。

tantalize[ˈtæntəlaɪz] *vt.* 逗弄；使干着急 *vi.* 逗弄人；令人干着急

[语境]Give the dog the bone—do not tantalize him.

把那块骨头给那条狗吧——别让它干着急了。

It's not her purpose to tantalize that guy, he is too bananas, not her type.

她并非要招惹那男人，他太疯，不是她要的款。

taxpayer[ˈtækspeɪə] *n.* 纳税人（积极词，略）

teenage[ˈtiːneɪdʒ] *a.* 十几岁的

[语境]Rock is the music of teenage rebellion.

摇滚乐是青少年的反叛音乐。

We have some interesting results from our survey on teenage hobbies.

对于青少年的爱好，我们做了一些调查，结果很有趣。

tenth[tenθ] *num.* 第十 *n.* 十分之一

[语境]We received only two tenths of an inch of rain during the entire month of June.

整个6月，我们这里的降水量只有0.2英寸。

He bought her a diamond ring on their tenth wedding anniversary.

他们结婚10周年纪念，他给她买了一枚钻戒。

toothache[ˈtuːθeɪk] *n.* 牙痛

[巧记]tooth(牙齿) + ache(痛)→牙痛

[语境] I have got toothache, so I must go to a dentist.

我牙疼,必须去看牙医。

A toothache racked my jaw.

牙疼使我的下巴难受极了。

transcendental [ˌtrænsenˈdentl] *a.* **先验的;卓越的;超越的**

[语境] Few men have had such transcendental capacity to stir the heart of people.

很少人有如此卓越的打动人心的才能。

It is entirely proper to classify Kant as a transcendental idealist.

把康德化为先验的唯心主义者是非常恰当的。

turkey [ˈtɜːkɪ] *n.* **火鸡,火鸡肉**

[巧记] Turkey *n.* 土耳其

[语境] It's traditional in England to eat turkey on Christmas Day.

圣诞节时吃火鸡是英格兰的传统。

People often drink white wine with turkey.

人们经常边吃火鸡肉边喝白葡萄酒。

tutorial [tjuːˈtɔːrɪəl] *a.* **辅导的;家庭教师的,个别指导的** *vt.* **个别指导**

[巧记] tutorial system 大学导师制

[语境] A planned tutorial programme was prepared by the senior mistress.

这个计划好的辅导方案是由那位高级女教师制定的。

TV = television(积极词,略)

U

unbelievable [ˌʌnbɪˈliːvəbl] *a.* **难以置信的**

[巧记] un(否) + believ(相信) + able(能够的)→不能够相信的→难以置信的

[语境] They work with an unbelievable speed.

他们以令人难以置信的速度工作。

That story is unbelievable.

那故事不可信。

uncomfortable [ʌnˈkʌmfətəbl] *a.* **不舒服的;不自在的**

[巧记] un(否) + comfortable(舒服的) →不舒服的

[语境] Planners seem a little uncomfortable with the current government guidelines.

规划师似乎不太接受现行的政府指导方针。

Visually the chair is very pleasing, but it's uncomfortable.

这椅子看上去很可爱,但它坐起来并不舒服。

underground [ˌʌndəˈɡraʊnd] *a.* 地下的,秘密的 *n.* 地铁 *ad.* 在地下,秘密地

[巧记] 反义词:overground(*a.* 地上的)

[语境] They caved in the roof of the underground passage with powerful explosives.

他们用强大的炸药把地下通道的顶部炸塌陷了。

The spy never told his family about his underground activities.

那个间谍从来不把他的地下活动告诉他的家人。

unemployed [ˌʌnɪmˈplɔɪd] *a.* 失业的;未动用的(积极词,略)

unforgettable [ˌʌnfəˈɡetəbl] *a.* **难忘的,不会忘记的**

[巧记] un(否) + forget(忘记) + able(能够的) →难忘的

[语境] The trip had been unforgettable experience for both of us.

那趟旅行是我们两人难以忘怀的经历。

He created many unforgettable characters in his novels.

他在他的小说中创造了很多令人难忘的人物。

unfortunate [ʌnˈfɔːtʃənɪt] *a.* 不幸,令人遗憾的(积极词,略)

unintelligible [ˌʌnɪnˈtelɪdʒəbl] *a.* **无法了解的;莫名其妙的**

[巧记] un(否) + intellig(明白) + able(能够的) →莫名其妙的

[语境] These words are usually unintelligible to those who are outside the specialty.

这些词语对那些外行人来说一般是晦涩难懂的。

His lips moved and some unintelligible sound came out.

他嘴唇微动,发出莫名其妙的声音。

大纲新增词汇

unknown [ʌnˈnəʊn] *a.* 未知的,不知名的

[巧记] un(否) + known(知道) →未知的

[语境] People usually infer an unknown fact from a known fact.
人们通常从已知的事实中推断未知的事实。
Motherhood was for her a journey into the unknown.
做母亲当时对她来说是一次未知的旅程。

unlikely [ʌnˈlaɪkli] *a.* 不太可能的

[巧记] un(否) + likely(可能的) →不太可能的

[语境] He is unlikely to make wild accusations without proof.
没有证据他不大可能胡乱指控。
It's theoretically possible, but highly unlikely ever to happen.
这从理论上说是有可能的,但是不太可能会发生。

[考点] be unlikely to do 不太可能……

unnecessary [ʌnˈnesɪsəri] *a.* 不必要的;多余的,没用的

[巧记] un(否) + necessary(必要的) →不必要的

[语境] This renders it unnecessary for me to do anything.
这使我无须做任何事情。
We shall have to trim away the unnecessary parts of the spending.
我们必须削减不必要的开支。

unpleasant [ʌnˈplezənt] *a.* 使人不愉快的;讨厌的

[巧记] un(否) + pleasant(令人愉快的) →讨厌的

[语境] They've been trying to push all the unpleasant jobs on me again.
他们一直想把所有讨厌的工作再次往我身上推。
Her manner seemed unpleasant at first, but she improved on further acquaintance.
起初她的举止让人很不愉快,但是经过进一步接触她改了许多。

unquestionable [ʌnˈkwestʃənəbl] *a.* 确实的;毫无疑问的

[巧记] un(否) + question(质疑) + able(能够的) →确实的

[语境] The witness showed unquestionable proof.

689

证人出示了确凿的证据。

He is a person of unquestionable principles.

他是个具有完美道德原则的人。

upside-down[ˌʌpsaɪd'daʊn] *a./ad.* 颠倒的(地),倒置的(地)

[巧记]upside(上面的部分) + down(到下面)→本来在上面的部分到了下面→倒置的

[语境]This is an upside-down cake.

这是一个倒放的蛋糕。

Uranus [jʊ'reɪnəs] *n.* 天王星

[语境]Uranus is unusual because it is tilted.

天王星非常特殊,因为它是倾斜的。

New discoveries about Uranus excited planetary astronomers in 1977.

1977年,对天王星的几项新发现使行星天文学家兴奋不已。

vaccination[ˌvæksɪ'neɪʃən] *n.* 种痘;接种疫苗

[语境]Smallpox can be contained by vaccination.

种牛痘疫苗可以控制天花。

Vaccination is a preventive against smallpox.

种痘是预防天花的方法。

Venus['viːnəs] *n.* 金星

[语境]Venus is of the same size as Earth.

金星跟地球差不多一样大。

videophone ['vɪdɪəʊfəʊn] *n.* 视频电话(积极词,略)

virtually['vɜːtʃʊəlɪ] *ad.* 实际上;几乎

[巧记]近义词:in fact 实际上

[语境]They were virtually impotent against the power of the large companies.

他们实际上无力与实力雄厚的大公司抗衡。

The job was virtually completed by the end of the week.

到周末时这项工作差不多完成了。

vocation [və(ʊ)'keɪʃən] *n.* 职业,行业

[巧记]同义词:profession, job, occupation

[语境]Her vocation is her work as an actress.

她的职业就是当演员。

She has no vocation for teaching.

她不适合教师这个行业。

[考点]辨析 profession, job, occupation, trade, vocation, career, work, employment

profession:以前常指要受过高等教育(尤指法律、医学和神学)才能获得的职业,现在一般指为谋生的职业,尤指从事脑力劳动和受过专门训练,具有某种专业知识的职业。

job:通常指一切有收入,不分脑力与体力运动,不论是否有技艺的、长期或临时的职业。

occupation:泛指任何一种职业,既不分什么行业,也不管是脑力还是体力劳动。

trade:指需要有熟练技巧、技能和体力的职业。

vocation:较正式用词,语气庄重,指长期从事,但不一定以此为主计的职业。

career:指经过专门训练,终身愿意从事的职业。

work:指任何种类的工作,也泛指职业。

employment:指受雇于他人,领取工资以谋生计,有较固定工作的职业

W

warning ['wɔːnɪŋ] *n.* 警告(积极词,略)

watchful ['wɒtʃf(ʊ)l] *a.* 警惕的(积极词,略)

wedge [wedʒ] *n.* 楔子,楔形 *v.* 楔牢,楔住,挤住

[语境]Put a wedge under the door so that it will stay open.

在门下面插个楔,好让门开着。

The box won't wedge into such a narrow space.

那盒子无法塞进那么小的地方去。

windy [ˈwɪndɪ] *a.* **多风的,刮风的**

[巧记] wind(风) + y(形容词后缀) →有风的

[语境] One spring it was very windy and dusty here.

有一年春天,这里风沙很大。

The north of China, unlike the south, is windy in spring.

北方不比南方,春天老刮风。

wretched [ˈretʃɪd] *a.* **不幸的,可怜的;卑鄙的,无耻的**(积极词,略)

Y

yeah [jeə] *ad.* **是**(积极词,略)

Z

zebra [ˈziːbrə, ˈze-] *n.* **斑马;人行道**

[语境] The lions devoured a zebra in a short time.

狮子一会儿就吃掉了一匹斑马。

There are several species of zebra.

斑马有好几种。

zoology [zəʊˈɒlədʒɪ] *n.* **动物学**

[巧记] zoo(动物园) + logy(学) →动物学

[语境] The library didn't stock zoology textbooks.

这家图书馆没有动物学教科书。

He's studying zoology at university.

他正在大学念动物学。

词组用法详解

A

a bit of 一点儿

I heard a bit of scandal about your friend.

我听到一点儿关于你朋友的流言。

a few 少许,一些

He spent a few months gadding about Europe before his exams.

考试前,他在欧洲漫游了几个月。

a great deal/a good deal 许多,大量

A good deal of housework can be mechanized.

大量家务活可机械化操作。

a great many/a good many 许多,大量

We have a great many to do at present.

我们当前有许多事情要做。

She has a great many distant relations.

她有许多远亲。

a lot/a lot of/lots of 大量,许多;非常,相当

There were a lot/lots of buffaloes in the North America 100 years ago.

100年前,北美有大量的野牛。

a little 一些,少许;稍许,一点儿

A little knowledge is a dangerous thing, but a little want of knowledge is also a dangerous thing.

没知识是危险的事,但不想求知也是危险的事。

a number of 许多

He made a number of inspections in this area.

他对这个地区进行了多次视察。

a variety of 多种的,各种各样的

A variety of Russian goods are forwarded through Sweden.

各种俄国货都是由瑞典转运来的。

about to 即将

That may be about to change.

这一切似乎好景不长。

above all 最重要,首先

Children should learn above all how to observe good manners at table.

小孩首先应学会餐桌礼仪。

accustomed to 习惯于

She has got accustomed to this sort of work.

她对这种工作已习惯了。

act on

1. 对……起作用

    The findings also suggest that short-term and long-term sleep loss may actually act on the brain in two different ways.

    这项发现也说明了,长期或短期的睡眠缺失实际上可以通过两种不同的方法对大脑起作用。

2. 按……行动,作用于

    In order for you to act on your objective, it must be actionable.

    为了使你能在你的目标上采取行动,这些目标必须能够执行。

add to 增加,添加,补充

The bad weather only added to our difficulties.

这种坏天气更增加了我们的困难。

add up to 总计,等于;意指

The numbers add up to 100.

这些数目合计为100。

after all 终究,毕竟

After all, what does it matter?

归根到底,那有什么关系呢?

after a while 过了一会儿,不久

After a while, I began to get bored with my job.

过了一段时间,我开始厌烦这份工作了。

again and again 反复地

This happens again and again.

这种情况一而再,再而三地发生。

ahead of 在……前,先于

Food and fodder should go ahead of troops and horses.

兵马未动,粮草先行。

ahead of time 提前

Her medical course was completed ahead of time.

她的医学课程提前完成了。

agree on/upon with 达成协议,意见一致

Are we all agreed on the best course of action?

我们是否都一致同意这一最佳措施?

aim at

1. 瞄准

   He aimed the gun at his own head.

   他用枪对准自己的脑袋。

2. 针对在,旨在

   The new treaty is aiming at improving relations between the two countries.

   这项新的协议旨在改善两国间的关系。

all along 始终,一直

This is because we knew it all along.

这是因为我们一直知道这个事实。

all at once 突然

All at once I stopped short.

我突然停住了脚步。

all over 到处,遍及

As it be, we have established trade relations with more than 100 countries all over the world.

就目前而言,我们已经和世界上100多个国家建立了贸易关系。

all of a sudden 突然

Then all of a sudden there was a crash of breaking glass.

接着,突然传来一阵玻璃的砸碎声。

all out 全力以赴

The team is going all out to win the championship.

这支队伍将全力以赴夺取冠军。

all right

1. 安全地(的);健康地(的)

    The car turned over but the driver was all right.

    汽车翻了,但是司机没有伤着。

2. 可以的;可接受的;令人满意的

    He mended my TV set all right.

    他把我的电视机修理得挺好。

all round 周围,处处

Visibility was good all round.

四周的视野都很好。

all the more 越发

I like the book all the more for its beautiful illustrations.

我因为精美的插图而更加喜欢这本书。

all the same 仍然,照样地

He's not reliable, but I like him all the same.

他是不太可靠,但我仍很喜欢他。

all the time 一直

Conditions are changing all the time.

情况始终都在变化。

anything but 根本不是,除……以外决不

His visit to Paris was anything but a success.

他的巴黎之行根本不成功。

apart from 除……之外

Apart from the injuries to his face and hands, he broke both legs.
他除了脸部和双手受伤以外,两条腿也断了。

apply...to 将……应用于;涂,抹

The rules of safe driving apply to everyone.
安全驾驶之规则适用于每个人。

approve of

1. 赞赏,同意

    The boss wouldn't approve of the plan.
    老板不会赞成这个计划。

2. 批准,通过

    The real trouble for Mr. Sarkozy is that, even if voters approve of the Libyan operation, they do not yet approve of him.
    对萨科奇来说,真正的麻烦是即使选民投票通过了对利比亚的行动,也不代表他们赞成他个人。

arm in arm 手挽着手;协同

I often see them strolling happily arm in arm.
我经常看到他们幸福地挽臂散步。

around the clock/ round the clock 昼夜不断地,连续 24 小时地

He studied around the clock for his history exam.
他夜以继日地准备历史考试。

as...as 与……一样

The old man looks as fresh as a young man.
这老年人看上去像年轻人一样生气勃勃。

as a matter of fact 实际情况,真相

As a matter of fact, I didn't have anything.
事实上,我什么也没有。

as a result 由于,因此

He didn't work hard; as a result he failed his exam.
他不用功,结果考试不及格。

as a rule 通常

As a rule, it's the gentleman that holds out his hand to invite a lady to dance.

通常,是男士伸出手来邀请女士跳舞。

as for/as to

1. 至于

   As for you, I don't think you have to go in person.

   你嘛,就不用亲自去了。

2. 就……而言

   There has been much gossip in commercial circles as to his resignation.

   关于他的辞职,在商界一直有很多流言蜚语。

as far as…be concerned 就……而言

As far as I am concerned, I'm not against your plan.

就我而言,我并不反对你的计划。

as far as/ so far as 只要;就……而言

I'll help you as far as I can.

我将尽我所能帮助你。

as follows 如下

Please amend L/C No. 205 as follows.

请按下述意见修改第205号信用证。

as if/as though 好像,仿佛;不妨

He was shaking with fright as if/though he had seen a ghost.

他吓得直哆嗦,就好像看见了鬼一样。

ask after 问候

He always asks after you in his letters.

他每次来信都问候你。

ask for 请求,要求

You should ask for a refund.

你应该要求退款。

as long as/so long as 只要,如果;既然

You may borrow the book as / so long as you keep it clean.

只要你不把书弄脏,你就可以借。

as regards 关于,至于

As regards the second point, we can discuss it at another meeting.

至于第二点,我们可以在下一次会上讨论。

as soon as 一……就……

I gave the alarm as soon as I saw the smoke.

我一看见冒烟,就发出了警报。

as usual 像往常一样,照例

As usual, there weren't many people at the meeting.

像往常一样,来开会的人不多。

as well

1. 同样,也

   Those drugs are given by injection as well as through the mouth.

   那些药品可以注射,也可以口服。

2. 倒不如

   You might as well go out and repossess cars or work for a collection agency.

   你还不如出去收回别人的汽车或为一家收回机构工作。

as well as

1. 除……之外,也,既……又

   Tom as well as Jack blamed me.

   不仅杰克,就连汤姆也责怪我。

2. 以及,又

   The tournament is open to amateurs as well as professionals.

   这次锦标赛不仅职业运动员可以参加,而且业余运动员也可以参加。

at a loss 困惑,不知所措

I am always at a loss to know how much to believe of my own stories.

我老是在困惑,对自己写的那些故事究竟应相信到什么程度。

at a time 每次,一次

Order! One at a time, please.

秩序!请逐个发言。

at a distance 隔开一段距离

The painting looks better at a distance.

这幅油画远处看起来好多了。

at all times 总是,无论何时

The rule is that someone must be on duty at all times.

按照规定,任何时候均需有人值班。

at all costs 无论如何,不惜任何代价

We must at all costs prevent them from finding out about the plan.

我们无论如何不能让他们探知这个计划。

at all 完全,根本

I certainly don't remember talking to you at all.

我当然完全不记得和你讲话。

at any rate 无论如何,至少

At any rate, the medical supplies will reach you within a week.

无论如何,医疗物资会在一周内到达。

at any time 在任何时候

Traffic regulations should always be kept to at any time.

任何时候都要遵守交通法规。

at best/at the best 充其量,至多

She is at best a second-rate singer.

她充其量是个二流歌手。

at first 首先

We didn't trust him at first, but his charming manner completely disarmed us.

我们开始时并不信任他,但他令人陶醉的举止完全消除了我们的疑虑。

at first sight 起初看,乍看

Believe in love at first sight.

相信一见钟情。

at hand 在手边,在附近

All is not at hand that helps.

有用的东西并不都是唾手可得的。

at heart 在内心,实质上

Wives say that men are invariably children at heart.

妻子们说男人实质上永远是孩子。

at home

1. 在家

   They would rather go fishing than stay at home.

   他们宁愿去钓鱼,也不愿待在家里。

2. 舒适,无拘束

   He feels like at home.

   他感觉很舒适,就像在家似的。

at last 最终,终于

Only in 1687 did he at last publish his new theory.

终于在一六八七年他发表了他的新理论。

at large

1. (囚犯)在逃,逍遥法外

   The soldier reported that a prisoner was at large.

   士兵报告说一名囚犯在逃。

2. 一般说来,随便地

   The people at large want peace.

   一般说来,人民是渴望和平的。

at least 最低限度,至少

We should at least have a try.

我们应该至少试一试。

at most/at the most 最多,至多

The freight shall not exceed ＄2,500 per ton at most, but we trust you will succeed in getting easier term.

运费最多不可超过每吨2500美元,相信贵方必能得到更为优厚的条件。

at no time 从不,决不

At no time and in no circumstances will China be the first to use nuclear weapons.

在任何时候、任何情况下中国都不会首先使用核武器。

at present 目前,现在

We have a great many to do at present.

我们当前有许多事情要做。

at random 随机地

The two groups are chosen at random, so the remedy should be the only systematic difference between them.

这两个组是随机抽取的,所以他们在系统中的唯一区别就在于是否接受治疗。

at times 有时

He can be a very tiresome child at times.

他有时候会是一个非常讨厌的孩子。

at the same time 同时;然而

Don't all speak at the same time.

大家别同时说话。

at the moment 此刻

The line's busy at the moment.

这会儿电话占线。

at the mercy of 在……支配下

His life was at the mercy of the king.

他的生命掌握在国王的手中。

at the cost of 以……为代价

He saved his daughter at the cost of his life.

他以牺牲自己的生命挽救了女儿。

at work 在工作,忙于

Ma was still at work when I got back.

我回来时,妈妈还在工作。

B

back and forth 来回,往返

He rocked back and forth in his rocking chair.

他坐在摇椅里前后摇晃着。

back down/off 放弃,让步,退却

I don't like that car sitting on my tail. Wave him to back off.

我不喜欢那辆车紧靠在我的车尾,挥手示意他倒车。

back up 支持,援助

The policeman wouldn't have believed me if you hadn't backed me up.

如果当时你不支持我,警察是不会相信我的。

based on 以……为基础

The theory is based on a series of wrong assumptions.

这一理论是以一系列错误的设想为依据的。

(be) sure of 确信

I am not sure of what he has said at the meeting.

他在会上说了些什么我不太清楚。

(be) friends with 对……友好,与……交上朋友

Don't be friends with baddy.

不要和坏人来往!

(be) made from 由……制造

The southerners prefer rice and the northerners prefer food made from flour.

南方人比较喜欢吃米饭,北方人爱吃面食。

(be) made up of 由……组成/构成

The cells are believed to be made up of at least two phenotypically distinct populations.

这些细胞至少有2种不同的分群,彼此形态各异。

be/get ready for 愿意;准备好

I have a lot of work to do to get ready for tomorrow.

我得为明天做许多准备工作。

be in the right 有理的

The retaliating countries would be in the right.

实施报复的国家是站在正义这一边的。

be/get used to 习惯于

Driving on the left is strange at first but you will get used to it.

沿着路的左侧驾车刚开始时有些别扭,可是习惯就好了。

You will soon get used to the weather here.

你很快就会习惯这里的气候。

bear/have/keep...in mind 记在心里

Accordingly, on guiding ideology, should "large part have something in mind, small part begin," save and make full use of limited space.

因此,在指导思想上,应该"大处着眼,小处着手",节省并充分利用有限的空间。

because of 由于,因为

Navigation is difficult on this river because of the hidden rocks.

因为河上有暗礁,所以在这条河上航行很困难。

before long 不久以后

I am afraid the gilt of the ring will wear off before long.

恐怕戒指的镀金层不久就会磨掉。

begin with 从……开始

Begin with this one and do the others afterwards.

先做这个,然后再做其他的事。

believe in 信仰,信奉;对……有信心

Do you believe in China's traditional herbal medicine?

你相信中国传统的中草药吗?

benefit from 收益于……

Did you benefit from the new way of doing business?

你是否从经营业务的新方法中获益?

beside the point 离题,不相干

You are absolutely beside the point. Please stop talking about it.

你已经完全跑题了,请不要再说了。

better off 富裕起来,(日子)好起来

He's much better off than before.

他手头比过去宽裕多了。

beyond/without question 没问题

He is without question the best man for the job.

毫无疑问,他最适合干这份工作。

bit by bit 一点点地,渐渐地

Little by little and bit by bit.

积少成多,积沙成塔。

boast of/about 夸耀,说大话

It is nothing to boast of.

这没有什么可夸耀的。

both...and 既……又……

He has both skill and dash.

他既有技巧,又有闯劲。

break away (from) 脱离,逃跑

Startled by the sudden whistle of the train, the horse broke away.

火车突然鸣笛,那匹马受惊脱逃了。

break down 分解,瓦解

You should break down your methods so that each method does a particular work.

你应当分解你的方法,让每个方法只做某一项工作。

break in

1. 强行进入,闯入

    The thief had broken in through a first-floor window.

    小偷是从一楼的窗户进入屋里的。

2. 打断,插嘴

    O'Leary broke in on his thoughts.

    奥利里打断了他的思路。

break into 闯入

Burglars had broken into while we were away on holiday.

我们外出度假时,小偷闯入屋内行窃。

break off 中止,中断

She broke off a piece of chocolate and gave it to me.

她掰下一块巧克力给我。

I decided to break off with him.

我决定同他绝交。

break out 突然发生,爆发

When did the war break out?

战争什么时候爆发的?

break through 突破

The sun broke through at last in the afternoon.

太阳在下午终于从云层后面钻出来了。

break up 打碎,拆散

Civil war could come if the country breaks up.

如果国家分裂就会爆发内战。

bring about 使发生

Science has brought about many changes in our lives.

科学为我们生活带来了很多变化。

bring forward

1. 提出

   Can you bring forward any proof?

   你能提出证据吗?

2. 把……提前

   The rain will bring forward the young crops.

   这场雨将促进作物幼苗的生长。

bring/come/go/put into effect 使生效;起作用

A new system of taxation will be brought into effect next year.

新的税收制度将于明年实行。

The new timetable will come into effect tomorrow.

新的时刻表明天生效。

bring/put into operation 使实施,使执行

The new system will soon be put into operation.

新系统即将启用。

bring out

1. 出现

   Jane never brings out her best dishes even when guests arrive.

   即使客人来了,珍也从来不把最好的盘子拿出来。

2. 呈出(某物);使(某物)显现出来

The new dress brought out her hidden beauty.

那件新衣服把她潜在的美展现出来了。

build up 增长;积累;增强

The pressure on the enemy is building up.

对敌人的压力在不断加强。

bring up

1. 教育,养育(孩子)

   My aunt brought up four children.

   我姑姑养了四个孩子。

2. 提及(提出)……

   Mr. Chairman, I should like to bring up the question of the re-organization of the committee.

   主席先生,我想提出改组委员会的问题。

burn out 烧掉;筋疲力尽

If he doesn't stop working so hard, he would burn himself out.

如果他继续这样拼命地工作,会累垮的。

burn up 烧尽

Let's burn up all this waste paper.

咱们把这些废纸都烧掉吧。

burst into (tears/laugh) 突然(哭/笑起来)

She burst into laughter/tears.

她突然笑(哭)起来。

by accident/ by chance 偶然,碰巧

He had a slip of tongue by accident.

他偶然说走了嘴。

I met him by chance yesterday.

昨天我无意中碰见了他。

by air (railway, sea, plane, bus, truck, etc.) 乘飞机(火车、轮船、飞机、公共汽车、卡车等)

I shall travel to New York by air this weekend.

这个周末我将要乘飞机去纽约旅行。

by all means 一定,务必

I told the waiter by all means to bring caviar and the cheapest dish on the menu.

我告诉服务员务必拿来鱼子酱和菜单上最便宜的菜。

by any means 无论如何

By any means, we should tell him frankly what we think of his proposal.

无论如何,我们应该直率地告诉我们对他的建议的看法。

by and by 渐渐地,不久以后

We'll meet again by and by.

我们不久又会再见。

by birth 在血统上;天生地

He is British by birth although he was born in America.

他虽然生在美国,但父母是英国人。

by comparison 比较起来

She is right: by comparison, football is only a game.

她是对的:相比之下,足球只是一种游戏。

by far 到目前为止,……得多

The economy is the number one issue by far.

到目前为止,经济是头等大事。

by hand 用手

A potter is making pottery by hand.

陶器匠正用手做陶器。

by heart 牢记,凭记忆

The children can repeat the poem they've just learnt by heart.

这些孩子能重述他们刚背过的诗歌。

by itself 单独地,独自地

The machine will start by itself in a few seconds.

几秒钟后,机器将自行启动。

by means of 用,凭借

We express our thought by means of words.

我们用词句来表达思想。

by mistake 错误地

I picked up your bag by mistake.
我错拿了你的书包。

by no means 决不

His judgment in this matter was by no means infallible.
在这件事上他的判断绝不是可靠的。

by turns 轮流地,交替地

We did the work by turns.
我们轮流干这活。

by the way 顺便提一下,另外

What happen to him, by the way?
顺便问一句,他后来怎么样了?

by way of 通过……方式;途径

The next flight doesn't go direct to Rome; it goes by way of Paris.
下一架班机不直接飞往罗马,中途经过巴黎。

C

calm down(使)平静下来

I won't see him until his anger has calmed down.
等他怒气消了,我再去看他。

call for 要求,需要

The situation calls for prompt action.
形势所迫,必须立即采取行动。

call off 取消,放弃

They wanted to get us to call off the strike.
他们想让我们取消这次罢工。

call on/upon

1. 访问,拜访

    I call on/upon just to say goodbye.
    我来仅仅是向你告别。

2. 号召

Call upon Owl, and we will be your guide.

召唤猫头鹰,我们将成为你的向导。

call up

1. 打电话

    The radio station had an open line on which listeners could call up to discuss various issues.

    这家电台开放线路,听众可打电话参与各种问题的讨论。

2. 召集,动员

    They were called up at the age of nineteen.

    他们十九岁时被征召入伍。

capable of 能……的;有……能力

He is capable of great things.

他担当得起大事业。

care about 关心

The children behave badly, but the guilt lies with the parents, who don't care about their behavior.

孩子们行为不端,但是这应归罪于他们的父母,他们不关心子女的行为。

care for 照管,关心;喜欢,意欲

He doesn't care for fish.

他不喜欢吃鱼。

carry on 继续,坚持下去;从事,经营

Let's carry on our discussion.

让我们继续讨论吧。

carry out 执行,贯彻

He will carry out his plan.

他要执行他的计划。

catch a cold 感冒

You catch a cold in summer when the air is not cold.

在夏天,天气不冷时,你也会感冒。

catch fire 着火,烧着

Paper is apt to catch fire.

纸容易着火。

catch one's breath 休息一下；歇一口气

With barely any time to catch their breath, the Rockets are now taking on one of the NBA's most experienced teams.

几乎没有喘息的机会，火箭队现在是 NBA 中最有经验的一支球队。

catch sb.'s eye 引人注目

What she did is in order to catch his eye.

她所做的一切都是为了引起他的注意。

catch/have/get sight of 看到，发现

Our eyes catch sight of a form in the blockhouse port.

我们看到碉堡发射孔里有人影。

catch up with 追上，赶上

I have to work hard to catch up with the other students.

要想赶上其他同学，我得特别努力才行。

can not help 禁不住，忍不住

I can not help smoking, because smoking calm my nerve, control anger and keep my weight down.

我忍不住抽烟，因为抽烟使我镇静，能控制愤怒，能减轻我的体重。

change one's mind 改变主意

For to change one's mind, or even one's policy, is a confession of weakness.

因为改变自己的思想，或者甚至改变自己的政策，无异于承认自己的弱点。

check in 办理登记手续

Is it time for us to check in?

现在可以办理登记手续吗？

check out 结账后离开；检验，核查

The hotel insists that guests check out of their rooms before 11 o'clock in the morning.

这家旅馆一定要客人在上午 11 点钟前结账后离开房间。

check up／(up) on 校对,检验,检查

An experiment was made to check up on the reliability of certain criteria.

已经进行了一项实验以检查某些标准的可靠性。

cheer up 兴奋起来

Don't look so blue and cheer up.

别那么垂头丧气,振作起来。

clear away 散去;收拾餐桌

Have you cleared away your books from the table?

你把你的书都从桌上拿开了吗?

clear up

1. (天气)变晴

    It is raining now, but I think it will clear up soon.

    现在还在下雨,不过我想很快就会放晴的。

2. 解释,澄清

    He cleared up the question of his absence in the presence of all his classmates.

    他当着全班同学的面澄清了他缺席的疑团。

come about 发生,产生

So how do new ideas come about?

那么新的创意从何而来?

come across 偶遇,碰到

Have you come across this problem?

你遇到过这个问题吗?

come off 成功,奏效

Her attempt to break the world record nearly came off.

她想要打破世界纪录,已接近成功。

come on 请,来吧,快点

Come on Doreen, let's dance.

来吧,多琳,我们跳舞吧。

come out

1. 出现,显露

The molten iron will come out.

铁水就要出来了。

2. 出版,发表

When will the dictionary come out?

那本词典什么时候出版?

3. 结果是,结局是

How did the movie finally come out?

这部电影最后的结局如何?

come round/around

1. 来访,前来

I'll come around later tonight.

我今晚会过来。

2. 苏醒,恢复知觉

He got faint, but soon came around.

他昏死过去,但不久就苏醒了。

come through

1. 经历,脱险

How did you manage to come through the Second World War without even a scratch?

你怎么经历了第二次世界大战还会安然无恙呢?

2. (电话)接通;(电报)收到

I was just leaving home when Smith came through on the phone from Nanjing.

我刚要离开家,史密斯就从南京打来电话。

come to oneself 苏醒,复苏

In a few minutes he suddenly came to himself.

过了一会儿他突然苏醒过来。

come true 实现,达到

His wish to be an actor has come true.

他想当演员的愿望实现了。

come up

1. 出现

It will be so great watching the Sun come up.

看着太阳冉冉升起将是十分美妙的事情。

2. 走上前来

Christmas is coming up soon.

圣诞节很快就要来到。

come up with 提出

He's come up with a great idea.

他想出了一个绝好的办法。

compare...to 把……比作

People often compare a little girl's face to a red apple.

人们常常把小女孩的脸比作红苹果。

consist in 在于,存在

A home does not consist in the quality of its architecture and decoration.

家之所以为家并不在于住所的设计与修饰。

come/go into operation 实施,执行

The new system comes into operation on June 1st.

新制度于6月1日实施。

consist of 由……构成,由……组成

The theory that the object of external perception, in itself or as perceived, consists of ideas.

这个理论认为一切外物无论是其本身或观察到的都存在于理念。

correspond to 相当于,对应,符合

The translation does not quite correspond to the original.

译文不切原意。

contribute to 为……出力/贡献

Can I contribute to multiple causes?

我能够捐助多个事业吗?

count in 包括,算上……

Don't count in me.

不要把我算在内。

count out 不包括

We'll have to count out Frank for next Sunday's trip.

我们下星期日旅行不得不把弗兰克排除在外。

count up 把……相加

I must count up how much money I've spent today.

我得算算我今天总共花了多少钱。

convince...of 使信服

He tried to convince them of the safety of travelling by airplane.

他想要使他们相信乘飞机旅行的安全。

cover up 掩盖,遮盖

No amount of lies can cover up reality.

谎言再多也掩盖不了事实真相。

cross out 删去,取消

You had better cross out the last name.

你最好把最后一个名字划掉。

cut back 削减,减少

They were forced to cut back production.

他们被迫减产。

cut off 切掉,剪去,删去

He cut off a small piece of bread and gave it to me.

他切下一小片面包递给了我。

cut short

1. 打断

   Impatiently he cut short what I was telling him.

   他不耐烦地打断了我的话。

2. 缩减

   I will cut a long story short.

   我就长话短说吧。

cut out 切去,删除减裁

Please cut out my overcoat according to this pattern.

我这件大衣请你照这个式样裁剪。

D

day and night 日日夜夜
He carefully attended to the wounded soldiers day and night.
他日夜细心照料伤员。

day by day 成天,天天
Day by day the disappointed lover peaked and pined.
这失恋的人一天天地憔悴下去。

deal with 处理,对付;讨论
The meeting will deal with these problems.
本次会议将就这些问题做出处理。

die down 渐渐消失,平息
These rumors will soon die down.
这些谣言不久就会逐渐消失。

dig into 探究
Our shop, in fact, was just beginning to dig into the problem.
事实上,我们的工厂刚刚开始研究这个问题。

die off

1. 相继枯死
   If the snowstorm does not blow over, the cattle will die off.
   如果暴风雪不停息,很多牲畜就要死掉了。

2. 渐渐消失
   We're afraid that the local wildlife is starting to die off.
   我们担心这一地区的野生生物正在开始(走向)灭绝。

die out 消失,灭绝
The English of today is very different from the English of 500 years ago. In time, some even die out completely.
现在的英语与500年前的英语已大不相同,有一些甚至会在今后完全消失。

dig out

1. 挖出

Rescue crews have been digging people out of collapsed buildings.

救援人员一直在倒塌的建筑物废墟中挖掘救人。

2. 查出

We are expecting to dig out some important facts.

我们希望能找出一些重要的事实。

dig up

1. 开垦

You will have to dig up the plant yourself.

你得自己把那株植物挖出来。

2. 查出,发现

His description fits perfectly the evidence dug up by Clyde.

他的描述和克莱德发现的证据正好吻合。

do away with 消灭,丢掉

I want them to do away with this feudal custom.

我希望他们废除这一封建陋俗。

do/try one's best 尽力而为

We'll do/try our best to solve this problem.

我们将尽最大的努力解决这个问题。

do without 没有……也行,将就

People can not do without food.

人没有食物不行。

draw in (汽车、火车)进站;吸引

It's stupid trying to draw in customers with prize and gift!

想用奖品和礼品引来顾客是件愚蠢的事!

draw up 写出,画出,草拟

We'll notify her to draw up a contract.

我们将通知她起草一份合同。

dress up 穿上盛装,打扮得漂漂亮亮

Her maid helped her to dress up for the party.

她的女仆帮助她穿上参加晚会的礼服。

drop by/in 顺便走访

Drop by/in and see us when you're next in London.
到伦敦时顺便来看我们。

drop out 逃学;离队出走

He says he has dropped out, and won't attend college any more.
他说他退了学,以后也不会去上大学了。

due to 由于

Due to circumstances beyond our control the lecture was cancelled.
由于无法控制的情况,讲座取消了。

E

each other 互相

The children ducked each other in the swimming pool.
孩子们在游泳池里互相把对方按入水中。

either...or... 或……或……,不是……就是……

Either dye or paints are used to color cloth.
不论是染料还是颜料都是用来染布的。

end up 以(某种身份、状态、境况)结束

We'll end up paying much more.
我们会花好多钱。

enjoy oneself 过得快乐

One can't enjoy oneself if he is too tired.
一个人如果太疲倦,就不能尽情享受。

even if/even though 即使,纵然

I wouldn't lose courage even if I should fail ten times.
即使要失败十次,我也绝不灰心。

every now and then 有时,时时,偶尔

Every now and then we visit our aunts.
我们偶尔拜访我们的阿姨。

every other 每隔一个的

She visited him in hospital every other day.

她每隔一天就到医院去看望他。

every other day 每隔一天

We have English lessons every other day.

我们每隔一天就有英语课。

except for 除……以外

But except for that, it's an excellent film.

但是除了那一点以外,它还是一部很优秀的电影。

F

face to face 面对面地

His ambition was to meet his favorite pop star face to face.

他一心向往的是要面对面地见见他喜爱的歌星。

face up to 大胆面对

Old people should face up to the fact that they are no longer young.

老年人应该勇敢地承认和面对不再年轻这一事实。

fall behind 落后

The major world powers are afraid of falling behind in the arms race.

世界各大强国均唯恐在军备竞赛中落后。

fall in love (with) 相爱,爱上

It is natural that he should fall in love with such a beautiful girl.

他爱上那位美丽的姑娘是很自然的事。

fall/run short (of) 缺少,快用完

We've run short of oil.

我们已快把油用完了。

far from 决不,决非;远离

He was far from impressive in his semi-final against Federer.

他在对抗费德勒的半决赛中表现平平。

feel like 想要

We all feel like a cup of tea.

我们都想喝杯茶。

figure out 算出,估计,推测

It didn't take the children long to figure out the correct answer.

孩子们没有花很多时间就算出了正确的答案。

fill in/out 填充,填写

The applicants have to fill in/out several forms.

申请人得填写几种表格。

find fault with 找岔子

He loved best to find fault with me.

他最喜欢找我的岔了。

find out 发现,查明,找出

He took a peep at the back of the book to find out the answers to the questions.

他偷偷看了一下书的后面,想找出那些问题的答案。

first of all 首先

First of all, you should know what profession suits you.

首先,你该知道什么职业适合你。

focus on 集中于

Today we're going to focus on the question of homeless people.

今天,我们主要讨论无家可归者的问题。

for example 例如

Many great men have risen from poverty—Lincoln, for example.

许多伟人从贫困中崛起,例如林肯。

for good 永久的,一劳永逸的

She left her country for good.

她离开了祖国,永不回来。

for instance 举例说,比如

For instance, one of our cargo ships sank last week in typhoon.

例如,我们的一艘货轮上星期在台风中沉了。

for sale 待售

All the exhibits for sale here are new products.

这里展销的都是新产品。

for sure 当然,一定;肯定,毫无疑问

If we could by any possibility manage to do it, we would for sure.

如果我们有办法做成那事,我们一定会做的。

for the better 好转,向好的方向发展

Would it be a change for the better?

形势是否会有所好转?

for the moment 暂时,目前

We're happy living in a flat for the moment but we may want to move to a house soon.

目前我们对于住公寓很满意,不过不久我们也许想住个独门独院的房子。

for the present 目前,暂时

He thought the matter might be left over for the present.

他认为目前这事也许被暂时搁置。

for the sake of 为了……

He argues for the sake of arguing.

他是为争辩而争辩。

for the time being 目前,暂时

Let's leave that for the time being.

暂时把这个问题搁一下。

free from 无……的,不受……影响的

He is free from prejudice to everybody.

他对所有的人都不带有任何成见。

free of 脱离,无……的

The department store delivers free of charge.

这家百货商店免费送货。

from now on 从今以后

I won't take any more of your sauce from now on.

从现在开始,我不会再忍受你那些无礼顶撞的话了。

from time to time 时常

He comes here from time to time.

他时常到这儿来。

from the first 从头

He set his face against the scheme from the first.
从一开始他就坚决反对这项计划。

G

get across 解释清楚,使人了解

He taught me how to get my ideas across.
他教我如何把自己的观点表达清楚。

get along (with) 相处;有进展,有起色

I get along well with my classmates.
我和同学相处融洽。

get at

1. 到达

   Don't leave the bottle where he can get at it.
   不要把瓶子放在他能够找到的地方。

2. 领会

   It is no easy thing to get at the meaning of every idiom in English.
   理解英语中每一个习语的含义并不是件容易事。

get away (from) 逃脱,离开

She struggled to get away from her attacker.
她挣扎着想摆脱那个侵犯她的人。

get down to 着手进行

I wish he'd stop mucking about and get down to some serious work.
我希望他不要再吊儿郎当,开始认真地做点工作。

get free 获得自由

The cat made a struggle to get free.
这只猫挣扎着想跑掉。

get hold of

1. 抓住

   He got hold of the rope, and we pulled him up.
   他抓住绳子,我们把他拉了上来。

2. 掌握

I'll explain, and you'll soon get hold of the idea.

我解释后你很快会理解这个想法。

get in

1. 收获

He took the entrance exam but didn't get in.

他参加了入学考试但未被录取。

2. 到达,进站

We would have come straight here, except our flight got in too late.

要不是我们的航班抵达太晚,我们本应直接到这里来的。

get in the way 成为障碍

The words get in the way.

欲言又止。

get off

1. 离开,动身,开始

We got off immediately after breakfast.

早饭后我们立即启程。

2. 下车,从……下来

Get off the bus after it came to a stop.

等车稳下再下车。

get on(with)

1. 继续做

Be quiet and get on with your work.

安静下来,继续做你的工作。

2. 上车

The people shoved to get on the bus.

人们你推我挤争着上公共汽车。

3. 在……方面取得进展

How is he getting on with that novel he is writing?

他正在创作的那部小说进展如何?

get out

1. 出来,出去,走开
   There were so many people in the doorway that we could hardly get out.
   门口那么多人,我们简直走不出去。
2. 开始被人知道;泄露
   To his surprise, the news soon got out.
   令他惊奇的是,消息很快就泄露出去了。

get out of 逃避,改掉

He tried to get out of paying his share of the bill.
他试图逃避支付账单上他那一份儿。

get over 克服,(从病中)恢复过来

She can't get over her shyness.
她无法克服她的羞怯心理。

get rid of 摆脱,除去

Frankly I can not imagine how any manager can afford to get rid of it.
坦率地说我不能想象哪个经理能摆脱得了它。

get through 结束,完成;接通电话

I can't get through to Danny.
我联系不上丹尼尔。

get together 集会,聚会

They get together once a year at Christmas time.
他们每年圣诞节时聚会一次。

get up 起床,起立;安排

What on earth will he get up to next?
下一步他究竟要耍什么花样?

give a bit 一点,少许

The boss took some matches, brushed a few in succession, and did not give a bit ammunition.
老板拿了些火柴过来,一连擦了几根,都擦不出一点火。

give away 泄露,暴露,出卖

His accent gave him away as a northerner.

他的口音让人听出他是北方人。

give back 送还,恢复

I gave the textbook back to him.

我将课本还给他了。

give in 投降,让步,认输

She's a gutsy player, she never gives in.

她是个勇敢的选手,从不屈服。

give off 发出,放出

The flowers give off a heady scent at night.

这些花晚上散发出醉人的芳香。

give out 分发,分派

There were people at the entrance giving out leaflets.

有人在入口处散发传单。

give rise to 引起,造成

So many things concurred to give rise to the problem.

许多事情同时发生而导致了这一问题。

give up 放弃,辞去;投降,屈服

I give up; tell me what the answer is.

我认输,告诉我答案吧。

give way to 让位于,被……代替

Give way to cars that come from the left.

给左边开过来的汽车让路。

go about

1. 从事,干

   Let's go about the work separately.

   这事咱们分头去做吧。

2. 闲逛

   It is dangerous to go about here.

   在这里到处走是很危险的。

go after 追逐,追求

Go after it with all that you are.

应全力以赴去追寻它。

go ahead 开始；前进，领先

Food and fodder should go ahead of troops and horses.

兵马未动，粮草先行。

go along with 陪同前往，随行

Can you go along with me?

你能与我同行吗？

go around/round 足够分配

Eventually we will not have enough water to go around.

最终，我们将没有足够的水供大家喝。

go by 经过，放过，过去

Time goes by quickly on vacation.

度假时时间过得真快。

go for 竭力想取得；喜爱，支持，拥护

I don't go for men of his type.

我不喜欢他那种人。

We'd better go for a doctor.

我们最好去请医生。

go in for 从事，致力于；追求，沉迷于

Which events is he going in for at the Olympics?

他将在奥运上参加什么项目？

They wanted me to go in for film work.

他们要我从事电影工作。

go into 研究，讨论，调查，审查

He went into a long explanation of the affair.

他对那件事长篇大论地解释起来。

go off

1. 爆炸，被发射

   A few minutes later the bomb went off, destroying the vehicle.

   炸弹几分钟后爆炸，炸毁了那辆车。

2. 离去，走掉

   He went off in a great hurry.

   他匆匆地离开。

go on (with) 继续,持续

Now (that) he is well again, he can go on with his English study.

既然恢复了健康,他就可以继续学习英语。

go on the stage 当演员

John gave up his teaching career to go on the stage.

约翰放弃了教书工作去当演员。

go out

1. 出去

    He reminded me to lock up the house when I go out.

    他提醒我外出时把屋子锁起来。

2. 罢工

    The workers went out for better pay.

    工人们为更好的待遇而罢工。

go over 浏览,读一遍;重说(读、看)

Go over your cabin thoroughly.

彻底仔细检查你的客舱。

She went over her lines before the first night of the play.

她在该剧首演前又练习了一次台词。

go to bed 去睡觉

My grandmother tends to go to bed early every day.

我祖母每天通常早睡。

go to extremes 走极端

They often go to extremes in their views.

他们在看法上经常走极端。

go through

1. 完成,做完

    How long will it take to go through the book?

    读完这本书要多少时间?

2. 检查,审查,搜查

    We shall go through these papers together.

    我们将一起审阅这些论文。

go up 上升;增长

Prices tend to go up recently.

最近,物价有上涨的趋势。

go with

1. 陪同前往

    We saw him going with his girlfriend.

    我们看到他与他女朋友一起走的。

2. 与……一致,与……调和

    That tie goes with your shirt.

    那领带与你的衬衫相配。

go without 没有,缺乏,将就;没有……也行

People can not go without food.

人没有食物不行。

good at 擅长于

She is no less good at swimming than Mary.

她和玛丽一样擅长游泳。

good for 有效,适用,胜任

These fruit knives are very good for stripping apple skins off.

这种水果刀削苹果皮很好用。

H

had better 最好还是,应该

We had better learn by heart as many sentence patterns as we can.

我们最好尽可能多背句型。

hand down 传下来又传给,往下

The life history of the individual is first and foremost an accommodation to the patterns and standards traditionally handed down in his community.

个人的生活史,首先就是适应他的社团中祖祖辈辈传下来的行为模式和准则的历史。

hand in 交上,递交

I handed my notice in on Saturday.

我周六递交了辞职信。

hand in hand 手拉手,联合,连在一起

The children walk down the street hand in hand.

孩子们手拉手地在街上走。

hand on 传下来,依次传递

The moral excellences are handed on from father to son.

那种美德是父子相传的。

hand out 分发,发给

I rustled up a few helpers to hand out leaflets.

我找到几个助手散发传单。

hand over 交出,移交,让给

He has resigned and will hand over charge of his office today.

他已辞职,将在今日办移交手续。

hang about 闲荡,徘徊,逗留

The library hasn't opened yet, so I have to hang about here.

图书馆还没有开门,所以我只得在这儿闲逛。

hang on 别挂(电话);紧抓不放

Hang on a moment, please.

请稍等。

hang on to

1. 紧握住

   Hang on to the strap. The bus is starting.

   抓住皮带,汽车要开动了。

2. 坚持下去

   John did not like his job, but he decided to hang on to it until he found a better one.

   约翰不喜欢他的工作,但他决定干下去,直到找到更好的工作。

hang up 挂断(电话)

All right, I'll call you back. Will you hang up, please?

好吧,我再给你回电。请先挂断电话好吗?

have a word with 和某人谈谈

I think I'll have a word with the man in private.

我想要和这人私下谈一谈。

have nothing/something with 与……无关/有关

Student B: Did it really have nothing with the team?

学生B：是不是与团队无关？

have…on 穿着……,戴着……

She had a purple dress on with a silver-white necklace.

她穿着一条紫色的连衣裙,配着一条银白色的项链。

have a cold 患感冒

My sense of taste isn't very good; I have a cold.

我的味觉不是很好,我感冒了。

have to/have got to 不得不,必须

Please be quiet. I have to study the book for a test tomorrow.

请不要说话了,明天要考试,我得看书。

have back 要回,收回

Let me have it back soon.

我要尽快将其收回。

head for 朝……走去

We saw him heading for us, so we stepped aside.

我们看见他向我们走来,就让到一边。

heart and soul 全心全意

He serves the people heart and soul.

他全心全意为人民服务。

help oneself 自取所需(食物等)

But in China, it is usual to help oneself to the food placed at the center of the table.

然而,中国人的习惯就是各人从餐桌中心的菜盘子里夹菜。

here and there 到处,处处

We searched here and there, but could not find her.

我们到处找她,但还是找不到。

hold back 踌躇,退缩不前

Don't hold back. Just go for it.

不要踌躇不前,努力去干吧!

hold on 稍后;别挂(电话);坚持下去

They managed to hold on until help arrived.

他们设法坚持住,直到有救援到来。

hold on to 紧紧抓住

I'd hold on to that house for the time being; house prices are rising sharply at the moment.

目前我不能出让那所房子,此刻房价正在急剧上涨。

hold one's breath 屏住呼吸

It's possible to hold one's breath for three minutes, with practice.

经过练习,屏住呼吸三分钟是可能的。

hold out 坚持,不屈服

We must hold out till victory.

我们一定要坚持到胜利。

hold up 举起,支撑,承载;阻挡,使停止

"Well, men," said the chairman, "I shall now proceed to put the matter to the vote. Will all those in favor hold up the right hand?"

"请大家注意,"主席说道,"我现在就把这件事交付表决,赞成的人请把右手举起来。"

Who knows how it will hold up?

天知道它会怎样,能不能扛住?

how about 如何,怎么样

How about going out for dinner?

出去吃晚餐如何?

hurry up 使赶快;迅速完成

Hurry up! Don't waste my time!

请你快一点,不要浪费我宝贵的时间。

I

if only 但愿,只要

If only he had known about it!

他那时要是知道这件事该多好!

in a hurry 匆忙,立即

She went to the telegraph office in a hurry.

她匆匆忙忙向电报局去了。

in a moment 一会儿

Please come in and wait for Jack. He'll be back in a moment.

请进来等杰克吧,他马上就会回来的。

in a position to 有能力做……

He wasn't in a position to help me.

他不能帮我的忙。

in a sense 从某种意义上说

In a sense she was misled by the advertisement's claims, and expected too much of the product.

从某种意义上说,她是受到了广告的哄骗,因此对此产品期望过高。

in a way 在某种程度上;从某一点看

In a way, I'm glad you made that mistake, for it will serve as a warning to you.

在某种程度上说,你犯那个错误我倒感到高兴,因为它可以对你敲警钟。

in a word 总而言之

In a word, the situation is serious.

总而言之,形势很严峻。

in addition to 另外,除……之外

In addition to giving a general introduction to computer, the course also provides practical experience.

课程除了介绍基本电脑知识外,还提供实际操作的机会。

in advance 预先,在前面

They will pay ＄100 in advance.

他们将预付出 100 美元。

in all 总计

That's £5.40 in all.

总共 5.40 英镑。

In any case 不管怎样,无论如何

In any case, you'll need to be at the station by nine.

无论如何你都要在九点钟前赶到车站。

in brief 简单地说

To begin with, I'd like to tell in brief the importance of the work.

首先,我想简要谈谈这项工作的重要性。

in case 假使,以防万一

In case of rain they can't go.

万一下雨,他们就不能去了。

in case of 假如发生,万一发生

Fire-brigades are standing by in case of an explosion.

消防队严阵以待,若有爆炸立刻出动。

in (the) charge of 负责

The Chancellor of the Exchequer is the minister in charge of finance in Britain.

英国财政大臣是负责财政的大臣。

in common 共同的,共有的

We have no interest in common.

我们没有共同的兴趣。

in contrast with... 与……相对比/相对照

In contrast with her sister, she is very tall.

与姐姐相比,她个子很高。

in danger 在危险中

The dam was in danger because of the rising flood.

洪水猛涨,大坝告急。

in debt 欠债,欠情

His extravagance explains why he is always in debt.
他挥霍无度,难怪总欠债。

in detail 详细地

He told us the accident in detail.
他详细地把事故讲给我们听。

in difficulty 处境困难

The swimmer seemed to be in difficulty, but managed to reach the shore in the end.
那游泳的人似乎力不从心,但最后还是设法游到了彼岸。

in effect 实际上,事实上

He said he graduated from Oxford, while in effect, he never went to college.
他说他是牛津毕业的,但实际上他从没上过大学。

in existence 存在的

This house has been in existence for many years.
这房子可有年头了。

in fact 实际上,其实

She pretends to have various abilities she doesn't, in fact, possess.
她自称有种种她事实上并不具有的才能。

in fav(u)or of 支持;有利于

Sentiment in the town is now in favor of a cut in tax.
市民赞成减税。

in front of 在……前面,面对

My view of the stage was blocked by the big hat of the woman sitting in front of me.
我的视线被坐在前排妇女的大帽子遮住了,看不见舞台。

in future 今后,从今以后

"I hope they'll be more cautious in future," he observed.
他说:"我希望他们今后能更慎重一些。"

in general 通常,一般来说

The class are, in general, very bright.
总的说来,这个班级的学生都很聪明。

in good/bad temper 心情好/不好

At times Joe was in good temper, at times bad.

乔的脾气有时好有时坏。

in half 成两半

The apple was divided in half.

苹果被分成两半。

in hand

1. 在掌握中

   With the whole IT picture in hand, map out how the information flows from start to finish.

   手边有了整体 IT 蓝图,下一步应规划信息如何从开头流向结束。

2. 正在进行

   We have still an hour in hand before the train leaves.

   火车开走前我们还有一个小时。

in hono(u)r of 向……表敬意,为庆祝……,为纪念……

A banquet was given in honor of the distinguished guests.

宴会是为了向贵宾们致敬而举行的。

in memory of 纪念

They dedicated a monument in memory of those who died in the great earthquake.

他们为悼念死于大地震的人们建造纪念碑。

in no time 立即,马上

I have a few dictionaries in hand. I can get the meaning of the phrase for you in no time.

我手头有几本词典,马上就可查到那个短语的意思。

in no way 决不

In no way am I responsible for what has happened.

我决不对发生的事情负责。

in one's way/in the way 妨碍,阻碍

Although he thought he was helping us prepare dinner, he was only in the way.

虽然他认为他在帮我们准备饭,但他只是碍手碍脚。

in order 整齐,秩序井然

I would have soon found the one I wanted if the books had been kept in order.

如果书籍摆放整齐了,我本可以很快地找到我想要的那本书。

in order (to/that) 以便

In order to maintain physical well being, a person should eat wholesome food and get sufficient exercise.

为了维持身体健康,一个人应该吃有益健康的食品,并经常锻炼身体。

in other words 换句话说,也就是说

In other words, she must give up singing.

换言之,她必须放弃唱歌。

in particular 特别,尤其;详细地

Among all the merchandise, I was interested in the cotton piece in particular.

在所有商品中,我对棉布特别感兴趣。

in person 亲自

She erred in failing to meet him in person.

她错在没有亲自与他见面。

in place 在适当的位置

I like to have everything in place.

我喜欢一切东西都在适当的位置。

in place of 代替

Joe had to work as blacksmith in place of his lazy father.

乔只得代替他懒惰的父亲去当铁匠。

in practice

1. 在实践中

   The idea sounds good but will it work in practice?

   这主意听起来不错,但在实践中行得通吗?

2. 实际上

   What does that mean in practice?

而实际上这又意味着什么呢?

in proportion to 与……成比例

His short legs were not in proportion to his long body.

他的短腿和他的身长不成比例。

in public 公众地

She was too proud to show her grief in public.

她十分骄傲,绝不当众流露内心的痛苦。

in question

1. 正在考虑的

   That is not the point in question.

   那不是要考虑的要点。

2. 正在谈论的,谈及的

   The job in question is available for three months only.

   所谈到的这一工作空缺为时仅三个月。

in/with regard to 关于

I am quite at sea in regard to his explanation.

他的解释使我如堕云里雾里。

in return (for) 作为回报,作为报答

He was always ready to help others, in return, he was liked by everyone.

他总是乐于助人,作为回报,大家都喜欢他。

in search of 寻找,寻求

They set off in search of the lost child.

他们出发去寻找走失的孩子。

in secret 秘密地,私下地

Last night, we held a meeting in secret.

昨晚,我们秘密地举行了一次会议。

in short 简言之,总之

In short, he is one of the most promising students I've ever known.

总之,他是我见过最有前途的学生之一。

in sight

1. 在望

The spokesman made it evident that no compromise was yet in sight.

发言人表示,目前还不会妥协。

2. 被见到

There was not a ship in sight.

看不到一艘船。

in some degree 在某种程度上

This restored wealth softened him in some degree.

不过这些恢复的财富却多少使他的心里轻松一点。

in spite of 尽管,不顾,虽然

In spite of his burns, he sprang up and rushed towards the fighting.

他不顾周身的灼伤,一跃而起,向激战的地方冲去。

in tears 流着泪,含泪,哭

When James heard of the news by telegraph, he cried Lou's name in tears.

当詹姆斯通过电报听说了这个消息后,他流着泪哭喊楼的名字。

in the dark

1. 在暗中

The little boy dreads going to bed in the dark.

这孩子不敢在黑暗中睡觉。

2. 秘密地

Her marriage to John was a leap in the dark.

她与约翰结婚是贸然行动。

in the distance 在远处

A bullfrog was croaking in the distance.

一只牛蛙在远处呱呱地叫。

in the end 最后

After many years of hard work, he won the award in the end.

经过许多年的努力,他最后终于获得了大奖。

in the face of 面对

In the face of the new evidence he had to climb down and admit he had been wrong.

在新的证据面前,他只得服输认错。

in the first place 首先,第一

Why did you choose basketball in the first place?

你为何首先选择篮球呢?

in the future 在将来

He does not care in the least what will happen in the future.

他对以后发生什么事一点也不在乎。

in the least 一点,丝毫

I was not in the least surprised, for I had expected as much.

我一点也没有吃惊,因为我早已料到会有那样的事。

in the long run 最终,从长远观点看

Sin never makes sense in the long run.

不合理之事终将毫无意义。

in the name of 以……的名义

He deposited the money in the name of his son.

他挂着他儿子的名(在银行)存款。

in time 及时地,适时地

He is believed to arrive in time.

相信他会按时到达。

in turn 依次,轮流

They answered the teacher's questions in turn.

他们依次回答了老师的问题。

in view of 鉴于,考虑到;由于

In view of the facts, it seems useless to continue.

鉴于这些事实,继续下去似乎是无益的。

insist on/upon 坚持,坚持认为

Liming Science and Technology Co. Ltd. will insist upon this policy, and will develop the more and better products so as to thank the users for their supports.

Liming 科技公司将坚持这一方针,开发更多、更好的产品来回报广大客户对 Liming 产品的厚爱。

instead of 代替

I made this cake specially, with brown sugar instead of white.
我特别地以红糖代替白糖做了这个蛋糕。

interfere in/with 妨碍,阻碍,干扰,干涉

I bitterly resent his attempts to interfere in my work.
我非常讨厌他企图干涉我的工作。

He tries not to let (his) business interfere with his home life.
他尽量不让日常工作妨碍他的家庭生活。

it goes without saying 不言而喻

It goes without saying that health is above wealth.
健康胜于财富这是不言而喻的。

J

just now 刚才,一会儿以前

You were rude to say that to your father just now.
你刚才对你父亲讲那种话太不礼貌了。

K

keep a distance with 与……保持距离

People always keep a distance with those who pull a face all day.
人们通常不喜欢那些终日拉着脸的人。

keep an eye on 留意

I'll keep an eye on the matter.
这事儿我留意就是了。

keep back

1. 隐瞒,保留

   The prisoner was keeping back vital information.
   该囚犯有重要消息不肯吐露。

2. 阻止,抑制

I would have been here sooner, but the rain kept me back.

我被雨所阻,否则早已经到了。

keep down 控制,压制,镇压;压低,放低(声音)

I hope the wind keeps down, or the sea will be too rough for sailing.

希望风不要再大了,否则,海面浪涛汹涌,无法航行。

keep house 管理家务

The principal roles of the wife are to keep house and raise the children.

妻子的主要任务就是打理家务、养育子女。

keep in touch 保持联系

We must keep in touch with each other.

大家要经常联系。

keep off 不接近,避开

That's dangerous. Please keep off.

那很危险,请勿靠近。

keep on 继续,保持

Turn left at the corner and keep on as far as the church.

到街角向左拐,一直向前走到教堂。

keep one's temper 忍住性子

To keep one's temper is not a sign of weakness, but an indication of self-possession and strength.

不发脾气并非表示软弱,而是说明自制和坚强。

keep one's word 守信用

One should keep one's word.

人应守信。

keep out of 躲开,置身……之外

You'd better keep out of these things.

你最好别卷入这些事。

keep up

1. 继续,坚持

   I hope the good weather will keep up.

   我希望好天气会继续下去。

2. 保持,维持

Keep up the struggle till you succeed.

继续战斗直到你们取得胜利。

keep up with 跟上,不落后

We must keep up with the times.

我们必须跟上时代要求。

keep pace with 与……保持一致

He was so unfit that he couldn't keep pace (with us).

他身体很不好,跟不上(我们)。

knock down 撞倒,击倒

He knocked his opponent down three times in the first round.

在第一回合中他把对手击倒了三次。

knock out 打昏,淘汰

He has now knocked out most of the other competitors.

现在他已击败了大多数的其他竞赛者。

L

laugh at 讥笑,嘲笑

Never laugh at other's dreams.

永远不要嘲笑别人的梦想。

lay down

1. 放下;使躺下

    The enemy laid down their arms.

    敌人放下武器投降。

2. 规定,制定

    He lays it down that the school should be kept clean and quiet.

    他规定,学校应当保持安静和干净。

lay off

1. 停止工作(活动)

    The doctor advised me to lay off cigarettes.

医生建议我戒烟。

2. 暂时解雇

The factory has laid off workers because of the drop in sales.

那个工厂由于销量下降而暂时解雇了工人。

lay out

1. 陈设;展开

She laid out all her new clothes on the bed.

她把她所有的新衣服都摊开在床上。

2. 花钱,花力气

He has laid out all his strength and is weary.

他使出了全部气力,非常疲倦。

lead to

1. (道路)通向

All roads lead to Rome.

条条道路通罗马。

2. 导致

Such a mistake would perhaps lead to disastrous consequences.

这样一种错误可能导致灾难性的后果。

lead the way 带路,引路

I'll lead the way. You just follow.

我来带路,你们跟着好了。

learn by heart 记住,背下

The children can repeat the poem they've just learnt by heart.

这些孩子能重复他们刚背过的诗歌。

leave alone 听其自然,不要去管

She wants to think things out quietly, so we had better leave her alone.

她要安静地考虑一下,最好别打扰她。

leave behind

1. 忘带,留下

He left behind an immortal example to all posterity.

他给后世留下了不朽的典范。

2. 使落后,丢在后面

　　The young athlete soon left the others far behind.

　　那位年轻运动员很快就把其他选手抛在后面。

leave out 省略,遗漏

　　He left that part of the speech out.

　　他把讲话中的那部分删去了。

leave word 留言

　　Please leave word with my secretary if you can't come.

　　你要是不能来,请给我的秘书留话。

let alone

1. 不理,不管(惹),不烦扰,不干涉

　　Let me alone!

　　别管我!

2. 更不用说,还不算

　　We can't afford a bicycle, let alone a car.

　　我们连自行车都买不起,更不用说汽车了。

let down 放下,降低;使失望

　　You can trust Brooks. He'll never let you down.

　　你可以相信 Brooks,他决不会使你失望。

let go 放开,松手

　　The bowler let go a couple of scorchers.

　　投球手投出了几个快球。

let in 让……进入,放……进来

　　Please open the window and let in some fresh air.

　　请把窗子打开,让新鲜空气进来。

let off 放(炮、烟火),开枪

　　They let off their guns at the British ships.

　　他们对英国船舶开炮。

let out

1. 使(火)熄灭

　　Don't let the fire out, will you?

　　别让火熄灭,好吗?

2. (非正)泄露秘密

Someone had let the news out.

有人把这消息泄露出去了。

line up 排队,使排成一行

I hate lining up in the cold to go to the cinema.

我非常讨厌在大冷天里排队等着看电影。

live on/by 靠……生活,以……为食

Most of Asians live on rice.

多数亚洲人以大米为主食。

live through 度过,经受住

He was among the few who managed to live through the enemy prison camp.

他是活着离开战俘集中营的几个人中的一个。

live up to 无愧于,不辜负

We will never fail to live up to what our parents expect of us.

我们决不辜负我们的父母对我们的期望。

look after 照顾,关心,照料

They don't look after themselves very well.

他们没有很好地照顾他们自己。

look at 看,注视

He looked at me with scorn.

他轻蔑地看了看我。

look back 回顾,回头看

I would like to look back on my high-school days, which were the happiest in my life.

我喜欢回顾我的中学时代,那是我生命中最快乐的时光。

look down upon 看不起

All people with a sense of decency will look down upon such conduct as that.

注重尊严的人都会轻视那种行为。

look for 寻找,寻求

Why are the police looking for you?

为什么警察在四处找你?

look forward to 盼望,期待

I'm looking forward to your visit next week.

我在盼望着你下周光临。

look in 顺便看望,顺便;访问

We shall be pleased to see you if you came to look in any time you're passing.

非常欢迎你路过时顺便进来坐坐。

look into 窥视,调查,过问

His disappearance is being looked into by the police.

他失踪一事警方正在调查。

look on 旁观,观看

John took part in the game, but the rest of us just looked on.

约翰参赛,而我们其余的人只是观看。

look out 注意,警惕

Tell the children to look out when they cross the main street.

告诉孩子们过大街时要当心。

look over 检查,查看,调查

I would like you to look over these documents.

我希望你检查一下这些文件。

look through 浏览,温习

I'll look your suggestion through before passing it to the committee.

我要先审查一下你的建议然后再送交委员会。

look up 查找,查阅,寻找,查出

Please look up a fast train to Leeds.

请查一下去利兹的快车。

look up to 尊敬,敬仰

I can be someone to look up to.

我能成为别人崇拜的人。

lose heart 丧失勇气,失去信心

Don't lose heart, whatever you do.

不管做什么,都不要丧失信心。

lose one's temper 发火,发脾气

He is prone to lose his temper whenever disagreed with.

人们和他持有不同意见时,他容易发火。

lose sight (of) 没看见;失明

Only a short-sighted man will lose sight of the importance of education.

只有鼠目寸光的人才会看不见教育的重要性。

M

make a difference 有影响,很重要

What you have told me may make a difference to my own opinion.

你告诉我的一切,可能影响我自己的看法。

make a fire 生火

He picked up sticks to make a fire.

他拾些小树枝来生火。

make faces/make a face 做鬼脸

You mustn't make faces in class.

上课不要做鬼脸。

make for 走向,冲向

Cleanliness makes for good health.

讲究卫生有助于增进健康。

make friends 交朋友,友好相处

Don't make friends with baddy.

不要和坏人来往!

make fun of 取笑,嘲弄

It is wrong to make fun of a cripple.

嘲笑残疾人是不对的。

make out

1. 填写(表格);开出(支票、账单)

   Please make out a bill for these goods.

请给这些物品开个账单。

2. 辨认出

It was difficult to make out the manager's handwriting.

经理的字迹很难辨认。

make one's way 前进,行进

It's not early. Let's make our way to the office.

时候不早了,我们去公司吧。

make the best of/make the most of 充分利用

We must make the best of the few natural resources we have.

我们一定要充分利用我们所拥有的一点自然资源。

make sense 讲得通,言之有理

This sentence doesn't make any sense.

这个句子没有意义。

make sure(of) 查明,弄确实

Go and make sure of the place and time.

去把时间和地点弄清楚。

make up

1. 编造

Tom makes up stories to amuse his little brother.

汤姆编故事逗他的小弟弟。

2. 弥补,偿还

Vitamin pills make up what you lack in your diet.

维生素丸可补充你食物中所缺乏的营养。

3. 化装,打扮

It didn't take her long to make up.

她很快就化好妆了。

make up for 补偿,弥补

Hard work can often make up for a lack of ability.

努力工作通常可以弥补能力的不足。

make up one's mind 决定,下决心

He makes his mind to study hard this semester.

他下定决心这学期努力学习。

make use of 利用

As to intelligence, the boy has more than he can possibly make use of.

至于那男孩的才智,多得他都用不完。

make way (for) 开路,让路

Make way, there! I need to get through.

让一让,我需要走过去。

mistake...for 将……误认为

She mistook him for the professor.

她把他错当成教授了。

mix up

1. 混合

   She mixed up flour and water.

   她把面粉和水搅匀。

2. 混淆

   Instead of helping her, his explanation only mixed her up.

   他的解释不但没帮她的忙,反而把她弄糊涂了。

more or less 或多或少,多少有点

I can earn 20 a night, more or less, as a waiter.

我当服务员一晚上能挣20英镑左右。

N

neither...nor... 既不……也不……

I could speak neither English nor French.

我既不会说英语,也不会说法语。

never mind 不要紧,没关系

Did you miss the bus? Never mind, there'll be another one in five minutes.

你没赶上公共汽车吗? 不要紧,五分钟后就来一辆。

no doubt 无疑,必定

There is no doubt about the correct thing to do.

对该做的正确的事情,不要有什么顾虑。

no longer 不再,已不

We want that nobody should try to take our test any longer; no more test of our patience and flexibility.

我们希望那些人不要再试探了,不要再试探我们的耐性和灵活性了。

no matter…无论……,不管……

He is game for anything no matter how dangerous it is.

无论这件事有多么危险,他都敢去做。

no more 不再

No more workers are being taken on at present.

目前不雇请更多的工人。

no more than 不过,仅仅

Our new foreign trade policy is no more than some general practice in international trade.

我们的新外贸政策只不过是国际贸易中的一些通常做法罢了。

no sooner…than…一……就……

No sooner had he returned, than he began to prepare for his next trip.

他一回来,就开始准备下一次旅行。

now and again 不时地,常常地

Drop in now and again.

有空过来玩儿吧。

now and then 时而,不时

A few cases of influenza cropped out every now and then.

不时出现一些流行性感冒的病例。

now that 既然

Now that you've seen the house, I'll show you the grounds.

屋子你已看过了,我领你参观一下庭园。

not only…but (also)…不仅……而且……

The students understood, they represent, not only themselves, but also the entire family; they compete, not only other people in the result, moreover superego in quality.

学生们懂得,他们所代表的不只是自己,还有全家;他们所竞争的不仅是在成绩上超越他人,而且是在素质上超越自我。

O

of course 当然

That was 40 years ago, but of course you wouldn't remember it.

那是40年以前的事,你自然想不起来了。

off duty 下班

He usually comes off duty at 5 p.m.

他通常下午五点下班。

on account of 基于,由于

He was granted special admission on account of his effort.

由于他自己的努力,他被破格录取。

one after another 一个接一个

They went into the classroom one after another.

他们一个接一个地走进教室。

on all accounts 无论如何

On all accounts you must finish the assignment tomorrow.

无论如何你必须明天完成作业。

on and off 断断续续,不时地

It rained on and off all day.

哩哩啦啦下了一天雨。

one another 互相

The Irish is a fair people; they never speak well of one another.

爱尔兰人是公平的人民,他们决不互相称赞。

on (an/the) average 平均起来;一般说来

We figured that we were losing on the average an hour's working time each day.

估计我们每天平均要损失1小时的工作时间。

on behalf of 代表……,为……代表

On behalf of my colleagues and myself I thank you.

我代表我的同事和我本人向你表示感谢。

on business 因公,因事

Mike is traveling on business.

迈克正在出公差。

on board 在船(火车,飞机)上

When all passengers were on board, the train pulled out of the station.

所有乘客都上车后,火车开出了车站。

on condition that 如果

I'll come on condition that John is invited too.

如果约翰也收到邀请,我就来。

on duty 值班,当班

The rule is that someone must be on duty at all times.

按照规定,任何时候均需有人值班。

on earth 到底,究竟

What on earth is the matter there?

那里究竟发生了什么事情?

on fire

1. 燃烧着

   He suddenly cried out that the storehouse was on fire.

   他突然叫喊仓库着火了。

2. 兴奋着

   The islanders were on fire and determined to fight against the attackers.

   岛上的人情绪激昂,决心与来犯者战斗一场。

on foot 步行

Seeing Venice on foot is best.

徒步参观威尼斯是最佳选择。

on guard

1. 警戒

   All this time, the mother is constantly on guard.

   在这段时间内,母亲一直处在警戒状态。

2. 值班

   Two soldiers must be on guard all night.

   必须有两个士兵彻夜站岗。

on no account 决不

We must on no account view problems superficially and in isolation.

我们绝不能表面地、孤立地看问题。

on one's guard 警戒着

I think it better, however, not to complain to Miss Bulstrode. One has to be on one's guard when dealing with that one!

可是我想还是不去向 Bulstrode 小姐抱怨。跟这个女人打交道,可要当心点。

on one's own 独自,靠自己

Although her father is in the firm she got the job on her own.

尽管她父亲在公司里,但她那份工作是靠自己得到的。

on purpose 故意,有意

I sometimes think that all his supposed mistakes are made on purpose just to annoy me.

我有时认为他犯的被信以为真的一切错误是在故意气我。

on sale 上市,出售;减价,贱卖

The latest model of this washer is now on sale in your shops.

这种最新型号的洗衣机目前正在你们的商店中出售。

on schedule 按预定时间

The train arrived on schedule.

火车正点到达。

on time 准时

The boss ordered that the work should be done on time.

老板吩咐工作必须按时完成。

on the basis of 以……为基础

On the basis of evidence we deduced that he was guilty.

根据这些证据我们推断他是有罪的。

on the contrary 正相反

It doesn't seem ugly to me; on the contrary, I think it's rather beautiful.

我觉得它并不丑,恰恰相反,它挺美。

on the ground of 以……为理由

We refused to publish the report on the grounds of cost.

因费用的关系,我们拒绝公布这份报告。

on the one hand 一方面

On the one hand, children need organized activities.

一方面,孩子们需要有组织的活动。

on the other hand 另一方面

On the other hand, he is a real despot.

在另一方面,他是个不折不扣的暴君。

on the road 在旅途中

Police have set up a roadblock on the road to London.

警察在通往伦敦的路上设置了路障。

on the spot 当场,在现场

He discussed business and concluded transactions with us on the spot.

他与我们谈判业务并当场成交。

on the whole 总的来说

My opinion is on the whole the same as yours.

我的意见大体上同你的差不多。

on top of 在……之上

We stood on top of the hill, drinking in the beautiful view.

我们站在山顶上,饱览这美丽的风景。

once again/more/over 再一次,又一次

He broke his words once again.

他又一次违背了诺言。

once and again 一而再,再而三

Why did she do that experiment once and again?

为什么她再三地做那个实验?

once for all 再也不,一劳永逸

Spending ¥1,800 of once for all in club will become Ordinary Member.

凡在本俱乐部一次性消费满¥1 800可成为普通会员。

once in a while 偶尔,有时

You have to pay the piper every once in a while.

你得时不时地承担一些费用。

once upon a time 从前

Once upon a time there was a giant with two heads.

从前有个两头巨人。

or else 否则,要不然

Stop smoking now, or else your health will be ruined.

别再抽烟了,否则你会毁了自己的健康。

or so 大约,左右

The oil wells will all run dry in thirty years or so at the present rate of use.

按现在的消耗速度,30年左右现在的油井就会干涸。

other than 除……之外

Does anybody other than yourself know this?

除你本人之外还有别人知道这事吗?

out of

1. 在……外,离开

   Jack was pushed out of the room by his companions.

   杰克被伙伴们推出房间。

2. 出于,由于

   He did it all out of kindness.

   他做这事完全出于好意。

3. 缺乏,没有

   Especially if you're living in a place where you have no information, information is your way out of poverty.

   特别是在缺乏信息的地区,信息是人们的脱贫途径。

out of breath 上气不接下气

He ran so fast that he was out of breath.

他跑得太快,气都喘不过来了。

out of control 失去控制

The plane got out of control and crashed.

飞机失去控制坠毁了。

out of danger 脱离危险

We were relieved to hear that she was out of danger.

听说她脱险了,我们的心才放下来。

out of date 过时的,陈旧的

This kind of machine is out of date.

这种机器过时了。

out of place 不适当的,不得其所的

His remarks are out of place.

他的话讲得不适当。

out of practice 久不练习,荒疏

I haven't played tennis for years, so I'm really out of practice.

我已经多年不打网球了,技术已经完全荒废了。

out of order 发生故障,失调

Our tractor is out of order.

我们的拖拉机坏了。

out of sight 看不见,在视野以外

We waved until the car was out of sight.

我们一直在挥手道别,直到汽车看不见为止。

out of the question 不可能的,办不到的

We cannot go out in this weather—it is out of the question.

天气这样糟,我们不能出去,这是完全不可能的。

out of the way

1. 不寻常的

    I didn't see anything out of the way in his talk.

    在他的发言中,我没听出什么新鲜的东西。

2. 已经解决的

Once all of that is out of the way, you obviously don't want more lines of code than you need.

当上面提到的这些问题都解决了的时候,你显然还希望代码不要有多余的部分。

out of touch 失去联系

We've been out of touch with Roger for years now.

我们至今已有数年未与罗杰来往了。

out of work 失业

He was out of work when the factory closed.

他在工厂倒闭后失业了。

owing to 由于,因为

Owing to engine trouble, the plane had to make a forced landing.

由于发动机出了毛病,飞机不得不进行迫降。

P

pass away 去世,逝世

She passed away in Shanghai on June 11, at the advanced age of 101.

她于六月十一日以一百零一岁的高龄在上海逝世。

pass on 传递;向前

Would you please pass the dictionary on to Mary?

请你把这本词典传给玛丽,行吗?

pass out 失去知觉,昏倒

She passed out when she heard the bad news.

她听到这噩耗后晕了过去。

pass over 省略;忽略

He has resigned and will pass over charge of his office today.

他已辞职,将在今日办移交手续。

pay attention to 注意

No attention was paid to his advice.

他的建议没有引起注意。

pay back 偿还，回报

I am sure that he will pay back every cent he owes you.

我敢肯定他会分文不差地把欠款还给你。

pay for 付款；偿还

How much did you pay for the book?

那本书你付了多少钱？

pay off 偿清；取得成功

You must pay off your old loan before you can obtain a new one.

你必须还清旧账，然后才能再借款。

pick out 选出，挑选

The child refuses to eat this fruit without first picking out the stones.

不把果核取出来，那个小孩就不会吃这水果。

pick up 捡起，拾起；(车船等)中途搭(人)/带(货)

He picked up the child and put her on his shoulders.

他抱起孩子，让她骑在自己的肩膀上。

play with 以……为消遣，玩弄

Don't play with fire.

不要玩火。

point out 指出，指明

This guide book points out the main facts of early American history.

这本导游手册讲述了美洲早期的重要史实。

pull down 拉倒，拆毁

They pulled down my old house and built five new ones.

他们拆除了我的旧房子，建起了五幢新房子。

pull in (交通车船)进站，靠岸

The train pulled in exactly on time.

列车准时进站。

pull off 完成(一件艰难的事情)

She pulled off a great coup in getting the president to agree to an interview.

她竟然办到了让总统同意接受采访。

pull out 拔出,抽出,取出;(交通车船)出站

The train pulled out exactly on time.

火车正点开出。

pull up 使停下

The car pulled up outside the inn.

轿车在旅馆外面停了下来。

put...into practice 加以实施

We've made our plans, and now we must put them into practice.

我们定好了计划,现在必须把它们付诸实施。

put across 解释清楚,说明

He could not put across his point of view to the audience.

他没能使听众理解他的观点。

put an end to 使……中止

We must put an end to the pointless conflict.

我们必须结束这毫无意义的冲突。

put aside 储存,保留

She's put aside a tidy sum for her retirement.

她存了一笔相当可观的钱以备退休之用。

put away 把……收起来,放好

She washed the cups and put them away.

她洗完杯子后便把它们收了起来。

put down 记下,写下

Let me put down your telephone number lest I forget it.

让我先记下你的电话号码,以免忘了。

put forward 提出

He put forward a plan for the committee to consider.

他提出一项计划交由全体委员审议。

put off 推迟,拖延

We've invited friends to supper and it's too late to put them off now.

我已邀请朋友来吃晚饭,现在取消已来不及了。

put on

1. 穿上,戴上

What dress shall I put on for the meeting?

我穿什么衣服去开会?

2. 上演

The local drama group is putting on "*Sister Jiang*" at the Capital Theatre.

当地的剧团正在首都剧场演出《江姐》。

3. 增加(体重)

He didn't want to put on more weight.

他不想增加体重。

put out

1. 扑灭;熄灭

They quickly put out the fire.

他们迅速将火扑灭。

2. 出版;发行;发布

They have already put out a new periodical.

他们已经出版了一种新的期刊。

put...to use 使用,予以利用

Instead of wrecking the valley, the water are put to use making electricity.

现在河水不但不在流域内肆虐,反而被人们用来生产电力。

put up

1. 举起,升起,提(价)

Put your hands up! You are arrested.

举起手来!你被捕了。

2. 为……提供食宿

I'm afraid I can't put you up.

恐怕我不能给你们提供膳宿。

3. 建造,搭起,支起

Many blocks of flats were put up in the 1990's.

许多公寓式建筑群都是20世纪90年代建的。

4. 张贴,公布

The principal put up the exam result.

校长公布了这次考试的结果。

put up with 容忍,忍受

I can't put up with noise when I am working.

我在工作的时候不能忍受喧闹声。

Q

queue up 排队

Please queue up and stand clear of the platform screen door.

请按箭头排队候车,勿倚靠屏蔽门。

quite a few 还不少,有相当数目

Our school library boasts quite a few rare books.

我们学校图书馆以藏有相当多的珍藏书而自豪。

R

rather than 而不,不顾

I tried to stand on my own two feet rather than turned to my parents.

我设法自立而不求助于我的父母。

refer to 查阅,提到,谈到

The new law does not refer to land used for farming.

那种新法律并不涉及耕种用地。

reflect on/upon 思索

We must seriously reflect on the influence of violence on TV upon children.

我们必须仔细考虑电视中暴力行为对儿童的影响。

regardless of 不顾,不管……如何

He continues speaking, regardless of my feelings on the matter.

他不顾及我在此事上的感情继续往下说。

rely on 依靠;信赖

If Helen says she will complete the job on time, you can always rely on her to deliver the goods.

如果海伦说她将按时完成任务的话,你可以永远信赖她,她会按时完成的。

remind sb. of 使想起,提起;提醒

This song reminds me of France.

我一听到这首歌就想起了法国。

rest on 依靠

Your success rests on your efforts.

你的成功有赖于你的努力。

result from 起因于

They know the positive result from it too.

他们也应该知道那会带来什么积极的效应。

result in 导致

The making of false statements could result in the invalidation of the contract.

提供虚假资料可能导致合同失效。

right away 马上,立刻

If war breaks out, we shall be called up right away.

如果战争爆发,我们将立即被征召服役。

ring off 挂断(电话)

I'll have to ring off now, someone is knocking at the door.

我得挂断电话了,有人在敲门。

ring up 打电话

If he comes, I'll ring you up.

他来了,我会打电话给你。

rub out 擦掉,拭去

She rubbed out those dirty marks on her white skirt.

她把白裙子上的污迹擦掉。

run across 偶然遇到

I ran across her in the public library yesterday.

我昨天在公共图书馆碰巧遇见了她。

run down 撞倒,撞沉

The ship ran down a small fishing boat.

这艘轮船撞沉了一条小渔船。

run for 竞选

Political leaders exploded a bombshell when they picked the young lawyer to run for mayor.

政界头面人物推举这位年轻的律师出来竞选市长,这真是个"爆炸"新闻。

run into 偶然遇到,撞见;碰撞

I ran into Bob yesterday on main street.

昨天我在大街上偶然遇到了鲍勃。

run out (of) 用光,耗尽

The hotel has run out of beer.

这饭店的啤酒已全部售完了。

run over 浏览,匆匆复习

The teacher ran over his notes before the lecture.

教师在讲课前先看一眼讲稿。

run through 匆匆地看

I'll just run through these newspapers, and then we'll go out.

我只看一眼这些报纸,然后咱们就出去。

S

see about 调查,查询

I've got to see about the car. It's been making a funny noise recently.

我必须检查一下汽车,近来它一直发出一种古怪的声音。

see after 照应,照顾

She promised to see after the children when their mothers were on the night shift.

她答应在孩子们的妈妈上夜班时照顾这些孩子。

see into 调查,检查

He said he would see into the matter himself.
他说他要亲自调查这件事。

see off 给……送行；送别

Shall we have a see off dinner party for her?
我们要不要为她办个送别晚宴呢？

see (to it) that

1. 负责，照料

   The doctor went to see that patient day about.
   这个医生每隔一天就去看那个病人一次。

2. 注意，留心

   See (to it) that children don't catch cold.
   留神别让孩子们感冒。

see through 看穿，识破

He's a poor liar, anyone can see through him.
他说谎不高明，任何人都能识破。

seek after/for 搜寻，寻找，寻觅

We shouldn't seek after comfort, personal fame, or gain.
我们不应该贪图安逸，追名逐利。

send for 派人请，召唤；索取

The child is running a high fever. We must send for a doctor at once.
孩子在发高烧。我们必须马上派人去请医生。

send in 呈报，提交，送来

After the scandal, he had to send in his papers.
出了丑闻后，他不得不辞职。

send off 寄发

Why haven't you got my letter? I sent it off last week.
你为什么还没有收到我的信？我上星期就寄出去了。

serve as 担任；起……作用

The general had served as a soldier in the earlier war.
在早期的战争中，这位将军曾当过士兵。

set about 开始，着手；出发

We set about our task at once with great enthusiasm.
我们立刻兴致勃勃地干起来。

set aside 宣布无效；驳回，废止

Let's set aside all formality.
这些客套咱们都不要讲了。

set back 推迟，延缓，阻碍

The problems arising in production set back his plan.
生产中发生的问题延迟了他的计划。

set down 记下，写下

Old Walter is setting down his memories of village life.
老沃尔特正在写他乡村生活的回忆录。

set fire to 使燃烧，点燃

They set fire to the city and massacred all the inhabitants.
他们放火烧了这座城市，而且屠杀了所有的居民。

set forth 提出，阐明

As set forth, he was a changed man from that moment.
如前所述，自那时起他就变成了另外一个人。

set free 释放

I think all caged birds should be set free.
我认为所有关在笼里的鸟儿都应该放出去。

set off 动身，出发；使爆炸，使爆发引起

That morning a new ship set out/off for London on its first trip.
那天早晨，有一艘新轮船首航去伦敦。

set out 动身，出发，开始；制定，打算

That morning a new ship set out/off for London on its first trip.
那天早晨，有一艘新轮船首航去伦敦。

set up 建立，设立，树立；资助，使自立，扶持

Plenty of foreign firms have set up factories here.
很多外国公司已在这里开办工厂。

settle down 定居，过安定的生活

He should get a house and settle down.
他应该买幢房子安定下来。

show in 领入
Some of his paintings are on show in the local art gallery.
他的一些画正在当地的一些艺术馆展出。

show off 炫耀,卖弄
He wrote in that style just to show off.
这种文体写文章,完全是为了卖弄文采。

show up 使显现,使醒目
Billy had been fasting against Cooper for three days before the debtor showed up.
Billy 为索债在 Cooper 门前静坐绝食三天,欠债人 Cooper 才露面。

shut down 关闭
The shop has shut down because of lack of trade.
那商店因生意萧条而停业。

shut out 排除
She had effectively shut him out by refusing to listen.
她拒不听他说话,并以此有效地将他排除在外。

shut up
1. 安静,闭嘴

   I wish she would shut up!

   她要是安静下来该多好!

2. 关严

   I shut my office up and went for lunch.

   我把办公室的门窗关好后就去吃午饭了。

sick of 厌烦
I was sick of their fun and games.
他们的嬉闹让我厌烦。

side by side 肩并肩,一个挨一个
The two children are walking side by side.
那两个孩子肩并肩地走着。

sit up 迟睡,熬夜
I want to sit up tonight and watch the late show.

今晚我不想睡觉,等着看深夜电视节目。

slow down 放慢速度

The machine slowed down and stopped.

机器逐渐减慢了转速,终于停住了。

so...as to 如此……以至于……;如此……以便……

The girl was so excited as to shout herself hoarse.

那个女孩兴奋得喊哑了嗓子。

so far 迄今为止

The scientist is doing experiments no one has so far attempted.

科学家们正在做一项迄今为止没人做过的实验。

so forth 等等

The water rate is the payment in Britain for water when it is supplied to houses and factories and so forth.

在英国,水税是指家庭、工厂等得到水的供应时所要交纳的款项。

so on 等等

She spends her day doing housework, watching television, reading, and so on.

她以做家务、看电视、看书等度过一天。

so that

1. 以便,为的是

   Put a wedge under the door so that it will stay open.

   在门下面插个楔,好让门开着。

2. 结果是,以致

   So pride motivates us to do well so that we gain respect.

   所以,自尊激励我们做得更好,从而能够赢得尊重。

so...that... 如此……以至于……

It is so quiet in the room that you can hear the drop of a pin.

房间里静得连(地上)掉根针都能听见。

sooner or later 迟早,早晚

He cheated Underwood and Underwood threatened to pay him back sooner or later.

他欺骗了 Underwood,Underwood 扬言迟早要对他进行报复。

speak for 替……讲话

I myself agree with you, but I can't speak for my boss.

我同意你的提议,可我的话并不能代表我的老板。

speak of 谈到

They spoke of the old days on the campus.

他们谈起昔日的校园生活。

speak out 大声说

If you have any objections, just speak out.

如果你有什么反对意见,就爽快地说出来。

speed up 使加速

I have found a way to speed up this process.

我已经找到了一个加速这个过程的方法。

stand by

1. 站在旁边;袖手旁观

   There were several people standing by when the accident happened.

   事故发生的时候有好几个人在场。

2. 支持,支援

   We'll stand by you through thick and thin.

   不管多么艰难困苦,我们都要支持你们。

stand for 代替,代表,意味着

UN stands for the United Nations.

UN 是联合国的缩写。

stand out 突出,显眼

The stonework stands out from the rest of the wall.

墙上的石雕工艺很显眼。

stand up for 为……辩护,维护

We stand up for the cause of liberty and justice.

我们拥护自由和正义。

stand up to 勇敢地面对,坚决抵抗

I wonder if he dare stand up to his boss.

我不知道他是否敢于反抗他的老板。

stand up 站起,竖起

The animal is able to stand up on its hind limbs.

这种动物能够用后肢站立。

step by step 逐步

He learnt the rules of the game step by step.

他逐步学会了游戏的规则。

step down 让位,下台

The manager had to step down on account of poor health.

那位经理由于身体不好,只能辞职不干。

step in 插入,介入

The police are reluctant to step in.

警察不愿插手干预。

step up 提高,加快,加紧

I hope you try to get them to step up production.

希望你们尽力使厂家增加生产。

stick to 坚持,忠于,信守

You must stick to your promise.

你必须遵守诺言。

such...that 那样的……以至

He told such funny stories that we all laughed.

他讲了这样滑稽的故事,把我们都逗笑了。

such as 像……那样的,诸如,例如

A symbol produced by a process such as handwriting, drawing, or printing.

通过诸如手写、绘制或打印之类的处理过程而产生的符号。

substitute for 替代;取代,代替

Can you substitute for the singer who is ill?

你能替一下那位得了病的歌手吗?

sum up 总结,概括

You have only 100 words in which to sum up his speech.

你只能用100个字来概括他的讲话。

T

take a/the chance

1. 冒风险

   We will take a chance to have the party outdoor.

   我们将冒险举行露天聚会。

2. 碰运气

   We may take a chance on her being at home.

   也许碰巧她在家。

take advantage of 利用,趁机

CPDOs take advantage of this anomaly.

CPDO 正是得益于这种异常现象。

take after 与……像

Your daughter doesn't take after you in any way.

你女儿一点都不像你。

take apart 拆开

It's easy to take a watch apart but difficult to put it together again.

把表拆开容易,装起来难。

take back 收回,带回

I forgot to take back my bicycle.

我忘了把自行车取回来。

take care 留心;保重

Take great care, I pray you!

要多加小心,我求求你!

take care of 照顾,照料;承当,处理,负责

They appointed her to take care of that old man.

他们委派她照顾那位老人。

take charge(of) 负责,看管

The department was badly organized until she took charge of it.

这个部门在她负责以前组织工作做得很差。

take delight in 以……为乐

Those who take delight in other people's pain will suffer retribution sooner or later.

把快乐建立在别人痛苦之上的人迟早要受到报应的。

take down 记下,写下

The reporters took down the speech in shorthand.

记者们迅速记下讲话的内容。

take effect 生效,见效

The prescribed medicine failed to take effect.

医生开的药没有见效。

take...for 误认为……,误以为……

I just took it for granted that you had been told about this.

我只是认为你已知道了这件事。

take...for granted 认为……理所当然

Don't take his help for granted.

不要认为他的帮助是应该的。

take in 接受,容纳;领会,理解;欺骗

I wonder if he's really taking it in.

我想知道他是否真正明白了。

take...into account 考虑到……

We should take into account the proposals of our parents and vice versa.

我们应该考虑父母的建议,反之亦然。

take...into consideration 考虑到……

Time factor is what we must first take into consideration.

时间因素是我们必须首先考虑的。

take it easy 别着急,慢慢来

Take it easy when you are on the stage.

上台的时间不要紧张。

take off

1. 拿走,取下;去掉

   I can't take the lid off, it's stuck!

这盖子卡住了，我拿不下来。
2. (飞机)起飞

It's exciting to feel the plane taking off.

感觉到飞机起飞令人兴奋。

take on 呈现,具有,装出;接纳,接受;承担,从事

The old factory has taken on a new look.

这家老厂已呈现出一派新面貌。

take one's time 不急不忙,从容进行

There are plans to take one's time, the principle of chaos; A budget is not poor, a practice undefeated.

有计划不忙,有原则不乱;有预算不穷,有实践不败。

take over 接管,接收

The strikers took over the factories.

罢工工人接管了工厂。

take pains 尽力,煞费苦心

Successful are those who are willing to take pains.

成功的人都是那些肯努力的人。

take part (in) 参加,参与

John takes part in many school activities.

约翰参加很多学校里的活动。

take place 发生,进行

The threatening strike did not take place after all.

可能来临的罢工终究没有发生。

take the place of 代替

It would be difficult to find a man to take the place of the secretary.

找一个代替秘书的人会很难的。

take turns 轮流

Susan and her brother take turns (at) doing the dishes.

苏珊和她的兄弟轮流洗盘子。

take up

1. 拿起;抱起

He took up telephone receiver and began to dial.

他拿起电话听筒开始拨号码。

2. 占去

I won't take up much of your time.

我不会占用你很多时间。

talk back 顶嘴

Don't talk back to your grandpa.

不要对外公顶嘴。

talk into 说服

She tried to talk him into adopting her plan.

她试图劝他接受她的方案。

talk over 商量,讨论

We must talk over the arrangements with them.

我们必须和他们详细商议这些具体安排。

thanks to 由于,多亏

Thanks to you, I was saved from drowning.

幸亏你,我才没有淹死。

that is to say 就是说,即

They left two weeks ago, that is to say, on March 21.

他们两周前离开的,也就是说三月二十一日那天。

the other day 前几天

I had rather an odd experience the other day.

前几天我有过非常奇怪的经历。

think better of 改变主意,重新考虑

You are right, I think better of him now after I have known him.

你说得对,了解他之后,我现在对他的印象好多了。

think of 想到,想起

I can't think of a better place for our party.

我想不出一个更好的聚会的地方。

think of...as... 把……认为是……

I don't really think of myself as a businesswoman.

我并没有真的认为自己是商界女性。

think over 仔细考虑

Try to think over the things from others' view.
尝试从旁观者的角度考虑事情。

throw away 扔掉,抛弃

He threw away the old sofa.
他把旧沙发扔掉了。

throw light on 使……显得清楚;阐明

Illustrations shed/throw light on the text.
图解帮助说明课文。

throw up 呕吐

The boy threw up his dinner again.
男孩又把吃的饭吐了。

time and again 反复地,一次又一次地

I read the poem time and again.
我一遍又一遍地读这首诗。

to a certain degree 在一定程度上

The new contract Law of China adopted it to a certain degree.
我国新合同法在一定程度上采用了该制度。

to a certain/great/some extent 在一定/很大/某种程度上

I agree with you to a certain extent.
我在某种程度上同意你。

touch on 关系到,涉及

I want to touch briefly on another aspect of the problem.
我想简单地谈一下这个问题的另一方面。

try on 试穿

Try on the hat to see if it fits you.
戴上这顶帽子试试,看是否适合你。

try one's best 尽力

We'll try our best to solve this problem.
我们将尽最大的努力解决这个问题。

try out 试验

We won't be able to tell what skills the man has until we try him out.
要等试用一个时期以后,我们才能知道这人有什么专长。

turn down 调低,关小

The housing sales have been turning down since the summer.

入夏以来,房屋的销售量日趋减少。

turn in 交出,上缴;转身进入,拐入

Turn in your homework, please.

请把作业交上来。

turn into 使变成

They turned the reading room into a laboratory.

他们把阅览室改建成了一个试验室。

turn off 关,关闭

Turn off the switch when anything goes wrong with the machine.

如果机器出故障,就把开关关掉。

turn on 打开,拧开

This tap is stiff; it won't turn on.

这个龙头太紧,拧不开。

turn out

1. 生产,制造

   They have been turning out great blades for 400 years.

   他们生产优质刀片已经有400年历史了。

2. 驱逐,使离开

   They were turned out of the hotel.

   他们被赶出了旅馆。

3. 证明是,结果是

   It turned out that he failed the examination.

   原来他考试不及格。

turn over

1. (使)翻转;调转

   Turn over or your back will get sunburnt.

   翻过身去,不然你的后背要被阳光灼伤的。

2. 仔细考虑

   He turned the new idea over in his mind.

   他仔细地考虑了这种新想法。

turn to 转向；求助于

1. 求助于

   I tried to stand on my own two feet rather than turned to my parents.

   我设法自立而不求助于我的父母。

2. （把注意力等）转向

   More and more people turn to computer science.

   愈来愈多的人从事计算机科学研究。

turn up 出现，发生

He didn't turn up until half an hour later.

半小时后他才出现。

under control 被控制住

The police kept the mob under control.

警察将暴徒制服。

under no circumstances 在任何情况下都不

Under no circumstances can we agree to such a principle.

在任何情况下我们都不能同意这一原则。

under the control of 在……控制之下

All schools are under the control of the Ministry of Education.

所有的学校都在教育部的管理之下。

under way 进行中

Consultations are under way.

正在进行磋商。

up to

1. 多达

   I can take up to four people in my car.

   我的汽车最多能坐四个人。

2. 直到

Up to now he's still quiet.

他直到现在仍保持沉默。

3. 在于……，取决于……

This is up to you.

这件事取决于你。

up to date 时兴的，切合目前情况的

The car is a beauty and quite up to date.

那辆车子很漂亮，是最新款的。

use up 用光，花完

By this time he had used up all his savings.

到这时，他的存款已全部用完。

used to (过去)总是

At one time they used to mine coal in these valleys.

从前，他们在这些峡谷中采煤。

W

wait on 伺候；等待

We waited on for another hour, but still she didn't come.

我们又等了一个小时，但她仍然没来。

ward off 避开，防止

I try to ward off fatigue by resting as much as possible.

为了防止疲劳，我尽可能多休息。

warm up 变热

Let's do some exercises to warm up a bit.

让咱们先做做操热一下身。

watch out (for) 戒备，提防

In the rush to go folkloric, watch out for collision of cultures.

在民俗化的热潮中，要提防不同文化的冲突。

wear down

1. 磨损，损耗

The point of the pencil had been worn down when I finished this letter.

写完这封信时铅笔已经磨得很短了。

2. 使疲劳

Looking after a high-spirited child can soon wear a person down.

照看一个精力旺盛的孩子,一会儿就能把人搞得筋疲力尽。

wear out 穿坏;(使)耗尽

Better to wear out than rust out.

【谚】与其锈坏,不如用坏。

what about(对于)……怎么样

I think this is a good idea. What about you?

我认为这是个好主意。你认为如何?

what if 倘若……将会怎么样,即使……又有什么要紧

What if I have no debts?

如果我没债务怎么办?

What if you stand in my shoes?

如果你处在我的立场你会怎么样?

whether…or 是……还是……,不管……还是

Get this job whether or not, I have no idea.

是否要这份新工作,我真拿不准。

wipe out 消灭,毁灭

The plague once could wipe out a village.

鼠疫曾一度可以夺走整个村庄村民的生命。

with respect to 关于

This is true with respect to English but not to French.

这一点在英语里属实而在法语里则不同。

with the exception of 除……外

All kinds of atoms, with the exception of hydrogen, has neutrons.

除了氢原子之外,一切原子都含有中子。

word for word 逐字地

He repeated that speech, word for word from memory.

他凭着记忆一字不变地复述那个演讲。

work at/on 从事

Is Tom still working at the new book that he promised?
汤姆仍在埋头撰写他曾允诺的那本新书吗?

work out 解决,算出;设计出,制定出

I've worked out your share of the expenses at 10 pounds.
我已经计算出你应分摊的费用是10英镑。

work up

1. 引起,激起

    I worked myself up to accept the challenge.
    我鼓起勇气接受挑战。

2. 逐渐向上,向上爬

    The young man works his way up to the top.
    那个年轻人努力使自己逐步晋升到最高职位。

worry about 担心

Today he does not have to worry about making a living.
现在他不用为生活发愁了。

would rather 宁愿,宁可

I would rather have the small one than the big one.
我宁愿要小的,不要大的。